PARLIAMENT
IN INDIA

TO THE MEMORY OF MY FATHER
and
TO MY MOTHER

PARLIAMENT
IN INDIA

by

W. H. MORRIS-JONES

*Professor of Political Theory and Institutions
in the University of Durham*

GREENWOOD PRESS, PUBLISHERS
WESTPORT, CONNECTICUT

Library of Congress Cataloging in Publication Data

Morris-Jones, Wyndraeth Humphreys.
  Parliament in India.

    Reprint of the 1957 ed. published by University of
Pennsylvania Press, Philadelphia.
    Bibliography: p.
    Includes index.
    1. India (Republic). Parliament. 2. Legislative
bodies--India. I. Title.
[JQ254.M6 1975]   328.54   75-29074
ISBN 0-8371-8382-0

This edition published in 1957 by University of Pennsylvania Press,
Philadelphia

Reprinted with the permission of University of Pennsylvania Press

Reprinted in 1976 by Greenwood Press,
a division of Williamhouse-Regency Inc.

Library of Congress Catalog Card Number 75-29074

ISBN 0-8371-8382-0

Printed in the United States of America

PREFACE

THIS book is intended to serve more than one purpose, more than one group of readers, both in India as well as outside. In Britain, certainly, there is interest in what is sometimes called 'the Indian experiment'. Can the institutions of parliamentary democracy take root in Indian soil? When power was transferred in 1947, had something of Britain's political experience been effectively communicated to India's new rulers; and, if so, would that something be enough to meet the exacting needs of the new republic? While Britain evidently has a peculiar concern for the political development of India, the pattern of world events in the last decade has imposed a similar curiosity on other countries of the West. Is India able to present to Asia a way of avoiding the uneasy 'choice' between the various forms of autocracy which appear to offer themselves? In particular, has she the political strength and skill to afford capable resistance to the most dangerous of these autocratic forms—that of Communist rule?

These questions are asked also inside India; the same uncertainties are felt there too. And with them are others with a slightly different emphasis. Can parliaments and politicians 'produce results'—in terms of improved living standards for ourselves, the Indian people? Can we fashion for ourselves honest government and upright administration? Have we yet discovered our political selves or do we play purely borrowed roles in our political behaviour?

The student of politics has further questions of his own. What is the exact mechanism whereby political institutions adapt themselves to new environments? What are the characteristics of this new attempt to combine cabinet-parliamentary government with federal structure and to add in an ambitious programme of state control and enterprise? How do national movements and their erstwhile allies adjust themselves to the roles of government and critic within an accepted framework of rules and conventions? For the Indian student these enquiries are supplemented by others. In many Indian universities there is something approaching a new awakening of political science. In the past the subject, though recognised and taught, lacked coherence; for between the study of modern European political philosophy on the one hand and the detailed and frequently too textual learning of Indian constitutional history on the other there fell the shadow of dependent status. Neither teacher nor student was able to convince himself that there was anything that could be called Indian political institutions; there were simply a

v

series of enactments and pronouncements emanating from the governing power, and the study of political institutions and behaviour meant,
if anything, the study of these things in so far as they could be observed
at work in far-away Britain. In consequence, the Indian student would
normally know much more of the working of Westminster and Downing
Street than of the Legislative Assembly in Delhi and the Viceroy's
Executive Council. It followed, too, that the observation of political
institutions often lacked the realism which more intimate contact might
have given, while it was at the same time frequently coloured by envy
(which made British politics too good to be true) or distrust (which
made them too bad to be believed). The achievement of independence
makes a balanced and rounded study of political science easier, and
there are indeed signs of a widely-felt desire for descriptions of what can
now be termed India's political institutions, for accounts at once more
lifelike than that which traditional academic exposition has provided
and more systematic and related to principles than could be obtained
from even the most perceptive press reports and comments.

Complete answers to these questions are not supplied in this book,
but an important part of the material required for such answers is here
set out, and on this basis I have felt justified in putting forward conclusions which at least suggest strongly the verdict which a more comprehensive study would reach. The limits of the present work may perhaps
be indicated at the outset. My study excludes, for the moment, the mani-
fold activities and the internal lives of the political parties—though I
have given an account of their organisation and behaviour in the legislatures. There is here no study of the civil services and the administrative
process at local, state and central levels; only in so far as legislatures
have to do with these matters—above all, through the operation of
parliamentary committees—have I touched upon them. I have also regarded much that is of interest in the working of cabinets as lying outside the scope of the present survey—though I have not been able to
avoid some comments on the role of Ministers in the assemblies of which
they are members. The omission of the courts and the judiciary was
more easily effected; even here, however, I have had to take note of instances where the working of parliament has come before the courts—
as in cases, for example, involving the position of the Speaker or the
privileges of members. Most difficult of all was the decision, reluctantly
taken, to say little on the electoral process which is a necessary preliminary to the very existence of legislatures. Yet to do that topic justice
would have entailed extensive first-hand observation or a co-operative
scheme of field studies; it would, in any case, have doubled the size of
the volume. For the most part, therefore, I took my legislators as I found
them, already past the hurdle of election; a study of their behaviour as
legislators throws some light on the stages by which they reached their

positions, but a study of the general election would perhaps do even more to explain their activities and characteristics in the legislatures. One more disclaimer: this book is in no way a guide to Indian parliamentary procedure; India's Erskine May will come later and must be prepared by someone who is continuously immersed in the day-to-day minutiae of parliamentary business.

The material used here is primarily the result of observations made and data collected during nine months' stay in India in 1953–54. I have made use of information relating to the whole period since 1947, but my main concern has been with the period since the inauguration of the new constitution in 1950 and the first general elections of 1951–52; it is above all an account of a part of the working constitution as it had developed by 1953–54. It is probable that many changes will take place even in the near future, but I believe that the main pattern of relationships and behaviour has been established and that changes will be restricted to modifications and developments of this established pattern.

The study devotes the greater part of its attention to the central Parliament (and there mostly to the Lower House). A tour covering all the 22 States possessing legislatures[1] was neither possible nor necessary, but I have made use of material gathered during visits to the assemblies of Bombay (classified in the Constitution as a 'Part A' State), Travancore-Cochin and Mysore ('Part B' States), and Delhi ('Part C' State). Since there is much uniformity between Centre and States in political behaviour and procedural arrangements, I have devoted no separate chapter to State legislatures.

Since Indian political institutions owe much to British experience, it has been difficult wholly to avoid at least implicit comparisons with British practice. Nevertheless, the attempt has been made, for it is certainly more important to measure political institutions and behaviour against national character and national needs. At the same time, it must be admitted that the two sets of tests are not unconnected. They are closely linked by the fact that many of the principles and standards of political philosophy which are embedded in British practice are widely shared by many of those who operate political institutions in India; and to that extent they constitute a part of 'national character and national needs.'

Many people have contributed to making this book possible and my debts are several and considerable:

to the London School of Economics, who granted me the year's study leave during which the work was prepared, and to my colleagues there who provided much encouragement in many forms;

[1] See pp. 100–101.

to the Rockefeller Foundation, whose generous travel grant made the collection of material possible;

to the late G. V. Mavalankar, Speaker of the House of the People up to his death in 1956, whose kind welcome ensured for me access to much valuable information and whose wise guidance must now be sorely missed;

to M. N. Kaul, Secretary of the House of the People, and his staff (in particular S. L. Shakdher, Joint Secretary), who placed every facility at my disposal and displayed great patience in answering the many questions I put to them;

to Ministers, members of legislatures and officials too numerous to mention, who found time—and always gracefully—to share with me their knowledge and judgment;

to friends in India (above all Sachin Chaudhury, Editor of *The Economic Weekly*) who have helped to nourish my interest and have shown me much that I might have missed;

to Dr. T. G. P. Spear, for reading most of the chapters and making useful suggestions;

to research assistants: Mr. K. Eaton, B.Sc. (Econ.), for extracting material, making sense of many statistics and making presentable many of the tables and charts; Sister Hedwige, Lecturer at Patna Women's College, who also extracted certain information; Mr. R. R. Setty, former Lecturer at Mysore University, who helped me with some of the members' biographies;

to typists: Miss Anderson and especially Miss E. Bond who deciphered patiently and intelligently;

above all, to my wife for her encouragement and help at all stages.

The responsibility for the result remains mine.

Durham
May, 1956.

CONTENTS

LIST OF TABLES

NOTES

2. *Terms*

(a) The use of the word parliament in the title of the book is inexact but convenient; it refers to the central Parliament and also to the State legislatures. In the text, I have distinguished between Parliament (the central legislature) and parliament (used to refer to legislative bodies generally).

(b) Before 1950 the units of India were provinces and princely states; since 1950 they have the uniform designation States.

(c) 'Centre' and 'Union' have been used interchangeably.

(d) During 1954, the desire to extend the use of Hindi led to the decision that the House of the People should be known as Lok Sabha and the Council of States as Rajya Sabha. Since these are simply Hindi translations of the English originals which remain in the English version of the Constitution, I have continued to use the latter.

CHAPTER ONE

THE NATURE OF INDIAN POLITICS

1. Introduction

THE dominating first impression of Indian politics which the foreign observer obtains is one of great complexity. A kitten has played with several threads, and since the ends seem to have disappeared it is difficult to know where to begin the work of disentangling. It is, of course, not only by her politics that India gives this impression; the enquirer whose interests are rather in religious mythology, or land tenures, or caste structure, or musical composition will quickly discover that intricacy is the key-note. The bewildering initial impact of an Indian bazaar on the tourist is not misleading.

Much of this impression is no doubt to be explained in terms of the strangeness and novelty of a different civilisation. The European senses fully the unity and distinctness of his civilisation when he moves outside it; just as, in a similar way, nothing causes an Indian to become more readily forgetful of the variety and divisions within India than a journey away from her shores. This strangeness of India to the Westerner is indicated by a well-known feature of European life in that country—the hated tendency for the whites to mix with their own kind; they seek the reassurance of the familiar, above all the familiar world of ideas. Of course, it is not to be denied that the exclusive clubs of the past owed much to a sense of superiority—however misplaced—and, even more, to a feeling that separateness was a political necessity, since only thus could the self-conscious corporate spirit of the rulers and the awe and respect of the ruled be safely preserved.[1] But even now when these corollaries of alien rule have disappeared, the search for the accustomed ways in an environment never wholly understood remains usual; the fact that the difficulty can be met by friendship with Westernised Indians serves only to underline the point. The Indian visitor to Europe has generally been in a stronger position, since his education in Western history and literature often warned him what to expect and made the new world more familiar. But it is true that the preparation was often misleading or at least less adequate than anticipated, and then the need to find a circle

---

[1] E. M. Forster's *Passage to India* still contains the last word on this particular subject, even if it is open to criticism on other aspects. See N. C. Chaudhuri, 'Passage to and from India', in *Encounter*, June 1954.

of one's own people became urgent; in any case, such advantage as there may have been is fast disappearing as school and college syllabi adjust themselves to national needs.

The degree of strangeness manifested by the various aspects of Indian life naturally varies with the extent to which they have felt the impact of Western influence. Most Westerners probably find a complete understanding of Indian music difficult, and it will take more than a little while for the European to master the ways of family and home life. Even in spheres where Western ways appear to have been all-conquering, the European may still be surprised. The analytical economist no doubt carries tools which will do their work with any kind of data, but his colleague, the applied economist, may have a series of shocks when he encounters, for example, the agricultural or even the industrial worker who does not respond to the usual incentives in the usual way, the employer who displays a seemingly odd reluctance to introduce labour-saving devices.

In the same way, the student of politics, too, is well advised to be on his guard. He should not assume, for instance, that institutions with familiar names are necessarily performing wholly familiar functions. He should be ready to detect political trends and forces in what he will be tempted to set aside as non-political movements. He should be prepared to find the behaviour of those who hold apparently familiar political positions conditioned by considerations which he would not normally associate with such places. Thus, to take only an obvious example, Gandhi was not primarily an individual eccentric and it was no accident that his evening prayer meetings were in effect an important part of Congress political machinery. Nor, as will be indicated more fully later, is it odd in terms of Indian politics that the leader of the Socialist Party should abandon 'politics' to dedicate his life to furthering and extending the work of the saintly Vinoba Bhave and his Bhoodan or Land-Gifts Mission.

The Western student of Indian politics who has at least reached the stage of realising that things are not always quite as they seem has a further temptation to overcome. Even after he has resisted the tourist's delight in imagining that he has found something 'just like it is at home', he may still seek to get his bearings in the strange world by establishing a series of intermediate reference points. Thus the British student will be inclined to say that he only needs to look across the Channel or over to America or back a little way in the history of his own country to find 'parallels'. Is it strange to find vivid contrast between the ways of life and the customs of the Punjab peasant and his counterpart in Travancore? Then we have only to remember that the United States contains within its boundaries the Californian fruit farmer of Italian origin, the Southern plantation owner and the prairie farmer who came from

Sweden. Does the whole texture and atmosphere of family life appear odd to one accustomed to the modern English home? But how the strangeness wears off when we think of the family in Italy or remember how our own grandparents spoke of the family in their day! Is it difficult to get used to the idea of a close interpenetration of religious thought and political behaviour? Surely not, if we stop for a moment and think of Spain and Ireland today, Wales yesterday or England last week. This method has its attractions (it may indeed be one of the ways we have to use in order to learn), and the comparisons may have a certain limited validity. But they are of necessity simplifications with a capacity to mislead. India is not any part of modern Europe, nor even any part of Europe in some chosen previous century; nor is it merely an undeveloped, primarily rural, agricultural country, nor merely a land where religions have left their deep marks; despite and because of Western influences, it is itself—a complex and even confusing but certainly distinct entity.

The sense of strangeness, then, is warranted. The complexity is not simply attributed by the unpractised eye of the observer; it is really present. It is the result, of course, of size and history. No country of its size and diversity of peoples could fail to be complex—unless, as is indeed by now conceivable, strong and ruthless power were able to impose simplicity. No country which has been subjected over a long period to a variety of deep influences on all aspects of its life[1] could be expected to remain simple. Our task here, however, is not to enquire into the causes of the complexity but simply to describe those aspects of it which bear on the character of Indian political life. This may be done by considering three topics: (a) the unity and diversity of India; (b) attitudes towards authority; (c) 'levels' of politics. Each of these topics frequently presents itself as a puzzling paradox to the student of Indian politics. Some understanding of the forces at work is desirable before we proceed to our study of a particular institution.

2. Unity

In formal political terms, the unity of India can be illustrated by reference to her constitution.[2] India is a Union of States,[3] and the indivi-

---

[1] Recognition of the importance of these outside influences does not imply endorsement of the view that 'whatever civilisation or social order flourished in India was the product of extra-Indian historical changes' (N. Chaudhuri, *Autobiography of an Unknown Indian*, 1952. The strictly autobiographical portions of Mr. Chaudhuri's book are thorough, valuable and fascinating; his views on Indian history, though sketchy and controversial, are always interesting.)

[2] *The Constitution of India* (Government of India, 1949). The Constitution came into force in 1950 and was first amended in 1951. Certain portions of the Constitution of particular relevance to the subject of this book are reproduced in Appendix I. See also Gledhill, *Republic of India*; Jennings, *Some Characteristics of the Indian Constitution* and *The Commonwealth in Asia*; Basu, *Commentary on the Constitution of India* (Calcutta, 1952).   [3] Art. 1 and the First Schedule.

dual constitutions of these States are set out as part of the Constitution of India[1] and as such can only be altered by the amendment procedure laid down in the Constitution.[2] The Parliament of India has exclusive power to make laws on the 97 subjects which appear on the 'Union List'—and these range from defence, foreign affairs and inter-state commerce to railways, civil aviation, patents and film censorship.[3] It has also the exclusive power to legislate on any matter not enumerated in the other two Lists of Concurrent and State Subjects—including the power to impose a tax not mentioned in those lists.[4] In case a State law is repugnant to a Union law, the latter prevails, unless the President gives special assent to the former.[5] Moreover, the Union Parliament is entitled, under a Proclamation of Emergency or on a resolution passed by a two-thirds majority of the Council of States, to invade the State List.[6] There is also an important provision empowering the centre to pass such legislation as may be required in order to give effect to international agreements.[7] Even more remarkable testimony to the constitutional unity of India is to be found in Articles 256 and 257 (1): 'The executive power of each State shall be so exercised as to ensure compliance with the laws made by Parliament and . . . [so] as not to impede or prejudice the exercise of the executive power of the Union, and the executive power of the Union shall extend to the giving of such directions to a State as may appear to the Government of India to be necessary for that purpose.'[8] The portions of the Constitution to which much attention has been directed in India are those which set out the 'Emergency Provisions'.[9] Of these the most noteworthy are not those which envisage threats to security but rather those that provide for the failure of constitutional machinery in the States and for a threat to the 'financial stability or credit of India or any part thereof'. If, for example, the President is satisfied from a report of a State Governor (who is appointed by him) that the constitutional machinery in the State has failed, he is empowered to assume to himself all the functions of the State, the powers of the State legislature may be exercised by the Union Parliament and any part of the constitutional machinery of the State may be

---

[1] Parts VI–VIII.   [2] Art. 368.
[3] Art. 246 (1) and the Seventh Schedule.   [4] Art. 248.
[5] Art. 254.

[6] Arts. 249 and 250. The Supply and Prices of Goods Act, 1950, is an example of an Act passed in pursuance of a resolution under Art. 249. Since there was, in 1950, only one House, the resolution 'to make laws with respect to certain matters enumerated on the State List' was simply passed by a two-thirds majority of that House (P.P. Deb., 12 Aug. 1950).

[7] Art. 253.

[8] There is a further provision enabling Parliament to confer powers and impose duties on States and States' officers. I am grateful to Mr. G. R. Rajagopaul, Joint Secretary, Ministry of Law, for pointing out instances of central Acts which 'give directions' and 'impose duties'.

[9] Part XVIII.

suspended.[1] Further clear indication of this constitutional unity is given by the absence of any dual system of courts (the judicial structure is an integrated whole competent to enforce Union as well as State laws) and the rejection of any kind of dual citizenship.[2] The financial provisions of the Constitution, even if no more than 'in accord with the general trend in other federations', do also play an important unifying role; 'the States, in view of their limited resources, must always look to the Centre for financial aid and thus will be following the dictation of the Union in all important financial and political matters'.[3] Finally, it is worth underlining[4] the fact that the Indian Union is far from being 'composed of indestructible States'; on the contrary, the States territories may be split up, reorganised, added to and reformed—and all this not by amendment of the Constitution but by simple law passed by Parliament.[5] In this way was the new State of Andhra created by the partition of Madras in October 1953.

Such a marked central bias, such a powerfully unified federal constitution, must clearly correspond to and flow from some firm and profound experience of unity. To realise that this is indeed the case, we have only to remember that India was, for about one hundred years, governed under a unitary system, and, further, that this period coincided with the rapid development of all means of communication. Centralisation, which was in so many ways for so long resisted in Britain, was effected, after a little hesitation, over the vast area of a sub-continent; the principle of hierarchy which was at least somewhat disguised at home was exported to India, there to shine in much glory. It is true that the princely states were, within certain limits, left alone, and that their area and population were considerable. Even there, however, it was on occasion difficult to know whether it was in the Palace, with the ruler and his ministers, or in the Residency nearby that the important decisions were taken—and the British Resident, for all the attachment and affection that he may have felt for the stately regime, was a member of the Indian Political Service accountable to the Viceroy of India. It is true also that towards the end of the period the process of transferring some responsibility from British to Indian hands had taken the form of a measure of provincial autonomy. 1919 already witnessed a partial delegation of power in certain subjects to elected provincial legislatures; the Act of 1935 introduced (with certain safeguards) full provincial autonomy with

[1] Punjab, P.E.P.S.U. (Patiala and Eastern Punjab States Union), Andhra and Travancore-Cochin have had periods of President's Rule, in 1951, 1953, 1954–55 and 1956 respectively.

[2] Art. 5.

[3] B. R. Misra, *Economic Aspects of the Indian Constitution* (Calcutta, 1952), p. 71.

[4] As did Mr. M. C. Setalvad, Advocate-General of India, in his paper on 'The Indian Federation' read to a conference on International Law held in Delhi in Dec. 1953.

[5] Art. 4 (2).

cabinets responsible to popular assemblies. But these latter-day innovations, most important as they were, could still scarcely efface or even
obscure the dominating political and administrative position of the
Indian Civil Service. Members of this *corps d'élite* occupied the leading
places from the district level—where they performed both administrative and judicial functions—up to the centre, where they were at once
the (permanent) secretaries as well as the members (or political heads)
of departments. They might be stationed at Trichinopoly or Peshawar
or Delhi, but they belonged to one service. They generally felt a responsibility for the welfare of the area placed in their charge, but they were
always accountable to a senior colleague placed a stage higher up 'the
steel frame'. They debated the pros and cons of centralisation and decentralisation,[1] but mainly from the viewpoint of administrative convenience.

Not all of the subjects of the Indian Empire, it is true, found it easy to
grasp the idea of an Indian nation. For the man in the village, even the
district town was still remote enough. But the politically relevant sections were naturally not so slow. It is noteworthy that the early stirrings
of modern political activity tended to be somewhat local in character:
witness the Bengal British Indian Society, the Servants of India Society
with its base in the intellectually lively centre of Maharashtra, Poona;
and, among religious reform movements, there was a distinctly Bengali
flavour about the influential Brahmo Samaj. But the national platform
came as soon as could be expected; in 1885, less than thirty years after
the Mutiny, the Indian National Congress held its first session, and the
work of creating a nation, rendered possible by common experience of
British law and order, was begun in earnest. The early demands of the
national movement were not such as to rouse all classes of the community, but they made as much sense to the professional and business
classes in Bombay as to their counterparts in Calcutta. The leaders of
the movement, for all the special appeal that they had in their own regions, were yet all-India figures. And when, with Gandhi, the roots of
the Congress were able to work downwards from the surface of society
to the different social soils below, the process was accomplished without
loss of national awareness; on the contrary, the fire of patriotism
burned more brightly than ever. There was a danger that in bringing
politics to the people, the leaders might find themselves prisoners of the
parochialism of the masses. If the demands had remained at the level of
the particular and the limited, this could indeed have happened. But the
cry of Swaraj captured the imagination of many levels of people, while
the interpretations given to it by district party workers enabled it to take
hold of many more. Above all, the symbolism of the spinning wheel and
the white cap, the disobedience march and the constructive programme

[1] As, for example, in the Report of the Decentralisation Commission (1909).

—all largely the products of Gandhi's exceptional political imagination
—gave a well-nigh universal rallying-point, where all could feel one and
from which it was possible for all to see a new world coming up over the
horizon. Nehru entitled his book *The Unity of India*, and Tagore sang[1]:

> Thou art the ruler of minds of all people,
> Thou Dispenser of India's destiny,
> Thy name rouses the heart of the Punjab, Sind,
> Gujarat, Maharashtra, Dravida, Orissa and Bengal;
> It echoes in the hills of the Vindhyas and Himalayas,
> Mingles in the music of Jumna and Ganges,
> And is chanted by the waves of the Indian Sea.

But if the framers of the Constitution had enjoyed the experiences of
unified rule and common revolt in the past, equally they were sharers in
certain common hopes and anxieties for the future; and the unitary
character of the Constitution flowed from both sets of factors. Many of
the anxieties came from a sense of uncertainty as to the strength of
centrifugal forces in the society—which we shall discuss presently; a
strong centre was in fact not only a reflection of an existing unity but
also a device designed to counter anticipated disunity.

One of the hopes of the constitution-makers was that with the 'surgi-
cal operation' of partition a source of weakness had been removed from
the Indian body politic. It had been evident for a decade that the
national movement had after all failed to gain the confidence of the
bulk of the Muslim community. It followed that if the Muslims remained as a political force in the state, it could only be at the cost of
radical concessions to their distrust, and a weak central government
would have been the first of such concessions. With the establishment of
Pakistan, Muslims would still be left in large numbers in India, but in a
politically deflated condition. The other potentially disintegrative forces
—'dynastic', communal and regional—could be contained and kept
under control, and in time further common experience of nationhood
and national reconstruction would reduce them to easily manageable
proportions. The policy of containment as well as that of national reconstruction demanded a strong centre.

So far as the threat to unity from 'dynastic' factors is concerned, it
can be said to have been completely overcome. The 562 princely states
have been securely integrated into the Indian Union.[2] No doubt

---

[1] This is now the Indian National Song. The verse given here (in Tagore's own translation) is still sung in its original form, including Sind, which is wholly Pakistan, and Punjab
and Bengal which have been divided.

[2] This should not perhaps be said of Kashmir so long as its future remains in dispute
between India and Pakistan. But although India still stands by the principle of a reference
to the people of the State to determine their future, in the meantime and especially since
the arrest of Kashmir's Premier, Sheikh Abdullah, and his replacement by Bakshi Ghulam
Mohammed, integration on economic, political and other lines has proceeded apace. On
the integration of the princely states in general, see the Government of India *White Paper
on Indian States* (1950) and Lumby, *The Transfer of Power* (1954), Chapter VI; on Kashmir,
Korbel, *Danger in Kashmir* (1954).

Congress leaders were deeply anxious during the summer of 1947. Paramountcy—the special relation of the rulers to the British Paramount Power—was not to be transferred to the new political leaders of India but was to lapse, so that the states were to become, as Lord Mountbatten put it, 'technically and legally independent'. The Minister of States, Sardar Patel, confessed in October 1949 that the situation in 1947 'was indeed fraught with immeasurable potentialities of disruption, for some rulers did wish to exercise their technical right to declare independence and others to join the neighbouring Dominion'.[1] The Butler Committee in 1929 had said that 'politically there are . . . two Indias. . . . The problem of statesmanship is to hold the two together.' But the makers of the new India believed firmly that India was politically one and that what was necessary was not a 'holding together' but a welding together.[2] By a judicious combination of tactful and persuasive public speeches on the one hand and a good deal of straight talking and shrewd bargaining on the other, a momentous political revolution was achieved. Kashmir presented (and continues to present) special difficulties, and the employment of force proved necessary in the cases of Hyderabad and Junagadh. But elsewhere the process suffered no serious check. From a modest request for accession to the Union in respect of Foreign Affairs, Defence and Communications and the conclusion of appropriate 'Standstill Agreements' governing administrative matters, the new Government moved steadily towards complete integration. A host of smaller states were simply merged into neighbouring provinces; a few were, for various special reasons, made into centrally-administered areas (or Part 'C' States); the rest—whether formed into unions of States or simply left as they were—became units of the new Republic, their constitutions part of the Indian Constitution, their powers the same as those of the former provinces, their status scarcely distinguishable except by the presence of a former ruler as Rajpramukh or Head of the State in place of a State Governor.[3] To consolidate the constitutional integration in financial, political and administrative terms takes a little longer; the backward condition of some of the states does not disappear overnight. But the confidence of Indian leaders appears to have been amply justified. There are surely political differences between Rajasthan and Bombay or between Punjab and P.E.P.S.U., but they are differences within a common order of political behaviour, no longer contrasts of regimes and political ways of life. It is not difficult to find in the former princely states a little nostalgia for the past, in some a certain wistful pride in the achievements of particular rulers or, more usually, their Ministers; and these attitudes are often combined with something approaching scorn

---

[1] Quoted in the White Paper, p. 123.   [2] *Ibid.*, p. 4.
[3] Even this distinction disappeared in the recommendations of the States Reorganisation Commission and in the subsequent States Reorganisation Bill introduced in Parliament in 1956. (See below, p. 24, n.)

for the newcomers to the political scene. But these sentiments have little independent political force[1]; the 'two Indias' have become very nearly one and the 'dynastic' threat is extinguished. The communal and regional threats we shall refer to below.

Of all the aspirations which dominated the makers of the Constitution, none was more important than that which centred on economic development. There might be very different ideas on the pace and methods of development, but there was unanimity on the priority to be given to raising the shockingly low living standards of the people. Everyone felt not only the suffering but also the shame which attached to India's poverty.[2] Some might see the solution in primarily Gandhian terms: the restoration of the village economy, making it more 'rounded' and balanced by the development of cottage industries. Others, their eyes glancing less at India's own past than at the world around them, simply saw what was required to enable India to catch up with others in the race for economic maturity: a 'normal' industrial revolution. What is important in the present context is that for all schools of thought alike,[3] the problem presented itself in all-India terms. The Indian economy was a unity, whether thought of as 700,000 villages or as an expanding pattern of steel works. Moreover, although different economic policies would no doubt in practice lead to quite different political consequences, there was very general agreement that Government direction and even participation would be called for, and that for this a strong centre was desirable. This did not entail too great a change of outlook for either rulers or ruled. The British Governments of India had not been noted for their economic enterprise, but at least whenever they felt that public control or even ownership was necessary (as they did, for example, with railways) they did not hesitate unduly on grounds of political propriety. Certainly, so far as the people were concerned, nothing was more natural than to 'look to Government'. The establishment of the Planning Commission in March 1950, charged among other things with the tasks of 'formulating a Plan for the most effective and balanced utilisation of the country's resources' and 'defining the stages in which the Plan should be carried out and proposing the allocation of resources for each stage', bore eloquent testimony to the new spirit. The pages of the

[1] This is not to say that the sense of distinctness has no influence when combined with other forces. It can, for example, reinforce anti-centre feelings; it can colour disputes and rivalries within unions of former princely states, such as Rajasthan and Madhya Bharat; it can affect the way in which some people approach the important question of the future reorganisation of states, supplying frequently a support for a conservative resistance to change.

[2] This in part explains the setting out of economic goals in the Constitution's *Directive Principles of State Policy*.

[3] I am not, of course, for a moment pretending to do justice to the rich variety of views on economic policy which are held in India. *The First Five Year Plan* (Government of India, Planning Commission, 1952) was at once a compromise between several of these and an expression of one.

Plan itself also indicate that the inherited economic unity of India is to be preserved and strengthened by unified political direction:

> In promoting capital formation on the required scale, in facilitating and in encouraging the introduction of new techniques, and in the overall re-alignment of the productive forces and class relationships within society, the State will have to play a crucial role. This need not involve complete nationalisation of the means of production or elimination of private agencies in agriculture or business and industry. It does, however, mean a progressive widening of the public sector and a re-orientation of the private sector to the needs of a planned economy.[1]

Again: 'The successful implementation of the Plan presupposes effective power in the hands of the State for determining policy and directing action along defined lines. . . .'[2]

This unified political direction, however, does not come easily; even with its central bias, Indian federalism imposes the methods of consultation and co-operation rather than those of dictation. 'In the field of policy', says the Plan, 'the Central and State Governments have to act in close co-operation with one another. . . . The implementation of the Plan depends vitally on the Central and State Governments conforming as closely as possible to the pattern of finance outlined.'[3] The Progress Report on the Plan for 1951–52 and 1952–53[4] makes the same point: 'Many vital parts of the Plan lie in the sphere of the States. The Centre can assist in many ways but, within the framework of the National Plan, the main responsibility for . . . [many schemes] . . . rests with the States. The Plan is a joint national enterprise in which the Centre and the States are partners, united in a common purpose and working with agreed policies in different fields of national development.' The sentence which follows that statement gives a hint of one of the difficulties: 'It is, therefore, important that both the Centre and State Governments should place their obligations towards the fulfilment of the Plan above all other claims.' This has to be read in conjunction with passages later in the Report, such as: 'Within this broad picture [of budgetary resources], there have been wide variations in performance not only between the Centre and the States but also as between the various States.'[5] Not only 'variations in performance' but even a certain amount of tough bargaining in which the States attempt to get as much Central aid for as little contribution to the whole—this is no more than is expected of federal arrangements, and is even characteristic of relations between local authorities and the central government in unitary

---

[1] *The First Five-Year Plan: A Summary*, p. 9.
[2] *Ibid.*, p. 2.
[3] *Ibid.*, pp. viii and 17.
[4] Government of India, Planning Commission, *Five-Year Plan Progress Report* (May 1953), p. ii.
[5] *Ibid.*, p. 7.

states. This kind of tension need not seriously impair the concept of economic unity. At times, however, it may develop attitudes and arguments which come very close to doing so. This may be illustrated by reference to a paper by Professor K. V. Rao on 'Centre–State Relations in Theory and Practice'.[1] His thesis is that the Constitution is already being operated in a manner and spirit contrary to the clear intentions of its framers and that there is a growing 'centralisation of initiative' which is reducing the States to mere 'administrative units'. He claims that the Planning Commission in particular has in practice become much more than a co-ordinating body, a veritable 'super-Cabinet'. Even the independent Finance Commission charged with the allocation of central grants is reduced, it is argued, to the position of a servant of the Planning Commission: 'instead of adopting an independent line of approach of allocating grants on the *inherent needs* of the Units depending upon their economic condition and need for funds for development, the Finance Commission assessed the needs as decided by the projects in hand and the *immediate necessity* for funds'[2]—as in effect already determined by the Planning Commission in its sanctioning of schemes. We are not here concerned with the debate regarding the nature of the impact of the Plan on government and administration[3]; it is simply necessary to point out that the concept of economic unity, firmly inherited from the British and enshrined in the Plan, is not free from attack.

The partition of India showed that an economic unity could be shattered on rocks of political antagonism and distrust. The mere existence of a centrally-biased Constitution and a National Plan might alone be insufficient to avoid further difficulties. But the two inherited political unities (which we have already indicated as important parts of the base on which the Constitution was founded) have remained largely intact: the unity of the higher administrative service and the unity of the principal political party. The structural pattern of the old I.C.S. has been repeated in the new Indian Administrative Service—the pattern, that is, of an all-India service which is called upon to staff not only posts at the Centre but also the more important positions at State and District levels—and this pattern is also maintained in a number of specialist all-India services. The members of these services continue to think much

[1] Read to the Annual Conference of the Indian Political Science Association in Dec. 1953 and published in part as an article in *The Indian Journal of Political Science*, Oct.–Dec. 1953.

[2] Italics in original.

[3] The reply of the Planning Commission on the particular point would no doubt be that it is a gross overstatement to speak of a loss of State initiative when the Plan is built up of State Plans and the schemes sanctioned are framed and proposed by the States. A view directly opposed to that of Professor Rao is expressed by Paul Appleby in *Public Administration in India: a Report of a Survey* (1953). See also the admirable *Report on Public Administration* (1951) by A. D. Gorwala. A balanced review of the problems is provided by M. Venkatarangaiya, 'The Pattern of Public Administration in the Five-Year Plan', in *The Indian Journal of Political Science*, July–Sept. 1953.

more in terms of the administrative unity of the country than would State-recruited services. Moreover, although they may not be as proudly aware of their distinctness and responsibility as were their British colleagues, yet it is remarkable how little the attitudes and frame of mind have changed. The cast of mind of the higher civil servant is still distinctive and he still tends, for reasons of taste and convenience, to restrict his social intercourse to the circle of his fellows; his sense of responsibility has remained very little dimmed in spite of some discouragement, especially at the State level, from unsympathetic or partial Ministers.[1] It is to be noted, too, that the area of influence of the members of this corps has increased rather than decreased. In spite of the chagrin caused in business and specialist circles, it has been primarily members of the I.C.S. who have been called upon to fill the top posts in new public undertakings such as the Airways Corporation and the new River Valley Corporations. In the same way, they hold places on the boards of other enterprises in which the state, by ownership of a portion of the shares, has taken control. Thus both in the traditional spheres of civil service activity—the districts, the State capitals and Delhi[2]—and in the new directions of governmental enterprise, as well as in any emergency work of vital importance (the re-establishment and reorganisation of government in Hyderabad and the reinforcement of administration in States such as Rajasthan are but two examples), it is this exceptional body of still exceptional men who are called upon. And their contribution is, by virtue of their training and outlook, a powerful unifying force. It is too soon to say just how much of this inheritance they are now passing on to the new recruits to the Indian Administrative Service.

At least as important as a force of unity is the party structure in Indian politics. This topic is considered in some detail in Chapter IV; at this point, a few preliminary observations will be sufficient. The party structure acts as a unifying force in two ways. In the first place, the important political parties are all-India parties. Out of 689 seats in the two

[1] Evidence is not easily set out, but frequent conversations with those concerned leave this unmistakable impression. For the politician's attitude to civil servants, see below, p. 152.

[2] They are traditional spheres, but there has been, of course, a very great increase in the amount of work at all levels and in its complexity. Mr. Paul Appleby (in his *Public Administration in India: a Report of a Survey* (1953), p. 1) has put the point well: 'In America we properly hallow the memories of the great leaders who at the time of our national beginnings coped with difficulties probably no greater than, if indeed equal to, those that would have been faced in India even in 1900. Yet . . . the times now are much more complex. . . . Not independence and self-government alone are the objectives, but such a government dedicated to achievement of mass welfare at a tempo never attained anywhere at the same stage of economic development. History provides no near precedent for what is being undertaken here.' Moreover, most of this additional burden seems to fall on the higher civil servants; it is only too easy to recruit a number of extra clerks, but additional personnel capable of exercising significant administrative discretion are scarce. This is indeed part of a more general impression that the outsider obtains in India: above a certain level, too much is depending on too few; below it, too little depends on far too many.

Houses of the central Parliament, 595 were in 1952 held by all-India parties. Even at the State level, of the 3,283 seats in all State assemblies no less than 2,660 were held by all-India parties.[1] With a few exceptions (for example, Jharkhand Party in Bihar, Ganatantra Parishad in Orissa, Akalis in P.E.P.S.U.) local State parties did not prove attractive to the electorate. Nor is this surprising. Indian federalism was born not of a coming together of independent states but of a loosening of control and power by a unified state, and the main political parties have their origins in the period of unity. If there had been more than two years of provincial autonomy before the war, it might have made some difference; it is certainly possible that now with independence won, State politics may be able to breed State parties, but the tendencies are not yet conclusively clear. The party structure may be seen as a unifying force in a second sense: not only are all important parties all-India parties but one all-India party in particular has an overwhelmingly dominant position. The Congress Party won 508 seats out of the 689 in the two Houses at the centre, and 2,247 out of a total of 3,283 seats in the State legislatures. Only in one State out of 22 with governments responsible to local legislatures has there been a non-Congress government in power; it was a minority Praja Socialist Party (P.S.P.) government in Travancore-Cochin dependent on Congress support.[2] The political scene is dominated by a party which inherits the traditions of a united national movement and reflects these in its rather centralised internal structure.

A nation often becomes aware of its unity less by introspection than by looking at its neighbours. The greater the internal variety and tension, the more consolation is to be obtained by concentrating attention on the contrast with outsiders; doubt about having anything in common with one's fellow citizens may be quickly set at rest by crossing a frontier.[3] In the years before independence, Indian emphasis on the unity of the country was primarily connected with a defence of the comprehensive character of the national movement against the supposed attempts of the British to exploit differences; since independence, unity has been stressed mainly to counter centrifugal forces. But the position of India *vis-à-vis* other nations also plays a part in the concept of unity. In India's case this is less a negative matter of hiding internal differences by accentuating external contrasts than a positive desire that a felt

---

[1] The figures would be even more conclusive if no account were taken of the large number of Independents. Election figures are set out below, Chapter II, Section 4.

[2] In Dec. 1954 the Congress withdrew its support and the Government fell in Feb. 1955, to be replaced by a Congress Government. Not all Congress Governments, however, are stable. See below, Chapter III, Section 1.

[3] Pakistan furnishes perhaps an exceptional example of this process. The gap which in almost every sense exists between Eastern and Western wings of the country explains much of the anxious desire to keep in view the contrasts with India. But the Western Pakistani appears to be more completely reassured by this method than his fellow citizen from the East.

national character should achieve international expression. One of the many irritations which attached to British rule was that which resulted from India's inability to show herself to the world as a distinct personality on the international scene. It is not surprising, therefore, that one of the first preoccupations of independent India has been the establishment and pursuance of a distinctive foreign policy. She has become aware of herself more than before as a part of Asia, and she is exploring to discover common political ground in that region. At the same time, she sees herself as a special part of Asia, peculiarly qualified, for example, to act as interpreter between Asia and the West. But a foreign policy may not only flow from a coherent national character; its pursuit in turn reacts back on the internal political situation.[1] In this respect nothing is clearer than that the foreign policies pursued by Pandit Nehru have not simply received widespread approval in India but have served to strengthen the sense of national unanimity and unity. Critics of the right who suspect tenderness and weakness towards Pakistan and critics of the left who distrust the Commonwealth and other links with the West have alike failed to make any deep and lasting impression.[2] This success enhances the unity it expresses.

To point out political and economic factors making for the unity of India is important, but is still not the whole story; it may be the less important part, even for a work concerned with political institutions. For while it is true that religion was the ground on which the political movement for the partition of the old India based itself, at the same time religion is also the ground on which much of the political coherence of the new India rests. The casual visitor who encounters the young Westernised Indian who is hazy about his gods and has even forgotten the more vivid stories from Hindu mythology may be tempted to believe that modern India is a post-Hindu civilisation in the sense in which modern Europe has been described as a post-Christian civilisation, living on its spiritual capital. But he would not need to go far to get his ideas corrected. It would be enough to penetrate into the same young man's home and meet his wife or, more convincing still, his mother. It would be enough to keep one's eyes open, even in the large cosmopolitan city of Bombay:

> We enter a winding street, lined with little one- and two-storey houses, like warped and tottering bird-cages, . . . and what look like garages or stables: the temples. Deep in the shadows, an altar is illuminated. Red and gold cloth behind the statuette, jewels, flowers, little glass trinkets, and in the narrow space before the altar a woman standing, motionless. Sometimes

[1] Two extreme possibilities are fairly familiar: the foreign policy (usually aggressive in tone if not in intent) which is designed to distract attention from contentious home policies; and the foreign policy which results in aggravating internal difficulties.

[2] I do not wish to suggest that Indian foreign policy is framed solely in order to produce these results.

the priest in a loin-cloth emerges from a dark corner to set two little sticks of burning incense down beside a low fountain in the little courtyard. . . . Little noise, and not a single smile. A temple bell rings, unmusically. One hears the shuffling of bare feet, the swish of pink, violet, and pale-green saris. . . . Here and there a man prays, squatting against a wall. . . . Everything is delicate, feline, miserable, precious, all at once. . . . A little further on, where the street turns and grows lighter, towards the black rocks and lowlands along the seashore, a group of seated men are listening to a man reading aloud. . . . It is part of the Mahabharata. Young and old, his hearers listen motionlessly to the book from which Gandhi read passages to his disciples every night. I do not know if I have ever seen anything more touching, or a group of men more simple and dignified in the act of hearing a poem.[1]

That is Bombay, but it could be any town of any size in any part of India.

In fact, religion—when once the outsider has learnt to recognise it— is everywhere: in the small family pilgrimages to Himalayan shrines, in the mass gatherings at holy places (the 1954 Allahabad Kumbh Mela was attended by about four and a half million people[2]), in the family and social celebrations of the festivals, in the cheap editions of sacred books read in the trains and by the lift-boys, in the glossy, gaudy pictures of a Krishna hung in a million tea and coffee stalls. It is not always easy to know what the impact of all this may be, for religion in India is not only most public but also most private. Denis de Rougemont, in the article just quoted, has put the point well: 'In this country where streets swarm dizzyingly, where . . . there are too many people everywhere; in this country which does not believe in the individual as an absolute, and seems dedicated to the collectivity, devotions and religion are individualistic.' The Hindu does not preach to the outsider; rarely does he even expound—and then only to a private circle. The religion is almost as inaccessible as it is obtrusive; but its impact certainly cannot be negligible. To repeat that it is the ground on which rests much of the political coherence of the country must not be taken to mean that India is a religious and not a secular state. Its influence is not so much direct—the openly communal political parties have not fared well—as indirect. In the first place, not only is religion everywhere but everywhere it is very largely the same religion: the variety of languages does not prevent the same sayings being recited, the same stories told from Amritsar to Cape Comorin; the regions may tend to have favourites among the gods and goddesses, but the pantheon is open to all. In the second place, although the religion does much to divide by caste, it does something to unite by occupation and even class; it will not be strange if among the men we

[1] From Denis de Rougemont, 'Looking for India', in *Encounter*, Vol. I, No. 1. Reprinted by permission.

[2] The Kumbh Mela takes place every twelve years. A good description of the 1930 gathering is given in Robert Byron, *An Essay on India* (1931), pp. 59–64. This often perceptive little book has received less attention than it deserves.

find at Benares, dipping prayerfully in the Ganges at dawn, there is the landlord, the teacher and the insurance agent. Religion in India, that is to say, has more than a power to divide; it has also the power to unite— by providing a common language across the different regions, by supplying a common way of thought and behaviour across certain social gaps.

3. Diversity

The centrifugal character of political forces is the oldest and the newest feature of Indian political life. The well-known failure of the earlier empires to establish effective and lasting control over the whole of the sub-continent was due in great part to the insufficiency of power at their disposal and to various internal weaknesses. But 'insufficiency of power' is a relative matter, and it is clear that the failure owed something to the strength of resistance of the small local kingdoms and their reluctance to be assimilated. Whatever the causes, the result of the failure was certainly that regional distinctness was firmly maintained. This distinctness was obscured during British rule and submerged in the national movement. With the achievement of independence it asserts itself once again.

British rule gave no precise recognition to the regions of India. In the early days of the Company it simply encountered kingdoms—the Moghul Empire, its provincial governors enjoying much independent political power, and a number of separate kingdoms mainly in the south. The Company extended its territories by treaties and conquests—at first only when necessity demanded, later whenever opportunity arose or could be created. When policy changed again and the remaining princes were confirmed in the areas they held, the result was to 'freeze' the map of India in the familiar curious pattern of red and yellow patches, few of which corresponded either to the ancient kingdoms or to the cultural regions. The whole was firmly held together until it became desirable to make concessions and yield some powers to nationalist discontent.[1] When this happened, it seemed natural to start the process at levels lower than the centre—by the introduction of local self-government and by measures of provincial autonomy.[2] This policy, combined with the desire to 'hold together' the princely states, led to the attempt in 1935 to create a federal constitution. The attempt broke on the intransigence of

[1] Or, as those concerned would have said, to give to certain groups of Indian subjects opportunities for the exercise of some responsibility and the enjoyment of some measure of association with the processes of government.

[2] The important dates are 1861 (formation or restoration of Provincial Legislative Councils), 1882 (Lord Ripon's Resolution on Local Self-Government), 1892 and 1909 (expansion of Provincial Councils) and 1919 (a measure of Provincial autonomy). Although these measures were accompanied by expanded councils at the centre too, they did not satisfy all sections of nationalist opinion (see also Chap. II). It has been suggested recently that the policy of conceding first the local levels was unwise. (See T. G. P. Spear, in *Asian* (then *Asiatic*) *Review*, April 1951.)

the states, but it nevertheless dictated the terms in which India's constitution-makers saw their problems in 1947.

It is worth while asking why the leaders of Indian nationalism, when they came to power and found the Muslim urge for separation removed by partition, still did not try to establish a unitary constitution. Did they themselves after all not quite believe all they had claimed about 'the unity of India'? Part of the answer is no doubt that in most work of constitutional construction, builders do not start from nothing; the foundations have been laid already and are not easily upset. However attractive might appear the constitutional experiments of other countries or the schemes of visionary political thinkers, they could not easily compete in influence with the simple fact that an elaborate and carefully worked out federal constitution for India already existed in the form of the 1935 Act. Nor was it simply a matter of taking what lay to hand; the problems which the 1935 constitution was designed to solve had not disappeared with the transfer of power. However optimistic the leaders might be with regard to the integration of the princely states, they would clearly have invited difficulties if they had offered only a unitary constitution; it was necessary at least to start with federalism, even if one cherished the hope that it would become increasingly unitary in character.

But it was not only the princes who had to be accommodated. The Acts of 1919 and 1935 may have been fiercely criticised for being timid and negligible concessions in relation to the demands made at the time, but they effected an important change in Indian political life: they introduced on to the stage the provincial politician. The provincial assemblies of the 1920s may not have been popular bodies and the fact that the nationalist movement's attitude to them as institutions was generally hostile no doubt robbed them of much value. But even at that stage they served to introduce the idea of provincial affairs, even the beginnings of a provincial platform. The provincial elections of 1936, fought on a wider franchise and vigorously contested by the Congress, deepened this experience to the point of transferring it from the margins of political life to the centre. Congress governments were formed in seven out of eleven provinces, and if they were in power for only two years it was nevertheless long enough to communicate to those concerned a lively sense of the value of provincial autonomy. Not only the holders of ministerial office during 1937–39 but also the members of the provincial legislatures during that period came to appreciate the scope and importance of government at the provincial level. It was unlikely that these men, when they came to form a significant proportion of the members of the Constituent Assembly in 1948–49, would allow much talk of a purely unitary constitution.

Yet it would be misleading to present India's federal constitution as

2—P.I.

a concession to the selfish political interests of princely states and of provinces which happened to be sufficiently strong at the time of constitution-making.[1] Rather, it was recognised that these interests corresponded (or at least bore some relation) to actual differences and variations between regions. There might be disagreement as to which areas really deserved the distinction of region and there would certainly be dispute about the regional boundaries. There might even be a feeling that to talk too much about regions savoured of a lack of patriotic sentiment. Yet no one could doubt that certain fairly well-defined regions with their own marked characteristics existed.

One of the extraordinary gaps in the literature of sociology in India is the absence of any study of these regional groups. Everyone knows they exist, but they are nowhere comprehensively described. The probable reason for this gap is significant; few people are sufficiently acquainted with their neighbours across regional boundaries. It is true that some of the big cities are cosmopolitan—in the sense that employment has attracted men from all parts of India: Madras much less than Delhi, Bombay or Calcutta. But it is striking to notice that, apart from the exigencies of work or business, few things cause the regional groups to mix. Outside office hours, the Bengali in business in Bombay, the Tamil in a government job at Delhi will meet almost invariably fellow Bengalis, fellow Tamils. At all-India conferences and gatherings, delegates when left to themselves quickly form regional groups—a little knot of Malayalees, a compact circle from Bihar. And, indeed, what could be more natural? It is, firstly and above all, a matter of language: a language other than one's own mother tongue has a dampening effect on social intercourse; Hindi (except in the regions where it is itself a mother-tongue—that is, in the north-central zone) is not yet widely used except perhaps in the more ordinary transactions; English is still available to many but, except for very few, it is not really fun.[2] With a language goes a way of speaking, a way of making jokes, a whole common world of

---

[1] It is true that they were what some would call 'vested interests'; vested interests certainly arise among political groups as well as from economic. It is the daily business of governments to reconcile them. I would go further and argue that, while it is not normally the business of governments to create them, even this can be a proper task. In any society, there will be certain energies of a political character which seek outlets. Whether these energies are considerable or insignificant varies from one period to another and from one society to another in accordance with a host of factors, including, for example, the extent and variety of ordinary employment opportunities. What is important for the political health of society is that its institutions should be such as will conveniently and usefully harness these energies and avoid their frustration. This is an important justification of federal constitutions and even of local institutions in a unitary state.

[2] It is instructive to see how a conversation often becomes either solemn or forced when English is imposed. Conversely, so to speak, it is noticeable how often English is resorted to when serious or technical subjects are discussed or when it is desired to convey an impression of knowledge, experience or achievement. It is generally admitted, moreover, that standards of English are falling quite rapidly; as a medium of instruction its place is shrinking, as a subject of study it has become less popular.

allusions and references so necessary to easy and enjoyable intercourse. As in Europe, only a tiny few are 'at home' in a language other than their own; a Gujarati girl married to a Punjabi will achieve this state—but such marriages between regions are rare. It is also a matter of a shared acquaintance with people and places and the possibility of communicating common memories of family and childhood. For the cultivated, it will be a matter of a common literary and musical heritage—though admittedly this is less important for some regions (Punjab, Gujarat perhaps) than for others. It is even a question of food—not unimportant where social intercourse is concerned. Even the European quickly learns to distinguish between the dishes of Kashmir and those of Madras, the cooking of Maharashtra and that of Bengal; the Indian's preference for his own region's food will often amount to a great distaste for that of others. Distinctive forms of dress (in part related to contrasting climates), festivals that have a peculiar regional significance, different codes of family and social behaviour, special attachment to regional heroes and episodes of the past—all this and much more goes to make vivid and profound the contrasts that exist between one part of India and another.

These regional differences have grown considerably in political importance since the transfer of power. The vigour of their political expression through provincial autonomy under the 1935 Act was subdued by a deeper loyalty to the struggle against alien rule. This check was removed by independence, and no equivalent substitute has yet taken its place. As we have seen, the federal Constitution is a centralised one, there is a National Plan for the development of the whole country's resources, there is a sense of India's place as a nation among the nations; but as binding forces these are still not so powerful as the battle for freedom. Regional awareness in political terms expresses itself partly through the tensions between the States and the Centre. We have already indicated an example in the case of the operation of the Plan. A number of other instances would be provided by a comprehensive administrative history of Centre–State relations; the difficulties in the way of coherent and effective policies with regard to food and refugees are only two of the better-known cases.

There can be no doubt that friction would have been more frequent as well as more serious if it were not for the all-India spirit of the leading administrators. Without access to the departmental files it is not easy to supply evidence of this influence, but one may be sure that their presence, for example at the frequent Centre–State departmental conferences,[1] makes it easier for decisions to emerge—and subsequently to be

[1] In answer to a question in Parliament on 2 Feb. 1949 the Minister of Agriculture paid tribute to the value of such conferences to informal co-ordination between Centre and the States. He stated that four such conferences had been held by his department during 1948. Other departments concerned with State or concurrent subjects have similar meetings.

implemented. There can be even less doubt that Centre–State relations
have been facilitated by the political omnipresence of the Congress
Party. When the party in power at the Centre is different from that in
command of a State, Centre–State relations do not simply become
difficult; worse, they provide an important arena for the expression of
party rivalry. India has largely been spared that problem during the infant years of its independence. The relations between Union and State
Ministers are at the same time relations between former colleagues of
the days of national struggle. Moreover, Nehru's position as President
of the Congress as well as Prime Minister helped greatly to smooth out
incipient quarrels.[1] Not only the course of a State government's actions
but even its very life has sometimes been largely decided and determined
by organs of the party at the Centre. It is uncertain how strong these two
checks on Union–State frictions can remain. Certainly Congress, even if
it retains control at the Centre, cannot hope to have for long its rule in
all the States. Already, in 1954, a Praja Socialist Government was installed in Travancore–Cochin—though this is hardly a test case, since
its members were at least former Congressmen and the Government
rested on Congress support in the State Legislature.

But the picture of the political expression of regionalism cannot be
conveyed simply in terms of Union–State relations. As already mentioned, the pattern of provinces and princely states which emerged under
British rule bore little relation to the cultural regions—though the formation in turn during the first half of the present century of the N.W.
Frontier Province, Assam, Bihar, Sind and Orissa was certainly a significant move in this direction. Moreover, the establishment of units on
a linguistic basis had not only been approved by the Montagu-Chelmsford and Simon Reports[2] but had been for long a point in the Congress
programme. The party had expressed its support for the idea not only in

---

[1] Nehru was Congress President from Sept. 1951 to Dec. 1954. In the manner of his
coming to the office and his leaving it, the strength of his position was revealed. In 1951,
Nehru had serious disagreements with the then President of the Congress, Purshottamdas
Tandon. Tandon was known to be conservative in social policies and insufficiently hostile
towards communal sentiments. When Nehru submitted to the All-India Congress Committee his resignation from the Working Committee, other members of the Working Committee quickly followed suit. When Tandon himself accepted defeat and resigned, Nehru
was at once chosen to take his place. In Oct. 1954, Nehru complained of an excessive burden of work and announced his intention to give up at least the party office. This he did in
December. Nehru's Working Committee recommended U. N. Dhebar as his successor, and
he was the only person nominated.
    The smoothing-out process could, from the viewpoint of Centre–State relations, work
in either direction. More usually, no doubt, the Prime Minister was able to use his Presidential prestige and influence to secure State acceptance for Central proposals. But it was
on occasion suggested that certain Chief Ministers of States had been getting too much of
their own way, largely because Nehru, in his capacity as President of Congress, had been
uncomfortably aware of their value to the party in the State. On the whole question of
party–government relations, see below, Chapter IV.
    [2] *Report on Indian Constitutional Reforms* (Cmd. 9109 of 1918), para. 246.
    Report of the Indian Statutory Commission (Cmd. 3569 of 1930), Vol. II, para. 38.

resolutions but also by basing its own organisation at least to some extent on such units: its constitution (since 1921) included Pradesh (or State) Committees for such areas as Kerala, Maharashtra, Tamil-Nad and Andhra. The 'Nehru' Report of 1928[1] strongly emphasised the desirability of creating new units on these lines, the policy had been included in the party manifesto, and in the Constitutent Assembly in November 1947 the Prime Minister on behalf of the Government accepted the principle underlying the demand. Given these two facts—that some of the peoples of India could be regarded as having already achieved a measure of autonomy in their homelands (the Biharis, the Bengalis, the Oriyas, etc.), and that linguistic units had been part of the national movement's programme, it is not surprising that the Constituent Assembly was faced at once with the demand that such units be created for all parts of India and that this should be done before the new Constitution was completed. Nor is it surprising that on the demand being refused, the issue has disturbed Indian politics and consumed considerable political energy. Nowhere is the impact of India's diversity and internal divisions on her political life clearer than in the history of the agitation among regional groups for their separate linguistic units. It merits a slightly closer examination.

This question has been the subject of three recent investigations. It was referred first by the Constituent Assembly to a Linguistic Provinces Commission which reported in December 1948.[2] Its conclusions were firmly against the formation of new units. It recognised that the demand had received important support in the past and that the subject had gathered around it much 'heat and passion and controversy'. It understood the case for the new units to rest on two alternative grounds: 'on the theory that these linguistic groups are sub-nations and as such contracting parties to the constitution . . .'or on 'the unwieldy size of the existing provinces, their heterogeneous composition and the administrative advantage which may result from bringing together people speaking one language, in imparting education and in the working of courts, legislatures, governmental machinery and democratic institutions'. The Commission found, however, that the sub-nation theory took

---

[1] *Report of the Committee appointed by the All-Parties Conference*, 1928. The Chairman was Motilal Nehru, father of Jawaharlal.

[2] The Commission is known by the name of its Chairman, S. K. Dar, retired Judge of the Allahabad High Court. Its report is published in *Reports of Committees of the Constituent Assembly (Third Series)*, 1950, at pp. 180–239. The Commission was limited by its terms of reference to the four possible Southern India units of Andhra, Karnataka, Kerala and Maharashtra, but the analysis it made has a wider relevance. Within that geographical scope, its terms of reference were wide: 'to examine and report on the formation of [these] new Provinces . . . and on the administrative, financial and other consequences of their creation'. Moreover, the tone of the press communiqué issued at the time suggests that the formation, of some at least of these new units, was expected: the Commission was 'to submit its report in time to enable the new States . . . to be mentioned in the First Schedule to the Draft Constitution before the Constitution is finally adopted'.

inadequate notice of the last two hundred years; the existing provinces had 'taken root and are now living, vital organisms' and whatever sub-nations might have once existed had now been assimilated with them. Moreover, since in no area do linguistic groups form more than 80% of the population, minorities cannot be avoided—and minorities in states created on specifically linguistic grounds would find matters far from pleasant. But above all, the Commission held, linguistic units will obstruct the spread of a national language and of national feeling—'nationalism and sub-nationalism are two emotional experiences which grow at each other's expense'—and Indian nationalism is too recent a growth (and too recently relieved of its main stimulus) to be able to stand such a strain. No doubt, in view of the intensity of feeling on the subject, to refuse the demands would cause much frustration; it was 'a grave risk', but one that had to be taken. Certainly there could be no question of new units being formed immediately: India was just recovering from partition, it was 'in the midst of an undeclared war with Pakistan', it had food and refugee problems to solve, its administration was 'depleted and over-strained'; and 'as if these anxieties were not sufficient, India is about to experiment with a new Constitution with autonomous States and adult franchise without the cementing force of a national language to take the place of English'.

The Dar Commission expressed the view that, in view of the dangers, it was not enough for India's political leadership merely to refrain from further support of the agitation; it had to 'rise to the occasion and guide the country to its duty', and for this purpose it should regard the changed circumstances as 'relieving it of all past commitments'. The Congress did promptly appoint its own committee[1] to go into the matter. It had the courage to accept the general view of the Dar report and it expressed once more the dangers to national unity implied in the encouragement of new loyalties. At the same time, it indicated the measure of feeling for the agitation by making two significant concessions: first, 'the case of Andhra can be isolated from others in that . . . there appears to be a larger measure of consent behind it, and the largest compact area likely to form part of this linguistic province is situated within one (existing) province'; second, it conceded that 'if public sentiment is insistent and overwhelming, the practicability of satisfying public demand with its implications and consequences must be examined'.

These concessions were naturally soon interpreted by those concerned as invitations to quicken the tempo of agitation. Congress ranks were divided on the issue, while of the other parties the Communists did not hesitate to make the demands an important part of their election campaigning in the south. In Andhra, in particular, feelings intensified to a

[1] The members were Sardar Patel, Dr. Sitaramayya and Pandit Nehru. Appointed at the Jaipur Congress session of Dec. 1948, it presented its report in April 1949 (Indian National Congress, *Report of the Linguistic Provinces Committee*, 1949).

point where government in the State of Madras became dominated and rendered difficult by the demands. The agitation approached a climax when one of the ardent devotees of the campaign began a fast unto death; the climax was reached when he died. Four days afterwards, on 19 December 1952, the Prime Minister announced to Parliament the Government's decision to form a State of Andhra by the partition of Madras. This was done and the new linguistic State of the Telugu people was born in October 1953. But this step brought little peace. The politics of Andhra since its formation have been stormy in the extreme; sub-regional tensions (anticipated by the Dar Commission) have now found scope for vigorous expression (on the question of the location of the capital, for example) and, when combined with deep caste divisions and a delicate balance among the political parties, produce an intricate tangle in which the common purposes even of Andhra become easily lost. Outside Andhra, of course, appetities—whether crude hunger for office and opportunity or idealised longings for liberation—have been considerably whetted. Party capital can still be made of all this by the Communists, while ugly rifts appear in the State Congress parties and even in their governments. The appointment of a fresh Commission in 1954[1] relieved the Union Government for a while of the necessity to take any further decisions, but the campaign by no means abated. On the contrary, protagonists and opponents of linguistic states alike marshalled every line of argument and every ounce of strength in order to influence the Commission in their direction. The result was a continued strain on party solidarity and on the smooth working of State governments. The Congress Working Committee considered the matter serious enough to warrant the issue of a directive banning party members from joining any agitation for linguistic states and permitting only the submission of memoranda and representations to the Commission. But this did little to lessen the strain. At most it kept up appearances—and not always was it successful even in that. In Madhya Pradesh, for example, the de- mand of the Marathi-speaking areas for a state of Maharashtra re- mained strong; two senior officials of the State Congress Party went so far as to prepare a memorandum alleging discrimination by the State government in favour of the Hindi areas—a document at once de- scribed by the Chief Minister of the State (also a Congressman, of course) as 'misleading, baseless, mischievous and anti-national'. In

---

[1] The announcement was actually on 22 Dec. 1953. It was made before an eagerly ex- pectant House and was well received. The members were Saiyid Fazi Ali (former Judge and lately Governor of Orissa), Sardar Panikkar (formerly Minister for a princely state and lately Ambassador to China and Egypt) and Pandit Kunzru (veteran independent parlia- mentarian). It was expressly charged to bear in mind the preservation and strengthening of the unity of India and the financial, economic and administrative problems affecting the whole country. It should also be noted that its survey was not limited to the possibility of linguistic states; it was free to consider any form of reorganisation, and its title was the Central Commission for the Reorganisation of States.

Bombay, too, considerable difficulties were encountered. The President of the State Party had to call for explanations from a large number of party members who convened a conference to support the division of Bombay State, the disintegration of Hyderabad and the inclusion of Bombay City in Maharashtra. Nor was the Congress Party the only one to be affected; similar rifts appeared in the Praja Socialist Party, especially on the question of the future of Bombay City.

The Commission reported in October 1955 and recommended radical changes. The distinction between Part 'A', Part 'B' and Part 'C' States was to disappear and the new pattern of units made big concessions to linguistic divisions.[1] These proposals, however, still fell short of the demands of powerful political groups. Unrest, ministerial resignations and even considerable violence followed. The Congress Working Committee and the Government felt obliged to make further concessions which were embodied in the States Reorganisation Bill, 1956.[2] It has been said that India must indeed be strong to be able to effect such reorganisation; but it is clear that the Government has been quite unable to resist the pressures of regional sentiment. These have operated somewhat independently of party and class divisions and have proved most powerful. Their victory is unlikely to reduce their vigour; on the contrary, inter-State rivalries and jealousies may be expected to develop further, unit selfishness *vis-a-vis* the Centre may well harden and the position of linguistic minorities in the new units may be for some time unenviable.[3]

[1] *Report of the States Reorganisation Commission* (1955). With the exception of three centrally-administered 'Territories' (Delhi and Manipur, already Part 'C' States, and the Andaman and Nicobar Islands, the Part 'D' State), India was to be divided into only sixteen States. This number entailed the disappearance of many units formed from previous princely states: Madhya Bharat, Saurashtra, Mysore, Travancore-Cochin, P.E.P.S.U., Ajmer, Bhopal, Coorg, Kutch, Himachal Pradesh, Vindhya Pradesh and Tripura. At the same time, three new linguistic States appeared: Kerala, Karnataka and Vidarbha.

[2] The Bill introduced in Parliament in March 1956 envisages fifteen States: Andhra-Telengana, Assam, Bihar, Gujarat, Jammu and Kashmir, Kerala, Madras, Madhya Pradesh, Maharashtra, Mysore, Orissa, Punjab, Rajasthan, Uttar Pradesh and West Bengal. This list corresponds closely to linguistic divisions. The Commission's Report has thus been modified in several ways: (i) Karnataka is retained but the name of Mysore is restored; (ii) Hyderabad is wholly absorbed by its neighbours; (iii) most important of all, the attempt to hold together Marathi- and Gujarati-speaking peoples in the State of Bombay is abandoned; and Maharashtra absorbs the previously proposed Vidarbha. As a result of the disappearance of Bombay State, the future of Bombay City became doubtful; despite Maharashtrian claims, the decision was taken to make Greater Bombay a centrally-administered territory. It thus joins Delhi, Manipur and the Andaman and Nicobar Islands as 'Union Territories'; the number of such units was brought up to seven by the addition of the Laccadive, Minicoy and Maldive Islands, Himachal Pradesh and Tripura.

[3] That inter-State rivalry is anticipated is perhaps shown by the proposal, simultaneously made in the Bill, to establish five 'Zonal Councils' of an advisory character, each comprising a number of States. It may be added that 1956 also witnessed the publication of a surprising scheme, put forward jointly by the Chief Ministers of West Bengal and Bihar, for the merging of their States; at the time of writing, however, little further progress in this direction could be reported and at least one of the Ministers concerned appeared to be anxious to drop the notion.

The regional feelings that gather around the question of language might be thought to be balanced and counteracted by the campaign for a national language. The Constitution has declared that Hindi is the official language of the Indian Union,[1] and there are many who are zealous in popularising and extending the use of the language. The movement for Hindi, however, encounters more difficulties than simply the resistance of the regional languages. In the first place, it comes into conflict with English as the only existing national language of India, and its progress in this struggle is not smooth. Correspondence on an all-India basis must still be conducted in English, and so must the proceedings of all-India conferences. Moreover, it will be some time before any Hindi newspaper can achieve the status and quality of the leading newspapers in English. Indian middle-class opinion is hardly firm in its views as to how far the replacement of English by Hindi is to be encouraged; when the Bombay Government recently attempted to debar children of Indian parents from admission to schools where the medium of instruction is English, it was the parents who protested loudest.[2] In the second place, there is not universal agreement as to the kind of Hindi that is to be propagated. It is to be in the 'Devanagari', not the Persian script, but how far words of Arabic and Persian origin are to be replaced by those derived or created from Sanskrit is a moot point; not infrequently does one hear the complaint that the new Hindi of the zealots is incomprehensible. And, finally, the conflict between Hindi and English has itself a regional significance and divides the north from the south; whereas Hindi is itself one of the languages of the north (and the others are not wholly remote from it), the southern languages belong to a quite distinct group. A few southerners have taken to Hindi, and no doubt the number will increase. For the present, however, the middle class in the south remains more at home in English.

Diversity has been discussed in terms of regional differences and enough has been said to show that there is here a serious problem of reconciliation of loyalties: political behaviour and thinking in national terms is not so firmly established that it can afford to allow unlimited opportunities of political expression to regional loyalties, but its weakness also means that it is unable easily to withstand the pressure. But if this were all that was entailed in India's diversity it would be a

[1] Art. 343. In pursuance of Article 344, the President of the Republic appointed on 7 June 1955 an Official Language Commission under the chairmanship of B. G. Kher, former Chief Minister of Bombay and High Commissioner in London. This Commission had the task of making recommendations to the President 'as to the progressive use of the Hindi language'. (The relevant Chapter XVII of the Constitution is at Appendix I. Article 344 contains provision for a rather novel use of a joint committee of both Houses to examine the Commission's recommendations.) It was reported (*Overseas Statesman*, 11 June 1955) that the Commission was markedly pro-Hindi in composition, even in its Bengali and Madras members.

[2] And the Supreme Court on 26 May 1954 upheld the protests and declared the orders unconstitutional.

straightforward problem in one dimension. This, however, is far from being the case. The divisions are in several dimensions at once. If geographical diversity is given first place and most space, it is less on account of its importance than because its effect on political life is more easily understood, more obvious and more easily documented.

Of India's social diversities, that which stems from religion has been the best known for its profound influence on politics. The independent form eventually taken by Muslim political aspirations found its logical conclusion in the partition of India and the formation of Pakistan.[1] Partition and the mass migrations which accompanied and followed it still left a substantial Muslim community of perhaps 35 millions in India, but it was difficult to see how it could resume independent communal political activity. The highest stakes had already been played for and won; moreover, the main leaders had moved to Pakistan, and in any case it was clearly wiser to try to placate and reassure the majority —already sad and angered by partition—by joining non-communal parties or by withdrawing wholly from the political scene.

The Constituent Assembly's Advisory Committee on Minorities had in August 1947 recommended that although separate electorates should be abolished, seats in legislatures should be reserved for Muslims (as also for Scheduled Castes and Indian Christians) for a period of ten years. But during the following year opinion—including Muslim opinion—had changed, and in a further report in May 1949 the Committee noted that 'although the abolition of separate electorates had removed much of the poison from the body politic, [even] the reservation of seats for religious communities, it was felt, did lead to a certain degree of separation and was to that extent contrary to the conception of a secular democratic State'.[2] The Constitution, accordingly, includes no such safeguards for religious minorities. But whether the Muslim citizen of India has already learnt to think of politics in purely non-communal terms is uncertain. There is, of course, that section which always adhered to the Congress; it has many representatives in the legislatures and even in ministerial position. The uncertainty is whether the allegiance of those who followed the Muslim League (but were yet unable or unwilling to go to Pakistan) has been effectively transferred so quickly, and, if so, which parties have proved attractive.[3] On this, definite evidence is naturally

[1] See W. Cantwell Smith, *Modern Islam in India*; Symonds, *The Making of Pakistan*; and, for the details of the final negotiations, Lumby, *The Transfer of Power*.

[2] The Report is published in *Reports of Committees of the Constituent Assembly (Third Series)*, 1950, at pp. 240–245. The institution of separate electorates is, of course, discussed in the main constitutional reports on India since 1917, and in K. B. Krishna, *The Problem of Minorities*. See also W. J. M. Mackenzie's 'Representation in Plural Societies' in *Political Studies*, Feb. 1954, on the general problem.

[3] The only State in which the Muslim League has remained as a political party is Madras, where Hindu–Muslim tension has seldom been pronounced. There the party contested 12 seats, mainly in Malabar, for the State legislature and was successful in 5. It also contested one seat from Madras for the House of the People and thus secured its one member of the central Parliament.

difficult to obtain. There are a few indications that the parties of the left have not gained—or at least not as much as might have been expected.[1] On the other hand, it is clear that Congress is concerned about its own failure to rally the minorities, including the Muslims.[2] There was considerable consternation when it became known that a conference of Muslims had been held at Aligarh in November 1953 and that the sentiments expressed had been distinctly communal and displayed distrust of the majority community.[3]

The other principal religious minorities are the Parsis, the Christians and the Sikhs. The Parsis, with their predominantly business and industrial interests largely centred on Bombay, have never been inclined to translate their community sense into distinctive political terms. The same is largely true of the Christians; the leaders of the community are at present probably more concerned to protect their religious and cultural institutions from the attacks of some extremist Hindus.[4] Only in Travancore-Cochin, where they constitute a very substantial and powerful minority of nearly 40% do the Christians act at all significantly as a political force. The Sikhs, on the other hand, while represented in all

[1] M. Venkatarangaiya's study, *The General Election in Bombay City* (1953), states that Congress secured the majority of Muslim votes in the City (p. 151), though of the 12 Muslim candidates who were put up (out of a total of 127 candidates), 6 stood for the Socialists and 2 for the Communists.

[2] In this connection, a party directive to Congress Legislature Parties in States issued in June 1954 (reported in the press on 25 June) is of interest. It admits that there is a 'growing feeling of uneasiness among minority communities', a sense of frustration, 'that they are not having a fair deal in the services and in the Congress organisation'. The directive therefore urges that 'adequate representation should be given to minority communities in the Congress organisation and other offices, which will . . . create a sense of security that their association with the Congress will advance their interest. . . .' This would help to counter 'the state of resentment that is growing apace'.

[3] Badarudduja, an ex-Mayor of Calcutta, presided over the convention and his address was at once protesting and suppliant in tone. He listed the oppressions of the minorities and the attacks on Islam which had led to 'economic paralysis, cultural death or disintegration and political helotage for Muslims'. He offered the co-operation of his community to the State, but begged for a 'square deal as an integral part of the Indian Nation'. The convention decided to form a new Muslim Party. Angry questions were put in the Indian Parliament and nothing further was heard of the Party.

[4] It has been reported that a volunteer movement was inaugurated in Delhi in July 1954 for the purpose of training Hindu religious workers to 'combat the menace of foreign missionaries'. Although the foreign missionaries provide a convenient pretext, the real intentions were evident in the speeches made on the occasion: conversions are to be 'checked' and efforts are to be made to 're-convert' the converted. Such a movement, anti-Christian in the guise of anti-foreign, has of course no official support. The Government of India, however, has its own policy towards foreign missionaries. It has been at least very sceptical about the value of missionary influence among tribal peoples (especially those of the N.E. border areas) and it has been disturbed by reports of missionaries' antagonism towards Indian culture. Its policy, reaffirmed in September 1955, is one of moderately discouraging neutrality. Pandit Nehru in his letter to the Primate of Sweden in 1953 stressed the view that the Indian churches 'need not rely too much on external assistance'. Missionaries already in India may continue to work 'unless they have come to adverse notice'; new arrivals for existing missions will be allowed to enter India if they are qualified and if no Indians are available; new missions will require special permission. (*India News*, 17 Sept. 1955.)

other parties (in the two states where they are numerous—P.E.P.S.U. and Punjab), have also had their own party, the Akali Dal. The community has, however, so suffered from the partition upheaval and from irresponsible political leadership that it has lost much political coherence in recent years.[1]

More important than the social diversity which flows from different religions is that which comes from cleavages within the Hindu fold. The political effects of some of these cleavages are to be seen on the surface of political life. The extent to which Madras politics is still dominated by the antagonism between Brahmin and non-Brahmin is well known, and no account of voting behaviour, legislature proceedings or even ministerial appointments would be complete unless considerable attention were given to this factor. Again, the lively tussles in the new State of Andhra between the coastal and interior sub-regions owe much of their vigour to the strong position of one particular caste in one of the areas. Caste-community factors play an important part in the non-Christian politics of Travancore-Cochin. All this is evident even to the spectator. But caste loyalties do not always operate on the surface; indeed, the bulk of their effect is, iceberg-like, below the surface. The outside observer least of all is likely to notice their power; he can only guess at their influence from their importance in social life as a whole. There is little doubt that this is steadily decreasing under the impact of education and industrialisation; there is as little doubt that it is still very great.

Most important of all the social–religious distinctions within Hindu society is that between those sometimes called caste Hindus and the others called untouchables, or Harijans (Gandhi's word for them, meaning sons of God), or the Scheduled Castes.[2] The Constitution has provisions for the reservation for a period of ten years of a number of seats for the Scheduled Castes and Tribes in Central and State Legislatures in relation to their population.[3] Under this system the community is assured of its due share of representatives in the legislatures, but they are voted upon by the electorate at large. In this way, though an element of communal distinctness is retained, there is a check on the pursuance of narrowly sectional programmes. The party of the untouchables, the All-India Scheduled Castes Federation, fared poorly in the General Elections. It put up candidates only for the reserved seats, but even there was rarely successful. This would appear to be not only due to the Harijan's loss of confidence in 'their own party' but also to antagonism from

1 Both sections of the split Akalis were soundly defeated in the P.E.P.S.U. elections of Feb. 1954 (see below, p. 107). The Sikhs conducted in 1955 a vigorous but untidy campaign for a separate Punjabi-speaking (i.e. Sikh majority) State.

2 The last term is derived from Schedule I of the 1935 Act. Their normal official designation before 1935 was Depressed Classes.

3 Part XVI gives the 'special provisions relating to certain classes'. It includes a clause (335) that 'the claims of the Scheduled Castes and Tribes shall be taken into consideration' in government service. This is the subject of detailed departmental instructions.

caste Hindu voters; it is said, for example, that the Socialists in Bombay lost votes among middle-class Hindus because of their electoral alliance with the S.C.F.[1] Also, it is unlikely that the almost complete absence of Harijan members elected to unreserved seats[2] is to be explained simply by there being no need to elect more than must in any case get elected to reserved seats; it is very probable that many caste Hindus would still find it difficult to bring themselves to vote for an untouchable.

But to understand this influence of caste on politics we have, as already suggested, to consider the place of caste distinctions in everyday life. To do this at all thoroughly would require a volume[3]; here it may be enough to refer to some striking facts given in the Report for 1952 of the Commissioner for Scheduled Castes and Tribes. The number of people in this status is immense: over 50 million in Scheduled Castes and nearly 20 million in Scheduled Tribes—with a further estimated 50 million whose status is almost as low, though their castes have not been 'scheduled'.[4] 'They live', says the Report, 'in ignorance, fear and centuries-old traditions, leading an impoverished and difficult existence.'[5] The practice of untouchability, which accompanies and helps to perpetuate the appalling economic conditions, is solemnly forbidden under Article 17 of the Constitution, but the Report finds that it 'still persists in the rural areas'.[6] The legislative measures taken in some States in order to give effect to the constitutional ban 'have not proved very effective'. Sometimes offences are not made cognisable, but 'even where such offences are made cognisable, these laws have not been of any material help to those for whom they were enacted. . . . Very few cases have been reported to the police . . . [because] the Scheduled Caste people have no courage to break the social barriers imposed on them.'[7] The Report gives instructive examples of the kind of social discrimination which is to be found. From a part of Punjab it is reported that in the absence of separate wells for them, the Harijans 'have often to wait for hours for caste Hindus to draw water for them and pour it into a pit alongside—for direct pouring into the untouchables' vessels would be

[1] M. Venkatarangaiya, op. cit., p. 152.

[2] For the whole of India, 'one Scheduled Caste candidate and one Scheduled Tribe candidate were returned to the House of the People to unreserved seats'. Of all the State Assemblies, 'two Scheduled Caste persons in W. Bengal and one in Travancore-Cochin were returned to unreserved seats'. (Reports of the Commissioner for Scheduled Castes and Tribes for the year 1952, pp. 49–50.)

[3] The best short account is found in J. H. Hutton, Caste in India (1946).

[4] In his Report for 1953, the Commissioner noted that 'every caste and community is running a race for being included in the list of backward classes', so great is the hope of gaining a few special privileges.

[5] Report of the Commissioner for Scheduled Castes and Tribes for the year 1952, p. 141.

[6] Ibid., p. 139.

[7] Ibid., p. 41. The passing of the Untouchability (Offences) Act, 1955, by the Indian Parliament is no doubt a further welcome indication of good intentions and even of determination to end the evils. The immediate effects of such legislation will, however, be limited in practice.

pollution'.[1] In the villages of Madhya Bharat, it is said, 'there are no in-stances of Harijans practising any other profession than those of their forefathers', while in Rajasthan 'cases still occur where Scheduled Caste people are not allowed to ride on horse- or camel-back within the village limits'.[2] The combination of social discrimination with economic backwardness is brought out pathetically in the passage which, after re-cording that in Madras there are by this time 'no disabilities in regard to the wearing of ornaments by Scheduled Caste women or in regard to the eating of ghee [butter], sugar and the like', adds: 'but they cannot afford all this due to their poverty'.[3] It is from Madras, too, that we get the following comprehensive picture:

> So far as access to shops, public restaurants and places of public entertain-ment and the use of wells, tanks [large ponds], bathing places, roads, etc., are concerned, except for a few advanced and enlightened Harijans, the majority are still afraid of making free use of public institutions. They fear that any claim of right on their part would wound the feelings of the caste Hindus on whom they are depending for their livelihood.[4]

That these fears are not wholly groundless is indicated by an account of an incident which shows at the same time a link between social discri-mination and political behaviour—though admittedly in an unusually extreme form: it appears that the Rajput landlords of parts of Madhya Bharat had been angered by the ending of the forced labour which they previously extracted and by the refusal of some Harijans to perform some of their traditional duties; the victory of untouchables at panch-ayat (village council) elections proved the last straw, and promptly 're-sulted in firings on the Scheduled Caste people in two villages'.[5]

These illustrations no doubt give but one side of the story. On the other side should be put all the influences—from the exhortations of leaders to the film and the motor bus—which work increasingly in an egalitarian direction. Caste may be losing its hold, but it is not happen-ing as quickly as Indian reformers would wish or as outside observers often imagine. And so long as it remains, it has to be taken into account; it can no longer be the job of either the Indian reformer or the foreign observer to overlook it. On the contrary, for both, the changes already effected must be less significant than the differences that remain. The bearing of these differences on political thinking and behaviour has three related aspects. They mean, in the first place, that political action may be directly conditioned by caste factors; one votes, makes appoint-ments, finds political association along caste lines, and also judges political proposals in terms of their influence on the position of one's caste. They mean, secondly, that even in the thinking of those who are less actively concerned with politics there is always present an element which is a competitor with national consciousness; that is to say, even

---

[1] *Ibid.*, p. 40.   [2] *Ibid.*, pp. 33–34.   [3] *Ibid.*, p. 31.   [4] *Ibid.*, p. 31.   [5] *Ibid.*, p. 39.

where caste sentiment is not strong enough directly to affect behaviour, it may still operate to hinder the emergence and then distort the shape of a national endeavour. Finally, the importance of caste differences is that they create their own deep gaps of social experience as well as contributing to the widening of gaps caused by other differences. Nowhere can the phrase that men who live differently think differently have a more profound meaning than in India. Caste is a community, not self-sufficient but rather connected and dependent on other similar communities; yet possessing, at least in its 'pure' form, its own distinctive customs and values.[1]

Religion and, within religion, caste are thus sources of social diversity with a special importance in India and for the study of Indian politics. But other sources of diversity, other differences with which the foreigner is perhaps more familiar, are by no means absent. On the contrary, class differences, for example, are unusually marked and they are also, as already suggested, reinforced by the regional and communal–caste differences. It will be hard to discover what there is in common between a wealthy Sikh businessman from Punjab and the landless Harijan from Tamil-Nad, between a Marwari financier and a Bengali Brahmin school teacher. It is, of course, easy to think of very sharply contrasted types of Englishman or Frenchman or American. But there are two points to note: first, in the Western examples there will be several places at which social experience has built substantial bridges across the gap, whereas in India such bridges are normally few; second, the gap itself is very much wider. Differences of class in India are not to be measured and grasped simply by the use of statistics showing the incomes of the various social groups; they would certainly demonstrate the existence of a large majority who live in conditions of more or less abject poverty and a small group enjoying exceptional wealth. But this is no more than even the most casual visitor already notices. More important is a different kind of dividing line which might not always correspond with money incomes. For example, if we think of our own society of somewhere between fifty or a hundred years ago, we are surely impressed by the importance, as a determinant of ways of thought and behaviour, of the employment of domestic servants in the homes of the upper and middle

[1] It seems possible that where it is perfectly accepted caste may continue to provide the individual with a valuable sense of security in a rapidly-changing world. The difficulty is that one of the things that is rapidly changing is precisely the extent to which it is perfectly accepted. The result, on balance, appears to be an accentuation of social tensions which harass the individual rather than a safe social harbour which shelters him. The question is discussed in G. Murphy, *In the Minds of Men: Study of Human Behaviour and Social Tensions in India* (New York, 1953). In a stable society, caste furnishes a source of solidarity and security and encourages a sense of dependence. In a period of marked social change— e.g. a movement of population to the towns— it can become also an added source of tensions, hostility and bitter despair. See also M. B. Nanavati and C. N. Vakil, *Group Prejudices in India* (Bombay, 1953).

classes. It is surely the disappearance of this institution, as much as any of the direct effects of social policy, which has brought about a striking uniformity in patterns of life; Disraeli's 'two nations' became one, not with Lloyd George's budget, nor even with the post-war welfare state, but simply when 'the family stopped having a servant' and father helped with the household work. In this sense, India is firmly 'Victorian'; the household of an officer in the civil or military services, of a substantial shopkeeper or businessman, of a landowner or professional man will include not one but several servants. Moreover, many whose incomes hardly permit this luxury will make other sacrifices to enable them to live as their status or their traditions demand, to keep themselves above the crucial line of social demarcation.[1]

To these more or less familiar economic class distinctions, we have to add still further factors before we have even an approximate idea of the diversities which bear on Indian politics. One of these is the contrast between town and country. More precisely in India's case, it is a contrast, first, between the village and anything more than a village; and, secondly, between small towns and big cities. It is true that much has happened to break down these contrasts. The big cities and industrial concentrations increasingly draw in from the rural areas workers whose families remain in the villages; visits are then made in both directions and two worlds meet. Again, the widespread development—above all, in the post-war period—of the motor bus has brought the district town within monthly or even weekly reach of the village—whereas it had tended to be a place of only annual pilgrimage. Yet the differences remain immense. Both aspects—the beginning of contact and the distance over which contact has to be established—can be illustrated by two simple pictures which happen also to have a political importance. The first is outside the imposing Parliament House in New Delhi: groups of villagers, who have come in to the city by horse-cart or lorry, stand awed and delighted by this marvel from a century so alien to their own. Second, inside the Parliament House waiting in the lobbies are also men from villages waiting to listen to their representatives or even to meet them; for adult franchise has brought the village into the world of politics, which was hitherto the preserve of the urbanised.

A mention must be made of two other distinctions. One is that between the Westernised Indian and others. This is, of course, very much a matter of degree and the range is great: at one end the few who have lived in the West and are as much at home in its customs as they are in their 'own'—or even more so; at the other end, the clerk who has a preference for American films or for wearing trousers in place of *dhoti*.

1 The more ardent members of the Communist Party naturally constitute an emphatic exception to this rule; it is not unusual for middle-class party workers to donate their incomes (above a bare minimum) to party funds and make a point of doing everything for themselves in an attempt to put themselves 'below the line'.

But whatever the form taken by Western influence, it has added its own special contribution to India's lack of homogeneity. A final distinction —but one by no means negligible—is that of age. In other words, there are in different generations different way of thought, on all subjects, including politics. There is nothing unusual in this. But, for politics in particular, there is now becoming evident in India a dividing line of special importance: 1947. That is to say there is a world of difference between the political attitudes of those who were old enough to be interested or active in politics before independence and those whose main interest and activity came later. The difference could probably be expressed or conveyed in several ways: the younger man may appear more constructive, less idealistic, more aggressive and so on. But it is clear that there is a contrast which is more marked than is usual between age groups.

The presence in Indian society of so many kinds of diversity, each of great importance, produces in political life a maze of cross-currents. The position has been well summarised by a recent writer:

> The absence of cultural homogeneity and the lack of social mobility . . . become sources of social tension. . . . India may or may not be, as some critics have maintained, many countries packed in a geographical receptacle, but she undoubtedly is a place where many centuries jostle together. Side by side in our country, especially among the Hindus, wide educational and cultural differences exist—differences accentuated by the rigid caste barriers; social life is cut up into many enclosures, and thought reared on such foundations gets fractured into particularisms.[1]

The clash of different social policies is, in all countries, seldom an exercise in reason and logic alone; even in the peculiarly homogeneous society of Britain we are accustomed to the pressures that sectional interests and limited experiences exert on political attitudes and programmes. In India, the diversity of experiences and loyalties is so great that it is sometimes a matter for wonder that coherent national policies are able at all to emerge. That they do is a tribute to the power of the forces making for unity which we noted earlier. But that the victory of unity over diversity is not at all to be taken for granted is shown by the continual appeals for a national view which are made by political leaders.

4. Authority

One of the manifestations of diversity which is an outstanding characteristic of Indian politics is the prevalence of faction.[2] It is indeed

---

[1] Asoka Mehta, *Politics of Planned Economy*, p. 31.

[2] In a speech in Delhi on 15 May 1954, Pandit Nehru placed his usual emphasis on the need for unity. He was explaining his retention of the position of Congress President along with that of Prime Minister: 'I did so because I found there was no other way out. Several weaknesses had crept into the Congress—dissensions, internecine quarrels, petty rivalries and bickerings. . . . We must remain united and ward off the evils of parochialism and casteism. . . . We must work hard to get things properly consolidated in India.'

a natural consequence of the multitude of cross-currents we have already described. Separate experiences and diverse loyalties make it difficult for common efforts to be maintained; cracks appear in the façade of unity and splits take place.[1] People find it easy to feel and believe that the other fellow is really impossible to get on with.

If it were invariably possible to relate factions to the social diversities we have mentioned, there would be no need to look further for an explanation. But in fact this is not so. Inability to work with others in the team often appears to be less the result of different loyalties than an independent characteristic with its own *raison d'être*. The suspicion that this is the case is strengthened by a connected feature of Indian politics which forcibly impresses the outside observer: a paradoxical or ambivalent attitude to authority. Authority in India appears to be subject at once to much more abusive criticism and much more effusive adulation than one is accustomed to elsewhere. Due respect combined with due criticism is the exception rather than the rule. The position of Ministers demonstrates this feature well. On the one hand, they are called upon to grace an enormous number of functions of all kinds, they are received with excited enthusiasm and heavy garlands of flowers, and their remarks are extensively reported in the following day's newspapers. On the other hand, both in public and private they are criticised in unmeasured terms, some of the smaller newspapers indulge in violent abuse, and scandal about them is always in demand. This is not the place to attempt a careful analysis of these attitudes. But a review of some of the factors that appear to be at work may throw further light on the nature of Indian politics.

Profound respect for authority has its grounds in several features of Indian life and history. To begin with the immediate past, it is clear that much of the enthusiastic awe in which the present leaders are held is derived from their prestige of yesterday, when they conducted the battle for liberation from British rule. The selfless sacrifices endured during that period are already losing much of their appeal—especially among the younger generation who look more to present performance—but they are still of some importance. But some of the respect is carried over from the British rulers themselves. Their devotion to duty and their pursuit of justice, their very remoteness and alien natures, helped to establish a widespread and firmly-rooted respect for government which was not damaged—was, indeed, even shared—by nationalist critics and

---

[1] I am not referring here to the kind of split which broke off the Socialists and later the Kisan Mazdoor Praja Party from the body of the National Movement. Clearly such splits were not only unavoidable; they were necessary, for a national movement hardly conformed to the requirements of an independent parliamentary democracy, where the need was for an opposition with an alternative policy. I refer rather to the kind of split which has taken place in almost every State Congress party; these have only rarely been prompted by differences over policy—though sometimes such differences have later been paraded for decency's sake. (In fact, even the K.M.P. split was not wholly free of this feature.)

opponents. The British in their turn had been able to build on suitable foundations; the pattern of Indian polity before the period of British rule—a pattern still discernible in the princely states until very recently —had as one of its clearest motifs an awe and devotion for the ruler. Moreover, the very structure of Indian Hindu society inculcated—partly but not exclusively through the caste system—a sense of status in all members. To be of noble birth and high caste no doubt entailed certain duties, but to be of lesser status certainly entailed the duty of respecting those placed above. Finally, any explanation of the place of authority in Indian society would have to take account of the family. In any society, the family is probably of such importance that the relations and attitudes which characterise it will find a place in the wider network of social relations. The extraordinarily central position of the family in Indian life makes it practically certain that the values it enshrines will overflow outside it to society at large. There can be little doubt that authority and status are the keynotes of Indian family life.[1] The places of elder brother, mother, mother-in-law and, above all, father are all clearly defined by custom and characterised by the possession of appropriate authority which attaches to them.

India, however, is undergoing a social transformation—which began before the political transformation and is yet far from completed. In such a period it is perhaps to be expected that there should be something of a revolt against old values. There is thus, as just mentioned, an impatience with the heroic leaders of yesterday unless they can show themselves useful today. There is also a more general reluctance to accept hitherto venerated authority. This attitude, when it encounters the older deeper feelings, reacts with some violence. This accounts for some of the abuse. But the matter is a good deal more complicated. Some of the feelings of resentment and bitter frustration seem to be the result of disappointed idealism.[2] The nationalist struggle had evoked such efforts and inspired such hopes that this was unavoidable; for some, that is to say, the post-independence Ministries are evident failures simply because the millennium has not arrived. Moreover, the nostalgia for the days of comradeship is all the stronger on account of the undisguised scramble for office and power. The unduly harsh and unsympathetic attitude towards authority also stems from the lack of

---

[1] The bulk of the novels and short stories written in the Indian languages (above all, of course, in Bengali) during the last half-century could bear witness to this. Some recently published accounts in English of Indian childhood and family life confirm the impression. See, for example, N. C. Chaudhuri, *Autobiography of an Unknown Indian*; N. Sircar, *Indian Boyhood*; S. Ghose, *And Gazelles Leaping*.

[2] This is not to say that there are not among certain sections—e.g. teachers—real grievances. These do not, however, account for the whole mood of disillusionment. One senior political leader with whom I discussed the question agreed; but he believed that the frustration was not a recent development: 'Frustration has become a habit of mind with our people.'

social cohesion. It is, in many ways, easier to respect authority exercised by a complete alien than when it is in the hands of someone from a neighbouring region or a different caste. Another consideration is the smallness of the *élite* in India. In the West the 'governing classes' of politicians and administrators are merged into and lost in the large body of the upper and middle classes; whereas in India the top layers of society are remarkably thin and the governing classes constitute an important proportion of them. The result is that M.P.s, Ministers, high officials are within easy reach and are known personally to those in these layers—a situation which makes contempt come easily and the retailing of scandal a popular pastime.

The inability to 'get on' with the other man, the reluctance to accept authority with due but not exaggerated respect, the preference among politicians for splits rather than compromises, the tendency among the educated classes to indulge in unconstructive and unreasonable criticism—all these are closely connected, and they play an important part in influencing, for example, the relations between governments and oppositions. They help to explain the importance of personal followings and personal incompatibilities in political groupings. In a country where the multitude of cross-currents in politics is conducive to the growth of faction, they reinforce that tendency. These characteristics may perhaps be described without unfairness as signs of political irresponsibility.[1] Should such a description be proper, its explanation is not difficult. It is a consequence, in the first place, of the long period of national struggle for independence which in such a high degree encouraged irresponsible utterance and behaviour; criticism could be careless because there was never any danger of the critic being invited to perform better. Moreover, in the countryside, the concentration of powers in the hands of the district officer was so great and his sharing of these powers so rare and minimal that it was scarcely surprising that he should have been called the 'man-bap' (mother and father) of his area; and since for most people 'government' meant the district officer, it was easy for a general impression to develop that responsibility was the exclusive possession of the rulers. But it seems also likely that irresponsibility may be related to more permanent features of Indian social life. It is, for example, clearly connected with the presence of so many strongly competing loyalties. A

---

[1] Mr. Paul Appleby, in his study *Public Administration in India* (1953), discusses, in relation to the work of administrators, what seems to me a similar feature. He lists as one of the factors making for disunity and incoherence in administration what he calls 'Lack of action-mindedness' (p. 4). But he attempts to avoid making the charge of irresponsibility: 'This does not imply sloth, lack of social consciousness or irresponsibility; it refers to a way of thinking about and addressing action problems. It may be related to the obverse side of the shield which is one of India's distinct virtues—a bent toward and capacity for speculative thought.' I find this not wholly convincing. Even Mr. Appleby goes on to say: 'It is certainly related to a history that provided little opportunity for large-scale action responsibility.'

man may be irresponsible in relation to State and Central politics simply because he has a high sense of responsibility to his caste or district.[1] It is also possible that the exercise by children of independent responsibility is less encouraged in Indian family life than it is in the West, and this may have its influence even on adult behaviour.

5. Levels of Politics

I have discussed a number of features of Indian social life and indicated the kind of influence they exert on Indian politics. Throughout this discussion it has been rather assumed that there is only one pattern of Indian political behaviour and that it is essentially the Western pattern with certain special modifications imposed by peculiar features of history and social life. The analysis, that is, has been similar to the kind one would expect to find in a book which set out to explain French or American politics to English readers. It is appropriate at this stage to introduce an element which appears to question this assumption, if not to render it invalid.[2] I refer to the presence in Indian politics of a manner of political thought and behaviour which it is difficult to regard simply as a local modification of some aspect of Western politics. It draws its inspiration from religious teachings and represents a development of an aspect of Gandhian politics. It leads its own life, alongside and not wholly unconnected with the world of 'normal' politics, but largely independent of it. It is possible to say that it is not politics at all; in that case the Western pattern (of course, with its modifications) is left in sole command as the only pattern of political conduct available. But it seems more in keeping with the facts to allow that it is politics, even if it is of a kind quite distinct from that of modern Europe.[3] It may not be misleading to say that Indian politics takes place at two different levels or in two distinct modes, the one Western and secular, and other religious and Indian.[4] At the same time, it must be confessed that it is difficult to see the two levels as alternative ways of politics available to India as a whole; 'spiritual politics' relies in many ways on the continuous practice of 'Western politics', whereas the latter owes little to the former.

[1] It is also a familiar point that nepotism often reflects a loyalty to family and clan in excess of loyalty to the state.

[2] The way in which I have expressed some of my reflections in this section owes something to a paper entitled 'The Idea of "Character" in the Interpretation of Modern Politics', read by Professor Oakeshott to the 1954 conference of the Political Studies Association of Great Britain.

[3] It appears that Professor Oakeshott (see previous note) might not agree with this. His view is that 'European political dispositions have been diffused outside Europe to such an extent that there is room for doubt whether there is a second political "character" of any significance now to be found in the world.'

[4] The word 'religious' is open to some misunderstanding. I should regard the activities of bodies such as the Hindu Mahasabha as falling clearly within the sphere of 'Western' politics; they compete with the use of similar methods for similar places. Perhaps 'spiritual' would be less ambiguous.

Yet it seems that the two ways can and do present themselves as alternatives to individuals contemplating political activity.

The foremost exponent of this other level of politics is Vinoba Bhave, and his entry into 'politics' was marked by his inauguration of Bhoodan Yajna or the Land-Gifts Mission in 1951.[1] The mission or movement consists simply in requesting those who own land to give a portion to those who have none. It appears to have started almost accidentally. Bhave, walking through the disturbed and stricken areas of Hyderabad in April 1951, was met at every point with the appeals of the landless for land. In one village where this happened, Bhave turned to those in the same village who had land and asked for donations of land. 'The people acceded to my request and I received my first land-gift that day. This is how the idea of Bhoodan came to me, and I tried it during my tour. It gave encouraging results. Within a period of two months I receive-about twelve thousand acres.' By April 1955, no less than 3,500,000 acres had been thus donated. And of that total, 120,000 acres had already been distributed to those who had none or little land before. For the work of collection and distribution he is aided by teams of voluntary workers in the various States.

Every pronouncement of Vinoba Bhave shows the way in which the movement combines spiritual and practical elements; the impulse is both spiritual and social, the consequences also partake of both worlds. 'We have accepted this work because we want to change and revolutionise society; and also because it will alleviate the miseries of the poor; and, further again, because we want to cleanse and purify our minds and hearts.' He justifies his work on the three grounds that 'it is in tune with the cultural traditions of India, it contains in it the seed of economic and social revolution and it can help in the establishment of peace in the world'. His teachings are full of references to Hindu mythology and are based on doctrines (such as non-attachment) which are part of India's spiritual heritage. He puts his creed in homely terms: 'If there are five sons in the family, I want to be considered the sixth. I claim one-sixth of the total cultivable land in the country.' At the same time, he relates his movement to the existing social conditions and existing movements.[2] 'I do not beg alms. I ask for the land as a right of the poor. I refuse to agree that my attempt . . . is contrary to the trends of history. New things can happen. . . . My mission is not to stave off a revolution. I want to prevent a violent revolution and create a non-violent revolu-

[1] Vinoba Bhave was for over thirty years a silent and little-known but devoted follower of Gandhi. A portrait of the man and a description of his work are given in 'Land Through Love', by Hallam Tennyson in *Encounter*, Dec. 1954, and the same author's *Saint on the March* (1955). A collection of his writings and speeches on his Land-Gifts Mission has appeared under the title *Bhoodan Yajna* (Navajivan Press, Ahmedabad, 1953) and it is from that booklet that I have taken the quotations used below.

[2] It is worth remembering that Bhoodan began precisely where the Communists had been most active among the peasantry.

tion.' But 'when a revolution in the way of life is contemplated, it must take place in the mind . . . and the present work is only the preparation of a psychological atmosphere'. That the movement has aims much wider than an approach to the land problem is made abundantly clear. 'This Bhoodan Yajna is an application of non-violence, an experiment in the transformation of life itself.' 'I firmly believe that India should be able to evolve, consistent with her ideals, a new type of revolution based purely on love. . . . We do not aim at doing acts of kindness but at creating a kingdom of kindness.'

It is worth while noting how Vinoba Bhave himself conceives the relation of his 'level of politics' to politics as more usually understood. He emphasises that his is a distinct sphere, though it contributes to 'normal' politics. 'As to the economic side of the land problem, society itself can look after it. . . . I have chosen as my work the creation of a moral atmosphere so that the problem might be solved peacefully. . . . I do not want to agitate for any legislative measure; mine is a moral movement. Whatever success I get is on account of this difference.' But though his mission may help the different activities of others, on a larger view it also makes them unnecessary. 'A law which follows a change in the moral principles of a people is just a formality of record. . . . In a non-violent social order, law is like the formal "The End" put at the end of a book. The end of the book does not depend on the affixing of that seal. Hence I am indifferent about legislation.' Vinoba often speaks of the importance of detachment from power, though he admits that political power can be an instrument of service. In the sphere of 'normal' politics, he sees the value of a system of government and opposition, but he would be happier if there could somehow be a basis and field of united activity as well as the debate of alternative policies. But the power in which he is mainly interested is a power that belongs to his own 'level of politics' and is envisaged as rendering the other variety obsolete. 'The power of the people is the opposite of the power of violence. . . . There is an element of violence in the power of the state, but inasmuch as this power has been entrusted to the state by the people its character differs from that of naked violence. . . . We, however, intend to go further and create conditions which will do away with the need to use even the power of the state.'

The success of the movement in the very short time it has been in existence is evidence of its undoubted appeal to many people in the country. One 'conversion' to Bhoodan which attracted special attention was that of the Socialist Party leader, Jayaprakash Narayan. He has abandoned the field of 'normal' politics and put his great mass appeal at the service of Vinoba Bhave. In an article written shortly afterwards, he has underlined the view of the connection between the two 'levels' of politics which we have already detected in Bhave's own writings. Thus, to the ordinary politician, Bhoodan is simply a well-intentioned and no doubt helpful movement of agrarian reform, which is at best preparing the ground. But in reality, says Narayan, it is a mass movement of conversion to a new climate of thought and new values of life. Since it aims to revolutionise man and society, it is an intensely and deeply political movement—but its politics are not those of parliaments and governments. It does not aim at capturing the state—the Communists do this, and what results is not a 'withering away' of the state, but the total state. The ultimate stateless society, in which people are able to manage their affairs directly, will only come by a change of mind brought about through the creation of conditions in which the people will rely more on themselves and less on the state. Bhoodan is the beginning of this larger movement.[1]

Many criticisms have, of course, been made of the Bhoodan movement. It has been said that many of the gifts were of land of little value or land which required much to be spent on it before it could yield results. It has been suggested that many landowners have been pleased to donate land which they feared they would in any event soon have to part with under legislative provisions, and that they were willing to forgo a future compensation payment in return for a greatly enhanced local prestige. Not always, it appears, has the machinery for the distribution of the land-gifts worked as the founder intended. Whatever the validity of these criticisms, it can certainly be admitted that in many cases neither the donor nor the receiver of the gift has had in his mind only those considerations which move Bhave himself. It would also be too much to claim that the spirit of Bhoodan is perfectly understood even by those who support it. In the parties of 'normal' politics, for instance, the emphasis is almost wholly on the value of Bhoodan as an auxiliary to the state.[2] None of this however, detracts from the fact that there is here an activity which is important in its results, which is peculiarly Indian in ethos, which is political but not in the accepted sense of the term. That this form of politics can exist side by side with 'normal' politics is perhaps a further sign of the strongly heterogeneous character of Indian society.

6. The Place of Parliament

Against this outline of the nature of Indian politics we may proceed to examine the particular institution of parliament in India. But before

[1] The article in which these themes occurred was published in *Bharat Jyoti*, Bombay, on 28 June 1954.

[2] Some of the truly Gandhian Congressmen may share Bhave's whole creed, but the tone of the Party's officials is unmistakably practical. The main circular from the All-India Congress Committee was issued in July 1953 and made support of the movement a duty of Congressmen; as a further letter of 20 Aug. 1953 put it, 'We should like to impress upon you the desirability of giving your full support to the Bhoodan Movement because it is the only practical way of solving the problem of land hunger in our country without having to spend millions of rupees on paying compensation to the land holders.' (*Congress Bulletin*, Aug.–Sept. 1953, p. 264.)

we do so, it may be well to mention here two familiar general lines of criticism to which the institution is often subject.

One of these appears at first sight to be related to the other 'level of politics' which we have just described. It alleges that parliamentary democracy, by virtue of being a Western institution, cannot be suited to India. Even after the winning of independence, there still remains to be accomplished the establishment of genuinely Indian political institutions. This view has nowhere been put forward with much skill or subtlety, but it nevertheless influences the outlook of many in India. It leads at least to the feeling that the political institutions of modern India are unworthy of notice; at worst, it produces, with the aid of much loose thinking, a sentiment of contempt and a series of ill-judged condemnations. Some illustrations of the view may be given from the writing of one of its more noteworthy exponents.[1]

India has chosen [he writes] to be a camp follower of the West and is taking pride in its godless secularism and in the paraphernalia of parliamentary democracy which it has decided to adopt. . . . It is a matter of great sorrow that the new Constitution does not breathe the principles of Truth and Ahimsa . . . [for] we know that the institutions of parliamentary democracy have failed to give happiness and peace to large sections of the world population who spend sleepless nights in fear of wars and party despotism . . .

He then describes some of the weaknesses of this form of government: the impossible task which it imposes on the elector; the sad elimination of the independent candidate and the growing rigidity of party discipline; the farce of non-co-operation between government and opposition; and the baneful influence of politicians on administration. It would have been better, the writer argues, if an attempt had been made 'to present to the world of political science some true Indian principles of political philosophy'. This could have been done by appointing a committee of experts to study the Hindu scriptures and epics and 'our vast history', with a view to discovering whether 'certain principles of our indigenous administration and government could not be replanted in our new Bharat [India]'. He concludes with five proposals which such a committee could even now consider:

The Heads of the Union and the States to be effective heads[2]; government to consist of talent from all parties; elections to be so devised as to reduce

[1] The passages are from 'Reflections on Parliamentary Democracy in India', the Presidential Address of Professor Bodh Raj Sharma to the Dec. 1953 conference of the Indian Political Science Association. I believe that Professor Sharma would be the first to admit that his views were shared by few of his colleagues.

[2] It is interesting to note that this proposal was also popular in discussions on constitution-making in Pakistan; it was argued that the American system of strong one-man executives was more Islamic than cabinet-parliamentary government. The committee of religious experts he suggests was of course actually used in the case of Pakistan—with somewhat unhappy consequences.

the powers of the bosses and of wealth; religious education to be compulsory and books on religion to be prepared by a committee of leaders of all religions with a view to the spiritual and moral regeneration of the community through self-control and the limitation of desires; nationalism to be subordinated to internationalism.

Although this view bears certain resemblances to the distinct 'level of politics' discussed earlier, it seems to owe most to a sense of resentment that anything should be borrowed from outside the culture of India.[1] It would perhaps scarcely be worthy of much attention were it not for the extent to which it is commonly (though very vaguely) felt. The question of the suitability of parliamentary democracy for India is no doubt a serious one. But it is unlikely that it will be correctly answered on the basis of hasty criticism of Western institutions and the inspection of those of mediaeval India. Rather is it to be answered—as in fact it is being answered—by experiment with readily available materials, by the attempt to operate and adapt those institutions with which recent political experience had made so many Indians familiar. The fact that parliament is in origin a Western institution is less significant than the fact that parliament in India has become an Indian institution.

The second line of criticism of parliamentary democracy—and one less restricted to India than the first—is related to many of the observations made above in considering diversity in India. The critics of this school believe that, while parliamentary institutions may work reasonably in homogeneous societies, they cannot do so in the absence of such conditions. The point is not so much that divisions on religious lines create permanent majorities and minorities instead of the fluidity of power which democracy demands,[2] as that the multitude of cross-currents of social loyalties will reduce parliament to a façade. The 'real' power struggle will take place anywhere but on 'the floor of the House', and parliament's proceedings will never be more than a formal recording of the results of tussles between the various groups of forces which have taken place privately outside. This criticism, like the first, tends to produce a conviction that the institutions are unimportant.

This view seems both plausible and naive: plausible because, as we have seen, India certainly does manifest a great degree of diversity and it would seem likely that the various forces could only find accommodation by means of fragmented negotiations; naive because in no parliamentary system is there a complete absence of such cross-currents and in no parliament are the party rooms and the lobbies less important than the 'floor' itself. But this view cannot be so quickly disposed of; it will in fact be a purpose of the following chapters to suggest an answer.

[1] In Bhave, on the other hand, there is no trace of resentment or contempt.
[2] This was a familiar, and largely valid, criticism—before partition.

CHAPTER TWO

THE COMING OF PARLIAMENT

1. The Experience

O N the 13th May 1952 the first session of the Indian Parliament opened in New Delhi. In the lives of the newly-elected members the day was certainly of great importance; many of them were taking their places in a representative assembly for the first time.[1] In the history of parliamentary institutions in India, too, the day marked the beginning of a new period. But with institutions, as also perhaps with individuals, we do well to maintain a certain scepticism when confronted with claims that they have begun wholly new lives. It is not easy to find in the new Parliament features that have no earlier beginning. The House of the People and the Council of States were new bodies, but a bicameral central legislature was thirty years old. Adult franchise was new, but the principle of election had been introduced over half a century ago.

Even the name of Parliament had been in use for two years. When the new republican Constitution of India was inaugurated on 26 January 1950 the existing legislature gave itself the title 'Provisional Parliament', and the adjective was forgotten in ordinary usage. To most of her citizens, indeed, India acquired a parliament even before this. The 'appointed day' of the transfer of power, 15 August 1947, would be chosen by many as the crucial birth-date. For on that day the Constituent Assembly became, under the terms of the India Independence Act, the legislature of the new Dominion. Yet the Constituent Assembly itself was built on older foundations—and the story is soon firmly back in the days of British rule.

It was a persistent complaint of India that Britain gave her concessions to Indian national sentiment too late and that she passed on always too little of her own constitutional heritage. The equally persistent comment of the British was that India was in too great a hurry. The Simon Commission, in the concluding pages of its first ('Survey') volume, stated: 'Indian political thought finds it tempting to foreshorten history, and is unwilling to wait for the final stage of a

---

The legislative experience of members is discussed in Chapter III, Section 2.

prolonged evolution. It is impatient of the doctrine of gradualness.'[1] In a similar tone, the Joint Committee on Indian Constitutional Reform emphasised the desirability of an evolutionary development: 'If the long collaboration of Englishmen and Indians is to result in the enactment of a Constitution which will work successfully under Indian conditions, we shall do well to discard theories and analogies and, instead, to base our scheme on the government of India as it exists to-day.' India could and should learn from the older Dominions:

> If the Constitutions of Canada, Australia, New Zealand and South Africa were framed on the British model, it was not because Parliament decided on theoretical grounds to reproduce that model in those countries, but because government in those countries had long been conducted on British principles and had already grown into general conformity with British practice. If these Constitutions, enacted over a period of more than forty years, differ from one another in certain points, those differences are not to be attributed to changes in British constitutional theory, so much as to variations in the experience and practice of the particular communities themselves. In India, too, there is already a system of government which, while possessing many special characteristics, is no less based on British principles, and is no less a living organism. . . . The safest hypothesis on which we can proceed is that the future government of India will be successful in proportion as it represents, not a new creation substituted for an old one, but the natural evolution of an existing government and the natural extension of its past tendencies.[2]

The comparative success of parliamentary government in independent

---

[1] *Report of the Indian Statutory Commission*, 1930 (Cd. 3568), I, 406. The Simon Commission Report was, of course, one of the most comprehensive surveys of Indian politics in the British period. It was also one of the most unpopular in the eyes of Indian opinion. Now when many of the issues with which it dealt are closed, it may be possible to revalue some of its general judgments. In this connection, the passage from which the quotation is taken is worth giving at greater length: 'Down to thirty or forty years ago India stood entirely outside the influence of the course of political ideas which at length produced democratic self-government in some other parts of the world. But in the last generation she has been swayed, at one and the same time, by the force of several conceptions which in Europe had followed a certain sequence. Thus, the struggle for power between rival religious communities, the rise of an intense national spirit, the spread of toleration, the growth of democracy, and the controversies of socialism, mark fairly well-defined epochs in European history. But in India, these various influences are contending side by side for the allegiance of the politically-minded. The growth of national self-consciousness is retarded by communal separation. The movement towards Western industrialism is countered by the return to the spinning wheel. The equality of Asiatic and European is proclaimed, while the clash of Brahmin and non-Brahmin, or caste and outcast, is intensified. Ultra-democratic constitutions are propounded, although the long process which was a necessary precedent to democracy in Europe, viz. the breaking down of class and communal and occupational barriers, has only just begun. Indian political thought finds it tempting to foreshorten history, and is unwilling to wait for the final stage of a prolonged evolution. It is impatient of the doctrine of gradualness.' Few people would now quarrel with this analysis and few would deny that the factors mentioned are still among the decisive ones in modern Indian politics.

[2] *Report of the Joint Committee on Indian Constitutional Reform*, 1934 (H.L. 6/H.C. 5), I, 8.

India can reasonably be attributed to the manner in which each stage in the evolution of political institutions was firmly based on what had gone before. On this method, there was at bottom less disagreement between Britain and India than on occasion appeared. Although Indian leaders sometimes framed their public demands in the form of absolute rights and universal principles, much of their thinking was in fact guided by a reliance on experience. Their estimates of the length of experience required were not the same as those of the British, and they were no doubt more reluctant to admit the need to introduce modifications for India. But their main quarrel with 'the doctrine of gradualness' came less from a distrust of experience than from an impatience with time.

The unmistakably evolutionary character of Indian political development as seen from the present day must not be allowed to obscure the reality of the changes that were made at different stages. Certainly, for the British administrators and statesmen concerned, each step appeared a giant stride—and for the most part along a poorly-lit path. Although few of them might have used Macaulay's well-known words, many would have echoed his sentiments: 'The light of political science and of history is withdrawn—we are walking in darkness—we do not distinctly see whither we are going. It is the wisdom of man, so situated, to feel his way, and not to plant his foot till he is well assured that the ground before him is firm.'[1] From the end of the nineteenth century, however, the statesmen were less assured of the firmness of the ground; they only knew that the risks of a step were less than the risks of standing still.

The story of the development of legislative bodies in India is of course only part of the constitutional history of British rule, and as such it is interwoven with other strands, above all with the relations between the home and Indian governments and with the interplay of unitary and federal forces. It is sufficient here to sketch so much of the legislature aspect as will indicate the experience which has been inherited by modern India's parliamentarians.[2]

Certain functions of government had been assumed by the East India Company in India long before any necessity was felt to distinguish between these functions. Authority rested with the Governor-General and his Council of officials, and in the Governors of the Presidencies (or Provinces) and their similar Councils. They made the laws and executed them. The Charter Act of 1833, while it centralised the law-making function in the Governor-General and Council, introduced the first element of institutional specialisation: the law-making meetings of the Council were differentiated from its executive meetings, and the

[1] Quoted in Coupland, *The Indian Problem*, p. 20.
[2] The student of Indian constitutional history is aided by the existence of excellent official documents. In what follows, I have relied chiefly on these and, in particular, on the Montagu-Chelmsford and Simon Reports.

Council in its legislative capacity was to be expanded by the addition of a fourth member who was to assist in the work of drafting the laws. This first move towards an Indian legislature was dictated not by political but by technical considerations. Politics entered a little more twenty years later: the legislative powers of the Presidency Councils had been taken away but the central government found that it could not conveniently possess the knowledge necessary to legislate for all parts of the country. The Charter Act of 1853 further distinguished the executive and legislative aspects of the Council, and the size of the Council-as-legislature was further increased by the addition of a representative of each Presidency, along with two judges. Certain differences of procedure for legislative purposes were also introduced; above all, the legislative meetings were made public and the proceedings published.

The changes that followed the Mutiny were more radical and were more evidently inspired by political rather than administrative convenience. The Indian Councils Act of 1861 was passed within three years of the end of Company rule and its replacement by the direct responsibility of the Crown. It is important, however, not to read too much into the calculations and hopes of the time. The Mutiny had no doubt been something of a shock.[1] But no one imagined it to be anything very different from what it was—an exasperated revolt of certain discontented sections. Certainly no one at the time could have been so misled as to believe that it represented an Indian national demand for participation in the business of government.[2] It is true that even several decades before the Mutiny a few British rulers of India had spoken of a day when alien domination would cease. But these were private dreams; it was not easy to see to whom power could be transferred nor how it could be done.[3] The impulse behind the Act of 1861 was different. In 1860, Sir Bartle Frere had put the matter clearly: 'The addition of the native element [to the Legislative Councils] has become necessary owing to our diminished opportunities of learning through indirect channels what the natives think of our measures and how the native community

[1] But it is well to be reminded that its effects were acutely felt only in a few areas and that for some it appeared simply as 'the late disturbance in the plains' (Woodruff, *The Guardians* (1954), p. 25).

[2] Nationalists love history but make poor historians, and Indian nationalists who saw in the Mutiny the first war of Indian independence were no exceptions. It is interesting in this connection to note that the 'History of the Freedom Movement' project begun in India in 1953 ran into some difficulty precisely on this point. The historian-Director of the scheme was reported in October, 1955 as resigning partly because he was unable to persuade the project Board that the events of 1857 were a sepoy mutiny and not a national war of independence. (He was also unpopular on account of discovering Hindu-Muslim communal sentiment before the creation of separate electorates by the British.) The whole Board was disbanded in December, 1955. A noteworthy recent addition to Mutiny studies is T. G. P. Spear's charming and scholarly *Twilight of the Moghuls* (1951).

[3] Indeed, the visions of the early nineteenth century become even more obscured after the Mutiny, the alternatives to British rule even less obvious. Three of the better known statements of the earlier period are quoted in Coupland, *op. cit.*, p. 18.

will be affected by them.' The Governor-General's Legislative Council was enlarged by the inclusion of further 'additional members'. The legislative powers of the Provinces were restored and five expanded Provincial Legislative Councils emerged. Moreover, although all the additional members were to be nominated, half of them were to be non-officials. Representation of the Indian public had begun, but the authors of the scheme did not see it as a departure from autocracy, let alone as a first step towards a different system of government. They saw it merely as the sort of device that any sensible autocrat would employ. Frere expressly compared the idea of the new Councils to that of 'the *durbar* of a native Prince . . . the channel from which the ruler learns how his measures are likely to affect his subjects, and may hear of discontent before it becomes disaffection'.[1] Not only was the majority of officials firmly retained; the functions were strictly limited to advice in relation to legislation. Lord MacDonnell explained that the Councils were simply 'committees for the purpose of making laws—committees by means of which the executive Government obtains advice and assistance in their legislation, and the public derive the advantage of full publicity being ensured at every stage of the law-making process. . . . The Councils are not deliberative bodies except with respect to the immediate legislation before them.'[2]

Thirty years later, in the Indian Councils Act of 1892, a further step was taken. In 1861, it had hardly been necessary to point out explicitly that the Councils were not envisaged as parliaments in embryo; by 1892, the disclaimer was expressly made. 'It is necessary', said Lord Dufferin, 'that there should be no mistake about our aims': the Act was not to be regarded as 'an approach to English Parliamentary Government'. 'India', he explained, 'is an integral portion of the mighty British Empire' and the Government of India was responsible not to any local legislatures but 'to the Sovereign and to the British Parliament'. All the same, a step was taken—and indeed the explanations would have been unnecessary otherwise. The Councils were further enlarged and their functions extended in such a way as to permit members to ask questions and to discuss (but not to vote on) the Budget. Lord Dufferin's account of the Government's intentions reveals a new kind of motive which has in it elements of something more than merely intelligent autocracy: the Councils are now designed 'to give a still wider share in the administration of public affairs to such Indian gentlemen as by their influence, their acquirements and the confidence they inspire in their fellow-countrymen, are marked out as fitted to assist with their counsels the responsible rulers of the country'.[3] More novel than this change of

---

[1] Quoted in *Report on Indian Constitutional Reforms*, 1918 (Cd. 9109) (Montagu-Chelmsford Report), p. 51.
[2] *Ibid.*, p. 53.　　　　　　　　　[3] *Ibid.*, p. 57.

emphasis was a change in the method of selecting these non-official members. They were to be nominated as in the past, but the nominations were to be made on the basis of recommendations put forward by various groups. It was a good deal more natural in 1892 than it may be now to think of representation in terms of classes and interests rather than individuals in a territorial constituency. It was even more natural to think in these terms in a country where social and other cleavages were so marked. As a Government of India dispatch of 1892 put it, Indian society was 'essentially a congeries of widely separated classes, races and communities with divergencies of interest and hereditary sentiment'.[1] The object of representation was that 'each important class shall have the opportunity of making its views known in the Council by the mouth of some member specially acquainted with them'. 'Class' and 'interest' were intended in several senses. The instructions accompanying the Act stated: 'Where corporations have been established . . . or where associations have been formed upon a substantial community of interests, professional, commercial or territorial', the Government might entertain 'their recommendations with regard to the selection of members in whose qualifications they might be disposed to confide'.[2] The Muslim community was listed among those groups for whom representation should be provided.[3]

Much that was implied in 1892 was made explicit in the Act of 1909 which embodied the Morley-Minto Reforms. The principle of election was no longer hidden but given legal recognition. Since, however, the new measure was still no more than an extension of an existing system, the 'constituencies' for the new elections were the groups and classes of 1892—universities, municipalities, trade associations, landholders and Muslims.[4] The much enlarged Councils were given greater powers, including the right to move resolutions and ask supplementary questions. Above all, the process of expansion now reached a point where the balance of forces in the Councils shifted appreciably: in the Provinces, non-officials were now in a majority, while even at the Centre the official majority was slender; in Bengal, the elected element alone constituted a majority. These changes only made it seem to the statesmen concerned all the more important to repeat and underline Lord Dufferin's disclaimer. Lord Morley assured the Viceroy of the British Government's 'cordial concurrence . . . [in] repudiating the intention or desire to attempt the transplantation of any European form of representative government to Indian soil'. 'The main standard and test' for any pro-

---

1 Quoted in Coupland, *op. cit.*, p. 24.   2 *Montagu-Chelmsford Report*, p. 60.
3 'Note on the History of Separate Mohammedan Representation' in *Report of the Indian Statutory Commission*, 1930 (Cd. 3568) (Simon Report), I, 183.
4 The authors of the Reforms 'agreed that in the immense diversity of interests and opinion in India, representation by classes and interests was the only practicable means of embodying the elective principle' (*Montagu-Chelmsford Report*, p. 64).

posal of reforms must be whether it gives 'new confidence and a wider range of knowledge, ideas and sympathies to the holders of executive power.'[1] This way of presenting the changes, as if they were intended to meet the rulers' administrative convenience rather than the political demands of the ruled, may not appear wholly convincing in the light of the agitation which was conducted by Indian nationalism at the time. It seems as if an attempt was being made to reassure those who feared that too big a step was contemplated. The same is true of the famous declaration by Lord Morley in answer to criticisms in the House of Lords: 'If it could be said that this chapter of reforms led directly or necessarily to the establishment of a parliamentary system in India, I for one would have nothing at all to do with it.'[2] A recent writer has confessed that it is 'difficult to understand what Lord Morley visualised' when he made this statement.[3] The authors of the Montagu-Chelmsford Report, too, felt 'constrained to say that despite his [Morley's] declaration the features of his reforms . . . do constitute a decided step forward on a road leading at no distant period to a stage at which the question of responsible government was bound to present itself'.[4] But that was written already ten crowded years later. In 1909 it was still easier to look backward than to see final goals. For one thing, although there might be much agitation and 'unrest', it seemed more likely that this had particular and removable causes than that it heralded an irresistible national movement. For another, it seemed as if there were insuperable difficulties to the operation of parliamentary institutions in Indian conditions. In a most revealing passage Lord Morley showed that he conceived of pressure for that end coming from Britain itself, not from India:

> Not one whit more than you [he wrote to the Viceroy] do I think it desirable or possible, or even conceivable, to adapt English political institutions to the nations who inhabit India. Assuredly not in your day or mine. But the *spirit* of English institutions is a different thing, and it is a thing that we cannot escape even if we wished . . . because British constituencies are the masters, and they will assuredly insist—all parties alike—on the spirit of their own political system being applied to India.[5]

The experience communicated and gained through these early Legislative Councils was limited but far from negligible. The electorate involved was still tiny, numbering little over 30,000 for all the Provincial Councils.[6] Even after the successive expansions, the numbers of

---

[1] *Ibid.*, p. 64.   [2] Quoted in *Simon Report*, I, 119.
[3] Sir P. Griffiths, *The British Impact on India* (1952), p. 318.
[4] *Montagu-Chelmsford Report*, p. 68.   [5] Quoted in Coupland, *op. cit.*, p. 26.
[6] *Report of the Franchise (Southborough) Committee*, 1919 (Cd. 141), p. 5. This figure has limited meaning, since the system of elections was mainly indirect. Most of the electors were already representatives—for example, members of municipal councils. The bulk of the 30,000 were Muslim voters who chose their members directly.

4—P.I.

Provincial Council members totalled only 318, of whom only about half were Indian non-officials; to this number must be added a mere 30 or so members of the Indian Legislative Council.[1] The powers and functions of the Councils were also limited by law and by political realities. Some of the limits were indications that the Councils were far from being parliaments in their relations with their executives; others, in the case of the Provinces, were reflections of the firmly unitary character of the constitution.[2] Nevertheless the Montagu-Chelmsford Report was able to conclude that the members had been given 'a real opportunity of exercising some influence on questions of administration and finance'.[3] The legislative record of 131 Acts passed by the Indian Legislative Council between 1910 and 1917, 77 of them without discussion, appears unimpressive. But these figures overlook significant committee discussions and, even more important, they do not indicate that the government had in fact cultivated the habit of consulting members informally before introducing proposed measures. The newly-granted power to move resolutions was used—and the fact that, out of 168, only 24 were accepted obscures the general effect of the motions. A sure indication of growing liveliness is given by the increasing use of questions: twice as many were asked in 1917 as in 1911. Budget discussions, the voting divisions and finally the introduction of an advisory finance committee added to the transformation. And similar developments took place on most of the Provincial Councils. The atmosphere may not have been wholly parliamentary, but the change as compared with the pre-1909 period—when 'a handful of officials and two or three complaisant Indian gentlemen sat round a table and read manuscript speeches in turn'[4]—was marked enough. Lord Meston's summary of the achievement up to 1919 appears just: in spite of 'much unreality in the business', 'futile disputation, growing impatience and irresponsible criticism', nevertheless the Councils

> familiarised an increasing number of intelligent Indians with administrative questions; provided them, through the right of interpellation, with facts which had previously been unavailable; enabled them by moving resolutions to put the official world on its defence and to elicit principles and motives for action which had previously been taken for granted; gave them a considerable influence in the conduct of affairs.[5]

[1] *Ibid.*

[2] Examples of the latter limits were: the need for Provinces to submit all their legislative proposals to the Governor-General for sanction and their inability to legislate on the large range of subjects already dealt with by the central Council. The modification of such provisions in later years belongs to the history of federation in India.

[3] *Montagu-Chelmsford Report*, p. 6.

[4] Ilbert and Meston, *The New Constitution of India* (1923), p. 91.

[5] *Ibid.*, p. 93. It has been thought worth while to include (Appendix II) a selection from Indian central legislature discussions on the financial statement or budget. These may indicate something of the changing tones of the emerging Parliament.

'Putting the official world on its defence' and exercising 'considerable influence' were, however, not enough for the post-war mood of political India. Something more was wanted, and some British statesmen—including even a few of those on the spot—did not fail to appreciate the situation. The Secretary of State wrote at the time: 'My visit to India means that we are going to do something, and something big. I cannot go home and produce a little thing or nothing; it must be epoch-making or it is a failure; it must be the keystone of the future history of India.'[1] The Declaration of 1917 had spoken not only of 'the increasing association of Indians in every branch of the administration' but also of 'the gradual development of self-governing institutions with a view to the progressive realisation of responsible government in India as an integral part of the British Empire'. Indian opinion expected much following this and was mainly disappointed by what emerged in the form of the Montagu-Chelmsford Report and the Act of 1919 based thereon.[2] Looking back at this distance of time, it can be seen that even if 'epoch-making' was too hopeful a term, the 1919 reforms did constitute the 'keystone' of subsequent constitutional development.

After 1917 it was not a question primarily of how to make the autocracy work more smoothly; it was a question rather of finding a way towards a transfer of power. That phrase was certainly nowhere used, but its meaning was implicit in the way the Report contrasted its purpose with that of previous reforms. There was now 'a new policy' and the authors beheld 'the colossal nature of the enterprise'. 'Hitherto we have ruled India by a system of absolute government, but have given her people an increasing share in the administration of the country and increasing opportunities of influencing and criticising the government'[3]; even the Morley-Minto Reforms were no more than 'the final outcome of the old conception which made the Government of India a benevolent despotism'.[4]

If the need for 'something big' was clear and the difference of kind between 1909 and 1919 quite evident, it was still not at all obvious which was the safest way forward. Britain would be 'letting go' bit by bit, but which bits first, and with what safeguards in case the new hands fumbled dangerously? To learn responsibility in the exercise of power, it was

1 Edwin Montagu, *An Indian Diary* (1930), p. 8.

2 Much of the disappointment was caused not by the Act itself but by other political developments such as the Amritsar incident which seemed to indicate that nothing would change after all. It must also be said that even if the reforms had 'gone further', as Montagu had hoped (*op. cit.*, p. 5), and even if there had been no Rowlatt Acts and no Amritsar slaughter, it is more likely than not that Gandhi's leadership would have taken the nationalist movement away from the quasi-parliaments and towards the techniques of non-co-operation.

3 *Montagu-Chelmsford Report*, pp. 5-6.

4 *Ibid.*, p. 69.

necessary that power be given and, therefore, risks taken.[1] But where and how? By stages—in which Sir William Duke and Lionel Curtis took prominent parts—it became clear that the great experiment would have to be started at the provincial level; even then it would have to be limited to a particular range of subjects. Provincial governments would be divided into two compartments: one of Indian Ministers responsible to elected legislatures for the 'transferred' subjects, the other of officials responsible to the Governor for the 'reserved' subjects.[2]

The Montagu-Chelmsford Report presented this conclusion only after its authors had given not only a brilliant historical review but had also undertaken a penetrating analysis of the nature of the problem. First, then, what was the goal? To all concerned, 'responsible government' meant the British parliamentary pattern,[3] and the Report went to the trouble of explaining what this implied: 'The electors send their men to the Councils with power to act in their name, and the Councils commit power to Ministers, over whom they reserve control in the form of the power of removing them from office. The elector controls his government because if his representative in Council supports Ministers of whom he disapproves he can at the next election change his representative.'[4] This account may be a classic statement of the liberal-radical theory of the nineteenth-century British constitution. As such, it had, even in its heyday, failed to win assent from non-liberal opinion. Moreover, by its omission of any reference to political parties, it showed itself increasingly in need of modification. In the context of its application to India, this inattention to the transforming role of parties was perhaps pardonable, since it was not easy in 1918 to discern an emerging pattern of political groups. But even here it was a dangerous omission, because it could (and to some extent did) lead to institutional arrangements which inhibited rather than encouraged the rise of parties. It can also be argued that although Montagu was personally optimistic and certainly determined to press on towards the final goal of an Indian Parliament, this

1 Montagu, *An Indian Diary*, pp. 136, 134: 'The reasons which make self-government impossible in this country now are not really distrust or unfitness or lack of ability or want of character. . . . What we want is a growth of those conventions and customs and habits of representative government without the acquisition of which democracy cannot stand. . . . It is this use of power which they must be taught, which they must learn by experience.' Montagu was of course ahead of British opinion in India; he had always to 'try and bring the Government of India with me.' (*Ibid.*, p. 55.)

2 On the emergence of the dyarchy idea, see (apart from the *Report* and Montagu's *Diary*) L. Curtis, *Papers relating to the Application of the Principle of Dyarchy* (1920). The story is, of course, told in constitutional and political histories of modern India such as A. B. Keith, *Constitutional History of India, 1600–1935* (1936), and R. Coupland, *The Indian Problem, 1833–1935*, being Volume I of *A Report on the Constitutional Problem in India* (1942–43).

3 Perhaps the only exception was Curzon who, although the author of this passage of the 1917 Declaration, apparently thought it meant something much vaguer (Coupland, *op. cit.*, p. 53).

4 *Montagu-Chelmsford Report*, p. 109.

theory tended to make the job seem even more difficult than it was. Be that as it may, there must be less disagreement with what the Report went on to say of responsible government:

> The system pre-supposes in those who work it such a perception of, and loyalty to, the common interests as enables the decisions of the majority to be peaceably accepted. This means that majorities must practise toleration and minorities patience. There must, in fact, be not merely a certain capacity for business, but, what is much more important, a real perception of the public welfare as something apart from, and with superior claims to, the individual good. The basis of the whole system is a lively and effective sense of the sanctity of the people's rights.[1]

As to the raw material that had to be worked upon in order that this goal should be reached, the Report saw two sets of facts about India as specially relevant. In the first place, in a land of great size and immense population, among whom 'the curve of wealth descends steeply', the vast majority live in poor villages in circumstances that limit vision severely. The rural population had come to put their grievances before their rulers, but it was still 'a revolution' from that to the new relationship with an elected representative. Interest in politics was confined to the urban minority—and even there it was necessary to distinguish between 'a core of earnest men who believe sincerely in and strive for political progress', 'a ring of less educated people to whom a phrase or a sentiment appeals' and 'an outside fringe "attracted by curiosity and finding diversion" in attacks "on a big and very solemn government, as urchins might take a perilous joy in casting toy darts at an elephant"'.[2] In the second place, it had to be admitted that Indian society was divided even more seriously than between town and country and rich and poor. The Report quoted from Lord Dufferin writing in the 'nineties: 'This population is composed of a large number of distinct nationalities, professing various religions, practising diverse rites, speaking different languages, while many of them are still further separated from one another by discordant prejudices, by conflicting source of usages and even antagonistic material interests.' It hastened to say that the colours of the Dufferin picture 'have since toned down' and to recognise that there was 'a new sense of unity'. Even so, however, India was still a country 'marching in uneven stages through all the centuries from the fifth to the twentieth'.[3] Despite all this, the Report boldly proclaimed that the time had come to disturb 'the placid, pathetic contentment of the masses' and to 'call forth capacity and self-reliance in place of helplessness, nationhood in place of caste or communal feeling'.

The reforms schemes and the Act of 1919, by envisaging a grant of responsible government in a certain field of government at the provincial level, entailed a joining together of the two processes of the transformation

[1] *Ibid.*   [2] *Ibid.*   [3] *Ibid.*, pp. 117–118.

of devolution into federalism and the development of parliamentary institutions. The Act and its rules contributed to the first process by giving definition and legal form to separate lists of provincial and central subjects and by an allocation of distinct sources of revenue.[1] The second process (with which we are here mainly concerned) was furthered in three main ways. First, representation was pushed further in the Provincial Councils. All the Councils were enlarged, the proportion of elected members was increased to not less than 70% and the property qualifications for the franchise were lowered to bring the number of provincial voters up to about $5\frac{1}{2}$ millions.[2] The authors of the Report wrestled with the question of separate electorates—and lost. They admitted that the system of communal electorates only perpetuated divided loyalties which hamper the development of a proper citizen spirit; they conceded that it encouraged minorities to be dependent,[3] and majorities to be complacent; all things considered, they felt the system to be 'a very serious hindrance to the development of the self-governing principle'. And yet, 'the hard facts' of distrust and lack of mutual confidence had to be faced, and, for the Muslims at least, the system 'must be maintained until conditions alter—even at the price of slower progress towards the realisation of a common citizenship'; it must even be extended—to the Sikhs.[4] In the second place, the list of provincial subjects had to be divided in order to define the area of responsible government. Law and order and land-revenue were subjects 'reserved' in the charge of the Governor and his Executive Council (now generally composed of two British and two Indian members) in accordance with the previous system. The other subjects were 'transferred' to the Governor, acting on the advice of Ministers in accordance with parliamentary practice. This transfer of powers was, not unnaturally, hedged about with safeguards: some of these provided for central intervention on, for instance, civil service matters and imperial interests; others provided the Governor with powers—of veto, certification, reservation, etc.—quite different from those of a strictly 'constitutional head'. Finally, although

[1] The task, said the Report, was 'the very reverse of that which confronted Alexander Hamilton and Sir John Macdonald', not, that is, the bringing together by means of a pact hitherto separate units, but rather of 'drawing lines of demarcation, cutting long-standing ties' (*ibid.*, p. 101).

[2] The Report had simply insisted that indirect elections, thought responsible for much of the unreality in proceedings, should be 'swept away', and that any limitations on the franchise 'should be determined rather with reference to practical difficulties than to any *a priori* considerations as to the degree of education or amount of income which may be held to constitute a qualification' (*ibid.*, p. 185). The details were worked out by the Franchise (Southborough) Committee (1919, Cmd. 141), which rejected literacy tests but stuck to property qualifications.

[3] Montagu's *Indian Diary* is full of references which show how he was angered by the passive attitude of minorities who leant on the government for protection, and how he was determined at least not to extend the principle of separate electorates (e.g., pp. 114, 118).

[4] *Ibid.*, pp. 186–190.

the great experiment of responsibility was to be performed at the provincial level, it was agreed that representation should be taken further even at the Centre.[1] In place of the small Legislative Council there was set up a bicameral legislature consisting of a Legislative Assembly of 145 members, of whom 104 were elected (on a franchise higher in property qualification than in the Provinces), and a Council of State of 60 members, 34 of whom were elected (on an extremely high property franchise).

A beginning was thus made and, like most beginnings, it was not easy. Under the most favourable conditions, dyarchy would have been 'a high test of human nature'[2] on all sides. Each side of provincial government would 'advise and assist' the other and neither would control or impede the other. Great tact and forbearance were called for from the participants and a fund of goodwill towards the enterprise on the part of public opinion.

In point of fact, as already mentioned,[3] conditions became distinctly unfavourable. Between early 1919 (when even the fiery Tilak was prepared to stand for election and almost all sections thought in terms of working the new scheme) and early 1920, 'the whole aspect of things had altered'.[4] The unpopular Rowlatt Acts, the awful sequel of the shooting in Jallianwalla Bagh at Amritsar, the Turkish Treaty which distressed Muslim opinion, the introduction of new extra-parliamentary techniques of political agitation and the increasingly evident nervousness and hostility of many of the British civil servants—all these played their part in spoiling the ground for the delicate seeds of partial responsible government. Yet, although it must have appeared at the time to British and Indian alike that dyarchy and the whole Montagu-Chelmsford scheme were an unqualified failure, when assessed as a deliberately temporary step towards an admittedly difficult goal they are seen as a qualified success.[5] Moreover there is not a great deal of disagreement between British and Indian authorities on the main characteristics of

[1] The Indian Legislative Council at the time had 68 members of whom 27 were elected. Montagu was biting in his comments: 'Nobody could have gone to the debate yesterday without realising what a farce it all was—that these 27 creatures should claim to be a representative institution' (*op. cit.*, p. 248). As we have already indicated, the Council had not been useless, but it had been fashioned as an extended 'durbar', not as an embryonic parliament. Hence Montagu's further comment: 'Their only chance, living at Delhi as they do, is to be surrounded by a really representative collection of people from all over India. This can only be done by enlarging and liberalising the Legislative Council. . . . Further, the Legislative Council as it stands is not meant to develop; Morley said so. We want to sweep away this dead wood and make something that is intended to develop.' (*Ibid.*, p. 117.)

[2] Ilbert and Meston, *op. cit.*, p. 138.

[3] Above, p. 51.

[4] 'Kerala Putra', *The Working of Dyarchy in India* (Bombay, 1928), p. 29 (the author was K. M. Panikkar).

[5] This kind of revision of opinion had happened before (Canada) and was to happen later (Ceylon, West Africa).

this period 1919–35, even if some aspects receive more emphasis from some writers than others.[1]

What then was the contribution of dyarchy to the development of parliamentary experience? The negative or limiting factors may be detected without difficulty. In the first place, experience went in not quite the right directions. The non-co-operation movement 'diverted the main stream of political activity' and many of the more and increasingly important leaders of Indian opinion abstained from participation in the reformed Councils.[2] The major party, the Swarajists (who were Congressmen), boycotted the first elections of 1923, and contested subsequent elections only to obstruct the exercise of power, not to obtain it. This had its effect on public attitudes towards the Councils: they were 'deprived of the interest and credit which they might have won from the public under normal conditions'. Equally, it disturbed the morale of the legislators who were 'kept in a state of nervous dread of the political agitation outside'.[3]

The idea of the reforms was to train men in responsibility—as Ministers, as legislators, as voters. At each level, there were serious difficulties in the way of realising this end. The responsibility of Ministers was hindered by the absence behind them of firm and organised majorities. Apart from the non-participating Swarajists, members belonged to ill-defined groups: 'the various groupings, with kaleidoscopic changes of nomenclature, composition and leadership, have not often been on anything but communal lines, and their communal character has tended to become more rather than less pronounced'.[4] Alongside this factor was the powerful presence of the bloc of officials in the Councils. They did not number more than 30%, but it soon became evident that the Ministers of the transferred half of the governments badly needed the support of these officials if the passing of their measures was to be ensured. So the Ministers became decreasingly responsible to an inchoate legislature and increasingly responsible to the compact and disciplined representatives of the reserved half of the governments.[5] This

---

[1] British official surveys are found in the Reports of the Reforms Enquiry (Muddiman) Committee, 1925 (Cd. 2360), and Simon Commission, as well as more briefly in the books of Keith and Coupland already mentioned. Indian studies include *The Working of Dyarchy in India*, by 'Kerala Putra' (Bombay, 1928), and A. Appadorai, *Dyarchy in Practice* (1937).

[2] *Muddiman Report*, p. 2.

[3] *Ibid.*

[4] *Simon Report*, I, 209. For this situation, incomplete responsibility and separate electorates have both properly taken their share of the blame. It is nevertheless doubtful if organised political parties could have been expected to develop so quickly even in the most 'ideal' conditions.

[5] Ministerial responsibility to the legislatures, wrote 'Kerala Putra', 'has been a myth' (*op. cit.*, p. 52). The same author demonstrated that in view of the bloc of nominated and official members, together with so many seats for special interests (Land, Industry, etc.), a party would have had to obtain, for example, in the Madras Council, no less than 75% of the 'general seats' (which were in turn subdivided according to community and included Muslim and Christian seats) in order to secure a council majority.

tendency was reinforced by the character of relations between the Ministers and provincial Governors. The intention of the reforms may have been to make Governors mere constitutional heads in relation to the transferred half, but in most cases this position was not established. Governors treated Ministers as advisors whose advice need not be taken. Moreover any hope of Ministers developing a system of joint responsibility was discouraged by the evident preference of most Governors for dealing with Ministers separately. Again, the division of subjects was such that Ministers found it necessary at several points to carry the reserved half with them if they were to proceed with their schemes.[1]

Nor is it difficult to see respects in which the legislators' sense of responsibility was inhibited. Their powers were at once considerable and inconclusive. They could pass legislation which might then be vetoed; they could make cuts in the budget which could then be 'restored'; they could reject government measures which would then be certified as passed. Add to this the absence of defined parties and the ambiguity of relations between the two halves of government and one has the ingredients of irresponsible parliaments. Nor was there much hope of responsibility being imposed on council members by their electors. Constituencies were generally very large; in most cases, contact between member and voters was slight and dependent on considerations other than those of policy and programme; and in any case main political interest centred elsewhere.

Yet, even if all this is true, it is not the whole story. During the period of dyarchy, four general elections were held and the percentage of the electors voting increased. No less than 93 public men had experience as Ministers, no less than 121 as members of Governors' Executive Councils. The number who gained experience as legislators at central or provincial levels cannot be less than 1,000 and is probably twice that figure.[2] Even the quality of the experience cannot be dismissed as negligible. It is true that the tone of legislatures was generally hostile to 'Government' as a matter of principle and, in so far as they made any distinction between reserved and transferred halves, more hostile to the former. In spite of this much was learnt in the Provincial Councils—and even in the Central Legislature. It was noted that the groupings in the Councils did gradually improve their organisations.[3] Debates were generally well attended, there was a high level of courtesy and genuine respect for the Chair, and proceedings were conducted in an impartial manner. Above

[1] One Minister, giving evidence before the Muddiman Committee, complained: 'I was Minister of Development—without the forests. I was Minister of Agriculture minus irrigation. . . . I was Minister for Industry without factories, boilers, electricity and water power, mines or labour, all of which are reserved subjects.' (Quoted in 'Kerala Putra', op. cit., p. 48.)

[2] Appadorai, op. cit., p. 72.

[3] Simon Report, I, 209: 'regular meetings of groups and the appointment of Whips have become more usual'.

all, perhaps, while it was no doubt frustrating to have to oppose without prospect of power, at least the techniques of opposition were mastered, and a good deal learnt in one way and another of the business of government. The supplementary question, the resolution and the cut motion in budget debates were all fully and not unskilfully exploited.[1] Committees, too, served a purpose: although government-dominated, Public Accounts Committees, Standing Finance Committees, Standing Committees for other departments and Special Committees (set up in response to questions or resolutions) made governments fully aware of public reactions and encouraged members to study aspects of administration.[2]

On the one side, therefore, governments, while not seriously threatened (owing to their reserve powers), were continuously 'exposed to challenge and comment' and were in fact considerably influenced in many of their actions by Council opinion.[3] On the side of the legislatures, what is remarkable, in view of the temptations to irresponsibility, is perhaps the extent to which the Councils (with one or two exceptions), so far from bringing the quasi-parliamentary government to a halt, did so far as possible play their roles constructively. A fair amount of useful social legislation was passed and a sincere attempt was in many places made to improve the conditions of the people. At the same time, the legislatures on the whole acted responsibly in matters of finance and law and order; if governments were reluctant to use their special powers, legislatures were almost as reluctant to force them to do so; budget cuts had fairly frequently to be restored, but in the provinces only once was a bill 'certified', and only twice or thrice was the veto employed.[4] Finally, even from the point of view of the electorate, the time of dyarchy was not time wholly wasted. If it is true that electoral contests were generally half-hearted affairs, at least in a few instances Ministers were defeated and the voters began to have the sense of power in their hands. And even if the centre of political gravity was in the non-co-operation movement, the Councils were not without their place of importance in public life: the public galleries were usually well filled, the debates widely reported and read. Parliamentary life had begun in India. There was, after all, some justification for the *Simon Report*'s impatience with

---

1 Appadorai (*op. cit.*, p. 82) gives these figures for one Province during the first nine years of reformed Councils: 3,801 resolutions on topics in the reserved half, 1,346 on those in the transferred half. The same author mentions 28 supplementaries on one occasion as not wholly untypical. Similarly in the first four years in Madras, 3,393 cut motions were admitted and 753 were discussed. ('Kerala Putra', *op. cit.*, p. 62.)

2 'Kerala Putra', *op. cit.*, pp. 67–69. See also *Simon Report*, I, 216 ff. See also below, Chapter VI, Sections 3 and 4, *passim*.

3 In one Council, in three years, of 109 resolutions passed, no fewer than 80 led to some government action ('Kerala Putra', *op. cit.*, p. 62). Appadorai even suggests that governments paid so much attention to legislature opinion that they became timid and failed to carry out measures that were needed (*op. cit.*, p. 112).

4 *Simon Report*, I, 217.

nationalist impatience: 'Political ideas are so rapidly assimilated by Indian progressives and the sense of novelty so quickly wears off that it is really necessary to pause and appreciate the extent of the transformation. Less then ten years ago there was not a province in India in which parliamentary institutions existed.'[1]

The process by which the next step (in the shape of the Act of 1935) was prepared was even more elaborate and complex than had been the case with the Montagu-Chelmsford scheme. Following the somewhat insipid report of the Muddiman Committee in 1925, the Simon Commission was appointed in 1927 and made its first visit to India in the spring of the following year. After exhaustive study, it published its Report in 1930. This was then commented upon in a Government of India Despatch of the same year. There followed the series of three Round Table Conferences in London, the last one in December 1932. A Joint Select Committee of both Houses in Westminster, appointed in 1933 to examine the Government's proposals which had been published in a White Paper, worked for eighteen months, and the resulting Bill was introduced into the Commons at the end of 1934. The Act was finally passed in August 1935.

This examination of the problem, like that undertaken in 1917–19, was naturally concerned with more than the development of legislatures. It also took place against a background of political events as turbulent as those that accompanied the earlier reforms. This is not the place to discuss either the constitutional details or the political history.[2] For our purpose, it is enough to summarise the main provisions and principal events.

The Simon Commission met with hostility from nationalist opinion from the moment when it was greeted at Bombay with black banners inscribed 'Simon, go back' to the final bitter condemnation of its Report. The Commission's main recommendation was the abolition of dyarchy in the Provinces and the complete transfer of all provincial subjects to Ministers responsible to enlarged legislatures elected on a greatly extended franchise. Separate electorates for the communities could not be abolished, for Hindu–Muslim tension had not decreased but increased since 1919.[3] So far as the Centre was concerned, the Report was more cautious. If the Provinces were to be given such 'new and heavy responsibilities', strength and stability must be preserved at the Centre. This

[1] *Ibid.*, I, 132. The Report pointed out that by contrast the old Morley-Minto Councils were presided over by the Governor-General and by Governors (whereas after 1921 there were nominated and then elected presiding officers), were still in form the old Executive Councils with some 'additional members' chosen to help in advice on legislation, and were not directly elected.

[2] See Keith, *op. cit.*, and Coupland, *op. cit.*

[3] The *Report of the Indian Central Committee* (1929, Cd. 3451) (a Committee of Indian members of the Central Legislature) had recommended considerable replacement of separate electorates by reserved seats.

was taken to mean that, until it was clear that the provincial experiment was succeeding, there could be not even a partial transfer of responsibility at the Centre. In the Commission's view, all that could be done at once was to re-fashion the central legislature on explicitly federal lines: both the Lower House, now to be called the Federal Assembly, and the Council of State should be chosen indirectly by Provincial Councils. The difficult but unavoidable problem of the relation between British India and the Indian states could be tentatively approached by bringing representatives of both together on a purely consultative Council for Greater India. The Government of India[1] was doubtful on the federal principle, feeling that with provincial self-government being developed apace everything should be done to preserve the unifying factors. On the other hand, it was prepared to go further than the Commission in the direction of a gradual transfer of responsibility at the Centre: the central government should be composed of officials and Ministers, and the numbers and powers of the latter should be permitted by convention to expand. Without the rigidity of dyarchy, a way of moving towards complete responsible government could be found.

In the outcome—following the three Round Table Conferences and the Parliamentary Joint Committee on Indian Constitutional Reform[2] —something of both views prevailed. Part II of the Act of 1935 made provision for the establishment of 'The Federation of India', including British India and the princely states. This depended, however, on the accession of a sufficient number of states to the Federation. As in fact this never took place, the federal part of the Act remained inoperative. It is, however, instructive in view of subsequent developments to see what was envisaged. The Simon Commission's vision of a federal Centre is realised—but with major 'centralist' modifications. The Upper House, the Council of State, was to consist of Rulers' nominees in the case of the states and of directly elected representatives for British India, each unit having a number of seats in proportion to its population. The Federal Assembly was to be similarly chosen, except that the British Indian seats were to be filled by indirect elections in Provincial Assemblies. Federal, Concurrent and Provincial Lists of subjects were elaborated and residuary powers were allocated by the Governor-General in his discretion. A proclamation of emergency would enable the federal legislature to legislate on any subject in the Provincial List. The federal executive was envisaged on dyarchy lines. There was to be a Council of Ministers, but certain subjects—notably defence and foreign affairs— were 'reserved' to the Governor-General aided by 'counsellors', and were not subject to vote. Moreover even in the 'transferred' field certain safeguards were inserted in the form of provisions for the Governor-

1 *Despatch* (20 Sept. 1930, Cd. 3700).
2 Cd. 3778, Cd. 3997, Cd. 4238; H.C. 5 of 1933–34.

General to 'act in his discretion' and to 'exercise his individual judgment'.[1] The former power extended from the 'reserved' subjects to control of the Reserve Bank, appointment of Ministers and summoning of the legislature, and power to declare an emergency. The latter power was mainly for exercise in relation to the Governor-General's eight 'special responsibilities': peace and tranquillity; minorities; civil servants; British commercial interests; backward areas; princely states; the financial stability and credit of the Federal Government; the effective execution of all federal orders.

Although the federal part of the 1935 Act did not come into force, the federal principle was established—in the sense that a division of powers and resources between Centre and units was given elaborate statutory form in the Federal, Provincial and Concurrent Lists, and also in that the Provinces were 'invested for the first time with a separate legal personality'.[2] Moreover the Provinces were moved forward from dyarchy to almost completely responsible parliamentary government. The 'almost' qualification was what nationalist opinion distrusted and disliked[3]: for although the whole range of provincial subjects was now transferred to the popular, responsible, ministerial side of government, certain safeguards were built up and placed in the hands of the provincial Governors. These were powers of 'discretion' and 'individual judgment' similar to those of the Governor-General at the Centre, not including any distinct 'subjects' but covering a number of aspects which might or might not in effect destroy the substance of provincial responsible autonomy. The considerable expansion of the provincial legislatures and—more important—of the provincial franchise which the Act provided were scarcely noticed in the great discussions that took place on the nature of the Act.[4] So opposed were the British and the Indian judgments of the Act that it is not easy to realise that they refer to the same document. The Indian view was shared by some moderate liberals and all ardent Congressmen. Sir C. Y. Chintamani wrote: 'I venture to describe the Government of India Act of 1935 as the anti-India Act. We are given a limp federation full of undesirable features, ill-balanced as between the States and the Provinces and denied powers which are vital to every government worth the name.' Congress leaders found it hardly necessary to study provisions in detail to see that they amounted to a 'slave constitution' and 'a new charter of bondage'. The British

---

[1] There was a nice distinction between these two powers. In the first case, Ministers were not entitled to give advice—though the Governor-General might seek it if he wished. 'Exercising individual judgment', on the other hand, implied that ministerial advice would be given, though the Governor-General could disregard it.

[2] Coupland, *op. cit.*, p. 133.

[3] Congress was, of course, even more disappointed at the federal arrangements which seemed to ensure that the rate of advance would be determined by the speed of the slowest elements—the princes.

[4] The table at the end of this section sets out the growth of assemblies and electorate.

view was that the Act provided for 'the passing of the centre of political gravity from British to Indian hands'—and this was the view of those who favoured such a step as well as of those who deplored it.[1]

Like the Act of 1919, that of 1935 began its life in difficult circumstances. Quite apart from the hesitation of the Princes to surrender some of their sovereignty through instruments of accession, so as to bring into effect the federal scheme, opposition to the 'safeguards' was such that even the provincial part of the scheme was threatened. The first hurdle was passed when all the parties decided to contest the elections to Provincial Assemblies which took place during the winter 1936–37. The Muslim League was prepared to work the provincial constitution 'for what it is worth'; the Congress wanted to win the elections only 'to combat the Act and seek the end of it'. But at least both parties produced documents that amounted to programmes, and at least the electoral campaigns were conducted with vigour. Moreover it was held a good omen for the future that the two main parties appeared to be on not unfriendly terms, that their programmes were not widely different and that they even established a common platform in some areas. And if British observers were sceptical as to how much the voters understood of the issues in detail, at least the appeal of Gandhi and the Congress was evident and over 54% of the electorate went to the polls. Congress won 711 of the 1,585 Provincial Assembly seats—and this in spite of contesting only 58 of the 482 separate Muslim seats. It won clear majorities in 5 of the 11 Provinces and was the largest party in a further 3.

Far from certain, however, was the question whether Congress would consider the conditions suitable for the acceptance of governmental responsibility. If the 'safeguards' were the decisive part of the Act, then popular ministries would be in a false position of responsibility without power and parliamentary experience was not worth buying at that price. For some months a battle for 'assurances' took place. In March 1937 the All-India Congress Committee resolution on office acceptance was passed. This was a compromise between two schools of Congress thought—those of the 'Left' under Pandit Nehru who were inclined to a non-co-operation policy of destroying the Act by causing its breakdown, those of the 'Right' who were eager to assume power and were content to try to work the scheme 'for what it was worth'. The terms of the resolution were that Congress ministries would be formed only in those Provinces where the leader of the party in the legislature 'is satisfied and able to state publicly that so long as he and his Cabinet act within the constitution the Governor will not use his powers of interference

[1] All quoted in N. Srinivasan, *Democratic Government in India* (Calcutta, 1954), pp. 62–64.

or set aside the advice of Ministers'.[1] The Governors were unable to give such assurances and minority ministries were formed. This position was clearly not one that either side wished to continue. In June the Viceroy issued a statement explaining the spirit in which the provincial constitutions would be worked, and in the following month the Congress Working Committee gave permission for Congress governments to be formed. Such governments at once took office in seven Provinces and in an eighth a year later; all these Congress ministries resigned in October–November 1939. Non-Congress governments in three Provinces remained in power from 1937 through the war, while similar governments took over from Congress in three Provinces during the war years. These years, then, from 1937 to 1939 (or, in some cases, later) were crucial years in India's experience of parliamentary government; what conclusions were suggested by this experience?

The record may be summarised under three headings: relations between Congress and other political parties; the performance of ministries; and relations between Congress ministries and their party headquarters. On the first of these, most British observers expressed some disappointment. Coupland, for example, impressed with the necessity for some improvement in communal relations if political advance was to continue within the framework of a united India, came to a firmly despondent conclusion:

All the provinces suffered more or less from the growth of communal antagonism, but in several of the Congress provinces it overclouded the whole picture. Owing . . . in particular to the high command's refusal to share power with the Muslim League, Hindu–Muslim discord became so bitter that, at the time the ministries resigned, it seemed, in the United Provinces and Bihar at any rate, that, without a drastic change of policy, constitutional government might soon become impossible.[2]

By the time Coupland was writing (1943) there may have been some Congressmen, too, who would in private have agreed that a coalition offer to Mr. Jinnah in 1937 might have saved a lot of trouble, and perhaps partition, later. B. P. Singh Roy certainly agreed that the Congress laid down impossible and fantastic terms for Muslim League co-operation when it was offered in the United

[1] B. P. Singh Roy, *Parliamentary Government in India* (Calcutta, 1943), p. 207. The author of this work was a member of a provincial legislature from 1921 and had a decade's experience as Minister. Other accounts from the Indian side of the working of the 1935 Act are to be found in P. N. Masaldan, *Evolution of Provincial Autonomy in India, 1858–1950* (Bombay, 1953) and in articles in the *Indian Journal of Political Science* (especially those of P. N. Masaldan in Oct.–Dec. 1941, D. Verma in April–June 1940, S. V. Kokegar in Jan.–March 1941 and B. N. Banerjee in July–Sept. 1941). The best account, however, remains that of Professor Coupland: *Indian Politics, 1936–42* (1943), being Volume II of his *Report on the Constitutional Problem in India*.

[2] Coupland, *Indian Politics, 1936–42*, p. 157.

Provinces.[1] Although events were to prove the Congress short-sighted, their attitude can at least be understood. The League was still small and it was not clear that Congress could not win away the Muslim masses. Moreover even though the League's manifesto had a progressive appearance, the party's social composition was thought to dictate a conservative legislative programme which would have conflicted with Congress radicalism. That these Congress calculations were mistaken became too quickly evident. As early as April 1938 the League stated its view that Congress ministries had failed to protect the minority, and it pointed to the riots in several Provinces. Jinnah's presidential address to the League in October contained more charges, and the bitterness of tone that marked later Indian history was distinctly heard: Congress, he said, was getting into 'the hands of those who are looking forward to the creation of a serious situation which will break India horizontally and vertically'.[2] A Muslim League 'Committee of Enquiry' prepared a list of Muslim grievances; a Congress offer to get the charges looked into by the Chief Justice (an Englishman) was rejected; and when Congress ministries resigned in 1939 Jinnah declared a 'Deliverance Day'.

Also in its relations with groups other than the Muslim League, Congress began to get a reputation for intolerance. Where it had clear majorities it insisted on 'going it alone'; where it was in opposition it was generally not content to be a purely parliamentary opposition. All this, of course, was but a natural consequence of the character of the party, of its aspiration to be an all-embracing national movement rather than one party among many. Sir Chimanlal Setalvad, Sir Cowasjee Jehangir, Dr. Ambedkar and others in a statement in October 1939 said that the record of Congress since 1937 'belies the hope that the present Congress leaders want to establish real democracy in India. The Congress governments resent any opposition and wish, like autocrats, that no opposition should exist. . . . Minority opinion is ignored with callous indifference. . . . Congress cannot bear rivals and cannot bear sharing credit.'[3] This was an unduly harsh verdict, but it was certainly echoed in British comments. Mr. Guy Wint, for example, noted not only the inclusion in Congress of all classes and its identification of itself with the Indian nation but also the fact that the movement had developed ahead of parliamentary institutions, whereas in the West, parties were generally more recent than parliaments; as a consequence, he wrote, 'Con-

---

[1] B. P. Singh Roy, *op. cit.*, p. 217. The terms apparently were, *inter alia*, that League members should join Congress, the League group in the Assembly should cease to function as a separate group and its members should obey Congress orders, the League should refrain from contesting by-elections and the League's Parliamentary Board should be disbanded.

[2] Quoted in B. P. Singh Roy, *op. cit.*, p. 242.

[3] *Ibid.*, p. 244.

gress's adoption of parliamentary ideas was to some extent fortuitous. . . . So long as a parliamentary regime means a Congress Raj, Congress is content with parliamentary institutions; the test would come if Congress faced the prospect of a prolonged exile from office.'[1] The point, of course, is that it is not reasonable to expect a nationalist movement to transform itself easily into a political party—and certainly not to expect this to happen before the achievement of independence. So long as the national struggle has not been won, 'exile from office' can be seen only as continued power in the hands of the alien oppressors or their agents.[2]

In most other respects, the record of the new ministries—Congress and non-Congress—was good. At the legislature level, the expanded assemblies worked well: 'The capacity already shown by Indian politicians to make an orderly and effective use of the traditional deliberative and legislative machinery of representative government has been confirmed.'[3] Of course, even at this level, there were some departures from British practice. The role of the new Speakers, for example, was conceived in a more 'American' than British way: the U.P. Assembly in particular passed a resolution that 'any member who is elected Speaker would not be handicapped in his public activities in consequence . . . and that he should be free to take part in political affairs outside the House at his discretion'.[4] Again, opposition groups—generally Congress —sometimes resorted not merely to obstructionist exploitation of procedure but also to 'walk-outs' of protest.[5] More important perhaps was the comment of some observers that assembly debates seemed dull; 'they lacked the spirit of reality, there was too often an air of listlessness, a feeling among members that the assembly did not count and that the true centre of political animation was to be found in the Congress committee rooms.'[6]

The legislative and administrative record of provincial governments

[1] Schuster and Wint, *India and Democracy* (1941), p. 167.

[2] B. P. Singh Roy (*op. cit.*, p. 350) puts the Congress attitude neatly: 'Every party and every group that stands aloof from the Congress tends knowingly or unknowingly to become a source of weakness to the nation and a source of strength to the forces ranged against it.' This is part of the nationalist equipment which has to be disposed of after independence if democratic government is to succeed. The record of the Congress Party in this respect since 1947 is—as will be indicated below—at least far better than that of, say, the Egyptian Wafd or the Pakistan Muslim League.

[3] Coupland, *op. cit.*, p. 80.

[4] Quoted in S. V. Kogekar, 'Indian Speakers and Party Politics' in *Indian Journal of Political Science*, July–Sept. 1939. Professor Kogekar defended this resolution as in keeping with Indian needs: to seek a non-party neutral—or even a member prepared to become one—would be to seek an incompetent Speaker, and this position would remain 'so long as the Indian Constitution is not backed by the irresistible sanctions which come of self-determination.' On the present position of Indian Speakers see below, Chapter VI, Section 1.

[5] D. Verma, 'Provisional Autonomy in the Punjab, 1937–39', in *Indian Journal of Political Science*, April–June 1940. Since 1947, Congress has been at the receiving end of such protests (see below, Chapter V).

[6] Schuster and Wint, *op. cit.*, p. 170.

5—P.I.

surprised most of the British observers. A good deal of valuable social legislation was passed, financial policies were seldom reckless and more often conservative, and governments were unexpectedly firm on matters of law and order. Governments, that is to say, did take the lead and did govern. Not all ministries were stable all the time, but most ministries were able to rely on adequately disciplined followings in the assemblies.[1] Relations between Governors and ministries were generally cordial, and between 1937 and 1939 only on very rare occasions and very few issues (such as the release of political prisoners) were disagreements so sharp as to be brought to a head. Even the relations between Ministers and the Services were better than had been feared. There may have been some attempted interference on the part of members and Ministers with the administration of justice, and also 'a tendency for Ministers to secure information from, and to use as their executive instrument not the civil service but the local party committees'.[2] Against this, on the other hand, must be remembered the novelty of office for most of those concerned and also the novelty for the Services of taking orders from men who belonged to a developed political organisation. In any case, what Coupland calls the 'one outstanding fact' remains: 'The Congress had at last become a constructive force in Indian politics.' The Viceroy himself referred at the time to 'a distinguished record of public achievement'.[3]

One aspect of Congress rule during 1937–39 deserves special attention —if only because several observers came to certain grave conclusions on the matter: the relation between Congress ministries in the Provinces and the Congress party machinery. There is no doubt that this relation was important and peculiar. It arose from the position of a nationalist movement in a situation of only partial transfer of power. As already mentioned, the question of office-acceptance was one on which there was disagreement within the party: was part of the prize to be taken or was it to be rejected in favour of a continued struggle for the whole? The victory of those supporting office-acceptance forced a difficult compromise on the Congress movement: whatever they might, as provincial governments, do to serve the people directly and on immediate issues could not be permitted to prejudice the larger aim of successful agitation for complete independence. In these circumstances, it is not

1 *Ibid.*, p. 154: 'At the time of the Round Table Conference the fear had been expressed that Indians (whose experience of politics had been in the legislatures rather than in the executive) would make the error of demanding that the assemblies should not only criticise and control the cabinets but that they should (as in France) extend their power so far as actually to share the responsibility of administration. But Congress cabinets once in office . . . were inclined rather to limit the rights of the legislatures. . . .' This is not to say, however, that many legislators did not learn a great deal about the business of government and administration through the various standing advisory committees of the assemblies.

2 *Ibid.*, p. 156.

3 Coupland, *op. cit.*, p. 157. Another aspect of the same question is less kindly put in Schuster and Wint (*op. cit.*, p. 153): 'many observers felt that Congress had come to mock but had stayed to bless'.

surprising that parliamentary democracy should have worked in ways different from those of the books. None of the members of the Congress Working Committee, the head of the party hierarchy, held ministerial posts in the Provinces. The movement's top leaders reserved their energies for the nation-wide organisation of the continuing struggle for independence. For them (as today for Communist parties) the parliamentary front was only one of many on which the fight was in progress. It is important to understand these attitudes, for failure to do so can suggest conclusions about the nature of the Congress which while valid for that period have only limited relevance to the present time.

The charges levelled against Congress behaviour and attitudes during this period are clear. Coupland writes of the 'totalitarian policy of the Congress high command' which weakened the application of the principle of responsible government and practically negated the principle of provincial autonomy; the provincial Ministers, that is to say, were responsible not to their legislatures, and through them to the electorate, but instead to the Working Committee sitting in Wardha or Delhi.[1] The same point is made by Schuster and Wint: 'of the assemblies Congress is able to say that before they were, it was'; 'the loyalty of its supporters is to party rather than to parliament' and 'thus the assemblies must serve Congress, not Congress the assemblies'.[2] A more recent British verdict echoes these.

Provincial autonomy [writes Sir Percival Griffiths] became distorted and the system of responsible government lost much of its virtue. The attitude of the Congress High Command protected the unity of the party and perhaps of India, but it prevented the development of political parties in the provinces. . . . The concentration of power at the centre bred an authoritarian approach to Indian politics. In the provinces, the necessary give and take of parliamentary life might have developed tolerance and respect for views of others, but these qualities were not likely to grow in the rarefied atmosphere of a Congress Central Committee with no responsibility for the government of the country.[3]

To these charges there is really no reply—except the adequate one that it is not reasonable to expect nationalist movements to behave as parliamentary parties. Only if Congress had possessed complete confidence in the intentions of the British Government and in its servants in India could they have allowed themselves to behave differently. And this confidence was wholly absent. Certainly, statements from Congress itself do not seek to hide their approach during this period. It is clear that Pandit Nehru spoke for many when he outlined the order of priority as he saw it in July 1937:

[1] Coupland, *op. cit.*, Chapter X.
[2] Schuster and Wint, *op. cit.*, p. 170.
[3] Sir P. Griffiths, *The British Impact on India* (1952), p. 340.

The opinion of the majority of the Congress today [he said] is in favour of acceptance of office, but it is even more strongly and unanimously in favour of the basic Congress policy of fighting the new constitution and ending it. . . . We are not going to be partners and co-operators in the imperialist firm. . . . We go to the assemblies or accept office . . . to try to prevent the Federation from materialising, to stultify the constitution and prepare the ground for the Constituent Assembly and independence, . . . to strengthen the masses, and, wherever possible in the narrow sphere of the constitution, to give some relief to them.[1]

In the following month he was to put the matter even more bluntly. 'It is manifest', he said in August, 'that the Congress is more important than any ministry. Ministries may come and go, but the Congress goes on till it fulfils its historic mission of achieving national independence for India'.[2] If these statements make clear the justification for what appeared to be 'totalitarian' ways, it must on the other hand be admitted that on occasion Congress leaders went very far in the direction of making a virtue out of what should have been no more than an unfortunate necessity. One of the most strikingly violent expressions of what amounted to anti-parliamentarianism came from Dr. Sitaramayya, a member of the Congress Working Committee at the time. 'If there is anyone', he told the All-India Congress Committee in 1938, 'who imagines that our [party] structure should be subordinated to the flimsy notions of democratic and parliamentary conventions, let that person remember that we are in a stage of transition. Those "goody-goody" notions of constitutional propriety are not applicable to the Congress in the present conditions.'[3] There is also the well-known statement of Gandhi's at this time: 'Congress is democratic in its internal administration but for the job of fighting the greatest imperialist power, . . . it has to be likened to an army. As such, it ceases to be democratic. The central authority has plenary powers enabling it to impose and enforce discipline on the various units working under it.'[4] It is to be noted that

---

[1] J. Nehru, *The Unity of India* (1942), p. 61. The Congress 1936 Election Manifesto had already made it clear that the party would, as B. P. Singh Roy says, try to have it both ways: Congress sought election both to end the constitution as well as to implement its constructive social programme under the constitution (*op. cit.*, p. 205).

[2] *Ibid.*, p. 75. It was on this occasion that he added a sentence which some people have since remembered: 'When that achievement comes in full measure, the Congress might well cease to exist.'

[3] Quoted in B. N. Banerjee, 'Democratic Theory in its Application to Indian Politics', in *Indian Journal of Political Science*, Oct.–Dec. 1943. Dr. Sitaramayya was justifying the action of the Working Committee in 'the Khare case'. Dr. Khare, Congress Premier in Central Provinces, resigned but was unable to persuade his colleagues to do so because, they said, resignations had not been ordered by the Congress Parliamentary Board (a subcommittee of the Working Committee responsible for supervision of the parliamentary front). Dr. Khare formed a new cabinet, but the Parliamentary Board condemned this independent move and secured Khare's replacement as Congress leader in the C. P. assembly. (See B. P. Singh Roy, *op. cit.*, p. 233.)

[4] Also quoted in B. N. Banerjee, *loc. cit.*

even these statements stress the peculiar and transitory nature of the circumstances of the partial transfer of power. At the same time, it may be admitted that habits of mind were formed and became somewhat set in this period—habits which were not so easily changed when the 'stage of transition' came to an end.

In view of the importance which at present attaches to relations between ministries and party committees,[1] it may be worth while outlining the 1937–39 position in a little more detail. How did the party leaders envisage the relation between ministries and various parts of the party hierarchy? The Congress theory in its most general terms is clear from what has already been said. It was expressed well, if naively, by Pandit Nehru. 'Ministers are responsible to their electorates, to their party in the legislature, to the Provincial Congress Committee and its Executive, to the Working Committee and to the All-India Congress Committee'; admitting that this might 'sound complicated and confusing', Nehru went on to say that in simple fact, 'the Ministers and the Congress parties in the legislatures are responsible to the Congress and only through it to the electorate'.[2] But precisely how was ministerial responsibility to the party to be ensured and expressed? On this, the leaders were not quite so clear. As Nehru explained, when on one occasion the A.I.C.C. had met to review the work of ministries, it was a difficult business because they had 'no rules or conventions for the purpose'.[3] Gradually, however, conventions were in fact established. In the first place, a line had to be drawn between principles and details:

It is clear that Congress Ministers have to follow Congress principles and govern themselves by the general directions issued by the Congress or the A.I.C.C. or the Working Committee. It is also clear that it is not possible or desirable to interfere in the day-to-day work of the ministries, or to call for explanations from them for administrative acts, unless some important principle is involved.[4]

Secondly, some Congress organs were more suited than others for the work of supervising the ministries. The A.I.C.C. and the Provincial Congress Committees were too large and too like mass meetings for the purpose. Local (e.g., district) Congress committees, on the other hand, covered too small an area and were too ignorant for the job; they could offer suggestions and make complaints but they had better do so quietly to the Provincial Executive Committee.[5] The key party organs were evidently the provincial executives and the central Working Committee. Finally, there were right and wrong ways of trying to supervise the ministries. While there was certainly no need for party committees to be

---

1 See below, Chapter IV.   2 J. Nehru, *op. cit.*, p. 81.
3 *Ibid.*, p. 78.   4 *Ibid.*, p. 78.
5 *Ibid.*, p. 83.

'silent and tongue-tied spectators' of ministerial performances, it was not appropriate for the party to attack its ministries in a destructive fashion. 'It is patent that for a Congress committee to condemn a Congress ministry is both improper and absurd. It is as if one Congress committee condemned another. The ministries, being the creation of Congress, can be ended at any time by Congress.' What is required is 'friendly criticism' and the avoidance of any 'embarrassment'.[1] It became obvious at a fairly early stage that the Working Committee and its Parliamentary Board were doubtful if supervision could be decently exercised by the provincial level committees, and that they preferred that everyone simply reported their complaints up to the centre and left it to the centre to do any controlling that might be necessary. In 1939 this preference was expressed in a direction: the P.C.C.s were told they were not to attempt to supervise ministries and they were prohibited from public discussion of any disagreements between ministers and provincial committees.[2] To sum up, Congress ministries were, in the course of their two years of office, rescued from the 'embarrassing' and often wrongly motivated attacks of the party's provincial organs, while being more firmly controlled in matters of general policy by the triumvirate (Patel, Azad and Prasad) of the Parliamentary Board.

Whether ministries could have been able in time to extend their area of autonomy is uncertain. In any event, the whole experiment of parliamentary provincial government was suspended in the Congress provinces with the resignations of all Congress ministries (on orders from the high command), as a protest against the failure of the British Government to consult Indian opinion before declaring her entry into the war. Congress returned to its more usual role of opposition, and the parliamentary front closed down. It is said that many Ministers were very sorry to have to quit office. To add that this can well be believed is not to attribute unduly selfish motives to the Ministers. The salaries they were permitted to receive were in any case controlled by a Working Committee directive. It was rather that although parliaments were only one front, some prestige did attach to ministerial rank; and that in two years there had grown a real sense of having accomplished something tangible and worth while in the way of public service. In this lies, of course, one of the positive achievements of the experience of the 1935 Act. The 'slave' constitution gave legislative experience to a very considerable number of politicians in the provinces[3]; it installed what were in effect fully responsible popular governments; it began to accustom all concerned to a

[1] *Ibid.*, p. 76. Also B. P. Singh Roy, *op. cit.*, p. 221.
[2] B. P. Singh Roy, *op. cit.*, pp. 221–222.
[3] Even the unchanged central assembly was no wasted institution. It forced an uneasy government to give explanations; it trained a small group of politicians—but trained them intensively—in the discussion of important and complex public issues; and, if it was not the heart of the political scene, at least it was preparing quietly so to become.

transfer of power. Above all, it gave experience precisely where it was needed; the men who began to learn governmental and parliamentary politics during 1937–39 were to a great extent the men who took over the total responsibility in 1947. Since there was in the post-war period no time for a gradual transfer of power, it was indeed fortunate that at least the two pre-war years had been well used. How much more difficult would the 1947 assumption of power have been had there not been the 'charter of bondage'! And how much easier it would have been if there had not intervened the wartime years of anger and frustration!

TABLE I.—DEVELOPMENT OF PARLIAMENT: SEATS AND FRANCHISE

CENTRE
1909–19
SEATS IN LEGISLATIVE COUNCIL

Nominated and ex-officio .		41
Elected—General . .	. 13	
Land . .	7 or 6*	
Muslim .	5 or 6*	
Commerce .	. 2	
Total elected . .	27	
Total Seats	68	

(Electorate 4,818)
* Alternate Elections
Southborough Report, 1919

1919–35

LEGISLATIVE ASSEMBLY			COUNCIL OF STATE		
Nominated . . .	41		Nominated . . .	.	27
Elected—Non-Muslim .	52		Elected—Non-Muslim . .	16	
Muslim .	30		Muslim . .	11	
Sikh . .	2		Sikh . .	1	
European .	9		Non-Communal . .	2	
Landholders .	7		European Commerce .	3	
Commerce .	4		Total elected . .	33	
Total elected .	104		Total Seats	60	
Total Seats . . .	145				

(Electorate 1,142,948*)	(Electorate 16,571†)
* In 1931	† In 1926

Simon Report, 1930 and *Lothian Report*, 1931

1935–47

LEGISLATIVE ASSEMBLY	COUNCIL OF STATE

The composition of both Chambers was similar to that of 1919–35. Although there was a slightly increased electorate, this was due to population increase rather than franchise extension.

1947–51
CONSTITUENT ASSEMBLY

General .	.	210
Muslim .	.	78
Sikh .	.	4
Total .	.	292

(Electorate*)
* Indirectly elected by Provincial Assemblies
Banerjee: 'The Constituent Assembly'

TABLE I.—*continued*

1952–

HOUSE OF THE PEOPLE		COUNCIL OF STATES	
Nominated—Non-scheduled .	8*	Nominated	16†
Scheduled tribes .	1	Indirectly Elected by State	
Elected—Non-scheduled .	390	Assemblies . . .	200
Scheduled castes .	72	Total	216
Scheduled tribes .	26		
Total	497	† Includes Kashmir (4)	

(Electorate 176 million)

* Includes Kashmir (6)

Report on the first General Elections in India, 1951–52 (Election Commission, 1955)

PROVINCES

1909–19

SEATS IN LEGISLATIVE COUNCILS (7)[1]

Nominated and ex-officio .		159
Elected—General .	69	
Land .	23	
Muslim .	21	
Commerce, etc .	17	
Total elected .		130
Total Seats . .		289

(Electorate 31,727)

Southborough Report, 1919

1919–35

LEGISLATIVE COUNCILS (8)[2]

Nominated . . .		183
Elected—Non-Muslim .	347	
Muslim .	179	
Sikhs .	12	
Anglo-Indian .	3	
Indian Christian .	5	
European .	11	
Landholders .	32	
Universities .	8	
Commerce .	43	
Total elected .		640
Total Seats . .		823

(Electorate 6,375,000*)

* In 1931

Simon Report, 1930 and *Lothian Report*, 1931

1935–47

LEGISLATIVE ASSEMBLIES (12)[3]		LEGISLATIVE COUNCILS (6)[4]		
General	817	Nominated . . .		29 to 38
Muslim . . .	482	Filled by Legislative Assembly .		39
Women . . .	40	Elected—General . .	118	
Anglo-Indian . .	12	Muslim .	56	
European . . .	26	European .	9	
Indian Christian . .	20	Indian-Christian .	3	
Backward Areas, etc. .	12	Total elected .	186	
Commerce, etc. . .	56	Total Seats . .		254 to 263
Landholders . . .	36			
Labour . . .	38	(Electorate 66,122)		
Universities . . .	8			
Sikhs . . .	34			
Total (all seats are elected) .	1,581			

(Electorate 41 million)

1946 Election Returns and 1935 India Act

1947–1951

Composition and Franchise as in 1919–35

TABLE I.—*continued*

1952

LEGISLATIVE ASSEMBLIES (22)[5]		LEGISLATIVE COUNCILS (7)[7]		
Nominated	11	Nominated . . .	.	69
Elected—Non-scheduled .	2,603	Indirectly elected by Local Authorities	.	125
Scheduled castes	477	Graduates	.	33
Scheduled tribes	192	Teachers .	.	31
		Legislative Assemblies	.	129
Total	3,283			
		Total	.	387

(Electorate 176 million)

ELECTORAL COLLEGES (3)[6]

90 seats

Report on the First General Elections in India, 1951–52 (Election Commission, 1955)

[1] Madras, Bombay, Bengal, United Provinces, Bihar and Orissa, Central Provinces, Assam.
[2] As in (1) plus Punjab.
[3] As in (2) plus Bihar, N.W.F.P., Orissa, Sind.
[4] Madras, Bombay, Bengal, United Provinces, Bihar, Assam.
[5] Assam, Bihar, Bombay, Madyha Pradesh, Madras, Orissa, Punjab, U.P., W. Bengal, Hyderabad, Madyha Barat, Mysore, P.E.P.S.U., Rajasthan, Saurashtra, Travancore-Cochin, Ajmer, Bhopal, Coorg, Delhi, Himachal Pradesh, Vindhya Pradesh.
[6] Kutch, Manipur, Tripura.
[7] Bihar, Bombay, Madras, Punjab, Uttar Pradesh, W. Bengal, Mysore.

2. The Argument

Whether or not the British Empire was won in a fit of absent-mindedness, such a mood seems to have had a good deal to do with the establishment of parliamentary institutions in India—at least in the sense that there has hardly been a full-scale debate on the subject. Among both the British and the Indians, views have varied at different times and among different sections, but more remarkable has been the extent to which the matter has been taken, one way or the other, for granted. We have seen in the preceding section how in fact the ground was prepared for parliamentary institutions. We must now review briefly the development of British, and especially Indian, ideas on the suitability for India of such institutions.

On the British side, as we have already noted, the initial assumption was that parliament was not for India. Those among the British leaders in India in the first half of the nineteenth century who thought in terms of a future end of British dominion did not say clearly who or what institutions they saw as their successors. But it can be safely assumed that, just as they saw themselves as inheritors of an autocracy, so it was to an indigenous autocracy—albeit of a reformed and enlightened kind—that they thought of bequeathing power. Even the radicals, whose whole faith lay in the institutions of representative government, could not see how it was possible to introduce them into India. James and John Stuart Mill hardly permitted themselves the rash luxury of even a tentative hope; only Macaulay went as far as that.[1] Even Macaulay and the other few radicals who turned their attentions to India felt that the only way was a 'strategy of indirect approach': the stumbling block was ignorance

[1] See Coupland, *The Indian Problem, 1833–1935*, pp. 18–22. Also Duncan Forbes 'James Mill and India', in *The Cambridge Journal*, Oct. 1951.

and superstition; remove these by Western education (plus the Gospel, added the Evangelicals) and then even India could march with the rest of the world.

But the Indian Whig aristocracy did not in fact emerge according to plan, and optimism about Indian political progress receded until the last third of the century,[1] when Gladstone's confident enunciation of liberal principles found a response in a few men like Lord Ripon; and by this time it was to the new middle professional classes that they looked for torchbearers for liberty. Yet it was perhaps not until Edwin Montagu that radical faith was consciously and carefully applied to the study of Indian conditions. 'The primary purpose of the Montagu–Chelmsford Report was to justify the assumption [that] the obstacles which British statesmanship had hitherto regarded as prohibiting a parliamentary system in India could somehow or other be overcome.'[2] At the same time non-radical British statesmen and administrators began to be somewhat more explicit than before as to what precisely these obstacles were. Lord Balfour had already in 1909 made the point that the British form of government was only suitable 'when you are dealing with a population in the main homogeneous, in the main equal in every substantial and essential sense, in a community where the minority are prepared to accept the decisions of the majority, where they are all alike in the traditions in which they are brought up, in their general outlook upon the world and in their broad view of national aspirations'.[3] It might be argued that this was an over-formidable list containing too many question-begging terms, but it indicated the lines on which future doubts would be expressed, and it supported an attitude of deep scepticism towards the view that institutions could be easily imported 'as you import a new locomotive'.[4] To assess the validity of this scepticism is not easy. It is tempting to notice that the sceptics were to be found among those who were opposed to any enthusiastic move towards a transfer of power; and to suggest that they were seeking intellectually respectable arguments to defend the *status quo*. It would be less crude and probably more accurate to say simply that it happens that political Conservatives are often philosophical conservatives; that is, those who were attached to Empire were at the same time those whose political philosophy was opposed to rationalist views of political institutions. An English philosophical conservative habitually thinks of political institutions as part of a tradition of life, not as devices designed to solve universal 'problems of government'; he would be sceptical about the possibility of exporting institutions even if he were desirous on immediate political grounds of doing so. Be that as it may, many British observers found, as they looked upon the Indian scene, more difficulties

---

[1] There were rare exceptions even in the darkest days; John Bright was one.
[2] *The Indian Problem, 1833–1935*, p. 54.   [3] *Ibid.*, p. 26.   [4] *Ibid.*, p. 81.

and more obstacles than the pessimists of the previous century had troubled to notice.

In the first place, there was certainly still ample ignorance and superstition. The peasantry had been quite untouched by Western education, and their vision was limited by grinding poverty and the remoteness of their villages from modern life. The fact that a tiny *élite* had been rescued from such conditions, so far from being a hopeful move in the direction of preparation for democracy, was, if anything, a further difficulty. For it meant a division in society so deep that here indeed was a tale of two nations. Could parliament fit such a situation without being a mockery? Moreover, added paternalists, could it be right to abandon the simple peasant to the wiles of the city lawyers? But, thirdly, this was not the only division in Indian society; there were also 'nations' of religious communities and, within communities, of castes. In the former case, the divisions were of an order that made majority rule the equivalent of permanent domination by one people over another; in the latter case, politics in the sense of reasoned debate on social and economic measures would be impossible, because all decisions would be determined by loyalties imposed by the fortunes of birth and the status it conferred. Parliamentary democracy was held to imply a discussion conducted by well-informed men who would have somewhat different interpretations of an essentially common good; in India, there could only be more or less clear and unanimous visions of several partial or sectional goods. This tendency would be enhanced by the importance of the family unit—yet another obstacle standing between the individual and his ability to conceive a goal of public weal. Finally, there were in the Indian temperament certain characteristics deposited by history and confirmed by the social system which were inimical to parliamentary democracy: at one and the same time an undue reverence for established authority and a stubborn uncompromising individualism.

This list has no claims to completeness, and each of the items merits a great deal of elaboration. Nor does this summary treatment imply that the points are without substance. Indeed, most of them have had already to be mentioned (in Chapter I) as factors of continuing importance in the nature of Indian political life. They serve here simply as an indication of the supports that were available for those disposed to be sceptical about the possibility for parliaments in India. The authors of the liberal-inspired Montagu-Chelmsford Report were aware of the points, but were determined to do all they could to overcome them—or at least to enable like-thinking Indians to overcome them. The authors of the Simon Report saw the same features—and tended to despair. In their 'Survey' the difficulties are unhesitatingly set out.[1] None of these, as far as they could see, would be easily changed. For example, 'any quickening

[1] *Simon Report*, Vol. I, especially Chapters 1–4.

of general political judgment, any widening of rural horizons beyond the traditional and engrossing interest of weather and water and crops and cattle, with the round of festivals and fairs and family ceremonies, and the dread of famine or flood—any such change from these imme-morial preoccupations of the average Indian villager is bound to come very slowly indeed.'[1] Or again, even if there are forces 'tending by de-grees to sap the rigidity of the caste system', nevertheless 'the spiritual and social sub-divisions of India, operating in a land where there is a deep respect for religion, and supported by ancient tradition and the canons of orthodoxy, are not likely to suffer very sudden or violent alteration, and nothing is more clear than that whatever change may come must come from the action of the people of India themselves'.[2]

When the authors of the Simon Report reached their 'Recommenda-tions',[3] the despair becomes in places most explicit. It was

> a difficult and delicate operation to transplant to India forms of government which are native to British soil. . . . The British parliamentary system has developed in accordance with the day-to-day needs of the people, and has been fitted like a well-worn garment to the figure of the wearer, but it does not follow that it will suit everybody. . . . British parliamentarianism in India is a translation, and in even the best translations the essential meaning is apt to be lost. We have ourselves in attending debates in the Assembly and provincial Councils been more impressed with their difference from than their resemblance to the Parliament we know.[4]

From this starting point, still many routes presented themselves. It would have been possible, for example, to preach the abandonment of democratic institutions altogether and the resumption of some authori-tarian form of rule patterned on Indian tradition—the extension to all parts of India, for example, of the monarchies of the princely states.[5] The Simon Report did not take that way; India, it believed, was 'gradu-ally moving from autocracy to democracy'.[6] On the other hand, the Report did not feel able to say much about the form democracy could take in India. It was content simply to explain a little further the grounds for doubt and leave it for Indian opinion to find its own way to a solu-tion. Thus the Report was at pains to show that at the provincial level, while in effect what was proposed was the British system, this was to be regarded by Indians as no more than a way of affording to them 'the opportunity of judging by experiment' whether that system was 'fitted to their needs and to the natural genius of the people'. No one should

---

[1] *Simon Report*, I, p. 15.   [2] *Ibid.*, I. p. 37.   [3] *Ibid.*, Vol. II.   [4] *Ibid.*, II, pp. 6–7.
[5] This was not an unusual idea among British administrators in India. A fairly recent example is provided in *Goodbye, India* (1946) by Sir Henry Sharp, in which the author asserts that Western democracy is ill-suited to the traditions and institutions of India and that a federation of oligarchies 'might prove the most durable solution'. In consequence of this view, he believes, of course, that whatever forms are adopted, 'the real power will come to be invested in some authority exercising a limited and benevolent despotism'.
[6] *Simon Report*, II, p. 14.

imagine that a fixed course had been set for Westminster. For instance, if in the Provinces something like the British party system fails to emerge but instead there is 'a system of shifting groups', then that will imply a constitutional position for provincial governments 'quite different from that of the Cabinet in the British system'. The main point was to realise that 'the British constitution is not a panacea which can be used at all times and in all places'.[1] If the Report wished to leave the provincial stage at least open for alternative ideas, it was, so to speak, even more decisively doubtful so far as the Centre was concerned. 'It appears to us', wrote the authors, 'that there is a serious danger of development at the Centre proceeding on wrong lines if the assumption is made that the only form of responsible government which can ultimately emerge is one which closely imitates the British system'. The only reason why that system, whose main feature is 'that the Government is liable to be brought to an end at any moment by the vote of the legislature', works reasonably well in Britain is that it is there bound up with an organised and stable party system 'which ensures the cohesion of elected members and their close contact with the electorate'.[2] Accordingly, 'the precedent for the Central Government in India must be sought for elsewhere', but the Report was not very clear as to where. It appears to have envisaged a very loose centre of an almost confederal type—'an association of units formed mainly for the purpose of performing certain functions on behalf of all'.[3]

The reluctance of the Simon Report to propose solutions is perhaps understandable. Indian politics was developing fast and its directions may not have been clear. Moreover it may be regarded as appropriately British to wish to see only the one immediate step ahead rather than to plan the whole journey in the light of a vision of the end. Yet, whatever the explanation, the fact remains striking: the Simon Commission, for all its doubts on the export of parliament to India, declined effectively to offer India any well-defined alternative; British statesmen were prisoners of their own traditions.[4]

[1] *Ibid.*, II, p. 147. It may be noted that while the Joint Committee of the British Parliament would not have disagreed with this statement, yet the tone of its Report is different in emphasis. There is less inclination to look elsewhere and more disposition to see the positive aspects: 'We cannot doubt that this apprenticeship in parliamentary methods has profoundly affected the whole character of Indian public life' (*Report of the Joint Committee on Indian Constitutional Reform*, 1934 (H.C. 5).

[2] *Ibid.*, II, p. 146.   [3] *Ibid.*, II, p. 18.

[4] Attention has been concentrated on the Simon Report, but it is fair to say that no other British source went any nearer to defining alternative forms of democracy. The work of Schuster and Wint (*op. cit.*), for example, was equally aware of the difficulties ('In concluding this survey it is impossible to suppose that the way is likely to be smooth' (p. 231)); in places, equally unhopeful about an Indian parliament ('Parliamentary democracy of the Westminster pattern will not suit India' (p. 439)); and equally reluctant to put forward any other pattern. Optimistic teachers of 'Comparative Government' may like to think that the growth of their subject in recent years makes such timid insularity impossible today, and constitutional problems in colonial territories have certainly provided ample challenge to inventiveness.

If we turn to Indian views of this matter, we find that their eyes have been almost equally fixed on the British model. For Indian nationalists from the beginning, to attain political maturity would be to obtain British political institutions. Their argument was straightforward and would have delighted Macaulay's heart, as it no doubt did delight Lord Ripon's. By education and imitation, they said, they had become as Englishmen, and as Englishmen they yearned for English political forms. 'From our earliest schooldays', said C. Sankaran Nair, in his Presidential Address to the Indian National Congress in 1897, 'the great English writers have been our classics. Englishmen have been our professors in colleges. English history is taught in our schools. We live now the life of the English'—except, of course, that the English governed themselves. The speaker went on to make that point: 'To deny us the freedom of the press; to deny us representative institutions, England will have to ignore those very principles for which the noblest names in her history toiled and bled.'[1] The tone became more insistent as the years went by, but the same point continued to be made. Another Congress Presidential Address, that of 1907 by Dr. Rashbehari Ghose, may be cited as an example: 'What we do demand is that our rulers should introduce reforms as steps towards giving us that self-government which is now the aspiration of a people educated for three generations in the political ideals of the West. . . . We want in reality and not in name to be the sons of the Empire.'[2] The fact that British political institutions were, in the minds of Indian leaders, a corollary of English education in its widest sense is nowhere made clearer than in the willingness, at least at the beginning and at least of some leaders, to limit the enjoyment of such institutions to those Indians who had received the benefits of such education.

> I was not aware [said Surendranath Banerjee] that any responsible Congressman had ever asked for representative institutions for one woman or for the masses of our people. We should be satisfied if we obtained representative institutions of a modified character for the educated community, who by reason of their culture and enlightenment, their assimilation of English ideas, and their familiarity with English methods of government might be presumed to be qualified for such a boon.[3]

When Banerjee spoke of the 'modified character' of the institutions which might be granted to India, he probably had in mind no more than

---

[1] Quoted in Andrews and Muhherjee, *Rise and Growth of the Congress*, 1938, p. 193. As that book states (p. 25), 'the authors of the Congress movement had great love for British parliamentary institutions'. They quote the remark of the famous Dadabhai Naoroji on his election in 1893 to the British Parliament as member for Finsbury: 'We hope to enjoy the same freedom, the same strong institutions which you in this country enjoy. We claim them as our birthright as British subjects.'
[2] *Ibid.*, p. 217.   [3] *Ibid.*, p. 160.

that legislatures could not at that stage and all at once be made sovereign bodies on the lines of the British Parliament; the qualification was,
that is to say, principally one of timing. But already there were other
Indian voices that spoke of modifications in a different and more fundamental sense. Sir Syed Ahmed Khan, founder of Aligarh (in 1877) as
an institution of higher education for Muslims, had already sounded
a note of distrust. In a speech delivered in the Legislative Council as
early as 1883 he had in effect explained the reasons for his doubts. He
said:

> In borrowing the system of representative institutions from England, it is of
> the greatest importance to remember those socio-political matters in which
> India is distinguishable from England. . . . In a country like India, where
> caste distinctions still flourish, where there is no fusion of the various races,
> where religious distinctions are still violent, where education in its modern
> sense has not made an equal or proportionate progress among all sections
> of the population, I am convinced that . . . the system of election, pure and
> simple, cannot be safely adopted. The larger community would totally over-
> ride the interests of the smaller. . . .[1]

This voice, speaking as it did the same language as the British conservatives, was never afterwards wholly silenced. At every stage, there were
some Muslim leaders who pressed for special safeguards for their position as a minority community, and in moments of special exasperation
or despair they would pronounce upon the utter unsuitability of parliamentary institutions of majority rule for a divided society. Mr. Fazlul
Huq's attack in 1924 on the whole idea of Western political institutions[2]
and many of Mr. Jinnah's statements after 1938 are examples of this
view. At the same time, it must be admitted that Muslim spokesmen only
very rarely if at all expressed their anxieties in the form of a positive demand for some different model of political institution. They—no less
than other Indians, and the British themselves—were limited in vision to
the British model.[3] The result was that Muslim political thinking may be
said to have moved almost in one jump from separate electorates to more
or less complete separation.[4] Such discussion as took place in India
before 1947 on, for example, fixed-term, composite executives on the

---

[1] The whole speech is given in Coupland, *The Indian Problem 1833–1935*, as Appendix
II.
[2] Given in the review of evidence in the *Muddiman Report*.
[3] The British were perhaps the least blind. It appears (Coupland, *The Indian Problem*,
p. 116) that Lord Peel at the Round Table Conference did at least throw out the suggestion
of the Swiss and American models; no one else took up the matter.
[4] There were, of course, intermediate stages in the shape of plans for great autonomy for
Muslim areas and a weak federal Centre. That was the attraction of the Cabinet Mission
Plan of 1946. The point, however, is that little thinking was done by Muslims along the
lines of finding (or devising) a form of institution that would safeguard minorities without
in effect separating them geographically.

Swiss model was the attempt of a few political science teachers to save a situation.[1]

The Muslim doubts arose from the fears of a minority at the prospect of majority rule, but other doubts, if anything still more fundamental, came to be expressed in the course of the 1920s and are associated with the influence of Gandhi. The liberal creed of Indian nationalism was in some measure displaced by the new philosophy and new techniques of a man who had absorbed English liberalism and then, in his South African career, passed to some extent beyond it. Gandhi was, not unnaturally, concerned more with moral principles and political techniques than with patterns of political institutions. He said and wrote enough, however, to make clear his general attitude on this question. The state as such was evil, and the self-realisation and moral development of the individual would be marked by its gradual disappearance through a process of decentralisation. More important for our present purpose was the fact that he did not share his liberal predecessors' enthusiasm for parliamentary institutions. In the first place this had been too much part of the slavish imitation of all Western ways. India would eventually have her own distinctive institutional path to tread. Gandhi's phrase, 'parliament is a prostitute', indicates clearly enough his hope that India's political forms would be such as would reflect and encourage higher moral qualities than those of the West.[2] Be that as it may, Gandhi's view had the effect of causing a number of Indians to cease waiting for an Indian replica of Westminster and instead to search for indigenous models more suited to the traditions and genius of her peoples. Of course, the influence of this line of thought must not be exaggerated. It came into none of the serious constitutional proposals put

[1] Several articles on the subject may be found in the *Indian Journal of Political Science* in the year following the failure of the Cripps Mission. Advocacy of the Swiss model is expressed in 'Coalition or Composite Cabinets' by E. Ashirvatham (July–Sept. 1942), where the author says that opinion had been 'hardening against the parliamentary type of government'; 'Type of Executive suited to India's Constitutional Development' by N. S. Pardasani (July–Sept. 1942); 'Workable Executives' by V. S. Ram and L. P. Choudhury (July–Sept. 1943). A more sceptical view is put in 'Composite Executives' by V. K. N. Menon (July–Sept. 1943), though he says that the idea had been widely current since the 1937–39 governments and adds that Mr. C. Rajagopalachari had approved the notion. Another article, 'Making Democracy Safe for India' by D. G. Karve (Oct.–Dec. 1942), urges instead a development of powerful parliamentary committees as a way of reassuring minorities.

[2] There is unfortunately no good study of Gandhi's political philosophy. I have been helped by reading the unpublished thesis, 'The Political Philosophy of Gandhi in Relation to the English Liberal Tradition' (University of London, Ph.D., 1955), of Mr. B. S. Sharma, but the view I have here taken is very different. Some of the contrasts between the Westernised Indian nationalists of pre-1917 and Gandhi are brought out vividly and emphatically in the last chapters of N. C. Chaudhuri, *Autobiography of an Unknown Indian* (1951). It was an unhappy fate that brought British optimism in the person of Mr. Montagu to the fore at the moment when Gandhi came to convert Indians away if not from liberalism (though that is Mr. Chaudhuri's somewhat exaggerated view)—at least from the love of liberal political institutions.

forward by Indians before independence. It was naturally not in evidence in the 'Lucknow Pact' of 1916.[1] It found no reflection in the 'Nehru' Report of 1928; in fact, that report expressly demanded for India the straightforward British or Dominion model of 'a Parliament . . . and an executive responsible to that Parliament'.[2] Anti-parliamentarianism failed to obtain expression even at the Round Table Conferences when Mr. Gandhi himself was present. Yet, throughout this period, the idea that India would move through independence not to a parliamentary regime but to an undefined but distinctly Indian 'Ram Rajya' was permeating certain particularly Gandhian sections of the Congress Party. It was sufficiently important to provoke the attacks of non-Gandhian nationalists. One of these, writing in 1928, detected 'danger' in the new attitude and reasserted the orthodox liberal–national view. The idea, he wrote,

> that what India wants is a constitution suited to her own genius . . . indicates either a reactionary mind which sees in democratic progress a challenge to interests, or a vague idealism generated by a faith in India's past greatness. Both attitudes are dangerous to the peaceful political evolution of India. What India wants, and what Britain has undertaken to give her, is nothing less than 'Responsible Government'. The assimilated tradition of England has become the basis of Indian thought.[3]

In the first section of this chapter we have seen that, despite the doubts of many, the British did afford to an increasing number of Indians experience of parliamentary forms. In 1947, when power was transferred, the shape of India's future constitution remained to be determined. The old Central Legislature disappeared and in its place was the Constituent Assembly. Elected indirectly by members of Provincial Assemblies, it was to be a temporary legislature as well as framer of the future. In England, the discussion might continue as between liberals with faith and conservatives with doubts. But in India decisions had to be taken. In the debates of the Constituent Assembly, therefore, we can find something approaching a real argument about parliamentary government.[4] It will be useful to examine some of these debates to see in particular how the four elements we have already noticed expressed themselves: the

[1] This was a compromise which, however important in the history of Hindu–Muslim political relations, was entirely within the parliamentary model; Congress conceded to Muslim fears not only separate electorates but also separate communal voting on certain issues in the legislature. See Coupland, *op. cit.*, p. 47.

[2] *Report of the All-Parties Conference* (1928), pp. 101, 161. For the Muslim reaction to this report, which proposed to drop the 'Lucknow' safeguards, see Coupland, *op. cit.*, p. 96.

[3] 'Kerala Putra', *The Working of Dyarchy in India* (Bombay, 1928), pp.v–vi; also pp. 111–116.

[4] This is not to say that this was (or appeared to the members to be) the most important topic under discussion. Only a small proportion of the 165 days spent during 1946–49 on constitution-making were devoted to the argument on parliamentary government as such. What follows does not purport to be an account of the framing of the Constitution; it is a very selective description of certain themes.

experience of quasi-parliaments, especially during 1937–39; the orthodox liberal–nationalist desire for full 'responsible government', the long-awaited genuine article of a British or Dominion parliamentary system; the Muslim anxiety for constitutional safeguards and modifications for minorities; the later fear of some nationalists that Western institutions would not suit India.

The opening address on the first day (9 December 1946) of the Constituent Assembly seemed to envisage that members would soon find themselves looking to countries other than Britain for their inspiration. The whole idea of a Constituent Assembly, said the Chairman, was unknown to Britain; 'we have to look to countries other than Britain to be able to form a correct estimate of the position of a Constituent Assembly'. He added: 'I have no doubt you will . . . pay greater attention to the provisions of the American Constitution than to those of any other.'[1] The Objectives Resolution moved by Pandit Nehru on 13 December was rather non-committal on models and forms of constitution, stating simply that 'all power and authority of the Sovereign Independent India, its constituent parts and organs of government are derived from the people'. Nehru's own speech made the point that 'whatever system of government we may establish here must fit in with the temper of our people and be acceptable to them', but he took care to leave the matter as open as possible: 'We stand for democracy [but] what form of democracy, what shape it might take is another matter . . . for this House to determine.'[2]

When the fourth session of the Assembly opened in July 1947, the issue of partition had been settled and constitution-making could begin in earnest. The main feeling of most members was that partition had made the job easier; the terms of the Cabinet Mission scheme—with 'sections' of the Assembly free to set up 'group' constitutions and so on—were left behind and a strong Centre became possible. Even forms of government might be affected because, so it was felt, India was 'now a homogeneous country'.[3] The first substantial indication of a lead in

[1] C.A. Deb., I, 3–4. The Chairman was Dr. Sachchidananda Sinha, a senior member, chosen to occupy the position pending the election of the Assembly's President a few days later.

[2] C.A. Deb., I, 57, 60. Attention at this time was of course on other questions—mainly on how the Cabinet Mission's proposals were to be interpreted, whether they would imply a weak Centre and whether the Assembly should go ahead in spite of the Muslim League's boycott. It was noticeable, however, that members found it difficult to avoid thinking in terms of a future parliament, as when Dr. S. P. Mukherjee said they were looking forward to the day when they would be able 'to declare this Constituent Assembly as the first Parliament of a Free and Sovereign Indian Republic' (C.A. Deb., I, 96).

[3] No speech captures the mood of release better than that of Mr. K. M. Munshi: 'I feel —thank God—that we have got out of this bag at last. We have no sections and groups to go into, no elaborate procedure as was envisaged, no double-majority clause, no more provinces with residuary powers, no opting out, no revision after ten years and no longer only four categories of powers for the centre. We feel free to form a federation of our own choice. . . . We have now a homogeneous country' (C.A. Deb., IV, 544).

the direction of parliamentary government came with the presentation to the Assembly of the Reports of the two Committees set up (in April 1947) to determine the 'Principles of a Model Provincial Constitution' and 'the Principles of the Union Constitution'. Sardar Vallabhai Patel, introducing the former report, said that the two Committees had met jointly for certain discussions, and he announced the decisions tersely: 'They came to the conclusion that it would suit the conditions of this country better to adopt the parliamentary system of constitution, the British type of constitution with which we are familiar. . . . The Provincial Constitution Committee has accordingly suggested that this constitution shall be a parliamentary type of cabinet.'[1] Patel was in any case a man of few words, but the fact that he could declare a vital principle in a sentence depended in large part on the crucial phrase: 'with which we are familiar'. Pandit Nehru a few days later introduced the report on the principles of the Union Constitution with even less attention to this particular aspect; it seemed that it could be taken for granted. In the event, it was not quite so easy, for the Muslim League members[2] at this stage came forward with criticisms. In the debate on Clause 12 of the Report on the Provincial Constitution Committee ('The Governor's ministers shall be chosen and summoned by him and shall hold office during his pleasure'), Muslim members put the case for a fixed-term executive, chosen by proportional representation election by the legislature—a form of Swiss composite executive. 'The English system of democracy does not suit India. . . . It is absurd to think that no sooner the constitution is framed, the religious groups will disappear and parties will be formed on political and economic principles'; only a fixed-term elected coalition would 'secure the confidence of every party in the cabinets'.[3] An irremovable cabinet of Ministers 'co-ordinated' by an effective provincial Governor would secure stable government, independent of the 'whim of the party'; 'the Swiss system is the best *via media* that can be accepted by us in this country'.[4] Although the motivation was evidently communal, the argument was put so far as possible in terms of governmental stability: 'you should protect the Ministers against the shifting parties and predilections of groups in the legislatures'.[5]

[1] C.A. Deb., IV, 579–580.

[2] Pakistan having been decided upon, the League boycott ceased and its members from constituencies in the new India attended the Assembly. The League acted as spokesman for the 35 million Muslims left in India—until its effective disappearance from the Indian political scene in 1948.

[3] Speech of Aziz Ahmed Khan (C.A. Deb., IV, 633).

[4] Speech of Begum Aizaz Rasul (C.A. Deb., IV, 635).

[5] Speech of Chaudhri Khaliquzzaman (C.A. Deb., IV, 650). It is interesting to notice that this theme, originated as a protection for a Muslim minority, seems to have become popular among Muslims for its other merits; it was not infrequently advocated in discussions of the proposed Pakistan Constitution during 1954–55, and always not as a protection for Pakistan's own minorities but as a protection for governments from the dangers of unstable associations of irresponsible politicians in the legislatures.

The argument was repeated when the Report of the Union Constitution Committee came before the Assembly a few days later.[1] To these criticisms, there were many different replies. The Muslim League proposals would 'fragment political life' and produce disunited ministries.[2] Government would tend to become weak, timid and inconsistent. The only way to effective government was by party government; 'if a party gets into power, it cannot implement its programme unless it is charged with the full executive responsibility of the government'.[3] Pandit Nehru forcefully endorsed this reply by saying that he could 'think of nothing more conducive to creating a feeble ministry and a feeble government than the business of electing them by proportional representation'.[4] Apart from this answer, there was also the hope that religious labels would now become less important and that 'a new alignment' would emerge. In that event, government could be expected to become in practice representative of all communities: 'there will be Christians, Muslims, Parsees in our governments'.[5] But, finally and decisively, there was the reply of experience of quasi-parliaments and the historic longing for the real thing. 'We have been brought up in an atmosphere which has been conducive to the establishment of what we are generally accustomed to term Parliamentary Responsible Government.'[6] Towards the end of the debate on this topic, a Muslim member confessed that theirs seemed a hopeless case: 'opinion in India is so much in favour of the British model that it is not practical politics to try to sing the praises' of other systems.[7] The Reports were passed.

More important than the failure of the League attack on the British parliamentary model was the gradual erosion, during the constitution-making process, of their safeguards, those 'modifications' of the system of representative government which the Muslims had enjoyed for so long. The Report on Minority Rights placed before the Assembly in August 1947 recommended the abolition of separate electorates and weightage in the electoral system. These had 'sharpened communal differences to a dangerous extent' and had 'proved one of the main

1 Thus Kazi Syed Karimuddin: there would be 'a plethora of parties' in independent India and in such a situation, parliamentarianism would result in instability of the French type (C.A. Deb., IV, 908). Mahboob Ali Beg argued that the British system was not really democratic: 'Parliament does not choose the Ministers; the electorate cannot throw them out'. But he also defended the idea of elected cabinets on the grounds that people did in fact continue to do their political thinking in religious terms (C.A. Deb., IV, 919).

2 Speech of K. M. Munshi (C.A. Deb., IV, 651).

3 Speech of N. V. Gadgil (C.A. Deb., IV, 640).

4 C.A. Deb., IV, 915.

5 Speech of Dr. Sitaramayya (C.A. Deb., IV, 647).

6 Speech of N. V. Gadgil (C.A. Deb., IV, 640). Also Seth Govind Das: 'We want responsible government. . . . The system of government in Britain must be followed here.' That system could not be blamed for the strife in India; in fact, the trouble was that the system had, properly speaking, 'not yet been put in operation' in India (C.A. Deb., IV, 637).

7 Speech of Hussain Imam (C.A. Deb., IV, 916).

stumbling blocks to the development of a healthy national life'.[1] On the other hand, reservation of seats was recommended for Muslims and Scheduled Castes and for Christians in certain provinces, though a suggestion that candidates for reserved seats should secure not a simple majority but also a certain percentage of their own community's vote was rejected. A minority attempt to introduce a constitutional provision for reserved places in cabinets was firmly turned down in favour of a general exhortation that minorities should be given opportunities in ministries and in the services.[2] Pakistan having been conceded, majority opinion was inclined to be somewhat fierce against pressures for minority safeguards. The tone was set by Sardar Patel's reply to one such plea: 'those who want that kind of thing have a place in Pakistan, not here', and the report adds '(Applause)'.[3]

At this stage, the Assembly in its constitution-making capacity adjourned—as Legislature, of course, it continued—while a Draft Constitution was prepared on the basis of the various approved reports. This document was then placed before the public for eight months. It would seem that this process caused a fresh expression of opposition of a new kind. The opposition during 1947 had been mainly communal and, to a much smaller extent, 'radical' and 'socialist'. When the Assembly came together to go through the Draft in November 1948, two new lines of criticism were apparent, and both were at once mentioned by Dr. Ambedkar, leading member of the Drafting Committee and in fact chief draftsman of the Constitution.[4] It was noticeable, in the first place, that he was at pains to distinguish the British from the American form and to defend the former.

There is nothing in common [he said] between the form of government prevalent in America and that proposed under the Draft Constitution. . . .

[1] C.A. Deb., V, 267. The Report is given as an Appendix to Vol. V of the C.A. Deb. It was said to have been approved 'by an overwhelming majority' of the Advisory Committee on Minority Rights, but this would not have been inconsistent with Muslim opposition on the Committee.

[2] The Report, of course, made several other recommendations which do not immediately concern us—including special nominations of Anglo-Indian members, the temporary protection of Anglo-Indians in certain employments and the appointment of 'minority officers'.

[3] C.A. Deb., V, 297. Much later, in 1949, the Minorities Committee found it necessary to present a further report. Patel, introducing the new report, said that the previous report of 1947 had been prepared 'when conditions were different and the effect of partition not wholly comprehended'. By late 1948, 'the Muslim representatives, some of them, had changed their opinions'. By waiting a little longer still, they found in mid-1949 'a considerable change in the attitude of the minorities'. When the majority proposed abolishing even reserved seats for Muslims (though keeping them for Scheduled Castes and Tribes), 'there was only one solitary vote' against the proposal out of the 40 members of the Committee (C.A. Deb., VIII, 269). In the Assembly debate on this report, one or two Muslims stuck to their traditional point, but the majority had concluded that this was no longer the way (C.A. Deb., VIII, 275 ff.).

[4] Criticisms of the balance between Centre and units, of the qualifications on fundamental rights, etc., are not our concern here and are left out of account.

What the Draft Constitution proposes is the Parliamentary system. . . . The President of the Indian Union will be generally bound by the advice of his Ministers . . . and the Ministers are members of Parliament. . . . The daily assessment of responsibility which is not available under the American system is, it is felt, far more effective than the periodic assessment, and far more necessary in a country like India. . . .

Secondly, Dr. Ambedkar revealed that there was discontent with the 'foreign' character of the Constitution, for he defended vigorously Western forms of government and poured scorn on the only Indian alternative of 'village republics'. There was, he believed, much false sentimentality about the ancient Hindu village polity and about the village of the present day. 'Village republics have been the ruination of India.' 'What is the village but a sink of localism, a den of ignorance, narrow-mindedness and communalism? I am glad that the Draft Constitution has discarded the village and adopted the individual as its unit.'[1]

Dr. Ambedkar was not mistaken in paying attention to these two lines of attack; they became very clear in the debate that followed. The first line drew its strength from rather diverse sources.[2] To some extent it shared the attitude which the Muslims had expressed earlier and for other reasons—and which, indeed, some of them again put forward. 'A removable parliamentary executive is at the mercy of hostile groups in their own party', living in fear of no-confidence motions and over-anxious to satisfy the 'legitimate and illegitimate' demands of their supporters.[3] Or, again, there was the fear that parliamentary government in India—with 'no conventions and no discipline'—would mean the crushing of all opposition.[4] More novel was the fear that the parliamentary system calls for more honest men and would therefore be more difficult for India: 'The parliamentary system must go. I have bitter experience of its working in the Provinces. In the Presidential system it is easy to find one honest President, but it is not so easy to find an army of honest Ministers and deputy Ministers and parliamentary secretaries and so on.'[5] Novel, too, was the argument that a separation of powers, of executive from legislative, would save the latter from corruption. The parliamentary executive which is part of the legislature 'is in a position to corrupt the House . . . to influence the votes of members by the

<hr>

[1] C.A. Deb., VII, 32–39. The bitterness of his remarks of course owes much to his position as leader of the Scheduled Castes Federation and his conviction that rural India is the stronghold of caste prejudice.

[2] Its importance in the Assembly as a whole must not be exaggerated. Indeed one of its spokesmen at one stage sighed—'I know that my voice almost appears as a voice in the wilderness'. (Prof. K. T. Shah, C.A. Deb., VII, 961).

[3] Speech of Mahboob Ali Beg (C.A. Deb., VII, 295).

[4] Speech of Kazi Syed Karimuddin (C.A. Deb., VII, 965).

[5] Speech of Ram Narayan Singh (C.A. Deb., VII, 249).

number of gifts or favours they have in their power to confer'.[1] There were also a tiny few who claimed that India needed a presidential strong man government. One of these said that 'power placed in the hands of the electorate might prove disastrous. . . . Any attempt to foist parliamentarianism on India will only spell our ruin and misery.'[2] The replies to all this were fairly brief. Dr. Ambedkar pointed out that even the Americans themselves had doubts about their own system, and urged that the legislature was in need of 'direct guidance and initiative from an executive sitting in Parliament'.[3] Alladi Krishnaswami Ayyar pointed out that the princely rulers could not be so easily fitted in as constitutional heads if the American pattern was followed. Moreover there was hardly a need to imitate a system which was born of peculiar circumstances and special distrusts, and which was even more difficult to operate: 'an infant democracy cannot afford to take the risk of a perpetual cleavage, feud or conflict or threatened conflict between the legislature and the executive'.[4] K. M. Munshi's reply was more elaborate. He put the Assembly two questions. First, 'What would make for the strongest executive consistent with a democratic constitutional structure?' On this, he thought that British experience was conclusive and noted that 'the British model has been approved by everyone, including leading American constitutional experts.' Second, 'What is the form best suited to Indian conditions?' Here, too, he considered that there could be little doubt; one had only to realise that experience with quasi-parliamentary institutions had become an essential part of 'Indian conditions'.

We must not forget a very important fact, that during the last one hundred years Indian public life has largely drawn on the traditions of English

[1] Speech of Prof. K. T. Shah (C.A. Deb., VII, 961). This point was felt by other members to have some force. For example S. L. Saxena admitted that he was uneasy. It was all very well but quite beside the point to look at England—'they have a tradition of 700 years'; more relevant was the fact that Indian experience of attempts on the part of Ministers to bribe legislators in one way or another had not been encouraging. He concluded, however, by saying that it was 'now too late to change' and they would simply 'have to be careful to develop traits' which would make the constitution work (C.A. Deb., VII, 963).

[2] This was Brajeshwar Prasad (C.A. Deb., VII, 373). He wanted provincial governments wholly abolished and all power vested in a President with four advisers—whose names he suggested! Such an omnipotant rule was what suited India—'what Plato advocated in his *Republic* has always been practised in India.' He also reviewed with admiration the achievements of Hitler, Mussolini, Kemal Ataturk and Stalin, and concluded with: 'the rule of the dictator is essentially democratic if he stands for the greatest good of the greatest number.' It was he who later (C.A. Deb., XI, 875) still further shocked his listeners with the violence of his views: 'If the will of ignorant and hungry people were ever to become the basis of government in India, it would mean the complete liquidation of all that is good and noble in Indian life. . . . The essence of democracy is the representation of the real will of the people as opposed to and distinct from the actual will. . . . I am opposed to federalism, provincial autonomy, parliamentarianism, adult franchise and fundamental rights'!

[3] C.A. Deb., VII, 968.
[4] C.A. Deb., VII, 985.

constitutional law. . . . For the last thirty or forty years some kind of responsibility has been introduced in the governance of this country. Our constitutional traditions have become parliamentary, and we have now all our provinces functioning more or less on the British model. . . . After this experience, why should we go back upon the tradition that has been built for over a hundred years and try a novel experiment framed 150 years ago and found wanting even in America?[1]

This defence of the British model and of political experience under British rule only served to provoke further the second line of attack, which had clearly been under preparation while the Draft Constitution was before the country. At this stage (i.e., late 1948), however, the attack was limited to few phrases in some of the speeches. Dr. Ambedkar's remarks on villages were held to be unfair, the Constitution was quite lacking in Gandhian outlook, it had even little in it that was really Indian, it was, as one member put it, 'a slavish imitation of—nay, much more—a slavish surrender to the West'.[2] This approach failed to result in any positive constructive proposals—except perhaps the suggestion that village panchayats should be used as an instrument for indirect elections to the legislatures. Nevertheless, the complaints continued. Indeed, they became loudest when it was too late to do anything, when all amendments had been dealt with[3] and the Constitution was finally about to be passed. This was, however, not inappropriate; the complaints were, after all, of the kind which lend themselves more to rhetoric than to serious proposals. Where were the villages, where was the spinning wheel, where the ban on cow-slaughter? Clearly, 'the ideals on which this Draft Constitution is framed have no manifest relation to the fundamental spirit of India. . . . What is there in the Constitution to be proud of?'[4] 'We wanted the music of Veena or Sitar, but here we have the music of an English band.'[5] 'If you look into this Constitution' said another speaker, 'it would be difficult for you to find anything Indian. . . . The British have departed but I regret to say that our countrymen have not forsaken the ways of their former masters. We will experience much more difficulty in bidding goodbye to the ways of the British than we experienced in bidding goodbye to the British themselves.'[6] To one member who protested that the Constitution contained no attempt to solve the day-to-day problems of the people, it had to be explained that

[1] C.A. Deb., VII, 984. The Draft Constitution had provision for State Governors to be elected by the voters, but this 'concession to the United States school of thought' was later removed (C.A. Deb., VIII, 426 ff.).
[2] Speech of Lokanath Misra (C.A. Deb., VII, 242).
[3] 7,635 amendments were tabled and 2,473 of them were moved (figures given in Dr. Ambedkar's final speech, C.A. Deb., XI, 972).
[4] Speech of Lakshminarayan Sahu (C.A. Deb., XI, 613–616).
[5] Speech of K. Hanumanthaiya (C.A. Deb., XI, 616).
[6] Speech of Ramnarayan Singh (C.A. Deb., XI, 639–642). He went on to add, a trifle wildly, that 'our country and our society need no government'. Yet in a way this was an authentic Gandhian voice.

the Constitution enabled them to do what they chose—and that that was all a constitution could do. But, apart from that, the replies were along lines already sufficiently indicated. The final reply to the debate was left to the main author of the Constitution. Dr. Ambedkar pointed out that it was 'futile to pass any judgment on the Constitution without reference to the part which the people and their parties are likely to play'; 'however good a constitution may be, it is sure to turn out bad if those who are called upon to work it happen to be a bad lot'. The Constitution made parliamentary democracy possible. Whether the possibility would be realised and maintained would depend on India's 'holding fast to constitutional methods', on transforming a political democracy into a social democracy and on resisting the temptations of hero-worship.[1]

3. Parliament in the Constitution

The previous section summarises some of the argument through the years, and in the Constituent Assembly in particular, on the general principle of parliament for India. But the Indian Constitution is one which goes into details.[2] Those provisions which relate to parliament—at Centre and State levels—have been given in full in Appendix I. A few comments on some of these will therefore be sufficient here.[3]

The Union Parliament consists not simply of one legislative body but of the President together with two Houses. The Upper House is called the Council of States, but its composition does not give equal weight to the units. It consists of twelve members nominated by the President as having 'special knowledge or practical experience in such matters as

---

[1] C.A. Deb., XI, 972–981. Constitutional methods he took to exclude not only revolution but also civil disobedience, non-co-operation and satyagraha. Social democracy was an urgent matter in a society based on inequality such as that of India—otherwise the contradictions between political democracy and social conditions would imperil the former. As for hero-worship, India was here in special danger, 'for in India Bhakti or what may be called the path of devotion or hero-worship plays a part in politics unequalled in magnitude by the part it plays in the politics of any other country in the world.' It was well to be grateful to great men but there must be 'limits to gratefulness'. 'Bhakti in religion may be a road to the salvation of the soul. But in politics, Bhakti or hero-worship is a sure road to degradation and eventual dictatorship.'

[2] This was criticised at the time by many members of the Assembly and has since been commented upon adversely by others (e.g., Sir Ivor Jennings, *Some Characteristics of the Indian Constitution* (1952)). The explanation is in part that it contains the State constitutions, in part that it is influenced by the 1935 Act and constitutes practically a handbook of administration. The general explanation of the latter feature offered by Dr. Ambedkar was that in India democracy was 'only a top dressing on soil which is essentially undemocratic' and the 'constitutional morality' of which Grote spoke was not yet diffused through the people; this deficiency required an elaborated constitution (C.A. Deb., VII, 38).

[3] Line-by-line reference to the Articles of the Constitution has not been given but pages of this section should be read along with Appendix I. Most of the topics are of course discussed at greater length in later chapters. The Appendix is taken from *The Constitution of India* (Delhi, 1949), with amendments incorporated. A brief summary of parliament in the Constitution is given in A. Gledhill, *The Indian Republic* (1951), Chapter 7. More detailed is D. D. Basu, *Commentary on the Constitution of India* (Calcutta, 2nd Edition, 1952).

literature, science, art and social service'.[1] The rest, up to a maximum of 238 (at present 207), are allocated by the Fourth Schedule among the various States in rough proportion to populations. From Part A and Part B States the members are chosen by State Assemblies by proportional representation with single transferable vote.[2] From Part C States members were similarly chosen by State Assemblies or, where they did not exist, by Electoral Colleges. The Council is not subject to dissolution but one-third of its members retire every two years. The age-qualification for members is placed at thirty years. During the early constitution-making debates, an amendment in favour of a single chamber was moved but defeated after hardly any discussion. The government view was put by Gopalaswami Ayyangar: 'The need has been felt practically all over the world wherever there are federations of importance.' Yet, in view of the Council's composition, he could hardly claim that it would serve as a defence for smaller States or even for States' rights in general. In fact, he restricted his argument to grounds which are independent of federalism: 'the most that we expect the second chamber to do is perhaps to hold dignified debates on important issues and to delay legislation which might be the outcome of passions of the moment'; it would 'also given an opportunity, perhaps, to seasoned people who may not be in the thickest of the fray, but who might be willing to participate in the debate with an amount of learning and importance which we do not ordinarily associate with a House of the People'.[3]

Whatever uncertainty there may have been on the purposes of an Upper House, there was at no stage any doubt that the House of the People would be the more powerful. Directly elected on the basis of adult suffrage, the House consists of not more than 500 members, each representing between 500,000 and 750,000 people,[4] and is subject to dissolution after not more than five years. The age qualification of twenty-five years is lower than for the Council of States but higher than for voting rights. Among proposals which were brought forward at some stage

---

[1] The original Draft Constitution showed more clearly the influence of the Irish Constitution and gave a more elaborate list of relevant avenues of experience.

[2] In the case of Jammu and Kashmir in 1951, representatives were chosen by the President in consultation with the State Government pending the establishment of a State Assembly (Constitution (Application to Jammu and Kashmir) Order, 1950). Since Jammu and Kashmir Legislative Assembly came into existence in 1954, this State too falls in line with the general practice (Constitution Order, 1954) and the first elections took place in Nov. 1954.

[3] C.A. Deb., IV, 927. When, in the later debate on the Draft Constitution, an attempt was again made to have only one House, Ananthasaynam Ayyangar defended an Upper House as a way of using harmlessly some of the country's political energy: 'It is common knowledge that in this country there is so much enthusiasm, and if for no other reason we must find opportunity for various people to take part in politics' (C.A. Deb., VII, 1198).

[4] Its strength at present is 499. Of these, 2 are Anglo-Indians nominated by the President. In the 1951 elections, the 6 Kashmir seats and the 2 for Andaman and Nicobar Islands and for certain Assam tribal areas were also filled by nomination. The remaining 489 were elected. On the population limits, see below, p. 95, n. 1.

of constitution-making but were fairly easily defeated were literacy tests for members, the use of proportional representation for general elections (rejected as being too complicated for the voter and tending to unstable governments) and the introduction of arrangements for the recall of representatives and for the holding of referenda.

The Constitution provides for the appointment of presiding officers (the Vice-President of the Union as ex-officio Chairman of the Council, an elected Deputy Chairman of the Council, elected Speaker and Deputy Speaker of the House) and their powers. It also provides for a separate secretariat for each House—this having been inserted as a consequence of a recommendation from a Speakers' conference. It further lays down certain general rules regarding the disqualification of members, though these have been elaborated by ordinary legislation—such as the Parliament (Prevention of Disqualification) Act, 1950, which released the appointments of Ministers and junior Ministers from the disqualification attaching to holders of 'offices of profit under the government'. It even goes so far as to establish certain general rules governing the conduct of business in Parliament, though Parliament has naturally been permitted to frame its own rules for most matters of procedure.[1] Certain 'powers, privileges and immunities of Parliament and its Members' are also stated in the Constitution. This topic was one of some difficulty. The 1935 Act had given simply freedom of speech and protection of members from proceedings arising out of the debates. Something more was now required to fit the status of a sovereign Parliament, and the Draft Constitution chose to copy the Australian Constitution: the powers and privileges of Houses and members could be defined by law but 'until so defined, shall be those of the House of Commons of the Parliament of the United Kingdom'. This explicit reliance on the British Constitution caused some doubts and misgivings, and several members urged that the Indian Constitution should be self-contained and that the powers and privileges should be defined and listed. It was explained to members that definition had been considered and found very difficult; that in any case 'the House of Commons is the assembly which has the widest privileges of all the assemblies of the world'.[2] It might have been (but was not) further explained that the peculiar and wonderful position of the Commons rests on the fact that it has the power of a court—the power to commit for contempt, that is to inflict punishment, and that precisely so long as it does not define its privileges and specify the offence, its action cannot be enquired into by the ordinary courts of law.

[1] In this connection, the language of debate is laid down as Hindi or English. Presiding officers are permitted by the Constitution to allow a member who cannot express himself adequately in these languages to use his mother tongue. 'Unless Parliament by law otherwise provides', the provision permitting English will be automatically deleted in 1965. No doubt several members will plead for an extension of its life.   [2] C.A. Deb., IV, 689.

In setting out the legislative procedure, the Constitution distinguishes between Money Bills and others. Ordinary Bills may be introduced in either House and must be passed by both Houses. The President's assent completes the procedure. This assent may be withheld once; but if the two Houses, after considering the President's recommendations, pass the Bill again, the assent must be given.[1] If an ordinary Bill is rejected by one House or delayed more than six months, or if the two Houses cannot agree on amendments, then the President may summon a Joint Sitting. Since the voting at such a sitting is by simple majority, and since the Lower House is twice as large as the Council, the Upper House has in effect no more than a delaying power of six months and can after that be overruled. Money Bills, on the other hand, may be introduced only in the House of the People. The Council may make recommendations within fourteen days, and these may or may not be accepted by the Lower House. The Constitution states the categories of Bill that may be considered Money Bills, but in cases of doubt the Speaker's decision is final.[2] The Constitution sets out the general procedure in financial matters including the annual financial statement, appropriation bills, grants and votes on account; it also lists those items which are charged on the Consolidated Fund and as such not submitted to vote of Parliament.[3] Finally, the Constitution establishes firmly the position and status of the Comptroller and Auditor-General as comparable to that of a Judge, and the system of audit under his authority covers States as well as Union Accounts.

The main provisions relating to the Union Parliament are reproduced, *mutatis mutandis*, in the Parts of the Constitution which set out the State constitutions. A few differences may, however, be noticed. The State legislature consists of the Governor[4] together with one or two Houses. In the Constituent Assembly there was considerable disagreement on the question of Upper Houses for States. In the event, those States with second chambers were allowed to keep them while the others remained unicameral; provision was at the same time inserted to enable second chambers to be created or abolished on the initiative of a two-thirds

---

[1] It may be added that Bills pending in Parliament do not lapse on prorogation.

[2] The definition is along British lines, but it may be noted that the definition in India includes Bills dealing with 'the regulation of the borrowing of money or the giving of any guarantee by the Government of India, or the amendment of the law with respect to any financial obligations undertaken by the Government of India'.

[3] Such items may, however, be discussed in either House.

[4] The State Governors, unlike the Union President, are not elected—though this was indeed the original intention and was abandoned in the face of some opposition. The introduction of Governors nominated by the President smacked too much of old days of bureaucratic centralisation; but the Government view was that an elected Governor might conflict with the Chief Minister, and the safest way to a constitutional head at State level was through nomination. Perhaps also the Government was not averse to a further measure of central 'pull'. In the Part B or former princely states, the Governor is replaced by the Rajpramukh or Ruler. But see above, p. 8, n.

majority of the State Lower House. Upper Houses, or Legislative Councils, where they exist are constituted in a complex manner: one-third elected by members of local authorities; one-third elected by members of the State Legislative Assembly; one-twelfth elected by teachers; one-sixth nominated by the Governor from persons in the fields of literature, science, art, co-operative movement and social service. Two important differences between States and Union are to be found in the legislative procedure. In the first place, even where there are two Houses of a State Legislature, there is no provision for a joint sitting; the Councils may delay for three months, but a second passing by the Lower House is sufficient to enable the Bill to go forward for assent. Secondly, there is in effect a central veto power on State legislation: the Governor may, like the President in the Union Parliament, withhold his own assent once only, but he may also reserve a Bill for the consideration of the President; in this case, it is possible for the President to continue indefinitely to withhold his assent.

4. The Election of Parliament

The first General Election for the Union and State Parliaments was held in 1951–52.[1] In the constitution-making discussions there had been some talk of proportional representation, and some hopes for a system of indirect elections based on village panchayats. But the main aspiration of the great majority was to see the introduction into Asia of free direct elections on adult franchise. In his final speech to the Constituent Assembly the President said that in making that decision they had indeed taken 'a very big step'. He went on:

I am not dismayed by it. . . . I know the village people who will constitute the bulk of this vast electorate. In my opinion, our people possess intelligence and common sense. They also have a culture which the sophisticated may not appreciate but which is solid. . . . They are able to take measure of their own interest and also of the interests of the country at large if things are explained to them.[2]

[1] The excellent official account is the Election Commission's *Report on the First General Elections in India, 1951–52* (Delhi, 1955). Articles on the elections include W. H. Morris-Jones, 'The Indian Elections' in *Political Quarterly*, July–Sept. 1952, and R. Park, 'Indian Election Results' in *Far Eastern Survey*, May 1952. Irene Tinker-Walker's 'Representation and Representative Government in the Indian Republic', an unpublished Ph.D. Thesis (University of London, 1954) contains a first-hand account of the elections, some of which has been published in articles on the elections in Himachal Pradesh, Travancore-Cochin and Rajasthan in the Summer 1953, Autumn 1953 and Spring 1954 issues (respectively) of *Parliamentary Affairs*. An interesting pamphlet study of the elections is Asoka Mehta's *The Political Mind of India* (Bombay, 1952). Other pamphlets or books include M. Venkatarangaiya's valuable *The General Election in Bombay City* (Bombay, 1953), B. R. Sharma's *Report on Elections in the Punjab* (Jullundur, 1952) and S. P. Singh Sud's *Elections and Legislators* (Ludhiana, 1952).
[2] C.A. Deb., XI, 989.

In the last sentence the President certainly touched the heart of the matter. Was the Indian electorate willing and capable to choose its representatives and was it presented with an understandable choice which it could make in a free and secret fashion?

The legal framework for the conduct of elections in India is in part provided by the Constitution itself. The Constitution, for example, lays down the manner in which the President of the Union shall be elected and also the Vice-President (Articles 54–58 and 66–71 respectively). It establishes certain general rules regarding the composition of and the qualification of members for both Houses of the Union Parliament (Articles 79–84 and 102–103) and for State legislatures (Articles 168–173, 190–191, 238 and 240). Most important, it provides that the superintendence, direction and control of preparations for and the conduct of all elections shall be vested in a permanent Election Commission independent of the governments of the day (Article 324). Finally, it lays down the principle of adult franchise (Article 326) and makes general provision for the reservation of seats for Scheduled Castes and Tribes and for the nomination of Anglo-Indians (Articles 330–333). This still left much to be done by ordinary legislation. Parliament filled the gaps with the Representation of the People Acts of 1950 and 1951 (later amended), while the Government under these Acts made two sets of statutory rules for the preparation of rolls and the conduct of the elections. It is understood that this mass of somewhat dispersed law will be codified before the second General Elections take place.[1]

The administrative framework began to take shape in 1950. Early in that year, the offices of the Election Commission were set up and the Chief Election Commissioner (Mr. Sukumar Sen) appointed. Over the period of the elections themselves, two full-time Regional Commissioners were also appointed. In all States, the governments appointed Chief Electoral Officers and, below them, Electoral Registration Officers, and these functions were performed as additional duties by existing government officers. In the same way, judicial officers were chosen to act as Revising Authorities to decide claims and objections to the draft rolls. Returning Officers and their assistants were found from administrative personnel. Presiding Officers and Polling Officers were supplied from a lower section of government employees. This whole administrative machinery was tested in polling rehearsals or mock elections held in every State during the late summer of 1951.

Nearly two years elapsed between the passing of the Constitution and the General Elections. But two years was not too long for the work that had to be completed. The delimitation of constituencies was in itself enormously difficult. The Constitution had set certain limits: not more than one member of the House of the People for every 500,000 people,

1 Election Commission, *op. cit.*, p. 6.

not less than one for every 750,000[1]; not more than one member of a State Assembly for more than 75,000 people. Upper and lower limits on the number of seats in State Assemblies are also laid down, as well as an upper limit of 500 for the House of the People. In addition, the Constitution's provisions regarding the reservation of seats for Scheduled Castes and Tribes had to be observed. The first task was the determination of population; the previous census of 1941 was considered too out of date and the Census Commissioner was charged with the preparation of estimates. On this basis, the Representation of the People Act, 1950, allocated House of the People seats to the States and also established the number of seats in State Assemblies. The latter was in every case an integral multiple of the former, so that a combination of State Assembly constituencies would generally constitute one Union Parliament constituency. Constituencies were normally single-member and were based as far as possible on existing district or other administrative units. In some areas the concentration of Scheduled Tribes permitted the reservation for them of single-member constitutencies, but for some tribal seats and all Scheduled Caste seats it was necessary to create double-member constituencies.[2] The proposals of the Election Commission were placed before the public for objections, and Parliamentary Advisory Committees for each State (consisting of M.P.s representing the State in Parliament) were invited to make their comments and recommendations. The final Delimitation Orders were subject to amendment by Parliament.[3]

No less difficult was the preparation of Electoral Rolls. Some preliminary steps were taken during 1948–49, but the electoral legislation passed in 1950 made the draft rolls largely unsuitable and work had to begin practically afresh. The new draft rolls were published in the autumn of 1950 and claims and objections received up to the end of the year. The chief difficulties arose with the large and somewhat floating population of displaced persons, with women voters who would give not their own names but only those of their male relatives, and with certain remote islands off the south-western coasts. Moreover, the authorities were able

[1] The latter limit was deleted by the Constitution (2nd Amendment) Act, 1952, since the population increase revealed in the 1951 census made it unworkable. It had already proved an artificial handicap to the task of delimitation.

[2] Of the 489 seats in the House of the People to be filled by election, 72 seats were reserved for Scheduled Caste candidates, 27 for Scheduled Tribes; they were arranged in 314 single-member constituencies, 86 double-member constituencies and 1 three-member constituency (which had reservation for both Tribes and Castes). Of the 3,373 State Assembly seats, 477 were reserved for Scheduled Castes, 192 for Scheduled Tribes; these were arranged in 2,124 single-member constituencies, 578 double-member, and 1 three-member.

[3] This procedure, according to the Commission (*op. cit.*, p. 57), 'did not work out smoothly or satisfactorily'. The Delimitation Commission Act, 1952, sets up instead an independent Commission of three (a retired Supreme Court Judge, a retired High Court Chief Justice and the Chief Election Commissioner), with two to seven associate members from each State drawn from members of the House of the People and State Legislative Assemblies.

to receive little help from the political parties, which were inexperienced in the work. All things considered, it was an achievement to enrol 49% of the total population as against an eligible proportion of 50·55%.

It had been these formidable administrative problems rather than doubts about the ability of the illiterate to vote which had seemed unsurmountable in the past. The Indian Franchise (Lothian) Committee's Report,[1] for instance, appeared more impressed with administrative difficulties of vast numbers than with the problem of the illiterate voter as such. They pointed out that even with the 1926 franchise, which consisted of only 10% of the adult population, half the Muslim and one-third of the Hindu voters of Bengal were illiterate. Nevertheless, with a literacy percentage of about 16½, the system of voting to be adopted did assume some importance. It was clearly impossible to ask the voter to mark his paper without assistance—and such assistance would at once have imperilled the secrecy of the ballot. The system adopted was one which had already been used in India: separate ballot boxes, each marked with the distinctive symbols of a candidate, are placed in the polling compartment; the voter is given a ballot paper which he does not have to mark but which he simply places in the box of his choice. Parties were invited to indicate their preferences in symbols and an allocation was made by the Commission to fourteen parties recognised as all-India parties.[2] Similar arrangements were made by State Chief Electoral Officers for other parties operating only on a State basis and for independents.[3] Since each voter was called upon to vote for his State Assembly as well as for the House of the People, each polling station required two sets of boxes for the two sets of candidates. Two and a half million boxes had to be made.

The elections certainly produced enthusiasm. In the first place, there was no shortage of candidates. The number of seats to be filled was 489 at the Centre and 3,373 in the States. For these, nomination papers were received for 2,833 and 23,287 candidates respectively. Even when some nominations had been rejected and others withdrawn, 1,874 contested the Centre seats and 15,361 the State seats. Only 93 candidates were returned unopposed and 41 of these were for reserved seats. Of course, the enthusiasm of many was misplaced; in spite of deposits (about £40 for Central, £20 for State elections), a total of 9,198 candidates had to suffer forfeiture—including 4,967 out of 6,520 optimistic Independents. In the

[1] 1932, Cd. 4086.

[2] In Feb. 1953 the Election Commission withdrew recognition as all-India parties from all parties which had failed to secure 3% of the total votes. This reduced the number to four: Congress; Praja Socialist Party; Communist Party; Jan Sangh (H.P. Deb., 3rd Session, 1953, Appendix II, Annexure I).

[3] The number of State parties has also been reduced since the elections: 39 were recognised in 1951; this has been reduced to 19, only 4 of which are recognised in more than one State.

second place, only considerable enthusiasm on the part of the administration could have ensured the establishment and adequate staffing of 132,560 polling stations. In many areas polling had to be spread over several days owing to shortage of personnel (the longest period was 25 days in one constituency), but at least every area, however inaccessible, was catered for—even if camels, elephants, porters and fleets of jeeps had to be used to transport the boxes and staff. Only in parts of one Himalayan constituency were the arrangements mishandled; there delay resulted in snow-bound conditions which made voting practically impossible. In addition, postal ballot papers were issued to nearly 300,000 voters—including armed forces, government personnel abroad and persons under preventive detention. Thirdly, even among voters there was more enthusiasm than had perhaps been generally anticipated. 105,944,495 persons—or 51·15% of the voters—cast their votes. The maximum percentage was 92·6 in one constituency, the minimum 10·1. Moreover, the process was orderly and peaceful in almost every polling station. The figure of 1,250 electoral offences reported—including 817 cases of impersonation—is remarkably small. There was, on the other hand, a spate of election petitions—338 in all, 314 of which were heard by Election Tribunals. These bodies were constituted by the Election Commission and were composed of a serving or retired High Court or District Judge as Chairman, a serving or retired District Judge and an advocate as members. Although 66 Tribunals were set up, the procedure was slow, and at the beginning of 1955 there were still 7 petitions still pending. Of the 307 dealt with, no less than 183 referred to improper acceptance or rejection of nomination papers—mainly because of the unnecessarily complex rules on the matter. In all, 156 petitions were dismissed, 128 allowed and 23 withdrawn.

The facts and figures of the electoral process are one thing; an assessment and judgment on the meaning of the elections quite another. A summary of the election results is given in Table II (pp. 100–101).

Certain statements can be made on the strength of these figures. It can be seen that while the Congress won an overwhelming majority of seats both at the Centre and in most of the States, its performance in terms of votes was less impressive. Neither in the elections for the House of the People nor in those for the State legislatures—except one, Saurashtra—did it succeed in securing an absolute majority of votes. In the absence of multi-number constituencies this result is, of course, not surprising; it was very easy for Congress to top the poll, but the total votes against it, divided among several parties, were generally greater than those for it. The discrepancy between seats and votes in the case of the Socialists and Communists has a different explanation. The Socialists put up many candidates and in consequence gathered votes but few seats; the Communists put up fewer candidates and concentrated on areas where they

7—P.I.

were already strong. It can be seen, too, that a substantial proportion of votes—rather more in State elections than in those for the Centre—were dispersed over a number of small parties and independent candidates. The election was an invitation to political adventure and no one could be quite certain that it would not be worth while. Some consolidation has already taken place since the election and more can be expected as issues become clarified and experience is acquired. A map showing how the parties fared in different parts of India[1] discloses readily the Communist strength in the south and in west Bengal. It also shows, less emphatically, the influence of the Socialists in the north-central States.

Analysis of statistics will not, however, tell us much about what the election meant to 'the average voter'. Most observers seem to be agreed that candidates were surprised to find such lively and intelligent interest on the part of apparently uneducated people. There appears to be little doubt, too, that the vote for Congress was not merely a vote of thanks for past glories and not merely a vote of loving trust in Pandit Nehru and the party of Gandhiji—though both these were important—but also a vote for the only party that could look for a moment capable of forming a reasonably stable and competent government. At the same time, this does not dispose of the doubt that votes may have been cast for quite other reasons. Nor does the fact that the real challenge to the Congress came evidently from the left rather than from the communal parties rule out the possibility that caste and community played a big part. One Indian political commentator went so far as to say that the votes were quite meaningless because the popular mentality was still authoritarian. This is clearly exaggerated, but how far and in what ways did the loyalties that emerge from the social structure affect the voting? The material for a thorough answer to this question simply does not exist. It can be said without question that in certain areas votes went where local landlords wanted them to go; this seems to have been particularly true of Rajasthan and Madhya Bharat. Again, certain regional parties were openly based on caste lines; thus, the Tamilnad Toilers' Party and Commonweal Party in Madras were based almost entirely on non-Brahmin sentiment in that State,[2] while the victory of the Jharkhand Party in Bihar was acknowledged as a victory for the organised tribal Adibasis. It appears too that not much sense can be made of the Congress Party's own internal difficulties in, for instance, Bihar, unless account is taken of caste factors. But caste is an iceberg; for the portion

---

[1] Such a map is given in the Election Commission's Report (*op. cit.*).

[2] Even within the Congress Party in Madras, Brahmin and anti-Brahmin feelings account for a very great deal of internal disagreement. It is presumed that a gain in anti-Brahmin strength within Congress during 1953–54 helped to persuade no fewer than 12 of the 19 Tamilnad Toilers' Party members in the Madras Assembly to cross over to the Congress benches in December 1954.

that is visible is much less than the part that is hidden. Two propositions can fairly safely be put forward. First, in most constituencies there was some voting which was decisively influenced by caste and communal loyalties; a Muslim or a Christian or a Nair or a Brahmin would, that is to say, attract votes by virtue of his community or caste alone.[1] Second, in most areas there were 'group leaders' of one kind or another in a position to command and offer the votes of their followers. Such group leaders might be village headmen or members of a caste panchayat, trade union officials or slum bosses.

Even when this has been said, the implications are not very clear. It would be incorrect, for example, to suppose that all such caste or group voting is blind or morally corrupting. In the best cases, it could in effect be a kind of indirect election in which the responsibility of the representative to interests in his constituency is more firmly ensured than might otherwise be possible. A group leader may be able to represent to a member of an Assembly the grievances and needs of his followers more effectively than they could themselves. Such a position is no doubt always open to corruption and is in any case far from the ideal of a vision of the common good grasped alike by voter and representative. On this, perhaps two comments suffice. One is that studies of elections in politically advanced countries have in recent years destroyed some illusions as to the extent to which such an ideal can be reached with adult franchise. The second is that the range of a person's vision is limited by general conditions of life and education as much as by sectional loyalties and that an attack concentrated wholly on the latter is likely to be misplaced. In any event, the Indian electorate did not betray the 'act of faith' of its leaders. No doubt there were the cases where superstitions became entangled in politics and peasant women wanted to garland ballot boxes as if they were idols. No doubt personalities and prejudices played an enormous part in the making of decisions—and no doubt 'making a decision' is a euphemism for the process in many cases. Nevertheless, the idea of a free choice penetrated downwards into layers of society which were hitherto unfamiliar with the idea and the political parties were educated in the politics of independence. The election was influenced by the domination of sectional visions, but the very holding of the elections may have been an important influence in the direction of widening those visions.

[1] Allegations that Congress 'exploited' caste loyalties need not be taken too seriously. All parties paid some attention to these factors in selecting candidates. In the Andhra elections of 1954 it was reliably reported that even the Communist Party was careful to work among certain castes only by means of party members drawn from those castes. It was further said that many who knew that their 'interests' pointed in one direction still voted in another in obedience to caste sympathy.

TABLE II—1951–52 ELECTION RESULTS
(a) *House of the People*

Party	No. of Candidates	Seats Won	Votes Polled	% of Total Votes
Congress	479	364	47,665,875	45
Communist	49	16	3,484,401	3·3
Socialist	256	12	11,216,779	10·6
K.M.P.	146	9	6,156,558	5·8
Jan Sangh	93	3	3,246,288	3·1
Other Parties	327	44	17,395,845	16·4
Independents	524	41	16,778,749	15·8
	1,874	489	105,944,495	100

(c) STATE

	Congress		Socialists		Communists		K.M.P.	
	Seats	Votes	Seats	Votes	Seats	Votes	Seats	Votes
PART 'A' STATES								
Assam	76	1,075,331	4	325,690	1	69,431	1	146,7921
Bihar	240	3,951,148	23	1,737,466	—	108,671	1	273,911
Bombay	269	5,556,334	9	1,330,246	1	159,994	—	559,492
Madhya Pradesh	194	3,281,983	2	660,883	—	24,460	8	276,723
Madras	152	6,998,667	13	1,312,703	62	2,591,341	35	1,793,629
Orissa	67	1,428,414	10	432,731	7	206,757	—	16,948
Punjab	96	1,830,601	—	224,608	4	251,713	—	—
Uttar Pradesh	390	8,032,455	19	2,032,594	—	155,869	1	954,196
Bengal	150	2,897,881	—	215,385	28	800,951	15	667,445
PART 'B' STATES								
Hyderabad	93	2,162,759	11	592,071	—	—	—	4,047
Madhya Bharat	75	938,919	4	145,843	—	39,600	—	6,510
Mysore	74	1,276,318	3	240,390	1	25,116	8	391,653
PEPSU	26	376,297	—	17,480	2	86,191	1	15,613
Rajasthan	82	1,286,953	1	136,464	—	17,181	1	16,411
Saurashtra	55	606,934	2	34,728	—	7,791	—	30,907
Travancore-Cochin	44	1,204,364	11	485,194	—	—	—	—
PART 'C' STATES								
Ajmer	20	101,441	—	1,094	—	3,494	—	—
Bhopal	25	117,656	—	1,744	—	—	—	—
Coorg	15	48,945	—	—	—	1,386	—	—
Delhi	39	271,812	2	12,396	—	2,591	—	13,646
Himachal Pradesh	24	85,079	—	2,664	—	—	3	26,471
Vindhya Pradesh	40	272,255	11	128,787	—	—	3	111,825
Kutch	28	72,834	—	4,462	—	—	—	—
Manipur	10	37,448	1	9,196	2	5,298	—	—
Tripura	9	36,167	—	—	12	55,603	—	—
Total	2,293	43,928,995	126	10,084,869	162	4,613,438	77	5,306,219

FOR NOTES TO THIS TABLE SEE p. 102.

(b) *Council of State* (indirectly elected from State Legislatures)

Party	Seats Won
Congress . .	146
Communist . .	9
Socialist . .	6
K.M.P. . .	4
Jan Sangh . .	1
Other Parties and Independents .	50
Total . .	216

NOTES:

(a) The size of the Council has been increased to 219 since the creation of Andhra in 1953.

(b) The figure of 216 here includes the 12 nominees of the President and the 4 nominees from Kashmir.

LEGISLATURES

Jan Sangh		Others		Independent		Total		
Seats	Votes	Seats	Votes	Seats	Votes	Seats	Votes	
								PART 'A' STATES
—	7,191	9	161,963	14	662,492	105	2,448,890	Assam
—	113,234	53	1,500,749	13	1,863,661	330	9,548,840	Bihar
—	4,876	18	1,594,726	18	1,917,574	325	11,123,242	Bombay
—	249,899	5	660,188	23	1,852,452	232	7,006,588	Madhya Pradesh
—	8,216	51	2,543,516	62	4,749,184	375	19,997,256	Madras
—	—	35	769,675	21	822,521	140	3,677,046	Orissa
—	277,616	22	1,211,643	4	1,182,408	126	4,978,589	Punjab
2	1,066,714	4	1,241,489	14	3,275,310	430	16,758,627	Uttar Pradesh
9	417,879	20	806,285	16	1,638,399	238	7,444,225	Bengal
								PART 'B' STATES
—	2,328	57	1,675,201	14	742,187	175	5,178,593	Hyderabad
4	193,627	13	404,755	3	258,156	99	1,987,410	Madhya Bharat
—	62,118	2	61,606	11	696,667	99	2,753,868	Mysore
2	37,494	21	401,678	8	419,725	60	1,354,478	PEPSU
8	193,532	33	714,723	35	896,178	160	3,261,442	Rajasthan
—	4,346	1	191,129	2	75,624	60	951,509	Saurashtra
—	—	16	557,080	37	1,151,555	108	3,398,193	Travancore-Cochin
								PART 'C' STATES
3	28,612	3	15,781	4	84,366	30	234,788	Ajmer
—	11,135	1	43,939	4	51,746	30	226,220	Bhopal
—	—	—	—	9	37,716	24	88,047	Coorg
5	114,207	1	24,142	1	82,922	48	521,766	Delhi
—	6,212	1	11,924	8	47,433	36	179,783	Himachal-Pradesh
2	67,330	2	43,702	2	57,900	60	681,799	Vindhya Pradesh
—	—	—	—	2	38,116	30	115,412	Kutch
—	—	16	79,283	1	8,105	30	139,330	Manipur
—	—	3	28,996	6	7,886	30	128,652	Tripura
35	2,866,566	345	14,744,173	332	22,620,333	3,370	104,184,593	Total

Notes to Table II.

(i) The Communists in Travancore-Cochin contested as Independents and combining with other Left groups in a United Front of Leftists secured 32 seats. In Hyderabad, their label was Peoples' Democratic Front which won 42 seats.

(ii) The 30 member bodies in Kutch, Manipur and Tripura are not legislatures but only electoral colleges chosen to select members for the central Parliament.

(iii) The number of seats in the Assam Assembly is 108, but in three constituencies no nomination papers were filed and no members chosen.

CHAPTER THREE

THE HOUSE AND THE MEMBER

1. The Balance of Power

NOT the most interesting but certainly the first necessary question to ask of a legislature is—who controls it? This in turn must normally entail an account of the party allegiance of its members. The position of the parties in the central Parliament following the elections of 1951–52 have already been set out above.[1] The outstanding features of the party pattern of both Houses can be listed shortly: first, the overwhelmingly dominant position of Congress; second, the very divided character of the opposition groups; finally, the comparatively large number of members returned as Independents and members of local parties of one kind or another. Nothing has happened since 1952 to remove any of these features, but the latter two have in some measure been modified.

By-elections account for little change. Of 19 by-elections which took place up to the end of 1953, Congress retained 10 of the 14 seats it previously held and failed to capture any of the other 5. All its 4 losses were gains to the Praja Socialist Party. This party also gained in terms of votes—as did the Communist Party—and both did so at the expense of parties other than Congress.[2]

More important were the changes affected by movements of parties and groups without reference to the electorate. Of these, the most noteworthy was the coming together of the Socialist Party and Kripalani's Kisan Mazdoor Praja Party, formed of dissident Congressmen in May 1951.[3] The two parties had fought the election separately, but as soon as the first session of the new Parliament began in May 1952 they decided to establish a parliamentary alliance. The objects may at first have been limited to securing parliamentary time and concerting lines of criticism in

[1] Pp. 100–101.

[2] As compared with the General Election, the percentage of total votes polled by the different parties showed the following trends: the Congress proportion remained steady, falling only from 48·4% to 48·3%; that of the P.S.P. rose from 16·4% to 24·6% and that of the Communists from 1·9% to 7·3%; the communal parties (Hindu Mahasabha, Jan Sangh and Ram Rajya Parishad) lost ground from 7·1% to 3%; so also did the other parties, from 7·9% to 4%, and the Independents, from 18·3% to 12·8% (figures taken from Indian National Congress, *Report of the General Secretaries, Jan. 1953–Jan. 1954*).

[3] Kripalani, a former Congress President, had attempted to content himself and others with a Democratic Front within the Congress, formed in 1950; by early 1951, it was clear that this was not enough.

debate, but further negotiations soon led to a complete merger of the two organisations on a nation-wide basis both inside the legislatures and in the country as a whole; the Praja Socialist Party was set up in August of the same year. The effect was to give a markedly greater coherence to the non-Communist opposition. This remains true in spite of the fact that the merger added a further element to the already imperfectly united Socialist Party leadership.[1] In the House of the People, certainly, the merger was an asset to the opposition and to the House itself. As leader in Parliament, Kripalani brought with him considerable personal prestige and status as well as capacity as a speaker—though admittedly of platform rather than parliamentary style. Asoka Mehta's entry into the House through a by-election in 1954 should have provided the P.S.P. group with other qualities required in leadership.

At the time when the K.M.P. and Socialists effected their initial parliamentary alliance to the left of Congress, an attempt was also made to bring about greater coherence of the right-wing elements. This attempt not only failed to develop into a general merger in the country as a whole; it has hardly been able to maintain itself in the House. The initiator of the grouping was Dr. S. P. Mukherjee, leader of the Jan Sangh, a new party hurriedly formed in 1951 following Dr. Mukherjee's resignation from the Cabinet and his dissatisfaction with the Hindu Mahasabha. He formed a group in the House of the People called the National Democratic Party. Its core was composed of the members of the Jan Sangh and Hindu Mahasabha, but it was able to attract a number of right-wing, primarily local parties such as Ram Rajya Parishad and some independents. At one time, in mid-1952, it may have numbered about 30. Towards the end of that year, however, it partly disintegrated when some of the independents found they could no longer follow Dr. Mukherjee's policy of hostility towards Pakistan. Dr. Mukherjee's death in 1953 not only removed an outstanding parliamentarian but seriously prejudiced the chances of a coherent rightist group. Mr. N. C. Chatterjee, an able Supreme Court advocate and member of the Hindu Mahasabha, has to some extent taken his place, but has not been able to rally the same measure of support.

1 The post-independence Socialist Party had a triumvirate leadership: Jaiprakash Narayan, the principal personality and formerly undisputed leader of the Congress Socialist Party days, but now, as we have seen above (p. 39), having abandoned Marxism for the Bhoodan philosophy and politics; Asoka Mehta, intellectual but also organiser, feeling his way towards an anti-Communist doctrine of 'constructive opposition'; Ram Manohar Lohia, individualist and even eccentric, following a doggedly middle line of no compromise with either Congress or Communists. The merger with the K.M.P. added the fourth leader, Acharya Kripalani. His Gandhian radicalism has not proved wholly undigestible since the socialist leaders were already in search of a philosophic alternative to Marxism. The divergencies in the leadership which manifest themselves sharply from time to time (as at the Nagpur Convention of the party in Dec. 1954, when Kripalani rather wearily resigned the Chairmanship in favour of the socialist 'elder statesman', Narendra Dev) would have been hardly less marked in the absence of the merger.

Towards the end of 1954, an attempt was made to create a parliamentary group of the left large enough to command recognition by the Speaker as the Opposition Party.[1] The initiative appears to have come from small non-Communist parties of the left, but the P.S.P. was naturally the largest element and Kripalani was chosen leader of the group. They gave themselves the name 'Union of Socialists and Progressives', but the Speaker was not convinced that they constituted a sufficiently homogeneous and stable organisation to merit recognition as a party. The group has, however, effected a futher integration of the non-Communist left and it has provided a useful parliamentary organisation for the tiny leftist groups and for some independents; it has claimed as many as 41 members.

These groupings, then, have modified two of the main features of the House as elected in 1952: the opposition is not quite as weak and undivided, nor is the number of unrelated local parties and unattached independents quite as large as the election returns alone could indicate. This, however, scarcely affects the dominating position of the Congress Party. The Government party has had to meet opposition arguments and has had to state its case, but it has not had to face a challenge of numbers. The record of the divisions in Parliament and the voting figures (given in Appendix IV) show two facts: first, the frequency of divisions in the House of the People has increased in comparison with the relatively placid days of the Constituent Assembly and Provisional Parliament; but, secondly, the numerical strength of the opposition to the Government has only once reached 100 in a House of 499 members.[2] If the Government Whips have been busy, the reasons must be sought elsewhere than in the threat of defeat.[3]

The post-1952 developments in the Upper House, the Council of States, have been similar. The composition in 1952 has already been given[4] and its features were those of the Lower House. The changes in the Council since 1952 have taken place partly through elections. These elections were not only by-elections as in the House of the People but also regular elections provided under the Constitution. The Council of States is not subject to dissolution; instead, one-third of its members retire every two years.[5] Since all the members of the Council of States in 1952 were newly elected, the retirement roster was introduced by ballot; members were divided into three groups to hold their seats for two, four and six years. The first elections accordingly took place in 1954. Of the 74 retiring members (4 of the 12 members nominated by the President also had to retire), only 43 were returned. The party positions, however,

---

[1] See below, p. 155, on the important question of recognition.
[2] Most of the largest opposition votes have been recorded in the course of the passage of Preventive Detention Bills.
[3] Their work is described in Chapter IV.
[4] P. 101.   [5] See above, p. 90.

changed less than the personnel. Congress recorded 10 gains and 1 loss, the net improvement of 9 reflecting the changed position in the State Assemblies which constitute the electorate for the Council.[1]

The changes in the groupings of Council members have been along lines similar to those in the House. The formation of groups has, if anything, been somewhat easier than in the House, since the Chairman of the Council has proved rather less exacting in his demands for certain qualifications of stability before granting recognition to groups. On the other hand, the pressure to combine is less in the Upper House, simply because it is the less important of the two chambers. Outside the Congress and Communist Parties, groups do exist for the purposes of demanding parliamentary time and selecting themes and speakers. But the composition of these groups is not constant and their influence outside the Council negligible.

Movements in the balance of power have been more evident in State Assemblies than at the Centre. Not only have election changes been more radical; the realignment of members once elected is also more important (at least in the politically less mature States) than it is in Delhi. For these reasons a brief review of the developments in some States will at the same time serve conveniently to illustrate the influence of some of the factors we noted in the first chapter on the working of parliamentary democracy. In three States, Assemblies elected in 1952 were dissolved and General Elections held again within three years. In P.E.P.S.U., stable government had been made difficult by the delicate balance of parties: in an Assembly of 60, Congress had 26 members, the Akali (Sikh) Party 22, Communists 3, K.M.P. 1, Jan Sangh 1 and there were 7 Independents. This unhopeful situation was at once aggravated by the baffling inconstancy and inconsequence of Sikh politics in an area of former princely states unaccustomed to parliamentary democracy.[2] At first, six Independents joined the Congress Party and, thus strengthened, the party formed a ministry. It was not long, however, before the farce began. On the very day when the ministry was formed, five members deserted. Within a month, they were followed by four

---

[1] The March 1956 elections resulted in even less alteration in party strengths in the Council, the only noteworthy change being an increase of Communist Party representation by 2.

[2] The peculiar quality of Sikh politics has nowhere been exhaustively examined, but it seems probable that the tendency to extreme factionalism may owe something to the highly developed and military clan organisation of the Sikhs in the eighteenth century, and even more to the need of the community from its very inception to define itself in relation to more than one bigger power. On these historical factors, see Khushwant Singh, *The Sikhs* (1953). The author explains lucidly the development of factions among the Akalis in the 1920s: a split first took place on the attitude to be taken to the Government and a further division, which cut across the first, arose out of different attitudes towards Congress (pp. 115, 139). Even the Communist Party in the Punjab has been influenced by Sikh factionalism (p. 147). This factionalism is reflected in 'the fiery confusion of thought so prevalent among Sikh politicians' (p. 143).

more—including a Minister—and the ministry resigned. Its place was taken by a coalition led by the Akalis and given the name of United Democratic Front. It soon became evident that the Front had little substance behind it, and that it could remain united only by interpreting democracy in eccentric ways. It showed, above all, a marked shyness in meeting the Assembly. The Constitution (Article 174) compels a meeting at least every six months, and the session that was summoned in November 1952 was one that could not well have been avoided. The next best thing was to adjourn it quickly. Only a few days after the opening of the session a little note passed from the Chief Minister to the Speaker—and a further respite was gained. A month later it was the Speaker who took the initiative, calling the Assembly without consulting the Minister. The Government was, however, equal to the occasion; on the eve of the meeting two members of the opposition were sworn in as Minister and Deputy Minister, a no-confidence motion was defeated and the Assembly again adjourned and subsequently prorogued. Meanwhile, the Election Tribunal was examining the unusually heavy crop of election petitions which had been filed in P.E.P.S.U. The seats of no less than 23 of the 60 members were in question. Moreover, of 17 petitions decided upon by early 1953, as many as 9 were upheld. The effect on government stability was made all the greater, because out of the 6 members of the Council of Ministers 3 were among the unseated, while a petition was still pending against another. It was in these circumstances that a Presidential Proclamation under Article 356 of the Constitution was issued in March 1953.[1] Under this order (originally for six months and later extended by Parliament for a further six months) the functions of government in the State were assumed by the Centre, the State budgets came before the Union Parliament and the administration in the State was afforded an opportunity to recover. From the elections of February 1954 an unambiguous pattern emerged. Congress won 37 of the 60 seats, the Communists gained 1 to give them 4, the Independents remained with a strength of 7, while the Jan Sangh and P.S.P. disappeared. The Akalis, who had enjoyed a lively series of internal disputes, entered the fight in two halves, Right- and Left-wing; they split their votes and secured only 12 seats between them.[2]

---

[1] A not unfair review of events was given by Dr. K. N. Katju, Union Home Minister in the debate on the Proclamation, House of the People, 12 March 1953.

[2] In terms of votes, the increased support for Congress is clear, but it was at the expense of parties other than the Akali:

		1952		1954
Congress	.	395,750		702,077
Akali	.	317,502	(Right)	324,699
			(Left)	120,210
Independents		369,294		336,485
Communists	.	33,235		96,697
Others	.	238,674		33,737

General Elections were also held in Travancore–Cochin during February 1954. The position after the elections of 1952 did not appear as unstable as in P.E.P.S.U. In an Assembly of 109, Congress secured only 45 seats. To this number, however, it was thought reasonable to add for all intents and purposes the 8 members of the Travancore Tamil-Nad Congress and a sufficient number of Independents. Here, however, the force of regional tension showed itself as powerful an unsettling factor as Sikh communal politics in P.E.P.S.U. The T.T.N.C. is a section of Congressmen whose only difference with the party arises from its support for the separation of the southern Tamil-speaking districts from the Malayalam-speaking remainder of the State and their merger with Madras. Their leader was given a place in the State Cabinet, but the tussle within the party continued; while the T.T.N.C. insisted on its own organisation outside the Assembly, other sections of the party strove to absorb it into the main body. The problem was considered important enough to merit the attention of the Congress Working Committee, but the appeal of that body that the matter should be put into cold storage until the whole problem of reorganisation of States came to be examined was not seriously listened to. In September 1953 the T.T.N.C. leader resigned from the Cabinet, and a few days later his party voted with the (primarily Communist) opposition to defeat the Government. The Chief Minister advised the Rajpramukh to dissolve the Assembly, and he continued in office until the elections were held.[1] The defeat of the Government, though caused by the intrusion of a regional tension, was followed by open and angry discussions among Congressmen.[2] The Government was accused of clinging to office and lowering the prestige of the party, and there were allegations of maladministration. Whatever substance these charges had, behind them were often different thoughts. On the part of some leading party personalities, there was simple disappointment and annoyance that since 1952 there had been not even one Cabinet change—so that they had remained excluded from office. The private resentment of a few, however, requires for its support a more general dissatisfaction; this was to hand in the shape of growing Hindu irritation at the increasing influence in the Travancore–Cochin Congress of the now prosperous Christian community. If still more was required to furnish ground for dissension, there was also the continuous difficulty of keeping the Cochin and Travancore

[1] This course of events was violently criticised by the Left, which argued that a Government could have been formed of the opposition groups and that the Rajpramukh should therefore have sent for the Leader of the opposition. British precedents were freely quoted on both sides and appeals were made across the straits to Ceylon, where Sir Ivor Jennings was invited to pronounce a judgment. The composition of the opposition was in fact very mixed, and it is unlikely that a stable government could have been formed.

[2] One report (*Times of India*, 13 Oct.) spoke of 'wild accusations flung through the newspapers whose columns are filled with statements and counter-statements often of the nature of personal attacks'.

wings of the State—and the Party—contented.[1] The Congress thus entered the election contest in a weakened condition, and even the energetic contribution of Pandit Nehru to the local campaign failed to enable the party to improve its position. Its proportion of the votes remained almost the same and it won 45 seats in an Assembly now of 118 members. Among the other parties, however, it had no likely allies. The Government at once resigned and a period of busy negotiation and active speculation followed. Apart from Congress's 45 seats, the Communists emerged[2] with 23, the P.S.P. with 19, the T.T.N.C. with 12, the Revolutionary Socialist Party with 9, and there were 9 Independents. The general expectation was that a leftist government would be formed with Congress in opposition. This belief was based on the election arrangement made between the P.S.P. and the Communist-led United Front of Leftists; both seemed to have made it clear that the Congress was the main enemy.[3] Yet although the U.F.L. offered to serve under a P.S.P. Chief Minister, and although there was much sentiment in the P.S.P. which favoured such a Leftist government, the outcome of discussions between the local P.S.P. and the National Executive of the party was different: the P.S.P. undertook, with its 19 members, to form a government alone, and with Congress support was able to do so. This Government proved stable; more, it showed itself to be capable, energetic and honest. It courageously refused to think or act in communal or regional terms and as a result won much respect in all regions and communities.[4] At the same time, it must be admitted that if the Communists, as the next largest single party after Congress, had been invited to form a government they might well have been able to do so— with the support of some P.S.P. members, who would thus have split

[1] The two formerly separate princely states were merged in 1949, and centuries of independent existence were not quickly forgotten. In Sept. 1951, 30 members of the Assembly from Cochin constituencies had resigned because the Cabinet contained no representatives of that area.

[2] The word is peculiarly appropriate; they had had to fight the 1952 elections under the label of Independents.

[3] It was later alleged by the Communists that the initiative for the alliance came wholly from the P.S.P., that the Communists stood down in favour of the P.S.P. and presented them with several safe seats and that the alliance was clearly understood to be a prelude to a Left Coalition Government.

[4] This is not to say that it was able to keep the T.T.N.C. quiet. On the contrary, that body became especially active in its attempts to impress the States Reorganisation Committee with the justice of its demand for a merger of the Tamil districts of Travancore-Cochin with Madras. In Aug. 1954, the P.S.P. Government was faced with a temporary but quite serious law and order problem arising out of the violent form taken by the agitation—said to be the result of the Communist Party having taken over the direction from the T.T.N.C. who had stirred up feelings they were unable to control. In any event, the police opened fire in several areas and at least four persons were killed. That a Socialist Government should use the police to fire on the people caused grave heart-searchings in the P.S.P. At a special party convention at Nagpur in Dec. 1954, a resolution declaring it unnecessary for the P.S.P. Government in Travancore-Cochin to resign on account of the firing was carried only by 303 votes against 217; and this in spite of the finding of a judicial inquiry that the firing was 'just and proper'.

their party. In any case, the P.S.P. Government did not last long. The Congress Party in the State became restive—partly because of proposed measures of radical land reforms—and asked the Party's Parliamentary Board in Delhi to permit them to withdraw support from the Government. The Board in December 1954 gave them permission to oppose any measure they thought undesirable, but warned them to consider carefully before taking steps which might lead to President's Rule. The local Congress Party did 'consider carefully'; it refrained from challenging the Government until the assembly members of the Tamil-Nad Travancore Congress imprisoned for their violent agitation[1] were released. It then secured 60 votes (out of the 118) for a motion of no confidence, and promptly accepted an invitation to form a government in February 1955. This Government was no stronger than its 1952 predecessor: it rested on 46 Congress votes, 12 of the unreliable T.T.N.C., and 2 or 3 former P.S.P. members (including the Speaker) who resigned from their party.[2]

The affairs of Madras also repay examination. The General Elections had failed to give Congress an absolute majority, and the other seats were divided among several parties and several Independents. In an Assembly of 375, Congress had 152, Communists 62 and P.S.P. 48. Other parties accounted for 51 and there were no less than 62 Independents—both largely due to the importance of caste sentiments. In the event, Congress was able to form a government; Mr. C. Rajagopalachariar, for whom no task was too difficult,[3] was prevailed upon to abandon once more any thought of retirement, was conveniently nominated by the Governor to the Upper House of the State and from that position managed to secure the support of an adequate number of Independents. With the formation of Andhra in October 1953, Madras was partitioned, and with it its Legislative Assembly. 140 seats were transferred to form the new Andhra Assembly. In the new diminished Madras Assembly, Congress still had no absolute majority, but its position was certainly eased by the departure of the bulk of the Communists. At the same time, this only gave greater freedom of movement to caste factions and personal rivalries.[4]

These difficulties in Madras were, however, insignificant by comparison with those encountered over the new border in Andhra. In the Assembly of 140, Congress had only 46 seats and were confronted by

---

[1] See previous note.

[2] It lasted just a year and fell in March 1956, apparently because of the defection of six discontented members of the Congress Party.

[3] He was the first Indian Governor-General following the departure of Lord Mountbatten in 1948, and subsequently held the position of Union Home Minister during the somewhat troubled pre-election years 1950–51.

[4] Their opportunities were further increased by the probably final retirement of 'C.R.' in early 1954. See also above, p. 98, n. 2.

45 Communists. The P.S.P. numbered 16; while there was a K.M.P. rump of 6 which had not been able to swallow the merger of the two parties. 14 members belonged to the Krishikar Lok Party, a peasant party formed in 1951 round the person of Professor Ranga, 2 represented the Scheduled Castes Federation and 11 were Independents. Intricate negotiations culminated in the formation of a Congress coalition ministry. Its Chief Minister was the leader of the P.S.P., but he resigned from the party on accepting the office. The P.S.P. group itself split, 10 supporting the ministry, 6 going into opposition with the blessing of the party's national executive. When the Government met the Assembly in November 1953, it appeared to have a voting strength of 80. On the election of a Speaker, it won by the comfortable margin of 86 to 48. The unpredictable character of party alignments did not, however, take long to reveal itself; on the following day the ministerial candidate for the Deputy Speakership secured 59 votes only against his opponent's 76. The brief ten-day session produced a series of unusual events: the K.M.P. rump of 6 dissolved itself, but one member opposed the decision and remained independently K.M.P., while the others became simply Independents; the crucial voting on the location of Andhra's capital got lost in the sands of several amendments; the K.L.P. group though considered attached to the ministry by the holding of one portfolio in practice voted in a rather wayward manner, the Deputy Chief Minister being constrained to remark that some of the legislators 'remain with the opposition in the morning and with the Government in the evening'; on the last day of the session the Government's dismay was completed by a 'snap' division by which an amendment was passed halving the Ministers' salaries. The Government was able to survive also the second short session of the Assembly in January 1954—and this in spite of the resignation from the Cabinet of the K.L.P. representative on the capital question. Press comment consequently began to speak about stability being assured. The 'wonderland' appearance of Andhra politics was, however, made once more amply evident during the May 1954 session. On the rousing Prohibition issue, on which Congress is committed, a Communist amendment for its abolition was carried; although this was, in the Andhra context, a matter of high policy and the defeat consequently serious, the Government simply announced that it would 'treat the resolution as recommendatory and not implement it'. On a number of occasions initiative passed out of the Government's hands and the Opposition was in effective control; a measure to establish a new university was in its passage changed almost out of recognition, the ministry being powerless to resist a long series of Communist amendments and actually suffering defeat on the two occasions when it tested its strength. The P.E.P.S.U. Government in 1952 avoided defeat by avoiding the Assembly; the Andhra Government in 1954 accepted

defeat but ignored it. The state of bliss was brought to an end by the Proclamation on 15 November 1954 of President's Rule, following the defeat of the Government on a motion of censure by 69 votes to 68. The Assembly was dissolved and fresh elections held in February 1955. In these, Congress was successful and a stable government was formed.[1]

Consideration of the three awkward cases of P.E.P.S.U., Travancore-Cochin and Andhra serves to illustrate the unsettling power of personnel, caste and regional factions. It may also have shown how the conventions of parliamentary government are on occasion imperfectly understood, here by a government, there by its critics. Since, however, the three States are admittedly far from typical, the examination of their post-election politics fails to give a useful guide to general trends. For these we may inspect by-election results of the 144 contests for State Assembly seats between the General Elections and the end of 1953. 74 were Congress seats and of these 45 were retained and 29 lost. Of the remaining 70 non-Congress seats, the party captured 29, its position remaining on balance the same. Of the 29 seats which Congress lost, no less than 15 went to the P.S.P., only 2 to the Communists, 5 to communal parties and 7 to Independents. This, taken alone, would suggest a consolidation of P.S.P. as Opposition. Reference to the voting figures, however, alters this impression considerably: only Congress and the Communists were able to poll a greater percentage of total votes than they had polled for their seats in the General Elections; moreover, only the Communists were able actually to increase their total poll for these seats.[2] The only firm conclusions that may be drawn from by-election results appear to be the continued power of Congress, the increased support for the Communists and the steady reduction in the numbers of Independents. Changes in party alignments in State Assemblies—other than those caused by by-elections—are not especially marked, but they do at least confirm the threat to the Independents. Its reality is appreciated

[1] In the debate on the Presidential Proclamation in the House of the People (20 Nov. 1954), the Communists claimed that they could have formed a stable ministry and should have been invited to do so. The P.S.P. also said that an attempt ought to have been made to find alternative government. The Union Government spokesman defended the temporary imposition of President's Rule on the ground that there was sufficient evidence that no stable alternative government could be formed; he refused a request to publish the State Governor's confidential report to the President on which action had been based; he admitted that it would be normal parliamentary practice for a defeated ministry to carry on until a new one was appointed, but said that this required a common understanding, as yet underdeveloped, between the political parties.

[2] As for the elections to the Centre discussed already (p. 103), the figures are from Indian National Congress, *Report of the General Secretaries, Jan. 1953–Jan. 1954*. The percentage figures show the following trends between 1952 and 1954: Congress, rise from 37·7% to 45·3% and Communists from 6·6% to 12·6%; P.S.P., fall from 17% to 15·4%, communal parties from 5·9% to 4·8% and Independents from 22·3% to 11·7%. The figures for the number of votes show a Communist increase of nearly 150,000 whereas all others polled less than for those seats in 1952—P.S.P. nearly 200,000 less, Congress over 50,000 less, Communal parties 86,000 less and Independents over 500,000 less.

by many Independent members who have accepted membership of the parties. Whether the motive has been hope for office and favour in the present or for election support in future is not always clear, but the trend is unmistakable. In Assam, for example, though there was only one by-election, Congress members in 1954 numbered 89 compared with 76 in 1952, while the Independents had shrunk from 14 to 9 and other parties lost 8. In Orissa, Congress gained two seats in by-elections but its strength in the Assembly rose from 67 to 75, the Independents again being reduced correspondingly.

The way in which parliamentary democracy works depends far more than we may like to admit on the balance of power between political parties. The inaugural period of parliamentary institutions in India has been presided over by one overwhelmingly powerful party. Perhaps the most important single fact about the elections of 1952—apart from the achievement of holding them—was that they gave Congress an absolute majority in both houses of the Union Parliament and in 18 out of 22 State Assemblies. It was well that it was thus. Nothing would have made the future of democratic institutions in India more uncertain than an initial period of unstable government. Even the few cases of unstable regimes may have been useful if they underlined the main lesson. Such trends as can be discerned do not lead to the supposition that this position will quickly pass away. Of course, the personal influence of Pandit Nehru is so great that if he were to withdraw his leadership from the party, its continued unity would then indeed be uncertain. Even the form of such a withdrawal would do much to determine the form of disunity. A simple withdrawal from the political scene would probably lead only to graver personal and other tensions in the party, whereas a deliberate attempt to move to the left would probably lead to a split in the party very largely on policy lines.[1] In the meantime, with stability assured, attention is free to concentrate on the growth of a coherent and responsible opposition. The weak and divided character of the opposition at the Centre and in most States has changed little and shows few signs of changing more. The K.M.P.-Socialist merger has helped matters somewhat, but the new P.S.P. is not yet a powerful magnet, and to see in it an alternative government still requires faith rather than political observation. The Communists are growing in strength but they can find no allies. The communal parties have fallen further since their thorough defeat in 1952, and the death in 1953 of Dr. S. P. Mukherjee, the creator and leader of the Jan Sangh, removed the one man who might have been able to transform these parties into a coherent nationalist conservative

---

[1] The talks between Nehru and P.S.P. leaders early in 1953 are supposed to have related to a possible coalition. The only terms acceptable to the P.S.P. were such as would probably have led to a split in Congress and perhaps the breaking away of a substantial conservative wing. Nehru was evidently not prepared at that time to risk so much.

party. The only gain in opposition coherence has come and will continue to come from the gradual disappearance of most of the small local parties and Independents.

2. The Members

One of the first published comments on the social and occupational composition of Indian legislatures was made by the authors of the Montagu-Chelmsford Report. They had made a study of the Councils under the Morley-Minto reforms and discovered that the legal profession was gaining ground, somewhat at the expense of the landowners. In the Indian Legislative Councils of 1909, 1912 and 1916, lawyers constituted 37%, 26% and 33% respectively of the total elected element. In the Provincial Councils their proportion was found to be 38%, 46% and 48% for the same years. Moreover these figures did not tell the whole story. So many of the 'constituencies' were 'special' ones restricted to specific groups; if these were excluded, the proportion of lawyers reached as much as 70%. The authors of the Report admitted that there was nothing very surprising or unusual in this, but they nevertheless felt that the political predominance of the lawyers was 'clearly not in the interests of the general community'.[1] They concluded that steps should be taken to ensure the election of other occupational groups. The separate electorates and reserved seats which we have seen to be characteristic of Indian legislatures in the British period were mainly the consequence of regarding Indian society as peculiarly divided, but it owed a little also to this particular desire to arrange deliberately for an even representation of all classes.

The present legislators of India are not only chosen to represent general territorial constituencies; they have been elected on an adult franchise which constituted a five-fold increase in the electorate over that under the 1935 Act. What kind of men are these new parliamentarians? What has been the influence of the introduction of adult franchise? Is there any appreciable difference between the members of the two Houses of the central Parliament? Or between members of Centre and State legislatures? Or as between the representatives of the different parties? An attempt is made in the following pages to present information about members of Indian legislatures under four main headings: age; education; previous legislative and local government experience;

[1] *Montagu-Chelmsford Report*, p. 72. The Report appears, however, to have been mistaken in believing that the predominance of lawyers was marked only after 1909. The municipality constituencies from the beginning provided the lawyers with opportunities. Dr. Tinker (*The Foundations of Local Self-Government in India, Pakistan and Burma*, 1954, p. 58 n.) has noticed that it was not the traditional landed proprietors but the new Westernised professional classes who entered the municipalities and through them went on to the Provincial Councils: 'Of the 43 members elected by municipalities from 1892 to 1909, 40 were lawyers.'

and occupation.[1] The material relates to four bodies. The Provisional Parliament of 1950–52 was the continuation of the Constituent Assembly which, since 1947, had been the Dominion Legislature. Its members had been chosen in several ways. The majority had been elected from the Provinces in July 1946 according to the method laid down in the Cabinet Mission Plan—that is, indirectly and on a communal basis by the elected members of provincial legislatures. Others, representing the princely states, had joined at various intervals later, and of these many were simply nominated by the rulers. The House of the People is directly elected by adult franchise. The Council of States, except for 12 nominated members, is elected indirectly from the State legislatures. Finally, Bombay Legislative Assembly is a Lower House of one of the larger and more advanced States.

We may begin with an account of the ages of the members. Table III shows the age composition of the four bodies:

TABLE III—AGE

Age Group	Provisional Parliament		House of the People, 1952		Council of States, 1952		Bombay Legislative Assembly 1952	
	No.	%	No.	%	No.	%	No.	%
20–29	6	2	24	5	1	—	16	5
30–39	54	17	110	22	35	16	49	16
40–49	96	31	144	29	58	27	80	25
50–59	76	24	135	27	60	28	51	16
60–69	50	16	39	8	38	18	13	4
70–79	8	3	1	—	11	5	1	—
Not known	23	7	46	9	13	6	115	36
Total	313	100	499	100	216	100	325	100

NOTE: Ages are given as at 1952. Percentages, in this and suceeding tables, are to the nearest whole number.

[1] The conclusions drawn are most tentative, since no claim can be made as to the completeness or accuracy of the material presented. It is based on a number of published collected biographies: *Provisional Parliament Who's Who* (1951); *House of the People Who's Who* (1952); *Council of States Who's Who* (1952); *Bombay Legislature Directory* (1953). The information given in these books was supplied by the members in response to requests from the Parliament Secretariat (in the case of the Bombay Directory, from the Bombay Legislature Congress Party). The data is not complete in all cases and some members failed altogether to supply material. Moreover the members were not answering the particular questions which here concern us; they have stressed their service to the national movement through various bodies and (though this is now less marked) through prison sentences. It has often been necessary therefore to make guesses, especially where 'occupation' was concerned. 'Occupation' is indeed a source of special difficulty. It is very common in India for a man to be engaged in several occupations at different stages of his life and even at the same time. A member may describe himself as a lawyer, a journalist and social worker, while at the same time indicating that he owns land and has considerable business interests. Private information has sometimes rendered guesses unnecessary, but not always.

If the first and second columns are compared with a view to assessing the influence of adult franchise, it will be seen that while the group 40–49 is still the most common, there has been a shift in favour of the younger men. The established politicians—venerable members of the nationalist movement and nominees of princely rulers alike—who still had a significant place in the Provisional Parliament are present in reduced numbers in the new Lower House; the percentage over 60 has shrunk from 19 to 8. The age composition of the indirectly elected Upper House, however, remains very similar. The Council of States is not entirely a body of elderly statesmen, but the over-60's account for 23% of the members and the 50–59 group occupy a slightly more prominent place than that of 40–49. Comparison of the State Assembly with the central legislature is made less easy by the large number of unknowns in the former. If it is assumed that their inclusion would make no big difference in the relation between the age groups, it can be said that the average age of State legislators is probably a little lower than that of those at the Centre.[1] It is also somewhat lower than in State Assemblies before the advent of adult franchise.[2]

Table IV gives information on the education of legislators.

TABLE IV—EDUCATION

	Provisional Parliament		House of the People, 1952		Council of States, 1952		Bombay Legislative Assembly, 1952	
	No.	%	No.	%	No.	%	No.	%
Graduated Abroad[3]	39	12	45	9	35	16	4	1
Graduated in India	171	55	246	49	105	49	103	33
College (Intermediate)	35	11	66	13	31	14	17	5
High School	23	7	60	12	16	7	35	11
Middle School	4	1	7	1	4	2	31	10
Primary School	8	3	8	1	3	1	29	9
Religious Education[4]	11	4	16	3	8	4	1	—
Private Education	9	3	8	1	6	3	1	—
Not known	13	4	43	9	8	4	94	30
Total	313	100	499	100	216	100	315	100

In all four Houses there is a striking proportion of graduates. As

[1] See below, p. 124 for Madras and p. 128 for Bombay City data which confirm this view.
[2] See below, p. 128, for Bombay before 1952.
[3] A small number of members, although not graduates, nevertheless received some of their education abroad. They have not been shown separately, but are included under 'College' or 'High School'.
[4] Religious education means education in Hindu or Muslim institutions.

between the three central legislative bodies there is indeed little contrast; only the rather high percentage of the present Upper House with overseas qualifications may be noted. The State Assembly, however, does appear to be significantly different. The contrast is again handicapped by the large number of members who gave no information, but in this case it seems probable that their inclusion would have the effect, if anything, of increasing the proportions of the less educated. It seems likely that while the number of central legislators who are equipped with no more than school education is in the neighbourhood of 10–15%, in the case of the States it may be as high as one-third. Madras statistics given below confirm this.

Reference has been made in the previous chapter to India's pre-independence experience of parliamentary or quasi-parliamentary institutions. This experience was decisive in persuading the makers of the Constitution to choose this form rather than others, and it may be considered that the success or failure of parliamentary government in India will depend in part on the extent to which this experience is being utilised and communicated. The previous legislative experience of the present members thus takes on a special significance. Legislators' experience of local government may conveniently be considered at the same time— especially in view of the fact that one of the important reasons for the stimulation of democratic local government in India was the rulers' belief that it constituted a sound training for the higher political responsibilities.[1] Both forms of experience are shown in the separate parts of the next table:

TABLE V—PREVIOUS EXPERIENCE OF LEGISLATORS

(i) Legislative Experience

	Provisional Parliament		House of the People		Council of States		Bombay Legislative Assembly	
	No.	%	No.	%	No.	%	No.	%
Old Central Assembly, pre-1947	39	13	18	4	15	7	0	—
Constituent Assembly— Provisional Parl. (1947–52)			108	22	34	16	1	—
State Legislature	82	26	124	25	79	37	58	18
No Legislative Experience	207	66	280	56	123	57	182	58
Not known	3	1	26	5	4	2	74	23
Total	313	—	499	—	216	—	315	—

[1] See Tinker, op. cit., p. 45.

(ii) Local Government Experience

	Provisional Parliament		House of the People		Council of States		Bombay Legislative Assembly	
	No.	%	No.	%	No.	%	No.	%
Municipality .	56	18	79	16	42	19	62	20
District Board	46	15	65	13	27	12	68	22
Panchayat .	2	1	2	—	2	1	4	1
None .	213	68	339	68	158	73	114	36
Not known .	3	1	26	5	4	2	74	23
Total .	313	—	499	—	216	—	315	—

NOTE: The figures in each of these tables overlap to some extent: several members have experience of both Centre and State legislatures, of both municipality and district board.

The first part of the table shows that between half and two-thirds of the legislators had no previous parliamentary experience. Among the central legislators there is a small but certainly invaluable group with previous experience of the old central assembly. A much larger group, amounting to between a quarter and a third, bring with them some useful experience of legislative work at the State level. There is no appreciable difference between the Lower and Upper Houses; some of the members of the latter have gathered much experience, but the proportions with no previous experience are practically the same. The State legislators are not so well equipped; while it is not surprising that their central experience is practically nil, it is worth noting that even the number with previous experience at the same level is less than one-fifth. (It is fairly safe to guess that few of the 'not known' group have previous experience.) In general, it may perhaps be said that adult franchise, despite its experimental nature, has succeeded in producing a reasonable balance between the retention of experience and the admission of new blood into political life. Considering the small size of the elected element in the former Central Assembly, it is important that as many as 33 of its members still have places in the present Parliament. In this, as in so many other respects, India has reason to be thankful that her expedition into independence, while certainly not less exciting and adventurous than others, is one that has been better planned and better equipped than most.

The extent to which local government experience finds its way into the legislatures is perhaps less important but still of interest. Men like Lord Ripon were convinced of the value of local government as a training ground for politicians. They were no doubt gratified when it happened that local government experience found an important place in the first Councils—and indeed this result was in large measure guaranteed by establishing municipalities as constituencies for the provincial indirect elections. Even after 1909 many members of the Legislative Councils 'were men who had made their name in local government'.[1] The maintenance of this feature was subsequently somewhat prejudiced by the policies of boycott and non-co-operation followed by the nationalist movement. Just as these policies may be said to have limited the use made of parliamentary opportunities at the Centre and Provincial levels, so they also at times kept able men away from local affairs. By the 1920s, 'local leaders gave their allegiance to the District Congress Committee . . . and local government, instead of serving as a school of political education, became a mere annexe to the national political stadium'.[2] Even so, however, local government experience is not negligible among modern legislators, and it is unlikely that this experience is even mainly restricted to the post-independence period. Between a quarter and one-third of the members of Parliament have served an apprenticeship on municipalities or District Boards. The State legislators are much more rooted in local government politics; perhaps over half their number come to State affairs from a district or municipality background. It may also be noted that whereas in the Centre municipality (i.e. medium-sized town and city) experience is rather more usual than district (i.e. small country town) experience, the opposite is true of the State. In all cases, the village panchayat is out of the picture; its members evidently stay in the village. The deliberations on rural affairs and the legislation for rural reconstruction are in other hands. It is tempting to wonder if any very different result would have followed if the attempts in the Constituent Assembly to introduce indirect elections based on panchayats had been successful.

Table VI gives the interests and occupations of members.

The categories available to us often fail to give an indication of a member's social position, and the ambiguity attached to 'Land' is particularly unfortunate. What is clear is that the professions are in all cases important and account for over half the members of Parliament. Within that group lawyers of course predominate. Also remarkable—and perhaps especially characteristic of India—is the size of the group which can only be described as engaged in social or political work. This feature is related to the family system in India, and these mainly non-earning persons are no doubt dependent on income from other members of the family engaged in business or, even more likely, in agriculture. Further comment on this table is unnecessary, except to point out that there is no evident and certain contrast in occupational composition to be found between the four bodies; as far as the evidence shows, the composition remains much the same whether it is State or Centre, before or

[1] Tinker, *op. cit.*, p. 89.
[2] *Ibid.*, p. 161.

TABLE VI—OCCUPATION OF LEGISLATORS

	Provisional Parliament		House of the People		Council of States		Bombay Legislative Assembly	
	No.	%	No.	%	No.	%	No.	%
Land Interests	41	13	122	24	50	23	46	15
Business Interests .	43	14	70	14	45	21	44	14
Land . .	20	6	93	19	33	15	32	10
Business .	25	8	49	10	28	13	38	12
Law . .	100	32	127	25	60	28	57	18
Press . .	33	11	38	8	20	9	8	3
Education .	26	8	34	7	21	10	19	6
Services .	16	5	10	2	11	5	6	2
Other Professions .	16	5	24	5	12	5	15	5
Public Work .	44	14	85	17	29	13	36	11
Not known .	33	11	39	8	2	1	104	33
Total .	313	100	499	100	216	100	315	100

NOTES:
(1) The first two categories overlap with those that follow. They have been included in an attempt to overcome the difficulties of 'double occupation'; the lawyer who reveals that he owns land, the editor who evidently has certain business interests find a place here as well as in their own professional categories. Even so, of course, the figures in these two categories ought almost certainly to be much larger. The great majority of members appear to be to some extent and in some way participating in business activity and/or dependent on the possession of a piece of land.
(2) The other categories also require explanation. 'Land' includes rent-receivers as well as working farmers. 'Business' includes the industrialist, the shopkeeper and the import-export agent. 'Law' covers the highly paid High Court advocate and also the penurious district pleader. The university professor and the primary school teacher find a place in 'Education'. Former army officers and civil servants account for the 'Services'. Doctors are the most prominent of the 'Other Professions'. 'Public Work' is perhaps the haziest of all: under this heading come most of the women members who describe themselves as 'social workers', many of the whole-time Communist Party workers, as well as a number of Gandhian followers engaged in political-cum-social service; the category therefore gives little idea of the source of income, but it is safe to say that in most of these cases (and, of course, in others too) membership of the legislature has become the main source.

after the extension of the franchise, by direct or indirect election. At the same time, it must be said that, if general impressions have any validity, certain contrasts can be found: first, the present members of Parliament do include among their number some men of less sophistication, of a lower social standing and lower income group than could be found in the pre-1952 (and certainly pre-1947) Assembly; second, the same remark could be made with even greater emphasis about the State legislatures. The relations between the categories 'land', 'law' and the rest may remain unchanged, but within each category there has been some broadening, mainly downwards.

For the purpose of comparing the main political parties under these headings, the members of the House of the People have been chosen. Table VII gives the comparison in terms of age:

TABLE VII—AGE COMPOSITION OF THE HOUSE OF THE PEOPLE

(BY PARTIES)

	Congress		Communist		Socialist		Hindu		Other Parties		Independent	
	No.	%	No.	%	No.	%	No.	%	No.	%	No.	%
20–29	13	4	2	8	1	5	1	14	4	13	3	7
30–39	75	23	12	50	7	33	—		7	23	9	21
40–49	99	30	7	29	7	33	2	29	10	33	19	45
50–59	111	34	3	12	3	14	3	43	5	17	10	24
60–69	30	9	—		3	14	1	14	4	13	1	2
Over 70 . . .	1				—		—		—			
Total giving information .	329	100	24	100	21	100	7	100	30	100	42	100

NOTE: Hindu means Hindu Mahasaba and Jan Sangh groups.

The main point to notice here is the striking, though not surprising, difference between the members of the well-established Congress Party and those of the newer parties. The Congress finds more of its members from the 50–59 group than from any other and only 27% are under 40. Among the Communists well over half are under 40, of the Socialists 38%.

No such marked differences are revealed in education:

TABLE VIII—EDUCATION OF THE HOUSE OF THE PEOPLE

(BY PARTIES)

	Congress		Communist		Socialist		Hindu		Other Parties		Independent	
	No.	%	No.	%	No.	%	No.	%	No.	%	No.	%
Graduated Abroad .	28	8	3	13	1	5	3	43	2	7	8	20
Graduated in India .	185	55	10	43	15	71	2	29	13	45	21	51
College (Intermediate) .	49	15	4	17	2	10	1	14	6	21	4	10
High School .	43	13	5	22			1	14	5	17	6	15
Middle School .	7	2										
Primary School .	5	1			2	10			1	3		
Religious Education .	14	4			1	5					1	2
Private Education .	4	1	1	4					2	7	1	2
Total giving information .	335	100	23	100	21	100	7	100	29	100	41	100

The large numbers of the Congress Party permit them to have some representatives of all kinds of education, while at the other extreme it is perhaps the small numbers of the Hindu parties which enable them to stand out prominently among the group with foreign degrees. But in general the differences do not appear significant. The smaller parties collected under the heading 'Other Parties' seem to have relied on rather less educated members, but among the rest the proportion of graduates varies only from the Congress's modest 63% to the Socialists' impressive 76%. The Communist members are neither better nor worse educated than the others.

Contrasts between the parties reappear when we turn to previous legislative and local government experience.

TABLE IX—EXPERIENCE OF THE HOUSE OF THE PEOPLE

(BY PARTIES)

(i) Legislative

	Congress		Communist		Socialist		Hindu		Other Parties		Independents	
	No.	%	No.	%	No.	%	No.	%	No.	%	No.	%
Old Central Assembly .	16	4					1	14			1	2½
Constituent Assembly—Provisional Parliament .	95	26			3	14	2	29	3	7	5	12½
State Legislatures .	106	29	1	4	2	10	2	29	3	7	10	25
No previous legislative experience . . .	180	49	23	96	16	76	5	72	27	61	29	72½
Total	363		24		21		7		44		40	

(ii) Local Government

	Congress		Communist		Socialist		Hindu		Other Parties		Independents	
	No.	%	No.	%	No.	%	No.	%	No.	%	No.	%
Municipality . . .	68	19	1	4	1	5	2	29	2	5	5	12½
District Board . .	58	16	1	4	2	10			3	7	1	2½
Panchayat . . .	1										1	2½
No Local Government Experience . . .	234	64	19	79	17	81	5	72	27	61	36	90
Total	363		24		21		7		44		40	

NOTE: See Note to Table V.

The most vivid contrast is between Congress and the Communists; whereas less than half the Congress members are new to work in legislatures, only one Communist has previous experience—and that is at State level. The other parties occupy a position midway between these extremes.

The contrast in legislative experience is hardly surprising given the nature of politics before the General Elections. The contrast is, however, hardly less marked in the case of local government experience. The large majority of non-Congress members have a political experience which is limited to party and other sectional or social organisations.

Finally we may set out the occupational composition of the House of the People by parties:

TABLE X—OCCUPATION IN THE HOUSE OF THE PEOPLE

(BY PARTIES)

	Congress		Communist		Socialist		Hindu		Other Parties		Independents	
	No.	%	No.	%	No.	%	No.	%	No.	%	No.	%
Land Interests . .	82	24	4	17	6	29			12	40	18	45
Business Interests .	55	16			1	5			6	20	8	20
Land . . .	62	21	4	17	5	24			9	30	13	32½
Business . .	37	11			1	5			5	17	6	15
Law . . .	103	30	2	8	5	24	4	67	4	13	9	22½
Press . . .	25	7	2	8	3	14	1	16	3	10	4	10
Education . .	22	6	4	17	2	10			3	10	3	7½
Services . .	8	2							2	7		
Other Professions .	15	4	2	8	1	5	1	16	2	7	3	7½
Public Work . .	67	20	10	42	4	19			2	7	2	5
Total giving information .	339	100	24	100	21	100	6	100	30	100	40	100

Our hesitation in drawing very definite conclusions from data on occupations has already been explained. Certain features nevertheless seem clear. A large proportion of Independents are known to be landed proprietors—and it was indeed primarily the influence which they derived from this which enabled them to contest successfully; this seems to be supported by our figures. Secondly, business interests, as one could expect, find no representation among parties of the left. Thirdly, the category of 'public work' has a special importance for the Communist Party; nearly half its members have no apparent occupation other than full-time party workers.

This material can be supplemented by data drawn from one of the few official State election reports available at the time of writing. The Madras Report contains much interesting information on age composition, educational qualifications and 'livelihood classes'.[1] The categories used differ somewhat from those given above, but the main conclusions seem to be confirmed. The following table gives the ages of the successful candidates in the Madras elections to the two Houses of the Centre and State legislatures:

[1] *Return showing the Results of the General Elections in Madras State*, Government of Madras, 1953.

TABLE XI—MADRAS: AGE OF MEMBERS

	House of the People		Council of States		Madras Legislative Assembly		Madras Legislative Council	
	No.	%	No.	%	No.	%	No.	%
25–34 . .	16	21	5	18	106	28	6	10
35–44 . .	28	37	9	33	155	41	19	32
45–54 . .	18	24	9	33	85	23	20	33
55–64 . .	12	16	2	7	27	7	13	22
65–74 . .	1	1	2	7	2	1	1	2
Over 74 .							1	2
Total .	75	100	27	100	375	100	60	100

For the two Lower Houses, the largest age-group is that of 35–44, but for the Upper Houses the next group of 45–54 is equally prominent.

Table XII shows the age composition of the Madras Legislative Assembly according to parties:

TABLE XII—MADRAS ASSEMBLY: AGE BY PARTIES

	Congress		Communist		Independent		Socialist or K.M.P.		Other Parties	
	No.	%	No.	%	No.	%	No.	%	No.	%
25–34 .	30	20	37	60	13	21	11	23	15	29
35–44 .	65	43	23	37	26	42	21	44	20	39
45–54 .	39	26	2	3	18	29	14	29	12	24
55–64 .	16	11			5	8	2	4	4	8
65–74 .	2	1								
Total .	152	100	62	100	62	100	48	100	51	100

A sharp contrast is revealed between the Communist Party and all others. No party can be described as a party of old men, but the Communist Party is distinctly a party of young men.

Table XIII compares the educational qualifications of the Madras members of Centre and State legislatures.

From this it appears that the better-educated candidates favour (or are favoured by) indirect election to Upper Houses. The contrast between the qualifications of the members of the State Assembly and those of members of the State Council is particularly marked. The most important feature, however, is the poor education which has been received by the majority of State Assembly members; and Madras is most unlikely to be inferior to other States in this respect. The majority of State

TABLE XIII—MADRAS: EDUCATION OF MEMBERS

	House of the People		Council of States		Madras Legislative Assembly		Madras Legislative Council	
	No.	%	No.	%	No.	%	No.	%
Degrees and Diplomas .	45	60	17	63	107	29	34	57
Intermediate (College) .	4	5	4	2	26	7	4	7
Matriculation (High School)	13	17			85	23	8	13
Middle School	5	7	4	15	60	16	4	7
Literate .	8	11	2	7	97	26	10	17
Total .	75	100	27	100	375	100	60	100

legislators are drawn from the meagrely educated sections and form a contrast to the members of the central Parliament. They are, no doubt, more like the people they represent. But the proportion of 'passengers' carried in State legislatures is for this reason high. The ministries are much less supported by informed criticism than at Delhi, and the parties' work of political training is heavy and difficult.

This impression could be checked by information relating to 'livelihood classes' and 'social groups'. The following figures are given in the *Madras Return*:

TABLE XIV—MADRAS: MEMBERS' 'LIVELIHOOD CLASS'

	House of the People		Council of States		Madras Legislative Assembly		Madras Legislative Council	
	No.	%	No.	%	No.	%	No.	%
I . . .	15	20	2	7	143	38	13	22
II . . .	3	4	1	4	6	2		
III . .				1	0			
IV . .	9	12	4	15	71	19	11	18
V . .	3	4			15	4	1	2
VI . .	8	11	1	4	20	5	4	7
VII . .	2	3			8	2	1	2
VIII . .	35	47	19	70	111	30	30	50
Total . .	75	100	27	100	375	100	60	100

NOTE: The eight categories used here are defined in the *Madras Return* as follows: I: Cultivators (or their dependents) of land wholly or mainly owned; II: Cultivators of land wholly or mainly unowned; III: Cultivating labourers; IV: Non-cultivating owners and agricultural rent-receivers; V: Principal means of livelihood from Production; VI: from Commerce; VII: from Transport; VIII: from other sources and miscellaneous sources.

TABLE XV—MADRAS: MEMBERS' 'SOCIAL GROUP'

	House of the People		Council of States		Madras Legislative Assembly		Madras Legislative Council	
	No.	%	No.	%	No.	%	No.	%
Non-backward classes . .	51	68	21	78	225	60	49	82
Unscheduled backward classes . .	10	13	5	18	84	22	11	18
Scheduled castes . .	13	17	1	4	62	16		
Scheduled tribes . .	1	1			4	1		
Total .	75	100	27	100	375	100	60	100

Although these categories are in several respects quite unsatisfactory, at least the high proportion of cultivators in the Madras State Assembly can be taken as bearing out to some extent the remarks made on education. The State legislatures—and especially the Lower Houses—contain a large number of members drawn from the class of small peasant cultivators, and a correspondingly smaller proportion from the professions.

The above sketch of the members of modern Indian legislatures would be rendered more valuable if a comprehensive comparison with the earlier legislatures were possible. Unfortunately, no published data appears to be available. Some information, however, has been gathered[1] and is presented in the following tables:

TABLE XVI—CENTRAL ASSEMBLY, 1944: OCCUPATIONS

Landowners	40
Lawyers, but mainly dependent on income from land	21
Lawyers	11
Businessmen	30
Other occupations . . .	17
	119[2]

TABLE XVII—COUNCIL OF STATE, 1944: OCCUPATIONS

Landowners	16
Lawyers	7
Businessmen	16
Other occupations . . .	5
	44[3]

---

[1] From private sources, based originally on official documents which seem to have disappeared.
[2] Including 18 nominated members.
[3] Including 11 nominated members.

A comparison of these two tables with those on occupations in present legislatures indicates some broadening of the social composition consequent upon the increasing size of legislatures and the popularising of politics which accompanied the advent of adult franchise. It is evident, however, that the elected member changes less rapidly than the electorate. Some of the traditional elements have no doubt suffered a setback in 'British India' areas, but this is somewhat obscured by their continued hold in the districts which were formerly princely states. There has been no massive invasion of Delhi by peasants and workers, only a slight admixture. In the State Assemblies, however, the new period has witnessed the arrival of large numbers belonging to the 'middle peasantry'.

NOTE: Although there is no comprehensive survey of the subject discussed in this section, a reference may be made to a few partial studies:

1. The first is a brief article ('The House of the People—its Personnel', in *Modern Review*, Calcutta, Jan. 1954) by Professor G. D. Srivastava. He, too, has had to rely on the published *Who's Whos*, supplemented by some personal enquiries. His figures do not agree in detail with those given here, but his general conclusions are similar. He shows that the popular age group is 40–50 and that the parties of the Left are younger than Congress. The proportion of members with previous experience of legislatures is higher among Congressmen (nearly half) than among parties of the Left (about 10%). Over 60% of the members are graduates and less than 7% have only elementary education; the differences between the parties in this respect are not significant. Professor Srivastava's occupation table is as follows:

	Congress	Parties of the Left	Others	Total
Agriculture:				
(a) Farmers	43	11	3	57
(b) Landlords	17	1	3	21
Business	37	4	7	48
Professions:				
(a) Law	110	11	11	132
(b) Education	22	5	5	32
(c) Journalism	25	4	4	33
Retired	20	1	7	28
Whole-time Public Workers	60	22	2	84
Miscellaneous	16	6	7	29
Unknown	35	—	—	35

2. Professor Venkatarangaiya's survey of *The General Election in Bombay* (Bombay, 1953) is a careful work but deals with Bombay City only. The data he collected relates not only to the elected members but to candidates—to 98 of the 127 City candidates for the State Assembly and to 15 of the 18 candidates

for the House of the People. He found that the age group 35–44 was the most common among candidates of all parties for the State Assembly seats, though in the case of Congress the next group, 45–54, was nearly as prominent. By contrast, this latter group was for all parties the most popular among candidates for the House of the People seats, indicating perhaps that parties preferred to put up more experienced men for the Centre. He found a similar difference in educational qualifications: although even for the State Assembly more than half the candidates were graduates, the proportion for the seats at the Centre was more than three-quarters. In education he found a difference between the parties, the Communist candidates for the State Assembly accounting for a proportionately large number of those with only primary or secondary school education. With regard to occupations he found a large number of professional and business people among the Congress candidates and an equally marked number of trade union workers among those of the Left parties. Congress candidates had more legislature as well as more local government experience than those of all other parties. (*Ibid.*, pp. 53–70.)

3. I am grateful to the Bombay University for permission to consult an unpublished thesis submitted for the degree of Ph.D. in 1953: 'The Bombay Legislature' by L. B. Wilson. The author collected by questionnaire a considerable amount of information relating to the Assembly and Council of that State before the 1952 General Elections. Some of his findings may be summarised as follows:

Age			% of Total Membership	Education	% of Total Membership
21–30	.	.	2	Degree and Diploma	69
31–40	.	.	22	College . . .	4
41–50	.	.	29	Secondary . .	22
51–60	.	.	31	Primary . . .	5
61–70	.	.	11		
Over 70	.	.	2		

Occupation			% of Total Membership	Income p.a.	% of Total Membership
Law .	.	.	41	Under £100 . .	18
Medicine	.	.	3	£100–£200 . .	24
Journalism .	.	.	3	£200–£400 . .	21
Education .	.	.	3	£400–£700 . .	6
Business	.	.	8	£700–£1,000 .	6
Agriculture	.	.	14	£1,000–£2,000 .	3
Social Work	.	.	17	Over £2,000 . .	7
Services .	.	.	2		
Miscellaneous	.	.	5		

A comparison of this information with that relating to the Bombay and Madras Assemblies after 1952 suggests that State legislators are younger, less highly educated and drawn to a smaller extent from the professional classes than they were before adult franchise and the expansion of the assemblies.

3. Times and Places

The Constitution of India requires that 'Parliament shall be summoned twice at least in every year' and that 'six months shall not intervene between its last sitting in one session and the date appointed for its first sitting in the next session'.[1] The table in Appendix III shows the opening and closing dates of the sessions, together with the number of days on which Parliament actually sat. The earlier years have been included for comparison, and it can be seen that the usual practice formerly was to have two sessions a year: one from late January or early February until the Budget was passed and the Delhi heat became difficult around the middle of April; and another after the rains had cooled the air in August and September. Occasionally a third session in November–December was added. By now, however, a pattern of three sessions has become normal; only the holding of the General Elections in 1952 prevents the table from showing this even more clearly. It is possible that the arrangement of the sessions may change; it has been suggested, for instance, that one session should be held during the monsoon rains of June–July, when the M.P.s are in any case unable easily to tour their mainly rural constituencies. Nevertheless, in whatever manner the sessions may come to be arranged, it is clear that the number of days in a year during which Parliament sits is unlikely to be reduced. As in other countries, the work of the Indian legislature has steadily increased. From 1921 to 1930 the number of days' sittings in a year was never more than 68; during 1931–38, it was never less than that, and in 1933 reached 97. The war years were naturally less active from this point of view, but the post-war period has witnessed again a big increase. The years 1947–49 saw the legislators busy in constitution-making—the non-legislative sessions are not included in the above figures—but from the inauguration of the new constitution in 1950 the trend is clear: Parliament meets for nearly 140 days a year. The Council of States commences its sessions at the same time as the House of the People, but it generally meets less often and may complete its work before the Lower House. The State Legislatures, though also subject to a six months rule,[2] do not meet as often as Parliament. Until very recently, a spring Budget session and a shorter autumn session were sufficient. During the last few years, however, a third session later in the year has been added in some States. Even so, the number of days' sittings annually is never very much more than half that imposed by the pressure of work at the Centre. From the point of view of work in the constituency and the pursuit of part-time occupations, the member of a State legislature is doubly fortunate compared with the M.P.: his presence is required in the State capital about three months a year, and in any event his constituency and home cannot

---

[1] Art. 85 (1).   [2] Art. 174.

be more than about twelve hours away; the M.P.'s 140 days' sittings entail his residence in Delhi for about six months and his constituency, home and other occupations may be as much as two or three days' journey from the Union capital.

Parliament is summoned and prorogued by the President of the Union,[1] the actual decision being taken by the Leader of the House in consultation with his colleagues, the Speaker and possibly leaders of opposition groups, and the summons being issued by the Secretary.[2] The first business of each session is the joint gathering of the two Houses to hear the President's Address, in which Parliament is informed of the causes of its summons.[3] This is a new institution for India; the Governor-General did not open the the sessions of the old Legislative Assembly. The President's Address is, of course, modelled on the Queen's Speech in the British Parliament, and its introduction is only one example of the way in which modern Indian parliamentary procedure has found more to suit its needs in British practice than in that of the former regime in India itself. The need for the President's Address was felt mainly because it underlines the responsibility of the Government to Parliament; for it consists of the Government's review of the international and internal situation and a statement of its general policy together with an indication of its legislative programme.[4] It was also felt appropriate that each session should begin with a solemn, even if simple, ceremony. The President is conducted in a small procession, led by the Secretaries and Presiding Officers of the two Houses, to the Central Hall of Parliament. The Address is delivered first in Hindi and then in English and no further business is done on that day.[5] Some days are then devoted to a debate on the Address—as many as five days of the Budget session, only two

[1] Art. 85 (2). The similar provision for the Governor or Rajpramakh's summoning of a State Legislature is in Art. 174 (2).

[2] *Rules*, Rule 3.

[3] Art. 87. For States, Art. 176. The Constitution (First Amendment) Act, 1951 restricted the occasions on which there has to be a President's (and Governors') Address to the first session after each election and the first session of each year. In practice, it was usual to retain the Address for each session until 1956 when it was dropped except for the first (or Budget) session.

[4] This is a striking example of the way in which an old and local custom can achieve by adaptation such a universal and modern meaning that it becomes suitable for imitation far away from the time and place of its origin.

[5] The Governors (in Part A States) or Rajpramukhs (in Part B States) deliver similar Addresses. On some occasions in a few States, the event has been marred by the ostentatious absence of members of the opposition and even by 'walk-out' demonstrations in the course of the Address. This has posed a problem for Presiding Officers. Since the meeting to hear the Address is not strictly a meeting of the House (or even a joint sitting where there are two Houses) there is no one 'in the Chair' and therefore no one whose function it can be to appeal for order. Some States seem to favour the provision of rules to deal with these cases, but the majority, while deploring these breaches of decorum, hope that conventions can be established and agreed upon between all parties. No serious incidents have occurred at the Centre, but the Prime Minister has stressed the fact that the President and Governors are symbols of the State and must be respected; dislike of Government policy should be expressed in other ways and at other times. (See H.P. Deb., 22 Feb. 1954.)

days of a shorter session. A motion of thanks is moved and seconded by two Government back-benchers and the debate takes place on a number of amendments moved by the opposition groups. The movers of the motions and other speakers have on occasion misunderstood the nature of the Address. One mover, for example, determined to make the most of this opportunity for oratory and anxious to underline the fact that the Address was 'no mere formality', went so far as to thank the President personally for his 'unerring guidance'. The Prime Minister later rose to correct the impression: 'It is the Government's Address, although the President delivers it. Some honourable members imagine that it is a private address of the President. It is nothing of the kind.'[1] The scope of amendments is wide and not strictly limited to the points actually dealt with in the Address; attention may also be drawn to omissions from the Address.[2] In view of the divided character of the opposition, it is not surprising that a large number of amendments is normally received. When they deal with important issues such as foreign policy and the food situation, for which separate days are known to have been allotted later in the session, their movers are usually persuaded to withdraw them. Thus, of 88 amendments moved in November 1950 only 15 were actually moved, and the discussion was thus concentrated on certain topics.[3] This does not happen invariably: in February 1953, 74 amendments were received; although the Deputy Speaker appealed for some selection and grouping to be made—for they were on a wide variety of subjects, as he put it, 'from China to Peru'—the House did not agree, and all 74 were moved and put.[4]

If the pressure of work has lengthened the sessions of Parliament, it cannot yet be said to have had the same effect on the number of hours the Houses sit during each day. At the inception of the Central Legislature, in 1921, the times were comparatively sedate and gentlemanly— from 11 a.m. to 5 p.m. with an ample luncheon interval from 1 p.m. to 2.30 p.m. These hours were maintained without change until the second session of 1948 when the start was advanced to 10.45 a.m. From 1951, the times have been more frequently changed. The decisions on this matter are in the discretion of the Chair but are naturally made after consulting the needs of Government business and the wishes of the members. Thus, in 1951, when the first session extended into the hot months of Delhi, the times were changed in the course of April and the House met from 8.30 a.m. to 1.30 p.m. These timings have proved popular with members and now tend to be the rule outside the winter months.[5] On the other hand, the 'winter' timings too have changed and

---

[1] P.P. Deb., 15 Nov. 1950.

[2] E.g., the observation from the Chair in H.P. Deb., 20 May 1952.

[3] P.P. Deb., 15–17 Nov. 1950.

[4] H.P. Deb., 13 Feb. 1953. Only one was pressed to a division.

[5] The Chambers are well air-conditioned and cool, but members obviously like to finish the work as soon as possible and perhaps enjoy a siesta.

1.30–6.30 p.m. or 2–7 p.m. are now the general practice.[1] It will be noticed, however, that in any event the sittings do not last for more than five hours.[2] It has sometimes been found necessary, towards the end of a session with much business unfinished, to extend the sittings very slightly. This always succeeds in causing a considerable outcry among the majority of members, the more serious of whom plead the need for time to study bills, reports and other papers, while others protest that social engagements are properly an important part of an M.P.'s life and should not be too much encroached upon. The Chair has agreed that sittings should not, if possible, be lengthened, adding the further reason that the quality of debate would tend thereby to suffer. It must be remembered, too, that Parliament normally meets on six days a week; Sundays are observed as holidays, but there can be no question as in England, of getting away on Friday evening for a week-end in the constituency.[3] The times of the sittings of State legislatures varies, but the total number of hours per day is normally between four and five. The Bombay Assembly, for instance, meets from 2–7 p.m. with a half-hour tea break, and a sitting of 12 noon to 3 p.m. on Saturdays; Travancore-Cochin generally observes the hours 11 a.m. to 1 p.m. and 2–5 p.m.

The Union Parliament meets in Parliament House in New Delhi. This forms part of a group of buildings constituting the governmental heart of the capital and planned by Sir Edwin Lutyens in 1919. Appropriately enough for that period, the Council Chamber (as it was then called) does not occupy the centre of the group. The view up Kingsway, the great central avenue, shows the Viceroy's House (now Rashtrapati Bhavan or President's House) in the centre, flanked and supported by the north and south blocks of the Secretariat, which housed the civil and military officers of the Empire; the Council Chamber was placed a little way to the right and off the crest of the hill. The building itself, however, is impressive, at once elegant and massive. Designed by Sir Herbert Baker and built in rose and cream-coloured stone, it is circular in shape, covers an area of six acres and is one-third of a mile in circumference. The plan of the ground floor is shown opposite.

It can been seen that the building houses three semicircular chambers, at present occupied by the House of the People, the Council of States and the Supreme Court. Between these chambers are three uncovered garden courts, while the centre of the building is occupied by the spacious Central Hall. This is used for the President's Address, as well

[1] The House thus sits little after dark. When it does so happen, it is indicated; until 1954, the sign was a gay, revolving circle of lights with the colours of the Indian flag; this has now been thought too frivolous and has been replaced by a sober single light.

[2] In September 1954 a new practice was introduced of a sitting of six hours from 11 a.m. to 5 p.m. with no lunch break but with a convention that the House shall not be counted between 1 p.m. and 2.30 p.m.

[3] With the introduction of the six-hour daily sitting, Saturdays ceased in 1954–55 to be ordinarily fixed for meetings.

as for any talk to members by a distinguished visitor. Its main importance, however, lies in its ordinary use—as the M.P.s' lounge. Here the
day's papers can be read, tea and coffee are served, and here take place
ceaselessly those conversations which supplement and support the formal debates in the Chambers. Surrounding all this are the office rooms—
of the Speaker of the House, the Chairman of the Council, the Secretariats of both Houses and of the Ministers of the Government. Here,
too, are found the Parliamentary Notice Offices (which receive notices of
motions, amendments, etc., handed in by the M.P.s) and the offices of
the Congress Party in Parliament. On the first floor are the galleries to

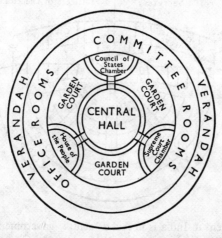

the Chambers, the Parliament Library and the Committee Rooms,
while there are two further floors occupied by the junior officers and
clerical staff of the Parliamentary Secretariats. For the internal decora-
tion of the building, materials have come from many parts of India—the
black marble for the Chamber columns from Gaya, white and coloured
marble from Makrana and different kinds of wood from Assam and
Burma. The Central Hall has panels, in which it is proposed that portraits of leading Indians will be placed; one of Dadabhai Naoroji, a
founder of Indian nationalism, is already in position, while one of
Mahatma Gandhi is hung above the dais. It is also proposed to decorate
the walls of the outer corridor of the building with murals depicting
episodes of Indian history and features of Indian life.

The shape of the Chambers dictates the seating arrangement of both
Houses. It has often been held that two kinds of shape are connected
with two forms of parliamentary democracy. The rectangular British
pattern is associated with clearly-defined Government and Opposition

confronting each other on opposite sides of the House. The circular Continental pattern on the other hand is associated with a parliamentary situation in which the Government, a coalition occupying a not very clearly demarcated central position, is flanked on both sides by its critics of Left and Right. Yet, in India, although both Houses are semicircular in shape and the seats follow the same pattern, the result is not at all the Continental arrangement. The plan of the House of the People illustrates the position:

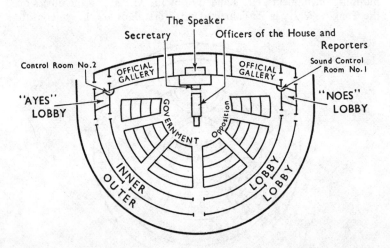

The Government in India is in fact a 'centre' government, but it does not sit on the centre benches; it sits, as does the Government in the House of Commons, on the Speaker's right, and it is confronted by the opposition groups whether of the Left or the Right.[1] In the House elected in 1952 the Congress Party normally occupied four of the six blocks of seats, thus spreading round to an almost 'Opposition' position. The Government itself, including the Deputy Ministers and Parliamentary Secretaries, occupies (at least during Question Hour) the first two benches of two or three blocks, its supporters behind and extending beyond into the fourth block. Often it seems as though the more independent members of the party prefer the third or fourth blocks where they can enjoy the feeling of being somewhat less than wholly committed.

[1] This leads to some apparently incongruous situations, as when, in the course of a debate on unemployment, the Maharaja of Bikaner, an Independent M.P., after making a speech in which he blamed the merger of the princely states for throwing many out of work, resumed his place next to the Communist group and began a most friendly conversation with one of their leaders! One is reminded of the saying from France that there is more in common between two Deputies, one of whom is a revolutionary and the other not, than there is between two revolutionaries, one of whom is a Deputy and the other not.

Here they begin to merge into the Independents and into the right and centre opposition groups who mainly occupy the fifth block. The Communists and P.S.P. sit in the sixth block, on the Speaker's left and directly facing the Prime Minister and his senior colleagues.

Equally important as a factor making the atmosphere of the Indian Parliament approximate, in spite of the shape of the Chamber, to that of the British rather than the Continental model is the absence of a rostrum. The dais in the centre is occupied by the Speaker with his Marshal at his side, while below him sits the Secretary. Each member speaks from his own seat and addresses his remarks to the Chair. The atmosphere of a genuine debate rather than a public meeting is thus retained. And the Chamber, though in fact large, is sufficiently compact to give a feeling of intimacy on all but the very poorly attended occasions.[1] Also important in this respect is the absence of microphones for individual speakers, for these would again tend to make speeches less informal. Instead there is a 'sound reinforcement' system similar to that of the new House of Commons.[2]

Outside the Chamber are two wide semicircular corridors equipped with comfortable seats and decorated with portraits of former Presiding Officers. These are the Lobbies—an Inner Lobby for M.P.s only and an Outer Lobby to which Press representatives with Lobby Passes can gain admission. Here take place conversations of a less leisurely nature than those that characterise the Central Hall, the hurried and urgent consultations between colleagues, the final checking of points before an intervention or a speech. Also on the ground floor and immediately to the right of the Speaker is the Official Gallery, placed near the Government front bench but technically outside the House. Here sit the officials of the ministries, watching the passage of their departments' measures and available for brief consultation if the Minister should desire it. In a similar position on the other side is the seldom occupied Special Box, reserved for visitors from abroad of ministerial or equivalent status.[3] Looking down on the Chamber are the galleries. The Press Gallery runs above the Speaker's Chair and faces the House. Over the Government

[1] There are not quite enough seats for all members. Formerly, the Chamber had only seats for 148; recent rearrangements now enable the accommodation of 461: 44 seats with desks, 363 without desks and 54 removable seats for specially crowded days. The seats are in the six blocks, each of 10 rows. The fact that only a small proportion of seats have desks is intended, along with a clear convention against bringing into the Chamber any papers or books other than those required for a contribution to the debate, to underline the nature of the House as a place in which to speak and listen, not to read.

[2] For members who still do not hear well, each seat has a concealed loud-speaker; when a peculiarly inaudible member is speaking, his colleagues will often be seen leaning forward in their seats with their ears close to these loud-speakers. Similar loud-speakers are provided in the Press Gallery and, on request, in the other galleries.

[3] Among those who were privileged spectators from this position during 1953–54 were Lord Swinton, British Secretary of State for Commonwealth Relations, the lady Health Minister from the Soviet Union and two former members of the Government of British Guiana, Dr. Jagan and Mr. Burnham.

back benches are the Diplomatic and Distinguished Visitors' Galleries, while opposite are the Speaker's Gallery and the Gallery for members of the Council of State.

The rest of the semicircle is occupied by the Public Gallery with a special section for ladies.[1] The question of broadcasting the proceedings of Parliament was at one time raised but opinion was firmly opposed to it, less because of certain constitutional and legal doubts than on the ground that it would encourage members to make speeches to the outside 'gallery'.

Most of these remarks apply equally to the Council of States. The Chamber of the Upper House is, however, smaller; originally planned to seat 86, it has now been expanded to accommodate 216, almost the present number of its members. There is one slight difference in the allocation of seats to members. As in the Lower House, the Government is to the Chairman's right and the opposition to his left. In the Council, however, the biggest opposition group was a Right-wing association of members, and they have been given the extreme left block; the Communists and P.S.P. have therefore to occupy a slightly more central position. In the States, the accommodation of legislatures varies in style. There are, in Bihar and Mysore for instance, magnificent new buildings full of light and grace, whereas in other States solid grey Victorian sobriety houses the Assemblies. In some States the Chambers are rectangular, in most semicircular; in some bare simplicity, in a few—as for instance when a former ruler's palace has been 'converted' for the purpose—stately luxury is the key note.

In some States, the sessions of the legislature are held alternatively in the different towns. Formerly this was done mainly for reasons of comfort. Thus, summer sessions of the Central Assembly were usually held in Simla, where the Government too moved to escape the impossible Delhi heat. This kind of practice is continued by Bombay, which holds a 'monsoon' session up the hill at Poona. But the practice in some States has also as a motive the desire to placate regional jealousies. The Andhra Assembly, for example, has already begun to hold sessions not only in the temporary capital Kurnool but also in Waltair in the 'rival' coastal zone of the State.[2] In Madhya Bharat not only the legislature but the whole machinery of government divides its time so as to keep both Gwalior and Indore content. In this connection, it is interesting to note that there is some suggestion that the Union Parliament itself should

[1] All the galleries, when filled to capacity with additional seats installed, hold 450 persons. Special passes are provided for each gallery. Admission to the Public Gallery is obtained through M.P.s who are ordinarily allowed two applications for passes for any one meeting.

[2] Comfort is not wholly absent as a consideration even here; a less pleasant spot than Kurnool is difficult to imagine. Lest I should be thought to be condemning the whole area of which it is a centre, let me add that it is possible that, if chosen as a permanent capital, it could be made habitable.

hold one of its three annual sessions away from Delhi. In South India, in particular, it is felt that the view of things as seen from the far north is incomplete, and that it would do Ministers and other members alike much good to have to spend a period in the south. Moreover, since Bangalore with its perfect climate for twelve months of the year is the site usually suggested, there is some sympathy for the idea even among Northerners. The move would, of course, have to include most of the Ministers and many officials and would be expensive in money and effort; nevertheless, it may well be considered worth while as a contribution to the unification of India.

4. Behaviour and Attitudes

'I, . . ., having been elected a member of the House of the People do swear in the name of God (or solemnly affirm) that I will bear true faith and allegiance to the Constitution of India as by law established and that I will faithfully discharge the duty upon which I am about to enter.' This oath (or affirmation) has to be made by every member before he takes his seat in Parliament. On his name being called by the Secretary, he proceeds to the table below the Speaker, takes the oath, mounts the dais to shake hands with the Speaker and signs his name on the Roll of Members. He is then a member of the House.[1] What is the nature of the duty he has undertaken and how is he expected to discharge it? Before answering this question in the subsequent chapters, we may take a general view of the conduct and attitudes of the individuals and groups that constitute a House. Although primarily descriptive of the House of the People, most of the comments are equally applicable to the Upper House and to State legislatures; some of the more striking differences are noticed in the course of the section.

Politicians, perhaps even more than teachers and as much as writers and artists, are men in love with their work. This is true of all countries, and in this India is certainly no exception. For the politician, politics is not an occupation so much as a way of living; not so much a task to be performed as a natural expression of the personality. No doubt most men are happy in the company of their colleagues and fellows, but nowhere is the enjoyment of professional community more marked than among politicians. The Indian politician—at least at the Centre—is in this respect in a peculiarly fortunate position; most members of Parliament not only work together but live together. In New Delhi, two large hostels are available primarily for M.P.s and their families. Even of those who live outside these hostels, a large proportion inhabit two streets of

---

[1] There is no elaborate House procedure for the checking of members' credentials; the Secretary relies on the information supplied by Returning Officers through the Election Commission.

flats specially allotted to M.P.s. There is thus never a dull moment; even when the House is not sitting, it is still possible and easy to drop in on the fellow member who lives in the same block or in the apartment across the road. The desire for professional talk, added to the love of conversation and social intercourse which characterises Indian life in general, is always easily satisfied. Most M.P.s are never left alone for a moment, and few of them would be happy if they were.[1]

Yet although for the politician, politics is everywhere and has no fixed hours, the sittings of the House naturally have a special importance. The Indian M.P. has in any case other reasons for attending besides interest. The pricking of conscience may play some part. The possibility of awkward questions from the constituencies is, so far, rather remote. More important by far is the force of party discipline; the members are there to support or oppose a government, and the party Whips[2] are there to see that they do so. The Constitution has also a word to say on attendance: 'If for a period of sixty days a member of either House of Parliament is without permission of the House absent from all meetings thereof, the House may declare his seat vacant.'[3] The House has therefore made arrangements for the scrutiny of applications for leave, though these are in practice almost invariably granted without much difficulty.[4] Last but not least there is a financial incentive: M.P.s receive a daily allowance 'for each day of residence at the place where Parliament meets'; and if one has taken the trouble to come to Delhi, it costs little to put in an appearance in Parliament House. Members who come to the House sign an attendance register in the lobby; at the same time the staff at the table keep an hourly count of the members actually present in the Chamber. The following table shows a contrast between the two which is only to be expected:

---

[1] This also means, unfortunately, that there is little time available for study or even for reading. Even during session periods, the Parliament Library is comparatively little used, except for the perusal of newspapers—and for still more conversation! It must be said that there are a few noble exceptions. It must also be confessed that the M.P. is no better nor worse than the middle class of India generally, among whom reading is still a largely undiscovered art and pleasure. The nature of family and social life and the design of houses have much to do with this; opportunity for silence and solitude is very rare. It is only fair to add that these conditions keep alive skill and ease of conversation, great hospitality and an absence of selfishness which the more private lives of the modern West have tended to destroy.

[2] See below, Chapter IV, Section 2.

[3] Art. 101 (4). For States, Art. 190 (4); the period here is also sixty days and, in view of the shorter sessions of State legislatures, the provision is therefore less important than at the Centre.

[4] Until 1954 the procedure was that the Speaker read out the application to the House and, in the absence of dissent, declared permission granted (*Rules*, Rule 228). Absence of even more than sixty days has been condoned. The large number of absentees during the session of Aug.–Sept. 1953 prompted the feeling that a proper scrutiny was called for. By a new rule introduced in Jan. 1954 the applications are first looked at by a Committee on the Absence of Members, which then reports to the House. Some time of the House as a whole has also been saved by this change.

TABLE XVIII—AVERAGE DAILY ATTENDANCE

	Average Daily Attendance (from Register)	Average Daily Attendance (from hourly counts)
Provisional Parliament, 1950–52 (membership rising from 285 in 1950 to 313 in 1951)		
Second Session	252	132
Third Session	241	109
Fourth Session	198	49
Fifth Session	178	62
House of the People, 1952–53 (499 members)		
First Session	432	247
Second Session	389	163
Third Session	371	144

These figures seem to show that in spite of the incentives to attend, members tend to become less active as the life of Parliament passes into middle and old age—fewer sign the register regularly, and of those a decreasing proportion spend their time in the Chamber.

The figures do not, however, show the variations in attendance. It is usual for attendance during Question Hour in the House of the People to be in the neighbourhood of 250, while a closely fought debate or a foreign policy statement will bring the numbers to over 400. At other times, the attendance may be meagre and near the quorum mark of 50.[1] In this respect, the galleries follow the House. The public gallery is crowded and alert during Question Hour and during big debates; the Diplomatic Gallery also fills for the Budget speech and the Prime Minister's speeches on the international scene. In the States, public attendance is generally greater than in Delhi, partly perhaps because the sessions are shorter. This is especially true of smaller States (though not so much of Delhi State, whose citizens are made blasé by the presence nearby of the Union Parliament). Travancore-Cochin is perhaps exceptional on account of the high level of education and widespread interest in politics; certainly the brief sessions at Trivandrum are throughout the day watched by a densely-packed crowd of mostly very young and keenly-attentive spectators. Those legislatures which have more than one place of meeting often find a significant difference in public interest; the Bombay legislature's Poona sessions are the delight of the student community in particular, whereas Bombay City's inhabitants for the most part seem to have other things to do.

It is, then, to a fairly crowded House and below fairly filled galleries

---

[1] The Constitution prescribes the quorum as one-tenth of the membership (Art. 100 (3)).

that the Speaker makes his daily entrance at the start of the sitting.[1] He is preceded and announced by the Marshal: 'Honourable Members, the Honourable Speaker'—spoken in Hindi.[2] The members rise in their places, the Speaker bows to the centre and to the two sides and all then resume their seats. The business of the day then begins. The scene which the spectator witnesses is generally orderly and dignified. At the same time it is a scene with some movement in it. The most colourful movement is that in and out of the Chamber by the liveried messengers, who bring notes and files to the Government front bench and to the Secretary's table, crouching low as they move in order to avoid coming between any speaker and the Chair. A more regular but less obtrusive movement is that of the reporters who sit at an extension of the Secretaries' table and take down the proceedings in shorthand, entering and leaving the Chamber in ten-minute shifts.[3] A certain amount of movement takes place among the members too. They enter and leave, rise to speak and move across to have a whispered word with a fellow member. A Minister may lean back to talk to a colleague or may even get up to speak to one of his staff in the official gallery—though this is rare and usually only during the discussion of amendments to Bills. Perhaps the most significant movement is the least noticeable of all: that of the Whips. The diplomatic work of these party managers is never finished; there is always something that requires to be said to some member of one's own flock or to a potentially friendly Independent or to the Whips of the opposition groups.

The task of establishing a code of parliamentary behaviour has not

1 The Speaker has the power to order the 'withdrawal of strangers' (*Rules*, Rule 300) and hold a sitting in private. This power does not appear to have been used. During the debate on certain clauses of the Representation of the People (No. 2) Bill, however, the Speaker said: 'I understand that it is the general desire of members that they meet informally and discuss the amendments to the Bill with the Minister of Law. . . . I have no objection to adjourn now'. The House then adjourned and continued its discussions in private. It is interesting to note that on the following day it became evident that there had been a misunderstanding and that some non-Congress members had thought that the 'private session' was open only to Congress Party members! The procedure, however, was repeated, the Deputy Speaker explaining: 'Though it is not a formal reference to a Committee of the whole House, it is as good as that.' (There is no provision for a 'Committee of the whole House' in the Indian Parliament.) And the Minister of Law added: 'Everyone is invited.' This was done a third time on the following day. The public was thus excluded from much of the discussion on this particular Bill. The procedure does not appear to have been used since. (P.P. Deb., 22–24 May 1951.)

2 Up to late 1952, only the Speaker was 'honourable'. On a member's protest, the Deputy Speaker instructed the Marshal that all were 'honourable' and the form was accordingly amended. (H.P. Deb., 20 Dec. 1952.)

3 The shifts are shorter for the more difficult Question Hour and also for the latter part of the day's sitting. The reporters transcribe their own shorthand, and an effort is made to have cyclostyled copies of the proceedings available for the table and for members who have spoken within 1½–2 hours of the end of the sitting. The reporters may co-operate informally with the members of the press gallery. Hindi speeches are taken down in Hindi shorthand. A large proportion of Hindi speeches—especially towards the end of the day— slows up the preparing of the proceedings.

been easy but, at the Centre at least, it has been achieved with some success. No doubt the existence of quasi-parliamentary institutions during the quarter-century before independence has been of decisive importance. For although the new Parliament of 1952 contained many members not merely new to Delhi but even without legislature experience of any kind,[1] it inherited very firmly a set of conventions established during the earlier period. The late Speaker, Mr. Mavalankar, who so ably guided the new parliaments from 1946 to 1956, has been able to benefit from the sure foundations laid down by his predecessors.[2] The raw recruit to parliamentary politics has been provided with clear guidance and has also been set a generally good example by his senior fellows. He quickly learns that there are rules to be observed. On arrival he is presented with a 'Handbook for Members' which supplies, among much other information, an outline of procedure and a list of Dos and Don'ts. Many of these have in fact been included as Rules of Procedure and Conduct of Business.[3] While the House is sitting, a member shall not read any matter except in connection with the business of the House, shall bow to the Chair when taking or leaving his seat, shall always address the Chair, shall not obstruct the proceedings or interrupt, and so on. These rules and conventions have usually been adopted in the States too. In some States, of course, they are of as long standing as at the Centre, and in a few cases, States have gone even further. Bombay, for instance, has provided its members with a lengthy list of conventions and a further list of expressions that have been held in Bombay to be unparliamentary,[4] and has referred its members to May's *Parliamentary Practice*.

Breaches of the rules and conventions naturally occur from time to time. Sometimes they arise from inexperience or oversight—as when the new member tries to read out his speech and has to be discouraged. Sometimes they follow from excitement or indignation, as when members forget to refer to each other indirectly as 'the Honourable Member', or when they fail at once to resume their seats when the Speaker rises to speak. More serious are those breaches of order which are deliberately made by way of protest or demonstration. The Speaker is of course equipped with powers to deal with such breaches. He can order the withdrawal of a member (i.e. from that day's sitting) or his suspension (i.e. for the remainder of the session) and he can adjourn the House or suspend a sitting for a period.[5] In case of a necessity to use force to

---

[1] See above, p. 117.

[2] For the position and function of the Speaker, see below, Chapter VI.

[3] E.g. Rules 246–252.

[4] The list makes amusing reading. It seems a little hard on members that they are forbidden the phrase 'throwing dust in the eyes of members' and the satirical use of 'divine jewel'. The ban on 'tongue diarrhoea' is more understandable; so also the exclamation 'To hell with the Government' and the description of the Commissioner of Police as the 'Chief Goonda (i.e. criminal, thug) of the State'!   [5] Rules 288–290.

implement his decisions, he can call upon his Marshal (called Sergeant-at-Arms in some States) or even on the Watch and Ward Staff of the House (who may be police deputed for the purpose). Although anger may be at first directed at the other side of the House, the Speaker's duty to preserve decorum quickly involves the Chair in the dispute and most of the ugly scenes have in fact eventually taken the form of protests against the Chair. Even at the Centre, 'walk-outs' of indignant individuals and of groups have taken place on occasion, the Communists being particularly attached to this method of drawing attention to themselves and giving emphasis to their view that the Chair is not impartial.[1] In State legislatures, this particular behaviour has been very much used —almost to the point of blunting its effectiveness; in many Assemblies it must by now be unusual for a session to pass without at least one walk-out.[2] So far as the use of force is concerned, occasions at the Centre have fortunately been rare. Since the election of the new Parliament, the Marshal of the House of the People has been called upon in this connection only twice; once his movement towards the recalcitrant member was sufficient to persuade him to promise to keep quiet, while on the other occasion the member had to be handled and forced out of the Chamber.[3] Some of the State legislatures have been rowdy more frequently. It appears, however, that only one incident perhaps deserves to be described as a riot: that occurred in Rajasthan, where parliamentary government if not a curiosity is at least a novelty.[4] Indeed, it is probably safe to predict that the generally high standards already to be found in Delhi and in the senior State capitals will spread elsewhere fairly quickly. Against this, it is true, must be reckoned the Communists' will-

[1] The House of the People has also witnessed what must be an unusual form of 'walk-out'—one staged by a Minister! During the debate on the Press (Objectionable Matter) Amendment Bill—on which there was considerable dispute—the 'walk-out' of the Communists on one day was followed by that of the Home Minister on the next. A press report of the incident (*Times of India*, 13 March 1954) reads: 'Two examples of scurrilous press writing quoted by the Minister were described by Mr. Anthony (Anglo-Indian nominated member) as harmless innuendoes whose import had been grossly magnified by Ministerial hypersensitiveness and ego. An elaboration of these remarks generated some heat and the Minister left the Chamber exclaiming "I can't sit here any more" to the accompaniment of derisive opposition laughter. He returned, however, a few minutes later.'

[2] It must be confessed that although the walk-out is a deliberate technique of protest, its use might not be so general if there was complete confidence in all Speakers. The Speakers' retention of party links makes this more difficult than is necessary. (On this, see below, Chapter VI, Section 1.)

[3] The first member was a Hindu Mahasabhite who would not accept the Speaker's refusal to admit his adjournment motion on the arrest of the Jan Sangh leader, Dr. Mukherjee; the other more stubborn M.P. was a Communist who created a scene during the debate on the controversial Preventive Detention (Second Amendment) Bill. (H.P. Deb., 18 July 1952 and 9 March 1953 respectively.)

[4] 'What happened on May 21 in the Rajasthan Assembly', said a press report (*Times of India*, 1 June 1954), 'has no parallel in the country's legislative history. Rajasthan legislators, on that evening, shook fists and screamed insults at the presiding officer, toppled over the desks and kicked away the chairs.' The incident ended when the Sergeant-at-Arms was ordered to remove a Communist member from the Chamber.

ingness to abuse political institutions for their own ends; but even this can be checked by the disapproval of public opinion.

The House, then, is generally well behaved, sober and serious. It is even—by comparison with the House of Commons at least—rather humourless. There are one or two members who are amusing and who make it their business to amuse; there are a few situations which never fail to raise a laugh—as when the Chief Whip makes one of his rare and brief interventions or a Minister repeats too often the plea that he requires notice to answer a question; and the wit of the Deputy Speaker[1] is an enlivening influence. On the whole, however, life on the floor of the House is rather earnest. There is a perceptible difference of atmosphere between the House and the Council. The Upper House is smaller in numbers and less pressed for time. It has to recognise that it is not the more important House; its smaller galleries are very seldom as crowded as those of the Lower House. The result is a less tense and more friendly tone of debate—to which the urbane and good-humoured personality of the Chairman contributes greatly. To listen to its deliberations is to listen to a very private and intimate discussion among members of a rather special club. This is not to say that the House of the People is ill-tempered or unfriendly. It is simply that it is busy and has serious work to do, and that it is the main arena of struggle. Seriousness, however, does not make for dullness. In fact, the House is dull neither to look at or to listen to. The gathering is a good deal more interesting to the eye than the generally dark-suited assemblies of Europe. The lady members naturally wear colourful saris, while the men's dress varies considerably. Some wear European clothes, Nehru's style of the elegant traditional North Indian long coat buttoned at the neck and tight trousers is followed by most Ministers and many members, while others, especially from the South, keep to the simple white shirt worn outside a white cloth *dhoti* tied in various fashions.[2] The style of speeches also varies considerably. No speeches are read[3] but a few members still adopt the tone and technique of the public meeting and declaim their phrases to the galleries, and this is indeed very common in the smaller State legislatures where the public attendance is large and the members unaccustomed to the style of debate. Even among those who have learnt how to talk in the House—in what is meant, after all, to be a discussion and not a series of

[1] Mr Ananthasayanam Ayyangar. On the death of Mr Mavalankar in Feb. 1956, he was unanimously elected to the Chair.

[2] The latter is practically universal in South Indian assemblies and appears as much a uniform as the dark suits of Westminster. It may be of interest to record, in passing, that the Prime Minister in 1954 issued guidance to Government officers on dress and favoured the buttoned tunic rather than the European open-necked coat and tie. (An enterprising New Delhi tailor on the following day advertised that he would undertake the necessary adjustments to European jackets!)

[3] There is no rule to this effect, but the practice has been effectively discouraged by the Chair. Certain ministerial statements and the Finance Minister's Budget speech are, of course, exceptions.

addresses—even here, there is room for much variation. It is a minority, so far, who can speak in a manner that is at once ordered and logical as well as graceful, and whose speeches have been given careful preparation beforehand. The majority is fluent without being impressive in manner. At the other extreme, there are some[1] whose style of delivery is so erratic and incoherent that they appear to invite interruption—and, indeed, sometimes appear to flourish on it to a point where it is difficult to see what they would have said if they had been left to speak undisturbed.

These comments on the speeches prompt a mention of the question of the language of debate. The Constitution provides that Hindi is the official language of the Union, but that for fifteen years (from 1950) English shall continue to be used for those official purposes for which it was being used before 1950. It also enables any State legislature to choose Hindi and/or a regional language as the official language of the State, again with the same proviso regarding English.[2] The Constitution further refers to the languages to be used in legislatures: in Parliament Hindi or English are to be used, in State legislatures the official language of the State or Hindi or English; in all cases, the presiding officers may permit a member who cannot adequately express himself in these languages to speak in his mother tongue.[3] In the Union Parliament, there has been very little difficulty arising out of languages other than Hindi and English. Shortly after the assembly of the new House a member asked the Speaker if translations would be provided of speeches made in a third language. The Speaker replied: 'Let us not raise imaginary difficulties'; genuine cases might arise and would be considered then, but ordinarily, he supposed, members 'will try to speak in a manner which is intelligible to other members'.[4] His hopes have been fulfilled, but there has been a tough tussle between the ardent North India advocates of Hindi and the non-Hindi-speaking members, especially from the South. On one occasion the occupant of the Chair, a member from Madras, asked a member who had begun in Hindi if he would kindly speak in English so that the Chair could follow.[5] Only two days later, the Railways Minister who replied in Hindi to the debate on the Railway Budget was asked by the Speaker to give a short summary also in English—'for the benefit of the large number of members from South India particularly'.[6] The same Minister was on a similar occasion advised by the Deputy Speaker that Minister's speeches had a special importance and should therefore be given in English.[7] On the other hand, when a Madras member asked for an English translation of an answer

---

[1] Including, I fear, some Ministers.   [2] Arts. 343 and 345.   [3] Arts. 120 and 210.
[4] H.P. Deb., 19 May 1952. During the first session, 496 members of the House of the People took the oath or made the affirmation; 259 did so in English, 220 in Hindi, 9 in Urdu, 4 in Malayalam, 2 in Telegu, 1 in Tamil and 1 in Oriya (Parliament Secretariat, Brief Summary of Work, First Session, 1952).
[5] H.P. Deb., 27 May 1952.   [6] H.P. Deb., 29 May 1952.   [7] H.P. Deb., 6 June 1952.

given in Urdu by the Education Minister to a question put in English, the Speaker remarked that members should really make efforts to learn Urdu or Hindi; translations were available for members some time later —admittedly too late from the point of view of putting supplementary questions.[1] Govind Das, one of the foremost proponents of Hindi, has been pressing that when questions are put in Hindi it should be made compulsory to answer them in Hindi. On one occasion, the Deputy Speaker replied that members must be given some time to learn Hindi; even the Constitution had given English fifteen years' lease of life and certainly 'point of bayonets' tactics would not help matters.[2] Classes in Hindi for those M.P.s new to the language have in fact been started, and some of the Congress Party members at least are enthusiastic. As a reciprocal gesture, some Northerners are making efforts to learn one of the Southern languages. Yet one may hazard the guess that it will not be until some time after 1965 that all members will be able to speak at all easily in Hindi.

Up to the present the proportion of speeches given in Hindi in the Union Parliament remains comparatively small, in spite of the efforts to increase its popularity.[3] There has, however, been some increase during the period since 1947. The following figures show the average number of minutes of Hindi speeches per day which the reporters of the House of the People have recorded:

TABLE XIX—LENGTH OF HINDI REPORTING PER DAY

Session	Average No. of Minutes of Hindi reporting per day
Before 1949	Less than 10 minutes
Constituent Assembly (Legislative)	
1949 Sixth Session . .	10
Provisional Parliament, 1950–52	
First Session . .	19
Second Session . .	13
Third Session . .	30
Fourth Session . .	46
Fifth Session . .	38
House of the People, 1952–54	
First Session . .	36
Second Session . .	35
Third Session . .	58
Fourth Session . .	39
Fifth Session . .	34

NOTE.—The length of the day's sitting has not been constant. Before 1951 they lasted 4¾ hours; after that, 5 hours. But there were, of course, a few extended sittings.

[1] H.P. Deb., 6 June 1952. The Education Minister, Maulana Azad, has always spoken in Urdu—the form of Hindustani or Hindi which is written in the Persian script and which contains a number of Arabic and Persian words.   [2] H.P. Deb., 30 March 1953.

[3] The announcements in 1954 that the House of the People would henceforward be known as the Lok Sabha and the Council of States as Rajya Sabha are illustrations of the campaign.

10—P.I.

It would appear that, except when topics of special concern to Hindi advocates are frequent (as in the Budget session of 1953), there is about half an hour's Hindi spoken in a five-hour day. It may be added that so far as the records of the House are concerned, speeches given in Hindi are published in Hindi—and since 1952 no English translation is given. At the same time a Hindi edition of the debates is being prepared alongside the English version.

In the States, English has already lost importance. In the States in Northern India such as Uttar Pradesh, the great majority of speeches are in Hindi. In most other States, too, the regional languages have come into their own. This is particularly evident where there is one main regional language. In Travancore-Cochin, for example, almost all the speeches are in Malayalam—which can be understood and spoken even by those whose mother tongue is Tamil; the Speaker, however, continues to make his remarks on procedure in English.[1] In Bombay, on the other hand, there are three regional languages and the best way to be understood by all is to speak in English. The cosmopolitan nature of the big cities also has its influence in keeping English alive in those assemblies which meet in Bombay, Madras and Calcutta.

It has already been noted that members of Parliament receive a daily allowance for their attendance. This arrangement, rather than the payment of a salary, was general in central and provincial legislatures during the period before 1947. Since the election of the new Parliament in 1952, this matter has been the subject of some thought and discussion; we may, therefore, begin a brief review of some general attitudes of M.P.s with an examination of their attitudes on this question of particular interest to them. The position on the eve of independence was that members received a daily allowance of Rs.45/-[2] for each day of parliamentary session or other parliamentary work. In addition members were paid a travelling allowance: one and three-fifths of the first-class fare to Delhi and back at the start and end of each session; one first-class fare to and from Delhi for any other parliamentary journeys. In 1949, the members greeted the approach of the new republic by sacrificing some of their allowance; the daily amount was reduced to Rs.40/-. Shortly after the elections of the new Parliament in 1952, a Joint Committe of both Houses containing representatives of all main parties was set up to consider whether it was desirable to change the system to a salary basis or to a combination of salary and allowances.[3]

[1] During the short ten-day session of the Travancore-Cochin Assembly in March 1954 there were, I believe, only two speeches in English, and one of these was by the nominated Anglo-Indian member. Otherwise, apart from the Speaker's remarks, English only arose in words and phrases here and there—such as 'on a point of order', 'deficit financing', and, every now and again in the course of a speech, 'Sir'.

[2] 1 Rupee = 1s. 6d.

[3] The Speaker announced the appointment of the committee on 6 June 1952. It reported a month later.

The Committee called for suggestions from M.P.s and received over two hundred proposals. It also considered foreign legislatures' practice. There was some disagreement in the Committee, but the eventual recommendation was against the introduction of any salary and for a further reduction in the allowance to Rs.35/– per day. The Communist representatives were the outspoken advocates of a salary; they suggested Rs.300/– per month plus a daily allowance of Rs.10/– per day. They emphasised the need to reflect the fact that an M.P.'s job was not only in Delhi but in his constituency too, and that it was an all-the-year job and not an affair of sessions. The Committee as a whole agreed to leave the travelling allowance unaltered and it rejected a proposal for free railway passes.

When, however, the Government tabled a resolution seeking to give effect to these proposals, there was something approaching a back-bench revolt; the back rows were not prepared for a second grand gesture of self-sacrifice. The Government took quick stock of the situation and decided not to press the matter. The report was stored away for a while. In the meantime, first-class accommodation on the railways was abolished during 1953; this gave a reasonable opportunity to re-open the whole question. In 1954, the House referred the problem back to the Joint Committee, with instructions to recommend new travelling allowances appropriate to the changed circumstances and also to re-examine the salary question 'in view of the further experience gained since the first report was presented.'[1] It was clear that a good deal of opinion had moved round in favour of a salary scheme. The Report[2] outlines the two opposing points of view. The salary school of thought stressed the need for a fixed income throughout the year to meet family obligations and to encourage political work in the constituencies. The allowances section of opinion pointed out that for thirty-three years the system had worked very adequately and also that a salary scheme would lead to neglect of work in Parliament. They also indicated that salaries would entail 'income-tax complications'.[3] The Committee felt that 'the arguments are so balanced that it is not possible to recommend any one view as applying universally to all members'. Members should therefore be free to choose either (a) a salary of Rs.300/– per month plus Rs.20/– per day, or (b) a daily allowance of Rs.40/– per day. The travelling allowances were to be adjusted to equal two second-class and one third-class fare for each journey. Once more, however, the back-benchers were not

[1] H.P. Deb., 27 March 1954. The Chief Whip who had had the difficult task of organising the Government retreat before back-bench pressure summarised his experience simply by saying that 'much water had flowed' since 1952.

[2] Parliament of India: Joint Committee on Payment of Salary and Allowances to Members of Parliament, Second Report, April 1954.

[3] What 'complications' would be entailed is not clear; certainly salaries would 'entail income tax'—and probably no more than that was meant.

satisfied. A meeting of the Congress Party in Parliament[1] was called to discuss the question. The Prime Minister indicated that he had an open mind on the subject and would leave it to the M.P.s themselves to decide. In these circumstances, it was inevitable that the 'self-sacrificers' would lose the day. The original proposal before the meeting was for Rs.300/- per month plus Rs.20/- per day; this was dropped in favour of Rs.400/- per month and Rs.21/- per day, and the option scheme was abandoned. The Bill finally passed by Parliament embodies these results of the Party meeting. It also included a free railway pass for the members, in addition to the continuation (meant for his family and servant) of travelling allowances in cash equal to one second- and one third-class fare for the sessions. The Ministers abstained from voting on the Bill, while the Communists attacked it as giving the M.P.s an income out of all proportion even to that of the middle class in general[2]; the great majority of members simply felt relieved at the prospect of being better able to withstand the pressure of Delhi's cost of living.

The salary question gave the ordinary M.P. a sense of his own power *vis-à-vis* the leaders. It can hardly be a precedent for other issues, since the Government in this case was not committed on a matter of high national policy. It may, however, have given greater confidence to some of the younger and more active back-benchers. Yet a great readiness to question, to suggest, to disagree will, it must be recognised, be reflected very little on the floor of the House; it will show itself largely within party circles. For the Indian M.P. is a strong party member. Despite regional attachments, despite class and caste affinities, party loyalty remains strong. Divergent views on policy and particular local emphases will, therefore, seek expression primarily within the councils of the party.[3] Every member represents a constituency and many members have particular 'interests' in whose furtherance they are concerned, but these loyalties have mainly to find their place within the loyalty to party. Clearly, this does not prevent the M.P.s' questions from having a regional or interest bias. A casual glance at one day's Question Hour is enough to illustrate the point: a Delhi M.P. asks about central aid for Delhi development schemes; a member from the Kangra tea-growing district enquires about the constitution of the Tea Board and the member from the coffee-growing State of Coorg wants to know about Government plans for the export of coffee; the M.P. who is President of the Federation of Indian Chambers of Commerce and Industry asks

[1] See below, Chapter IV, Section 2.
[2] H.P. Deb., 14 May 1954, and C.S. Deb., 19 May 1954. The measure was 'piloted' by the Government Chief Whip in his capacity as Minister for Parliamentary Affairs—or, as he had described himself, as 'Minister for Members'; in this case, however, his task was rather to gauge the strength of back-bench feeling and, having done so, to stand aside and let it have its way.
[3] This process at present takes place mainly within the Congress Party. The Party's machinery of State Groups and specialised Standing Committees is described below, Chapter IV, Section 2.

whether, and if so how, the Government proposes to associate men with experience of industry in the management of State Enterprises; and a trade unionist questions the ministry on the wages paid to employees of the Government Presses.[1] Nor does party loyalty mean the suppression of these particular 'sectional' concerns in the course of debate; even from a party point of view the best contribution a member can make may often be of this kind; and, indeed, the Whips will choose their parties' speakers mainly on these grounds. Thus if the debate is on the Control of Shipping Bill, members from both sides of that particular industry will expect to be able to speak; a discussion on the Coir Industry will naturally constitute an opportunity to members from Travancore-Cochin, where that industry is largely concentrated.[2] 'Pressure groups', though not elaborately organised, certainly exist, and it would probably be difficult to discover any significant 'interest' which was not directly or indirectly represented in the House. The 'group' will work unobstrusively but it will naturally use all legitimate means to press its case. One clear example is provided by the Federation of Indian Chambers of Commerce and Industry. This body is directly represented in Parliament in that both its President and Secretary are members, one Independent, the other Congress. It will have its views expressed on the floor of the House and through party channels. It will be called upon (or it will itself ask to be allowed) to give evidence before Select Committees handling Bills in which it is interested. It will also be consulted on a wide range of subjects by the appropriate ministries of Government, the consultations taking place through departmental committees, deputations and verbal representations, or correspondence. In the same way constituency pressure also exists and seeks several ways of expressing itself. This pressure is on the whole rather weak at the Centre. It is true that M.P.s receive letters and that on any day of the session there will be groups in the corridors of Parliament House who have come in the hope of pressing their member to some action or representation on their behalf.[3] The

[1] H.P. Deb., 8 March 1954.

[2] The Whip's choice of speakers is discussed also below, Chapter IV, Section 2. It sometimes happens that members not directly connected with the particular business feel that they are unfairly excluded. On the Coir Industry Bill debate, for instance, a member was prompted to ask the Chair whether there was any convention that only directly interested M.P.s were able to 'catch the Speaker's eye'; he was assured that this was not the case (H.P. Deb., 17 Nov. 1953). The Speaker is, however, much guided by the lists put in by the Whips, and the complaint indicates that the Whips had given clear priority to members from coir districts.

[3] The pressure, whether by correspondence or by interview, is difficult to assess and appears in any case to vary a great deal from member to member. The pressure bears some relation to the responsiveness of the M.P.: a few members have a heavy burden of correspondence which they conscientiously try to deal with; others receive few letters and do not reply even to those. The main opportunity for constituency pressure arises when the member returns home at the end of the session. He then has to receive a fairly constant stream of visitors. But many of their requests will be of a personal nature. The M.P., that is, will be asked to use his influence to find suitable employment in Delhi for this man's son or that man's cousin. A few matters that can be regarded as questions of policy may also be raised, but it must be remembered that, above all in rural constituencies, the policies that touch the people tend to be the responsibility of the State Governments.

main constituency pressure, however, is at the State level and is exerted on and through the State member of the legislative assembly (M.L.A.); in this case, too, it operates through questions, speeches, representation on Select Committees on Bills and above all through party channels.

Perhaps the most searching questions that can be asked in order to reveal the character of a parliament and the attitudes of its members are those that concern the relations between private member and the Government and between Government and Opposition. Lord Campion has recently made a brief but penetrating analysis of this matter so far as Europe is concerned by pointing out some of the contrasts between the British and French models of parliamentary organisation and behaviour.[1] The exploration of these questions in the Indian context will show that parliament in India appears to have characteristics which belong to both models; in some respects it might even be said that there is an Indian model which represents a position somewhere between the two.

Lord Campion first enquires into the relations between the Government and Parliament, or the Government and the private member. 'The British Cabinet', he writes, 'is not only responsible to Parliament, it is part of Parliament, whereas elsewhere some hankering after the doctrine of the separation of powers (which is strictly incompatible with parliamentary government) tends to make the association . . . to be from outside, or half in and half outside.' In the Continental parliament the situation of 'Ministry versus the Chamber' is normal and predominant, and is reflected in several rules of procedure. Thus, in Norway, a member who becomes a Minister hands over his duties as a member to a substitute. It is often a rule that a Minister may speak in either House—as if it were a courtesy granted to a stranger—whereas the British Minister must 'belong' to one House and has rights only where he belongs.[2] The French Minister is an alien in the House—unable to serve on its committees, unable to move amendments in his own name, and so on.

The position in the Indian Parliament is in this respect by no means identical with that of Westminster. One important difference is that Ministers are given by the Indian Constitution the right to speak in and otherwise take part in the proceedings of either House.[3] This does help to create a feeling of their being, if not strangers, at least somewhat less than members—as well as somewhat more. For the constitutional provision is no formality; Ministers who are members of one House do in

---

[1] Lord Campion, 'European Parliamentary Procedure', in *Parliamentary Affairs* (Spring, 1953). The procedural aspects in particular are set out in greater detail in Campion and Lidderdale, *European Parliamentary Procedure* (1953). See also Lidderdale, *The Parliament of France* (1951).

[2] South Africa follows the Continental model in this.

[3] Art. 88.

fact have to spend a great deal of their time in the other.[1] To some extent the need for a Cabinet Minister to operate in both Houses is lessened by entrusting some work to a junior colleague in the other House; but, so far at least, this practice, though increasing, is by no means general. The Minister who pilots a Bill through the House of the People of which he is a member will, some weeks later, appear on the floor of the Council of States to repeat his performance. In the same way, the Minister who answers a batch of questions on production or legal matters in the Council of which he is a member will probably appear a few days later to answer a similar series put by members of the Lower House.[2] The Prime Minister and his senior colleagues certainly have to be careful to divide their time between the two Houses and aid the transaction of important business in both. These arrangements, while they give a certain amount of flexibility and enable a shortage of members of ministerial quality to be overcome, place a great burden on the Ministers and result in their being more easily regarded by members of both Houses as of very different and distinct status.

By itself, however, this constitutional provision would not have a very pronounced effect on relations between members and government. More important is an attitude of distrust of the Government inherited from the days of nationalist antagonism towards the alien government of the British. Old habits of thought die hard, and it often appears as though this particular old habit of distrust has been carried over into the new period and transmitted into a variant of the 'hankering after the doctrine of the separation of powers' which Lord Campion detects in France. An excellent illustration of this feature is supplied by an exchange between the Speaker and certain members which took place towards the end of 1950. The Speaker felt called upon to remark on the distrust displayed even by members of the Government party.

> Members should not jump to the conclusion that the Government want to keep anything away from them. . . . That seems to me to be a remnant of old memories, ignoring the character of the Government we have now. . . . We must change our approach towards the Government. (An Hon. Member: What about the Government changing its approach?) Whatever may be the mistakes of Government, we are now a sovereign House and the Government is responsible to the House. (An Hon. Member: It is not.) If they are not, I should say the House is weak not to drive them out. (An Hon. Member: It is for you.) It is not for the Speaker. It is for the majority to be strong and insistent, and I am sure that any government which claims

[1] In the Ministry of 1952 after the General Elections, out of 15 Cabinet members, 5 were of the Council; of the 6 Ministers of Cabinet rank, none were from the Council; of the 14 Deputy Ministers, 3; of the 4 Parliamentary Secretaries, 1—making a total of 9 Council members out of a Ministry of 39.

[2] Questions are grouped in each House so that certain departments are covered on certain days. Since Question Hour is at the same time in both Houses, the Secretariats coordinate this allotment of days for different departments to avoid overlapping.

to be democratic and responsible to the House is bound to respond to what the House says.[1]

This distrust is further aggravated by the lack of mutual respect between politicians and civil servants. This, too, is a relic of the past when the civil service was an arm of that foreign administration which put in prison a large number of those who are now the leading politicians. The result is that a member who becomes a Minister is still felt in some way to have gone over, if not to 'the other side', at least to a position of potential antagonism. The classic expression of this view was given by the member who confessed: 'When I hear a word of praise from the Ministers about their Secretaries and staff, I feel they are lost to the country'.[2]

One of the questions Lord Campion asks in order to demonstrate the relations between Government and Parliament is—who chooses the Government? On this point there is little difference, so far at least, between India and Britain. The Government of India is chosen by the electorate, which on the whole votes for a party; it is not chosen as the result of negotiation between ill-defined and freely-deciding parliamentary groups.[3] The Nehru Government between 1947 and 1952 was deliberately not a one-party government, since the Constituent Assembly (Legislative) and the Provisional Parliament had not been chosen directly by the people, and in any case it was felt desirable to start the post-independence period with a broad leadership.[4] By the time of the General Elections, however, the non-Congress Ministers had resigned, and after the elections there was no question of anything but a one-party ministry.[5] On another question—who controls the Government?

[1] P.P. Deb., 20 Dec. 1950. At the same time, the Speaker and his staff have in a number of ways had to assert the independence of Parliament and have thus done something to accentuate the sense of cleavage and distinctness between Government and Parliament. On this see also below, Chapter VI.

[2] The M.P. concerned was one with a long record of service for the Congress Party from 1921 to 1946, and he had been imprisoned on no less than six occasions for participating in Congress activity. Although the remark was made shortly after independence (C.A. (Leg.) Deb., 17 March 1948), the attitude it reflects is still a force in the minds of members.

[3] He would be too bold who would predict the party structure of India in a score of years. But it seems to me that the trend towards the disappearance of small parties will continue. If this proves correct, it will also follow that the choice will tend to remain with the electorate; it can be no more than a tendency—as the 1954 elections in Travancore-Cochin showed. (See above, p. 109. Who 'chose' the P.S.P. Government?)

[4] See the Prime Minister's statement in the House (C.A. (Leg.) Deb., 8 March 1948) when he spoke of the consequences—'much argument in the Cabinet' but also 'extreme friendliness and co-operation'.

[5] The important resignations were: Dr. S. P. Mukherjee (later to found the Jan Sangh) on 19 April 1950 on the issue of the 1950 Agreement with Pakistan, and with him K. C. Neogy; Dr. Mathai on the relation between himself as Minister of Finance and the Planning Commission; Dr. Ambedkar (who then resumed leadership of the Scheduled Castes Federation) on 11 Oct. 1951 on the slow progress of the Hindu Code Bill, on foreign policy, and other issues; Baldev Singh on 13 May 1952. A brief note on the changing structure and composition of the central ministry since 1948 is given in a Note at the end of this chapter.

—the Indian answer is not so clear. In Britain the Government is controlled partly by its own supporters, but also, says Lord Campion, by a homogeneous Opposition; in the Continental model, governments are usually controlled by the two wings—Right and Left—of the Opposition; also by the fact that even the parties supporting the government have 'one foot in the Opposition'; and, finally, by a committee system which is designed to produce a distinctive 'Chamber point of view'. Here, again, India presents something of both worlds. The committee system in India is considered later; at this point it is enough to say that in the nature of the committees established as well as in the scope and tone of their work, the system goes beyond that of Britain and in some respects comes near to that of the Continent.[1]

The relations between Government and opposition in India present several special features. The most obvious is, of course, the predominant strength of the Congress Government. This is a strength not of numbers alone. It is a strength of relative unity compared with the disparate elements of the opposition. It is also a strength of experience; as we have seen,[2] the bulk of legislative—let alone executive—experience is to be found in the Congress Party. This tends to make opposition criticism often unrealistic and out of touch with administrative reality; it also tends to predispose the Government to be scornful of the opposition's contribution. An important consequence of this is that the Ministers often feel that they bear a heavy burden in isolation; some feel that few points of use are made from the opposition benches or even from their own party, and the discussion that must precede policy is a discussion restricted to a few colleagues in the ministry with the help of the senior officials.

The relations between Government and opposition are also influenced by the past of the Congress Party. This, too, contributes to feelings of peculiar resentment on both sides. The Congress struggles to make the psychological adjustment of climbing down from its position as a national liberation movement, while the opposition is irritated by its inability to change its mood overnight. The situation is complicated by the fact that many of those on the opposition benches are former members of Congress; this adds special tones to the attitudes on both sides. It may be added that the presence of the Communist Party as a prominent part of the opposition tends further to slow the transformation; confronted with the Communists, the Congress feels more easily justified in

[1] See below, Chapter VI. Lord Campion points out that just as the role of the Opposition in Britain 'may seem to us to go some way towards disproving the charge of autocracy' which is often levelled against us on the Continent, so also 'the French system of committees does at any rate do something to make good the Assembly's need of political leadership' which is often felt in Britain to be the main defect of the Continental parliament. The Indian committee system may go beyond that of Britain, but not to this degree; political leadership is still provided by a homogeneous government.

[2] Above, p. 122.

its retention of the national mantle. To put the matter at its worst, all this tends to make for unresponsiveness in the Government and irresponsibility in the opposition.[1] The criticism should certainly not be exaggerated; there are on both sides of the House members who listen to the opposite benches with attention and with minds open to the ideas of others. Moreover, although it is indeed important that good habits be cultivated in these formative years of Parliament, there are signs at the Centre that the position is already improving; the impatient Minister is disappearing and the irresponsible critic may follow him.[2] The process will no doubt be a little slower in the States.

The Indian pattern, then, is not that of a government confronted and controlled by a strong and homogeneous opposition. Nor can it really be said that it is the French pattern of a government managing to exist by keeping at bay two wings of opposition which threaten continuously to engulf it; there are two wings of the Indian opposition but they make no real threat as yet.[3] In the peculiar circumstances still prevailing in the Indian party system, the Indian Government is not effectively controlled; it is simply influenced by the desire to retain its past popularity in the country as a whole and by the need to take some account of movements of opinion among its own rather varied supporters.[4] The latter influence is perhaps weaker now than it was before the General Elections; certainly open criticism from within the party is less marked now than in the Provisional Parliament. From this point of view, there was more opposition when there were no opposition groups.[5]

---

[1] It is interesting that many M.P.s who were members of the old Central Assembly (as well as some independent press observers of the old legislature) compare the present Parliament unfavourably with the old. Although the Government of those days was alien and remote, they say, its members took very careful note of all criticism (as the files show), replied minutely to the points of the Opposition and were conscientious in their attendance and attentiveness alike.

[2] A newspaper comment expressed the familiar complaint: 'In a new Parliament, few are more unhelpful than the petulant Minister whose face puckers with irritation when details are asked for, who rails at the opposition or silences the rank and file of his own party, sinking back into his seat with a sense of achievement and conscious of the mechanical majority behind him' (*Statesman*, 26 Jan. 1954). Some Ministers have made the caricature almost a portrait. The Prime Minister has normally set a good example. On one occasion, for instance, the seriousness with which he treated opposition comment was said (*Hindustan Times*, 23 Dec. 1954) to have 'created a profound impression': when Communist members made certain allegations with regard to affairs in Pondicherry, he left the House to put through a special trunk call and returned to communicate his information to the critics.

[3] The P.S.P. Government in Travancore-Cochin was perhaps in this position, its movements being influenced by the need neither to outrage its Congress 'supporters' nor to give too many opportunities for telling criticism from the extreme Left.

[4] Governments are, of course, also influenced by their own sense of mission and duty, and this is particularly strong in the case of a former national movement.

[5] The Aug. 1951 session of the Provisional Parliament, one M.P. remarked at the time, would become famous for the number of occasions on which the Government bowed to opinion expressed by Congress M.P.s on the floor of the House. Several bills were introduced, subjected to heavy criticism in debate, held over for a while and finally considerably amended from their original form (e.g. Part C States Bill, P.P. Deb., 25 Aug. 1951).

In this context it is worth noting the extent to which recognition and rights are accorded to the opposition in Parliament. In the House of the People the Speaker has maintained a distinction between Party and Group which was made in the old Central Assembly. In a House of 140 a body of 12 qualified for recognition as a Party, while 9 was sufficient to constitute a Group. In the new Parliament the Speaker has felt that the tests, at least for Party status, should be stiffened, and in fact three qualifications are now regarded as necessary before recognition as a Parliamentary Party can be accorded: a number equal to the quorum of the House (50)—for it must be able to 'keep the House'; a certain unity of ideology and programme—so as to avoid encouraging mere associations of convenience; and the possession of an organisation outside the House as well as inside. By these tests, only Congress has been able to achieve recognition, even the P.S.P. and Communists being too small. Groups are given recognition more easily and the Communist Party has been accorded Group status. The position in the State Assemblies naturally varies. In some cases, even where the Centre's tests have been applied, Party status is achieved by one or more group. In other cases, State Speakers have waived the tests; in Uttar Pradesh the small P.S.P. group has been given Party status and its leader recognised as Leader of the opposition. Sometimes disagreement within the opposition ranks prevents recognition even when the Speaker is ready to give it. In West Bengal the opposition numbers 81 in a House of 158, but it is much divided; the largest group is the Communists (30), but the rest of the opposition (51) objects to any recognition being given to them.

In any event the difference in the privileges given to Parties and to Groups appears on the surface to be not very marked. Groups as well as Parties are consulted on the arrangement of the business of the House.[1] Both are equally considered from the point of view of opportunities to speak, and both are allotted blocks of seats in the Chamber. The differences remain two: first, only Parties (i.e. only the Congress Party at present) are given office accommodation in Parliament House; second, Groups have only an uncertain and limited right to be consulted on important issues of policy. It is the latter point which has greater importance than at first sight appears. The Government may in practice consult the opposition Groups, but this is a very different matter from being continuously aware of the existence of a Leader of the Opposition who is the head of an alternative government; and in fact the practice is that there is little consultation.[2] Everyone in India is anxious to see a stronger

[1] See below, pp. 217–219.

[2] The spectator from the gallery will often notice the Government Chief Whip moving over to talk to leaders on the other side of the House (and there is also similar consultation in the lobbies and offices), but the matters dealt with are mainly procedural, though the Whip may also 'sound' some of those on the other side on some questions of policy. The Prime Minister has set up a very informal foreign affairs group which contains members from the other side. It may be true that consultation would be freer and easier if the Communists were not present.

TABLE XX—STRUCTURE AND

	1947–48	1948–49	1949–50
1. PRIME MINISTER & EXTERNAL AFFAIRS Minister of State for External Affairs Deputy Minister for External Affairs	NEHRU—(a)———	(a) ——— Keskar (a) —	
2. DEFENCE Minister of State Deputy Minister Deputy Minister	BALDEV SINGH–		
3. EDUCATION NATURAL RESOURCES & SCIENTIFIC RESEARCH Minister of State for Natural Resources Deputy Minister of State for Natural Resources & Scientific Research	AZAD ———		
4. HOME STATES INFORMATION AND BROAD-CASTING Minister of State for Information & Broadcasting Deputy Minister for Home Affairs	}PATEL	{ PATEL Diwakar	———————→
5. TRANSPORT RAILWAYS Minister of State for Railways Deputy Minister for Railways & Transport	}AYYANGAR	AYYANGAR Santhanam———	
6. HEALTH Deputy Minister	KAUR———		
7. COMMUNICATIONS Deputy Minister	KIDWAI——— 	Lal———	(see 11) ———→ ———————→
8. FINANCE Minister of State Deputy Minister	MATHAI——————→		DESHMUKH———
9. LAW MINORITY AFFAIRS Minister of State for Law Minister of State for Minority Affairs	AMBEDKAR———		Biswas ———
10. LABOUR Deputy Minister	RAM ———		
11. FOOD & AGRICULTURE Minister of State Deputy Minister	DAULATRAM———	——————→	MUNSHI———
12. REHABILITATION Minister of State Deputy Minister	Saksena— (b) ———	(b) ——→	Jain (b) ———
13. INDUSTRY & SUPPLY WORKS, MINES & POWER COMMERCE WORKS, PRODUCTION & SUPPLY Deputy Minister for W.P.S. WORKS, HOUSING & SUPPLY Deputy Minister for W.H.S. COMMERCE & INDUSTRY Minister of State for C. & I. Deputy Minister for C. & I. PLANNING, IRRIGATION & POWER Deputy Minister for Planning Deputy Minister for I. & P. PRODUCTION	MUKHERJEE——— GADGIL——— NEOGY ———	——————→ ——————→	MAHTAB (see below) ————(see below)——→ PRAKASA (see 3)
14. MINISTER WITHOUT PORT-FOLIO			RAJAGOPALACHARI
15. Minister of State for Parliamentary Affairs		Sinha	

(a) Plus Commonwealth Relations.   (b) Plus Relief.   (c) Health & Communications combined.
    (d) Transport & States combined.   (e) Defence & External Relations combined.

PERSONNEL OF CENTRAL GOVERNMENT

1950–51	1951–52	1952–53	1953–54	29.1.55
		——— (e) ———	——— (e) ———	→
——— (see 4) ———→	Chanda———			Mahmud
	AYYANGAR	NEHRU (e)	——— (e) ———	KATJU
Himatsinjhi	Majithia———	Tyagi		→
		Chandra		→
PRAKASA	}AZAD———			→
				Malaviya
	Malaviya———			→
RAJAGOPALACHARI	}KATJU———		(see 2)	PANT
AYYANGAR (d)				
	Keskar———			→
	Datar———			→
——— (see 2) (d) ———→	}SHASTRI———			→
	Alagesan———			→
——— (c) ———	Chandrasekhar———			→
KAUR (c) Bahadur	RAM———			→
Tyagi———	Shah ——— (see 2) ———→ Guha			→
	}BISWAS———			Pataskar
——— (see 7) ———→	GIRI Abid Ali———			DESAI
	KIDWAI P. S. Deshmukh Krishnappa———			JAIN
Rao				→
——— (b) ———→	Bhonsle———		JAIN (see 11)	Khanna
GADGIL Burgaohain (see below)				
MAHTAB Karmarkar	SWARAN SINGH Burgaohain KRISHNAMACHARI Karmarkar———	→		
	NANDA———			Mishra
	REDDY———	Hathi———		→

NOTE.—Members of the Cabinet are given in CAPITALS. Ministers of State (who are of Cabinet rank but not actual members) and Deputy Ministers are in ordinary type.

and more coherent opposition; it is easy to see that it may become stronger, but it is not easy to see it operating as one homogeneous force under one leader. The recognition policy laid down by the Speaker is intended to help the process, without encouraging alliances based on no principle. Nevertheless, in the meantime, Government itself suffers by the lack of contact with the opposite benches. It might be better—even now, before the next elections bring their new configuration of parties—to attempt to encourage the opposition Groups to agree upon one Leader solely for the purpose of consultation on policy with the Government. Such a Leader would not, of course, be able normally to express a general and coherent opposition view, and the practical usefulness of his comments might at first be very limited. This would matter less than the fact that the Government would begin to learn the habit of consultation and the opposition would begin to feel a share of responsibility.

NOTE on the Structure and Composition of Governments (see p. 152, n. 5)

An attempt has been made in the table, pp. 156–7, to set out the changes in the structure and personnel of the Central Government.

It will be seen that the arrangement of portfolios has changed considerably from time to time, so much so that few of them have remained unaltered throughout the period. Some of the changes have been effected to meet the needs of the available personnel; the temporary combination of Transport and States under Gopalaswamy Ayyangar in 1950–51 is an example of this kind. Others have resulted from special temporary needs—such as a Minister for Minority Affairs, later combined with the Law portfolio before it eventually disappeared. Others, again, have arisen out of the developing nature of State activity; the portfolios of Production and of Planning, Irrigation and Power are obvious examples of this kind.

The structure of the Government has also undergone changes. The first post-independence Government consisted of 14 members of the Cabinet and 1 Minister of State. In the following years the number of Ministers of State (of Cabinet rank but not members of the Cabinet) was increased, and Deputy Ministers were introduced. On the eve of the General Elections of 1952 the Cabinet numbered 13, Ministers of State 6 and Deputy Ministers 7. Subsequently while the numbers of the Cabinet and Ministers of State have remained practically the same, the number of Deputies has been doubled—an indication of both the pressure of ministerial duties and the importance of creating an intermediate level of Government leaders, many of whom are younger men with chances of promotion. The same factors, it may be added, are also responsible for an increase in the numbers of Parliamentary Secretaries.

The changes in the personnel of the Government have been in part due to death or retirement—as with Patel, Ayyangar, Kidwai. Sometimes Ministers have left to become State Governors—as did Prakasa, Munshi and Diwakar. Finally, there have been the resignations on grounds of policy. These have been of two kinds. The first group occurred during 1949–51 and meant the break-up of the post-independence coalition cabinet: Mathai, S. P. Mukherjee, Neogy, Ambedkar and Baldev Singh were all men whose previous political connections with Congress were not strong. After the General Elections of 1951–52 the Government was a Congress Government. Even so, however, there have been resignations on grounds of policy: those of Giri and Krishnamachari (the latter's subsequently withdrawn) are the important examples.

In the States' Governments, too, similar changes have taken place. The rearrangements of portfolios have been very frequent and in most cases the changes appear to have been determined by personal factors.[1] While it is unnecessary to set out this part of the story, it may be useful to show the changes of personnel as a guide to the stability or otherwise of State rule. The following table shows the membership of some State Governments during each of the seven years since 1947:

TABLE XXI—MEMBERSHIP OF SOME STATE GOVERNMENTS SINCE 1947

1. Assam

	1947–48	1948–49	1949–50	1950–51	1951–52	1952–53	1953–54
Bardoloi	+	+					
Medhi	+	+	+	+	+	+	+
J. J. M. Roy	+	+	+	+	+	+	+
R. Das	+	+	+	+	+	+	+
M. Mazumdar	+	+	+	+	+	+	+
R. Brahma	+	+	+	+	+	+	+
O. K. Das	+	+	+	+	+	+	+
M. M. Tayyebulla	+	+					
Bora			+	+	+	+	+
Sarma					+	+	+
Chaudhury				+	+	+	+
B. Mookerjee					+	+	+

2. Bihar

	1947–48	1948–49	1949–50	1950–51	1951–52	1952–53	1953–54
S. K. Sinha	+	+	+	+	+	+	+
A. N. Sinha	+	+	+	+	+	+	
S. Mahmud	+	+	+	+			
J. Chaudhury	+	+	+	+			
R. Singh	+	+	+	+	+		+
B. Verma	+	+	+	+	+	+	+
K. B. Sahey	+	+	+	+	+	+	+
B. Jha	+	+	+	+			
A. Q. Ansari	+	+	+	+			

[1] See C. Jha, 'Grouping of Portfolios in State Cabinet with Special Reference to Bihar', in *Problems of Public Administration*, edited by B. B. Majumdar. Professor Jha is able to show that the arrangement of portfolios is certainly not based on any discernible principle.

2. Bihar—continued

	1947–48	1948–49	1949–50	1950–51	1951–52	1952–53	1953–54
D. N. Sinha					+	+	+
M. P. Sinha					+	+	+
S. P. Mandal					+	+	+
D. Singh					+	+	
M. Shafi					+	+	+
S. M. O. Munemi					+	+	+
B. Paswan					+	+	+
H. Mishra					+	+	+
R. C. Sinha						+	

3. Bombay

	1947–48	1948–49	1949–50	1950–51	1951–52	1952–53	1953–54
B. G. Kher	+	+	+	+			
M. Desai	+	+	+	+	+	+	+
M. D. Gilder	+	+	+	+			
D. N. Desai	+	+	+	+	+	+	+
U. L. Mehta	+	+	+	+			
L. M. Patil	+	+	+	+			
G. Nanda	+	+					
M. P. Patil	+	+	+	+	+	+	+
G. D. Vartak	+	+	+	+			
G. D. Tapase	+				+	+	+
J. N. Mehta		+	+	+	+	+	+
Naik-Nimbalkar		+	+	+	+	+	+
B. S. Hirey					+	+	+
S. H. Shah					+	+	+
Y. B. Chavan					+	+	+

4. Madhya Pradesh

	1947–48	1948–49	1949–50	1950–51	1951–52	1952–53	1953–54
R. S. Shukla	+	+	+	+	+	+	+
D. P. Mishra	+	+	+	+			
D. K. Mehta	+	+	+	+	+	+	+
S. V. Gokhale	+	+	+	+			
R. K. Patil	+					+	
W. S. Barlingay	+	+	+	+			
R. Agnibhoj	+	+	+	+			
P. K. Deshmukh	+	+	+	+	+	+	+
A. M. Kakade	+	+	+	+			
G. N. Kale		+	+	+			
D. Gupta					+	+	+
B. A. Mandloi					+	+	+
N. C. Singh					+	+	+
M. S. Kannamwar					+	+	+
B. Biyani					+	+	+
S. Tiwari					+	+	+

5. Madras

	1947–48	1948–49	1949–50	1950–51	1951–52	1952–53	1953–54
O. P. R. Reddiar	+			+			
T. S. S. Rajan	+	+	+	+			
M. Bhaktavatsalam	+	+	+	+			+
B. G. Reddi	+	+	+	+			
Gurupadham	+						
H. S. Reddi	+		+	+			
K. Chandramouli	+	+	+	+			

5. *Madras—continued*

	1947–48	1948–49	1949–50	1950–51	1951–52	1952–53	1953–54
T. S. A. Chettiyar	+						
K. M. Menon	+	+	+	+			
K. V. Rao	+						
A. B. Shetty	+	+	+	+	+	+	+
V. Kurmayya	+						
P. S. Kumuraswami Raja		+	+	+			
B. Parameswaram		+	+	+			+
N. Sanjiva Reddi		+	+				
C. P. Reddi		+	+				
J. L. P. R. Victoria		+	+	+			
Rajagopalachari					+	+	
Subramaniam					+	+	+
K. V. Naidu					+	+	
N. Ranga Reddi					+	+	
V. C. Palaniswami Gounder					+	+	
M. V. K. Rao					+	+	
U. K. Rao					+	+	
Nagana Goud					+	+	
N. Sankarra Reddi					+	+	
Manickavelu Naicker					+	+	+
K. P. K. Nair					+	+	
Raja R. Sethupathi					+	+	+
S. P. B. Rao					+	+	
D. Sanjeevayya					+	+	
K. K. Nadar							+
S. S. R. Padayachi							+

6. *Orissa*

	1947–48	1948–49	1949–50	1950–51	1951–52	1952–53	1953–54
H. Mahtab	+	+					
N. Kanungo	+	+	+	+			
L. Misra	+	+	+	+			
L. R. S. Bariha	+	+	+	+			
S. Tripathi	+	+	+	+	+	+	+
R. K. Bose	+	+	+	+			
N. K. Choudhury			+	+	+	+	+
P. M. Pradhan			+	+			
R. Rath					+	+	+
D. Sahu					+	+	
S. Soren					+	+	+
K. C. Banhj Deo					+	+	+
S. Mohanty							+
K. P. Nanda				+			

7. *E. Punjab*

	1947–48	1948–49	1949–50	1950–51	1951–52	1952–53	1953–54
G. Bhargava	+	+	+	+			
Swaran Singh	+						
Partap Singh	+						
Ranjit Singh	+		+	+			
P. Singh Azad	+	+	+	+			
G. Kartar Singh	+		+	+			
C. K. Gopal Dutt	+						
S. I. Singh Majhail			+	+			
Lenha Singh Sethi			+				
Bhim Sen Sachar		+			+	+	+
Ch. Lehri Singh		+			+	+	+

11—P.I.

7. *E. Punjab—continued*

	1947–48	1948–49	1949–50	1950–51	1951–52	1952–53	1953–54
G. Singh Bajwa		+			+	+	+
Ujjal Singh		+			+	+	+
Ram Sharma					+		
Jagat Narain					+	+	+
Ch. Sundar Singh					+	+	+
Partap Singh Kairon					+	+	+
J. Singh Mann		+					
N. Singh		+					
P. Chand		+					

8. *Uttar Pradesh*

	1947–48	1948–49	1949–50	1950–51	1951–52	1952–53	1953–54
G. P. Pant	+	+	+	+	+	+	+
H. M. Ibrahim	+	+	+	+	+	+	+
Sampurnanand	+	+	+	+	+	+	+
Hukom Singh	+	+	+	+	+	+	+
N. A. Sherwani	+	+	+				
G. Lal	+	+	+	+	+	+	+
A. G. Kher	+	+	+				
C. P. Gupta	+	+	+	+	+	+	+
L. B. Sastri	+	+	+	+			
K. D. Malviya	+	+	+				
A. Zaheer				+	+	+	+
Hargovind Singh				+	+	+	+
Cheran Singh				+	+	+	+
M. L. Gautam					+	+	+
K. Tripathi					+	+	+
V. N. Sharma					+	+	+
A. G. Kher				+			

9. *W. Bengal*

	1947–48	1948–49	1949–50	1950–51	1951–52	1952–53	1953–54
B. C. Roy	+	+	+	+	+	+	+
N. R. Sarkár	+	+	+	+			
K. S. Roy	+						
H. N. Choudhury	+	+	+	+			
P. C. Sen	+	+	+	+	+	+	+
J. N. Panja	+	+	+	+	+	+	+
B. C. Sinha	+	+	+	+			
N. B. Maity	+	+	+	+			
N. D. Mazumdar	+	+	+	+			
K. Mukherjee	+	+	+	+	+	+	+
B. Mazumdar	+	+	+	+			
H. C. Naskar	+	+	+	+	+	+	+
Mohini Mohan Barman	+	+					
Syama Prasad Barman			+	+	+	+	+
R. Ahmed			+	+	+	+	+
S. K. Basu					+	+	+
K. N. D. Gupta					+	+	+
R. Ray					+	+	+
P. Bose					+	+	+
A. K. Mukherjee					+	+	+
I. D. Jalan					+	+	+
R. Roy					+	+	+

10. *Hyderabad*

	1949–50	1950–51	1951–52	1952–53	1953–54
M. K. Vellodi	+	+			
Nawab Bahadur	+	+			
M. Seshadri	+	+			
C. V. S. Rao	+	+			
B. R. Rao	+	+	+	+	+
V. Koratkar	+				
V. B. Raju	+	+	+		
P. Gandhi	+	+	+		
D. G. Bindu			+	+	+
K. V. R. Reddy			+	+	+
V. Vidyalankar		+	+	+	+
G. S. Melkote			+	+	+
Nawab Jung			+	+	+
Chenna Reddy			+	+	+
A. Rao Ganamukhi			+	+	
J. R. Chandergi			+		
S. Dev			+	+	
D. S. Chauhan			+	+	
G. R. Ekbote					+

11. *Jammu and Kashmir*

	1948–49	1949–50	1950–51	1951–52	1952–53	1953–54
Abdullah	+	+	+	+	+	
Ghu Mohammad Bakshi	+	+	+	+	+	+
M. A. Beg	+	+	+	+	+	
Budh Singh	+	+				
G. M. Sadiq	+	+	+			+
S. L. Saraf	+	+	+	+	+	+
G. L. Dogra	+	+	+	+	+	+
P. M. Khan	+	+	+			
M. Qasim						+
D. P. Dhar			+			

12. *Madhya Bharat*

	1949–50	1950–51	1951–52	1952–53	1953–54
G. K. Vijayavargiya	+				
L. Joshi	+				
J. L. Shriva stava	+	+			
S. Pandviya	+	+	+	+	+
K. Virulkar	+				
Premsingh	+		+	+	+
S. H. Ali	+	+			
Sunnulal	+	+			
M. Gangwal		+	+	+	+
M. Mehta		+	+	+	+
V. V. Dravid			+	+	+
S. Tajoo			+	+	+
S. M. Jain				+	+
N. R. Dixit				+	+
T. Jain		+			
P. S. Rathov		+			

13. *Mysore*

	1948–49	1949–50	1950–51	1951–52	1952–53	1953–54
K. C. Reddy	+	+	+			
H. C. Dasappa	+	+	+			
K. T. Bhashyam	+	+	+			

13. *Mysore—continued*

	1948–49	1949–50	1950–51	1951–52	1952–53	1953–54
H. Siddaiya	+	+	+			
T. Mariappa	+	+	+			
R. Chennigaramiah	+	+	+			
T. Siddhalingaiah		+		+		
Hanumanthaiya				+	+	+
Siddaveerappa				+	+	+
A. G. R. Rao				+	+	+
T. Channiah				+	+	+
K. Manjappa				+	+	+
R. N. Gowda						+
J. M. Shariff	+					
Chandresekharaiya	+					
P. S. Chetty	+					

14. *Rajasthan*

	1948–49	1949–50	1950–51	1951–52	1952–53	1953–54
H. Shastri	+	+				
S. Ram	+	+				
P. N. Mathur	+	+				
S. Dhadha	+	+				
R. H. Singh	+	+				
B. Baya	+	+				
N. Kachhwaha	+	+				
P. Bafna	+	+				
V. Tyagi	+	+				
R. D. Goyal	+	+				
T. R. Paliwal			+	+		+
M. L. Sukhadia			+	+	+	+
B. Nath				+	+	+
B. L. Pandya				+	+	+
R. K. Vyas				+		
N. R. Mirdha				+		
A. L. Yadav			+	+	+	+
R. K. Joshi				+	+	+
J. N. Vyas				+	+	+
K. Arya				+	+	+
J. K. Chaturvedi				+		
B. S. Mehta				+		
M. D. Mathur				+		
B. S. Sharma				+		
N. L. Joshi				+		
J. Singh				+		

15. *Saurashtra*

	1948–49	1949–50	1950–51	1951–52	1952–53	1953–54
U. N. Dhebar	+	+	+	+	+	+
D. Dave		+	+	+	+	+
R. U. Parikh	+	+	+	+	+	+
G. Kotak	+	+	+	+		
M. Shah	+	+	+	+	+	+
K. Modi				+	+	+
G. C. Oza				+	+	+
R. M. Adani				+	+	+
B. Mehta	+					
S. Gandhi	+					
J. Parikh	+					

16. *Travancore-Cochin*

	1948–49	1949–50	1950–51	1951–52	1952–53	1953–54
C. Keshavan .			+			
T. K. N. Pillai	+	+	+			
P. G. Menon .	+	+		+	+	
A. J. John .	+	+	+	+	+	
N. Kunjuruman	+	+				
E. J. Philipose	+	+				
T. M. Varghese				+	+	
Kalalhil				+		
V. Madhavan				+	+	
K. Kochukuttan				+	+	
A. C. Nadar .				+	+	
K. V. Nair .					+	
A. T. Pillai .						+
P. S. N. Pillai						+
A. Atchuthan						+
P. K. Kunju .						+
E. E. Warrior	+					
K. Aiyappan .	+					
T. A. Abdulla	+					
A. Mascrene .	+					

It will be seen that in many States, Cabinet changes have been frequent. Sometimes these are the results of changes in the party complexion of the Government—as in Travancore-Cochin in 1953–54. Sometimes the changes are signs of movements within the ruling Congress Party—as in Rajasthan and Madras. Even in the stable States, such as Bombay and Uttar Pradesh, the 1952 General Elections occasioned some ministerial changes.

CHAPTER FOUR

PARTIES AND PARLIAMENT

A PARLIAMENT of Independents, however improbable, is not wholly inconceivable; what cannot be imagined is that they would for long remain independent. An Independent member of the Indian Parliament, questioned as to the way he worked in the House of the People, replied without hesitation: 'The first thing you have to understand is that a number of us Independents have formed a group.' The great majority of members, however, do not have to create parties; they are elected in a dual capacity as representing both a constituency and a party, and they are part of a group before they reach Parliament House. To describe the working of Parliament—even in strictly procedural terms—without first analysing the life of each group which makes up the whole would be certainly difficult and surely misleading.

Parliamentary groups vary in character according as they approximate to one or other of two theoretical models: first, the group whose political world is identical with or at least no greater than the world of Parliament itself, and whose activity is confined to the Chamber and its precincts; second, the group which is no more than a part of a larger political organisation. The main groups in Indian legislatures are of the second type, and we have therefore first to examine the relation of these parliamentary groups to the parties to which they belong. The comparative study of political institutions has already shown that there is room for much variety even in this second type; the parliamentary group may be anything from an obedient wing of the main body to its very heart. Even the limited comparisons which can be made within British political life point to some measure of contrast.[1] We should therefore not assume that the pattern of each party in India is identical, nor that it is unchanging.

1. Party Organisation and the Parliamentary Party

There are sufficient reasons for devoting first place and most of our attention to the Congress Party. Its dominating parliamentary position ensures that the internal rules and conventions it develops have a decisive bearing on the working of parliament in India. Secondly, these rules and conventions serve willy-nilly as models for many of the other parties. Finally, as the senior and largest political party, it has left com-

[1] At least in theory; actual behaviour varies less. See R. T. Mackenzie, *British Political Parties* (1954), and Bulmer-Thomas, *The Party System in Britain* (1953).

paratively little in its constitution to the mercy of *ad hoc* arrangements, and the relations between its several parts are open to public scrutiny and comment.

The Congress Party has, in the course of its seventy years' existence, changed its character in radical fashion, and its constitution has had to try to reflect this changing nature.[1] Although the movement was initiated in 1885, it was not until 1899 that it gave itself a formal constitution.[2] The object of the Congress was 'to promote by constitutional means the interests and well-being of the people of the Indian Empire'. The organisation was in a rudimentary stage: the Congress itself was a body of 'delegates elected by political associations or other bodies, and by public meetings', and it was to meet two or three times a year. There was an Indian Congress Committee of 45 members chosen on the basis of recommendations from the Provinces and consisting of a fixed number from each Province. Provincial Congress Committees were to be organised 'for the purpose of carrying on the work of political education, on lines of general appreciation of British rule and of constitutional action for the removal of its defects'. There was also a 'British Congress Committee' in England 'to represent there the interests of the Indian National Congress'.

Following the development of nationalist sentiments and the breakaway of the 'extremists' in 1907, the new constitution of 1908 restated the objects of the Congress:

(i) the attainment by India of self-government similar to that enjoyed by the self-governing members of the British Empire and participation by her in the rights and responsibilities of the Empire on equal terms with those members; (ii) the advance towards this goal to be by strictly constitutional means by bringing about a steady reform of the existing system of administration and promoting national unity, fostering public spirit and developing and organising the intellectual, moral, economic and industrial resources of the country.

At the same time, the movement's organisation was elaborated. The All-India Congress Committee emerges at the top of a hierarchy which now reaches down through Provincial to District and even Taluka Congress Committees. The Congress itself is to meet annually, and the delegates now have to pay a Rs.20/– fee (reduced to Rs.10/– in 1915), half the

[1] See N. V. Rajkumar, *Development of the Congress Constitution* (Delhi, 1949).

[2] There were, of course, resolutions before this date which set out various rules of procedure. One of these, No. XIII of 1888, is of peculiar interest: it was 'resolved that no subject shall be passed for discussion by the Subjects Committee or allowed to be discussed at any Congress by the President thereof, to the introduction of which the Hindu or Mohammedan Delegates as a body object unanimously or nearly unanimously'. The popular tendency to attribute communal politics to the British—and in particular to the introduction of separate electorates in 1909—would seem to overlook evidence of this kind which shows that the national movement was very aware of the importance of communal sentiments.

proceeds of which were to be sent to London for the use of the British Committee.

The transformation of the Congress at the end of the First World War is reflected in the new constitution of 1920; a refined liberal pressure group of middle-class gentlemen sets out to be a mass movement with a single clear aim: 'the attainment of Swarajya (independence) by the people of India by all legitimate and peaceful means'. The Provincial Congress Committees, now organised on the basis of linguistic areas, are delegate bodies chosen so that one member represents 50,000 inhabitants. The A.I.C.C. expands to 350 members, and the daily direction of the political struggle is entrusted to the new Working Committee appointed by it. The British Committee disappears and the funds are divided between the A.I.C.C. and the P.C.C.s. The rather substantial fees of the pre-war period give way to a simple 4-anna subscription. Gandhi's influence was also evident in certain amendments of the 1920s. An attempt was made in 1924 to replace the 4-anna path of entry by a 'yarn franchise': 'no one shall be a member of any Congress Committee or organisation who does not wear hand-spun and hand-woven *khaddar* at political and Congress functions and does not make a contribution of 24,000 yards of evenly-spun yarn per year of his or her own spinning'. This harsh test was a year later allowed to be simply an alternative to the money subscription. The last pre-independence Congress constitution, that of 1934, made further attempts to increase the mass following while retaining the more difficult qualifications for an *élite* within the organisation. Thus, Primary Committees were set up for enrolment purposes. At the same time, those elected as delegates had to perform, for six months prior to election, some manual labour 'equal in value to 500 yards per month of well-spun yarn of over 10 counts and equal in time to 8 hours per month'. The most interesting change in the higher levels of the organisation related to the Working Committee: this was to be no longer chosen by the A.I.C.C., but instead to be appointed by the President of the Congress. The debating society had become a disciplined political power.

With the achievement of independence, the object of Congress had to be restated. 'If the Congress had achieved all its objectives there would be no purpose in its continuing,' Pandit Nehru remarked on one occasion.[1] 'But it has achieved only one objective—no doubt, a major objective. The other major objective has been economic. . . .' Article 1 of the new constitution of the party states that 'the object of the Indian National Congress is the well-being and advancement of the people of India and the establishment in India, by peaceful and legitimate means, of a Co-operative Commonwealth based on equality of opportunity and

[1] Speech at the Political Conference of Tamilnad Congress workers in Oct. 1954 (*Congress Bulletin*, Oct.–Nov. 1953).

of political, economic and social rights and aiming at world peace and fellowship'. It was, however, less the restated object than the conquest of power which changed the character of the Congress after 1947. For one thing, of course, the transformation of a national movement for independence into a political party, at least potentially one among many, demanded radical adjustment of ideas on the part of the leaders—and especially those whose work, in legislatures for example, brought them in continuous contact with other parties. For the organisation as a whole, however, this aspect was less important than another: even if Congress were now 'only' a political party, it was—and much more obviously—*the* political party, the only one that mattered as an instrument of power. In consequence, the character of the party became heterogeneous in a new way.

Already before 1947, Congress had under Gandhi's guidance developed two sides to its nature: it was a broad political movement with the usual functions of agitation and education; it was, at the same time, a social service organisation through which 'constructive work' could be done to improve the lot of the downtrodden. It was Gandhi's idea that after 1947 this second aspect alone should remain. Congress should cast aside its political personality and blossom forth as a 'Lok Sewak Sangh', a society for the service of the people. The political field should be left to new and purely political organisations. This did not happen. The Congress which had demanded the transfer of power had to accept the power transferred. The two personalities had been welded into one over the years and could not now be divorced.[1] To these two personalities, the achievement of unquestioned power now added a third: the party as government. It is no doubt a great over-simplification to say that 'in pre-Independence days it was those who were ready to suffer and sacrifice who joined the Congress'[2]; since Congress represented a moral as well as a political ideal and offered a number of alternative forms of action, it attracted a wide variety of idealists and rebels. It is certainly true, however, that 'since Independence, because of the lure of offices, self-seeking people too entered the portals of this organisation'.[3] The

[1] The possession of this social service aspect makes it difficult for the leaders to accept the end of the national movement. Even Pandit Nehru, who understands and welcomes the need for opposition, is reluctant to admit that the corollary must be the reduction of the Congress to a 'mere' political party. In a speech delivered in 1954 he said: 'The Congress necessarily has to function as an electoral organisation, but that is not its only or its most important task. It has been our proud privilege to be soldiers in a mighty national movement which brought freedom to this country. We cannot allow Congress to shrink now into just an electoral organisation. . . . Our party organisation must be something more than a party. It must win confidence and respect by patient and self-sacrificing service, and thus live in the hearts of our people.' (Report in *The Statesman*, 23 Jan. 1954.) This is, indeed, a real problem: India has a great need for nation-wide social service organisations to undertake social welfare work which the State cannot wholly cope with; yet the only substantial body already experienced in the task is the leading political party.

[2] *Report of the General Secretaries of Congress, October 1951–January 1953*, p. 25.

[3] *Ibid.*

rush of this kind was all the greater because it was evident that Congress had no real rivals. Moreover, in India employment opportunities are out of gear with the demands created by the educational system; the political world too thus becomes overcrowded. Many of the references to India as a one-party state are grossly unfair and misleading, but at least in this respect the phrase has a validity: Congress was widely understood to be the high road to influence, office and power. The development of this third facet of the Congress Party must be seen not only from the viewpoint of the man seeking a career; it has another aspect as seen from the position of the leaders. To a Congress Minister, the party organisation appears as a support for the policies of the Government. This situation is not, of course, peculiar to India; rather it is normal. Yet it had a special importance in India. For one thing, it was a novel position for an Indian political party. For another, the programme of national reconstruction which had to be undertaken called for widespread public understanding and mass effort if it was to be successful.[1] It seemed as if Congress had not only to provide a road to power but also to constitute itself an arm of the administration.

These developments have brought with them a number of difficulties and problems of organisation. Some of the most troublesome of these relate to membership of the party. The constitution of 1948 was in effect a new one; yet it has had to be amended in 1950, 1952 and 1953—and on each occasion the question of membership has been central. In 1948 the demand for entry to the Congress was heavy, and the leadership was anxious to have a broad basis of support in the country for its measures. The doors were thrown open and party workers vied with each other to produce, in one way or another, impressive figures of numbers recruited. The result was a mass intake so large that the organisation was barely able to digest it. Nearly 30 million primary members were enrolled by the end of 1949, and even the more exacting categories of qualified and effective members numbered several hundred thousands. In these circumstances, not unnaturally, strange things happened. 'In certain cases', the official report admits,[2] 'fraudulent enrolment was apparent. One district made history by enrolling 400,000 effective members. In certain villages enrolment exceeded the adult population and in a few cases even exceeded the total population of the village.' The management of the party's elections proved practically impossible and serious abuses were quite common. The same official report puts the matter very mildly when it remarks that 'indeed it was a bold venture to make this attempt to hold elections on a mass scale through non-official agencies and with inadequate re-

---

[1] The relations between the British Labour Party and the trade union movement during 1945–51 may afford some basis of comparison.

[2] *Report of the General Secretaries, January 1949–September 1950*, p. 78.

sources'.[1] In 1950 a fee for primary membership was reintroduced and fixed at the relatively high level of one rupee. At the same time, a qualifying period of two years as primary member was laid down as one of the conditions of 'effective' membership. Two years later, the fee was reduced to 4 annas and the two-year qualifying period removed.

Of greater interest to our present study is the impact of the changed character of Congress on the relations between the different organs of the party and on relations between these organs on the one hand and those of the state on the other. The party institutions were set out in its constitution[2] and must first be briefly described. Both primary and active members of the party are organised in party constituencies of not less than 500 primary members and corresponding so far as possible to areas with a population of 100,000. Each constituency is entitled to elect one delegate to the Annual Session of the Congress, but only active members may be candidates in these elections.[3] This body of delegates is the core of the party and numbered, in January 1953, for example, 3,561. The country is divided into twenty-six areas called Pradeshes, which generally but not invariably correspond to the States created in the Indian Constitution.[4] The delegates within the Pradesh area constitute the Pradesh Congress Committee, while below the Pradesh there

[1] *Ibid.*, p. 82. The careful preparations and conduct of the General Elections two years later may have owed something to the leaders' chastening experience of the party elections. They owed much more, of course, to the work of the administration. The party's own elections in 1952 were again not well conducted. *The Report of the General Secretaries, January 1953–January 1954* reveals that 'lots of complaints regarding the irregularities and malpractices in the Congress elections poured into the All-India Congress Committee office.... The office looked into these complaints and sent special representatives to investigate.... The investigation in Bihar showed that of a total of 2,100,000 primary members there, no less than about 1,000,000 were irregularly enrolled.

[2] *Constitution of the Indian National Conference* (as amended in July 1953) and *Rules for Various Articles of the Congress Constitution* (1953).

[3] The conditions for active membership are much more exacting than those for primary membership and show the continuing importance of Gandhian tenets. Thus while a primary member need only pay four annas and declare that he is over 18, accepts the object of the party and belongs to no separate political party, an active member has to pay one rupee and sign an eight-point declaration: 'I am of the age of 21 or over; I am a habitual weaver of hand-spun and hand-woven Khadi; I am a teetotaller; I do not observe or recognise untouchability in any shape or form; I believe in equality of opportunity and status for all, irrespective of race, caste, creed or sex; I am a believer in inter-communal unity and have respect for the faith of others; I devote part of my time regularly to some form of national, community or social service otherwise than for personal profit, or to some constructive activity [here 20 alternatives are listed, including the organisation of peasants or labour or students, adult education, village sanitation and the uplift of women] and will send periodical reports on my work . . .; I shall collect ten rupees annually and pay it towards the Congress Reserve Fund.'

[4] The Congress Pradesh has always taken more account of linguistic differences than the administrative State has done; Andhra had its Pradesh in the party structure before it gained its recognition as a State. The party structure may thus point the future pattern of States in India; the present State of Bombay is divided for party purposes into no less than four units—Maharashtra, Gujerat, Karnatak and Bombay City. On the other hand, sometimes the party structure has fallen in line with changing State divisions; the former Pradesh of Kerala was in 1952 divided into two, one for Travancore-Cochin and one for Malabar.

are similarly constituted District and Mandal (or Taluka) Congress
Committees.[1] The delegates in every Pradesh meet to elect from among
themselves one-eighth of their number as members of the All-India Congress Committee. They also meet in this way to choose the President of
the Congress, whose term of office—and that of all the Congress committees—is two years. 'The highest executive authority of the Congress',
charged with the implementation of policy and responsible to the
A.I.C.C., is the Congress Working Committee. This body, often referred to as the 'Congress High Command', consists of the President
and twenty members nominated by him. These must include the
Treasurer and one or more General Secretaries, and will ordinarily be
drawn from members of the A.I.C.C. The Working Committee enjoys
wide powers by constitutional provision and by conventional practice.
Among its functions is the setting up of the Parliamentary Board consisting of the President as Chairman and five other members. This Board
is to 'regulate and co-ordinate the parliamentary activities of the Congress Legislature Parties'. For the purpose of conducting election campaigns and selecting candidates for Centre and State legislatures, the
Board (with the addition of five members elected by the A.I.C.C.) constitutes itself into the Central Election Committee.

It is with these organs then that we are concerned if we wish to enquire into the relations between Congress as government and Congress
as party. The story may begin before a government is actually chosen,
for certain features of the party as a candidate for power have a bearing
on its subsequent behaviour. The elections of 1952, the first to be held
on adult franchise and the first after independence, were not only a
headache to the administrator; they were, for all parties, an adventure
into the unknown. The Congress realised that a great deal depended on
how it chose its candidates. On the one hand, if its prestige and strength
were going to return it in overwhelming numbers to the legislatures, it
was important that its men should be of such a calibre as would make
them valuable members of such bodies, able to contribute to the debate
of policies and to furnish the personnel of governments. On the other
hand, if there was to be a serious challenge from the other parties, it
would be wise to choose men of influence in the constituencies. Again,
in the selection of candidates a due balance had to be maintained between the reward for services given and sacrifices made in the past and
the admission of fresh youthful zeal needed to rejuvenate the party.
'Candidates', said the Central Election Committee, 'should be chosen
with great care and should be men and women of integrity who, by their
past record and present professions, have shown that they believe in and
act up to the principles and objectives proclaimed on behalf of the Con-

[1] In some of the areas of former princely states, District Committees had not yet been
established in early 1954.

gress. In particular, care should be taken that the choice of suitable candidates is not affected by the predominance of any group or clique in the area.'[1] The procedure for selection certainly demonstrated this intention to choose with care. Applications were invited by the Pradesh Congress Committees from candidates for both Centre and State legislatures. Applicants did not need to be members of the party—'The test', Pandit Nehru said, 'must be "integrity first, integrity second and integrity third", integrity and ability.'[2] The Pradesh Congress Committees set up Election Committees which consulted with district party leaders, sometimes interviewed candidates and finally made recommendations to the Central Election Committee. The list of candidates thus recommended was made known and appeals and objections were also to be sent to the Central Committee. This machinery, however, was almost thrown out of gear by the pressure of work. For the 3,769 seats in all legislatures, about 25,000 applications were received. What was worse, they were quickly followed by over 100,000 appeals and objections. 'Thousands of letters and hundreds of telegrams poured into the [Delhi] office every day'[3]—there to be scrutinised along with the recommendations. The volume of applications illustrates well the extent to which Congress was generally accepted—in spite of the uncertainties of adult franchise—as the way to importance. The fact that less than one in six could be chosen meant inevitably a number of disappointed men. Yet the procedure can perhaps also be blamed, since it presented unrivalled opportunities for that factionalism among Congressmen which was above all to be avoided.[4] The broad avenues laid down for complaints and objections did not greatly aid the selection, but they did tend to ensure that disappointment should quickly become discontent. Thus, before the perhaps unavoidable tension between government and party could begin, the ground was prepared by an antagonism between the chosen (most of whom were to be legislators, and many Ministers) and the rejected (who would be expected to continue as party devotees).

In fact, of course, difficulties between the Congress Government and the Congress Party had been encountered long before the election. To

[1] Resolution of 14 July 1951, quoted in *Report of the General Secretaries, October 1951–January 1953*, p. 13.
[2] Quoted in M. Venkatarangaiya, *The General Election in Bombay City*, p. 33. One chapter of the book is devoted to the selection of candidates.
[3] *Report of the General Secretaries, October 1951–January 1953*, p. 15.
[4] Rather more high-powered interviewing and rather less documentation and hearing of 'evidence' might have been better. One respected Congressman was reported to have observed: 'Evidence, oral and documentary, is being piled up; at least some of it is reported to be forged. Every attempt is being made to drag the reputation of one's rivals into the mud. The ghastly part of it all is that such complaints are patiently heard and registered. Nothing can be more degrading. No one's reputation is safe in such circumstances. And such a habit grows. This game of mud-slinging will continue after the elections. To me this seems to lead to disintegration.' (Mr. Sampurnanand, quoted in Venkatarangaiya, *op. cit.*, p. 39.) The prophetic sentences at least have proved true.

go no further back than the transfer of power and to speak first of the position at the Centre,[1] it is only necessary to recall the protests made by Acharya Kripalani during his period of office (1947–48) as Congress President. Here, he complained, was a Congress Government which took vital policy decisions without consultation with the elected head of the party itself. When the Presidentship went, in 1949, to Dr. Sitaramayya, relations appeared to calm down considerably—probably less on account of any increased consultation than because the clash of temperaments was less marked, the Doctor's sphere of interests did not overlap so much with those of the government and the stature of the Prime Minister was growing apace. Nevertheless, there was held a Secret Session of the A.I.C.C. in May 1949 for 'a frank discussion on the activities of Congress Ministries and the possibilities of developing intimate contact between the Ministry and the Congress Organisation' —and there is no reason to suppose that attention was devoted to the position in States to the exclusion of that at the Centre. In any event, it is not clear that any great change was effected by the meeting: 'An over-all survey was made and the practical difficulties that were experienced in working out the Congress programme through administrative and legislative methods were placed before the Conference. There was a genuine attempt to assess the situation and to make suggestions for taking recourse to better constructive efforts.'[2] It may not be wrong to suppose that the party's non-governmental leaders were told the facts of ministerial life and went away, still sadder but at least also somewhat wiser men. The period that followed—from September 1950 to October 1951—might be called without facetiousness the *annus horribilis* of the Congress and without over-dramatisation its year of serious crisis. So preoccupied, indeed, was the party with its internal strains and stresses[3] that it had little time to worry about relations between government and party. The election of the orthodox Tandon as President of the Congress, the closeness of the contest between him and the more radical

[1] The Congress Provincial Governments of 1937–39 were notoriously subject to instructions from the High Command at Delhi. (See R. Coupland, *The Indian Problem*, Chap. X.) Their position, however, was quite special. They were influenced by the Working Committee partly because the main party leaders were on that committee and not in the governments, and partly because not even ministerial Congressmen could feel that the conduct of government had any importance by the side of the national struggle for freedom. See above, pp. 67–70.

[2] *Report of the General Secretaries, January 1949–September 1950*, p. 30.

[3] The *Report of the General Secretaries, September 1950–October 1951* is a significantly brief document compared with others in the series. Yet it does not hide the situation. 'A little over a year has passed since the Congress met at Nasik under the presidentship of Shri Purushottamdas Tandon. This period has been one of great stress and anxiety. . . . The Congress has weathered many a storm. . . . Fissiparous tendencies developed within the Organisation. Several prominent Congressmen from time to time expressed dissatisfaction at the manner in which the Organisation was functioning. Fears were also expressed that undesirable elements were creeping into the Congress' (p. 1).

Kripalani,[1] the death (in December 1950) of Sardar Patel, who had done so much to hold together the different forces—all this sharpened what were perhaps inevitable clashes of political view. But the resolution of the party's internal difficulties at the same time did much to ease party-government tension. In May 1951, Kripalani, after an attempt to create within Congress a Democratic Front, resigned to establish his own Kisan Mazdoor Praja (K.M.P.) Party. Even more important were the events of September of that year. Pandit Nehru determined to bring matters to a head by submitting his own resignation from the Working Committee. This direct challenge to Tandon succeeded; other resignations from the Committee quickly followed and finally Tandon himself resigned. The A.I.C.C. then elected Nehru President without contest.

Only a few years ago, the possession by one person of the two positions of Prime Minister and Congress President would have been thought both improper and impossible. Yet it has proved possible, has been widely accepted as natural and has certainly made life easier for both the Government and the party.[2] The success of the new arrangement owes much to Pandit Nehru's ability and capacity for work, and even more to his popularity in the party and in the country as a whole. At the same time, it may indicate the reduced importance and influence —as an independent body—of the Congress Party; it may be taken, in other words, as a sign of the final transformation of a national movement into a political party. Certainly it is not easy to see how the former practice could return even should it be for some reason desired. The world of the party by itself no longer holds the centre of the stage; a glance at the list of members of the Working Committee reveals no names of possible future Presidents—other than those of men who are already Union or State Ministers. When a party is in power, the centre of political gravity shifts from the party organs to the Cabinet.[3]

---

[1] There were three candidates. Of the 2,600 valid votes, Tandon got 1,306—only 6 more than the 50% necessary for election on the first count. Kripalani secured 1,092 and Shankarrao Deo 202, and it is likely that on a second count the votes of the latter would have gone mainly to Kripalani. (*Report of the General Secretaries, January 1949–September 1950*, p. 83.)

[2] There may be some critics of the arrangement. Pandit Nehru in his Presidential Address to the Congress in Jan. 1953 said that 'he agreed entirely with those friends and comrades who objected to the high offices of Prime Minister and Congress President being held by one and the same person . . .'. Yet one cannot help suspecting that this was more in the nature of a tribute to a past idea. He indicated the bulk of Congress opinion when he went on to say: 'but he could not say "No" to so many of his valued colleagues.' (The *Report of the General Secretaries, January 1953–January 1954*, p. 2.) He had been re-elected, again without contest, at the end of 1952.

[3] These lines were written before Pandit Nehru announced (in Oct. 1954) his desire to be relieved of some of his several responsibilities and in particular of the party presidentship. It does not seem, however, that they require revision. Pandit Nehru's chosen successor as President is a sincere and devoted Congressman, but not a man who is likely to question the boundaries laid down by the Prime Minister between party and Government.

The establishment of a link at the apex of government and party has proved decisive. It is, however, by no means the only link. There had from 1947 always been some Ministers who were members of the Working Committee, but the party had jealously insisted that the proportion of Ministers (State as well as Centre) should never exceed one-third. In September 1952 the limit was removed. The Working Committee for 1953, for example, contained among its 21 members no less than 10 Ministers—4 of the Union Cabinet, 6 Chief Ministers of States.[1] Moreover, it is quite usual for one or two other members of the Union Ministry to be invited to attend meetings where topics falling within the sphere of their departments are to be discussed. The monthly meetings of the Working Committee, held as they are at the Prime Minister's residence and under his chairmanship, are very far from being assemblies of party bosses or political agitators out of touch with the responsibilities of government. Of the items on the agenda, often as many as half have no connection with internal party affairs—and in terms of time taken, party matters are almost certainly more quickly disposed of. The main attention is on matters of national policy and developments in State politics, though the discussion is naturally in predominantly party terms and thus differs from that which takes places on identical subjects in the Cabinet.[2]

This overlapping of membership between party and governmental or State organs is one of the ways in which tension can be most easily lessened, and the system is to be found also below the level of Working Committee. It is not always easy in a democracy to get party committee members into the legislative or executive organs of government, but it is always possible to keep those party members whose main sphere of activity is governmental in touch with party life. To some extent this would no doubt happen even in the absence of special arrangements. During 1952–53, however, the Congress introduced in its constitution a new category of associate membership which is designed specifically to achieve this end. Under the new rules, all Congress members of the Union Parliament are associate members of the Pradesh and District

---

[1] This proportion becomes even more impressive if it is added to that of the remaining 11, 3 were the General Secretaries (and these were M.P.s), 2 more were M.P.s, leaving only 6 who were party leaders pure and simple, in fact Presidents of Pradesh Congress Committees.

[2] Cf. H. Morrison, *Government and Parliament*, p. 10: 'At the formal Cabinet meetings with the Cabinet Secretariat present, the cruder aspects of party electoral and parliamentary tactics and the internal problems of the party in power are not discussed more than is necessary.' Some examples of Working Committee agendas may be of interest. The Sept. 1953 meeting (in fact, three meetings lasting in all about seven hours over a weekend) heard a review of the international situation by the Prime Minister and discussed, among other topics, the political situation in Travancore-Cochin and in Andhra, the terms of reference of the States Reorganisation Commission, an analysis of by-election results, legal and administrative reforms contemplated by the Government and the abolition of Legislative Councils in the States.

Congress Committees in their constituencies.[1] Those of the M.P.s who are on the Executive of the Congress Parliamentary Party[2] are further awarded associate membership of the A.I.C.C. In a similar way, Congress members of State Legislative Assemblies are associate members of District Congress Committees, while those who are on the Executive of a Congress Legislative Party in a State are in addition associate members of the Pradesh Congress Committee. These arrangements are no doubt useful, though time and space are surely limiting factors, especially for the member of the Union Parliament; the sessions get longer rather than shorter, and his region can only be visited in the recess.[3] On the other hand, the Congress Party during 1953 began a campaign to get its M.P.s more acquainted with their constituencies. Apart from its value from the point of view of explaining party policy and gathering public opinion and popular grievances, the campaign owes something also to the desire to bring the party legislator closer to the party organs in the States and Districts. 'We thought that such a programme would create the necessary enthusiasm among the Congress Party workers in the States.'[4]

Relations between party and parliamentary groups at the Centre can be understood by following further the extent of overlapping membership. The Congress Party in Parliament has 11 office-bearers and an Executive Committee of 20, and almost every one of these occupies a place on some committee in the party hierarchy. More significant is the extent to which the office-bearers of the party in Parliament are office-bearers of the Congress organisation (see p. 178).[5]

In these circumstances it is not surprising that the party's Parliamentary Board (which in 1953 consisted of 3 of the above, 2 Chief Ministers of States and 1 other Union Minister) should have had to spend very little of its energies on problems of liaison at the Centre. It needed in any case all the time it could afford for the consideration of these problems in the various States.

It will not be too much to say that, apart from the time of the troubles in 1951 to which we have already referred, the most crippling defect of

[1] There is a proviso that no M.P. can be an associate member unless he has been a primary member for two years and is now an active member. Associate members of party committees have no right to vote.

[2] See below, p. 187.

[3] Those with constituencies near Delhi are better placed. But it is also a matter of personal temperament; Mr. Kidwai, Union Food Minister until his death at the end of 1953, would no doubt have been active in the party politics of his State even if it had not been U.P. and thus on the doorstep of Delhi. Mr. Kidwai was a member of the Executive Council of the U.P. Pradesh Congress Committee.

[4] *Report of the Congress Party in Parliament for 1952–53*, p. 14. It is not easy to judge whether it has been wholly successful in this part of its object. Some local party officials appeared pleased but others were less impressed by the visitors from Delhi.

[5] This was the position in 1953. There is no reason to suppose that the overlapping will be much less marked in future.

Name	Office in the Congress Party in Parliament	Office in the Congress Party
Pandit Jawaharlal Nehru .	Leader	President
Maulana Azad . . .	Deputy Leader	Senior Member of Working Committee
Satyanarain Sinha .	Chief Whip	—
Harekrushna Mahtab .	Secretary General	—
Balwantray Mehta .	Secretary	General Secretary
Shiva Rao . .	Secretary	—
Amarnath Aggarwal .	Secretary	—
R. R. Morarka . .	Treasurer	—
U. S. Malliah . .	Deputy Chief Whip	General Secretary
D. K. Borooah . .	Deputy Chief Whip	Member, Working Committee
Amolak Chand . .	Deputy Chief Whip	—

the Congress since the transfer of power has been quarrelling within the States and in particular between State Ministers on the one hand and Pradesh Congress Committees on the other. Already by 1949, a number of cases had arisen which were serious enough to damage State government and necessitate the active intervention of the party's central organs. Congress affairs in West Bengal had reached such a state in 1949 that the Working Committee had to hear representations from sections of the party in the State, and Pandit Nehru courageously visited Calcutta to study and try to deal with the explosive situation.[1] In Madras, one group of Congressmen levelled charges against the Congress Government of the State—and did so in the public forum of the Madras Legislative Assembly. The Working Committee ordered an enquiry but could find no case worth further investigation. The critics were not so easily silenced and again moved a motion in the Assembly; only a threat of disciplinary action caused them to withdraw.[2] East Punjab, recovering with difficulty from the chaos of partition and its accompaniment, found stable government denied to it by party dissensions. Dr. Gopichand Bhargava formed the first government after being unanimously elected leader of the party. But within a fortnight a vote of no confidence in him by the party was carried and he was replaced by Mr. Bhim Sen Sachar. The Congress Parliamentary Board instructed the new Premier on the composition of his Cabinet and for the sake of unity insisted on the inclusion of Bhargava. Very soon, however, Bhargava made complaints to the Board and secured signatures for a memorandum condemning the Premier's actions. The Board then instructed the

[1] 'Explosive' is meant literally; this was the occasion when a bomb was thrown while Nehru was addressing a crowd.

[2] Even this proved temporary. The attacks began again in 1950 and Mr. Prakasam, the leader of the group, eventually joined Kripalani's K.M.P. Party. It was he, however, who in 1953 was persuaded to head the Congress Ministry in the new State of Andhra (see p. 111 above). At the end of 1954, he rejoined the Congress.

Premier to seek a vote of confidence from the party. On his failing to achieve this, he resigned and Bhargava returned.[1] During the same year, similar troubles disturbed Uttar Pradesh and Travancore-Cochin, leading in the first case to the expulsion of a group by the Working Committee and in the second to a dissident bloc which eventually joined the K.M.P.

The party's leaders tried to tackle the problem from both sides. On the one hand, the Working Committee directed that Pradesh Congress Committees were not to pass no-confidence motions against their Congress Ministries; any complaints should be brought to the notice of the Parliamentary Board. Similarly, party members in Assemblies who had grievances against Ministers should refer in the first instance to the Leader of the Party in the Assembly and if necessary to the Board. On the other hand, attempts were made to persuade State Ministries to take their parties into greater confidence. At a conference in 1949 of Presidents and Secretaries of Pradesh Congress Committees, 'it was felt necessary that the P.C.C.'s and legislative parties must have closer contact established through a liaison office. Regular joint sittings might be arranged', and important Bills could be discussed in this way before they were introduced in the Legislatures.[2] The Congress President of the day issued a directive to all P.C.C.s and Chief Ministers suggesting that the State Governments should place before the P.C.C.s their legislative programme and proposed administrative measures, and obtain recommendations and co-operative assistance. He further thought that heads of P.C.C.s might be made ex-officio members of legislative parties and that State Governments might open a complaints section for party members.[3] It is not surprising that very little came of these suggestions, some of which perhaps show little understanding of the nature of ministerial responsibility.

The departures and the expulsions from the party, especially during 1951, removed only a few of the critics. Certainly the more recent period has witnessed a continuation of similar difficulties. The dissensions may be attributed to several causes. In an earlier chapter the divisions of Indian society have been indicated as facilitating faction; the intense and newly-released struggle for power within the party since independence finds it easy to attach itself to these divisions. The instability of Congress rule in Rajasthan,[4] for example, can be traced to a combination of at

[1] Since the General Elections, Mr. Sachar has been Premier again.
[2] *Report of the General Secretaries, January 1949–September 1950*, p. 60.
[3] *Ibid.*, p. 61.
[4] In Nov. 1954 Rajasthan obtained its sixth Congress Cabinet since the State was formed in 1949, its third since the General Elections of 1952. This time the change was supervised by party headquarters. First, the central Parliamentary Board 'advised' the Chief Minister to seek a vote of confidence from the Congress Party in the State Assembly. Then one of the party's General Secretaries went to Rajasthan and arranged the secret voting which went against the Chief Minister.

least four factors: a class tension due to the recent entry into the party
of several of the feudal landowners who have preferred to jump on the
wagon instead of obstructing it; a caste tension between Rajput and Jat
which to some extent coincides with the class tension; regional rivalries
between Congressmen from the different areas of Jaipur, Udaipur,
Jodhpur—formerly separate princely states; and personal antagonisms.
'The opposition to the jagirdars', i.e., landlords', entry into the Congress', wrote an observer, 'is motivated by a strange amalgam of
factional and radical considerations. It is not easy to indicate where
radicalism shades off into caste feelings and considerations of factional
advantages.'[1] The variety of causes is paralleled only by the variety of
forms which the dissensions may take. Sometimes Cabinets have been
constituted so as to contain representatives of different groups; in these
cases, disputes occur within the Cabinet and lead to resignations or
threats of resignation. Punjab may be cited as one example. Following
disagreements in the Cabinet, the Chief Minister, Mr. Sachar, dropped
one of his colleagues, Mr. Sharma. The latter at once charged Mr.
Sachar with autocracy and the ministry as a whole with nepotism and
corruption, charges as promptly denied by the Chief Minister, who
accused Mr. Sharma of dishonesty. The battle took place on the floor of
the Assembly and presented, as one editorial comment put it, 'a spec-
tacle that must sadden those concerned to uphold parliamentary standards. . . . The public is left wondering whether all that Ministers do is
to fight among themselves.'[2] Under guidance from Delhi, the rebels
were expelled from the party. A similar incident in Bhopal a few months
later brought the Congress General Secretary to the spot and resulted in
suspensions from the party of an ex-Minister and his following. In other
States, the tussle takes place not in the Cabinet but between the Cabinet
and the Parliamentary or Assembly Party—probably because the
Cabinet has been composed of one group to the exclusion of others. Of
this variety, Madras and Delhi States supply good illustrations. In
Madras, one Congress member of the Assembly gathered the signatures
of a number of others to a document expressing want of confidence in
the Chief Minister. An attempt was made to enlist the support of the
President of the Pradesh Congress Committee, but this was not successful. Instead, the matter was taken to the Parliamentary Board which
strongly backed the Chief Minister. In this case, a threat of disciplinary
action proved sufficient. In Delhi State, on the other hand, things went
further. Signs of discontent appeared in October 1953 when a meeting
of the Assembly Party was demanded and Ministers were severely criticised for evasive answers to a number of questions such as the issue of
liquor licences and the presentation of purses to Ministers. In March

1 *The Times of India*, 12 June 1954.
2 *The Times of India*, 12 Oct. 1953.

1954, after a brief lull, fighting broke out again and the Party Leader in the Assembly suspended one member. The Parliamentary Board undertook an investigation and ordered that the suspension order should be kept pending until Pandit Nehru had had an opportunity to hear both Ministers and critics. In June 1954 the order was confirmed, and the Congress President took advantage of the occasion to deliver some general advice on behaviour and discipline.[1]

The most bitter struggles, however, seem to be those that take the form of conflict between the ministry on the one hand, with or without the support of the Assembly Party, and the leaders of the Pradesh Congress Committees on the other. Here the two classic cases of recent years are furnished by Mysore and Hyderabad. In Hyderabad the conflict between the political parties was, during 1953, quite overshadowed by the battles that took place between the ministry and the leadership of the Pradesh Congress Committee, battles that in this case—most unusually—owed something to an ideological cleavage between Right (in the Government) and Left (in the party organisation). The main participants were called to a meeting of the Parliamentary Board in Delhi in October, and the P.C.C. President, Swami Ramanand Tirth, was invited to state all his charges. The Board found that although these charges had been given great publicity, in the press and in the public speeches of the P.C.C. leaders, they lacked substance, and those concerned were reprimanded for behaving with lack of discipline and decorum.[2] Yet, as has happened not infrequently, it required even more pointed intervention on the part of Pandit Nehru before the voices of dissent were stilled. Only after he had visited the State and ordered a secret vote in the Legislature Party and in the P.C.C. was a semblance of peace restored. The troubles in Mysore have been of a similar character and have proved if anything even more resistant to treatment.[3] As usual, the Party's General Secretary visited the State and conferred with both leaders, Mr. Hanumanthaiya, the Chief Minister, and Mr. Veeranna Gowda, P.C.C. President, and as usual Pandit Nehru sent letters indicating his displeasure at the public washing of the Mysore party's dirty linen. The only perhaps novel feature of the Mysore wrangles was that which occurred following one of the customary stormy scenes at a

[1] Within two years, however, the critics had won; the Chief Minister was deposed in 1956. An interesting feature of this sequel was that the Speaker of the Assembly was chosen as Party Leader and accordingly stepped down from the Chair to the front bench! This perhaps illustrates the paucity of political talent in some smaller States. It certainly shows that an Indian Speaker need not abandon all hope of a party political career (see also below, p. 269 n.).

[2] *Congress Bulletin*, Oct.–Nov. 1953, pp. 318–321.

[3] By a nice coincidence, the first press cutting I made on arriving in India is one dated 7 Oct. 1953 and headlined 'Mysore Congress Chiefs' Conflict'; the last is dated 30 June 1954 and reads: 'Deep-rooted Differences among Mysore Congressmen; Mediation Efforts Fail.'

party conference: one delegate rose and said that 'after hearing the speeches it seemed to him that they were all power-mad, and that it would be in the best interests of the country if both Mr. Hanumanthaiya and Mr. Veeranna Gowda vacated their offices'.[1]

That this unhappy impact of party disputes on the business of government at the State level is not due to any indifference on the part of the Congress leadership has already been made clear. If instructions and advice were enough, the problem would long ago have been solved. A circular letter from the A.I.C.C. office in September 1953 is only one example: 'We have noticed with regret that even prominent Congressmen indulge in mutual criticism and bickerings publicly through press and platform. . . . Differences are quite likely to crop up among Congressmen on important issues of public importance . . . but this should not of itself give occasion to dissensions and personal vilifications. . . . Public controversy should be avoided at all costs.'[2] On more than one occasion, the leadership has set out in programme form the relations which it considers should obtain between the ministry, the Assembly Party and the Pradesh Committee, and has made suggestions to aid smooth working. The Cabinet, it has been explained, must work as a team; members should by all means—preferably by informal social contacts and discussions—thrash out their differences, but they must co-operate in action. The Chief Minister is Leader of the Party; he must lead the whole party and not only a group, and in return must be treated by all as the Leader. Contact between ministry and Assembly party must be so close and continuous that government policies are understood and backed by the members while they at the same time have ample opportunities—through party meetings and party specialist committees—to express their views and those of their constituents. Members of the Assembly party (and this applies to members of the Central Parliament too) must visit their constituencies oftener so as to popularise Congress policies and keep in touch with what the people are thinking; they should be careful, however, not to interfere with the district administration or attempt to exercise their influence on officials.[3] Ministers should have regular meetings with the leaders of Pradesh and District Congress Committees, and, after a two-way exchange of ideas, the latter should support the party government, remembering at the same time that the Ministers are responsible not to the party alone but to the Assembly as

[1] Report in *The Hindu*, 1 May 1954.
[2] *Congress Bulletin*, Aug.–Sept. 1953, p. 269. The A.I.C.C. addresses letters not only to P.C.C.s but to the Leaders of Assembly Parties.
[3] It is interesting to note that this has recently been extended to the Congress members of the Council of States and State Legislative Councils. These members, being indirectly elected, have no territorial constituency; they have been asked by the A.I.C.C. to select an area in which they will concentrate their activities as if it were their constituency (Report in *The Times of India*, 29 June 1954).

a whole and to the people of the State.[1] The formulae are agreed to and applauded; and the practice changes little.

There is, then, a marked contrast between the smoothness which has generally characterised the relations of party and government at the Centre and the difficulties which are so general in the same relations at the State level. Why should this be so? A major part of the answer would seem to be that smaller places have smaller men. The calibre of State Chief Ministers in the former provinces is usually high,[2] but the same cannot be said for those States which were formerly ruled by the princes. The Congress leaders in the latter areas are for the most part very new arrivals in the business of responsible government. They tend, therefore, to be more susceptible to all the pressures of a divided and factional society which we have already discussed. Although this may be sufficient as an explanation, attention may be drawn to one vital difference between the arrangements at the Centre and those of the States. We have already seen that a dominant unifying factor at the Centre was Pandit Nehru's tenure of the top positions in both party and government. The imitation of this pattern at the State level is expressly forbidden by Pandit Nehru and the Working Committee. Even if it so happens that one man should be elected Leader of the Assembly party (and therefore Chief Minister) and also President of the Pradesh Committee, he must choose one and resign the other. This position arose in Madras in 1954, when Mr. Kamaraj Nadar, P.C.C. President, was chosen as Leader of the Congress Assembly party in place of Mr. Rajagopalachariar; he had to resign from the presidentship. A case in Hyderabad was even more striking. There one of the members of the Cabinet other than the Chief Minister was elected President of the P.C.C.; even this joint tenure was not permitted. It may be true that in some States there are not the men who can safely carry the two responsibilities and be allowed to enjoy the two sets of powers. It may be, too, that with some, even, there would be a danger of the party becoming too much a slave of the government, or the government a tool of the party.[3]

---

[1] These points have been taken from two sources: *The Report of the General Secretaries, Jan. 1953–Jan. 1954*, pp. 120–122; and the press report (*The Times of India*, 17 June 1954) of Pandit Nehru's note to Delhi Congress leaders.

[2] Indeed, it is here, more than in the Union Cabinet, that one has to look for future successors to the combined throne of Prime Minister and Party President.

[3] The former situation is already alleged by some. Thus Mr. Tandon, former Congress President, is reported to have declared: 'I do not feel the same joy in hoisting the Congress flag as I used to, because the Congress of today is not the same as it used to be. The Congress Ministers have forgotten the people and are in love with palaces. The Congress Party has become the slave of the Government' (*The Times of India*, 10 June 1954). To others, especially outside the Congress Party, the opposite danger naturally seems greater. One of the most frequently made allegations is that Congress Governments appear unable to distinguish between government and party and are willing to make the former work for the latter. It seems always to be said, for instance, that Congress State Governments make elaborate preparations to welcome the periodic grand sessions of the A.I.C.C.—preparations which are more suitably the responsibility of the P.C.C. (E.g., letter in *The Statesman*, 28 May 1955, on the A.I.C.C. meeting in Orissa.)

As a hard-and-fast general rule, however, it has little merit, while in some cases its application may have encouraged a tension which otherwise might not have existed and which has done more harm than good.[1]

The attitudes and practices of the other parties on this question can be dealt with very briefly. To be out of power simplifies so many matters—among them the relations of the party organisation to the party in the legislature. The only party besides Congress which has had to do with governing is the Praja Socialist Party. In the cases of both Andhra and Travancore-Cochin, the National Executive of the P.S.P.[2] had important decisions to take, and these decisions influenced considerably the outcome in these States. In Andhra, they refused to permit Mr. Prakasam, the local P.S.P. leader, to lead a coalition government with the Congress; he had to leave the party to do so. In Travancore-Cochin, the National Executive firmly discouraged a coalition with the Communists and guided the local party towards assuming the sole responsibility for government, though with the support of Congress in the Assembly. There is as yet too little evidence available to say what influence the National Executive has continued to exercise over the P.S.P. Government in Travancore-Cochin, but it would appear that the latter has enjoyed virtual autonomy. In the Union Parliament, the P.S.P. group is small, numbering only 37. This fact, combined with a general tendency among young parties of the Left to regard parliamentary activities as a minor part of their work, meant that the centre of political gravity within the party was at party H.Q., rather than in the Parliamentary Party. Nevertheless, this situation has been changing. By the middle of 1954 not only the Chairman, Kripalani, but also the former Socialist party leader, Asoka Mehta, were in the House of the People. With the departure of Jai Prakash Narayan from party politics,[3] this left only Dr. Lohia of the well-known national leaders outside Parliament. The P.S.P. headquarters remains in Bombay, the traditional base of the Indian Socialists, but the initiative has passed to Delhi. The Parliamentary Party may continue to receive policy directives, but its influence on these directives is now important and its interpretation of them in any case independent. The protests that are heard against this tendency only underline its force.[4] The trend is, moreover, common to all the parties. It is,

---

[1] It is to be noted that Pandit Nehru's 1954 abdication from the party throne was based on pressure of work, not on political or constitutional propriety.

[2] The organisation of the P.S.P., though naturally less developed than that of the Congress and weak in party managers, is similar to that of the 'parent' party. (The Socialists were a distinct group in the Congress from 1935 until 1948, when they became a distinct party. The K.M.P. was formed of former Congressmen in 1951, merging with the Socialists in 1952.)　　　　　[3] See above, pp. 39, 104 n.

[4] At the P.S.P. annual conference in Dec. 1953 it was alleged that 'the Parliamentary section, instead of working as a limb of the Party, is working as if it were an independent organisation. The Parliamentary section thus going its own way, the other sections . . . very naturally tend to follow in its footsteps, with the result that the provincial offices, bereft of all contacts, initiative and authority, are reduced to the status of mere post offices' (Report in The Statesman, 1 Jan. 1954).

for instance, no accident that the leader of the Hindu Mahasabha in the House of the People, Mr. N. C. Chatterjee, was in 1954 elected President of that party. Only in the Communist Party is there some resistance to the change; the parliamentary front is only one, and by no means the most important, of the many fronts along which the party conducts its struggle. The 'guidance' which the parliamentary representatives receive from the Politburo is no doubt 'the line', and not lightly disregarded. Yet even in the case of this party, it is noteworthy that its leader in Parliament is an important member of the Politburo, while there are half a dozen of the M.P.s who are on the Party's Central Committee. Moreover, the Party H.Q. has been moved to Delhi, primarily to enable easier consultation with the parliamentary group. Also, much of the party's research work is now done under the control of the parliamentary group, which thus serves the organisation as a whole. And one of the notable sights of New Delhi is the large board which proudly indicates 'The Office of the Communist Party in Parliament'.

This general trend has a wider significance and a meaning that is unmistakable: for the parties, for political life as a whole, Parliament has become the focus of attention.

2. The Parliamentary Party

In considering the working of the party groups inside Parliament, most attention can again properly be given to the Congress Party. Although there were Congress representatives in the old Central Legislature, and although they were naturally well organised as a group, the modern arrangements of the party date from the post-war establishment of the Constituent Assembly, and above all from the transformation of that body, in August 1947, into a Dominion Legislature. The title of 'Congress Party in Parliament' could come, of course, only after the inauguration in 1950 of the new Constitution and the consequent change from Constituent Assembly (Legislative) to Provisional Parliament. With the elections in 1952 and the setting up of the House of the People and the Council of States, the present organisation of the party finally took shape.[1]

The Congress Party in Parliament is a body of some 527 members of the two Houses. It consists of M.P.s elected as Congress candidates though there are also provisions for the admission of others such as Independents. All members are pledged to follow the principles and policy laid down by the Congress, as well as to conform to the rules, resolutions and instructions of the Party in Parliament. They must also undertake to resign their seats when called upon to do so by a competent party authority, and they pay an annual subscription of Rs.175/- (about

[1] These various constitutional stages have been described in Chapter II. The material that follows is drawn from The Constitution of the Congress Party in Parliament, the annual reports of the Party and from interviews.

£13) of which Rs.50/-is earmarked for the party library and research work. The organisation has eleven office-bearers: Leader, Deputy Leader, Chief Whip, three Deputy Chief Whips, Secretary-General, three Secretaries and Treasurer. The Leader is elected by the Party in Parliament for the full term of the Parliament. The Chief Whip is nominated by the Leader, and the Deputies are nominated by the Chief Whip with the approval of the Leader. The others are elected annually. The constitution also provides that one of the Deputy Chief Whips and one of the Secretaries shall be a member of the Council of States.

General meetings of the party are held as often as necessary, and according to the constitution at least once a month during sessions. At the annual general meeting the office-bearers are elected and the accounts presented. At the first meeting of each session the Leader generally outlines the important work of the session. Of the other meetings, some are held on the requisition of not less than 50 M.P.s. The meetings of the general body are such large assemblies that discussion is not easy; they tend to be used for three main purposes. They are, in the first place, the occasions on which the Leader can deliver addresses on general topics, such as the Five-Year Plan or the international situation, or convey to every member directly some new emphasis which has to be given to their work. They are also used when it is desired to give members an opportunity to hear talks by distinguished visitors from abroad. Finally, they serve an important morale purpose: whether requisitioned by a group or advised by the Whips, they enable members to 'let off steam' and Ministers to explain their policies on particular subjects.

The considerable increase in the size of the party following the election of the new and expanded Parliament of 1952 led to the institution of a new level between the general meeting and the executive committee. By an amendment of 1952 there was introduced the General Council. This is elected by the members sitting in State groups and choosing 20% of their number; it consists of 108 members. According to the constitution it must meet at least once a week during sessions, but the Secretary-General[1] revealed that it had actually met only four times during the 1952 Budget session, whereas the general body had met as many as twelve times. For discussions of the party policy and the methods of its implementation through the departments of government the General Council is clearly better suited than the assembly of over 500. It would seem, however, that the need for frequent meetings of the general body continues to be felt; during the January–May session of 1954 it met thirteen times—and more than half the meetings were devoted to addresses by the Prime Minister on foreign affairs. It may be that the General Council has not yet firmly established its place, but tends rather to be squeezed out between Executive Committee and general body.

[1] In an address at Indore in Sept. 1952.

Ministers are often among those elected to the Council, but they can in any case be invited to attend even if not members; no discussion of the Five-Year Plan or the food situation would normally take place in the absence of the Minister responsible for the subject. The Council is also a convenient forum for the consideration of the broader features of the party's organisation in the two Houses; it has, for instance, discussed the committee structure of the Party in Parliament.

The direction of the party is in the hands of the Leader and the Executive Committee. This Committee consists of the 11 office-bearers, plus 21 elected members, 15 of whom are chosen by party members of the House of the People and 6 by those in the Council. These may include a few Ministers, but normally not more than a few. It is interesting that in 1952 the general meeting sought to dispense with elections by asking the Leader to choose his own team. Pandit Nehru at first declined but later, after inviting and receiving some suggestions for inclusion, did nominate his Executive Committee. This Committee meets frequently. It prepares the ground for the General Council and the general meetings of the party and it considers matters of discipline and organisation. Above all, it studies the progress of parliamentary business in some detail. The constitution of the Party in Parliament lays down that, so far as possible, all important government motions, Bills and resolutions should be placed before the Executive Committee in advance of their consideration by Parliament. There is even a sub-committee which considers the amendments which have been suggested and advises the Executive Committee. Some of this examination of Bills and amendments may duplicate discussions in departmental and government committees, but it is designed for different ends. It is meant, for one thing, to ensure that ministerial and party thinking do not diverge too much; measures will be examined from the point of view of their conformity to the party's policies and with an eye on the possible reactions of different elements in the party. A further important function of this examination is to prepare the party members for the reception of a particular measure and ensure that their contributions, in debate and by way of amendments, shall be constructive and not contrary to the purpose of the measure concerned. It is, of course, this Committee which also considers non-official resolutions and works out what the party attitude should be. In all its work, the Committee owes much to the presence of the Whips and the Secretaries and to the links that most members have with the Congress organisation outside Parliament.

One of the most interesting recent developments has been the establishment of party Standing Committees. In part, they are a replacement for the all-party Standing Advisory Committees of the old Central Assembly which were abolished in 1952.[1] They are primarily study

[1] See also below, pp. 308–311.

groups. Each M.P. is asked to indicate his main fields of interest, and the Executive Committee nominates the Standing Committees in the light of this information. Most M.P.s appear to be on only one committee, though some are members of two. The number of such committees is not fixed, but they correspond more or less to the departments of government, and in 1954 there were twenty-six. Their size varies greatly, indicating partly the directions in which members are interested, partly the judgment of the Executive Committee. It appears, for instance, that not all those M.P.s who indicated Planning or Agriculture as their main interests have been permitted to sit on those committees. Even so, while the Planning Committee has 62 members and that on Agriculture 58, the Transport Committee numbers only 13 and that on Natural Resources and Scientific Research only 15. An attempt is also made to keep a due balance in membership between the two Houses. The committee members are expected to make a special study of their subject, to examine the measures proposed in that field and to be ready to speak on them in the House and to sit on the Select Committees[1] of the House when the Bills are discussed. At the same time, the Standing Committees are sometimes used by Ministers to try out ideas which they are in the process of formulating and to prepare party opinion for adjustments of policy. On the other hand, it would be misleading to present the committees simply as aids to the party and government, a form of exploitation of the back-bencher; they are at least as important as channels for complaints and suggestions which the M.P.s themselves may want to make or which they at least desire to pass on from others. Some examples of topics discussed may be useful. Thus, the Commerce and Industries Committee discussed textile control, handicrafts for foreign markets and Bills on the control of royalties and the collection of commercial statistics. The Railways Committee considered the Railway Budget and relevant portions of the reports of the Public Accounts Committee, as well as the schemes for the re-grouping of railways and the building of locomotives. Sometimes committees have held meetings to hear talks by specialists. The External Affairs Committee heard the Indian Ambassador to Egypt describe the situation in that country, while the Defence Committee arranged talks on the Indian Air Force and on the Japanese Army.

The effectiveness of the committees depends on the members, on the Minister of the related department and especially on the committee convenor who is nominated by the Chief Whip. Frequency of meetings may not tell the whole story of a committee's work, but they give some indication: during the period from June 1952 to April 1953 (when Parliament was in session about six months in all), the Planning Committee met 19 times, that on Education twice. Apathetic members, a weak convenor and an unco-operative or otherwise preoccupied Minister spell an

1 See below, pp. 230–232.

ineffective committee. On the whole, however, the committees have proved valuable. In the first place, from the party point of view, the committees strengthen and improve its parliamentary performance; on any subject there is a team of party M.P.s who can be expected to have given some thought to the matter. The committees, that is, do something to reduce the big gap in ability and knowledge between Minister and member and perhaps a little to lessen the burden on Ministers of parliamentary debate; as one party office-bearer put it, 'each member is able to contribute his mite to the second line of parliamentary defence. It has been our experience that members of the party reply to criticisms levelled by the Opposition without the intervention of the Minister.' In their role as a training ground for M.P.s the committees can do a great deal—and there is certainly much to do. Up to the present, they have perhaps done more to raise the level of the really backward M.P. rather than to produce teams of advanced specialists; there no doubt are certain specialists in the party, but they have become so without the help of 'post-entry training'.

The achievement of the committees may be viewed, in the second place, as an aid to the administrative process. It is here that so much depends on the temperament of Ministers. The Minister who is receptive to suggestions and sensitive to currents of thought and opinion can learn much of value from a committee, and will encourage the convenor and members in their work. It might be thought that the good Minister in this respect will be the one whose background has been dominated by life in party politics; though there is some tendency for this to be the case, there are several exceptions—on the one hand, strong party men who feel sure they know already all the ideas or complaints that could possibly come through party channels; and on the other, former professional men, whose connections with the party have been slighter, who are happy to be able to check their own views and impressions with those of the back-bencher. There is no doubt that ideally the committees are especially important in India, where geography and social structure conspire so easily to place a gulf between the *élite*—ministerial and official —and the mass. There is, moreover, no department whose subject is of so technical a nature that the lay member has nothing at all to contribute. In practice, however, performance has been very uneven. It will be enough to describe how the good committees work; the ways of the bad ones can then be easily imagined. In a good committee the convenor, after informal discussion with several members, will select one or two particular topics for consideration. He will then call for material or guidance notes from the ministry, from the research section at the A.I.C.C. office and from any other possibly helpful source. At a preliminary meeting of the committee he will outline the task and, if possible, allocate the preparatory work among the members. At a further meeting—after an interval during which the convenor has been in touch with his colleagues and ensuring that they are working along the right lines—the results of the study will be brought together and discussed. Finally, the Minister will be invited to attend a meeting to hear the result of the committee's deliberations and give his comments. This kind of thing, it must be confessed, happens rarely, and the committees are therefore less effective than they might be.[1] At the same time, it would be misleading to judge a committee's usefulness or influence simply by the number of occasions on which its representations have led to a distinct modification of policy—though there are a few such cases. Rather, the committee's work and its influence should be more indirect and continuous, an influence—and only one among many—on the method of approach to problems on the part of Ministers and their advisers. In this connection, it is interesting that the opposition parties were quick to detect possible dangers. During the debate on the Appropriation Bill in 1952[2] one of the topics listed for discussion was expressed as follows: 'The recent steps taken to identify the administration with the Congress Party; for example, the Planning Commission being present at Congress Party meetings and Working Committee meetings, and the constitution of special group committees of the Congress Parliamentary Party at which officials are present to take advice.' The Prime Minister rejected the charges: the Planning Commission met representatives of all parties, not only the Congress; as for the study groups of the Party in Parliament, they were a useful institution which other parties would do well to imitate, and he would gladly attend such committees as dealt with the subjects for which he was particularly responsible; and it was untrue that officials were present to take advice from the party. Nevertheless, in the special circumstances of the Congress Party, the dangers are real, and it is well that the opposition was alert. The attendance of officials at meetings of the Standing Committees is in fact very rare, though it may have happened on occasion that a Minister was accompanied by an official adviser who could better answer some questions of detail which members wished to put.

There is no doubt that the keen party M.P. appreciates the Standing Committees. It gives him an important feeling of contributing to the process of government, especially if the Minister appears to be grateful for suggestions and conscientious in his replies to complaints. If the M.P. makes use of the opportunities wisely, it enables him to gain a reputation for a command over a particular subject. If he is ambitious, he will realise that it can be made into a route that leads to junior minis-

---

[1] This is one reason why steps have been taken by some M.P.s (with the encouragement of the Parliament Secretariat) to establish an Indian Parliamentary Group which has organised study circles on particular subjects.

[2] H.P. Deb., 4 July 1952.

terial posts. The committees show up the lazy and the stupid; they also make it possible for the bright to shine.

The Congress Party in Parliament has organised its members not only into Standing Committees for the study of particular subjects but also into State Groups. These groups are used, as we have seen, for the election of the General Council. Their real importance, however, is as a channel for special local representations to departments. Thus the Travancore-Cochin State Group will discuss the slump in the coir industry and attempt to suggest remedies. The convenor of the group will then probably see the Minister concerned and press the urgency of the matter, and put forward the group's proposals for consideration. The complaints of the peasants in Himachal Pradesh will come to the ears of the M.P.s from the State and will be passed on to the Ministry of Agriculture. Every group will put forward claims on behalf of its State for new railway lines, fresh community projects and government-sponsored industries, thus supplementing and reinforcing representations already made by the State Governments. It may not always be possible for the group to restrict itself to topics that are wholly the responsibility of the Central Government, but even the discussion of State subjects is not wasted since it increases the awareness at Delhi of the problems being confronted at the various State capitals. When a Bill of special interest to a particular State is before the Houses, the group will consider its attitude and choose those it considers best fitted to speak on the subject. The convenor will pass the names on to the Whips.

The State Groups are, of course, far more natural units than the Standing Committees; they are groups in which M.P.s would in any event tend to gather. They will contain former colleagues from State politics, friends from neighbouring districts, above all people who speak the same language. Indeed, so strong is the sense of regional community that it is not unusual for a State Group (or at least its convenor) to consult with opposition M.P.s from the same area before submitting points to the Ministers. The size of the group varies considerably: that from U.P. numbers over 80, while there are at the other end several ones and twos. Generally, however, they constitute a fairly compact and very intimate circle, in almost continuous social contact (in the Central Hall, for example) and freely discussing not only points on which representations may be made but also politics in general and the more exciting pieces of local gossip in particular. It is therefore not surprising that the State Groups are an important link in the party's organisation and a particular asset to the Whips; no one will know the mood of the members better than the State Convenor, and no one is in a better position than he to be able to assess the character of each member of his flock, distinguishing the sycophant and the rebel, the zealot and the sleeping partner.

The smooth working of the Congress Party in Parliament depends in some measure on the effectiveness of the secretariat and office. The general meetings, the General Council and above all the Executive Committee have to be adequately serviced with prepared agenda and systematic records. The activities of the Standing Committees and State Groups have to be watched and controlled. The office of the Party in Parliament, however, goes beyond these routine secretarial functions in three directions. In the first place, it has set up a Bureau of Parliamentary Research with a staff of half a dozen research officers. This Bureau works in co-operation with the research staff at the party headquarters or A.I.C.C. office, but its role is rather different. It is designed to serve the needs of members, and therefore concentrates on preparing 'talking points', collecting material relevant to measures before Parliament and in general on short-range, specific questions rather than on long-range, more fundamental enquiries. It has, for instance, prepared a series of small pamphlets outlining for each State the meaning for that area of the Five-Year Plan, another series describing the policy of the Government in relation to certain questions of Foreign Policy and a third on such topics as Labour Policy, River Valley Schemes and the Food position. On a smaller scale, and for a more immediate purpose, it prepared for the 1954 Budget session a brief note on the nature of deficit finance. A second direction in which the secretaries and staff have been active concerns the campaign to develop constituency work among members. Questionnaires have been prepared with the intention of making the members establish closer acquaintance with local difficulties and complaints, and in the hope that the channels of communication in both directions between Parliament and the people can be cleared. It is worth noting that the most important questionnaire was distributed not only to M.P.s but also to members of State Legislative Assemblies (M.L.A.s), in an effort to co-ordinate this aspect of the work of both. The party has also experimented, not unsuccessfully, with sending teams of M.P.s on talking tours of areas removed from their own; this assists, as one member put it, in 'fostering a feeling that India itself is our constituency.' Finally, the party secretariat has undertaken certain responsibilities as a central co-ordinator of all State legislature parties. At the time when the A.I.C.C. was meeting at Indore in September 1952 it was decided to convene a meeting of Congress legislators from all the Assemblies, as well as the Parliament. This proved a useful occasion for certain practices of the Centre—the Standing Committees, the roles of the Whips, and so on—to be explained and advocated to the States. The convention also discussed work in the constituencies and relations with Pradesh Congress Committees. One of the results of the meeting was the establishment in the offices of the Party in Parliament of a Legislative Co-ordination Section. It is the duty of this section to arrange a continuous exchange of information about the conduct of parties in legislatures—both among the State Assembly parties and between Centre and States. One of the steps so far taken has been the deputation by State legislature parties of members of their staff for training at the secretariat of the Party in Parliament.

The work of the Whips in relation to the House as a whole is mentioned elsewhere.[1] We have noticed, however, that they are at the same time important office-bearers of the Party in Parliament. It would, indeed, not be incorrect to say that they serve the House mainly through serving the Government and the party in power; for it is by organising the Government's majority that they are able to perform their main function of ensuring the smooth passage of business through Parliament. They are, no doubt, 'the usual channels' through which the Government party negotiates with the opposition parties and with the officers of the two Houses, but they would not be able to serve in this capacity if they were not already important members of Government and party.

The institution of the Whips is central to the working of the British form of parliamentary cabinet government. It is an institution whose working brings so close together the Executive, the Legislature and the party that it is difficult to know where one ceases and the other begins; its character is one of subtlety, its instruments persuasion and conventions, its methods compromise and adjustment. It might be possible for one country to copy without comprehending the electoral laws or the legislature standing orders of another; no plausible imitation of the British system of Whips would be possible, however, unless the spirit had been thoroughly grasped. In India this has been achieved. The new Parliament has perhaps been fortunate in its first Government Chief Whip. Mr. Satya Narayan Sinha brings to his task a rich political experience. As a party member, he was President of a District Congress Committee for seventeen years, Secretary of a Pradesh Committee for five and a member of the A.I.C.C. since 1925. As a legislator he had experience at State level from 1926 and then at the Centre from 1934. It was as early as 1937 when he first performed the functions of Whip. But perhaps the qualifications of personality are more important, and it appears to be generally agreed that he is both shrewd and persuasive, both purposeful and humorous; it has been said that while every conversation with him hides a negotiation, at the same time every negotiation becomes a conversation.

In India the Chief Whip is a Minister of Cabinet rank with the title of Minister for Parliamentary Affairs.[2] Although not a member of the

---

[1] Eg., pp. 218–219, below.

[2] The Chief Whip was given explicit ministerial status during 1949 with the title ' Minister of State'. In 1950 he was 'Minister of State for Parliamentary Affairs', while his present title was introduced in 1952.

13—P.I.

Cabinet, he is the chairman of the Cabinet's Parliamentary Affairs Committee, which determines the measures to be brought before the legislature and the order in which they are to be introduced and considered.[1] He is also a most important member of the Business Advisory Committee of the House of the People, as his Deputy in the Council of States is of the similar Committee of the Upper House. These committees, on which opposition groups are represented, decide the allocation of available time among the various measures which the Government proposes to introduce. The work of being 'stage manager' for the Government is, however, by no means finished when these committees have done their work. In the first place, the debate cannot be left to chance; the party must have its speakers ready. The Chief Whip submits his party's list of speakers to the Speaker of the House.[2] To be able to do this, he must know his members. This is one of the reasons for providing the Chief Whip with a number of assistants. In addition to the three Deputies, one of whom is in the Council, there are nine Whips in the House and four in the Council, and these Whips are responsible for a 'bloc' of members from a particular 'zone' of the country. The Chief Whip, when selecting the party's speakers, will be guided by the desire to choose men who will be able to handle the particular subject and by the anxiety to have various parts of the country fairly represented. The Whips will therefore get in touch with the Convenors of the Standing Committees and of the State Groups and will then make their suggestions to the Chief Whip. A similar procedure takes place when the party has to nominate some of its members to sit on the Select or other Parliamentary Committees.[3] The best known function of the Whips, of course, arises when a division of the House takes place, and the members vote for or against a motion. Although in the central Parliament, Congress has majorities that are comfortable to the point of luxury, the party has nevertheless thought it wise to cultivate the habit of disciplined voting. The familiar system of ordinary, one-, two- and three-line whips is used to indicate the extent

[1] The Committee is a small one and is believed to include the Home and Law Ministers. As in Britain, the whole structure of Cabinet Committees changes from time to time and is not completely known to the public. Occasionally, however, information on particular committees is divulged; the Prime Minister, for instance, told the Provisional Parliament the composition, functions and work of the Economic Committee (P.P. Deb., 13 Mar. 1950, I, 1, 799).

[2] However, as the Speaker has had to explain to dissatisfied members on several occasions, the Chair is in no way bound by the Whips' Lists; they are simply an aid to enable the Speaker to keep up the level of the debate and give a fair chance to all. (E.g., P.P. Deb. 7 Dec. 1950 and 27 Feb. 1951; H.P. Deb., 6 June 1952 and 20 Dec. 1952.)

[3] In the case of Select-Committees on Bills, it is usual for the Congress Members, once elected, to meet as a group to discuss the party's attitude to the particular measure. Congress M.P.s on other committees—e.g., Estimates Committee—neither meet separately nor function as party members on the Committee; they are then simply members of Parliament confronting the administration. (See below, Chapter VI.)

of urgency attaching to the vote. Specimens of whips issued are given below.[1]

CONGRESS PARTY IN PARLIAMENT
(House of the People)

24–25, Parliament House,
New Delhi.

Whip No. 10.   8 April 1953.

The Khadi and other Handloom Industries Development
(*Additional Excise Duty on Cloth*) *Bill,* 1953

Members of the Congress Party are requested not to move any amendment to the above Bill, and if any amendment is moved by non-party members, it should be opposed.

SATYA NARAYAN SINHA
(*Chief Whip.*)

CONGRESS PARTY IN PARLIAMENT
(House of the People)

24–25, Parliament House,
New Delhi.

Whip No. 9.   31 March 1953.

Members of the Congress Party are requested to be present in the House this evening throughout the sitting, as there will be a Division on Demands for Grants in respect of Ministry of Home Affairs & States.

S. N. SINHA
(*Chief Whip*)

CONGRESS PARTY IN PARLIAMENT
(House of the People)

24–25, Parliament House,
New Delhi.

Whip No. 13.   18 April 1953.

The Finance Bill

Members of the Congress Party are requested to be present throughout the sitting this afternoon from 4 p.m. onwards, as there will be a division on the Finance Bill.

for Deputy Chief Whip

The Whips are, of course, responsible for discipline in a much wider sense than voting for the Government. The constitution of the Congress Party in Parliament includes several rules for the party member: he must send to the party office a copy of any motion, amendment or Bill which he proposes to move or introduce, and can proceed only if the party allows; he must not raise any important issue outside the scope of the

---

[1] No three-line whip is included and they have in fact been so far used only very rarely up to the present.

Order Paper without permission; he is not to move a motion for the adjournment of business without Executive Committee approval; and contravention of these rules or the deliberate disregard of any whip renders the member liable to expulsion from the party. The Whips are there to see that these rules are obeyed. The member is also expected to obtain the consent of the Whips for any absence from the House while it is in session and for any departure from Delhi. Nevertheless, the imposition of discipline is by no means the whole story. Perhaps the most important function of the Whips is to communicate to the Leader the mood of the party M.P.s and record the most minute and subtle changes of sentiment and opinion. Here, again, the team of assistants is necessary. They must be in continuous contact with members—on the floor of the House, in the lobbies, in the Central Hall. The Chief Whip himself has tried to describe this ceaseless work: 'The Whips are not only shock-absorbers, but also indicators of the Party; they are not only advisers to the Leader, but also the binding-force in the Party; they are not only barometers of the different regions and opinions, but also the counsellors of members.'[1] It is not unusual to hear the charge that Congress in Parliament is a sternly and rigidly disciplined party. Those who complain thus are generally unable to recognise discipline as one of the necessary features of coherent parliamentary conduct. Very often the protest is simply a form of complaint against the large Congress majority; certainly it is seldom made by Congressmen, most of whom suffer from no sense of frustration.[2] Indeed, while voting behaviour is admittedly closely controlled, Congress M.P.s are in practice allowed to state a variety of different points of view on the floor of the House, provided naturally that their speeches imply a general support for the Government and make no serious challenge. Within the Congress Party in Parliament, members have adequate opportunities for making suggestions and pressing their points of view.[3] In fact, the non-Congress M.P. who likes to portray the

[1] A speech given at a conference of Congress Party Whips in Sept. 1952. In his capacity as adviser to the Leader he will normally during session meet the Prime Minister not only for one set interview daily but also several times in the course of the day for brief consultations. His advice may be on internal party matters (as Whip to Leader) or on the progress of Government business (as Minister for Parliamentary Affairs to the Prime Minister). On his capacity as a 'shock-absorber', I must also add the story, said to be true, of a chat between the Chief Whip and the Prime Minister. 'I have found out how to describe my work, Panditji.' 'How is that?' 'Do you know why the carpet in your office is always so clean? Because there's a mat outside on which everyone wipes his shoes before entering. I am the door mat which prevents the dirt from reaching you.'

[2] This is less true at the State level.

[3] It is worth noting that the effort of the intelligent Whip is directed above all at the training rather than merely the disciplining of the member. At the 1955 All-India Whips' Conference (a new institution, at present mainly Congress), the Government Chief Whip put the point thus: 'Congress Whips at the Centre and in most States have had on the whole an easy time owing to preponderant majorities. . . . But this is just the time when we can afford to be less political and more positive in our functions. We should devote our energies to improving the quality of the legislators in our charge.' (*India News*, 29 Jan. 1955.)

Congress member as docile and helpless will on other occasions protest that he has too many special opportunities for influencing Government policy.

The organisation of the other parties in Parliament is based on similar lines to that of the Congress. Since, however, they are so small and have none of the problems of a Government party, their arrangements are very much simpler and generally more informal, even in some cases to the point of being ill-defined. The P.S.P. Parliamentary Group consists of 37 members, of whom 10 are in the Council. The direction of the group comes from the eight chosen office-bearers who form the Executive Committee: a Leader, Deputy Leader, Secretary and Whip in each of the two Houses. The group is small enough to make meetings of the whole body easy and frequent, and informal contact is naturally continuous among the members of each House. The question of forming State Groups of course does not arise, but even the specialisation of members on different subjects raises difficulties. Individual members have been asked to concentrate on particular fields of interest, but it has not been found possible yet to constitute formal study circles. Only when this has been done will the party be in a position to attempt the same kind of approach to ministries—for both information and discussion—which the Congress Party Standing Committees have been able to make. Up to the present, certainly, the P.S.P. group has felt that the absence of any access to Government sources of information has been a handicap. To understand the difficulty, it is necessary to bear in mind that in India non-official research bodies, agencies, etc., are far less developed than, say, in England, and information from sources other than the Government unusually difficult to obtain. Also, the party itself cannot yet have any large research organisation of its own—either in Bombay or in Delhi. Moreover, it is not only small but also comparatively inexperienced; it is not in the position of a former government, now for a while in opposition but equipped with the knowledge derived from office. It is therefore not surprising that P.S.P.—and other opposition groups too—should regret the passing of the Standing Advisory Committees of the old Assembly. As already mentioned,[1] the Prime Minister has set up a purely informal Foreign Affairs group on a non-party basis, but it is doubtful if the solution can lie in that direction without obscuring ministerial responsibility. The best that opposition groups can do at present is probably to make the most of their opportunities on the Parliamentary Committees, and attempt to build up their own Standing Committees on special subjects. It is worth mentioning on the other hand that one of the advantages of smallness is that individual opposition members have greater opportunities for speaking on the floor of the House than can be the case with the Congress back-bencher.

[1] Above, p. 155 n.

The Communist Party in Parliament is a group of forty. One of the peculiarities of its organisation is that of this number only about a dozen comrades are instructed to work continuously in Parliament. The remainder is organised so that, while they have periods in Delhi, they spend also a great deal of their time outside—on the party's other 'fronts'. Such members of the group as are present in Delhi meet weekly during the sessions, but the leading members are in more or less continuous consultation. The group has begun to devote more attention to research than it did at first, and its members are instructed to specialise in certain subjects and study in conjunction with the research staff, which is also organised in several 'subject' sections. The other parties and groups are even less elaborately organised; indeed, it is mainly for particular issues and in order to be able effectively to command a share of precious parliamentary time that they come together at all.

We have already seen that since 1952 the Congress Party in Parliament has attempted to act as a co-ordinator and adviser for the various Congress parties in State legislatures. There is, in consequence, some uniformity of practice at Union and State levels. The fact that some States have very large Assemblies (and party groups) while others are comparatively tiny results naturally in differences of scale and elaboration. In Bombay the Congress Party in the legislature has a strength of 330, comprising 272 in the Assembly of 316 and 58 in the Council of 72. The sessions in States are of course much shorter than at the Centre, but so long as they last, the whole group meets weekly.[1] So also does the 16-member Executive, nominated annually by the Leader. The Leader has also instituted a system of meeting the members from each district in turn; this usually means a daily meeting during sessions. The party has set up study groups on different subjects, but the short sessions made serious work difficult. Discipline in the Bombay Party is very effective, but appears to be achieved without much difficulty.[2] It keeps together a party in which regional tensions are always threatening (the Whips are careful to keep a balance between regions in their choice of speakers and nominees for committees—and the Chief Whip is, conveniently, from no region of the State but from Andhra!) but it extends beyond voting behaviour and leads to a certain uniformity of speeches on the floor of the House. In Travancore-Cochin, the Congress group numbers forty-five. This body may meet even more frequently than weekly during the brief sessions. For instance, during a ten-day session in March 1954 it

[1] In view of what was said in Section 1 of this chapter, it is interesting to note that in Bombay not only are there the usual links between party and legislature party (e.g., Leader is member of Working Committee, many M.L.A.s are members of P.C.C.) but the Presidents and Secretaries of the four Pradesh Congress Committees covering the area of the State (Maharashtra, Gujerat, Karnatak and Bombay City) are invited to attend meetings of the legislature party, though not entitled to vote.

[2] It could not of course wholly withstand the States Reorganisation crisis of 1955–56.

met three times. It has an Executive, but so far attempts to build up study groups do not appear to have been successful. In those States where the leading politicians lack experience of parliamentary democracy, the business of the legislature group is managed much more informally, often more crudely and always in an atmosphere where personalities count for a great deal. There the whips are issued as whispers in the corridors and lobbies, and the Whips who issue them at last look less like polished diplomats and more like party bosses.

CHAPTER FIVE

PROCEDURE AND PRIVILEGE

THE procedure of a parliament is no doubt a reflection of political traditions and of the disposition of political forces; it is at the same time capable of influencing political behaviour and thus moulding the traditions and amending the dispositions. The procedure of the British House of Commons is unintelligible except when read in the context of the country's political history and in the light of particular conflicts and clashes; yet it has shaped the behaviour of generations of politicians and done much to set the tone of public life. To those who regard democracy as a particular social structure, parliamentary procedure cannot be of great interest. At most, they will try to judge it efficient or not as a means to that end, and probably the procedure they would approve if 'the right people' were in office would not be the same as that which they would favour if the balance of power were reversed. As soon as we see democracy differently, as a particular way of reaching political decisions rather than a possible way of reaching particular decisions, then the significance of procedure is at once enhanced. It becomes a vivid—though no doubt complicated—expression of a pattern of political ideals, and we can judge it as such. We ask whether it allows scope for minority views and whether it encourages a full and frank exchange of opinions; we see if it helps to make rulers responsible and to what extent it permits dominant intentions and aspirations to be clearly expressed.

The procedural character of a legislature depends very much on the constitutional context in which it is placed. A fundamental distinction is drawn between legislatures of the 'American' Presidential-Congressional type in which executive and legislature are separate and those of the 'European' Cabinet-Parliamentary model in which the two powers of government are integrated. This distinction cuts across that which is also made between Federal and Unitary systems, and is, for a consideration of procedure, the more important. The Indian Constitution is federal—or at least has federal elements[1]; yet what matters more from our present viewpoint is that she chose the Cabinet-Parliamentary in preference to the Presidential-Congressional form. As we have already seen, however, there is variety even within the range of parliamentary legislatures, and a further distinction is drawn between those that follow

[1] See pp. 3–5 above. Professor Wheare (*Federal Government*, p. 28) has used the term 'quasi-federal' to describe the Indian Constitution.

the British and those that approximate more closely to the Continental model.[1] We saw that in some ways Parliament in India displays 'Continental' features, and we shall note others of a similar kind in the following chapter. So far as procedure is concerned, however, Indian legislatures belong, as one would expect, to the British rather than to the French variety. The rules and conventions, that is to say, are designed to enable the House as a whole to retain the initiative rather than rely on the formulation of issues by committees. The process of general debate is therefore carefully regulated and always takes place on a precisely defined question. Also, the procedure encourages the gradual building up of a case for and against the Government rather than a series of direct challenges and decisions by way of votes of censure and confidence.[2]

In what follows little attention is given to the detailed exemplification of these general features of British parliamentary procedure. We shall instead try to see the special Indian modifications of the general model and note some of the innovations that have so far been devised.[3]

1. The Evolution of Procedure

Although legislative bodies in India have a long history of gradual development,[4] parliamentary procedure may be said to have begun at the Centre and in the Provinces in 1921.

The 'Manual of Business and Procedure' of the first Indian Legislative Assembly reflects with some exactness the development then reached by that institution. On the one hand, the rules were now more elaborate than those which had served adequately the needs of the Morley-Minto Councils. The Legislative Councils had continued to be regarded as no more than enlarged versions of the Governor-General's Executive Councils; the new Assembly was a distinct legislature with two houses.[5] On the other hand, a glance at the new Manual is sufficient to show that the Assembly was still far short of the status of a sovereign parliament. The sources of the new procedure were three. In the first place, the Act of 1919 itself contained several provisions relating to the legislature. Its composition, the duration of life of its two chambers, its general powers

---

[1] Above, pp. 150–155.

[2] See Campion, *op. cit.*, and Campion and Lidderdale, *op. cit.*, pp. 10–11.

[3] A good account of British procedure is Eric Taylor's *House of Commons at Work*. I should underline what I have already said in the Preface. First, this is not a handbook on Indian parliamentary procedure. Second, I am not primarily concerned to make comparisons between India and Britain. At the same time in this chapter and the next, comparisons have been particularly difficult to avoid; the two systems have so much in common that it has seemed worth while to avoid much detailed description by a brief reference to Commons procedure which is already explained in other books.

[4] See Chapter II, Sec. 1.

[5] The change was, of course, even more marked in the Provinces, where dyarchy had transferred a portion of the provincial range of subjects to Ministers responsible to the new legislatures.

and limitations were all set out in the Act. Moreover, the Act further laid down certain rules more closely affecting matters of procedure. Thus, the President of the Assembly was for four years to be appointed by the Governor-General and thereafter to be elected by the Assembly subject to the approval of the Governor-General; members of the Executive Council were to be ex-officio members of one of the two chambers and to have the right to attend and speak in the other; certain measures (including, for example, those affecting 'the public debt or public revenues or imposing any charge on the revenues', 'religion or the religious rites and usages of any class of British subjects', 'the relations of the Government with foreign Princes or States') could be introduced in the legislature only with the Governor-General's sanction; budget procedure was to include certain non-votable items and the Governor-General could authorise certain necessary expenditure if the legislature refused demands; the Governor-General could withhold his assent to Bills, disallow Acts passed and certify Bills which had been rejected; members were to enjoy freedom of speech and were not liable to proceedings in the courts by reason of their speeches and votes. Although much was in this way stated in the Act of 1919 itself, the Act provided for the two other sources of procedure, the Rules and the Standing Orders. The 'Draft Rules' of Business for Provincial Legislative Councils and the Indian Legislative Assembly as approved by the Joint Select Committee[1] were made by the Governor-General in Council under Article 67 (1) of the Act and with the sanction of the Secretary of State in Council. These 'Indian Legislative Rules' were at once influenced by those of the previous Councils and at the same time the basis for all subsequent procedure. Numbering some fifty rules, they provided for legislative and Budget procedure, questions, motions, quorum and so on. Finally, a set of Standing Orders regulating more minutely the procedure of the Assembly was made by the Governor-General under Article 67 (6) of the Act (and subsequently in minor respects amended by the Assembly with the Governor-General's consent).[2]

Since the federal portions of the 1935 Act never came into operation, the changes in rules of procedure which followed the Act were relatively unimportant. A comparison of the 1945 edition of the Manual with that of 1926 reveals few significant alterations.

When the Constitutent Assembly (Legislative) began its work in 1947, it took as its Rules 'the Indian Legislative Rules in force immediately

---

[1] Cmd. 814 of 1920. The Provincial Rules were practically identical with those of the Central Assembly (differing mainly because the provincial legislatures under the 1919 Act were unicameral and required no rules for the transmission of Bills between chambers). The pattern of uniform procedure throughout India was thus firmly established (see below, Chapter VI, Sections 1 and 2). The only scope for procedural variety occurred in those princely states which had representative institutions, such as Mysore and Travancore.

[2] In the Provinces, Governors issued similar Standing Orders for the Councils.

before the establishment of the Dominion of India, as modified and adapted by the President of the Constituent Assembly of India in exercise of the powers conferred by sub-section (3) of section 38 of the Government of India Act, 1935' and its Standing Orders were similarly based.[1] The modifications and adaptations thus effected were substantial. The most important arose out of the transformation of the Governor-General into a constitutional head of state. The former powers of disallowance, certification and restoration (of grants refused by the legislature) were simply removed. So also was the rule requiring the Governor-General's consent to the putting of questions or moving of motions on such matters as tribal affairs and relations with the princes and foreign countries. Certain powers in relation to the legislature which had previously been exercised by the Governor-General were not removed but transferred: that of arranging for the election of the presiding officer to the President of the Constituent Assembly, that of alloting the time of the legislature for non-official business to the Speaker. Apart from these fundamental changes in the rules were other not less interesting. The rules relating to Bill procedure largely disappeared since there was now only one chamber, the Constituent Assembly (Legislative). A new form of oath was introduced and the quorum provision omitted. The language rule was modified: previously members of the Assembly could speak in English or, by permission, in any Indian vernacular; now they were entitled to speak in English or Hindi or, by permission, in another Indian language. New provisions were introduced to permit motions of no confidence and to allot days for the stages of the Finance Bill. A previous rule limiting the power of the presiding officer to delay procedure on Government Bills was removed. Finally, there were changes of terminology: 'Member' (i.e. of the Executive Council) became 'Minister'; 'The Governor-General in Council' became 'The Government of India'; the Assembly's 'President' becomes 'the Speaker'.

During the autumn session of 1948 the Speaker appointed a Committee of nine members under his Chairmanship to examine the Rules and suggest further amendments.[2] He invited members to submit their comments and suggestions, though it appears from his remarks made in a statement to the House a year later that few responded. In any event he and his staff as well as the Committee had been giving much thought to the matter. The Speaker's statement of December 1949 revealed that he had taken action in two directions.[3] In the first place, he had considered certain points to be of sufficient importance to merit inclusion in the Constitution itself. He had therefore brought his proposals before

---

[1] *Constituent Assembly (Legislative) Rules of Procedure and Standing Orders*, pp. 1 and 13. The powers under the Act of 1935 were of course conferred on the Governor-General but, on the transfer of power, Orders gave these powers to the President of the Constituent Assembly.

[2] C.A. (Leg.) Deb., 3 Sept. 1948.   [3] C.A. (Leg.) Deb., 20 Dec. 1949.

the Drafting Committee engaged in the preparation of the Constitution and he was glad to say that 'the more important points now form part of the Constitution of India'. Among these were the President's Address to Parliament, the revised financial procedure including Votes on Account, Votes of Credit, Appropriation Bills and the Consolidated Fund, and the important Article 105 which gave to Parliament the power to define its own 'powers, privileges and immunities' and declared that until so defined they should 'be those of the House of Commons of the Parliament of the United Kingdom.[1] There were many other changes to be made; his second line of action, therefore, had been to prepare, after consultation with the Government, a further series of modifications and adaptations to the existing Rules. On the inauguration of the new Constitution in 1950 both the relevant Articles as well as the amended Rules —now the 'Rules of Procedure and Conduct of Business in Parliament' —came into force.

The Rules of 1947 were the result primarily of the omission of now repugnant provisions; the Rules of 1950 were mainly marked by elaborations of existing provisions or the introduction of wholly new elements.[2] Of the matters now worked out in greater detail, Question Hour procedure, the admissibility rules for Questions, the procedure of Select Committees, the Divisions of the House and the General Rules for speaking were foremost. The new elements in the Rules were partly the result of the provisions of the new Constitution: the President's Address, the new financial arrangements and a fresh chapter on privileges. Other changes, unconnected with the new Constitution, were of no less importance: the introduction of the Estimates Committee, the Short Notice Question and the 'Half an Hour Discussion.'[3] If these changes appeared to be in the direction of strengthening the House *vis-à-vis* the Government, some other alterations, smaller but of equal significance, seemed to be designed for the same end: all Bills involving expenditure to be accompanied by a Financial Memorandum; the Chairman of a Select Committee to be any member of the Committee appointed by the Speaker—not, as before, the Law Minister *ex officio*; the reports of Select Committees to be presented to the House not by the Minister in charge of the Bill but by the Chairman of the Committee; the Finance Minister to consider the suggestions of the Estimates Committee in deciding the form in which the Budget is presented; the Chairman of the Public Accounts Committee to be no longer the Finance Minister *ex officio* but any member of the Committee appointed by the Speaker.

A third transformation of the Rules took place with the election of the

[1] See also below, pp. 245–255.

[2] The Rules of 1950 incorporated both the 'Rules' and the 'Standing Orders', and the distinction disappeared. It should be added that the arrangement and order of the new Rules appear to have been a big improvement on the old.

[3] All these matters are considered in greater detail in this chapter or in Chapter VI.

two new Houses of Parliament in 1952. The introduction of a bicameral legislature necessitated several changes—in particular the inclusion of provisions for joint committees and for an appropriate Bill procedure. At the same time, the opportunity was utilised to bring in further changes unconnected with the establishment of two Houses. The most important of these concerned the development of the Lower House's committee system: two new committees—the Business Advisory Committee and that on Subordinate Legislation—appear; a third, the Rules Committee, becomes formally recognised; while the procedures of the Public Account Committee and of Select Committees are elaborated. This development of committees represents—as we shall see more fully when we consider the committee structure in detail[1]—a further reinforcement of the House, very largely designed to enable it to stand up to the Executive and exert more control over it. The removal in 1950 of the Law Minister from chairmanship of Select Committees on Bills is in 1952 carried a stage further: neither the Law Minister nor the Minister in charge of a Bill is to be an ex-officio member of the Select Committee. Moreover, a new set of rules defines the powers and conduct of Parliamentary Committees in general.

These changes have been the result almost entirely of the initiative of the Speaker and his Secretariat. Before 1951 few members took much interest in the development of procedure, and the informal Speaker's committee was firmly guided by its chairman. Even after the formal establishment of the Rules Committee in 1952, the proposals put forward by the Speaker or Secretary have almost without exception been agreed to. This represents a considerable achievement and bears witness to the energy and devotion of those concerned. Although it is indeed fitting that the establishment of procedure should be primarily the work of those whose position enables them to make a continuous study of the subject, Assemblies have yet in practice often insisted on exercising considerable influence on the rules and orders; that this has not happened in India (where Parliament is not exactly short of lawyers) shows the confidence that most members have in the Speaker. The power to effect these changes was given to the Speaker (and the Chairman of the Council of States) by the Constitution. It is, however, in the nature of a temporary power. The Constitution lays down that it is each House which is to make its rules; it is only until such rules are made that the Speaker is authorised to make 'modifications and adaptations' to the previously existing rules.[2] While the power has lasted, it has given the Rules of Procedure great flexibility, and several changes—some of considerable importance—have been made with great ease. Since 1952 alone, there have been three occasions on which significant alterations have been made.

[1] See below, Chapter VI.
[2] I.e., to the Rules of 1947–50 which were in turn modifications and adaptations of the pre-1947 rules. The Constitutional provision is Art. 118.

In April 1953 a definite period was set aside for Private Members' business, Ministers were excluded from membership of the Public Accounts and Estimates Committees and, most important, a new and extraordinary Committee on Government Assurances was set up. In August of the same year, a completely new procedure in connection with Private Members' Bills was devised and a new Committee for the purpose introduced. At the same time the powers and functions of the Estimates Committee were very considerably expanded and a new procedure introduced for the discussion of matters of urgent public importance. Only a few months later, in January 1954, the scope of citizens' petitions was much enlarged,[1] a further committee on the absence of members established, the jurisdiction of the Committee on Private Members' Bills extended to cover resolutions and provision made for secret sessions of the House. The result of all this activity is, of course, that the present Rules bear very little resemblance except in broadest outline to those with which the Speaker began in 1947. The changes have in many cases followed on informal experimentation and have been formalised only when results were successful. In all cases, the amendments and additions have arisen out of the work of the House and its needs as felt and formulated by the Speaker and his staff. The House has thus been able rather smoothly and very quickly to adjust its manner and methods of work as new tasks and new attitudes have revealed themselves. At the same time, this happy state of affairs is unlikely to last for long and soon no doubt the House will assert its constitutional power to 'make its own rules'; one consequence will probably be a certain rigidity and difficulty of change as compared with the past.[2]

Although the new Rules are largely the result of close daily observation of procedure in the House and a certain amount of experiment, it should not be concluded that the process has been haphazard or without guiding principles. On the contrary, it has been perhaps peculiarly conscious and deliberate, and its results reflect at every point the central ideas of those who have been responsible for the changes. At the outset, intentions were, as we have suggested, concentrated on the elimination of the

[1] The Committee on Petitions will now have to examine and report on petitions connected not only with Bills but (subject to certain restrictions) on any business before the House or of general public interest. It remains to be seen what use will be made of this provision.

[2] Already in 1954 there were signs of a certain restiveness in some sections of the House and especially among the opposition groups. In Feb. 1954, one opposition M.P., Mr. More (who was defeated in the contest for the Speakership in May 1952), petitioned the President to move the Supreme Court (under Art. 143) and obtain its opinion on the validity of the present Rules. Mr. More contended that the power exercised by the Speaker was intended to be purely transitional and of a very limited character, and that the Speaker has exceeded his authority in making completely new rules and continuing the amending process for a long period. The fact that the Speaker is advised by a Rules Committee nominated by him does not amount, Mr. More argued, to the Speaker performing a function of the House under its delegated authority.

distasteful portions of the old Rules which gave special powers to the Governor-General, limited the powers of the House and in general were unsuited to a sovereign parliament. This simple negative attitude was obviously of itself insufficient and the need for positive principles was quickly felt. Such principles would no doubt gradually emerge from experience, but it was considered that examination of an existing model could provide useful suggestions and probably save time. Since the complaint before 1947 had been that the Delhi Assembly fell short of the House of Commons and that India had been given an inferior article, it was natural that Westminster should have been chosen for this purpose. Visits to London and correspondence with the staff of the House of Commons helped greatly in achieving a clearer idea of the line of advance. A cursory examination of the present Rules is, however, sufficient to show that the use of the model has been discriminating. Such an examination will also show that the marked feeling of distinctness in India between House and Government (whose general causes and character we have already discussed[1]) has been given clear expression. At this point a few examples will suffice.[2]

In many respects, then, the procedure and practice of the Indian Parliament is taken from that of the British. Some parts—and, indeed, the general outline—came from Westminster via the old Central Assembly; India, that is, began with British procedure, though it was severely modified in accordance with the conceptions held by the British Government as to what was suitable for Indian circumstances of non-responsible government. It was not Commons' procedure, but it could be recognised as derived from that model rather than from that of, say, the French Chamber. There was a time for Questions, a similar Bill procedure, similar general rules for making speeches. Other parts came from Westminster directly and were taken soon after independence. These portions were designed to demonstrate the characteristics of a sovereign parliament and in particular to reduce the dominance of the Ministers under the old regime. The introduction of the Consolidated Fund and connected elements of financial procedure, the establishment of an Estimates Committee and the release of the Public Accounts Committee from government control are all examples of this second stage. Finally, the House of Commons continues to be a guide in many matters of refinement. In a very large proportion of amendments, an important argument for change has been that the new rule would incorporate Commons' procedure.[3] Although this would be derided by some xenophobic Indians as further evidence of the slavish imitation of the

---

[1] Above, Chapter III, Section 4.

[2] The contents of the rest of this chapter, as well as of Chapter VI, can be viewed simply as further illustrations.

[3] E.g., 'Secretary explained that the proposed rule was analogous to a rule of the House of Commons'; 'It was explained to the Committee that it was an accepted convention in

West, it is in fact nothing more than the sober judgment of technical experts that it is worth while relying in many ways on the experience of similar technicians of procedure who happen to have been longer at the job.

The makers of modern Indian parliamentary procedure have respect for experience provided it is relevant experience. Their post-independence examination of Commons' procedure persuaded them that in some respects India's own quasi-parliamentary experience deserved to be followed in preference to that of Westminster. Thus India has considered but not accepted the institution of Standing Committees for Bills; she continues to follow the system of *ad hoc* Select Committees chosen for each Bill which is to be sent to committee. Again, she has no Committee of the Whole House and, in particular, no Committees of Supply and Ways and Means. It is recognised that many of the Commons' procedures which owe their origin to peculiar historical circumstances have been adapted to serve modern needs; others, however, are felt to have been imperfectly adapted and to be more cumbersome than alternative methods that can now be devised. Thus it has not been thought necessary to take over the system of money resolutions. In other cases, again, Commons' procedure is regarded as containing useful devices but doing so in what would for India be an unnecessarily antiquated and indirect form. At the end of the day's business in the Commons, when the motion is moved that 'the House do now adjourn', what happens in practice is that for half an hour a member is allowed to raise a matter of public grievance or complaint and obtain the Minister's considered reply. In India, the idea has been thought worth following, but the form is direct: the Rules provide for 'Half an Hour Discussions'. Similarly, explicit provision is made for ministerial statements.

Finally, there are ways in which Indian procedure has moved away from both its own past and the Commons' present. The establishment of a Business Advisory Committee and the strengthening of the Estimates Committee are examples of wholly new developments of existing practices and institutions. The Committee on Government Assurances is an example of an innovation.

The procedure of the Upper House is briefly referred to later. Its rules, too, are the result of 'modifications and adaptations' made by the Chairman of the Council. These were mainly effected for the new Council of 1952—there being no Upper House during 1947–52—and

the House of Commons that . . .'; 'The proposed rule is designed to make our procedure more elastic and in conformity with the practice in the House of Commons'; 'The Speaker of the House of Commons had always ruled that . . .'. It is of some interest that on one rule English practice was explicitly found irrelevant; in India the rules are framed under a written Constitution interpreted by the Courts. Even in this case it was 'suggested that it would be better to have a rule in conformity with the practice in England, leaving it to the Courts, if ever occasion should arise, to pronounce upon the matter'.

have not been developed subsequently to the same extent as those of the House of the People. The evolution of State legislatures' procedure has followed stages similar to those we have described. The process has, of course, varied as the starting points of the different States varied. Those States which were formerly Provinces with Legislative Assemblies and Councils have followed an almost identical line of development from the same starting date of 1921. They, too, of course, had representative councils of a kind even before that time.[1] The position in the former princely states showed no uniformity. In the politically undeveloped areas, no popular representative institutions of any kind existed; they had to be created when the accession and integration of states took place in 1947–50. In others, such institutions had sometimes a long history. In Travancore, for instance, a nominated Legislative Council set up in 1888 became partly elective in 1908 and mainly elective in 1921. In 1948 the state introduced adult franchise ahead of the Indian Union. Mysore was even more advanced. Its Representative Assembly dated from 1881 and two 'Houses' were in existence from 1907.[2] In all cases, however, important procedural changes were necessary corollaries of the advent of responsible government. These changes have been very much modelled on those at the Centre. The lead of the Parliament Secretariat in Delhi is generally closely followed in the States, while the Conference of the Speakers of all legislatures under the Chairmanship of the Speaker of the House of the People is a further unifying force.[3]

2. The Parliamentary Day

When the Speaker enters the House the order of business is already settled. Each member has been given the List of Business for the day (or, sometimes, covering two or more days). Portions of two such lists are reproduced below:

HOUSE OF THE PEOPLE

LIST OF BUSINESS
November 16, 17, 18 and 19, 1953
[1-30 P.M.]

OATH OR AFFIRMATION

Members who have not already done so to make the prescribed oath or affirmation of allegiance to the Constitution.

---

[1] See above, Chapter I.

[2] Government of Mysore, *Report of the Committee on Constitutional Reform in Mysore*, 1939.

[3] See below, Chapter VI, Sections 1 and 2. Most States like to show with pride how far they have been able to walk in Delhi's procedural footsteps. A few, on the other hand, show pride in their independence and point out directions in which Delhi's Rules have not been imitated. Some have even entered into direct correspondence with Legislatures abroad (in U.K. and the Dominions), but this has been discouraged.

14—P.I.

QUESTIONS

Questions entered in the separate lists to be asked and answers given.

EVIDENCE RELATING TO REPORT OF PUBLIC ACCOUNTS COMMITTEE

Shri B. Das to present Volume II—Evidence relating to the Fifth Report of the Public Accounts Committee (1952–53) on the Appropriation Accounts (Railways) and (Posts and Telegraphs), 1949–50.

PAPERS TO BE LAID ON THE TABLE

*1. **Secretary** to lay on the table a copy of the statement showing the Bills passed by the Houses of Parliament during the Fourth Session, 1953, and assented to by the President.

2. **Shri Jagjivan Ram to lay on the table, under sub-section (3) of section 5 of the Indian Aircraft Act, 1934, a copy of the Ministry of Communications Notification No. 10–A/34–50, dated the 6th September, 1952, together with an explanatory note.

***3. **Shri C. C. Biswas** to lay on the table, under sub-section (2) of section 9 of the Delimitation Commission Act, 1952, a copy of the Delimitation Commission, India, Final Order, No. 2, dated the 15th September, 1953.

***4. **Shri Arun Chandra Guha** to lay on the table a copy of each of the following papers in accordance with sub-section (3) of section 35 of the Industrial Finance Corporation Act, 1948:—

 (i) Fifth Annual Report of the Board of Directors of the Industrial Finance Corporation of India on the working of the Corporation during the year ended the 30th June, 1953; and

 (ii) statement showing the assets and liabilities of the Corporation at the close of the year and the Profit and Loss Account for the year.

***5. **Shri Arun Chandra Guha** to lay on the table a copy of the Report of the Rehabilitation Finance Administration for the half year ended the 30th June, 1953, in accordance with sub-section (2) of section 18 of the Rehabilitation Finance Administration Act, 1948.

---

 * To be laid on Monday, the 16th November, 1953.
 ** To be laid on Tuesday, the 17th November, 1953.
 *** To be laid on Wednesday, the 18th November, 1953.

LEGISLATIVE BUSINESS

The Rehabilitation Finance Administration (Amendment) Bill.

1. **Shri C. D. Deshmukh** to move that the Bill further to amend the Rehabilitation Finance Administration Act, 1948, be taken into consideration.

Also to move that the Bill be passed.

(*Amendments printed on separate list to be moved*)

The Sea Customs (Amendment) Bill.

2. **Shri C. D. Deshmukh** to move that the Bill further to amend the Sea Customs Act, 1878, be taken into consideration.

Also to move that the Bill be passed.

(*Amendments printed on separate list to be moved*)

The Coir Industries Bill.

3. Further consideration of the following motion moved by Shri D. P. Karmarkar on the 7th August, 1953, namely:—

"That the Bill to provide for the control by the Union of the Coir Industry and for that purpose to establish a Coir Board and levy a customs duty on coir fibre, coir yarn and coir products exported from India, be taken into consideration."

Shri D. P. Karmarkar to move that the Bill be passed.

(*Also further consideration of the amendment for reference of the Bill to a Select Committee moved by Shri V. P. Nayar, on the 7th August, 1953.*)

The Ancient and Historical Monuments and Archaeological Sites and Remains (Declaration of National Importance) Amendment Bill.

4. **Maulana Abul Kalam Azad** to move that the Bill to amend the Ancient and Historical Monuments and Archaeological Sites and Remains (Declaration of National Importance) Act, 1951, as passed by the Council of States, be taken into consideration.

Also to move that the Bill be passed.

The Calcutta High Court (Extension of Jurisdiction) Bill.

5. **Dr. K. N. Katju** to move that the Bill to extend the jurisdiction of the High Court at Calcutta to Chandernagore and the Andaman and Nicobar Islands, as passed by the Council of States, be taken into consideration.

Also to move that the Bill be passed.

The Travancore-Cochin High Court (Amendment) Bill.

6. **Dr. K. N. Katju** to move that the Bill further to amend the Travancore-Cochin High Court Act, 1952, as passed by the Council of States, be taken into consideration.

Also to move that the Bill be passed.

The Live-Stock Importation (Amendment) Bill.

7. **Shri P. S. Deshmukh** to move that the Bill further to amend the Live-stock Importation Act, 1898, as passed by the Council of States, be taken into consideration.

Also to move that the Bill be passed.

The Repealing and Amending Bill.

8. **Shri C. C. Biswas** to move that the Bill to repeal certain enactments and to amend certain other enactments, as passed by the Council of States, be taken into consideration.

Also to move that the Bill be passed.

The Cantonments
(Amendment) Bill.

9. **Shri Mahavir Tyagi** to move that the Bill further to amend the Cantonments Act, 1924, as passed by the Council of States be taken into consideration.

Also to move that the Bill be passed.

The Indian Railways
(Amendment) Bill.

10. **Shri Lal Bahadur** to move that the Bill further to amend the Indian Railways Act, 1890, as passed by the Council of States, be taken into consideration.

Also to move that the Bill be passed.

The Special
Marriage Bill.

11. **Shri C. C. Biswas** to move the following:—

"That this House concurs in the recommendation of the Council of States that the House do join in the Joint Committee of the Houses on the Bill to provide a special form of marriage in certain cases, and for the registration of such and certain other marriages and resolves that the following members of the House of the People be nominated to serve on the said Joint Committee (names of persons to be mentioned at the time of making the motion)."

NEW DELHI,
The 11th November, 1953.

M. N. KAUL,
Secretary.

HOUSE OF THE PEOPLE

LIST OF BUSINESS
December 11, 1953.

PART I

GOVERNMENT BUSINESS
[*From* 1-30 P.M. *to* 4 P.M.]

A Supplementary List showing Government Business is being issued separately.

PART II

PRIVATE MEMBERS' BUSINESS
[*From* 4 P.M. *to* 6-30 P.M.]

Private Members' Bills to be introduced

The Universities
(Extension of Jurisdiction to other
State or States) Bill.

1. **Shri Sivamurthi Swami** to move for leave to introduce a Bill to extend the jurisdiction of a university of any State in India to other State or States linguistically connected or for any other purpose and to provide for matters connected therewith.

Also to introduce the Bill.

The Indian Railways
(Amendment) Bill.
(*Omission of sections
71A, 71B and amendment of sections 71C,
71D, etc.*)

2. **Shri K. Ananda Nambiar** to move for leave to introduce a Bill further to amend the Indian Railways Act, 1890. (*Omission of sections 71A, 71B, and amendment of sections 71C, 71D, etc.*)

Also to introduce the Bill.

The Government of Part C States (Amendment) Bill. (*Amendment of sections* 1, 3, *etc., and omission of section* 23, *etc.*)

3. **Shri Dasaratha Deb** to move for leave to introduce a Bill further to amend the Government of Part C States Act, 1951. (*Amendment of sections* 1, 3, *etc., and omission of section* 23, *etc.*)

Also to introduce the Bill.

The Government of Part C States Bill. (*Amendment of sections* 1, 3, *etc., and omission of section* 23, *etc.*)

4. **Shri Biren Dutt** to move for leave to introduce a Bill further to amend the Government of Part C States Act, 1951. (*Amendment of sections* 1, 3, *etc. and omission of section* 23, *etc.*)

Also to introduce the Bill.

The Government of Part C States (Amendment) Bill. (*Amendment of sections* 1, 3, *etc., and omission of section* 23, *etc.*)

5. **Shri V. P. Nayar** to move for leave to introduce a Bill further to amend the Government of Part C States Act, 1951. (*Amendment of sections* 1, 3, *etc., and omission of section* 23, *etc.*)

Also to introduce the Bill.

The Indian Trade Unions (Amendment) Bill. (*Insertion of new section* 15A.)

6. **Shri K. Ananda Nambiar** to move for leave to introduce a Bill further to amend the Indian Trade Unions Act, 1926. (*Insertion of new section* 15A.)

Also to introduce the Bill.

The Training and Employment Bill.

7. **Shri Diwan Chand Sharma** to move for leave to introduce a Bill to make provision for employment and training for employment and to establish a comprehensive youth employment service.

Also to introduce the Bill.

The Unemployment Relief Bill.

8. **Shri A. K. Gopalan** to move for leave to introduce a Bill to provide relief to unemployed workers.

Also to introduce the Bill.

The Unemployment Relief Bill.

9. **Shri V. P. Nayar** to move for leave to introduce a Bill to provide relief to unemployed workers.

Also to introduce the Bill.

The Chartered Accountants (Amendment) Bill. (*Amendment of sections* 2, 4, *etc.*)

10. **Shri C. R. Narasimhan** to move for leave to introduce a Bill further to amend the Chartered Accountants Act, 1949. (*Amendment of sections* 2, 4, *etc.*)

Also to introduce the Bill.

PRIVATE MEMBERS' LEGISLATIVE BUSINESS

The Indian Cattle Preservation Bill.

11. ***Further Consideration** of the following motion moved by Seth Govind Das on the 27th November, 1953:—

"That the Bill to preserve the milch and draught cattle of the country be taken into consideration."

Seth Govind Das to move that the Bill be passed.

The Monogamy Enforcement Bill.

12. **Pandit Thakur Das Bhargava** to move that the Bill to enforce monogamy and to prohibit and penalise future bigamous marriages and to declare them illegal, be taken into consideration.

Also to move that the Bill be passed.

* Seth Govind Das to continue his Speech.

The Prevention of Bigamous Marriages Bill.

13. **Shri H. V. Pataskar** to move that the Bill to provide for the prevention of bigamous marriages, be taken into consideration.

Also to move that the Bill be passed.

The Hindu Divorce Bill.

14. **Shri H. V. Pataskar** to move that the Bill to provide for a right of divorce among all communities of Hindus in certain circumstances, be taken into consideration.

Also to move that the Bill be passed.

The Dowry Restraint Bill.

15. **Shri Fulsinhji B. Dabhi** to move that the Bill to restrain the custom of taking or giving of dowry in marriages, be taken into consideration.

Also to move that the Bill be passed.

The Control of Export and Standardisation of Handloom Cloth Bill.

16. **Shri S. V. Ramaswamy** to move that the Bill to control the export and the standardisation of handloom cloth, be taken into consideration.

Also to move that the Bill be passed.

The Punishment for Adulteration of Foodstuffs Bill.

17. **Shri Banarsi Prasad Jhunjhunwala** to move that the Bill to provide for punishment of those found guilty of adulteration of foodstuffs, be taken into consideration.

Also to move that the Bill be passed.

The Prevention of Juvenile Vagrancy and Begging Bill.

18. **Shri M. L. Dwivedi** to move that the Bill to make provision for prevention of juvenile vagrancy and begging, be taken into consideration.

Also to move that the Bill be passed.

The Dowry Restraint Bill.

19. **Shrimati Jayashri Raiji** to move that the Bill to provide for restraining the taking or giving of dowry in connection with marriages and for matters incidental thereto, be taken into consideration.

Also to move that the Bill be passed.

The Indian Penal Code (Amendment) Bill. (*Amendment of section 302.*)

20. **Shri Syed Mohammad Ahmad Kazmi** to move that the Bill further to amend the Indian Penal Code, 1860 (*Amendment of Section* 302), be circulated for the purpose of eliciting opinion thereon by the end of February, 1954.

The Muslim Kazis Bill.

21. **Shri Syed Mohammad Ahmad Kazmi** to move that the Bill to provide for the appointment of persons to the office of Kazi and for performing and keeping a record of marriages and for the appointment of Tribunals for trying and deciding cases of divorce and dissolution of marriage amongst Muslims, be circulated for the purpose of eliciting opinion thereon by the end of February, 1954.

The Indian Penal Code (Amendment) Bill. (*Amendment of sections* 53, 121, 132, *etc.*)

22. **Shri Rohini Kumar Chaudhuri** to move that the Bill further to amend the Indian Penal Code, 1860 (*Amendment of Sections* 53, 121, 132, *etc.*), be circulated for the purpose of eliciting opinion thereon by the end of February, 1954.

The Parliament Library Bill.

23. **Shri Diwan Chand Sharma** to move that the Bill to provide for building up an up-to-date and a comprehensive Library for Parliament, be taken into consideration.

Also to move that the Bill be passed.

The Military Pensions Bill.

24. **Dr. N. B. Khare** to move that the Bill to regulate the grant of ordinary pension, disability pension, family pension and special pension to military personnel, be taken into consideration.

Also to move that the Bill be passed.

The Indian Penal Code Amendment Bill. (*Insertion of new section 294B.*)

25. **Shri Nageshwar Prasad Sinha** to move that the Bill further to amend the Indian Penal Code, 1860 (*Insertion of new section 294B*), be taken into consideration.

Also to move that the Bill be passed.

The Indian Registration(Amendment) Bill. (*Insertion of new section 20A.*)

26. **Shri Satis Chandra Samanta** to move that the Bill further to amend the Indian Registration Act, 1908 (*Insertion of new section 20A*), be taken into consideration.

Also to move that the Bill be passed.

The Children's Protection Bill.

27. **Shrimati Sushama Sen** to move that the Bill to provide for protection, maintenance, custody, education and employment of children, be taken into consideration.

Also to move that the Bill be passed.

The Indian Livestock Improvement Bill.

28. **Shri Jhulan Sinha** to move that the Bill to provide for the improvement of livestock in India, be taken into consideration.

Also to move that the Bill be passed.

The Indian Registration (Amendment) Bill. (*Amendment of section 21.*)

29. **Shri S. V. Ramaswamy** to move that the Bill further to amend the Indian Registration Act, 1908 (*Amendment of section 21*), be taken into consideration.

(*Amendment printed on separate list to be moved.*)

Also to move that the Bill be passed.

The Prevention of Cow Slaughter Bill.

30. **Shri Nandlal Sharma** to move that the Bill to prevent the slaughtering of cows in India, be taken into consideration.

Also to move that the Bill be passed.

The Suppression of Immoral Traffic and Brothels Bill.

31. **Shrimati Maniben Vallabhbhai Patel** to move that the Bill to provide for and consolidate the law relating to suppression of immoral traffic in women and brothels, be taken into consideration.

Also to move that the Bill be passed.

The Code of Criminal Procedure (Amendment) Bill. (*Omission of sections 268, 284 and 309 and amendment of section 286, etc.*)

32. **Shri Khub Chand Sodhia** to move that the Bill further to amend the Code of Criminal Procedure, 1898 (*Omission of sections 268, 284, and 309 and amendment of section 286, etc.*), be taken into consideration.

Also to move that the Bill be passed.

The Women's and Children's Institutions Licensing Bill.

33. **Shrimati Maniben Vallabhbhai Patel** to move that the Bill to regulate and licence institutions caring for women and children, be taken into consideration.

Also to move that the Bill be passed.

The Code of Criminal Procedure (Amendment) Bill. (*Amendment of sections 496 and 497.*)

34. Pandit Thakur Das Bhargava to move that the Bill further to amend the Code of Criminal Procedure, 1898 (*Amendment of sections 496 and 497*), be taken into consideration.

Also to move that the Bill be passed.

The Unemployment Relief Bill.

35. Shri Hirendra Nath Mukerjee to move that the Bill to provide relief to unemployed workers, be taken into consideration.

Also to move that the Bill be passed.

The Payment of Wages (Amendment) Bill. (*Amendment of sections 2 and 17 and insertion of new section 27.*)

36. Dr. N. B. Khare to move that the Bill further to amend the Payment of Wages Act, 1936 (*Amendment of sections 2 and 17 and insertion of new section 27*), be taken into consideration.

Also to move that the Bill be passed.

The Code of Criminal Procedure (Amendment) Bill. (*Amendment of section 435.*)

37. Shri Raghunath Singh to move that the Bill further to amend the Code of Criminal Procedure, 1898 (*Amendment of section 435*), be taken into consideration.

Also to move that the Bill be passed.

The Sri Kashi Viswanath Mandir Bill.

38. Shri Raghunath Singh to move that the Bill to provide for the better administration and governance and for the preservation of the Sri Kashi Viswanath Mandir known as the Golden Temple of Banaras be taken into consideration.

Also to move that the Bill be passed.

The Women's and Children's Institutions Licensing Bill.

39. Shrimati Uma Nehru to move that the Bill to regulate and licence institutions caring for women and children be taken into consideration.

Also to move that the Bill be passed.

The Code of Civil Procedure (Amendment) Bill (Omission of section 87B.)

40. Shri H. V. Pataskar to move that the Bill further to amend the Code of Civil Procedure, 1908 (*Omission of section 87B*) be taken into consideration.

Also to move that the Bill be passed.

The Child Marriage Restraint (Amendment) Bill. (*Amendment of sections 2 and 3.*)

41. Shri S. V. Ramaswamy to move that the Bill further to amend the Child Marriage Restraint Act, 1929 (*Amendment of sections 2 and 3*) be taken into consideration.

Also to move that the Bill be passed.

The Indian Penal Code (Amendment) Bill. (*Amendment of sections 312 and 314.*)

42. Shri S. V. Ramaswamy to move that the Bill further to amend the Indian Penal Code, 1860 (*Amendment of sections 312 and 314*) be taken into consideration.

Also to move that the Bill be passed.

The Prohibition of Manufacture and Import of Hydrogenated Vegetable Oils Bill.

43. Pandit Thakur Das Bhargava to move that the Bill to provide for the prohibition of manufacture and import of hydrogenated vegetable oils be taken into consideration.

Also to move that the Bill be passed.

The Titles and Gifts from Foreign States (Penalty for Acceptance) Bill.

44. Shri C. R. Narasimhan to move that the Bill to provide for penalties for acceptance of titles and gifts from foreign States be taken into consideration.

Also to move that the Bill be passed.

The Handloom Industry (Improvement and Protection) Bill.

45. Shri S. V. Ramaswamy to move that the Bill to provide for the improvement and protection of the handloom industry be taken into consideration.

Also to move that the Bill be passed.

The Special Marriage (Amendment) Bill. (*Amendment of section 2.*)

46. Shri S. V. Ramaswamy to move that the Bill further to amend the Special Marriage Act, 1872 (*Amendment of section 2*) be taken into consideration.

Also to move that the Bill be passed.

The Child Marriage Restraint (Amendment) Bill. (*Amendment of sections 2 and 4.*)

47. Pandit Thakur Das Bhargava to move that the Bill further to amend the Child Marriage Restraint Act, 1929 (*Amendment of sections 2 and 4*) be taken into consideration.

Also to move that the Bill be passed.

The Indian Arms (Amendment) Bill. (*Amendment of sections 1 and 26 and insertion of new sections 17A and 34.*)

48. Shri Uma Charan Patnaik to move that the Bill further to amend the Indian Arms Act, 1878 (*Amendment of sections 1 and 26 and insertion of new sections 17A and 34*) be taken into consideration.

Also to move that the Bill be passed.

The Essential Supplies (Temporary Powers) Amendment Bill (*Amendment of section 7 and substitution of section 9.*)

49. Pandit Thakur Das Bhargava to move that the Bill further to amend the Essential Supplies (Temporary Powers) Act, 1946 (*Amendment of section 7 and substitution of section 9*) be taken into consideration.

Also to move that the Bill be passed.

The Prohibition of Manufacture and Sale of Vanaspati Bill.

50. Shri Jhulan Sinha to move that the Bill to provide for the prohibition of manufacture and sale of vanaspati in India be taken into consideration.

Also to move that the Bill be passed.

The Suppression of Immoral Traffic and Brothels Bill.

51. Shrimati Uma Nehru to move that the Bill to provide for and consolidate the law relating to suppression of immoral traffic in women and brothels be taken into consideration.

Also to move that the Bill be passed.

NEW DELHI;   M. N. KAUL,
The 8th December, 1953.   *Secretary.*

In any Assembly the arrangement of business is a delicate and important matter. The bulk of the time of the House is required by the Government, but some time must be set aside for Private Members; and even in the time allotted to Government business the wishes of the opposition groups have to be taken into account. Since 1953 the last two and a half hours of the Friday sittings are normally allotted for the transaction of Private Members' business.[1] Such business may consist of

[1] New Rule 24.

Resolutions or Bills, and which of the two is to be dealt with on a particular Friday is left to the Speaker to decide. On days devoted to Private Members' Bills, precedence is given according to the stage already reached by the Bills, but among Bills at a similar stage of progress precedence is decided by ballot.[1] On Resolution days, precedence is determined by ballot. Towards the end of 1953 it was decided that there should be a Committee on Private Members' Bills and Resolutions.[2] The Committee, nominated by the Speaker, was primarily intended to recommend time limits for the various Bills and Resolutions, since it had been found that some M.P.s who were fortunate in the ballot tended to hold the floor Friday after Friday.[3] This part of the work of the Committee has gone smoothly. Bills have been classified in two categories, by tests of public importance and urgency and in the light of possible Government-sponsored legislation. As among the Bills given priority, a fixed number of hours for the completion of all stages is laid down.[4] The Committee was, however, also asked to examine in particular Private Members' Bills seeking to amend the Constitution. The Committee took this matter very seriously and laid down certain general principles. One of these stated that 'The Constitution should be considered as a sacred document—a document which should not be lightly interfered with and should be amended only when it is found absolutely necessary to do so. . . . Such amendments should normally be brought by Government.' The Committee found that four Bills of which Private Members had given notice sought to amend the Constitution; it examined them and recommended that none of the four should be allowed to be even introduced in the House.[5] This report was accepted by the House but only after some uneasiness had been felt by many members.[6]

Apart from the half-day on Fridays, the rest of the time of the House is allotted to Government business. The decision as to which Bills are to be introduced and further proceeded with is determined by the Cabinet and in particular by its Parliamentary Affairs Committee under the Chairmanship of the Chief Whip or Minister for Parliamentary Affairs.

[1] Rule 25, as amended in 1953. Bills to be introduced now have precedence over others —a concession to members' pressure.

[2] *Rules*, New Chapter VIA. The Committee was appointed on 1 Dec. 1953 and its jurisdiction, at first restricted to Bills, was in Jan. 1954 extended to Resolutions. The Deputy Speaker is Chairman.

[3] Seth Govind Das and his Indian Cattle Preservation Bill proved particularly tenacious. So also Mr. Gopalan's Resolution on Unemployment.

[4] See Reports of the Committee on Private Members' Bills and Resolutions. In the five months of its existence up to May 1954 the Committee met 12 times and issued 8 Reports. It examined and classified 56 Bills, placing 13 in 'Category A'. It decided to recommend an upper time limit of four hours for any Bill or Resolution, and it fixed a particular number of hours for 15 Resolutions.

[5] *Ibid.*, First Report.

[6] H.P. Deb., 11 Dec. 1953. The Communists found some support for their view that the Committee appeared to be determined that only the Government should initiate Constitutional changes.

The further decision as to the order in which they are to be taken up is a matter for consultation between the Leader of the House—in practice, the Chief Whip will negotiate—and the Speaker, and the List of Business is prepared accordingly by the Secretary. This decision, however, is dependent to some extent on how much time is to be devoted to each stage of each Bill. For the settlement of this problem a Business Advisory Committee was established from 1952. Consisting of fifteen members from the main parties nominated by the Speaker and meeting under his Chairmanship three or four times a session, the Committee allocates time for the various Government Bills. The Chief Whip is, of course, an important member of the Committee and he will state which Bills, in the view of the Government, merit most attention. The agreed conclusions of the Committee are then announced in the House by the Speaker. The Committee has worked well and has reduced by a considerable amount the discussion by the House as a whole of the allocation of time. This achievement does not mean, however, that all difficulties in the arrangement of business have been overcome. Trouble continues to arise in two ways. In the first place, the order of business is not kept constant and members who prepare themselves for one Bill complain that they find another has been moved forward in its place.[1] These last-minute changes are in part the fault of Ministers whose other engagements and tours undertaken at short notice sometimes cause them to be absent when their Bills come up for discussion. Most of the alterations, however, are the consequence of the House itself not adhering to its programme; unfinished business caused by some unexpected intervention today is carried forward to upset the plans for tomorrow. Apart from the troubles of day-to-day arrangements, there is usually also an end-of-the-session rush. Members have, for example, pressed for a foreign affairs debate towards the end of a session; yet they are often unwilling to accept the consequences. They generally resist any curtailment of time agreed upon for the other items, they are averse to any extension of the session and they are usually most hostile to any suggestion that the House might sit a little longer than its five-hour day. Somewhat surprisingly, they often choose instead to do without the Question Hour for as many days as may be necessary.[2]

Normally, however, it is with Question Hour that the day's business

---

[1] Before 1952, the complaints came from all sides of the House; e.g. P.P. Deb., 28 April 1951. Since 1952, it is a frequent point of the opposition groups; e.g., 23 Nov. 1953.

[2] E.g., H.P. Deb., 17 Dec. 1953, when the Prime Minister, as Leader of the House, put the problem before the members: the session was due to end on 24 Dec., but he had agreed to a debate on foreign affairs; it seemed to him that they would have to sit later or curtail debate on other items. In the result, Question Hour on 22–24 Dec. was used for ordinary business in order to avoid sitting beyond the hours of 1.30–6.30. This marked hostility to long hours is said by some to be a reaction against certain days of 1952 when the House, after sitting its normal 8 a.m.–1 p.m., met again in the evening from 4–7 p.m. Optimists believe that the House will eventually be willing to accept a seven-hour day.

begins. This institution is as highly developed in India as it is in Britain, and in this important respect the Indian Parliament is distinguished not only from those of Continental countries but even from some of the older Dominions.[1] It is generally the most interesting part of the day's proceedings—less on account of the actual answers given (though these may contain important statements) than because of the battle of wits that can take place between the questioning members and the Minister. This is the time when the lively M.P. can make his mark; it is, equally, the time when Ministers can make or mar their reputations.

Questions for which an oral answer is wanted are 'starred' by the questioner, and members are each allowed a ration of three such questions per day.[2] Any others are supplied with written answers only; the same happens to questions intended for oral answer but not in fact reached in the allotted time. Different days are set aside for the various ministries, and members state the date on which they require an answer from a particular Minister.[3] Ministries are in practice placed in three groups so that each Minister's turn (in the House of the People[4]) comes twice a week. A typical week's allotment of days is given below:

ALLOTMENT OF DAYS FOR ANSWERING QUESTIONS DURING THE SIXTH SESSION OF THE HOUSE OF THE PEOPLE

Tuesday 16 February	Wednesday 17 February	Thursday 18 February	Friday 19 February
Prime Minister External Affairs Commerce and Industry Information and Broadcasting Irrigation and Power Planning Production Rehabilitation Works, Housing and Supply	Communications Food and Agriculture Health Labour Railways Transport	Defence Education Finance Home Affairs Law Natural Resources and Scientific Research States	Prime Minister External Affairs Commerce and Industry Information and Broadcasting Irrigation and Power Planning Production Rehabilitation Works, Housing and Supply

[1] Sir Anthony Eden, in his tour of the Commonwealth, is said to have felt more at home in the Indian Parliament's Question Hour than he had in the Australian Parliament.

[2] The rules relating to Questions are given in Chapter VII (i.e., Rules 38–58) of the *Rules*. For the practice relating to Questions, I have consulted the appropriate sections of the two series of volumes of 'Decisions' and 'Observations' from the Chair.

[3] Members have been guided in the sometimes complicated matter of which Minister is responsible for what; the Parliament Secretariat has published a 50-page pamphlet which gives the answer in some detail.

[4] See above, p. 151. His turn in the Council of States is arranged not to coincide.

ALLOTMENT OF DAYS FOR ANSWERING QUESTIONS—*continued*

Monday 22 February	Tuesday 23 February	Wednesday 24 February
Communications	Defence	Prime Minister
Food and Agriculture	Education	External Affairs
Health	Finance	Commerce and Industry
Labour	Home Affairs	Information and Broad-
Railways	Law	casting
Transport	Natural Resources and	Irrigation and Power
	Scientific Research	Planning
	States	Production
		Rehabilitation
		Works, Housing and
		Supply

A member wishing to question the Finance Minister thus knows the days available, and he also knows that he must give ten days' notice for his question.

The admissibility of questions is decided by the Speaker, and he is guided by a list of twenty-two conditions which have been stated in the Rules of Procedure.[1] Even so, the work is laborious—the Secretariat has a special Questions Branch which helps to determine for example whether a question should be disallowed on the ground that it has in substance already been answered. It is also sometimes difficult; questions which relate to public corporations and universities and those which touch on the sphere of State responsibilities have to be carefully examined before being admitted. In cases of uncertainty, the Speaker asks the department concerned for the relevant papers and then makes his judgment.[2] Copies of all questions are in any case sent to the ministries concerned as soon as they have been edited in the Parliament Secretariat, and an opportunity is given to the ministries to point out, for instance, that the question is a repetition of one already answered or that the information it seeks is already available in a published document. These comments are laid before the Speaker when he comes to decide on admissibility. Ministries may not make any suggestions or pleas to the Speaker on admission or disallowance; it is always open to

[1] Rule 47. A question shall not, for example, ask for an expression of opinion, relate to a matter which is not primarily the concern of the Government of India, make or imply a charge of a personal character, etc. Two fairly recent additions to these conditions are that a question may not refer discourteously to a friendly foreign country and may not seek information regarding Cabinet discussions.

[2] As a general rule, questions which refer to any of the following are admitted: action taken on an All-India basis, even if done by each State; events of All-India importance, even if occurring in the States; matters in respect of which the Government of India makes grants or gives advice. The Speaker also exercises his discretion in deciding whether oral or written replies are suitable and very many 'starred' questions are in fact transferred to the list of 'unstarred'.

them to answer a question by a refusal to supply information on the grounds that the expenditure of time and labour involved in collecting the information will not be commensurate with the result or that it is not in the public interest to disclose the information or simply that the information is not available. In a few cases, it may happen that a ministry feels that it would be against public interest that a certain question should even be asked—if it relates, for example, to delicate negotiations still in progress; the Minister of Parliamentary Affairs would then be asked to approach the member concerned and try to persuade him to withdraw the question.

Questions are asked in the order in which they appear in the List of Questions—and that, in turn, is the order in which notice is received.[1] The members put their questions by standing and calling out the question number as given in the List. Part of a typical List of Questions in the House of the People is reproduced below:

HOUSE OF THE PEOPLE

'Questions for Oral Answers'

to be asked at a sitting of the House to be held on

Monday, the 8th March, 1954

SMUGGLING AND CATTLE LIFTING

*745. Sardar Hukam Singh: Will the **Prime Minister** be pleased to state:

(a) whether there is any co-ordination and co-operation in checking smuggling and cattle lifting at the border check posts of the two Punjabs: and

(b) the number of cattle heads lifted from Indian territory by Pakistanis during 1953–54 and the number returned?

U.S.-PAKISTAN MILITARY ALLIANCE

*746. Th. Lakshman Singh Charak: Will the **Prime Minister** be pleased to state whether there has been any difference in the normal movement of people from Pakistan to India and *vice versa* since reports of the talks on U.S.-Pakistan Military alliance appeared in Press?

1 Requests from Ministers that, within a day's List, questions should be grouped according to the Ministers to whom they are addressed have not been granted. It was pointed out that if the order according to ministries was kept constant, questions to certain Ministers would never be reached by the end of Question Hour and the replies would invariably be written. On the other hand, if Ministers took it in turn to be at the head of the List, there would be a rush of questions to particular departments on particular days.

CYCLE INDUSTRY

*747. Shri Bahadur Singh: Will the Minister of **Commerce and Industry** be pleased to state:

(a) the annual production of cycles by the Punjab Cycle Manufacturers;

(b) whether the Tariff Commission has received representations from these manufacturers asking for protection to this industry;

(c) whether the Tariff Commission has considered those representations; and

(d) if so, what is the decision?

CHANDERNAGORE

*748. { **Sardar A. S. Saigal**:
 Shri Tushar Chatterjea:
 Shri M. S. Gurupadaswamy:

Will the **Prime Minister** be pleased to state:

(a) whether the Jha Commission has submitted its report on the future Administration of Chandernagore;

(b) what are the recommendations in the report; and

(c) when these recommendations are likely to be implemented?

MANAGER, TECHNICAL INSTITUTE, FARIDABAD

*749. Shri V. P. Nayar: (a) Will the Minister of **Rehabilitation** be pleased to state whether it is a fact that the Manager, Technical Institute, Faridabad, has applied for a monthly remuneration, over and above the contract terms?

(b) What has been decided regarding the salary to be paid to the Manager?

PALM *Gur*

*750. Shri Jhulan Sinha: Will the Minister of **Commerce and Industry** be pleased to state:

(a) the total annual expenditure over the monthly publication *Tad Gur Khabar*;

(b) the areas where it is distributed; and

(c) the expansion of the Palm *gur* Industry as a result of the superintendence of and direction given by the Palm *Gur* section of the Ministry?

U.N. COMMISSION ON RACIAL DISCRIMINATION

*751. Shri S. N. Das: Will the **Prime Minister** be pleased to state:

(a) whether there has been any widening of the terms and scope of the U.N. Commission of Inquiry on the racial discrimination in South Africa; and

(b) the nature of work that the Commission has decided to do since the U.N. General Assembly passed the resolution to continue the Commission?

MAHATMA GANDHI SAMADHI

*752. Shri Krishnacharya Joshi: Will the Minister of **Works, Housing and Supply** be pleased to state:

(a) whether a new model of the Samadhi of Mahatma Gandhi at Rajghat has been prepared and completed by the C.P.W.D.; and

(b) if so, when the work of reconstruction of the Samadhi at Rajghat will begin?

DEVELOPMENT SCHEMES IN DELHI

*753. Shri Radha Raman: Will the Minister of **Planning** be pleased to state:

(a) the aggregate amount sanctioned by Government to the Delhi State for various development schemes;

(b) the amount already drawn;

(c) the number of development schemes submitted against the sanctioned amount;

(d) the number of schemes so far accepted; and

(e) how long it will take to accept the other schemes?

HANDLOOM WEEK

*574. Dr. Ram Subhag Singh: Will the Minister of **Commerce and Industry** be pleased to state:

(a) whether it is a fact that a Handloom Week was recently observed throughout the country under the auspices of the All India Handloom Board;

(b) whether it is also a fact that some grants were made to all the States for observing this week; and

(c) whether some grants were also made to those co-operatives which participated in observance of that week?

COAL PURCHASE BY PAKISTAN

*755. Shri M. R. Krishna: Will the Minister of **Commerce and Industry** be pleased to state:

(a) whether it is a fact that the Pakistan Government are gradually lessening the purchases of coal from India; and

(b) what reasons were given by the Pakistan Government for this action?

ARID ZONE RESEARCH

*756. Shri S. C. Samanta: Will the Minister of **Irrigation and Power** be pleased to state:

(a) whether it is a fact that the Jaswant College at Jodhpur has been associated with the arid zone programme of the UNESCO;

(b) if so, when; and

(c) what are the advantages derived by this college by such association?

MANUFACTURE OF FOUNTAIN PENS AND INK

*757. Shri K. P. Sinha: Will the Minister of **Commerce and Industry** be pleased to state:

(a) whether it is a fact that a new plant for the manufacture of fountain pens and ink is to be set up at Bangalore;

(b) what would be the total expenditure involved in setting up this plant.

In spite of a number of disallowed questions and a number of transfers from Starred to Unstarred Lists, the number of questions admitted for oral answer (usually 35–45) is always much greater than the number that are actually answered within the Hour (normally 20–25).[1] The reply is read out by the Minister; if it is lengthy or complicated, the answer will be that 'a statement is laid on the Table of the House'; in that case an exception is made to the rule that answers are not available before the oral reply is given, and the questioner is permitted to see the statement fifteen minutes before Question Hour begins.[2] As soon as the reply is finished, supplementary questions may begin, precedence being given to the original questioner. The control of supplementaries is a delicate affair; the tests that apply to questions apply equally to supplementaries, but to apply these tests on the spur of the moment, and to do so without giving undue protection to the Government or undue licence to the members, calls for skill and quick judgment. In India, generally, the practice is to allow six or even more supplementaries.[3] A harassed Minister can

---

[1] The margin is sometimes useful if many members are absent, but the absentees often exercise their right to authorise another member to put the question for them.

[2] The intention, of course, is to give him a reasonable opportunity to prepare his supplementary questions. In some States (e.g. Delhi State) the practice is carried much further: in order to help members to frame their supplementaries, all answers are printed along with the questions and shown to members one day beforehand. This is generally presumed to be a transitional procedure which will disappear as members gain in experience. In all cases, the answers are released to the press only when Question Hour has finished.

[3] The Council of State is even more liberal towards the members (or hard on the Government) and supplementaries may often continue for about five minutes. The Council is of course better able to afford the time, since its members and the questions they put are fewer than in the House of the People. It is also worth noting that the Speaker's task of controlling Question Hour is a good deal simpler now than it was in the inexperienced first year of the new Parliament.

15—P.I.

always check the barrage by replying that he requires notice, but abuse of this device gives as bad an impression as a vague or hesitant answer. Usually it is at once evident which Ministers have a real grasp of their subject—and which have not.[1]

At the end of the Question Hour, the temperature of the House may rise or fall according to the business that follows. Some possible procedures will almost certainly maintain interest and even excitment. There may, for example, be a Short Notice Question. Although subject to the same tests as ordinary questions, the Short Notice Question (i.e. a question which has been allowed in spite of a notice of less than ten days) will be of special interest because it will have fulfilled the further condition of referring to an urgent matter of public importance. Again, there may be a Motion for the Adjournment of the business of the House for the purpose of discussing a definite matter of urgent public importance.[2] Such motions were quite commonly allowed in the old Central Assembly. The Government of those days recognised that there was a fairly constant sense of frustrated opposition to many of its policies and it was prepared to permit occasions for the expression of such feelings. With the advent of fully responsible government, however, the Chair has felt that acceptance of such motions should be rare. They amount to proposals to depart from an agreed order of business, and this should be accepted only in cases of genuine national emergency or by way of implying practically a motion of censure on the Government.[3] In consequence, the tests for admission have been applied with severity, and motions have been disallowed because the matter was not sufficiently important or not really urgent or more suitably ventilated by a Short Notice Question or a Half an Hour Discussion. In fact, only one Adjournment Motion of this kind has been admitted in the House of the

1 The inexperienced Junior Minister can, of course, be excused his initial blunders. He is often rescued from discomfort by his senior colleague. The Prime Minister himself sometimes joins in, and nothing does more to raise the excitement of the House than to see the P.M. spring to his feet in indignant support of a suffering friend.
2 The relevant part of the *Rules* is Chapter IX. The matter has also been the subject of several Decisions and Observations from the Chair.
3 The most important of several rulings is one of 1950 (P.P. Deb., 21 March 1950). The Speaker outlined the development in the House of Commons and pointed out that from having at one time been frequently admitted, they were now severely restricted. 'The test of urgency . . . is best expressed in the old dictum of Speaker Peel in the Commons. He said: "What I think was contemplated was the occurrence of some sudden emergency either in home or foreign affairs. . . ." During the period 1921–39 the annual average of such motions admitted by the Speaker was 1·5.' He then reviewed Indian practice. 'Successive Presidents of the Central Legislative Assembly including myself had considerably relaxed the rule of admission. . . . The Government then was not responsible to the Legislature, nor were they amenable to its control. There was therefore good ground . . . to allow opportunities of admission of all important questions. Since 15 Aug. 1947, the entire constitutional and political set-up has changed. The Ministry is fully responsible to this House and Members now have ample opportunities for discussing various matters. . . . We can no longer look upon an adjournment motion as a normal device for raising discussion on any important matter.'

People since 1947.[1] At the same time, while disallowing these motions, the Speaker has often permitted Ministers, if they wish, to make statements on the subject, in order briefly to set out the facts and indicate government attitude or policy. No questions or discussion are allowed to follow such statements, though a member may, of course, give notice for a later date of a question or request for discussion.[2] There is, finally, one more item of business which may intervene between Question Hour and the main work of the day: the laying of papers on the Table of the House. This procedure is required in respect of certain documents by the Constitution itself, in other cases by the Rules and conventions of Parliament and in some cases by Acts of Parliament.[3] In all cases the procedure is simple and brief: the papers have in fact already been forwarded to the Parliament Secretariat; on the appointed day the item is listed in the order of business and the Minister merely reads out the title of the paper concerned. In this way, the documents are made public and any M.P. or citizen who is interested is able to consult them.

Reference has already been made to special opportunities provided for discussions. Although these periods of discussion do not take place until the end of the main business, they arise out of the earlier part of the proceedings and may therefore be considered here. The first kind of opportunity is the Half an Hour Discussion, a peculiarity of the Indian Parliament introduced in 1950 and designed to perform a similar function to the half-hour at the end of each day in the Commons. It was felt that while the attempts of the Chair to prevent supplementary questions during Question Hour from becoming a miniature debate were justified, and while it was desirable that that period should be mainly utilised to secure information, nevertheless there was a felt need for a short discussion on some matters. A questioner who wishes to pursue a little further an answer he has been given is therefore given the right to request a half-hour discussion.[4] Three days' notice is normally required and the member must have the signatures of two others to his request. He also states

---

[1] H.P. Deb., 18 Feb. 1954. The mover was the Independent M.P. Dr. Lanka Sundaram. The motion was to draw attention to an alleged inconsistency on the part of the Government in allowing on the previous day a discussion in the Council of States on a subject which on the same day had been ruled out in the House of the People. The intention, said the mover, was to demonstrate that there was no co-ordination among Ministers, between Government and Parliament or between Council and House. The motion was pressed to a division and lost by 66 votes to 259. The incident reflected more than anything else the resentment which is quickly felt by the Lower House of anything that seems like preferential treatment of the Council. But on this aspect, see below, Section 5.

[2] The same rule applies to all special 'Statements' which Ministers may make. Provision for such Statements is made in a separate rule (No. 286) and they are generally called by the Speaker at the end of Question Hour.

[3] E.g. Annual Financial Statement, Ordinances and Proclamations (under Arts. 112 (1), 123 (2), 352 (2), etc.); despatches and State Papers quoted by Ministers (under Rule 261). On the provisions regarding subordinate legislation, see below, pp. 311–313.

[4] See Chapter VIII of the *Rules*. The procedure was known to some Provinces earlier; it has since been imitated by many States.

briefly why he considers the matter important. The Speaker then decides whether he will allow the discussion. By a recent amendment, he may not 'admit a notice which may, in his opinion, seek to revise the policy of Government'.[1] The discussion, if admitted, can take place on Wednesdays and Fridays at the end of the normal day's sitting. The member who has given notice makes a brief speech setting out the grounds of his dissatisfaction and the Minister concerned makes a brief reply. The discussion is then thrown open to members who have given notice of their wish to speak, and the Minister is allowed the final word. These occasions prove of considerable general interest and are much appreciated by the M.P.s.

A procedural peculiarity (by House of Commons standards) of the Half an Hour Discussion is that there is no specific motion before the House and there is no decision or vote to be taken at the end. The same is also true of another form of Discussion recently introduced. The strict refusal to admit adjournment motions and the limited nature of the Half an Hour Discussion—from the viewpoint of time available and the breadth of the issues allowed—left members still feeling that further special opportunities were required. During the Budget session of 1953 many members were eager to discuss, at some length and in critical spirit, the events in Jammu, where there was an agitation for the closer union of Kashmir with India. The Deputy Speaker held a conference with the leaders of various parties and groups and an agreed procedure was arrived at for 'Discussions on matters of urgent public importance for short duration'.[2] The procedure is similar to that for the Half an Hour Discussions except that no notice is required, no particular day is allotted and the time allowed may be up to two and a half hours. In many ways, therefore, the new form of discussion has simply replaced the old use of the Adjournment Motion. The difference that there is no specific motion and no decision to be taken does, however, tend to free the debate and remove the tenseness usually associated with Adjournment Motions. In any case, the latter remains still available for exceptional emergencies in which something approaching a vote of censure is required.

These special procedures are naturally in addition to the more usual provisions for Motions and Resolutions.[3] Ordinary motions and resolutions have to some extent been replaced by the newer forms; in so far as they remain, they are primarily used by the Government—except, of

---

[1] The intention is to prevent or at least discourage the attempt to bring forward for this brief discussion very large issues of policy. The wording of the amended rule is unhappy, but the practice is in fact reasonable.

[2] The Deputy Speaker announced the procedure in the House of the People (H.P. Deb., 30 March 1953) and it was subsequently incorporated in the *Rules* as a separate Chapter VIIIA.

[3] *Rules*, Chapters XI and XII.

course, in the case of resolutions appearing in Private Members' Business. It may also be mentioned that there are special rules for Motions of No Confidence.[1] In particular, leave to make such a motion is only granted if 50 members rise in their places to signify their support.

Although it is very unlikely that the most important function of Parliament is to pass laws, nevertheless the bulk of the time of a legislature is spent on the consideration of Bills.[2] The life of a Bill, however, begins long before it is introduced in Parliament. It begins, of course, in a ministry and has the form of a proposal for legislation to implement a policy. Even at this early stage, consultation takes place between the initiating ministry and the Ministry of Law. The latter will give general advice, in particular on the existing state of the law on the subject and on any constitutional implications. The proposals are then prepared, together with the background facts of the subject, in a Summary which is then submitted to the Cabinet (or one of its Committees) for approval. Only after approval has been granted will the initiating ministry send the proposals to the Ministry of Law with a memorandum indicating precisely the lines of the legislation required and a request that a Bill be drafted. The work of drafting involves its own skill, but it can certainly be made easier if the initiating ministry has made its requirements clear. In any event, however, several conferences between the draftsmen and the officials of the initiating ministry will probably be needed and several drafts may have to be prepared before all concerned are satisfied with the legal form and administrative content of the Bill. The process deserves not to be hurried, but in this it seldom gets what it deserves. Before the Bill can be printed and made ready for Parliament it must be accompanied by several other documents: by a Statement of Objects and Reasons for the Bill signed by the Minister responsible; by the sanction or recommendation of the President wherever this is required by the Constitution[3]; by a financial memorandum where expenditure is involved; and by a further memorandum where powers of delegated legislation are proposed.[4]

The Constitution has laid down that Bills other than Money Bills may originate in either House.[5] Money Bills must be introduced in the Lower House and, although the Council may make recommendations

[1] Rule 179. The first to be moved since 1947 was a motion of no confidence in the Speaker moved in December 1954. See below, p. 269 n.

[2] Statistics showing the actual distribution of time in the House of the People are given in Table XXIII, p. 321.

[3] Arts. 3, 117, 274, 349. These Articles refer to the boundaries of States, Money Bills and the use of English for fifteen years for certain official purposes.

[4] The memoranda are required by the *Rules*, 70 and 71 respectively. I am grateful to some of the officers concerned for a part of the information contained in this paragraph; they are, however, in no way responsible for any of the statements made.

[5] Art. 107 (1). Money Bills are defined in Art. 110 (1) and the matter is decided by the Speaker (Art. 110 (3)). See Appendix I.

(provided it does so within fourteen days), the House of the People may reject them and the Bill may yet be considered passed.[1] In the case of other Bills disagreement between the two Houses is resolved by a Joint Sitting at which the Speaker of the House normally presides.[2] Since the procedures of both Houses are practically identical, and since in fact the majority of Bills are introduced in the Lower House, it will be enough to describe Bill procedure in the House of the People. A joint sitting can hardly be described; the party composition of the two Houses is so similar that disagreements on Bills have not occurred and no Joint Sitting has been held. An example of a Bill is reproduced in Appendix V.

The first stage of a Bill in the House is its introduction.[3] What is important is that the proposed legislation is made available to members, and study of the measure can begin. What happens in the House is simply a Minister's formal motion for leave to introduce the Bill. By convention, no discussion takes place at this stage, though it has happened that members have taken the opportunity to raise a point as to whether a Bill is *ultra vires* of the Constitution.[4] Once the Bill is introduced (and normally after an interval of at least two days), the subsequent stages can follow at any time. The member in charge of the Bill makes one of four motions: that it be taken into consideration, or that it be referred to a Select Committee of the House, or that it be referred to a Joint Committee of the Houses with the concurrence of the Council, or that it be circulated for the purpose of eliciting opinion on it.[5] The discussion on any of these motions is of a general nature: 'the principle of the Bill and its provisions may be discussed generally, but the details of the Bill shall not be discussed further than is necessary to explain its principles.'[6] If the motion for consideration is moved, an amendment proposing one of the other three alternatives may be moved. If the member in charge moves for reference to a Committee, an amendment proposing its circulation may be moved. If a motion for circulation is carried and the Bill is duly circulated, the member in charge must then normally move its reference to a Committee.[7]

---

[1] Art. 109. [2] Arts. 108 and 118 (3) and (4).

[3] Chapter X is the part of the *Rules* covering legislation.

[4] The convention not to oppose a Bill at this stage was broken for the first time on 23 Nov. 1954; a division was forced on the Preventive Detention (Amendment) Bill, its introduction being carried by 146–36.

[5] When sent to Committee or circulated, a time limit by which the Bill must be returned to the House is usually stated.

[6] Rule 75 (1).

[7] The Delimitation Commission Bill, for example, was originally to be taken at once into consideration, but the Government accepted an amendment that it should be circulated for a period (H.P. Deb., 9 July 1952). At the end of the period the member in charge then moved its reference to a Select Committee (H.P. Deb., 12 Nov. 1952). Again, the same procedure occurred about the same time in connection with the Constitution (Second Amendment) Bill (H.P. Deb., 8 July 1952 and 11 Nov. 1952).

The practice in the Indian Parliament is that only a few Bills are referred to Select Committees[1] (and even fewer to Joint Committees). This procedure is used only with Bills of exceptional importance or unusual complexity. The size of Select Committees varies from 20 to 30, but the Select Committee on the Estate Duty Bill, 1952, numbered 35. The names of members are included in the motion itself. There is no nucleus of members who generally sit on Select Committees; each Committee is freshly chosen for each occasion. The practice is that the Minister for Parliamentary Affairs usually offers about one-quarter of the places to the opposition groups and chooses the rest, after consultation with the party's convenors,[2] from among those of his own party who are known to be interested in the subject. The Chairman is appointed by the Speaker from among the members and is usually a member of the majority party. The conduct of the Committee is in his hands subject to the Rules of the House and the more detailed directions which the Speaker has issued to the Chairmen of Select Committees. The principle of the Bill has already been settled and the attention of the Committee is concentrated on the details and on any amendments that may be moved in Committee. Select Committees may appoint sub-committees to investigate particular points; they also have the power to call for the attendance of persons and the production of papers. In many cases, of course, outside bodies take the initiative and ask to be called as witnesses. The Committees' proceedings are confidential and press and public are not allowed.[3] The reports are, of course, published (along with any minutes of dissent) as soon as they have been presented to the House[4]; in some cases, the evidence and the proceedings during the examination of witnesses may also be published.

When a Bill has been reported on by a Select Committee or a Joint Committee, the House has to agree that it be taken into consideration before the clause by clause consideration is taken up. Each clause is considered in turn and put to the vote of the House. It is at this stage, immediately after a clause is placed before the House, that amendments to clauses may be moved. Amendments of which members have given notice are duplicated in lists as they are received. Below is the seventh of several lists of amendments to the Press (Objectionable Matter) Amendment Bill, 1953. This particular list contains only two brief amendments, but the lists are often lengthy:

---

[1] The practice in States is sometimes the same; in other cases, reference to Select Committees appears almost usual.

[2] See Chapter (IV), Section 2.

[3] The proceedings may not be referred to in the House—e.g. an observation from the Chair in the House on 12 May 1951.

[4] The Draftsman of the Ministry of Law who has prepared the Bill attends all the meetings of the Committee.

List No. 7.

HOUSE OF THE PEOPLE

Notice of Amendments
The Press (Objectionable Matter) Amendment Bill, 1953
(*To be moved at a sitting of the House*)

17. **By Shri Frank Anthony:—**
That the Bill be circulated for the purpose of eliciting opinion thereon by the 15th April, 1954.

Clause 5

18. **By Shri Khub Chand Sodhia:—**
In page 2, line 9,—

(i) *omit* "The competent authority or"; and
(ii) *omit* "other".

NEW DELHI,   M. N. KAUL,
The 27th February, 1954.   *Secretary.*

Naturally, if the Bill has already been examined by Select Committee, many of the amendments will have been already considered, but there may still be many others to be moved—including those that may arise as a result of disagreement with the Committee's recommendations. The fact that a Bill has been sent to Committee does not, therefore, ensure a short clause-by-clause stage; all that can be said is that it will normally be shorter than if the Bill had been taken at once into consideration.[1] Amendments to the clauses are subject to conditions of admissibility— they must in particular be relevant and within the scope of the Bill—and the Speaker is given by the Rules the power to select amendments. In practice, although a very large number of amendments is very often moved, the Speaker has not exercised the power of selection. The number of amendments is large partly because of the fragmented character of the opposition; the Speaker is unwilling to undertake the responsibility of making selections partly because it is difficult to know in advance which amendments are likely to be most important.[2] In consequence, the clause-by-clause stage is often laborious. Each clause is normally moved separately, and each amendment (except those that are withdrawn) also must be put and agreed to or negatived.[3]

[1] The Estate Duty Bill, 1952, was a measure of extraordinary complexity and subject to much controversy. It was sent to Select Committee and considerably amended during the twenty-one meetings of the Committee. Nevertheless it was discussed on the floor of the House for a total of 92½ hours. (See H.P. Deb., 15 Sept. 1953.)

[2] The confidential nature of the proceedings of the Select Committees adds to the difficulty.

[3] The Ajmer-Merwara Tenancy and Land Records Bill contained more than 200 clauses and there were many amendments to almost every clause. In order to save the time of the House, some members suggested that all the clauses and agreed amendments should be put collectively. The Speaker observed: 'It would not only save time, but also the constant

The final or 'third reading' stage of any Bill is reached only after the clauses (with amendments), the schedules if any, the enacting formula, preamble if any, and the title of the Bill have all been put (in the form that they 'stand part of the Bill') and agreed to by the House. The third reading is the motion that the Bill (where necessary, 'as amended') be passed. On this motion the discussion 'shall be confined to the submission of arguments either in support or rejection of the Bill. In making his speech a member shall not refer to the details of the Bill further than is necessary for the purpose of his arguments which shall be of a general character.'[1] Since, however, it is also a decision of the House that there shall be no repetition, it is in fact only rarely that there are speeches at this final stage; the general principles have been discussed already and the details have also been examined.[2] When a Bill is passed by the House, it is transmitted to the Council for concurrence. It will there pass through a similar procedure[3] before being presented to the President for his assent. Up to 1954 the assent of the President has been refused only once—and then on purely technical grounds and clearly on the advice of the Ministry of Law.[4]

This procedure for the discussion of Bills has not proved unsatisfactory. The growing volume of legislation—coupled with the disinclination of members to sit longer hours—is, however, now beginning to pose certain problems. If the House is to retain its opportunities for questions and general discussions unrelated to Bills—and it would certainly be an incalculably serious loss if these were to be curtailed—it would seem that one of two alternative courses must be taken: either time in committee must be used to replace time in the House; or the debate in the House must be limited by the imposition of rules of closure.

physical exertion on my part that it involves, namely to get up and sit after every motion. But I think the present procedure is necessary to check up the amendments relating to each clause—unless, of course, there are no amendments to certain clauses, which can then be put collectively.' (P.P. Deb., 5 April 1950.)   [1] Rule 114.

[2] The only possibilities are, in the case of a Bill of some importance, that there might be a case for a final general summing up on both sides, or, in the case of a Bill much amended in the course of debate, general remarks on its new form. E.g. the following ruling of the Speaker: 'In the third reading, no speeches are allowed ordinarily. . . . The position is that at the third reading, the discussion is restricted to such amendments or changes that have been made during the clause-by-clause stage. That is the general rule. The member's idea is that he can make an extensive speech again as if he was speaking on the consideration motion; but that is not permissible.' (P.P.Deb., 29 Feb. 1952.)

[3] There appears to be one curious difference. The Rules of the House state that if a Bill originating in the Council has been referred to a Select Committee of the Council it cannot be referred to a Select Committee of the House. The Council, which had a similar rule for some months, deleted it in Sept. 1952 with the result that a Bill which has already been before a House Select Committee could be sent to a Committee of the Council (*Rules of Procedure in the Council of States*, Rule 123).

[4] The House of the People (H.P. Deb., 5 April 1954) was told by the Speaker that the President had refused assent to the P.E.P.S.U. Appropriation Bill passed by Parliament on 8 Mar. The ground for refusal was that the Proclamation, under which Parliament (during the imposition of President's Rule in P.E.P.S.U.) had been empowered to legislate for that State, had been revoked on 7 Mar.

The House seems reluctant at present to adopt either of these measures. Yet the consequence is that Parliament tends to constitute a 'bottleneck' so far as legislation is concerned. It not infrequently happens that each session begins with a heavy load of Bills carried forward from previous sessions, as well as those freshly introduced. For example, the last session of 1953 was confronted not only with 19 new Bills but with 27 pending from previous sessions, of which nearly half were Bills introduced in 1952.[1]

Proposals for a system of Standing Committees for Bills, which would enable amendments to be more completely disposed of away from the floor of the House, have often been put forward, and as often rejected as unnecessary. It is understandable that members value the opportunity to put forward their own amendments in public, and, so long as the Select Committee system obtains, no limitation of the amending process on the floor of the House will be easy. Large Standing Committees, in which most of the interested members were able to take part and whose proceedings were public, would seem to go a long way towards a solution. In the absence of this device, there is, in fact, a tendency towards the limitation of the debate. Certain rules are, of course, of long standing. The closure can always be moved at any stage[2]; the Speaker, if he feels that there has been reasonable debate, will then put the motion 'that the question be now put', which, if carried, means that discussion ends and the matter under discussion is at once put to the House. But the use of the closure, if out of keeping with the conventions of the House, is naturally most unpopular. Apart from the closure there have been special rules for ensuring the conclusion by a definite date and time of the discussions on Demands for Grants, and, more recently, on the Finance Bill.[3] Until 1952, however, the Speaker's powers were otherwise limited.[4] In the new Rules of the House of the People a fresh power has been included: 'Whenever the debate on any motion becomes unduly protracted, the Speaker may, after taking the sense of the House, fix the hour at which the debate shall conclude (and) the Speaker shall at such appointed hour . . . proceed forthwith to put all such questions as may be necessary to determine the decision of the House on the original question.'[5]

---

1 *Hindustan Times*, 16 Nov. 1953.
2 Rule 256.
3 Rules 185 and 193. On financial procedure in general, see below Section 3.
4 'With respect to other Bills, I have no right to fix a time limit even for the Bill as a whole. With this restriction, I feel very much embarrassed if any honourable member thinks that I am allowing too much time. That is my position and the position of anybody who may be in the Chair.' (P.P. Deb., 21 Sept. 1951.) Again: 'The procedure of the House is that in a Bill I am bound to call every honourable member wishing to speak. If the House thinks that there has been sufficient discussion, it is open to any honourable member to say that the question may be put. Otherwise it is not competent for me to prevent members from speaking.' (P.P. Deb., 11 April 1950.)
5 Rule 257. In Aug. 1953 the powers were further increased: the Rule was amended to give the Speaker power to fix time limits for 'any or all stages' of the Bill.

As a matter of convention, this procedure was already in force[1]; even now after the institution of the rule, it is very largely a matter of informal negotiation and settlement between the leaders of the various groups. It does, however, seem to happen with growing frequency. There is, that is to say, a drift towards the limitation of debate rather than towards the use of committees. This may indeed solve the problem of time, but it is difficult not to feel that it does so at greater cost than the system of Standing Committees. In the first place, it means that Bills are in general less fully considered. Secondly, it tends to result in a saving of time in the debate on principles and not in the more mechanical consideration of amendments. Finally, amendments that might be accepted by the Government in committee tend to be rejected when moved on the floor of the House.

A word may be added on the actual system of reaching a decision when the question—whether it is a motion in connection with a stage of a Bill, any other kind of motion or a resolution—is put before the House.[2] The Speaker puts the question—for example, that the Bill be taken into consideration—and invites those in favour to say 'Aye' and those against the motion to say 'No'. He then says: 'I think the Ayes (or the Noes) have it.' If this opinion is not challenged, he repeats twice: 'The Ayes (or the Noes) have it', and the decision is taken. If his opinion is challenged, he has two courses open to him. He may ask the Ayes and the Noes to stand in turn in their places, and on a count being taken, he declares the decision. This is the less usual form of voting, but it has been used on some occasions.[3] The more usual—and lengthier—process is the 'Division' proper. The bells are rung for two minutes throughout the building and members run from the Central Hall and other rooms to file through the 'Division Lobbies' on either side of the Chamber. Their names are marked off by the Division Clerks (members of the staff of the secretariat), who then hand the lists to the Secretary; the totals are presented to the Speaker and announced by him.[4]

[1] E.g. 'I concede that under the rules there can be no guillotine on any legislative programme, but I had stated the decision (to close the debate) as representing the general will of the House. It was a matter of agreement and I have been reminding hon. members every now and then that they may please remember that the guillotine would be applied at six o'clock. If the hon. member is very particular about stating the rule, I may tell him that I am going to accept closure at six o'clock.' (P.P.Deb., 22 Dec. 1950.)

[2] Rule 287.

[3] It can be used if the Speaker feels that the challenge is somewhat light-hearted and not wholly serious. It was employed for example when the Communist Party forced a vote on an unexpectedly minor issue. (H.P. Deb., 18 Nov. 1953. In this particular case, so the story went, there was a tea party being given to a distinguished visitor from abroad in one of the Parliament House refreshment rooms. A Minister was overheard to explain to the visitor that the Government were in no way inconvenienced by the Opposition, which was so weak. The remark was passed round without delay and some of the Opposition decided to show that they could at least spoil a tea-party!) Normally, under this system, names are not recorded, but in this case they were.

[4] A division involving 400 voters will take about 20–25 minutes. There are rules permitting the member who loses his way to correct his vote. A recent introduction is a rule permitting the vote of a member to be challenged on the ground that he has a personal,

Divisions are naturally comparatively uncommon in the present Parliament. A record of divisions is given in Appendix IV. It will be seen that, apart from two busy days in the Provisional Parliament in 1951 and a few extra trials of strength at the beginning of the new Parliament of 1952, the frequency of divisions is about two in a month. An analysis of the minority vote would show that the voting patterns among the opposition groups are far from constant.[1] The largest musters of opposition opinion occurred on 23 December 1953 (on Preventive Detention), when the vote against the Government reached 91 and on 7 September 1954 with a total of 106.

3. Financial Procedure

The essentials of the Indian Parliament's financial procedure are laid down in the Constitution.[2] The central principles are those that have achieved classic expression in Britain: 'The Crown demands money, the Commons grant it, and the Lords assent to the grant. But the Commons do not vote money unless it be required by the Crown; nor impose or

pecuniary or direct interest in the matter. The Speaker's decision on this is final. (These rules, it may be added, also permit membership of Select Committees to be similarly challenged and decided.) The system of division lobbies is usual in State Assemblies too. It should perhaps be mentioned that press reports appearing some time ago said that an electric push-button vote-recorder was on its way from Germany to Calcutta. If true, it is to be hoped that the legislators for whose convenience it is intended, have heard how in Finland the members found that, by the careful use of match sticks in the buttons, their votes could be cast for them even in their absence!

[1] One example of a splitting of the voting power of the opposition may be given. On 14 Dec. 1953 there was before the House a Government motion to accept the invitation of the Council of States to join a Joint Committee to consider the Special Marriage Bill. Dr. Lanka Sundaram moved an amendment intended to protest against the procedure—as part of the quarrel between the two Houses (see below Section 5). The amendment was supported by the Left and the Right, but the mover withdrew it after the subject had been debated. A vote then took place on the original motion. The Right opposition was in no difficulty, for it opposed both the procedure and the actual Bill itself. The Left, however, was in a dilemma; they wished to support the measure, but they were severely critical of the procedure. After hurried consultations, they decided that the withdrawal of the amendment left them no opportunity to express their convictions; there took place, therefore, an unusual event—the movement of the Communist M.P.s across the floor to join in the 'Ayes' lobby with the Government, thus isolating the Hindu Mahasabha, Jan Sangh and some Independents. The vote was 181 to 27. (H.P. Deb., 14–17 Dec. 1953.)

[2] Arts. 112–117 (see Appendix I). In this section I am concerned only with financial procedure in Parliament. The working of the Financial Committees of Parliament is considered below, Chapter VI, Section 3. The subject of financial control in general is treated in P. K. Wattal, *Parliamentary Financial Control in India* (Simla, 1953). It includes, of course, not only the preparation of the Budget and the work of the Audit Department but also the difficult problem of relations between the Ministry of Finance and the other ministries. This question received much public attention in India during 1954, largely because it was reported that the Finance Minister had threatened to resign on account of his disagreement with his colleagues on this subject. The issue arose on the Prime Minister's invitation to the Auditor-General designate to investigate the system of budgeting and control, and on some of the reported findings of this officer—especially perhaps those recommending that the Financial Advisers attached to ministries should no longer be answerable to the Finance Ministry and that spending departments should be given wider powers of internal financial discretion.

augment taxes, unless the taxation be necessary for the public service as declared by the Crown through its constitutional advisors.' The executive, that is to say, can neither raise nor spend money without the authority of Parliament; this authority rests with the Lower House; but it is exercised only on the initiative of the executive. In the language of the Constitution, 'The President shall in respect of every financial year cause to be laid before both the Houses of Parliament a statement of the estimated receipts and expenditure of the Government of India for that year, referred to as the "annual financial statement"'—or more generally, the Budget. This statement distinguishes between money required to meet 'expenditure charged on the Consolidated Fund of India' and other expenditure; the former includes the salaries of the President, Presiding Officers of Parliament, the Auditor-General and the judges, and while open to discussion in Parliament is not voted upon[1]; the other estimated expenditures are submitted to the House of the People in the form of Demands for Grants and may be passed, refused or reduced by that House. When the Grants have been made, an Appropriation Bill is introduced which provides for the appropriation out of the Consolidated Fund of moneys needed for both kinds of expenditure. The Constitution provides that similar procedures shall be employed for Supplementary Grants (when the sum authorised proves insufficient), Additional Grants (when a new service is undertaken) and Excess Grants (when more has been spent than was authorised). Finally the Constitution gives powers to the House of the People to pass Votes on Account pending the completion of the ordinary procedure and Votes of Credit to meet uncertain needs, and to make Exceptional Grants.

It is to an unusually crowded House of the People with overflowing galleries that the Finance Minister presents his Budget and makeş (usually reads) his Budget speech.[2] The presentation takes place usually at 5 p.m. on the last day of February and, by a special rule, there can be no discussion of the Budget on that day. The members go away to study the Statement and speech whose contents have, of course, up to then remained a closely guarded secret.[3] The Budget itself is a fairly compact

[1] Before 1947 the salaries of Ministers and certain civil servants as well as the whole expenditure on Defence was non-votable.

[2] The relevant part of the *Rules* is Chapter XIV. For elucidation of several points in this section I am indebted to Mr. S. L. Shakdar, Joint Secretary, Parliament Secretariat. His article, 'Two Systems of Financial Procedure' (*Parliamentary Affairs*, Summer 1953) draws attention to the main differences in this respect between the British and Indian Parliaments.

[3] The question of whether there had been a Budget 'leakage' was raised in the House of the People in 1954 (H.P. Deb., 5 Mar. 1954). It appeared that some copies of 'Part B' of the Budget speech—the part containing the tax proposals—had in fact been distributed in error to a few press representatives about an hour before the speech was delivered. Fortunately, the mistake was detected in a few seconds and the copies were promptly returned. At the same time a similar question was being raised in the Delhi State Assembly. There a Minister had, in an answer during Question Hour on the day before the Budget was presented, disclosed certain figures from the estimates; the Speaker ruled that the breach was a technical one without any serious consequences and that no further action was necessary.

document of some twenty-five pages, but can hardly be understood without simultaneous study of the Minister's speech (usually 1½ hours) and, if possible, the 200-page Explanatory Memorandum on the Budget.

It may be as well at the outset to note certain general features of the Indian Budget and budgetary procedure. It is, in the first place, a budget in two parts: as in several Continental countries also, in India the Railway Budget has for several years been separated from the General Budget. The two Budgets are similar in form and are treated similarly by Parliament. There are thus separate Demands for Grants for Railways and a separate Appropriation Bill. In what follows there is no description of the process of passing the Railway Budget, but it has to be borne in mind that a similar procedure to that of the General Budget is being repeated with respect to Railways.[1] The Indian Budget, in the second place, is not simply the taxation proposals of the Government but a statement of estimated expenditure and estimated revenue.[2] Moreover, it is not dealt with in separate 'Committees of the whole House' as in England but in ordinary sittings with the Speaker continuing in the Chair. Although the Budget is voted upon only by the Lower House, it is also presented to the Council of States; no Budget speech is made in the Council, but the papers are laid before it. A general discussion on the Budget in the Council is also allowed, and is usually timed to precede (and thus to contribute to) the main debate in the House of the People.

The general discussion that takes place on the Budget some days after the Finance Minister has made his speech is a relic from times when the Central Assembly could do little more to the Budget than discuss it generally. The Houses discuss the Budget as a whole and any question of principle involved in it. No motion is moved and members are discouraged from raising matters of detail or specific grievances.[3] It is an occasion on which each House is able to express its mood, and the

---

[1] The Railway Budget is generally presented in the third week of February and is at each stage one step ahead of the General Budget. In recent years a number of public corporations have been created by Acts of Parliament and they have been permitted separate budgets. The Budget of the Damodar Valley Corporation is presented to Parliament and the State legislatures concerned (Bihar and Bengal), and the voting by Parliament and these legislatures is confined only to the share of the respective Governments in the project. As the Governments of Bihar and Bengal are financed by loans from the Centre for meeting their share of expenditure of the project the provisions for loans in the Central Budget is also voted by the Centre. The detailed Budget of the D.V.C. is not voted by either Parliament or those State legislatures. On public corporations, see below, Chapter VII, Section 3. The States have, of course, no Railway Budgets, but their General Budgets are subject to procedures in the Assemblies similar to those of the Central Parliament.

[2] That is, the Indian Budget Day introduces the whole financial procedure, whereas in England it is the day on which the Commons turn attention from 'the Estimates' to the financial proposals, from expenditure to revenue. There are also several differences in the actual preparation of the Budgets of England and India—such as the use and importance of Revised Estimates in India. (See Wattal, *op. cit.*, p. 67.)

[3] E.g. rulings given on 26 May 1952 (H.P. Deb.: 'So far as specific points or grievances are concerned, members will have an opportunity later. . . . A general survey of the administration would be in order now.') and on 4 March 1953.

Government may learn how particular proposals will be received during the subsequent stages. Ministers are expected to attend regularly and the Chair has on occasion drawn attention to this convention.[1] It is also an opportunity for discussing those items which are 'charged on the Consolidated Fund' and therefore non-votable.

When the general discussion is completed, the way is clear for the business of voting the grants. The Demands for Grants are prepared by the ministries in the same form: Part I is a statement of the total estimated expenditure requiring the vote of the House ('charged' or non-votable expenditure being shown separately); Part II gives the sub-heads; Part III the details under the sub-heads; and in respect of each, four columns of figures showing, in the case of the 1954–55 Budget for instance, the actuals from the accounts of 1952–53, the Budget Estimate for 1953–54, the Revised Estimate for 1953–54 and the Budget Estimate for 1954–55. The Demand is made in a motion 'that a sum not exceeding Rs.x be granted to the President to defray the charge which will come for payment during the year ending 31st March 1955 in respect of [the subject of demand]'. To this motion three kinds of amendment, called 'cut motions', are possible. The most drastic is the refusal of supplies—'that the Demand be reduced to Rs.1'; this has not been used in India since independence. The second possibility is the economy cut—that the Demand (as a whole or a particular item) be reduced by a specific sum. This is also, if not unknown, at least very rare; in order to be able to mention a specific sum by which the Demand should be reduced, more knowledge and more appetite for detailed study are required than most M.P.s possess. In practice the only form of amending motion used is the 'token cut'— 'That the Demand be reduced by Rs.100'. On this any grievance or request for information or suggested reforms may be brought to the attention of the particular Minister concerned. The Demands of each ministry are taken up in turn and, in consultation with both sides of the House, the Speaker allots a definite period for each. The cut motions, though numbered serially as received in the Secretariat, are grouped according to the Demands to which they refer. Usually, the Speaker puts the Demands and the Cut Motions together before the House and then the discussion begins. The Cut Motions are almost invariably moved only by opposition members, the Congress Party having effectively discouraged Cut Motions from its own supporters. At the same time, since this is an important opportunity for expressing local grievances and requests, the Party makes full use of a special procedure

[1] The Budget of March 1952 was a 'caretaker Budget' in the sense that a new Parliament was being elected. Nevertheless, the Chair observed: 'I would like a larger number of Ministers to be here. . . . Some of the Hon. Ministers are taking notes for others, but why should not the others be here unless they are out of town ? . . . They should be here to hear the Budget speeches' (P.P. Deb., 3 Mar. 1952). Some M.P.s who were also in the old Central Assembly have remarked that the non-responsible members of the Government of those days were never absent from their places during the Budget debate.

recently devised whereby M.P.s submit to the Ministers—usually, in the case of Congress members, through their State Groups[1]—ten-line memoranda containing those local and particular pleas. In giving notice of a Cut Motion the mover will state the subject to which he wishes to draw attention. As in the case of amendments to Bills,[2] the divided nature of the opposition leads to a very large number of Cut Motions, and the desire of each opposition member to submit the complaints of his constituency is a further factor making for lengthy lists of such motions. A typical list of a few of the Cut Motions moved in connection with the 1954–55 Railway Budget is given to illustrate some of the topics raised:

HOUSE OF THE PEOPLE

DEMANDS FOR GRANTS IN RESPECT OF RAILWAYS—1954–55
List of Motions of which notice has been received to be moved under Rule 226 (3) of the Rules of Procedure at the sittings of the House to be held on the 8th and 9th March, 1954.

MOTIONS
Demand No. 1

Shri V. Boovaraghasamy to move:—
443. That the demand under the head Railway Board (pages 1–2) be reduced by Rs.100. (Passenger's amenities.)

Demand No. 8

Shri N. D. Govindaswami Kachiroyar to move:—
444. That the demand under the head Ordinary Working Expenses—Operation other than Staff and Fuel (pages 41–46) be reduced by Rs.100. (Inadequacy of passenger amenities.)

Shri K. Ananda Nambiar to move:—
445. That the demand under the head Ordinary Working Expenses—Operation other than Staff and Fuel (pages 41–46) be reduced by Rs.100. (Failure to abolish absentee-middleman-vendor-contractors on Railways.)

Demand No. 9

Shri K. Ananda Nambiar to move:—
446. That the demand under the head Ordinary Working Expenses—Miscellaneous Expenses (pages 47–55) be reduced by Rs. 100. (Refusal to pay arrears of pay for suspended period in the cases of employees reinstated after acquittal by courts disregarding the recent Bombay High Court judgment.)

[1] See above, p. 194.
[2] See above, p. 232.

Demand No. 9A

Shri K. Ananda Nambiar to move:—

447. That the demand under the head Ordinary Working Expenses—Labour Welfare (pages 57–62) be reduced by Rs.100. (Improvement of the Railway Colony High School in Golden Rock to accommodate more students.)

Demand No. 15

Shri V. Boovaraghasamy to move:—

448. That the demand under the head Construction of New Lines—Capital and Depreciation Reserve Fund (pages 76–78) be reduced by Rs.100. (Opening of new railway lines in Tiruchi and Tanjore Districts, Southern Railway.)

Demand No. 18

Shri K. Ananda Nambiar to move:—

449. That the demand under the head Open Line Works—Development Fund (pages 91–94) be reduced by Rs.100. (Opening of a road connecting the Golden Rock Colony with Melekalkandar Kottai by constructing a passage through the colony walls.)

Shri K. Ananda Nambiar to move:—

450. That the demand under the head Open Line Works—Development Fund (pages 91–94) be reduced by Rs.100. (Construction of an over-bridge at the Golden Rock Railway Station in order to facilitate the crossing railway lines for people going to Senthannirpuram.)

NEW DELHI
The 6th March, 1954.

M. N. KAUL,
Secretary.

Each cut motion may refer to only one subject and not to the Demand as a whole.[1] The Chair has made appeals to members to make an agreed selection of cut motions for discussion in order to give coherence to the attack,[2] and to some extent this is now being done. In any event, when the end of the allotted time is reached, the Speaker puts all the Demands regardless of whether they have in fact been discussed or not. Supplementary Demands are subject to the same procedure, except that where a new service is proposed the discussion may include the principles

[1] E.g. 'Only one subject will be allowed under one cut motion' and 'When a cut motion is moved, all arguments must only relate to the particular subject with which it deals' (P.P. Deb., 4 Mar. 1952). These and other restrictions, originally conventions expressed as Decisions of the Chair, have subsequently (Nov. 1954) been incorporated into the *Rules*. The refusal of supplies in the form of the reduction to Rs, 1 is now called the 'disapproval of policy' cut.

[2] E.g. P.P. Deb., 27 Mar. 1951.

16—P.I.

involved, since the House will not already have had an opportunity to discuss them.[1]

A recent (1950) introduction into Indian financial procedure is the Vote on Account. This device avoids the necessity to complete all the Budget discussions before the new financial year begins on 1 April. The House instead passes a Vote on Account which provides the Government with the authority to draw funds for a period of two months. The House is thus enabled to continue its examination of the Budget until towards the end of April. The Vote on Account is not usually debated, since its object is simply to permit the real debate to be carried on.[2]

The final stage in the voting of supplies is the passing of the Appropriation Bill.[3] This procedure, too, is new to India. It follows from the introduction in the new Constitution of the Consolidated Fund. Before 1950, the passing of the Demands was formally completed by the laying on the Table of the House a Schedule of authorised expenditure signed by the Governor-General. The new procedure is more in keeping with a sovereign Parliament, but its purpose is similar: to give legal effect to the demands as voted and to authorise the issue of moneys for those purposes from the Consolidated Fund. The attitude towards the debate on the Appropriation Bill has undergone some change already and affords a good illustration of the wise experimental flexibility of Indian Parliamentary practice. In 1950 the Speaker said that the Bill was 'in a sense formal legislation', but it gave another opportunity for suggestions and comments.[4] By 1951 an attempt was being made to establish a convention whereby the Bill was 'treated purely as a matter of form'.[5] In 1952

[1] 'The general principles followed in regard to cut motions on Demands for Supplementary Grants are as follows: That cut motions must be restricted to the particulars contained in the estimates on which supplementary grants are sought and to application of the items which compose those grants; that a question of policy cannot be raised on demands for supplementary grants in so far as such demands refer to schemes which have already been sanctioned by the House; that with respect to a new service for which previously no sanction has been obtained, questions of policy may be raised, though they must be confined to the item on which the vote of the House is sought' (H.P. Deb., 8 Dec. 1952). Supplementary Demands in India may arise more than once and the amounts involved have often been very large.

[2] Thus, on 12 Mar. 1951, the Speaker explained: 'In this procedure, since full discussion follows, the grant of supply for the interim period on the Motion for Voting on Account is always treated as a formal one just like a Motion for leave to introduce a Bill. . . . Hon. Members will have a full opportunity to discuss the Demands for Grants in a detailed manner from 26 Mar. to 10 April.' On that occasion, the Vote on Account was for one month only. The Speaker added, by way of further explanation: 'I do not see what useful discussion can be had on one month's supply, when eleven months' supply is going to be discussed and when there had already been ample General Discussion for four days' (P.P. Deb., 12 Mar. 1951).

[3] More precisely, Bills; the Railway Appropriation Bill is passed separately first.

[4] P.P. Deb., 24 Mar. 1950.

[5] Thus, the Speaker: 'I should invite the attention of the hon. Members to a convention that has been agreed to. I am not prepared to say that no observation is permissible on this Bill. . . . But after a discussion of fourteen days . . . I think it will hardly be fair to the House as a whole to repeat the same arguments now. . . . I would not say that the hon. Member has no right to speak, but I am shutting my eyes so that nobody is able to catch them. I shall put the Motion straightaway to the House.' (P.P. Deb., 16 April 1951.)

the Speaker was firm to the point of severity: 'There is no debate on an Appropriation Bill—not by rules but by convention of the House firmly established. . . . The hon. Member can make use of some other opportunity; not this one.'[1] With the newly-elected Parliament, some concession to the opposition groups was thought desirable; the Speaker therefore invited them to let him have a list of any points they wished to raise at that stage. 'The whole idea is that there should not be any repetition of the debate on the Demands for Grants. . . . If there be any really new points which require elucidation or consideration, certainly I will consider them.'[2] In the following year, the concession was so utilised as almost to throw the machinery out of order; the Chair said:

> When I made the suggestion, I naturally expected only particular subjects to be submitted on behalf of particular groups. I now find that individual Members also have sent in points, and apart from those which I received yesterday . . . there is a very large number of further points here today. . . . It was not my intention that so many points should be brought up.[3]

The way out of the difficulty has been twofold. On the one hand, the general position has been formulated in a Rule of the House:

> The debate on the Appropriation Bill shall be restricted to matters of public importance or administrative policy . . . which have not already been raised while the relevant Demands for Grants were under consideration [and] the Speaker may require members desiring to take part to give advance intimation of the specific points they intend to raise, and he may withhold permission for raising such of the points as in his opinion appear to be repetitions. . . .[4]

At the same time, the convention has been developed in a more organised way. The Speaker suggested that 'the National Democratic Party, the Communist Party, the Praja Socialist Party, and Independents may have one subject each and the Unattached Members one subject, thus making a total of five subjects for discussion'.[5] The debate on the Appropriation Bill has thus become a short and well-organised discussion of about three to four hours.

With the passing of the Appropriation Bill[6] the authorisation of expenditure by Parliament is completed. There remains the approval that

---

[1] P.P. Deb., 5 Mar. 1952.

[2] H.P. Deb., 3 July 1952.

[3] H.P. Deb., 8 April 1953.

[4] The Rules Committee felt that 'the scope of discussion on Appropriation Bills had become crystallised and it was thought proper that it be incorporated in the Rules'. The intention was to facilitate the prior selection of fresh and important points.

[5] H.P. Deb., 8 April 1953.

[6] It is a Money Bill and goes through the Council of States subject to the same rules as other Money Bills. See above, pp. 92, 229–230.

has to be given to the Government's proposals for raising the necessary revenue. These proposals are embodied in the Finance Bill and this Bill is introduced in the House of the People at the conclusion of the Finance Minister's Budget speech. The Finance Bill follows the usual Bill procedure. After its early introduction, it is not taken further until the supply work is finished. A motion is then usually made for its reference to a Select Committee, and the debate on this is generally very wide. The Select Committee examines the proposals in detail, and it is not unusual that it recommends considerable reductions in taxation which are accepted by the Government. The provisions of the Finance Bill, since they describe tax changes, must come into operation not when the Bill is finally passed but from the moment of its introduction; a declaration at the end of the Bill states 'that it is expedient in the public interest' that certain clauses of the Bill should 'have immediate effect under the Provisional Collection of Taxes Act, 1931'. If, as a result of its passage through Parliament, the Finance Bill becomes changed and the tax levels reduced, the excess revenue collected in the meantime by the Government has to be refunded.[1]

There are, then, four main opportunities on the floor of the House for the discussion of the finances of the Government. The General Discussion on the Budget is intended for a review of financial policy and questions of broad policy. When the Demands for Grants are made the debate become narrower, being 'limited to each head of the Demand and, where cut motions are moved, still further limited to the particular subject on which the motion is made'.[2] The position as regards the Appropriation Bill has been adequately described. The discussions on the Finance Bill are not restricted at all as to subject—on the 'acknowledged principle that any subject can be discussed and any grievance ventilated', when authorising the taxation of citizens. In all these debates, the Speaker has the power not only to fix time-limits for speeches but also (in consultation with the Leader of the House) to allot time for the various stages and put before the House whatever questions may be necessary to conclude the particular business on time. In practice, the distribution of time on the Budget in the two Houses is roughly as follows:[3]

[1] The Indian Provisional Collection of Taxes Act, 1931, authorises collection for only sixty days in anticipation of the passing of the Finance Bill. Presidential assent must therefore be given to the Bill before the end of April. Parliament, in other words, has two months in which to complete its whole financial procedure. The British procedure, which allows as much as four months, is more leisurely and allows members to make a more thorough study of the business. On the other hand, there is not much anxiety in India to imitate Westminster on this point; Delhi's summer, unlike that of London, is only too punctual and is well under way by the end of April.

[2] The Speaker, in the course of a general explanation of the new procedure (P.P. Deb., 24 Mar. 1950).

[3] Figures taken from Shakdar, *loc. cit.*

	House	Council
Railway Budget : General Discussion . .	3 days	2 days
Demands for Grants .	3 days	—
Appropriation Bill .	About 2 hours	1 day
General Budget : General Discussion . .	4 days	3 days
Demands for Grants .	15 days	—
Appropriation Bill . .	1 day	1 day
Finance Bill . . .	4 days	1 day

4. Privilege

On no aspect of the life of Parliament has India since her independence modelled her ways more carefully on those of Britain than in regard to the privileges of the Houses and their members. The Constitution itself prefers not to attempt to describe those 'powers, privileges and immunities' but instead says simply that until they are defined by law, they 'shall be those of the House of Commons of the Parliament of the United Kingdom'.[1] They have remained undefined by Indian law, while those of the House of Commons are, of course, nowhere codified but are part of the Common Law of the land, and have to be pieced together from a wealth of precedents.

The status of Indian legislative bodies from the viewpoint of privileges and immunities had been a matter of concern to Indian legislators and in particular to Indian Presiding Officers almost from the inception of the 1921 Assemblies. The position up to 1935 was that, while the Assemblies tried to pretend that they had privileges analogous to those of the House of Commons and persuade others to respect them as if they were supported in law, whenever actual cases arose it was only too clear that privilege was neither part of the 'law of the land' nor had it been statutorily conferred; if newspapers offended against supposed privileges, there could be no question of calling the editors 'to the Bar of the House'. When the Joint Parliamentary Committee in London was considering in 1933 the next instalment of reforms for India, the Presiding Officers of Indian legislative bodies sent a memorandum in which they urged that since they were helpless to deal, for instance, with press abuse, they should have conferred upon them the powers, privileges and immunities of the Commons. The 1935 Act fell short of their hopes in this respect. It protected the freedom of speech in legislatures and empowered the legislatures to make laws whereby the courts would be able to punish persons refusing to give evidence before legislature committees.

[1] Art. 105 (see Appendix I) and, for States, Art. 194. This reference to the British Parliament is not without precedent. Canada (British North America Act, 1867, Section 18), Australia (Commonwealth of Australia Constitution Act, 1900, Section 49) and Ceylon (Ceylon (Constitution) Order in Council, 1946, para. 27) had already used Westminster as a convenient reference point on this same matter; the Indian provision is indeed taken directly from the Australian Act.

Beyond that, it carefully left matters as they were. It did indeed empower legislatures to attempt the definition of their privileges by law, but it expressly forbade the conferring on any legislature 'the status of a court or any punitive or disciplinary power other than a power to remove or exclude persons infringing the rules'.[1] In Bengal, an attempt was in fact commenced and a Bill defining privileges was drafted. In some respects it simply elaborated the few powers bestowed by the 1935 Act; in others, however, it went clearly beyond them. It sought, for example, to give the Speaker power to demand the attendance in the legislature of members arrested on criminal charges.[2] The Bill had not been proceeded with when the war suspended normal political life.

Following independence, the question of privileges again became open to discussion. The fact that many M.P.s and M.L.A.s were being arrested and detained under Preventive Detention orders lent even a certain urgency to the matter. At the same time, legislatures could not very well set about defining their privileges until it was settled what the Constitution itself would have to say. The terms of the Constitution have already been stated; what was asked for in 1933 and refused in 1935 was taken in 1950—a status equivalent to that of the House of Commons.[3] Nevertheless, there have been two schools of thought as to what should now be done. One view is that the Indian Parliament (and State legislatures) should still avail themselves of the now unrestricted power to define their privileges by statute law. The other view holds strongly that such a course is unnecessary and indeed would be unwise. The latter view, which has strong support at the Centre and in some States, has up to now prevailed. It concedes that to define the Indian Parliament's privileges as 'those of the House of Commons' permits some ambiguity, since the privileges of the Commons are themselves undefined and only to be discovered by the study of actual cases.[4] It argues, in the first place, that the probable interpretation of the Constitution would be that as soon as a legislature enacts a law defining its privileges, those of the House of Commons at once cease to be available. An attempt to define would therefore lead to a likely curtailment of powers and privileges. It is also pointed out that the most important privilege is the right to punish for contempt or a breach of privilege. This power has been firmly established by the Speaker of the House of Commons, and he may issue a

---

[1] Government of India Act, 1935, Sections 28 and, for Provinces, 71.

[2] Bengal Assembly Powers and Privileges Bill, 1938, Clause 8.

[3] When an international questionnaire was circulated in 1950 to ascertain the position of different parliaments in relation to privileges, the reply from India simply quoted Article 105 of the Constitution and added that the answers prepared by the House of Commons should be regarded as the answers of the Indian Parliament.

[4] A case which has had to be carefully studied in India in connection with preventive detention of M.P.s is that of Captain Ramsay. See Report of the Committee of Privileges of the House of Commons, 9 Oct. 1940; the Memorandum prepared by Lord Campion for that Committee illustrates well the uncertainty that can arise.

warrant on these grounds without further specifying the nature of the breach committed. In India, so long as privileges remain 'those of the House of Commons', the Supreme Court would probably uphold this power and protect it against restriction even by the Fundamental Rights. If the privileges were codified, however, if they were set out and defined in an Act of Parliament, the courts would at once feel entitled to enquire into the constitutionality of such privileges. On balance, therefore, it is far safer to rely on the article of the Constitution which refers to the House of Commons.

Forecasts regarding political institutions in India are risky, but it is fairly safe to say that parliamentary privilege is likely to cause some difficulty in the future. For one thing, the whole question of privilege is one which even in more settled parliamentary regimes is being subjected to a certain amount of re-examination. It must be admitted that the history of privilege in England is most intimately bound up with the rather special story of the struggle of parliament to free itself from the power of the executive; the fact that the institution began its life as the High Court of Parliament is a further fact to be borne in mind—even if this was more a convenient excuse than a direct cause of many privileges. Countries like Australia inherited the historical memory as well as the institution. But now in Australia and—though naturally to a lesser extent—in England it is asked whether some of the privileges are not out of date.

It is here that some attempt has to be made to distinguish between those privileges which, whatever their origins, can still be seen as necessary for the proper working of the institution and others whose justification in terms of the modern constitution is less obvious. Clearly the immunity of members from civil and criminal proceedings arising out of things said in parliament must be protected if there is to be free debate. Again, each House must be able to exercise disciplinary powers over its members. Doubts arise mainly in regard to the power of the House to punish non-members for contempt of the House; for the consequence of this power is that citizens may be sent to prison without a trial before a judge in an ordinary court of law. One of the most striking cases of the assertion of parliamentary power of this kind occurred in 1955 when the proprietor and the editor of the *Bankstown Observer* were imprisoned on a warrant issued by the Speaker of the Australian House of Representatives for breach of privilege of the House. The High Court of Australia refused applications for writs of *habeas corpus*, holding that since the constitution makes the privileges of parliament those of the British House of Commons,[1] the courts were in no better position

[1] At least 'until declared by the Parliament'. Some of the Australian State legislatures have in fact broken away from reliance on the House of Commons model and have enacted their own codes of privilege; only Victoria and South Australia have adopted the wide privileges of the Commons.

than English courts would be to look behind the warrants issued by the Speaker. The Judicial Committee of the Privy Council decided that the judgment by the High Court was 'unimpeachable' and refused to grant leave to appeal. In the public discussion that took place in Australia, it was felt by many that, leaving quite on one side the merits of the particular case,[1] it was doubtful if such powers ought to be exercised wholly by a body like parliament without even the possibility of appeal to the ordinary courts and an open trial. At least one English authority has asked whether this Australian reconsideration would not 'afford a convenient opportunity to review the matter in England also'.[2]

If there are some doubts in England and Australia, it is not surprising that there should be more in India. Resentment at having to follow Westminster is the least valid and probably the least important of the reasons. Nor is the mere fact that India's Constitution is written a serious obstacle; the Australian judges have shown that they can and do regard 'the unwritten custom of several centuries of English history [as], so to speak, scheduled to the written constitution of Australia'.[3] The question concerns political wisdom more than technical ingenuity: is there any longer the same need for parliamentary privilege? At whose expense is parliamentary privilege asserted in the modern democratic state? And, in the context of the Indian Constitution, is parliamentary privilege more fundamental than the Fundamental Rights? These are the important questions which lie behind the controversy as to whether the privileges of Indian legislative bodies should now be defined by law; for, once defined by law, the privileges become unambigiously subject to the Constitution and it will be the duty of the Supreme Court to determine cases where privilege and Fundamental Right conflict.[4]

The staunchest defence of the *status quo* whereby the Indian legislatures enjoy the ample privileges of the British House of Commons comes not unnaturally from the officers of the Parliament. The strongest criticism of the *status quo* has been put forward in the Report of the Press Commission.[5] The former tend to think in terms of the defence of the legislature against the executive and believe that the representative assemblies of the people require the support of the fullest historic claims of the Commons. They hold the view that it is wise to imitate

1 The two men were found by the Committee of Privilege of the House to have sought to intimidate and silence a member by publishing imputations of corrupt conduct.
2 Professor H. Street, 'Parliament and the Courts' in *The Listener*, 24 Nov. 1955.
3 *The Times*, 25 June 1955.
4 This does not mean that the Supreme Court at present cannot find itself called upon to do this, only that until the privileges are defined the Court has to try to reconcile legislative supremacy of the British model with Fundamental Rights of the American model—an unenviable task. See below, p. 254, for an example of this kind of case.
5 Government of India, 1954. See also the chapter contributed by C. V. H. Rao, formerly Editor of the 'Indian Nation', to *The Indian Parliament*, edited by A. B. Lal (Allahabad, 1956).

the modern Commons attitude of modest caution and disinclination to 'extend' their privileges, but they are equally insistent that it is a matter of discretion resting with the Speaker and the legislature. The critics on the other hand, while recognising that privileges and immunities are essential if legislative bodies are to be able to function effectively,[1] have concluded that limits should be set by law in order to avoid ambiguity and to establish that privilege is not beyond inspection by the courts.[2] In a word, the critics may be said to prefer that the area of privilege be determined by the courts in the context of citizen rights than by the legislature in its discretion. It is difficult not to feel the force of this view in the Indian context. For, in the first place, most modern privilege cases seem to consist in conflict between legislature and the public rather than between executive and legislature. In the second place, the cabinet system implies that the executive can normally through party allegiance control the legislature. For these reasons the old context of privilege may be said to have given way to a new one. In these circumstances, excessive emphasis on privilege could even become a weapon in the hands of an intolerant party cabinet in control of an obedient legislature.[3] Even without that extreme danger, there is still the not negligible fact that new legislatures may be too easily tempted to be over-zealous in protection of their privileges and too prone to limit narrowly the operation of legitimate criticism. Already the Report of the Press Commission[4] has commented on 'the oversensitiveness of some legislatures to even honest criticism'.

Some of the more interesting cases that have arisen since the inauguration of the new Constitution in 1950 may be briefly described. They show that, generally speaking and certainly so far as the Centre is concerned, Parliament through the Speaker has displayed a wise attitude of caution; it has been reluctant to proclaim breaches of privilege except in serious cases, and it has not attempted too quickly to assert and exercise its powers. On several occasions in 1950, members tried to raise supposed questions of privilege on the floor of the House; the Speaker insisted on most occasions that members should first see him in his chamber, since the questions were not really of privilege at all and only wasted the time of the House.[5] The procedure to be followed if the

---

[1] E.g., Report of the Press Commission (p. 430): 'No one disputes that Parliament and State legislatures must have certain privileges and the means of safeguarding them so that they may discharge their functions properly'.

[2] *Ibid.*, p. 421.

[3] See also Rao, *loc. cit.*, p. 46.

[4] The Commission naturally looked at the problem from the point of view of its impact on the Press—as the Speaker of the House of the People promptly pointed out in his address to the Speakers' Conference on 3 Jan. 1955. But the Commission contained only a small minority in any way connected with the Press and does not appear to have been too biased in favour of the Press.

[5] E.g., P.P. Deb., 10 Mar. 1950 and 30 Nov. 1950.

Speaker has been first persuaded that there may be a question of privilege is laid down in the Rules of Procedure.[1] At the end of Question Hour, the member wishing to raise the point makes a short statement of the case and asks for leave to raise the matter. If there is any objection to leave being granted, the Speaker asks those in favour to stand. If less than twenty-five members rise, leave is refused. If leave is granted, then the House may consider and decide the matter or a motion is moved (usually by the Leader of the House) to refer it to a Committee of Privileges nominated by the Speaker. This Committee reports to the House, which then determines the action to be taken.[2] During 1950, three incidents concerning privileges occurred but none was referred to Committee. On one occasion a member who was conducting a fast on the banks of the Jumna in Delhi (in protest against the low wages of sugar factory workers) was picked up by the local authorities and taken back to his family. He was at the same time externed from Delhi. The externment order raised a question of privilege. The Prime Minister and Home Minister admitted that the police authorities had not behaved correctly and expressed the apologies of the executive. The House was divided in its views and some members pressed for a Committee; after a useful luncheon adjournment, however, a motion that the apologies be accepted and the matter dropped was accepted.[3] The other two cases concerned the press. One newspaper published some of the conclusions of the Select Committee on the Finance Bill before thay had been reported to the House, but its full apology was accepted.[4] Another published certain remarks made in the House which the Chair had ordered to be expunged and not to form part of the proceedings; the Chair avoided declaring whether a breach had been committed, but said that it was 'highly regrettable', though not so serious as to be pursued beyond a warning.[5]

The first major case requiring reference to a Committee of the House occurred in 1951 and concerned the conduct of a member. It was referred not to the Committee of Privileges but to a special Committee on the Conduct of a Member.[6] The procedure throughout was in fact closely modelled on that of the House of Commons in 'the Boothby

---

[1] Chapter XV.

[2] In April 1953 a new Rule was added setting out how judges and magistrates are to inform the Speaker whenever a member is arrested on a criminal charge or imprisoned or detained.

[3] P.P. Deb., 28 Feb. 1950 and 1 Mar. 1950.

[4] P.P. Deb., 27 Mar. 1950.

[5] P.P. Deb., 12 Dec. 1950.

[6] The Speaker remarked: 'There is a Committee of Privileges constituted under the Rules. Yet it is within the powers of the House to constitute other special committees. . . . It is a moot question to be considered as to whether any such conduct as alleged is really a breach of privilege or something different. . . . The practice in the House of Commons has been to constitute a special committee. . . . It is better to keep the Committee of Privileges apart.' (P.P. Deb., 6 and 8 June 1951.)

Case'.[1] The Prime Minister moved and the House passed a motion to set up a Committee

(a) to investigate the conduct and activities of Shri H. G. Mudgal, M.P., in connection with certain dealings with the Bombay Bullion Association which include canvassing support and making propaganda in Parliament on problems like option business, stamp duty, etc., and receipt of financial and business advantages from the Bombay Bullion Association and (b) to consider and report . . . whether the conduct of the hon. Member was derogatory to the dignity of the House and inconsistent with the standards which Parliament is entitled to expect from its Members.[2]

The Committee's procedure was that of a 'Court of Honour' rather than a Court of Law. It was not, that is, bound by technical rules. It received 'directives' from the Speaker and heard evidence; the Attorney-General opened the case and attended many of the meetings; Mr. Mudgal and his counsel were present except when the Committee deliberated. At the end of July, the report was submitted to the Speaker. The Committee found that Mr. Mudgal had received, and expected to continue to receive, sums of money for services rendered to the Bombay Bullion Association in the way of putting certain questions, moving certain amendments, arranging interviews with Ministers, etc.[3] The members of the Committee were unanimous in finding that 'Shri Mudgal's conduct is derogatory to the dignity of the House and inconsistent with the standards which Parliament is entitled to expect from its members.'[4] Some members felt that a code of conduct of M.P.s could and should be formulated, and a draft of such a code prepared by one member was in fact circulated on the Speaker's orders to all M.P.s. On 24 September 1951, the Prime Minister moved a resolution in the House to expel Mr. Mudgal. After being allowed to speak and on being asked to withdraw for a vote to be taken, Mr. Mudgal quickly wrote out his resignation and handed it to the Chair. This, however, only led to an amended

[1] See Owen Clough, 'The Boothby Case' in *Journal of the Society of Clerks-at-the-Table in Empire Parliaments*, Vols. XI and XII, 1942–43, pp. 90–116. The Indian case is similarly described in detail by S. L. Shakdher in 'The Mudgal Case' in the same *Journal* Vol. XX, 1951. Mr. Shakdher points out some of the differences in procedure between the two cases, in particular the greater powers conferred on the Speaker in India to regulate the work and organisation of the Committee.

[2] P.P. Deb., 6–8 June 1951.

[3] It seems that the Bombay Bullion Association had hardly received their money's worth when the arrangements were abruptly brought to an end. But this is of course no more relevant to the questions of principle involved than the suspicion that Mr. Mudgal at first saw little wrong in his behaviour. It is interesting in this connection—and perhaps not unilluminating—to refer to the entries after Mr. Mudgal's name in the *Who's Who* of the Provisional Parliament: 'Educated New York College, New York and Columbia University. . . . Editor and feature writer of *The American Banker* published in America, for three years; Editor-in-Chief, *The Negro World*, published in America. Returned to India in 1937 after 17 years abroad.'

[4] The Reports, Evidence and Proceedings are given in 'Committee on the Conduct of a Member' (Parliament Secretariat, 1951).

resolution which declared that he had 'deserved expulsion' and that the language of his letter of resignation constituted a 'contempt of the House which only aggravates his offence'.[1]

The first occasion for a reference to the Committee of Privileges arose on the arrest of Mr. Deshpande, Hindu Mahasabha M.P., in March 1952. The question raised was whether the arrest and detention of a member while the House was in session constituted a breach of privilege. The Committee found that privilege did not extend to arrests and detentions under the Indian Preventive Detention Act, 1950. 'The Constitution authorises preventive detention in the interests of the State, and it is well settled that "the privilege of Parliament is granted in regard to the service of the Commonwealth and is not to be used to the danger of the Commonwealth"'—that is, for '"the protection of the community as a whole"'. The arrest did not constitute a breach of the privileges of the House, and the Speaker had been informed as quickly as possible.[2] Another case, shortly afterwards, concerned the arrest of a Communist M.P. who was at once released on bail. The only issue there was whether there was a duty on the part of the magistrate to inform the House. The Committee found no difficulty, after consulting Erskine May and some British cases, in concluding that this duty only obtained when a member has been committed to prison and detained without bail.[3]

An interesting case arose out of a debate in the House. One member, Dr. Satyanarain Sinha,[4] in the course of his speech alleged that a preceding speech by a Communist M.P. had been taken from an article by a Russian Communist.[5] He added certain further allegations and referred to other documents, whereupon the Deputy Speaker remarked: 'If any hon. Member refers to any document or reads any extracts from it on the floor of the House, he must place it on the Table of the House.' Dr. Sinha on the following day laid certain documents on the Table. A few days later the Communist Party leader in the House wrote asking the Speaker's consent to raise a question of privilege. The contention was that Dr. Sinha's remarks were calculated to lower the prestige of the particular Communist member and thereby that of the House in the eyes of the public, and further that the documents laid were false, fabricated and forged. The Speaker referred the case to the Committee of Privileges. The Committee found no breach of privilege; Dr. Sinha's charges

[1] P.P. Deb., 24 Sept. 1951.
[2] Committee of Privileges, *The Deshpande Case* (Parliament Secretariat, July 1952). Four members of the Committee (one Hindu Mahasabha, one Communist and two Socialists) did not agree that preventive detention should be treated as if it were penal detention; they held that immunity of arrest for M.P.s should extend to such cases; and they held that there had been undue delay in informing the Speaker.
[3] Committee of Privileges, *The Dasaratha Deb Case* (Parliament Secretariat, July 1952).
[4] Not to be confused with his namesake, the Minister for Parliamentary Affairs.
[5] Dr. Sinha's charge was uncertainly stated: 'I have compared the speech and found that it was word for word—I would say the general line—from an article written by one Lemin in February'.

were perhaps exaggerated but his documents were genuine. Both parties to the dispute had been too hasty.[1] The Committee had at the same time to decide a related question. Some days after the Sinha case had been referred to the Committee a press report appeared in which a Communist M.P., Mr. Sundarayya, was said to have remarked at a meeting that 'the Committee of Privileges had now almost completed its investigations and Dr. Sinha was finding it difficult to get out of the situation'. Mr. Sundarayya gave a different version of this speech; he had only said that the Committee 'will be going into the whole matter and now it will be for Dr. Sinha to prove his allegations, which will be a very hard job for him to do'. The Committee declined to decide between the two conflicting reports, but pointed out that, since in fact the Committee had at that time not met, there was no case of inaccurate reporting of the proceedings of a Committee but rather a purely incorrect statement. They recommended no further action, but pointed out that 'it is highly desirable that no person including a member of Parliament or Press should without proper verification make or publish a statement or comment about any matter which is under consideration or investigation by a Committee of Parliament'.[2]

Similar cases have arisen also in the States. Two Bombay cases may be mentioned as illustrations. One of these concerned the arrest of a member without warrant during a session. Since, however, the arrest was made under the ordinary law on charges involving offences for which, under the Indian Penal Code, a person is liable to be arrested without warrant, the Committee found no difficulty in saying that membership of the House conferred no immunity.[2] The other case arose out of an editorial comment in *The Times of India*. Questions had been allowed and put in the House to the Minister of Finance and Prohibition on the granting of liquor permits to magistrates and judges. The questioner asked whether the Government was 'aware of the feeling in the public that granting of liquor permits to Magistrates and Judges is likely to influence judicial decisions in prohibition cases'—to which the reply was 'No'. Supplementaries secured the names of the judges who were fortunate enough to get permits. The editorial comment followed two days later—under the heading 'Contemptible'. The questions asked 'were nothing short of a degrading design to lower their Lordships in public esteem. . . . The singling out of magistrates and judges for public

---

[1] Committee of Privileges, *The Sinha Case* (Parliament Secretariat, Dec. 1952).

[2] Committee of Privileges, *The Sundarayya Case* (Parliament Secretariat, Dec. 1952). Mr. Sundarayya, though a member of the Council of States, gave evidence before the Committee of Privileges of the House of the People. See below, p. 261.

[3] Bombay Legislature Department, Report of the Privileges Committee in the matter of breach of privilege arising out of the arrest without warrant of Shri R. S. Patel, M.L.A. (Dec. 1953). Two members of the Committee, while agreeing with the main finding, felt that the arrest in this case was *mala fide* and that the House should protect its members in such cases.

obloquy cannot but be part of a deliberate pattern.' The questions should have been disallowed, since they violated the conditions laid down for the admissibility of questions, and they were 'mean and petty'. 'The entire performance in its malice and vituperation is unworthy of the Legislature of what was once a premier State. But perhaps it is too much to expect elementary good manners and good taste from those who know no standards and observe none.' The Committee of Privileges, after hearing the editor and his counsel, considered that the questions did not amount to any contravention of the Constitution which bans 'discussion' of the 'conduct of a Judge in the discharge of his duties'; further that they were not contrary to the provisions of the rules regarding questions; finally, that the criticism in the editorial 'exceeds the bounds of decency, reason and fair comment' and 'is calculated to undermine the prestige and authority of the House'. The editor and paper were held guilty of contempt and therefore of breach of privilege of the House. The House endorsed the findings and carried out the Committee's recommendation to disapprove of the conduct of the editor and, in the absence of a published unconditional apology, to withdraw the press facilities given to the paper.[1]

Only in one or two cases has any kind of conflict appeared between the Speaker as defender of the privileges of the House and outside authority. One instance worth mention—though indeed the matter did not come to a head—occurred in West Bengal when the Speaker of the Assembly granted temporary permission to two Communist M.L.A.s to remain on the Assembly premises in order to avoid arrest under the Preventive Detention Act. It appears to be generally agreed, however, that the desirability of allowing a member to continue to perform his duties towards his constituency cannot be allowed to confer a general immunity from arrest. The only immunity permitted by established practice in Britain is that arrests cannot be effected within the precincts of the Chamber while the House is actually sitting. Another instance of some importance led to a case in the Allahabad High Court. The Speaker of the Uttar Pradesh Assembly, in the exercise of his powers to maintain order, had to instruct that the leader of the Opposition be removed from the Chamber. He further suspended the member from the remainder of the day's sitting and referred the matter to the Committee of Privileges. The Committee agreed that the member had behaved in a disrespectful manner and a resolution of the House then suspended him for the rest of the session. The member thereupon brought an action in the High Court against the Speaker, on the ground that double punishment had been awarded in contravention of one of the Articles on Fundamental

---

[1] Report of the Privileges Committee in the matter of Breach of Privilege by the Editor, Printer and Publisher of *The Times of India*, Bombay (Bombay Legislature Department, Mar. 1953). One M.L.A., an Independent, disagreed, finding the comments fair and reasonable.

Rights in the Constitution. The Court dismissed the member's application. It held, first, that disciplinary action for a breach of parliamentary rules was not 'punishment' as intended by the chapter on Fundamental Rights, and therefore the question of double punishment did not arise. Secondly, the resolution passed by the House was an internal matter which the Courts have no power to scrutinise.[1] Although the judges were thus far agreed, there was not complete agreement in their comments on the general position. One view was that in reconciling the privileges of Parliament as set out in Articles 105 and 194 with the rest of the Constitution it had to be taken that the framers had not intended the privileges to be overruled by the Fundamental Rights; others were of the contrary view that the Fundamental Rights were more fundamental.[2] One of the best known privilege cases arose out of action taken by the Speaker of the Uttar Pradesh Legislative Assembly in referring to the Committee of Privileges a criticism of his own conduct published in the Bombay newspaper *Blitz*. The Committee held the author and the editor guilty of breach of privilege and recommended the imprisonment of the editor. The Assembly approved the report and a warrant for the arrest of the editor was issued. He was arrested, flown from Bombay to U.P. and detained. Within a week of his being arrested, a *habeas corpus* application was presented to the Supreme Court raising *inter alia* the point that the detention was contrary to Article 22 of the Constitution which requires the production of the arrested person before a magistrate within 24 hours of arrest. The Court upheld this contention and ordered the release of the editor.[3] The Assembly took no further action.

This brief review of a few privilege cases serves to show the kind of problem that has arisen in the period since independence. It also shows that those responsible for the protection of Parliament's privileges have on the whole proceeded cautiously.

5. *Relations between the Two Houses*

It is the habit of institutions to give birth to loyalties, and when two institutions are placed side by side it is easy for clashes to occur and feelings to run high. In a federal state, for example, no amount of skilful vision of labour can prevent a sense of competition from arising between the centre and the units; even if the jurisdictions of each are demarcated with precision, there is always room for charges of unfair encroachment. The same is true of relations between Legislature, Executive and Judiciary—unless the three are highly integrated. This tension is often desirable, and indeed some institutions have been deliberately established

---

[1] Art. 122 (2) or, for States, 212 (2) (see Appendix I).
[2] Raj Narayan Singh *v.* The Speaker of the Uttar Pradesh Assembly (1953).
[3] Petition No. 75 of 1952.

with a view to creating a 'separation' and 'balance' of powers. The existence of antagonism between two Houses of a Parliament should occasion no more surprise, and is in fact encountered in the political history of more than one country. Independent India has enjoyed the operation of a bicameral legislature only since the General Elections of 1952. Nevertheless this short time has proved long enough to enable the development of almost bitter rivalry between the two Houses. That this has happened so quickly and in spite of the dominating position of one party in both Houses bears striking witness to the power of institutions to inspire fresh attachments of sympathy and devotion.[1]

The Council of States is an indirectly elected House with powers similar to but in certain respects less than those of the House of the People.[2] The party composition of the two Houses is very similar[3]; indeed it would have required a very curious system of choosing the Council to have produced a great contrast between the two in the present state of political forces in India. Even the social compositions of the Council and House resemble each other rather closely—or at least do not differ in any way sufficiently to make them possess distinct characters.[4] The Council of States is neither significantly older nor significantly more experienced or more specialist than the Lower House. It contains some experienced parliamentarians, a few lawyers of high standing and a few statesmen of wide experience; so does the House of the People. Some of the Council members are quiet, elderly men of mature wisdom and moderate views; the opposition benches, however, look if anything slightly younger than those of the House of the People and would certainly be unwilling to admit that they were less noisy.[5] The Vice-President of the Republic in his capacity as Chairman of the Council succeeds wonderfully in conveying to the proceedings a tone of friendly urbanity, but the realities of party strengths are little affected and party organisation in the Council is no less developed than in the House of the People. The Upper House is a Council of States of the Union and its members are elected by the State Assemblies. This, however, does not seem to have made the floor of the Council a battleground between Centre and States; a defence of 'States-rights', an expression of regional demands, is just as likely to be heard in the other House.

[1] Lest this be thought too innocent a way of putting the matter, let it at once be admitted that other factors play an important part. If a Lower House begins to agitate for the abolition of the other, the defence offered by the members of the latter is not unconnected with the prospect for them of a loss of employment. It is also true that a quarrel between the two Houses can be made to afford opportunities for some parties in the opposition to embarrass the Government.

[2] See Chapter II, Section 3 and Appendix I.   [3] See above, pp. 97–98.

[4] See Chapter III, Section 2. I have not been able to test the truth of the view that a large number of members of the Council were campaign organisers during the General Election who were subsequently rewarded by being nominated for the Upper House.

[5] This is not to say that there are not, among the Socialists in particular, men of real ability.

Nor is the procedure of the Upper House such as would appreciably distinguish it from the House of the People. As we have already seen, it has nothing to do with the Demands for Grants and only limited powers over Money Bills.[1] Since it is smaller and less worried by the pressure of work on limited time, its debates are less frequently subject to strict control through time limits. It has less need to use Select Committees for the same reasons—and also for the reason that important or difficult Bills have usually been subjected to that treatment in the House. The Council devotes not only two and a half hours weekly to Private Members' business but the whole of each Friday—even doing without Question Hour on that day. It has the same Half an Hour Discussion procedure as the House but, instead of the longer Discussion period also provided in the Lower House, the Council has adopted the House of Lords' procedure of moving 'for papers'; the effect, however, is identical. The Council's Question procedure did indeed begin as a somewhat distinctive institution; at its inception in 1952 it had the rules of the old Council of State (not States), which permitted a *total* of three questions on only two days —perhaps half an hour a week. The members, not unexpectedly, refused to stand for this, and within two months a regular Question Hour with a maximum of three per member had been conceded.[2]

Composed of men similar to those who sit in the House of the People, the Council has, not surprisingly, failed to evolve a distinct role for itself. It might well be useful for what is discussed in one place to be discussed further in the other, but the value is very limited when the same things are discussed in the same way. The Council provides neither for technical revision nor for a wider and more leisurely debate. The following table is of interest:

	No. of Bills received from House of People and passed by Council	No. of Amendments passed by Council to such Bills
First Session .	25	1
Second Session .	16	—
Third Session .	26	1
Fourth Session .	5	—
Fifth Session .	15	1[3]

[1] At first, the Council's procedure provided only for 'the consideration and passing' of Money Bills. By an amendment to the Rules in Sept. 1952 three stages were introduced: consideration; clause by clause examination; and finally the motion—taken from Eire— 'that the Bill be returned'.

[2] See Council of States Manual, Part I, Rules of Procedure and Conduct of Business.

[3] The three amendments were accepted by the Lower House. The complaint of the Council is that the Government is always in such a hurry to get the Bills passed that there is insufficient time for the minute examination which revision demands.

Amendments, no doubt, do not tell the whole story; an examination of the debates, however, fails to reveal any more subtle contribution on the part of the Council. On the other hand, two points are to be noticed. First, the Government has made an effort—and indeed has found it most convenient and useful—to introduce first into the Council an increasing number of its Bills:

	No. of Bills first intro- duced in Council
First Session .	4
Second Session .	3
Third Session .	11
Fourth Session .	11
Fifth Session .	8

Second, there are a few recent signs that the Council may be beginning to 'try its wings' as a forum for grand and soaring debate. Perhaps for the first time, one of its discussions, on foreign affairs in late August of 1954, appears to have impressed observers considerably.[1] It is always possible, therefore, that the Council will succeed in fashioning a distinctive role for itself. That, however, is rather a matter for speculation.[2] What is quite certain is that it has started its career as far as possible on the same lines as the House of the People, that it feels consequently inferior and somewhat frustrated, that it has striven for more equal status and that it has provoked the most violent reactions among some members of the Lower House. Some of the cases of dispute are worth examination.

The first major public clash between the two Houses occurred during the Budget session of 1953. The issue was in some ways small but passions were thoroughly roused on both sides. On the 29 April 1953 the Council of States took up for consideration the Income Tax (Amendment) Bill, 1952, as passed by the House of the People. The Bill had been certified as a Money Bill by the Speaker, but in the course of the debate

[1] I rely on the usually good judgment of the *Statesman's* political correspondent: 'There was a touch of greatness in the tone and content of the Rajya Sabha (Council of States) debate last week on foreign affairs which may serve the other House as a useful example. . . . For once it was a delight to sit in the Press Gallery.' The writer drew attention to the valuable contributions of Dr. Ambedkar, Dr. Ramaswamy Mudaliar and Mr. Krishna Menon. He also paid tribute to Dr. Radhakrishnan's 'directional skill'; 'he chose the participants with extreme care . . . and, though outside the discussion, he seemed part of it, alert but flexible, strong and at the same time forgiving' (Overseas *Statesman*, 4 Sept. 1954).

[2] It may be of significance that out of the 31 new faces in the Council as a result of the first elections of one-third of the members in March 1954, 5 were of persons with prominent positions in States: 2 ex-Chief Ministers, 2 ex-Ministers and 1 Pradesh Congress Committee President. If there is anything like a trend to move up from State to Centre by way of the Council, it could happen that 'States' rights' would be heard of more frequently in the Upper House.

in the Council some members argued that it was not. The Law Minister, Mr. Biswas,[1] who is not only a member but the Leader of the Council, in replying to these doubts permitted himself to say that the Council would be reassured if it were told categorically that the Speaker had applied his mind to this question and issued the certificate after a full and fair consideration of the matter.[2] On the following day, a member of the House of the People sought to move a motion that the remarks of the Law Minister were unjustifiable and inconsistent with the dignity of the Speaker. The Chair observed that the Law Minister might be present in the House on the following day when the motion could be brought up for discussion.[3] The Council responded quickly to the situation and passed a resolution 'that this Council is of the opinion that the Leader of the Council be directed not to present himself in any capacity whatsoever in the House of the People' when the matter was brought up in that House.[4] The Law Minister was present in the House of the People when the Deputy Speaker read out a message from the Chairman of the Council. The Chairman said that 'it was nobody's intention, least of all that of the Leader of the Council, to cast aspersions on the integrity and impartiality of the Speaker. It is our anxiety in this Council to do our best to uphold the dignity of the Speaker and the privileges of the other House as we expect the other House to protect our interests and privileges.' The Law Minister said he associated himself with those remarks, and the Deputy Speaker said he thought that further discussion was not called for. The members of the House had, however, heard of the resolution just passed by the Council and were not prepared to let the matter drop. The Law Minister at this stage withdrew and the Deputy Speaker eventually gave in to pressure and read out the resolution passed by the Council.[5] Members angrily asserted that Ministers were responsible to the House and doubted the propriety of the Council's resolution. Subsequently, however, further apologies from the Law Minister and an intervention by the Prime Minister appealing for an end to the hostilities, persuaded members to drop the matter.[6]

Meanwhile another dispute was gathering momentum off the floors of the two Houses. It appears that some members of the Council had soon formulated the idea that, in order effectively to carry out its general discussion of the Budget and its debate on the Appropriation Bill, it was necessary that the Council should either have its own Estimates and Public Accounts Committees[7] or that its members should be included in

[1] The incident is sometimes referred to as 'The Biswas Business'.
[2] C. S. Deb., 29 April 1953.   [3] H.P. Deb., 30 April 1953.
[4] C.S. Deb., 1 May 1953.   [5] H.P. Deb., 1 May 1953.
[6] H.P. Deb., 6 and 7 May 1953. It is of incidental interest to note that the Prime Minister revealed that the Speaker has invariably taken advice from the Law Ministry before certifying Bills as Money Bills. Opposition members were not slow to point out that it looked as if some Ministers did not know enough about the work done in their department.
[7] These Committees are discussed below, Chapter VI, Section 3.

the existing two Committees of the House of the People. In January 1953 the proposals of the Council's Rules Committee with regard to the Public Accounts Committee were sent to the House of the People; they suggested a Joint Committee and added that since there were already 15 members on the House Committee, the simplest method would be to add 7 from the Council. The Rules Committee of the House met to consider these proposals and had before them a resolution of the Public Accounts Committee which stated its opinion that a Joint Committee or a separate Council Committee on the subject would be 'against the principles underlying the Constitution' and therefore unacceptable.[1] The Rules Committee agreed with this view: the House had special responsibilities in financial matters; it cannot share these with anyone else; the responsibilities of the Council in financial matters required no such measure; and the particular rules suggested by the Council were objectionable.[2] The most that could be conceded was that the Council could, if it wished, set up on its own not a Public Accounts Committee but an *ad hoc* Committee to guide them in the discussion of financial matters. The question was brought into the open when the Prime Minister moved in the House a motion on the subject. This was not to establish a Joint Committee, but to 'recommend to the Council of States that they nominate seven members to associate with the Public Accounts Committee of this House'.[3] The Prime Minister found unaccustomed allies in the Socialists and even the Communists.[4] Nevertheless there was much uneasiness in the House and much support for the views of the Rules Committee.[5] Replying to the debate, the Prime Minister argued that the financial powers of the House were in no way threatened as the Public Accounts Committee imagined; that the British precedents which had been quoted were not relevant; the Council of States was not the House of Lords and the fears of some members were the result of suspicions which 'flowed from some distant background knowledge of

[1] That Committee had further suggested that the Speaker be 'requested to take all necessary steps to safeguard the privileges of the House and the Public Accounts Committee and to make it quite clear to the Council of States that their suggestion is unconstitutional, tending to interfere with the rights, privileges and prerogatives of the House of the People in financial matters over which this authority is supreme'.

[2] It had been suggested, for instance, that the Chairman of the Joint Committee should be elected by the Committee (instead of nominated by the Speaker), that the quorum should contain a quorum of Council members and that the Committee should be autonomous (instead of working under the Speaker's guidance).

[3] H.P. Deb., 12 and 13 May 1953.

[4] The Communist leader explained, not unreasonably, that while they were not in favour of a second chamber, so long as it existed they were in favour of giving it work to do. It was, however, probably unnecessary for him to confess that his party was 'not wedded to constitutional pedantry'.

[5] One member expressed a part of the uneasiness when he said: 'Today it is the Public Accounts Committee; tomorrow it may be the Estimates Committee.' Another alleged that 'what the Constitution prevents the Council from doing this motion enables it to do in an indirect way'.

English history'. Nevertheless he agreed further to postpone the question. The motion was finally passed in December 1953 and the Council members joined the new Committee in May 1954.[1]

Similar difficulties have occurred with regard to the problem of Joint Committees. In this case, too, the Council suggested rules to which the House took objection. Joint Committees have in fact been set up for a few Bills, but when in December 1953 the proposal for a Joint Committee came from the Council the House again became indignant, speakers referred to 'the subversion of the Constitution', 'acts of discourtesy' and the Deputy Prime Minister promptly moved the adjournment of the debate.[2] Two days later the Prime Minister took part, and once more appealed to members to be reasonable; the invitation came from the Council simply because the Bill concerned originated there. Somewhat sullenly, the House agreed.[3]

Even greater excitement was caused by an incident in 1954. The Hindu Mahasabha leader in the House of the People, Mr. N. C. Chatterjee, was reported as saying in the course of a public speech that 'the Upper House, which is supposed to be a body of elders, seems to be behaving irresponsibly like a pack of urchins'. The question of privilege was raised in the Council and the Chairman instructed the Secretary to ascertain the facts. The Secretary's letter asking Mr. Chatterjee whether the reports were correct was in turn raised in the House on the following day. The Prime Minister argued that there could be no harm in the Secretary's letter and pointed out that in Sundarayya's Case in 1952 a member of the Council had helped an investigation of the House. The Speaker, however, held that the letter was more 'in the nature of a writ' and favoured the reference of the particular issue, as well as the general problem of procedure in such cases, to a joint meeting of the Privileges Committees of the two Houses. This was agreed to by the Council of States, the Chairman taking advantage of an opportunity to say that the Council's action was in conformity with the practice of the British Parliament and that of India.[4] By the end of the year the two Privilege Committees, sitting together, had been able to work out an acceptable procedure for cases where a member of one House commits a breach of the privileges of the other.

In view of these disputes it is hardly surprising that there should be a body of opinion in the House of the People which favours the early abolition of the Council. The debate on the subject which took place in

---

[1] H.P. Deb., 24 Dec. 1953. The House was reassured that the Committee remained a Committee of the House under the Speaker's control (H.P. Deb., 10 May 1954), while members of the Council, though somewhat disappointed with the compromise, were relieved to be told that they were full members of the Committee (C.S. Deb., 13 May 1954).
[2] H.P. Deb., 14 Dec. 1953.
[3] H.P. Deb., 16 Dec. 1953.
[4] H.P. Deb., 12 and 13 May 1954, and C. S. Deb., 11 and 14 May 1954.

the House showed that there were some members of the Congress party who were of this view—as well as the Leftists.[1] The arguments on both sides were fairly familiar. Against the Council, it was urged that the Council was a 'stronghold of reactionary elements' and 'a device to flout the voice of the people'. There was more validity to the very different arguments that the Council performed no useful function. The Government mainly contented itself with pointing out that two years was hardly an adequate trial period. Other speakers were perhaps nearer the possible lines of future development when they said that the Council might be retained but differently chosen. On this point, however, there has so far been little constructive thought. What is certain is that peaceful coexistence is difficult if the two Houses continue to desire to perform the same functions.[2] Moreover, if their roles are not soon distinguished, the tradition of rivalry will become established and the Council will continue to attract a large number of persons who would have even more readily found themselves in the House of the People. The practice of rivalry is a most wasteful exercise of political energies and one without even by-products of value. It can only serve to lower Parliament as a whole in public esteem.

The position of second chambers in the seven States which possess hem is even less happy.[3] Although they are composed of members chosen in five different ways,[4] they have not been more successful than the Council of States in creating for themselves a distinctive role. Generally, however, the Councils aspire to no position of rivalry; they meet very much less than the State Legislative Assemblies and achieve very little. The Bombay Council may be given as an example. In 9 sessions held between 1950 and 1954, only 2 Bills were first introduced in the Council—and those were in 1950. In the same period the Council passed 219 Bills received from the Assembly and suggested amendments to 7 of them. In some States the movement for the abolition of the Councils is well advanced and the Congress Party Parliamentary Board has left the question to local decision. The Constitution lays down that only the Central Parliament can pass the law to abolish the Councils, and it may do so only if the Legislative Assembly of the State passes a resolution to that effect by a majority of its total membership and a two-thirds majority of those present and voting.[5] These conditions have already been fulfilled in some States. In Bombay, for instance, the resolution

---

[1] H.P. Deb., 2 April 1954. The discussion was on a Private Member's Resolution moved by a Socialist member.

[2] One member spoke about 'the mad drive towards equalisation of powers and functions'.

[3] There are Legislative Councils in six (of the nine) Part 'A' States: Bihar, Bombay, Madras, Punjab, Uttar Pradesh and West Bengal; and in one Part 'B' State, Mysore.

[4] Art. 171 (3) (Appendix I).

[5] Art. 169 (see Appendix I).

was debated for two days and during that time no member spoke in favour of retaining the Council. The Chief Minister simply put the case for and against and left the decision to a free vote of the House; 213 members of the Assembly voted for the abolition of the Council, none against, while 6 abstained.[1]

[1] Bombay Ass. Deb., 12 and 14 Dec. 1953.

CHAPTER SIX

OFFICERS AND COMMITTEES

REFERENCE has already been made to an important feature of the Indian Parliament—its self-consciousness as a Legislature, distinct from and even standing against the Executive. This attitude is most clearly expressed through the officers of Parliament and through the Parliamentary Committees. In an old and firmly established institution whose relations with neighbouring institutions are clearly defined and unquestioned, the task of its officers is usually limited; problems of internal order and external harmony are normally solved by appropriate adaptations of accepted codes. The case of the Indian Parliament is different. Although its origins may be traced back several decades, the changes since 1947 have been radical. In this situation, the influence of the Speaker and his staff has been exceptional. The political leaders have been preoccupied with policies; the institutions have been moulded by their officers.

1. The Speaker

The institution of the Speaker in India is a good deal older than the title; while the title was assumed only in 1947, the institution dates from 1921 and was established by two very different men during the 1920s.[1] The first President of the Central Legislative Assembly was Sir (then Mr.) Frederick Whyte. He was not elected by the House but nominated by the Governor-General of the day for a period of four years; in these first years the foundations of procedure and conduct were laid. Indian opinion wanted nothing better than to be able to follow the ways of the House of Commons; and, within the constitutional limits prescribed by the Government of India Act, 1919, and under the guidance of Sir Frederick Whyte, himself a former member of the House of Commons, the members of the Assembly were enabled to do so. It may be that a nominated Englishman as Speaker was inevitable and even suitable at the time. Yet with the entry into the Assembly in the General Elections of 1923 of the Swarajist Party (a group within the Congress), such a situation would not have been easily tolerated for long. In fact, the Government had in any case intended that an elected President should be chosen when Sir Frederick Whyte's four-year term ended. Since the

---

[1] For much of the historical information in this and the following sections, I am especially indebted to Shri M. N. Kaul, Secretary of the House of the People, and in particular to his three articles, 'Growth of the Position and Powers of the Speaker', 'Dignity and Independence of the Chair' and 'Parliament under Mr. Mavalankar' (*Hindustan Times*, 24 and 31 Jan. and 7 Feb. 1954).

Swarajists did not command an absolute majority in the House, it was perhaps with some surprise as well as with jubilation that they found their candidate elected by 58 votes to 56, defeating the rival candidate who enjoyed official support. President Vithalbhai Patel held office from 1925 to 1930 and did more than any of his successors before 1946 to assert and consolidate the independence of the Chair.

On more than one issue President Patel came into conflict with the Government, and on each occasion fought with tenacity for his independent powers. One of his first battles was for a separate staff under his control. Even Sir Frederick Whyte had favoured such a measure, though he had not felt able to press his views with insistence. The Government, too, conceded the principle, but resisted change on grounds of economy and efficiency; the Assembly continued to be served by a staff which formed part of the Legislative Department, a branch of the Government under the Law Member of the Government.[1] President Patel raised the issue soon after his election, but his position was much strengthened in 1927, when he was re-elected to the Chair with the unanimous support of both official and non-official members—itself a tribute to the reputation he had already established. In a famous statement to the House, he announced in effect his open campaign for independence: 'As President, elected by the Assembly, I am responsible to the Assembly and to no other authority.' In 1928 the House carried a motion for the formation of a separate Legislative Assembly Department under the President, and after reference to London the new regime was inaugurated in the following January.[2] Another assertion of independence related to his power to admit or disallow motions. Even at the commencement of his tenure of office he refused to admit a Government motion to take into consideration a Public Security Bill which had been reported upon by a Select Committee.[3] He maintained his position in spite of a Viceroy's address to the House on the subject, and even wrote to the Viceroy protesting against his criticisms of the Chair. Towards the end of his period in office, he succeeded in asserting the authority of the President over the maintenance of order and security in the precincts of the House. The Government at first held that it had to be the judge of what measures were necessary, but Patel thereupon ordered the closing of the galleries. After negotiations an agreement was reached: Government control of

---

[1] It may be mentioned at this point that the old Council of State was also serviced by the same department. Moreover, although a separate independent department was created for the Assembly, the Council continued to employ the old arrangements until it came to an end in 1947. When the new Council of States was established in 1952, it was given its own separate secretariat distinct from the Government departments—and distinct also from that of the House of the People.

[2] The Department was legally in the portfolio of the Governor-General but the *de facto* control rested unambiguously with the President.

[3] He based his decision on the ground that discussion would not be possible without reference to the Meerut Conspiracy Case, which was *sub judice*.

the outer precincts was unchanged but the inner precincts were placed in charge of a Watch and Ward staff, some of whom were police officers deputed by the Government, but all of whom were responsible to the President.[1] Perhaps President Patel's most striking action was in defence of respect for the Chair on the part of members. It appears that on one occasion reports reached him that the official members (that is, of the Government) freely commented in disparaging terms on some of his decisions. He thereupon raised the matter in the House and requested the Leader of the House to give members an explanation of the position. On receiving an ample apology, he treated the matter as closed.

The resignation of President Patel in 1930 coincided with the withdrawal also of most Congressmen from the Assembly, and the centre of political gravity, which had in any case never very surely rested in the Assembly, now certainly moved away from it. A succession of Presidents during the 1930s and 1940s maintained the gains which Patel had made, but the period of consolidation gave way to a new period of development only in 1946 with the election of Mr. Mavalankar, the present Speaker.[2] His election itself was an event of some excitement. He was opposed by the Government, which decided, somewhat strangely, to put up a nominated member to contest the election. The Government nominee was assured of Muslim League support, and the Government appeared to be confident of the result. In fact, Mr. Mavalankar won by 66 votes to 63.[3] In the recent development of the position of Speaker, the personality of the man who held the position of Presiding Officer from the last days of the Central Assembly of 1946, through the Constituent Assembly (Legislative) of 1947–49 and the Provisional Parliament of 1950–52, to the House of the People of 1956, has naturally played an important part.[4] In the House he was stern and

[1] The Speaker's control has more recently been extended to all security arrangements.

[2] Following Patel's resignation, the Chair was occupied by Sir Muhammed Yakub (1930–31), Sir Ibrahim Rahimtoola (1931–33), Mr. Shanwukham Chetty (1933–34) and finally for a long tenure by Sir Abdur Rahim (1935–45).

[3] It has been recently revealed (in public statements by M. N. Kaul and Dr. Khare on 10 and 11 Jan. 1954 respectively) that a sufficient number of official members of the Government were persuaded to vote for Mr. Mavalankar. It also appears (from the same sources) that the Government was so anxious to discover which of its members had disobeyed the Whip that they made efforts to secure the ballot papers; these had, however, been destroyed by the Secretary in anticipation of such attempts.

[4] Mr. Mavalankar began with the career of advocate but in the early 1920s became a prominent worker in the Congress movement, for which he was on more than one occasion imprisoned. He was active in local affairs and for some years President of Ahmedabad Municipality. He was Speaker of the Bombay Assembly in the period 1937–39. The Chair in the House of the People is also occupied from time to time by the (elected) Deputy Speaker and by the (nominated) members of the Panel of Chairmen. Their impact on the House has naturally been less than that of the Speaker, though the round and cheerful figure of the Deputy Speaker presided over the House during the long absence through illness of the Speaker in 1952–53. As already mentioned, on the death of Mr Mavalankar in February 1956, Mr Ananthasayanam Ayyangar, previously Deputy Speaker, was unanimously elected in his place.

conducted the proceedings with almost forbidding firmness, though not without permitting himself from time to time the luxury of exercising his sense of humour. He had a skilful lawyer's capacity for disentangling procedural puzzles and stating the issues clearly and at short notice; at the same time, he knew when and how to postpone a decision to give time for more leisurely consideration. Above all, he had the ability to catch the sense of the House and respond to the movements of sentiment and emotion among the members.

The important functions of the Speaker in the House of the People have already been indicated in the preceding pages. The maintenance of order and decorum and the smooth conduct of business; the decisions on the admissibility of questions and motions; the establishment of the scope of different kinds of debate and their regulation[1]—all this and more is already obvious from a few hours in the galleries or from a perusal of a day's proceedings in the House. And if matters appear to proceed smoothly, it is usually because a difficulty has already been well handled in the past. The influence of the Speaker in his own chamber is no less significant. We have already noted that the present Rules of Procedure are practically the creation of the Speaker—usually tentatively tried out in conventions, compared with those of the House of Commons and, if found suitable in practice, incorporated in formal terms.[2] His chairmanship of the Business Advisory Committee is central to the planning of the House's work and to the fostering of reasonably harmonious relations between the Government and the opposition groups. The emerging policy of the House on matters of privilege—the cautious consolidation and resistance to ambitious extensions—is largely of the Speaker's making.[3] The working of the whole range of Parliamentary Committees (which we consider further below) is conducted under the guidance of the Speaker, who in some cases has issued special directives and who is on every occasion the person to whom a worried Committee Chairman would go for advice.

The very constitutional framework within which the House operates

[1] It has not been unusual in India for the Chair to interrupt speeches in order to get clear the point which the members are making. This, however, is largely a matter of personal temperament, and some occupants of the Chair are fonder of this form of participation in the debate than others.

[2] 'We freely refer to and follow British precedents in so far as they represent experience about human affairs . . . and are the outcome of the evolution of democracy through centuries' (Mavalankar, 'The Development of Parliamentary Procedure in India', *Asian Review*, Jan. 1953). The Speaker added that there was no need to imitate 'outward forms'; in fact, however, there is a good deal of discussion among the Speakers of various legislatures on the subject of the introduction (or, where it already exists, in some States, the retention) of the Mace. The objections to it appear to be that it is un-Indian and that it is a symbol of force; on the other hand, some Speakers claim to have found a similar symbol used in ancient India and they say it stands not for force but authority.

[3] It must be added that the Speaker, while no doubt checking the exaggerated anger of the wilder members, has been zealous in the defence of the powers of the House in relation to what are felt to be the encroachments of the Council.

owes much to the Speaker's influential advice. Many of the provisions of the Constitution which relate to Parliament were indeed the direct results of the Speaker's recommendations. This can be said, for instance, of the inauguration of each budget session with a Presidential Address and the radical transformation of financial procedure. More important, the vital sections on privileges were the consequence of his intervention. It may also be noted that the outcome of the fight of President Patel for an independent secretariat is now, largely thanks to the Speaker's insistence, included as a part of the Constitution.[1]

Since the institution of the Speaker is in general so much modelled on that of Britain, attention is naturally drawn to certain differences. Of these, the position of the Speaker in relation to party politics is the most interesting. In the early days, under the guidance of the first President, the British model was accepted and generally followed; there was, that is, a complete severance of the Speaker from party politics. Moreover this position was more or less maintained during the whole period up to independence. With the advent of popular governments in the Provinces in 1937 the question became slightly more open, but on the whole there was agreement that impartiality and the appearance of impartiality demanded sincere attempts to break previous political connections.[2] After 1947, however, the situation changed.[3] Now every Speaker almost without exception was a Congress politician of some prominence. Among their number there were some who did not simply fail to live up to the standard of the agreed model, they declined to accept the model as suitable for India. Such Speakers argued that the nature of the national movement had been such that to sever relations from it on being chosen Speaker was neither possible nor necessary; if it were rigidly enforced, men of quality would not come forward for the position; and, in any case, so it was said, impartiality in the Chair does not depend on the nature of the Speaker's outside activities. Between this new school of thought and the older orthodox view, the Speaker of the House of the People has followed a middle course. He has held that Speakers must be recruited from men of political experience, in order that democracy may be consolidated. This certainly involved not imposing any drastic rule or convention of abstinence and severance. On the other hand, he has stressed the danger of Speakers developing an unconscious bias which imperils their impartiality, and of their losing the confidence of minority parties. He has urged therefore that even if party membership is retained,

---

[1] Art. 98 (see Appendix I). For this purpose, the Speaker summoned in 1949 a special session of the Conference of Presiding Officers of all Indian legislatures to support his efforts. (This institution is mentioned below, p. 270.)

[2] See, however, p. 65 above.

[3] Already in 1946 Mr. Mavalankar performed the symbolic act of discarding the Speaker's wig which had been worn until then; he appeared—and continued to appear—in the little white 'Gandhi' cap of the Congress.

participation in active politics of a kind that may be controversial—especially if related to matters that could come before the legislature—should be avoided. 'Though it is conceded that the Speaker in India should stand apart from party strife, it is maintained that he should not keep himself entirely aloof from politics as the British Speaker does.' As a first step, he has evolved the formula that 'though the Speakers may continue to be members of their parties, they should not attend party meetings where various subjects are discussed nor should they actively participate publicly in controversial matters that are likely to come up for discussion before the House'. According to this view, the final aim is unchanged: 'In course of time, we shall be able to evolve from this a sound convention on the lines of the British speaker.'[1] The Speaker has been able to get his views accepted to a limited extent among the presiding officers of State legislatures, but there are still many Speaker-politicians.[2] As memories and attachments to the national movement gradually lose their former power, however, there is no doubt that non-participation will become more general. Already there is a realisation that the practice, held by all Speakers to be desirable, of not contesting the Speaker's seat in the General Elections, can only develop along with the convention of non-participation.[3]

The lead given by the Speaker of the House of the People does not in any way entail a silent or neutral attitude on certain general public

[1] Mavalankar, *loc. cit.*
[2] In some States there have been opposition attempts to remove the Speaker from the Chair. This is usually an expression of Communist obstruction, but they are sometimes able to play on a more general suspicion of partiality. The first motion of no confidence in the Speaker of the Central Parliament was moved on 18 Dec. 1954. It was condemned by the Prime Minister as 'vicious', and he described the opposition responsible for it as 'incompetent and frivolous'. Over 50 members stood to indicate their support to the admission of the motion for discussion, but the opposition accepted defeat on a voice vote without pressing for a division. The main grievance was the remark of the Speaker that he would give more credence to facts put forward by the Government than by others. But the background appears to have been dissatisfaction with the Speaker's almost absolute refusal to allow adjournment motions; it was said that he had allowed only 1 out of 89 in three years. The incident was unfortunate, but it was hardly a serious setback to the institution of the Chair. The behaviour of some State Assembly Speakers, on the other hand, has on occasion seemed partial. A striking illustration not of partiality but certainly of political Speakership was provided by events in Delhi State in Feb. 1956. Dissensions among the Congress Party members of the State Assembly suggested the need for a new leader as Chief Minister; the Speaker accepted nomination, was duly elected and descended from the Chair to take over the leadership of the Government benches!
[3] The way the issue most frequently presents itself to the Speakers is as follows: If I am to be asked to give up party politics, I must be assured of my future career as a Speaker; this means (a) that my party must have a convention that they will normally nominate me again as a candidate for a constituency and for re-election to the Speakership, and (b) that there must be a convention between the parties not to contest the Speaker's seat; until these assurances are established, I cannot be expected to commit political suicide by losing touch with my party organisation and my electorate. (It may be noted that at the Centre at least there is a firm convention that, although the Speaker may not enter a debate or put a question, he can represent his constituency's needs by private communication with the Government.)

questions. The Speaker, for instance, has not hesitated to give his views in public speeches on such burning issues as the formation of linguistic states. Usually, however, he has restricted himself to remarks on the broad features of the developing political life of the country. Thus he has on occasion spoken of the importance of building up a strong but responsible opposition, of the meaning of secular democracy and the value of social work in local areas.[1] Above all, he has played a prominent part in the formulation and expression of a specifically 'Legislature' point of view. In this connection, the changing role of the Speakers' Conference is significant. This institution is as old as the Legislative Assemblies but it has recently assumed a new meaning. In 1921 the Presiding Officer of the Central Assembly carried out a tour of Provincial Assemblies, as a result of which a Conference of all Presiding Officers was called in Delhi in the same year. The meeting was designed to discuss procedural problems encountered in the different Assemblies, to exchange experiences and ideas, and, where possible, to reach agreed conclusions which would ensure the development of procedure throughout India on more or less uniform lines. The Conference at once proved valuable and met frequently though not at regular intervals.[2] The proceedings have from the start been confidential, but the practice has developed of giving the Opening Address and the gist of some of the discussions in the form of statements to the press. The original function of the Conference has been retained, and in the post-independence period the guidance which the less experienced Speakers from some States have received has been of exceptional worth. Most of the procedural difficulties discussed are submitted from the States; definite decisions on these are recorded in resolutions only if there is complete agreement. The Chairman and guiding spirit is the Speaker from Delhi, and the Conference Secretariat is supplied also from Delhi. In this way procedural development is everywhere kept on similar lines; Delhi in no way lays down orders or gives instructions, but the advice it offers on the basis of its experience is followed as far as possible. It must be admitted, however, that the position of Speaker in some States is hardly as strong as that at the Centre. In many cases they have much more difficult Houses to control—with shifting party alignments, unstable majorities, and so on. Not in all cases by any means are the Speakers themselves sufficiently withdrawn from the

[1] E.g. a speech reported in the press in Feb. 1954: 'In one-party rule there is a danger of democracy degenerating into autocracy. A strong opposition is most essential. Both the party in power and the opposition should have the welfare of the country at heart, and by means of discussion and compromise evolve what is best for the country. In a democracy, all criticism should be inspired by a sense of responsibility and practicability of suggestions.' (*Statesman* 20 Feb. 1954.)

[2] Conferences were in 1921, 1923 (two), 1925, 1926 (two), 1928, 1929, 1932, 1933, 1938, 1939. None were held during the war years. The post-war series had been held in 1947, 1949 (two), 1950, 1951, 1953, 1954, 1955. The place of meeting is now varied; the 1951 Conference was held in Trivandrum, that of 1953 in Gwalior, 1954 in Kashmir and 1955 at Rajkot. The idea is to extend the knowledge of various parts of the country and also in part perhaps to strengthen the morale of certain legislatures and their staff.

hurly-burly of stormy State politics to be able to command respect from all sides. Above all, not all Governments are as prepared as that of Pandit Nehru at the Centre to allow the Legislature to develop any form of independence of the Executive.[1] It is in this connection that the Conference has begun to assume a new meaning—as a united expression of specifically Legislature rights and interests.[2] It is, that is to say, not simply procedural puzzles but deeper problems of the status and powers of the Speakers, above all *vis-à-vis* governments, that now press for discussion; the conference of technicians is developing, so to speak, a professional *esprit de corps*.[3]

Behind this *esprit de corps*, as we have already suggested, there is something like a distinctive political theory which emphasises not the separation but certainly the distinctness of the powers of Legislature and Executive. In the somewhat fluid state of political institutions in India, the importance of such emerging attitudes is not to be under-estimated; even if the prevailing pattern of political power allows only a limited scope for its expression, it may well come to be decisive at a later stage. The opening address of the Speaker to the 1953 Conference gives one of the clearest expressions to this view.[4] A central passage may be quoted in full:

Unless Parliament is in a position to assert its independence as against the executive, there can be no hope of real democracy or Parliamentary Government; and it becomes more difficult where the members are organised as parties. This question is both important and delicate in the present set-up, when the political life of the country is not impersonal, is not wholly organised on the basis of programmes, and almost all the Legislatures have a comfortable majority for only one party and the opposition is so much divided in ideologies, parties and persons. Majorities are undoubtedly an advantage to push through a programme, but there are also dangers. . . . Having very large majorities, the administration tends to become stiff, uncompromising and sometimes unresponsive even to reasonable criticism. . . . Political life has yet to be organised and based solely on programmes

[1] In regard to some States, this way of putting it errs on the side of mildness; some Chief Ministers, with monster majorities and well-managed followers, are not disposed to regard the Legislature Officers as other than the staff of one more department of government: they are to be firmly controlled. I am informed on good authority that such Ministers have tried to put pressure on the Speakers—to disallow, for example, inconvenient amendments.

[2] An attempt is naturally made to represent the Legislature's rights as bound up with those of the citizen body. On the occasion of the 1955 Speakers' Conference at Rajkot, the Speaker of the Saurashtra Assembly called upon his fellows to realise that they were not merely presiding officers but 'custodians of the democratic rights and privileges of the people'. As already suggested in the discussion on privilege, this kind of claim, while no doubt intended in good faith to be asserted as against the executive, may in practice come to be more significant as a weapon against, for example, the press and the judiciary.

[3] There have recently been proposals for the creation of an Inter-Legislature Association of Indian parliamentarians. Though intended primarily for the discussion of policies, it may also reinforce the tendency.

[4] E.g., as reported in *The Times of India*, 25 Oct. 1953. This was, of course, by no means the only theme of the address.

and it will take a long time before conditions settle down. . . . The independence of the Speaker and the Legislature Secretariat is therefore a matter
very vital and essential not only for a proper discussion, freedom of speech
and free expression of opinion, but for the very existence of legislatures as
really democratic bodies and not merely handmaids to the executive. . . .
[In relation to legislative control over finances,] I feel that no control by the
elected representatives of the people over the transactions of governments
can ever be too much. . . . [In general,] the Legislature is the head which
acts through the Government, and the Government has, therefore, to show
proper courtesy and consideration for the Legislature.

From one point of view, these opinions may be regarded as standing in
the traditions of President Patel confronted with an alien executive; they
are equally important as an expression of a present trend in political
thinking.

2. The Secretariat

The Secretariat serves the House and its Speaker. But, as in the case of
the Speaker, its importance is not only in its routine functions but in its
wider, 'political' significance in the present circumstances of the Indian
Parliament.

The establishment of a separate Central Legislative Assembly Department was, as we have seen, effected after some difficulty in 1929.[1] This
department continued to serve the Constituent Assembly (Legislative)
during 1947–49 and became, in 1950, the Parliament Secretariat, subsequently the Lok Sabha (or House of the People) Secretariat.[2] Its staff,
formerly appointed by the Governor-General in consultation with the
President of the House, are now appointed by the Speaker and serve
under him. They are chosen from men already considered suitable by the
Public Service Commission, but the decision rests with the Speaker—or,
in the case of junior staff, with the Secretary. Indeed, when in 1948, a
special Selection Board of the Government Secretariat suggested that it
should extend its authority over Assembly Department appointments
the Speaker at once observed that his Secretariat 'should not in any way
—in the matter of appointment, discipline, control or in any other matter

[1] Constitutionally, the same is now the position of Secretariats of State legislatures (Art.
187, see Appendix I); in practice, many State legislature Secretariats are administratively
under the control rather of Ministers (usually the Finance Minister) than of the Speaker.
[2] The title of Parliament Secretariat was actually retained even after the Council of State
came into existence in 1952; it would appear as if there was a reluctance to part with a designation which underlined the greater importance of the Lower House. The change was
quietly effected without loss of dignity in 1954 when the Hindi titles were introduced. The
two Secretariats are now called Lok Sabha and Rajya Sabha Secretariats, even when referred to in English speech or correspondence. The Rajya Sabha Secretariat is similar in
organisation to that of the Lok Sabha. It is, however, naturally smaller (it has 15 gazetted
officers and a total administrative staff of 140); it has a less ambitious programme of research and publications; and, while it shares its members' attitudes towards the House of
the People, it has not the same policy importance as the Lok Sabha Secretariat.

—be subject to the jurisdiction of the executive',[1] and this stand was accepted. The salaries and conditions of service are settled by the Speaker in consultation with the Finance Ministry. The convention is firmly established that the budget of the secretariat, though subject to scrutiny by the Finance Ministry, is not discussed in the House, though members may make suggestions and recommendations privately to the Speaker.[2]

The staff of the Secretariat numbers over 250 and is organised in several branches. Its routine work may be divided into those functions which it performs in preparation for meetings and those which it carries out by way of record and reference subsequently. In the preparation of business, the Questions and Legislative Branches are the most important, the former sifting the questions submitted and minuting each for the decision of the Speaker, the latter preparing the amendment lists and the general order of business. Two Committee Branches, one for the two financial committees alone, perform similar preparatory functions for the several committees of the House. The proceedings of the House (and many committees) are taken down by the staff of the Reporters' Branch. Stencilled copies are available within two hours of the end of the day's debate and are sent for his corrections, if any, to each member who has spoken. The work of preparing the Debates for press is done by a separate Publications Branch; the Debates are published in two parts, one giving the Questions and Answers of the first hour, the other the remainder of the proceedings, while Appendices are also printed which contain the lengthy statements laid on the Table of the House. Since 1949 a Hindi edition of the Debates has been prepared alongside the English edition. The Debates are not, however, the only regular routine publications. Each House has also its Bulletin. Part I is a daily publication and is a brief record of the proceedings. A specimen copy is given below:

HOUSE OF THE PEOPLE

PARLIAMENTARY BULLETIN—PART I
[Brief record of Proceedings]

December 15, 1953

No. 232

1. Oath or Affirmation
One member made affirmation in English.

---

[1] Kaul, *loc. cit.*

[2] In 1948 the Government appointed an Economy Committee to examine the staffing of Government departments. The Committee raised the question of its being permitted to investigate the Assembly Department. The Speaker agreed, but on two conditions: the report would be a private one to the Speaker and would not form part of the official report; it would be for the Speaker alone to consider how far the recommendations could be implemented. These conditions were accepted. (Kaul, *loc. cit.*)

18—P.I.

2. Starred Questions

Fifty-three starred questions (Nos. 940–947 and 949–993) were put down on the order paper. Original notices of starred questions Nos. 975 and 982 were received in Hindi.

Thirty-three starred questions (Nos. 940–942, 944–947, 949–961, 964–968, 971, 973, 975–978, 980 and 981) were orally answered and supplementary questions were asked on all of them. Replies to the remaining questions (including starred questions Nos. 943, 962, 963, 969, 970, 972, 974 and 979 of which the questioners were absent) were laid on the Table.

3. Unstarred Questions

Twenty-three unstarred questions (Nos. 419 to 441) were put down on the order paper. Original notices of unstarred questions Nos. 424, 426 and 440 were received in Hindi. Replies to unstarred questions were laid on the Table.

4. Message from the Council of States

Secretary reported a message from the Council of States that the Council, at its sitting held on the 10th December, 1953, had agreed without any amendment to the Industrial Disputes (Amendment) Bill, 1953, passed by the House on the 30th November, 1953.

5. Leave of Absence

Shri Chandikeshwar Sharan Singh Ju Deo was granted leave of absence from all the meetings of the House for the current session.

6. Paper laid on the Table

The Deputy Minister of Finance laid on the table a copy of the Second Annual Report of the Consultative Committee of the Colombo Plan.

7. Statement by Minister of Home Affairs and States

The Minister of Home Affairs and States made a statement regarding the elections in P.E.P.S.U. and Travancore-Cochin.

8. Government Bills introduced

   (1) The Delivery of Books (Public Libraries) Bill, 1953.
   (2) The Salt Cess Bill, 1953.
   (3) The Press (Objectionable Matter) Amendment Bill, 1953.
   (4) The Government of Part C States (Amendment) Bill, 1953.

9. Government Bills passed

(I) *The Indian Tariff (Third Amendment) Bill,* 1953

Shri D. P. Karmarkar concluded his speech in reply to the debate on the motion for consideration of the Bill moved by him on the 14th December, 1953.

The motion for consideration of the Bill was adopted and the clause by clause consideration was taken up.

Clauses 2 and 1, the Enacting Formula and the Long Title were adopted.

The motion that the Bill be passed was moved by Shri D. P. Karmarkar.

The motion was adopted and the Bill was passed.

(II) *The Forward Contracts (Regulation) Amendment Bill*, 1953
(as passed by the Council of States)

The motion for consideration of the Bill was moved by Shri D. P. Karmarkar. Shri Tulsidas Kilachand spoke on the motion.

Shri T. T. Krishnamachari replied to the debate.

The motion for consideration of the Bill was adopted and the clause by clause consideration was taken up.

Clauses 2, 3 and 1, the Enacting Formula and the Long Title were adopted.

On the motion moved by Shri D. P. Karmarkar, that the Bill be passed, the following members took part in the debate:—

(1) Shri Radhelal Vyas
(2) Shri T. T. Krishnamachari

The motion was adopted and the Bill was passed.

10. Government Bill under consideration

The Minimum Wages (Amendment) Bill, 1953

On the motion for consideration of the Bill moved by Shri V. V. Giri, the following members took part in the debate:—

(1) Shri M. S. Gurupadaswamy
(2) Shri Amarnath Vidyalankar
(3) Shri T. B. Vittal Rao
(4) Shri Kamakhya Prasad Tripathi
(5) Shri B. S. Murthy
(6) Dr. Virendra Kumar Satyawadi
(7) Shri K. A. Damodara Menon
(8) Shri Mangalagiri Nanadas
(9) Shri Debeswar Sarmah
(10) Shri Khub Chand Sodhia
(11) Pandit Suresh Chandra Mishra
(12) Shri Ahmed Mohiuddin
(13) Shri P. C. Bose
(14) Shri Pisupati Venkata Raghaviah *(Speech unfinished).*

The discussion was not concluded.

(The House adjourned till 1.30 P.M. on Wednesday, the 16th December, 1953.)

M. N. KAUL,
Secretary.

Part II is published almost as frequently; it contains general information likely to be of interest to members. Here is a typical Council Bulletin Part II:

COUNCIL OF STATES

COUNCIL BULLETIN—PART II
February 24, 1954

No. 787
Agreements entered into between the Governments of India and U.S.A.

Members are informed that copies of the following Agreements entered into between the Government of India and the Government of the U.S.A. under the Indo-U.S. Technical Co-operation Programme, 1953–54, received from the Ministry of Finance, are available in the Library for reference purposes:—

1. Second Supplement to Operational Agreement No. 1—Project for acquisition and distribution of fertilizers.
2. Provision of Engineering Services for Damodar Valley Corporation.

No. 788
Tea and Coffee Buffets near the Council Lobby, Parliament House
Buffets for serving tea, coffee and light refreshments to the Members are functioning on either side of the passage leading from the central entrance of the Council Lobby to the Central Hall.

No. 789
Opinions on the Hindu Minority and Guardianship Bill, 1953
Copies of "Paper No. II—Opinions on the Hindu Minority and Guardian-ship Bill, 1953", as introduced in the Council of States, were circulated to Members on the 22nd February 1954.

No. 790
The Air Corporations (Amendment) Bill, 1954
Copies of the Air Corporations (Amendment) Bill, 1954, as introduced in the Council of States were circulated to Members on the 23rd February 1954.

No. 791
Bill passed by the House of the People
Copies of the Government of Part C States (Amendment) Bill, 1953, as passed by the House of the People, are being circulated to Members today separately.

S. N. MUKERJEE,
Secretary.

In addition, there is the Journal of the House, a sessional record and practically, in effect, a collection of the Part I Bulletins of the session. Among the special sessional records kept (mainly by the Table Office of the Secretariat) are various sets of statistical information,[1] and the com-pilations of Rulings and Observations from the Chair.

This routine work is no doubt exacting, for it demands always pre-cision and often speed.[2] The Secretariat in Delhi, however, has gone far

[1] E.g. statements showing time involved in various kinds of business; statistical informa-tion relating to Questions; brief summaries of work relating to Legislation; time involved in various stages of Bills (see Chapter VII and Bibliography).

[2] I may be permitted to pay a personal tribute to the Secretariat Staff, whom I found in-variably co-operative and efficient. They compare very favourably with those of Govern-ment departments—perhaps because they are a more compact organisation, more easily capable of feeling that they are a team with a worth-while job to do. At the same time, it must be said that their officers set a good example and, by such means as lectures to staff on the work of Parliament and its Secretariat, help to instil an unusual keenness.

beyond the performance of mere servicing. It has established in the first place a Research and Reference Branch which is primarily intended, along with the staff of the Parliament Library, to cater for the needs of members. In the absence of developed party and non-official research agencies, this is a potentially most valuable undertaking. Up to the present, however, it is only a tiny minority of M.P.s who place their demands for information. The Research section has, rather, had to take the initiative itself; it prepares brochures on what it considers members ought to want to know. In this connection it has been especially busy in setting out information on parliamentary procedure in other countries, especially Britain.[1] It prepares notes and bibliographies on important Bills and it has started a record of important cases decided in the Supreme and High Courts.[2]

The senior officers of the Secretariat are, of course, the advisers as well as the servants and teachers of the members. They are always available for consultation on a wide variety of problems: why their questions have not been admitted; how their amendments might best be formulated; when would be the best opportunity to raise a discussion on a particular subject; what were the implications of the afternoon's ruling, and so on. The Secretariat has also done much to form the Indian Parliamentary Group, which is a further means whereby the education of members and their self-consciousness as a distinct body can be developed.

The Secretariat in Delhi is also the guide for all State legislature secretariats. The custom has recently started of holding a Secretaries' Conference at the same time as the Speakers' Conference, and here methods of work are discussed. Apart from the annual Conferences, however, Delhi is becoming a centre for training and reference. Secretariat staffs from the States are sent to Delhi for several weeks to learn the system of organisation, and there is from many States a constant series of references on points of procedure which Delhi with its greater resources and experience is better able to handle. Certain officers from the Delhi Secretariat have on occasion been sent to State capitals to assist in arranging the work of local departments on suitable lines.[3]

Above all, the Secretary, with his staff, is the adviser to the Speaker.

[1] E.g., 'Privileges of the House of Commons', 'Parliamentary Practice in Commonwealth Countries', 'The U.S. Budget and Accounting Act, 1921', 'Question Time in the House of Commons', and even compilations of 'Rulings of the Chair in the House of Commons'.

[2] It has even published—because no one else appeared likely to do so—a list of publications of all the Ministries of the Central Government.

[3] Even Nepal has come within the orbit of the Delhi Secretariat; it received an adviser at the time of the inauguration of its new Assembly in 1954. What may possibly be regarded as the logical end of growing uniformity—viz., a single All-India Parliamentary Service—has been mooted but by no means as yet generally accepted. Mr. Kaul, Lok Sabha Secretary, in a public speech at the time of the 1953 Secretaries' Conference, said: 'We have to see that there is uniformity of procedure, organisation and administration in the various parts of The Grand Parliament of India'—i.e. in all the legislative bodies of India.

Although the Secretariat is strictly non-political—and must be so in order to be able to serve all parties—it would be reasonable to assume that the Secretary, while primarily a technical adviser and permanent head of an administrative department, shares and supports the general views about the position of the Legislature which we have seen are held by the Speaker. In fact, since the Secretary of the House of the People has on a few occasions given public expression to his opinions, we are not obliged to rely on assumptions; there is sufficient evidence to show that his influence is certainly exercised in the same direction. He has, for example, commented on the system whereby the President of the Republic is elected by the votes of all the members of Central and State legislatures:

> The total strength of members of all our legislatures is 4,058—and this may be increased when the constituencies have been freshly delimited. This body is, in essence, what I call the Grand Parliament of India, and in my opinion it was a mistake not to have actually summoned this body at the time of the Presidential Election. The recording of votes at various centres and sending them through the post does not emphasise the real unity of India through its various legislatures. The old symbols are disappearing, and the importance of new symbols of unity should be appreciated. The meeting of all members in one place would have had a great psychological effect.[1]

Parliament, however, is no mere symbol. It is there that 'power in the last analysis resides', and the task is to consolidate and develop the power of Parliament. 'I have repeatedly asked myself the question: Where does the line of future development lie, and in what way can Parliament become effective in the true sense of the term?' His answer would no doubt include the jealous maintenance of the powers of the Speaker and the independence of his Secretariat. But above all,

> I have come to the conclusion that the most effective line of development in the sphere of parliamentary activity is the formation of parliamentary committees. Parliament discusses policy, but unless there are committees which can discuss details and where those who run the administration have to give evidence, where matters can be thoroughly examined, Parliament's control tends to become feeble.[2]

Committees have the great advantage that they do not function in a party-political atmosphere; rather, attention is concentrated on the control of the executive. If only the members of Parliament are organised 'to apply this time fully, what a potent force and influence our Parliament will become!'[3] On the occasion of the celebration of the silver jubilee of the independence of the Parliament Secretariat from Government

---

[1] Speech at the Madras Press Club, reported in the press on 21 Oct. 1953.
[2] Kaul, *loc cit.*
[3] *Ibid.*

control, the Secretary allowed himself to express a vision of the future:

> I feel confident that one day, when our country becomes richer and greater, there will rise near Parliament House stately buildings in which will be housed the Parliamentary Committees, not one or two but twenty. Each will have its separate set of rooms, each will be assisted by its own secretarial staff. Not only secretarial staff but, as in the United States, expert advisers and research workers. Just imagine the vast vista that opens out: an expansion of the parliamentary sphere of investigation and control over the Government.[1]

When institutions are in a state of rapid development, visions may quickly become realities. A review of the committees of Parliament will indicate how far this has already happened.

3. Financial Committees

If it is true that a legislature may be known by the committees it keeps, it is reasonable to expect that financial committees in particular should have a special importance. The House of the People is not as large as the House of Commons (and, of course, the State Assemblies are much smaller), but it is still too big and too inexpert a body to be able, as a whole House, to exert any effective financial control over the Government. That function is performed by the Public Accounts Committee and the Estimates Committee. An examination of their work to date will show not only how financial control is exercised but also how far legislature-consciousness or even the mentality of separation of powers has developed.

The Public Accounts Committee is, in name at least, an institution of some age. Although it took the British Parliament a very long time to create this particular device, it was transplanted quickly into the soil of India's quasi-parliamentary institutions. Public Accounts Committees were set up both at the Centre and in the Provinces under the Montagu-Chelmsford reforms, the first Committees being constituted in 1923. They were generally small bodies of about 8–10 members and they met invariably under the chairmanship of the Finance Member of the Executive Council. It was also always the rule that the Committees were serviced by a secretariat drawn from the Finance Departments. Although these features indicate at once that the Indian Public Accounts Committee was only in a very qualified sense a committee of the legislature, an attempt was made to model it on British lines. The 'Memorandum on the work of Public Accounts Committees in India', prepared by the Auditor-General in India during this period[2] and intended for the purpose of explaining 'to members of Public Accounts Committees

---

[1] Speech to the Secretarial Staff at the Central Hall of Parliament House (*Statesman*, 11 Jan. 1954).
[2] New Delhi, 1927. The Auditor-General was Sir Frederic Gauntlett.

throughout India the nature of the duties entrusted to them', devoted much of its space to explaining how the Westminster Committee worked. Indian Committees were invited to emulate the standard set by the British Committee, which had helped to secure that the gap between estimated and actual expenditure was reduced to as little as 1½%. At the same time the author expressed the duty of the Committee as being 'to ascertain that the money granted by the Legislature has been spent by the Executive "within the scope of the demand"'. He added that this involved, for instance, checking whether anything that could be described as 'a new service not contemplated in the demand for grants' had been undertaken by government; it involved also ensuring that moneys had been spent with 'due regularity'—'that is, in accordance with those rules of sanction and appropriation which are laid down by superior authorities to be followed by subordinate authorities'. It is fairly evident from these phrases that the British model was in fact modified for India. The 'terms of reference' were more confined within a purely technical scope—as indeed one would have expected from a committee controlled by the Finance Minister and staffed by his officers. Even the Auditor-General, on whose reports the Committee has so much to rely, was, as the Simon Report said, 'not in any sense a servant of the legislature' but 'an officer appointed directly by the Secretary of State in Council and holding office during His Majesty's pleasure'.[1] In the circumstances of the time, this provision more easily implied his association with the executive than his independence. Nevertheless, while it cannot be said that the Public Accounts Committee worked in the same atmosphere and with the same scope as its British counterpart, this does not mean that it performed no useful function. It did act as some sort of check on financial propriety and it certainly gave very valuable experience to its members.[2]

No change in the nature of the Committee took place on the transfer of power in 1947. The parts of the Indian Legislative Rules relating to the Committee remained unchanged under the Constituent Assembly. With the introduction of the new Constitution in 1950, however, a new period began. Under the Rules of Procedure and Conduct of Business of the Provisional Parliament (that is, the former Rules modified and adapted by the Speaker), the Chairman was no longer the Finance Minister but a member of the Committee appointed as such by the Speaker. At the same time, the work of servicing the Committee was transferred from

[1] *Simon Report*, I, 376.
[2] The Simon Report seems to have overstressed the similarity of the Indian Committee to that of Westminster and underestimated the differences. For instance, the crucial feature of the Chairmanship of the Finance Minister is simply described as having 'sometimes embarrassing results'. The Report also accepts the Government of India's verdict that the Committee was 'industrious and efficient' and its scrutiny of expenditure 'jealous, detailed and enthusiastic' (I, 373–74). No doubt the Committee did all it could but its context was against it, and it is too much to claim that it was effective except within narrow limits. For a study of the British Committee, see B. Chubb, *Control of Public Expenditure* (1952).

the Ministry of Finance to the Parliament Secretariat. The change of control was emphasised by the inaugural meeting. The Committee for the year 1950–51 was elected on 10 April 1950; on the same afternoon a meeting was called, which the Finance Minister and Comptroller and Auditor-General attended by invitation and which the Speaker addressed. And when the Chairman a year later presented the first report of the Committee to Parliament, he confirmed that the change had been real: the Committee, now unambiguously a Committee of Parliament, was able 'to function in a freer atmosphere and to offer its criticism in an unrestricted manner'.[1]

The work of the Public Accounts Committee can be understood only in connection with that of the Comptroller and Auditor-General. The Constitution devotes one chapter[2] to this office. It not only lays down the provisions which ensure, as for judges of the Supreme Court, security of tenure and independence; it also provides that the duties until prescribed by Parliament shall be those already exercised under the 1935 Act. In fact, there are certain peculiar features of the duties of the Indian Comptroller and Auditor-General which deserve special notice. In the first place, although his title was changed by the Constitution from mere Auditor-General, the alteration was one of name only; the Indian Auditor-General is not in reality a Comptroller. That is, he is not in a position effectively to control the issue of public money, The public revenues of India are lodged not in one central account but in some 300 local treasuries. Moreover, certain departments are authorised to draw money without limit. Therefore, 'the responsibility for keeping within the amount sanctioned in the budget is entirely that of the executive'.[3] As the Comptroller himself complained, 'it is impossible in the existing circumstances to keep track of the up-to-date progress of expenditure'.[4] However, the importance of this defect should not be exaggerated. Control designed to prevent unauthorised issues in excess of grants is less valuable than audit proper—the check after the event to ensure that such issues have not taken place. An effective audit should suffice to impose an adequate sense of responsibility on the spending authorities. The second peculiarity of the Indian Auditor-General is that he is responsible not only for audit but also for keeping the accounts. Economy was the reason for the combination of these two distinct functions which should properly be separated, and economy is the reason given for the continuance of the system. This question has been the subject of a special report of the Public Accounts Committee,[5] following frequent

[1] Speech of Mr. B. Das, P.P. Deb., 29 Mar. 1951.
[2] Chapter V of Part V, Articles 148–151.
[3] Wattal, *Parliamentary Financial Control in India* (Simla, 1953), p. 167.
[4] Quoted in Wattal, *op. cit.*, p. 168.
[5] Public Accounts Committee, 1952–53, *Third Report* ('Exchequer Control over Public Expenditure'), Dec. 1952. This Report was based on that of a sub-committee which investigated the subject.

protests by the Auditor-General himself. The Committee strongly endorsed the Auditor-General's plea for a separation of accounting and
auditing functions and recommended accordingly that 'separate Accounts Offices for the various Ministries and the major spending departments . . . should be set up as soon as possible'.[1] Finally, it must be
noticed that the office of Comptroller and Auditor-General is one with
jurisdiction over States as well as Union. The audit of the accounts of
both Union and States is made, by the Constitution's Seventh Schedule,
one of the Union list of subjects. This centralised audit power is generally accepted as desirable. On the other hand, the keeping of State
accounts which is attached to it is a function which, it is felt, would be
more appropriately performed separately by the States. These special
features apart, the work of the Comptroller and Auditor-General is that
of auditing government accounts in order to assure Parliament that the
moneys it has voted have been spent as intended. The Constitution
(Article 151) provides that his report on Union accounts 'shall be submitted to the President who shall cause them to be laid on the table of
each House of Parliament', and that his report on State accounts should
similarly go to the Governor or Rajpramukh for laying before the State
legislature. These audit reports constitute the basis on which Public
Accounts Committees can function.[2]

The detailed duties of the Public Accounts Committee are set out in
the Rules of Procedure of the House of the People.[3] It is to examine
'accounts showing the appropriation of sums granted by the House for
the expenditure of the Government of India, the annual Finance Accounts of the Central Government and any other accounts laid before
the House as the Committee may think fit'.[4] It has to satisfy itself: '(a)
that the moneys shown in the accounts as having been disbursed were
legally available for and applicable to the service or purpose to which
they have been applied or charged; (b) that the expenditure conforms to
the authority which governs it; and (c) that every re-appropriation has
been made in accordance with the provisions made in this behalf under
rules framed by competent authority'. Its functions have also been extended to include the examination of the accounts of 'State Corporations, Trading and Manufacturing Schemes and projects', as well as of

[1] The Comptroller and Auditor-General subsequently announced (e.g. *Statesman*, 18
June 1955) that separation had been effected in three central departments and was being
done also in West Bengal.

[2] In India no binding dates have been fixed for the submission of the audit reports and
delays have on occasion been considerable.

[3] *Rules of Procedure* (Oct. 1952 edition), Rules 196–197. Similar rules govern the working of Public Accounts Committees in the States.

[4] Finance Accounts set out receipts, disbursements and cash balances; Appropriation
Accounts give a comparision of the grants made by Parliament for particular purposes
with the actual expenditure on those purposes. Apart from the Appropriation Accounts
(Civil), there are separate Appropriation Accounts and Audit Reports for Defence, Posts
and Telegraphs and Railways.

'autonomous and semi-autonomous bodies, the audit of which may have been conducted by the Comptroller and Auditor-General either under the directions of the President or by a statute of Parliament'.

This statement of duties of the Committee should not give the impression that the scope of the Committee's work is unambiguous and not open to dispute. There are in fact two problems of scope, neither of which is capable of final solution but for both of which working understandings at least are desirable. First is the problem of the area of governmental activity to be covered by audit. In the case of public corporations, the position has so far been generally satisfactory from an audit viewpoint, but parliamentary vigilance will perhaps always be required to ensure that the statutes establishing corporations continue to include proper safeguards. The Damodar Valley Corporation Act, for instance, provides that the Central Government appoints the auditor in consultation with the Comptroller and Auditor-General, and the rules framed under the Act in fact stipulate that the auditor shall be an officer appointed by the Auditor-General. But it has been thought by some that it would be safer not to leave it to the rules but to ensure that the parent statute itself guarantees audit by the Auditor-General and the presentation of his reports to Parliament,[1] Even more delicate and difficult is the case of private companies formed by the Government of India for the management of Government industrial undertakings. This matter was already briefly noted by the Committee in its first report following its new constitutional status as a Parliamentary Committee: 'We attach considerable importance to the necessity of safeguarding against any whittling away of Parliamentary control by the participation of Government in private companies.'[2] The Committee returned to the question more thoroughly in their important Third Report (1952–53) already referred to above. They had before them an exceptionally strong statement from the Comptroller and Auditor-General in which he went so far as to describe the formation of private companies financed from the Consolidated Fund as 'a fraud on the Companies Act and also on the Constitution'. He pointed out that it was scarcely proper either to pretend that the President or Secretary of a Department were 'persons' as intended by the Companies Act or to take money from the Consolidated Fund for such concerns. He feared that so far as audit was concerned his own

[1] This was the view of the Committee itself. 'As regards the audit of other Corporations financed either entirely or partly by the Central Government, we share the views held by the Comptroller and Auditor-General that his functions and responsibilities should be defined in explicit terms in the Statute itself providing for the setting up of a Corporation. We would also recommend that before statutory Corporations involving financial commitments by Government are created, the Comptroller and Auditor-General should be consulted in regard to the provisions for accounting and audit control.' (Public Account Committee, 1950–51, *Report on the Accounts of 1947–48* (*Post-Partition*) (Mar. 1951), p. 5.) See also Wattal, *op. cit.*, p. 163.

[2] *Report on the Account of 1947–48* (*Post-Partition*), p. 5.

control might be ousted, since he would certainly have no automatic right to audit the accounts of such companies; and even if he were invited to do so, the invitation would come from the company instead of from Parliament and, more important, his report would also be submitted to the company, thus by-passing Parliament and the Public Accounts Committee. The Committee endorsed this view in its Report.[1]

The second problem of scope concerns not the area of audit and inquiry but rather its character and degree. The 'terms of reference' as given in the Rules quoted above appear fairly narrow and technical. In practice, however, Public Accounts Committees tend to range beyond the technical. This is to some extent true of the British Committee; it is even more true of those in India. The interests of the members, the knowledge that Parliament as a whole cannot effect any real probing of the administrative machine, the politician's distrust of the bureaucrat, even a hankering after the sensational disclosure of scandals—all these factors prompt a desire to pass from technical irregularities into the realm of 'waste', 'extravagance', 'lack of adequate administrative controls' and even 'unsuitable organisation'. The boundary lines between the technical and the political are in the nature of the case ill-defined. So long as the Public Accounts Committee was controlled by a Finance Minister and serviced by his staff, the parliamentarians could be kept safely—even too safely—away from the business of the executive machinery. Once a non-official chairman is chosen and the staffing provided from the Parliament Secretariat, the barriers protecting the administration are almost down; at least the battlefield is extended and the executive has to pursue ingenious manœuvres rather than rely on any 'Maginot Line'.

The Public Accounts Committee consists of 15 members elected annually by the House of the People by proportional representation with single transferable vote, and the Chairman is appointed by the Speaker from among the members. In a committee of this kind, much depends on the calibre of the membership and in particular of the Chairman. Members must be able and keen and there must be at least a nucleus of men with some experience of the work. In Mr. B. Das, Parliament has found a man with a long parliamentary life (he entered the Central Assembly in 1923 and has been a member since), considerable experience of Public Accounts Committee work and a keen interest in public finance. His main assistant has been Mr. T. N. Singh, an enthusiastic and able former journalist and teacher of economics. Other members include a few with considerable business experience and training in economics. It is also clear that an attempt has been made to maintain continuity of

---

[1] Public Accounts Committee, 1952–53, *Third Report* (*Exchequer Control over Public Expenditure*) (Dec. 1952), pp. 3–4. The Auditor-General's statement is published as Appendix I to that Report.

membership as a way of ensuring a pool of experience. If the membership of the Committee since the new Constitution is examined, it can be seen that of the 15 members elected in 1950–51, no fewer than 11 remained for the following year. Even after the elections some continuity was secured: the 1952–53 Committee included 7 of the 1951–52 Committee, and 6 of these had been members of the 1950–51 Committee. This is a not unimportant achievement when it is remembered that there is some keenness on the part of members to get on to committees and when the Congress party is anxious to train as many people as possible in some aspect or other of committee work. The calibre of the members may be indicated by noting that two of the members of the 1952–53 Committee resigned to take up ministerial office. The party complexion of the Committee is a matter of little importance, but it may be recorded that the composition of the 1952–53 Committee was Congress, 10; Independents, 3; Socialist, 1; Communist, 1. The whole troublesome issue of permitting members of the Council of States to be chosen for the Public Accounts Committee has already been discussed in Chapter V, Section 5.

The Committee's work is based on the audit reports of the Comptroller and Auditor-General and until these reports are before it, the Committee cannot begin to function.[1] When they are ready, a preliminary discussion takes place between the Chairman and the Auditor-General and copies of the reports are circulated to all Committee members. A meeting of the Committee is then called—usually in July—in order to settle the programme of work for the year. This may be preceded by an inaugural meeting at which an address of a general nature is given. The Speaker, for instance, delivered an address to the 1950–51 and 1951–52 Committees, the Auditor-General to the 1952–53 Committee. The preparatory business done, the Secretariat notifies the ministries concerned of the Committee's programme so that they may 'keep themselves in readiness'.[2] Members peruse the Accounts and Reports and may frame questions or requests for information, which are sent to the Secretariat. Material furnished by the ministries in response to Secretariat requests is circularised to the members and to the Auditor-General. The stage is thus prepared for the examination by the Committee of witnesses from the ministries and departments.[3]

[1] Delay in the preparation of the audit reports led the Committee to suggest in 1952 that preliminary reports drawing attention to any grave irregularities might be given to the Committee in advance of the full report.

[2] See 'Rules of Procedure of the Public Accounts Committee' given in *Financial Committees, 1952–53*, prepared by the Parliament Secretariat. These Rules, prepared in 1952, embody mainly long-standing practice. The present paragraph is largely based on these Rules.

[3] It should be mentioned that of course each ministry has had an opportunity at an earlier stage of answering as to matters of fact and even offering explanations; relevant portions of the audit report are sent to ministries in draft for their comments before the report is finally prepared.

The meetings of the Committee are private. The examination of witnesses is generally begun by the Chairman, other members being free to put their own questions as the examination develops. The Comptroller and Auditor-General is invariably present. The line of examination has probably been discussed with him and he acts as an adviser to the Committee. His position is sometimes one of translator—explaining the officials to the politicians and vice-versa. On occasion, he has felt it necessary to protect official witnesses from over-aggressiveness on the part of Committee members; at other times, he has joined in and reinforced a criticism of a ministry made by members. A perusal of the proceedings of the Committee reveals other points of interest. It is clear, for example, that much time during the examination of witnesses is spent in members obtaining information on the organisation of departments; they feel that the inner ways of the administration have been for so long a closed book that this is an opportunity not to be missed. Members are generally uninhibited and prepared to make comments on quite major questions of organisation. The proceedings have been—in these first years of independence—at times quite acrimonious, but already there is an improvement as each 'side' becomes accustomed to the other, less distrustful and more co-operative. It is also noticeable that the proceedings become more economical in terms of time and more effective, as members acquire experience and confidence; they can get to the point more quickly and they are not so easily side-tracked by hares of prejudice and partisanship. Yet although the Committee is changing, moving away from certain attitudes, it is by no means a complete change; the Public Accounts Committee certainly remains very conscious of itself as Parliament's watch-dog and guardian of the people against official negligence or corruption.

Some extracts from the proceedings will serve to illustrate most of these points. The following, for example, taken from the examination of the accounts of the Prime Minister's Secretariat, illustrates the Committee as an information room and the Auditor-General in the role of restrainer over the members:

SHRI T. N. SINGH (*Member*): The Prime Minister is a public man. He has got so many other public activities. In addition, he is the President of the Congress. I do not think your Secretariat comes into the picture at all, so far as his activities as the Congress President are concerned?

SHRI B. N. KAUL (*principal Private Secretary to the Prime Minister*): No.

SHRI M. L. DWIVEDI (*Member*): The Prime Minister enjoys a position better than that of other Ministers, and so he has a general control over all the Ministries. Is it not so?

SHRI B. N. KAUL: I would not put it like that. He is the Prime Minister ...

SHRI M. L. DWIVEDI: Has he got any supervisory functions over other Ministries or not?

SHRI B. N. KAUL: The Minister-in-charge of each Ministry is responsible for the affairs of that Ministry. Under the Cabinet system of Government, the Minister is the highest person in charge of a Ministry. He is directly responsible to the Prime Minister. The Prime Minister's Secretariat cannot supervise the work of Ministries, each of which is in charge of a Minister.

SHRI V. P. NAYAR (*Member*): Cannot the Prime Minister sit in judgment over the other Ministers?

SHRI B. N. KAUL: He can. Ultimately the Prime Minister is responsible.

SHRI V. P. NAYAR: Has he not got control over the various Ministries?

SHRI B. N. KAUL: He exercises it through his Ministers. The Prime Minister's Secretariat has no control over the other Ministries.

CHAIRMAN: This Secretariat is not similar to the other Secretariats.

SHRI B. N. KAUL: So far as the work entrusted to any particular Ministry is concerned, the Minister in charge has got complete control over that Ministry. The Minister in charge is the final supervisory authority of that Ministry. Nobody can interfere with that.

SHRI DATAR (*Member*): Can you as the head of the Prime Minister's Secretariat call for Reports from the various Ministries?

SHRI B. N. KAUL: I do not call for any Reports from anybody.

SHRI DATAR: Does the Prime Minister receive Reports from anybody?

SHRI NARAHARI RAO (*Controller and Auditor-General*): May I say again —as a senior official, formerly a Secretary to Government, and not as the Auditor-General—a few things in this connection? The internal organisation and the way in which business is regulated between the Ministries concerned and so on ar eordinarily regarded as a secret which is not to be discussed at all. They are not allowed to be seen by anybody who is not concerned with the Government itself. And here we are trying to go into details, if I may say so with all respect, which really ought not to be discussed— how the internal work is done as between the Ministers, to what extent orders are issued by each Minister, what Reports the Prime Minister gets— these are not matters for the Public Accounts Committee.

SHRI M. L. DWIVEDI: I raised the point because I had come to know that in a certain Secretariat, clerks and officers go to sleep on chairs and there is nobody to supervise them.

SHRI B. N. KAUL: The Superintendant of the Branch concerned is supposed to supervise the clerks.[1]

Another extract will show how from financial matters to questions of general organisation generally seems a small step. In this case, the Auditor-General in some measure supported the members' probing:

SHRI T. N. SINGH (*Member*): I will raise the general question of the Telephone Factory itself. That relates to the general working of the factory. You

[1] Public Accounts Committee, 1952–53, *Seventh Report on the Appropriation Accounts (Civil) 1949–50*, etc., Vol. II—Evidence, pp. 20–21.

have got before you, I think, the balance sheet of the company, etc. For the period 1949–50 you have shown a net profit on the total sales of Rs.19·21 lakhs, whereas the net profit on the total sales of Rs.84·5 lakhs for the period 1st February 1950 to 31st March 1951 was only Rs.17,000. That means a terrible reduction in the profits. What are the reasons for it? Then the question is also about the valuation of the assets taken over by the company after the liquidation and the liquidation of the liabilities of the company to the Government. What interest is being paid on the liability which the company owes to Government? Also whether the liability has been liquidated so far? Then we find that the cash in hand and at the bank was the very heavy amount of Rs.73·87 lakhs in addition to the deposit of Rs.30 lakhs which means over a crore. Is such a large amount of working capital justified? Is it necessary at all, when the total turnover for a period of 14 months does not exceed about Rs.84 or 85 lakhs?

SHRI NARAHARI RAO (*Auditor-General*): We have started a new method of Government enterprise by nationalising Government industries. Sindri has been converted into a private limited company but there is no private capital. Money has been found from the Consolidated Funds and yet it is termed as a private company. I am doubtful about the validity of it. Some of the reasons are good. In running a business concern of that magnitude we cannot run it as an ordinary Government Department or Office. It has to be run as a business concern. Somebody must have responsibility and authority in the matter. But it is unnecessary to make it a private limited company without having all other characteristics of a private company. Parliament will itself lose control in respect of a concern which has been declared a private limited company because it falls within the purview of the company law. The proper course is to place the whole thing on a proper basis by an Act for regulating such concerns. There is general agreement on the importance for not whittling away Parliamentary control.

CHAIRMAN: I think he should reply question by question. Otherwise we will get lost.

SHRI T. N. SINGH: All right, Sir. What were the reasons for the non-surrender of the amount?

SHRI R. NARAYANASWAMI (*Joint Secretary, Ministry of Finance*): The matter had to go to the Standing Finance Committee and I think it went very late and by the time details could be obtained it was too late for surrender.

SHRI T. N. SINGH: You could not get time even up to the 20th March to surrender?

SHRI A. V. PAI (*Secretary, Ministry of Communications*): The decision was taken in January.

SHRI NARAHARI RAO: Surely when the change was made sometime in February—1st February—the surrender should have been made by the end of March. Somebody failed to do it. Let us leave it at that.

CHAIRMAN: That raises the general question I raised: whether Ministries have got competent machinery to administer commercial concerns. The

Posts and Telegraphs are under you: it is a complete separate organisation. Here about telephones, we have got a Production Ministry. We want to know what is the proper method—whether the Production Ministry can take up all manufacture. We do not know which Ministry controls a particular industry now—changes have been so quick. We want you to assist us to come to a definite conclusion—whether every Ministry will deal with industrial concerns or they will be controlled by one Ministry. It is a general question that we are going to investigate in this Session of the Public Accounts Committee. But you assist us so far as the Telephone Factory is concerned. Will it be under an individual Ministry?

SHRI A. V. PAI: It is under the Ministry of Communications.

CHAIRMAN: Will the Communications Ministry also specialise in industrial manufacture and development, etc.?

SHRI A. V. PAI: No decision has been taken so far. It has not been transferred to Production.

CHAIRMAN: My point is whether an individual Ministry will deal with a few schemes, e.g., the Health Ministry dealing with drugs like Penicillin, etc., and the Communications Ministry dealing with the Telephone Factory or whether all these will come under the control of the Ministry of Production.

SHRI NARAHARI RAO: May I suggest that that question could be more appropriate for the Production Ministry?

CHAIRMAN: But if my friends of the Communications Ministry can help us by giving their opinion, then that Ministry can have the courage to say that all industries should be concentrated under it.

SHRI A. V. PAI: We will find out what is the best course. In this particular case, Telephones, it is entirely under the Posts and Telegraphs Department. The experts are all of the Posts and Telegraphs Department. For co-ordination it is much better that it remains under the Communications Ministry—both the Factory and the Posts and Telegraphs.

SHRI S. N. DAS (*Member*): In view of the fact that the Production Ministry is now set up, has the question of transferring this Department, i.e. the telephones, been considered by Government?

SHRI A. V. PAI: It has been considered to some extent, because the Production Ministry asked us whether we would have any objection to this being taken over by them. We gave them reasons why in the interest of co-ordination we thought it better that it remained where it was.

SHRI S. N. DAS: Has it been considered at higher level?

SHRI A. V. PAI: It has not gone to the Cabinet.

SHRI U. C. PATNAIK (*Member*): How is it more convenient to have it under the Communications Ministry?

SHRI A. V. PAI: The main reason is—easier co-ordination. If it is under a different Ministry, the co-ordination has to be at a higher level; now the co-ordination is within the Ministry, which is easier.

19—P.I.

SHRI NARAHARI RAO: I think there is a good deal to be said in favour of leaving the Telephone Factory under the Communications Ministry because—this is my provisional view only—they know what they require. They are the technical experts and they have to look after the telephones, keep abreast of modern conditions and so they would be in a better position to look after the Factory; they know precisely what they want. If it is put under somebody else's control, I think the whole thing may go wrong. But the Production Ministry might have a say in the matter of general conditions of labour or other things like housing and so on which should be conformed to in all Government-sponsored industries. We do not want to have different policies in regard to non-technical matters not solely concerning your Ministry, but which are of common concern. That, I think, is probably what you have in mind. That would be satisfactory.

PANDIT MUNISHWAR DATT UPADHYAY (*Member*): These remarks also apply to the production of every article.

SHRI NARAHARI RAO: Quite so. For instance, if Railways want locomotives to be manufactured, should the manufacture go to the Production Ministry? It would lead to chaos.[1]

The following extract on the subject of the Bhakra-Nangal Dam illustrates one of the fairly rare cases where the questioning (by the Communist member) took on a clearly political character:

SHRI V. P. NAYAR (*Member*): I would like to know whether this idea of consultation with the American engineers, and import of American experts originated from the Department, or at the Ministerial level. Was it a Cabinet decision or was it something that originated in your Ministry?

SHRI S. D. KHUNGAR (Chief Engineer and Secretary to the Government of Punjab, P.W.D., Irrigation Branch): The idea was that the Punjab Government wanted specialists, and we asked for Americans of course with guidance of the Centre. The idea first originated with the Punjab Government, who approached the Control Board in the matter; and the negotiations were done with the concurrence of the Centre.

SHRI V. P. NAYAR: My question has not been answered. I shall put the question more specifically. Did you ask for American Engineers?

SHRI S. D. KHUNGAR: Yes, we asked for them.

CHAIRMAN: The Punjab Government cannot take foreign experts without the approval of the Central Government. So, everything was done with the consent and sanction of the Secretary to the Ministry of Irrigation and Power. In that case, the question will go over to Shri Khosla.

SHRI A. N. KHOSLA (*Additional Secretary, Ministry of Irrigation and*

---

[1] Public Accounts Committee, 1952–53, *Seventh Report on the Appropriation Accounts (Civil) 1949–50*, etc., Vol. II—Evidence, pp. 26–28. A moment earlier, the Auditor-General had ventured to comment to the witness: 'The point which has given rise to all this is that you are not ready with an explanation, which shows that you did not examine the Audit Report in time. . . . I hope it will not happen again' (*ibid.*, p. 25).

Power): The memorandum came from the Punjab Government. We examined it and we put it on to the Central Cabinet, saying that we will require about 75 Americans for the purpose.

SHRI V. P. NAYAR: Probably you are aware that the maximum development of hydro-power and irrigation has been in Russia for the last two decades at any rate. For instance, the Volga Dam project and . . .

SHRI A. N. KHOSLA: The Dneiper Dam is a relatively small one, compared with the American installations.

SHRI V. P. NAYAR: I am not referring to the Tennessee Valley System . . .

SHRI A. N. KHOSLA: I am referring to the other projects which are much bigger.

SHRI V. P. NAYAR: You will find in the statistics of development of hydro-power for the last twenty years in the world, and also of the enhancement of irrigation facilities, that the maximum acreage has been irrigated under the new canal systems in the Soviet Union and not in America. Likewise, the maximum development of hydro-power may have been only 1 million kilo-watts a few years ago, but during the ten years preceding this date, the maximum development has been in Russia and under more or less Asian conditions too. Did you for ever think that a study of the Soviet system was necessary before you thought of importing Americans?

CHAIRMAN: I think the technical data are not available in India without consulting engineers and experts for study.

SHRI V. P. NAYAR: It has been made clear that the idea of importing Americans originated in the Department and not at the Ministerial level. The Department specifically asked for American consultants. I would like to ask: Have you made a study of the comparative development of hydro-power in the world, before starting the work in India?

SHRI A. N. KHOSLA: Generally speaking yes, excepting the Soviet Union of which we have very little information.

SHRI V. P. NAYAR: Did you ever try to get that information?

SHRI A. N. KHOSLA: I do not know where that information is available.

SHRI V. P. NAYAR: It was categorically stated that an attempt was made to study the whole procedure in all the countries, in Europe and America. I should say that they have forgotten the maximum development of hydro-power that has taken place in the world.

CHAIRMAN: The difficulty is because of our knowing very little about Russia. As a student of political science, I can say that American aid was taken by the Russians, besides German experts also. Technical details about Russian development are not available with our engineers and technicians.

SHRI V. P. NAYAR: He says that he does not know anything and at the same time he does not give us the facts. When I asked him about the Volga Dam he said that that is a very small project. He himself has admitted that he knows very little about it. That being so, how can he say that it is a very small one? Do you know the extent of the Tsimilin-Skaya sea?

SHRI A. N. KHOSLA: I do not.

SHRI V. P. NAYAR: Do you know that it is the biggest artificial sea in the world?

SHRI A. N. KHOSLA: I do not know that.

SHRI V. P. NAYAR: Then you please don't say that it is a small system that obtains in Russia. When the question was put as to why other nationals are not imported, the reply was given that right from the beginning, they are following the American system. That is why they are denied the opportunity now to get better technicians at cheaper rates. They cannot utilise Englishmen or Frenchmen or others, because they are using the American system. We were thinking that this importation of American experts was done at the Ministerial level. But we find that the Ministry has been guided by the experts in the matter. The Committee must note that.

CHAIRMAN: The Committee notes the fact that our technical experts are not apprised fully with what has taken place in Russia.[1]

Finally, one extract which shows the sensitiveness of the Committee in regard to its rights; it shows the Auditor-General as defender of the officials in this case:

CHAIRMAN: Now, your Ministry has advised our Secretariat that certain reports about Hirakud cannot be furnished to this Committee because they have not been supplied to you. How is that? These reports ought to have reached you.

SHRI A. N. KHOSLA: The report is not yet final.

CHAIRMAN: That does not matter. If you have received a part of the report, it ought to be submitted to this Committee. This is a Committee of Parliament to look into the progress, and why should any Secretary withhold any report from us?

SHRI A. N. KHOSLA: The Secretary has to obtain the advice of the Minister. Because it is an interim report submitted to the Government of India in the Irrigation and Power and Finance Ministries, and has not received final consideration of Government it has not been made available. But it can be supplied in its present form, if desired.

CHAIRMAN: Who withheld it, or decided that it should not be furnished to us?

SHRI A. N. KHOSLA: It is between the two Ministers. But it can be supplied, if required.

CHAIRMAN: We are not concerned with the Ministers. Your letter is signed by an Under-Secretary and the reason given is that the final report has not been received and so your Ministry is unable to supply it at present to Parliament. Whether the report is final or interim matters little. The point is, do you recognise this Committee as a Committee of Parliament?

SHRI A. N. KHOSLA: We certainly do, Sir.

[1] Public Accounts Committee, 1952–53, *Seventh Report on the Appropriation Accounts (Civil) 1949–50*, etc., Vol. II—Evidence, pp. 120–21.

CHAIRMAN: No Minister of Government can interfere with the discharge of its duties by this Committee. You stated just now that the Finance Minister and the Irrigation Minister decided not to submit this report to the Public Accounts Committee.

SHRI A. N. KHOSLA: It is not a decision that way. If a request comes from the Public Accounts Committee that we have to supply that report, we will certainly do it.

CHAIRMAN: No Financial Adviser—not even the Finance Minister—has ever till now said that a certain document should be withheld from a Committee of Parliament. Secretaries to Government have got this privilege: they can say that a certain document is confidential. But when an Under-Secretary to Government writes to us categorically in the strain of the letter I read out just now, I feel rather insulted.

SHRI A. N. KHOSLA: What we meant to convey was that the report was not final and therefore . . .

CHAIRMAN: Whether it is interim or final report, it has to be made available to a Committee of Parliament which looks into the working of the Government of India Ministries. When I receive such a reply as this my mind goes back to twenty-five years back when the Secretaries to the Government of India used to refuse information sought by us.

SHRI NARAHARI RAO: Though I do not think it is entirely within my province—I have been only assisting you generally—it seems to me that when a report is received by Government and they have not yet considered it, or the report is only an interim one, it is desirable to wait for their final action and to ask the Government to let the Committee have the report as well as the action taken by them. Otherwise, this Committee might make itself into an executive body and usurp the functions of the Government itself. From that point of view I do not see anything improper in what the Finance and the Planning Ministers have decided. The only request that we might make is that they should not delay this matter further and that we must have very urgently a copy of the final report and action taken on it, or proposed to be taken by Government.[1]

When the examination of witnesses is completed, the Committee may discuss the lines of its report. Here, as in the initial stages of preparing questions for witnesses, the skill and ability of the Secretariat, together with the advice of the Auditor-General, are central to the work. The reports of the Committee are, in form, recommendations to Parliament. In practice, Parliament as a whole does not find time to devote a set period to a debate on the reports. News of the contents—or at least of the more sensational portions—does, however, reach the members quickly, and occasions easily present themselves when members can in questions and

[1] Public Accounts Committee, 1952–53. *Seventh Report on the Appropriation Accounts (Civil) 1949–50*, etc., Vol. II—Evidence, pp. 151–152.

other ways make use of points taken from the reports. The press, too, is quick to seize on any criticisms of the Government which have been made by the Committee. The reports are, above all, addressed to the ministries and departments.

A review of the work done by the Public Accounts Committee in the first few years after the new constitution shows that the Committee has settled down well and is becoming industrious.[1] In 1950–51, 13 meetings were held lasting 29 hours; in 1951–52, 20 meetings lasted 59 hours; in 1952–53, 31 meetings lasted 81 hours. In the first year one, in the second year two, while in the third seven reports were presented. The explanation of the increased 'output' is partly that the Committee and its Secretariat were doing more and better work. It is also in some measure due to a new method employed in 1952–53, when five sub-committees were set up for particular tasks. Three of the seven reports for that year are in fact reports of sub-committees. The sub-committees number generally three or four members and there is considerable keenness among those selected. One of the sub-committees—that on the Hirakud Dam Project —not only put in 102 hours of committee work but also spent some time on a visit to the site itself.

It is easier to give this record of work done than to assess its importance and value. The Public Accounts Committee is in no way executive and its usefulness has to be measured only in terms of its influence on Government departments. There is no doubt that some of its reports have been of high quality. The Third Report (on Exchequer Control) has already been mentioned several times. The Sixth Report on the Hirakud Dam Project was another very competent document. It brought to light some serious cases of financial irregularity, and even if it is true that the ministry was already in the process of making some changes, the Committee's report administered a 'shock treatment' which certainly speeded reforms. The report impressed observers with its sober and factual character, and its publication performed a valuable public service. The total effect of the Committee on the departments is difficult to gauge with any degree of accuracy. A perusal of the statements of action taken on the recommendations of the Committee tells little, since the departmental replies are of a somewhat set and uncommunicative character: 'recommendation noted', 'explanatory memorandum sent to the Committee', 'necessary instructions have been issued' and, of course, 'matter

---

[1] The Parliament Secretariat publishes each year a review of the work of the Financial Committees. The Public Accounts Committee's Reports are published and the reports usually contain, as an Appendix, a statement of the recommendations and a further statement showing the action taken by the Government on previous recommendations. The verbatim record of evidence heard by the Committee was formerly published but suspended in 1942; from 1952–53, publication has been resumed and some separate Volumes of Evidence have appeared. Evidence given before sub-committees, however, is not printed. It may be added that the Rules of the Committee provide that there shall be no Minutes of Dissent to the Reports.

under consideration'. It is certainly rare for a Committee recommendation to be rejected,[1] but it has been a fairly frequent complaint of Committee members that the Government, while saying it agrees, in fact does nothing. For example Mr. T. N. Singh at one meeting protested: 'We have been noticing that every year it is said that action has been taken, meaning thereby that circulars have been issued . . . saying that in future such and such rules should be observed, etc. And yet we come across the same type of mistake every year. I would like to know if the Department has done anything more than issuing a circular.'[2] Nevertheless, there is some exaggeration in this, and it is the opinion of the Committee and of officials alike that the administration does pay attention to recommendations.[3] The fair conclusion is that the Public Accounts Committee is succeeding in three main directions: first, it underlines and brings to public notice defects which the administration is aware of but which it has not yet wholly remedied; second, the mere existence of the Committee and the Auditor-General serves to remind officials that their actions are subject to scrutiny on behalf of Parliament—and the fact that the scrutiny is *ex post facto* makes no difference here; last, but in India by no means least, the work of the Committee serves to bring official and politician together and train both—the former in responsiveness to public opinion, the latter in the task of constructive criticism.[4] The work of Public Accounts Committees in the States is a good deal less effective. For one thing, in most States the Committee is still dominated by the Finance Minister and his officials; for another, it is not so easy to find able men for the job. Even so, however, the achievements just listed for the Committee at the Centre can be held to apply to at least some extent in the smaller sphere of State administration.

If Indian parliamentarians were happy by the change in the character of the Public Accounts Committee in 1950, they rejoiced even more at

[1] This happened, however, in the case of one of the rather broad and ambitious recommendations of the Hirakud Dam Report which had stated that 'there should be a full-fledged, high-level General Administrator in charge of the project as a whole.' The ministry evidently felt it was really beyond the province of a Public Accounts Committee to lay down the organisation of a project in that way. It was reported in the press (1 Jan. 1955) that the Ninth Report of the Public Accounts Committee, which strongly criticised certain Government of India purchases of jeeps in London, prompted an equally strong defence by the Finance Minister of the officials concerned who did not, he said, deserve the condemnation they had received from the Committee.

[2] *Seventh Report*, Vol. II (Evidence), p. 25.

[3] In fact the administration cannot easily escape the Committee's persistence. In this connection it is an important feature of the financial committees of the Indian Parliament that they have already developed the habit of following up certain cases. Thus the Public Accounts Committee, having by its Sixth Report, 1952–53, on the Hirakud Dam Project provoked certain Government action, returned in its Eleventh Report, 1953–54, to examine the adequacy of that action. When, as mentioned in a previous note, the Government replied to criticisms made in the Committee's Ninth Report, 1953–54, on the jeep contracts, the Committee took up the reply in their Fourteenth Report, 1954–55.

[4] The importance of ceasing to be content with purely negative criticism has been one of the constant themes of the Speaker in his addresses to the Committee.

the birth of a completely new financial committee in that same year: the Estimates Committee of the House of the People. Previously, from the time of the Montagu-Chelmsford reforms, there had been a committee of the Assembly called the Standing Finance Committee,[1] and similar committees in most of the Provinces. These committees were composed of a majority of elected members, but they were invariably presided over by the Finance Ministers and staffed by officials of the Finance departments.[2] The Montagu-Chelmsford Report was quite clear that these committees would work under limitations; they would be purely advisory and would serve mainly 'to familiarise elected members with the process of administration and to make the relations between the Executive and the legislature more intimate'.[3] In the Provinces their influence varied considerably according to the attitudes of the different governments. Their intended functions were to scrutinise proposals for new expenditure, advise on supplementary estimates and consider and initiate proposals for retrenchment. In most Provinces, however, their scope became extended and there was always 'a distinct tendency to encroach on the sphere of administrative policy'. At the Centre the committees' activities were, at least until after 1935, more confined. The point of view of the governments appears to have been that, however great a nuisance the committees were, they were worth while because they educated the members and they enabled the executive to know in advance what lines of criticism to expect in the Assembly. The claim of the Simon Report that 'the Executive has rarely, if ever, ignored its advice'[4] is worth noting— even if the explanation in part is that the Government only brought before the Committee those items of expenditure on which it was prepared to follow Assembly advice.

In any event, in the years following independence back-benchers expressed an anxiety to see a real Estimates Committee established, many of them feeling that such a committee would be a sign of a sovereign parliament.[5] The matter was debated in the Constituent Assembly (Legislative) soon after the transfer of power.[6] The Finance Minister reviewed the history of the Standing Finance Committee and explained

---

[1] From 1924, when railway finances were separated from the general budget, there was a separate Standing Finance Committee for Railways.

[2] There were also Standing Advisory Committees for most departments. These are referred to briefly below, pp. 308–311.

[3] *Simon Report*, I, 369.   [4] *Ibid.*, I, 371.

[5] There had been talk of an Estimates Committee in 1938. But at that time what the nationalist Opposition wanted was a 'retrenchment committee' that would cut the big salaries, reduce expenditure and lower taxation. The suggestion of an Estimates Committee came from one of the European non-official members. The Finance Member of the Government agreed to the idea and put forward a scheme for the consideration of all parties. The Committee was to elect its own Chairman, but its Secretary was to be an official of the Finance department and the estimates to be discussed by the Committee were to be selected by the Finance department. The Opposition did not agree to this and nothing further was done.   [6] See C.A. (Leg.) Deb., 17 Nov. 1947.

how its functions had developed by conventions. The Committee scrutinised recurring expenditure of Rs.100,000 and over, non-recurring expenditure of Rs.500,000 and over, all supplementary estimates and all new items involving policy; in addition it assisted the Finance ministry on any matters the Minister might refer to it. The Minister went on to say that it seemed to him that the Standing Finance Committee was in many ways a stronger committee than the House of Commons Estimates Committee which has to take Government policy for granted, is able to consider estimates only when expenditure has begun and has to restrict itself to the examination of a few fields of Government spending. But members were not satisfied. Some of them felt that what was good enough for the House of Commons would be good enough for India; as one member put it, 'Now that we are free, we can have it!' Some were prepared to concede that the Estimates Committee could for a while be presided over by the Finance Minister. Others drew attention to Britain's wartime Select Committee on National Expenditure and pointed out that it had done very well in a situation which had one significant resemblance to that of independent India, namely, the absence of a real Opposition in Parliament. Others again would be satisfied with the old Standing Finance Committee, provided its powers were increased and the ministry took the Committee fully into confidence. In the event, the Estimates Committee suggestion was dropped for the time being and the Standing Finance Committee was continued.

In 1950, with the inauguration of the new Constitution and the transformation of the Public Accounts Committee, the matter was raised more insistently, the Speaker and his Secretariat now acting as the spearhead of the attack. It appears that official opinion in the Finance ministry was opposed to the formation of an Estimates Committee, presumably fearing that a too-powerful parliamentary committee might have a crippling effect on Government departments.[1] But the parliamentary view prevailed and the Finance Minister himself welcomed the setting up of an Estimates Committee. He thought its suggestions and criticisms would be useful to the Government and he felt that its very existence would 'act as a deterrent on extravagance in public expenditure.'[2] The first Estimates Committee was elected on 10 April 1950. At the same time, the Standing Finance Committee was not abolished until all the Standing Advisory Committees disappeared in 1952 after the General Elections.[3] During the period of the Provisional Parliament (1950–52),

---

[1] At the same time there seems to have been another school of official thought which, on the basis of a study of the British pre-war Estimates Committee and on the strength of British Treasury opinion, formed the view that an Estimates Committee would be a useless body. Presumably, both views could be held together in a nightmare vision of a powerfully troublesome committee that served no useful purpose.

[2] P.P. Deb., 28 Feb. 1950.

[3] See below, p. 310, for an account of the ending of the Standing Advisory Committees.

therefore, the House had three financial committees: Public Accounts, Standing Finance, Estimates. It is not surprising that on occasion it was felt that there was some confusion of duties; each committee, said the chairman of the Estimates Committee in 1951, was 'beating the air in a different direction'.[1]

The work of the Public Accounts Committee has already been described. The function of the Standing Finance Committee continued to be, as before, simply to make available to the Government the view of some representative members on certain specific proposals for fresh expenditure; the Committee was set up on the initiative of the Government, worked under the Finance ministry and was in effect a Government committee. The Estimates Committee was in its status clearly unlike the Standing Finance Committee. It was to be a Parliamentary Committee like the Public Accounts Committee, working under the direction of the Speaker, staffed by the Parliamentary Secretariat and reporting to the House. The exact scope of its functions was, however, not so easy to define. The general idea of an Estimates Committee was explained by the Finance Minister in 1950. It would act as 'a continuous economy committee'. That is to say, it would not be concerned with specific proposals but with 'the question of economy over the whole range of public administration'. They would examine the estimates of the various departments not with a view to changing the expenditure already undertaken for that year but to give guidance to the Government as to the proposals to be made for the following year. The Estimates Committee, the Finance Minister said, would not be concerned with matters of policy, which were the responsibility of the Government; rather, 'within the framework of policy', they would 'see that only the minimum expenditure is incurred for fulfilling the objectives of Government'.[2]

As with the Public Accounts Committee, certain provisions concerning the duties of the Estimates Committee are to be found in the Rules of Procedure of the House of the People.[3] The Committee is to 'examine such of the estimates as may seem fit to the Committee and to report what, if any, economies consistent with the policy underlying those estimates may be effected therein, and to suggest the form in which the estimates shall be presented to Parliament'. But if in the case of the Public Accounts Committee the line between 'financial irregularity' and 'waste and extravagance' is difficult to maintain, certainly in the case of the Estimates Committee it is easy to move from economy to efficiency, from administration to policy. Apart from suggesting the form in which estimates shall be presented to Parliament and recommending economies within a given policy framework, the Estimates Committee has

1 P.P. Deb., 21 Mar. 1951.   2 P.P. Deb., 3 April 1950.
3 Rule 198 with fourteen sub-rules.

regarded its scope as including the whole field of administrative organisation and even proposals for adjustments and alterations of policy designed to secure increased efficiency in administration. Even in Britain, where relations between Government and Parliament are well established by firm conventions, the operations of the wartime National Expenditure Committee caused some doubts as to whether it was not trespassing into policy matters and infringing the principle of ministerial responsibility.[1] The Indian Committee is to a large extent inspired by the example of the National Expenditure Committee and is guided by men who wish to build up the legislature as a substantial counter to a dominant executive. In the Estimates Committee, with its almost un-avoidably flexible terms of reference, they have found a very suitable instrument.

The Estimates Committee is larger than the Public Accounts Committee, being composed of up to 25 members.[2] They are elected by the House of the People from its members by proportional representation and the term of office is one year. The Committee works under the guidance and control of the Speaker and is staffed by the Parliamentary Secretariat; in addition, the Chairman of the Committee during the important initial years 1950–54 was the Deputy Speaker. These arrangements have provided a strong and purposeful direction of the Committee's work.[3] As with the Public Accounts Committee, an attempt has been made to build up at least a nucleus of experience. No fewer than 20 of the 25 members for 1951–52 were members of the 1950–51 Committee, and even after the General Elections it was possible to secure that 9 of the 1952–53 Committee had served in the previous year, 6 of them for two years; as many as 19 of the 1953–54 Committee had been members of that of 1952–53. Seventeen of the 1952–53 Committee were Congress Party representatives, and of the remaining 8, 2 were Independents, 1 Communist, 1 Socialist and 4 from small parties. The Committee has been keen in attendance, the average number present being 18. One somewhat curious feature of its composition deserves notice: there is no overlapping of membership between this Committee and the Public Accounts Committee. This is strange since it is admitted on all sides that the work of the two Committees requires fairly careful co-ordination. This point has been made by the Speaker himself in one of his addresses to the Committees. It was made by the Chairman of the Public Accounts Committee when he was invited to speak at a preliminary meeting of the

---

[1] On the British Committee, see Chubb, *op. cit.*, Chapter 9.

[2] The increased size of the Public Accounts Committee following the addition of members from the Council of States has since 1954 brought the numbers of the two Committees close together.

[3] The Speaker has taken considerable interest in the Committee, sometimes attending its preliminary meetings and always keeping in touch with its work through his almost daily contact with the Chairman and Secretariat.

Estimates Committee in 1952. It was also made by the Chairman of the Estimates Committee in the course of a speech in the House when he specifically suggested that the membership of the Committees should to some extent overlap and the House should arrange to elect to one committee two or three members of the other. The suggestion was not carried out, the Minister of State for Parliamentary Affairs (in his capacity as Chief Whip of the Congress Party) intervening in the debate to say: 'For reasons which I shall try to explain to the Hon. Member outside the House, it is not possible for us to accept that suggestion.'[1] It is believed that the party's reasons for opposing overlapping membership included its desire to satisfy the demand of back-benchers for committee positions and its anxiety to give training facilities and experience to as many party members as possible. Co-ordination between the two Committees therefore rests only on the fact that they share a common Secretariat.[2] It may be added that Estimates Committees in the States have up to the present been of a rather different character in that in most cases they continue, as do the Public Accounts Committees, to be presided over by the Finance Minister.[3] They are thus less than full Parliamentary Committees in the sense intended at the Centre, though they are serviced by the legislature secretariats. In any case, it is probably wise that until members of State committees acquire some experience they should be guided by Finance Ministers, and so long as this arrangement continues there is a further co-ordinating link between Estimates and Public Accounts Committees.[4]

The methods of work of the Estimates Committee were to some extent provided for in the Rules of Procedure of the House. To a greater degree they are to be found in the Committee's own rules, approved at its first meeting in 1950 and subsequently elaborated. Even so, much remains determined by conventions worked out by the Committee itself, or rather by its Chairman and Secretariat with the approval of the Speaker.

---

[1] P.P. Deb., 21 Mar. 1951.

[2] The same arrangement exists in the House of Commons, but there a further connection is established by the practice of making the Chairman of the Estimates Committee a member of the Public Accounts Committee. It was this problem of co-ordination that prompted in England Lord Campion's suggestion of a single Public Expenditure Committee. This idea was considered in India also, but there too it failed to attract sufficient support.

[3] One exception is the State of Andhra which went, so to speak, one better than the Centre and chose the leader of the Opposition as Chairman of the Estimates Committee; this, however, was in the nature of an *ad hoc* political concession. Travancore-Cochin is one of the States which in late 1954 followed the lead of the Centre and passed new rules providing for a non-ministerial chairman.

[4] There is no doubt that in time—and in most States quite soon—the central pattern will be reproduced everywhere. Already the Speakers' Conference has encouraged this development. Moreover, the Speaker of the Indian Parliament has begun to organise all-India conferences of Chairmen of Estimates and Public Accounts Committees. These are clearly intended to become regular institutions parallel to the Speakers' Conference and will serve to bring about greater uniformity of procedure in the conduct of parliamentary financial committees throughout the country.

The Committee, usually elected in June, begins its work in July and continues to meet as necessary—and so far as possible during off-session periods—until the following May. Its first task is to make a plan of work for the year. From its inception the Estimates Committee has followed the advice given by the Speaker and the Finance Minister (and the practice of the British Committee), and has selected only a few ministries for examination. In its first session, the Committee had not assessed the magnitude of the task and it chose five ministries, of which it was able during the year to examine only three.[1] The Committee quickly learnt that if its examination was to be thorough, it was further necessary that it should concentrate not merely on a few ministries but even on a few subjects within a ministry or a group of ministries, and a rule to this effect was agreed to in 1951. The approach of the Committee has subsequently become clearly one based either on projects within a ministry or on topics and aspects common to several; there is no question of examining item by item the whole estimates of any ministry.

The Estimates Committee cannot proceed directly from a perusal of the bare estimates to an examination of witnesses and, unlike the Public Accounts Committee, it has no equivalent of a ready-made audit report on which it can base its work. The second step it has to take, therefore, is to procure from the ministry under examination certain further information against the background of which it will be able more usefully to consider the estimated expenditure of that ministry. The Rules of the Estimates Committee in fact set out most elaborately the form in which ministries are to 'furnish material in support of the Estimates'. In all there are nine headings under which ministries are asked to give information, and they include the organisation (with charts) and functions of the ministry, detailed descriptions of schemes and projects undertaken, and explanations for variations, if any, between actual expenditure in past years and current estimates.[2] The volume of material submitted to the Committee is very bulky, and probably the amount can be reduced as officials get to understand better the kind of information the Committee requires.[3] In addition to this routine information, the Committee prepares questionnaires which indicate particular points on which further information is needed. In the first year, the preparation of the questionnaires was somewhat casual, the Chairman and all members submitting their questions and the whole list being forwarded to the ministries. In the second year, a special sub-committee was charged with this task.

[1] In the second year it chose only one, but was unable to complete a report on that on account of the arrears of work from the first year.

[2] The Finance Minister was present at the Committee meeting when these headings were formulated. He pointed out the difficulties in the way of preparing so much information, but the Committee did not accept his objections.

[3] The Parliament Secretariat began by publishing a volume of material supplied by one ministry, but this practice was afterwards abandoned.

Finally, from 1953 onwards, a new procedure was devised which integrated the initial formulation of questions with the subsequent investigations. Even in the first two years, the Committee had worked through 'study groups' for various topics. These groups had examined the written material and prepared the way for the oral examination of official witnesses. In the second year, these study groups had been used for the further purpose of conducting on-the-site enquiries in relation to some of the major river valley projects. Now, from 1953, the groups were designated sub-committees and made responsible for all the work in relation to selected topics; that is, they framed the questions, studied the material supplied by the ministries, examined witnesses and drafted reports. This thorough organisation of sub-committees saved much time of the full committee and enabled a much more effective investigation of the estimates. In 1950–51, the Committee had 52. meetings lasting 167 hours; in 1951–52 activity was reduced—partly because of the preoccupation of members with the elections, partly because of the heavy calls on the Chairman's time as Deputy Speaker during the illness of the Speaker—and 15 meetings lasting 41 hours were held. In 1952–53, with the introduction of sub-committees, more and better work was done, although the Committee itself met for only 55 hours in 21 meetings.

The examination of witnesses is on lines similar to those already described above for the Public Accounts Committee. If anything, the wider scope of the Estimates Committee, together with the absence of any 'interpreter' such as the Auditor-General, has served to make relations between the Committee and witnesses at times more difficult. Both sides of the table are new to the job and time is needed before ways of putting questions and ways of answering them are satisfactory. Already, however, there is more skill and less tension than was evident in the first years. Also, as members become better informed through the work of the sub-committees, questioning in full Committee is more to the point and less time-wasting.[1] When the examination of material and witnesses has been completed, the Committee considers its draft report. An interesting feature of Indian procedure is that an advance copy of this document, marked 'secret', is at once sent to the ministry concerned for verification of factual details and for any action which the Minister may wish to take in advance of the presentation of the final Report to Parliament; copies of this draft report are also sent to the Ministry of Finance and the Prime Minister, as well as to the Speaker. Corrections may

[1] It is unfortunately not possible to give illustrations from the proceedings of the Estimates Committee, since these are not published. It is intended eventually to do so, but it is felt at present that publication—and consequent press publicity—would cramp the style of both members and witnesses. It may be mentioned that the proceedings for the very first meeting of 1950 were published and were numbered 'Volume I, No. 1', but perhaps this particular issue was considered not the best advertisement for the Committee; in any event, the series stopped at once. Apart from the Reports, the Committee publishes only its brief minutes and a record of government action on its recommendations.

then be made by the Chairman before the Report is presented to the House.

Some interesting cases have come to light which illustrate the kind of problem that may easily arise in relations between the Committee and the Government. Early in 1951 a Minister asked to see the proceedings of the Estimates Committee containing the evidence given by a chairman of a public corporation working under the ministry. The Speaker decided that the proceedings were confidential until and unless laid on the Table of the House, and the request was refused.[1] On another occasion a Minister, on receiving a report of the Committee, protested that it contained inaccuracies and that if it was released to the press, he would have to counter it publicly. The reply he was given was that the report had been sent to his ministry for correction and that errors remaining were not the fault of the Committee; that any report presented to Parliament was public property and could be freely commented upon in the press; that, on the other hand, it was undesirable for the Minister to comment in advance of discussion in the House; that, finally, the opportunity for ministerial comment would come when the House found time for a debate on the report. Since that incident it has been the practice that, in the event of major differences between Government and the Committee, informal discussions are held. On at least one occasion the Prime Minister considered it advisable to preside over the discussions. These incidents seem to indicate that while the Estimates Committee has no more than a power to make recommendations, a Government that wishes to maintain its popularity with the House will need to give good reasons for not following the recommendations. On the other hand, if a rash or inexperienced Estimates Committee makes ill-considered suggestions, such good reasons may not be so difficult to find.

The Estimates Committee in its first four years presented the following reports:

1950–51	First Report	Ministry of Industry and Supply.
1950–51	Second Report	Reorganisation of the Secretariat and Departments of the Government of India.
1950–51	Third Report	Ministry of Commerce.
1950–51	Fourth Report	Ministry of Works, Mines and Power.
1951–52	Fifth Report	The Central Water and Power Commission and Multi-Purpose River Valley Schemes.
1952–53	Sixth Report	Ministry of Food and Agriculture.
1953–54	Seventh Report	Ministry of Food and Agriculture.
1953–54	Eighth Report	Damodar Valley Corporation.
1953–54	Ninth Report	Administrative, Financial and Other Reforms.
1953–54	Tenth Report	Ministry of Food and Agriculture.
1953–54	Eleventh Report	Ministry of Information and Broadcasting.

[1] This kind of difficulty may afford another reason (see previous footnote) for not wishing to publish the proceedings. If, however, a decision is taken to publish in future, the difficulty could be overcome, as it is in England, by permitting witnesses to give evidence off the record.

While the Second Report is a slim document of 16 pages, most of the others are substantial booklets of over 50 pages, while the Ninth has 84 pages. Clearly there is not here the space to analyse these reports in detail nor to trace the exact extent to which their recommendations have been implemented.[1] Some indication of the tone and attitude of a few reports and a general idea of the Government response may, however, be given.

The First Report contained three main types of recommendation. One group of recommendations concerned improvements in the form of presenting the estimates. These were favourably considered by the Government and a number of improvements were fairly promptly introduced.[2] A second kind of recommendation was that aimed directly at securing economies in administration and avoidance of losses through negligence. This category included reductions of staff and salaries, curtailment of expenditure on touring and telephones, and measures for the speedy disposal of surplus stores to avoid deterioration. The Government replies on these points tended to take the form of undertakings to investigate or assurances that adequate measures had already been taken to prevent recurrences of previous errors and losses. A third type of recommendation went much further and proposed various changes of organisation. For instance, the whole organisation for the purchase of stores abroad should be overhauled and a State Purchase Corporation set up. Again, certain directorates should be closed down and others merged. Most important of all, a series of proposals were made to effect the better planning and conduct of a number of State enterprises such as the Sindri Fertiliser Factory, the Machine Tool Factory, and State Salt Factories. The Government replies here either announced the appointment of investigating committees or expressed the belief that certain Cabinet decisions would secure what the Committee intended.

---

[1] The latter is, in addition, no easy task. As already mentioned, the Committee's Secretariat publishes separately booklets giving the action taken by the Government on the Committee's recommendations. Many of the Government's replies are in the nature of promises to consider and investigate, and the final result of the recommendation is not immediately obvious. The only attempt at an assessment of the Indian Estimates Committee known to the present author is that made very early by Mrs. Hicks in the *Economic Weekly* (Bombay, 21 July 1951) and in *Public Finance Survey: India* (United Nations, 1951). Mrs. Hicks was full of praise for the work of the Committee, but in at least one respect she wrote too soon: the Government may have appeared at first to accept the recommendation to abolish the Enforcement Directorate, but it later changed its mind and rejected the suggestion. There is also the difficulty of knowing to what extent government action is really the result of a Committee recommendation, even if it appears to follow it; *post hoc* may not be *propter hoc*, but it may be convenient to let it appear so.

[2] This may have been because the suggestions were clearly reasonable or because the executive felt that this kind of topic was obviously one on which the wishes of a legislature committee ought to be followed. It was perhaps helped by the coincidence that the member of the Committee most closely associated with this set of recommendations, Mr. Tyagi, was appointed Minister of State for Finance (under the Finance Minister) just when the recommendation was being published by the Committee; he was in the position of being asked to implement his own proposals.

The Second Report was in some ways a less orthodox and more interesting document. It concentrated attention not on one ministry but on one aspect of governmental organisation—namely, the secretariat and problems of overlap between several ministries—and it constitutes in effect an organisation and methods report. The recommendations regarding amalgamation of ministries, departments and branches were of a general character. They were followed by quick Government action to regroup and reconstitute certain ministries, but it would be incorrect to attribute this mainly to the Estimates Committee; schemes to this end were in fact already under preparation by the Reorganisation Wing of the Ministry of Home Affairs. The Committee formed a conclusion that the establishment of several ministries included several unnecessary senior appointments which were not justified, and it recommended the abolition of the posts of Additional Secretary, Deputy Director-General and, in some cases, Joint Secretary. Here the Government replied that some of the posts had already been abolished and others were fully occupied, but they undertook a further examination of establishments. The Committee favoured a return to the pre-war system of ensuring that officers deputed from States to the Centre returned to their States on completing their tenure period. A scheme along these lines, the Government replied, was about to be implemented. Other recommendations included requesting officers earning high salaries to surrender all income over Rs.3,000, more efficient systems for handling correspondence and simplified systems of drafting, and economies through the pooling of typists and messengers. The official replies again took the form of accepting in principle subject to a closer investigation or explaining why a particular proposal would not prove desirable.

One of the most valuable reports of the Estimates Committee was that on the River Valley Schemes in general. The Committee attacked a complicated question with enthusiasm and skill and did so at the right time. The Government was forced to appoint the high-level Rau Committee to examine some of the criticisms and recommendations relating to the Damodar Valley Corporation, and the improvement which subsequently took place in the administration of that scheme and others owes a great deal to this Fifth Report.[1] It may not have been accurate in all particulars—and for that, much of the blame belongs to the departments who supplied the Committee with incorrect information—but it showed a sound grasp of organisational principle and put the responsible ministry and corporations under salutary critical fire. In the first place, the Committee stated clearly the need for a three-tier organisation for the Valley Schemes:

[1] The Eighth Report on the Damodar Valley Corporation does little more than underline some of the conclusions of the earlier report and press for action. It also devotes attention to rebutting the Rau Committee's Report where it disagrees with that of the Estimates Committee.

20—P.I.

The first tier should consist of the Cabinet, which on the advice of the Ministry of Natural Resources and Scientific Research, the Planning Commission and the Central Water and Power Commission will give policy decisions. The functions of initiating and making plans should vest in the C.W.P.C., which would act as fact-finding and initiating agency. They would collect data, make plans and frame estimates. It should be the responsibility of the Ministry and the Planning Commission in consultation with the C.W.P.C. and the Ministry of Finance to give these plans and estimates final shape. The third tier is the creation (by Statute of Parliament) of semi-autonomous organisations with well-defined functions and powers, which would be charged with the responsibility of constructing the project on the lines of approved plans and within the estimate framed.[1]

They went on to stress the importance of a properly integrated scheme in which all aspects are co-ordinated. They advised three-men Boards for the projects and suggested a procedure for deciding on modifications to plans. They favoured a careful Government watch on the progress of schemes and urged that Government directions to the Board should be issued formally. Parliamentary control should be safeguarded by quarterly progress reports laid on the Table of the House. They put forward recommendations as to the methods to be used for making appointments of different grades and contracts of different values. They even went into the question of provision of training facilities for engineers and of adequate repair workshops.

If anything, the Ninth Report was an even more remarkable survey. At the conclusion of nearly five years' work, the Committee felt that they should bring together in one document their views on a number of administrative and financial questions which they had tentatively or implicitly expressed in their other work. One of the most interesting parts of the Report contains an analysis of financial procedure in the administration, explains how methods appropriate to the pre-war government are inappropriate in the new context of a welfare state and suggests new procedures. The Committee were convinced that many losses were incurred because schemes were approved and begun without adequate preparation of technical blueprints and detailed estimates. With regard to grants and loans to States, too, there was too haphazard a procedure, leading only to delay, uncertainty and friction; State governments should submit consolidated proposals well in advance and a Centre–State conference should determine definite allocations for various schemes. The Committee expressed itself as generally dissatisfied with the management of State undertakings; instead of being run by civil servants who conduct them as if they were mere extensions or branches of ministries, they should be entrusted to men of experience in business and industry who should be recruited into an all-India 'Commercial and Industrial

[1] Fifth Report, p. 69.

Service' for the purpose. The Committee added recommendations on the establishment of an Institute of Cost and Works Accountancy, the extension of Organisation and Methods Divisions, the separation of accounts and audit,[1] effective action in disciplinary cases, decentralisation to State governments, delegation to junior officers, and methods of inter-departmental consultation. Most of the Committee's remarks on these points are at least usefully provocative even if they tend to overlook difficulties and see only one side of the problem. A couple of recommendations which show the Committee at its most ambitious and least realistic are those which read: 'No government servant who at the time of retirement . . . is in receipt of pay of Rs.500 per mensem and above shall take employment in any private business which comes within the sphere of responsibility of the Department in which he worked during three years before retirement'; and 'early steps should be taken to examine the question of prescribing the ceilings on salaries in private employment consistent with the policies and principles adopted for the public sector'.

These summaries of a few reports may be enough to indicate the quality of work done by the Estimates Committee. It has of necessity lacked experience and expertise, but it has found an effective way of working and has tried, with some success, to produce reports of a constructive character. The reports are without doubt pieces of simple, vigorous writing indicative of earnest and thoughtful purpose. If it is clear that the Committee has a few hobby-horses which it loves to ride, it is also clear that it is capable of hard and sober analysis coupled with imaginative insight. It is not easy to be certain as to the extent to which its reports are followed by the Government, but it is evident that the Government recognises the Committee as a powerful force not to be neglected.[2] There are even on record a few cases where spending departments have submitted proposals for expenditure to the Estimates Committee for their comment before making a final decision. The indirect influence of the Committee—working through the House and the parties as well as through public opinion generally—is probably even more important than its direct influence on the Government. Its development has been rapid, and now that it is sensing its own power and becoming more confident it is likely to increase still more in importance. To a very real

---

[1] This is an example not so much of wasteful overlap of effort by the Estimates and Public Accounts Committees as of one Committee reinforcing a recommendation of the other.

[2] 'As soon as I took over the Revenue and Expenditure side of the Finance Ministry', said Mr. Tyagi, 'I issued instructions to my Ministry and deputed one of the Joint Secretaries to take stock of the recommendations, tabulate them Ministry-wise, negotiate with the Ministry concerned on every item and submit me a fortnightly report. . . . My Ministry will take all possible steps to implement the recommendations.' (P.P. Deb., 29 Mar. 1951.) Similarly, the Finance Minister himself: 'We have every intention of treating the Estimates Committee as an ally. . . .' (P.P.Deb., 10 April 1951.)

extent, this type of committee, inspired as it is by the idea not simply of economy nor even of efficiency alone but also of acting as a check against an oppressive or arbitrary executive, achieves a special political significance as a substitute for a real Opposition. Indeed, it may well be that in an underdeveloped country—in which there is a wide measure of agreement not only on goals but also on methods—this kind of arrangement may be more suitable. In the immediate future, at any rate, it is if not the only source of constructive opposition at least a most important component of such an opposition. Finally, it must be noted that the Estimates Committee, perhaps even more than the Public Accounts Committee, performs two tasks of quite special importance in India. In the first place, it is a most valuable training-ground for members of the House. As a consequence, debates can become better informed and a pool of experience is made available from which governments can recruit fresh members.[1] In the second place, the reports of the Committee have a great educative value inside the House and also outside. They can help greatly to build up that layer of informed public opinion which is so urgently needed if the gap between rulers and ruled is to be closed.

Of the Estimates Committees in the States, it may suffice to say that up to the present their stature has been much less than that of the Committee at the Centre. Nevertheless, as they develop men of calibre and work themselves independent of their governments, they will no doubt perform on the smaller State scale the functions already described as being carried out at the Centre. Certainly they will continue to receive, through the Speaker and his staff, every encouragement to follow the model in New Delhi.

4. Other Committees

While the financial committees described in the previous section are no doubt the most important part of the Indian Parliamentary Committee structure, an account of this structure cannot be concluded without a mention of some others.

Reference has already been made to the distinctive system of Standing Advisory Committees in the Indian pre-war Assemblies, and the character of the Standing Finance Committee in particular has already been discussed. It was probably the most important and certainly the most active of all these advisory committees, but at least committees of some sort were in existence for each department or ministry.[2] Most of the committees numbered 10 members and the Chairman of each was

---

[1] There have been several promotions from the Estimates Committee to ministerial rank, of which those of Mr. Tyagi and Mr. Guha are only the most important.

[2] In reply to questions in the House, information was given that most of the advisory committees met 4–5 times in the course of 1948, whereas the Standing Finance Committee met 11 times. There were in all seventeen Standing Committees for the various ministries during 1948.

the Minister concerned. Rules to regulate the constitution and procedure of these committees were passed when fresh elections to the committees took place after independence. Their pre-war character was somewhat modified. The rules determining which matters were to be brought before the committees left the initiative and discretion mainly in the Minister's hands, but 'major questions of general policy' and 'legislative proposals' were now to go to the committees, whereas in pre-independence days there had been added the qualification—'on which the Minister desires the advice of the Committee'. However, it was expressly stated that the functions of the committees were purely advisory. The proceedings were to be strictly confidential and only brief reports indicating subjects discussed and conclusions reached would be circulated to members of the Assembly. Meetings were to be summoned by the Secretary (an official of the ministry concerned) at such times as the Minister might decide, but not less than twice a year. Pandit Nehru, in moving the election of new committees, said that the 'standing committees of the past' had met only twice a year and had been rather formal affairs; he hoped the new committees would meet oftener and that they would survey the whole scene of a ministry's work; he promised the full co-operation of the ministries.[1]

These committees, then, continued their existence into independent India, and it appeared as if the Indian Parliament might develop a powerful system of committees parallel to the departments of Government and, little by little, coming to exercise a control on ministerial policy and even perhaps on the process of administration. Such a development would, of course, have been in a different direction from that of the British Parliament, a direction pointing more towards France or the U.S.A. This has not happened. Each year, as the time arrived to elect fresh committees, a short debate took place on their work. It became clear that the views of Ministers and back-benchers were diverging. In 1948, members demanded wider powers for the committees—especially the Standing Finance Committee—and called for a more co-operative attitude on the part of Ministers.[2] In the following year, similar pleas were heard again, and Mr. Ananthasayanam Ayyangar (Deputy Speaker and later Chairman of the Estimates Committee) pressed for several changes that would have had the effect of strengthening all the committees and making the Finance Committee in particular something like an Estimates Committee.[3] In the first year of the new Constitution, differences of opinion became very clear. From the ministerial side, it was pointed out that a system of powerful committees on departmental lines belongs to a type of government quite different from that of the Commonwealth. India had adopted the British pattern in which ministerial

---

[1] C.A. (Leg.) Deb., 19 Nov. 1947.   [2] C.A. (Leg.) Deb., 31 Mar. 1948.
[3] C.A. (Leg.) Deb., 23 Mar. 1949.

responsibility was the crux of the matter; that responsibility must not be confused or challenged by parallel committees of the legislature.[1] Among back-benchers views were divided. Some were disappointed with the Standing Committees, revealing that they were often poorly attended and that members could not really grasp adequately the points put quickly before them by the officials. Others, however, felt that the committees were valuable. They argued that there was no sense in copying Westminster where in any case a government was checked by an experienced Opposition. The defects in the committees could be put right so that they would train and educate members and in time become a strong and healthy check on government. In particular, the demand was raised that the committees should be staffed by the Parliament Secretariat instead of by the ministries.[2]

So long as there was no clear Opposition in the House, the Standing Committees could manage to remain in existence—even if there was some restiveness on the part of both Ministers and back-benchers. After the General Elections, however, the situation changed. The House now contained opposition groups, and among them the Communist Party. In these circumstances, was there any sense in continuing to have advisory committees with whom projects would be confidentially discussed? The Government decided firmly that there was not; the committees should be abolished. The opposition and Independents criticised this move as retrograde and undemocratic, but the Prime Minister was not deterred. He explained that these committees had been formed in quite different conditions and that they would now have 'no meaning'. They belonged to a different system of institutions from those now in existence, and in any case they had proved of very little use in recent years. He indicated that he was quite prepared to have informal conferences with members of the opposition from time to time.[3]

The abolition of the Standing Advisory Committees has been a relief to Ministers and a disappointment to members of the House outside the Congress Party.[4] The view of the officers of Parliament is that the change is for the better.[5] They believe that a Cabinet type of government

[1] This was not the unanimous view of Ministers. The Finance Minister of the day, Dr. Matthai, spoke in defence of the Standing Finance Committee and said he found it useful.
[2] P.P. Deb., 24 Mar. 1950.
[3] H.P. Deb., 4 July 1952. It is not easy to obtain precise information as to the extent to which such informal conferences have been held subsequently. It is believed, however, that the Prime Minister has on a few occasions invited certain members of the House to private discussions on foreign policy.
[4] Members of the Congress Party in Parliament may hardly notice the change, for the party's own subject committees (see Chapter IV) serve the same purpose.
[5] This was certainly the case in 1953–54. More recently, however, Mr Ananthasayanam Ayyangar has confirmed that he at least remains in favour of the Standing Committees: at the Seminar on Parliamentary Democracy held in New Delhi in February 1956, he spoke of the desirability of reviving this institution and of the value of such committees for the scrutiny of Government measures prior to their introduction in Parliament. In his new position as Speaker he may be able to exert some pressure in this direction, but it is certain that ministerial resistance will be strong.

responsible to Parliament could never have permitted the Advisory Committees to become an effective force—regardless of whether Communists were present or not. Moreover, so long as these committees were staffed by the civil servants of the ministries, they would never have become instruments of Parliament. With the removal of these committees, therefore, energies on the parliamentary side have been concentrated on building up a new structure of committees, not parallel to the departments of government but cutting across them, not serving in an advisory capacity to Ministers but working under the direction and control of the Speaker and serviced by the Parliament Secretariat. The two financial committees are the centre of this new system; some of the other components may now be mentioned.

During the session 1953–54 there were in existence eleven Parliamentary Committees. These committees are now the subject of a special series of Rules of the House.[1] They are committees chosen by the House or nominated by the Speaker; the Chairman is appointed by the Speaker from among the members; the Committee is staffed by the Parliament Secretariat. They are in effect of two kinds. Some are committees concerned purely with problems of internal management of the House.[2] Seven of the eleven committees are of this kind and the more important have already been discussed in earlier chapters: Business Advisory Committee, Committee on Petitions, Committee of Privileges, Rules Committee, House Committee, Library Committee and Committee on Private Members' Bills. The remaining four, on the other hand, are designed to work as controls on the executive. Two of these are the financial committees; the others are the Committee on Subordinate Legislation and the Committee on Government Assurances.

The Committee on Subordinate Legislation was first nominated by the Speaker on 1 December 1953. The idea of such a committee was discussed between the Speaker and the Minister of Law as early as mid-1950, and a good deal of time was spent by the Secretariat in studying (and making known to some members) British experience from the 1929 Committee on Ministers' Powers down to recent assessments of the work of the Commons' Select Committee on Statutory Instruments.[3]

---

[1] Rules of Procedure 263–285. At the Speakers' Conference in Jan. 1955, the Speaker of the Union Parliament urged upon the Speakers of State Assemblies the importance of consolidating the structure of Parliamentary Committees. Special Rules of Procedure emphasising their distinctively parliamentary character could help, and State Assembly Rules should be brought into line with those of the House of the People. 'Parliamentary Committees' do not include several 'bodies on which members of Parliament are represented' —such as the Central Advisory Board of Education, the Central Silk Board, the Court of the University of Delhi and the Central Advisory Committee of the National Cadet Corps. There were during 1953–54 thirty such bodies.

[2] The Council of States has similar committees.

[3] The Parliament Secretariat had compiled booklets of 'Select Documents' of British and Indian material for both Public Accounts and Estimates Committees. These gave an account of the working of the British Committees and drew attention to some of the

Provision for such a committee was laid down in the Rules of Procedure in 1952.[1] The general function of the Committee is to see and report to the House 'whether the powers delegated by Parliament have been properly exercised within the framework of the statute delegating such powers'. The Committee is nominated by the Speaker and consists of ten members under a Chairman appointed by the Speaker.[2] It has powers similar to the financial committees to appoint sub-committees having the powers of the main Committee and to require the attendance of persons and production of papers and records.[3]

There is in fact a great deal of delegated legislation in India[4] and it is of several varieties. Not all delegated legislation has had to be laid on the Table of the House, because Parliament, at the time of passing an Act under which ministerial orders have been issued, was not sufficiently vigilant to ensure this. In some cases, however, the parent Act has insisted that the power it delegates to departments to issue elaborating legislation shall be subject to the provision that such rules must be laid on the Table. Even so, there is no uniformity of procedure: some orders are laid after they have come into effect, others come into effect after they have been laid on the Table for a certain period, and so on. The Rules of Procedure of the House already set down two important provisions independent of the establishment of the Committee. One rule (No. 71) States that 'a Bill involving proposals for the delegation of legislative power shall further be accompanied by a memorandum explaining such proposals and drawing attention to their scope and stating also whether they are of normal or exceptional character'. Another (No. 222) reads:

> Each 'regulation', 'rule', 'sub-rule', 'bye-law', etc., framed in pursuance of the legislative functions delegated by Parliament to a subordinate authority and which is required to be laid before the House (hereinafter referred to as 'order') shall, subject to such rules as the Speaker may in consultation with the Leader of the House prescribe, be numbered centrally and published in the *Gazette of India* immediately after they are promulgated.

The exact terms of reference of the Committee on Subordinate Legislation follow these rules. The Committee is to examine the orders and consider nine points[5]:

developments to date in India. The Secretariat now did the same for the Committee on Subordinate Legislation, summarising the Donoughmore Report and subsequent developments and providing also a bibliography on the subject of delegated legislation.

[1] Rules 215–226.

[2] It has subsequently been expanded to fifteen.

[3] The Government may decline to produce a document only on the ground that its disclosure would be prejudicial to the safety or interest of the State.

[4] No statistics indicating the volume are available.

[5] It will be noted that this list differs from that in the case of the British Select Committee; the terms of reference of the Indian Committee are in effect wider, but they still stop the Committee short of a consideration of the merit of an order.

(i) whether it is in accord with the general objects of the Act pursuant to which it is made; (ii) whether it contains matter which in the opinion of the Committee should more properly be dealt with in an Act of Parliament; (iii) whether it contains imposition of taxation; (iv) whether it directly or indirectly bars the jurisdiction of the courts; (v) whether it gives retrospective effect to any of the provisions in respect of which the Act does not expressly give such power; (vi) whether it involves expenditure from the Consolidated Fund or the Public Revenues; (vii) whether it appears to make some unusual or unexpected use of the powers conferred by the Act pursuant to which it is made; (viii) whether there appears to have been unjustifiable delay in the publication or laying it before Parliament; (ix) whether for any reason its form or purport calls for any elucidation.

The Committee reports such matters as it thinks fit to the House.

The Committee's First Report was published in March 1954 and revealed a most unsatisfactory position. Only one Bill introduced in the House since 1952 complied with the Rule laying down that an explanatory memorandum should accompany proposals for delegated legislation—and even in that case the memorandum was quite insufficient and inadequate. They recommended in strong terms proper adherence to the Rule. In the second place, the Committee examined the bewildering variety of provisions under which delegated legislation is issued, and was disturbed at the high proportion of Acts which required no more than that orders issued under the Act should be published in the official *Gazette* before coming into effect. They recommended that uniformity be secured by ensuring that Acts shall always lay down that orders be laid on the Table of the House for thirty days before coming into force. The Committee has been in existence for only a short time but it has made an able and workmanlike start to its important task.

Having delivered its major attack in the general terms of the First Report, the Committee has subsequently followed this up with a detailed examination of statutory orders. It examined 90 orders in its Second and 131 in its Third Report. It was found necessary to draw attention to several features of orders deemed undesirable: curtailment of the jurisdiction of the courts; indefinite, complicated and ambiguous wording; contravention of the provisions of the parent Act; undue delay between the publication of an order and its being laid on the Table of the House. The Speaker, congratulating the Committee on its first year's work, told its members that they were 'the only protectors of the people against the "new despotism" getting aggressive'; it was their job 'to direct the rule-making power in proper channels'. At the same time, they were not to see themselves as necessarily hostile to the administration; they were rather its 'collaborators, co-operators and friends', saving the civil servants, as it were, from their worst selves.[1]

[1] The address of the Speaker is given as an Appendix to the Committee's Third Report (May 1955).

The Committee on Subordinate Legislation is modelled on a House of Commons committee. The Committee on Government Assurances appears to be a wholly Indian invention—and perhaps one which would be unlikely in Westminster. This remarkable Committee was first set up by nomination of the Speaker on 1 December 1953.[1] It is noteworthy for two reasons. In the first place, it is the only Committee of the Indian Parliament which is presided over by a leading member (Mrs. Sucheta Kripalani) of the opposition. In the second place, the whole conception of the Committee is novel. The terms of reference read boldly: 'The functions of the Committee are to scrutinise the assurances, promises and undertakings, etc,, given by Ministers from time to time on the floor of the House and to report on (a) the extent to which such assurances have been implemented; and (b) where implemented, whether such implementations have taken place in the minimum time necessary for the purpose.'

The Committee originated in back-bench pressure in the first days after independence. Members wanted to know whether there existed any machinery to check up on the vast numbers of promises and undertakings which Ministers were in the habit of making in reply to questions and in debate. The office of the Government Chief Whip—later that of the Minister for Parliamentary Affairs—accordingly undertook to make statements to the House (based on data collected from all ministries) showing 'action taken by Government on assurances, promises and undertakings during the session'. It was in 1953 decided, mainly by the Speaker and his Secretariat, that this function was more properly performed by a Parliamentary Committee. In the nature of the work, it is the Secretariat rather than the Committee that is busy. Each day's proceedings are examined for phrases that amount to assurances. Statements and reports are then watched for 'implementations'. From time to time the Committee reports on the gap between promise and fulfilment.

It is too soon to say a great deal about the effect of the Committee. In its First Report, published in May 1954, it set out a list of 34 standard forms of assurance, including everything from the firm 'I shall inform the Hon'ble Member' to the vague 'I am reviewing the position'! It fixed two months as the normal period for implementation and recommended that when a ministry finds this period too short it should report the particular difficulty to the Committee. Finally, it set out a table, ministry-wise, of assurances given but not implemented, so that the House and public might know thereby which were the biggest culprits! The Second Report announced that out of 2,875 assurances given in the eight sessions of the House, 1952–54, 760 remained unimplemented and of these 61 had been outstanding for over two years. This may appear naïve, but it is a beginning of an institution which may become im-

1 At first 6 members were appointed; the numbers were brought up to 15 in 1954.

portant in itself and which certainly illustrates the atmosphere of legislature-consciousness which has already been mentioned. The whole structure of Parliamentary Committees reflects and at the same time reinforces this mood of watchfulness over the Government. It provides the student of politics with an interesting if slight modification of parliamentary government of the British type. More important, as already suggested, it saves the Indian Government with its large majority from the worst temptations of autocracy.

CHAPTER SEVEN

THE ACHIEVEMENT OF PARLIAMENT

ANY account of parliament in India must have a somewhat un-finished appearance, for it can be no more than an account of 'the end of the beginning'. Yet this is not to say that no conclusions can be reached on developments to date. It should be evident from the preceding chapters that a pattern of parliamentary politics has emerged in India. This itself is a great deal. Recall the doubts and fears; contemplate the circumstances and environment of independent India in post-war Asia; it can then be realised that a sufficient achievement of parliament in India is that it exists. It is not an author's egocentricity that prompts the remark that it is significant that a book of this kind can be written; rather, the mere fact that there is an institution, working in a regular manner and therefore susceptible of orderly description, is itself noteworthy.

Nevertheless, the existence of parliament in India is no guarantee of its continuance; for that, it is necessary that it should serve certain purposes, that it should work, in the sense not merely of following a regular pattern but of satisfying reasonable expectations. The qualification that the expectations should be reasonable is perhaps particularly important in India, for as we have seen[1] it has not been uncommon for political leaders there to expect, or seem to expect, more from political institutions than they can ever give. This is probably a natural consequence of a period of nationalist struggle against alien rule when everything appears to await the big political event, and men become victims of a 'deep delusion' and

'. . . . expect
All change from change of constituted power.'

The man who complained of the Indian Constitution that it did not 'solve the day-to-day problems of the people'[2] has to learn that neither constitutions nor the political institutions they provide can of themselves feed hungry mouths. It is equally important, of course, that in learning that lesson he should not fall into the opposite error of imagining that political institutions have no bearing at all on 'the day-to-day problems'. Their role may be only that of help or hindrance, but even this can be decisive.

What questions, then, may properly be put to test the success of parliamentary government in India? The functions of a parliament can no

1 Above, pp. 88–89. 2 *Ibid.*

doubt be variously defined and listed, but perhaps the following four would be widely accepted as central. A parliament must in the first place both sustain and control a leadership in such a way as to encourage initiative without permitting arbitrary governmental actions. Second, it must furnish channels through which grievances and aspirations can be heard by those in authority. Third, it must provide a platform on which public policy can be debated so that alternative courses may be adequately considered. Finally, it must afford opportunities not merely for the expression of given public opinions but also for the education of relevant sections[1] of the people so that they may have opinions worth expressing. How parliament in India answers to these tests may be fairly clear from what has gone before, but it may be useful if the conclusions are drawn out more explicitly.[2]

1. Ventilation of Grievances

The opportunities for the ventilation of grievances are several but there is no doubt that the most important is Question Time, the liveliest part of the parliamentary day. The figures (see following page) covering sessions of the Provisional Parliament and the House of the People are of interest. There is clearly a brisk business in questions.[3] Not all the questions put can be said to ventilate grievances and hopes; a large number, very properly, are designed to evoke statements of general policy from Ministers. Nevertheless, the proportion of 'ventilation questions' is quite high. If, for example, we list the topics in any one session on which a large number of questions were put, we can see that they include several topics which lend themselves to this kind of question. Thus, in the Autumn Session of 1953 more than twenty questions were put on the following: Cotton Textiles; Handloom and Khadi Industry; Postal Employees; Army; Sugar; All-India Radio; Scientific Research; Coal and Collieries; Railway Accidents; Roads; and, top scorer of all and a good example of a ventilation topic, Railway Lines and Links.

Question time is not the only opportunity. Adjournment Motions are

[1] The use of this phrase is meant simply to indicate that it is not necessary that parliamentary democracy should develop political opinions in all its citizens, but only that it should try to secure that the opinions of those whose interests are in politics should be developed opinions. Grievances and aspirations (mentioned in the second function), on the other hand, may belong to all.

[2] In the following pages the statistical material is given without detailed references. It has all been obtained from records published by the Parliament Secretariat and listed in the Bibliography.

[3] There may even be something like a competitive spirit among a few members to see who can put most questions. The Parliament Secretariat seems to encourage this by publishing for each session the names of those members who submitted the largest number of questions (e.g. Fourth Session, 1953, 181 from Mr. Raghunath Singh), those who had the largest number admitted (75 from Mr. Dwivedi), and those who succeeded in putting the largest number of supplementaries (139 from Mr. Dwivedi). This may assist keenness, but it also puts a premium on questions for questions' sake.

TABLE XXII—QUESTIONS IN THE HOUSE

	Provisional Parliament					House of the People			
	2nd Session: 31 July– 14 Aug. 1950	3rd Session: 14 Nov.– 22 Dec. 1950	3rd Session: (cont.) 5 Feb.– 9 June 1951	4th Session: 6 Aug.– 16 Oct. 1951	5th Session: 5 Feb.– 5 Mar. 1952	1st Session: 13 May– 12 Aug. 1952	2nd Session: 5 Nov.– 20 Dec. 1952	3rd Session: 11 Feb.– 15 May 1953	4th Session: 3 Aug.– 18 Sept. 1953
No. of Question Hours .	9	26	95	44	22	54	32	66	35
No. of Questions (Starred and Unstarred) received in Session	1,062	2,533	8,696	3,627	695	6,467	4,271	8,234	4,842
Ditto: Daily Average	118	97	92	85	35	120	133	125	138
No. of Questions (Starred and Unstarred) allowed in Session .	681	1,247	4,137	2,066	402	2,999	2,182	3,670	2,163
Ditto: Daily Average	76	48	44	44	19	56	68	56	62
No. of Supplementary Questions put in Session .	978	2,631	9,355	4,337	1,443	4,870	3,497	6,877	3,664
Ditto: Daily Average .	109	101	98	96	65	90	109	104	104
No. of Short Notice Questions received .	53	71	336	190	42	205	127	209	189
No. of Short Notice Questions allowed .	19	11	47	34	5	24	35	28	43

NOTE: As already stated above (p. 225) the number of questions answered orally in the House is about 20–25 daily, and the number of supplementary questions usually permitted to each main question about six.

nowadays only very rarely admitted by the Speaker, but the giving of notice of such a motion and the few minutes required to dispose of the motion (e.g. by a ruling from the Chair with or without a ministerial statement of explanation or policy) serve well enough to draw the attention of the House and the public to grievances which are considered by those who raise them as both important and urgent. Many of the adjournment motions have a general political point but others refer to particular grievances. In the list of such motions for the Budget Session of 1953, examples of the former are: 'U.S. decision to neutralise Formosa' and perhaps also 'Strike by mail van workers in Calcutta'. Certainly, however, examples of the latter type are more numerous and include: 'Minimum wage structure in tea plantations', 'Police firing on displaced persons in Punjab', 'Issue of licences for import of dyes', 'Prohibitory order banning processions in Delhi' and 'Stoppage of electric works in six Andhra districts and consequent unemployment of 2,500 workers'. The Half an Hour Discussions also afford opportunities for ventilating grievances; in the session just quoted, such opportunities were taken when topics like 'The bidi industry' and 'The International Wheat Agreement' were put forward. In addition to these occasions which are expressly provided for the purpose, other times by convention come to be used in the same way. The most important occurs when the Demands for Grants are before the House. As already mentioned,[1] this is the recognised chance for local pressures to express themselves. Individual members will put forward local district claims and complaints, while groups of members from the different States will get together to frame regional demands. Finally, it should not be forgotten that even in the debates on Bills it is often possible to press home the interests of a section of the population; the members from Assam do not lose their opportunities with a Bill like the Tea Bill, 1952, nor would members from Bengal and Punjab allow the Administration of Evacuee Property (Amendment) Bill, 1952, to pass through its stages without the benefit of their comments.

Opportunities are thus not wanting and in fact are adequately employed.[2] Against this, two considerations may quite reasonably be urged. First, it may be said that there is no strong Opposition able on the basis of a grievance to create an effective stir in Government circles. Second, it can be argued that relations between member and public are so weak

[1] Above, pp. 239–241.

[2] For completeness 'sake mention must be made of petitions. The Rules of Procedure provide for the submission of petitions relating to Bills; such petitions are examined by a Committee on Petitions which can direct that they be circulated as papers along with the Bills to which they refer. The arrangement has been little used to date and is one which is obviously open to abuse. It may be worth recording that in 1952 the only Bill which provoked petitions was the Preventive Detention Bill; 65 petitions with 388 signatures were presented. In 1953, a few Bills prompted single petitions, in some cases with only one signature.

that it is only too easy on the one hand for real grievances and injuries and legitimate pressing demands to go unheard, while on the other a great deal of noise may be made out of ill-founded rumour or on behalf of interests already able to look after themselves. These views contain a little truth, but not enough. For one thing, the Opposition ready to take up a grievance is a mixed blessing; it is not always the most worthy cause that looks good for political 'investment'. Moreover, these criticisms overlook the fact that the absence of a strong Opposition can be—and in India is—associated with a lively internal organisation of the major party through which many complaints and demands can find their way upwards. The Congress Party's organisation for this purpose is improving and is likely to continue to improve. It is true that the member of Parliament in Delhi is kept there by long sessions and is bound to become somewhat isolated from his constituency. On the other hand, 'constituency contact campaigns' are conducted to overcome this tendency and many if not most members are by some means or other kept in touch with local affairs.[1] In any case it must be remembered that so far as the mass of the people are concerned, the member that matters is not the one in Delhi but the one in the State parliament.[2] Contact in that case is much easier because the State Assembly sessions are short and the member is for most of the year at home. Moreover, complaints and hopes may arise not only from localities and individuals but from 'interests'. It is not easy to form a picture of the operation of 'pressure groups' in the parliaments of India,[3] but it does appear that many of the significant interests—sugar cultivators, railway unions, teachers, etc.—do in fact have fairly recognised spokesmen among the members.

2. Legislation

Parliament is the legislature, and indeed the bulk of the Assembly's time is spent on the discussion of Bills. The following table, while not an exhaustive analysis of parliamentary time,[4] is sufficiently complete to give a reliable picture of the dominating position of Government Bills:

[1] The intense sociability of all Indians and of Indian politicians in particular is a great asset here. So also is regional clannishness and family solidarity. The result of all these factors is that the M.P.s' quarters in Constitution House, New Delhi, resemble busy waiting rooms, bursting with friends and relations who have come up to town to stay for anything from a day to a year. There is much talk and it is impossible that the member will not learn a great deal about things back home.

[2] The complaint of many Delhi M.P.s is that they can't be quite as important to their constituencies as the members of State Assemblies because they have so little to offer—apart from railway lines. All the 'important' subjects are State, not Centre, responsibilities.

[3] Some would say that inaccessibility of information is already a sign that such groups are adequately organised.

[4] Question Hour is not included. Private Members' Resolutions are included, but not Private Members' Bills. The latter, however, account for very little of Parliament's time—perhaps about four hours a session—and have all been unsuccessful. The times spent in discussing the Budgets of States (Punjab and P.E.P.S.U.) temporarily under President's Rule are also excluded.

TABLE XXIII—DISTRIBUTION OF PARLIAMENTARY TIME (HOURS)

	Provisional Parliament						*House of the People*		
	1st Session: 28 Jan.–20 Apr. 1950	*2nd Session: 31 July–14 Aug. 1950*	*3rd Session: 14 Nov.–22 Dec. 1950*	*3rd Session: (cont.) 5 Feb.–9 June 1951*	*4th Session: 6 Aug.–16 Oct. 1951*	*5th Session: 5 Feb.–5 May 1952*	*1st Session: 13 May–12 Aug. 1952*	*2nd Session: 5th Nov.–20 Dec. 1952*	*3rd Session: 11 Feb.–15 May 1952*
Motions of thanks to the President's Address and amendments thereto . . .	9	8	12	—	9¾	6	14	—	19¾
Adjournment motions . .	5¼	¼	¼	1¼	1	¼	1¾	2	2½
Statements by Ministers . .	1½	½	¾	1½	¾	—	1½	1¼	1
Debate on motions . . .	2½	17¾	7¾	13¾	15¾	—	7	18	3
Government Bills . . .	125	3	71½	241½	183	45	283	84	123
Government Resolutions .	¼	4½	—	5½	8¼	—	—	21¼	3¾
Private Members' Resolutions .	7	—	3¾	7½	3¾	4¼	7¼	3¼	7¾
General Budget, General Discussion	12¾	—	—	14	—	8¾	15	—	20½
Demand for Grants, including Grants on Account and Supplementary Grants . .	47¾	2½	5	64	4¼	4½	66	1	70
Railway Budget, General Discussion	8¾	—	—	11	—	5	11¼	—	13¼
Demands for Grants on Railway Budget, including Grants on Account and Supplementary Grant	8¼	—	2¼	15	2¼	¾	10¼	—	12

There would be no meaning in any figure giving the average amount of time spent by the House on each Bill; some Bills occupy in all their stages only a matter of minutes,[1] while others take hours. It can be said that Parliament chooses wisely—it does, that is, spend time on those Bills which deserve it. Some of the measures on which a great deal of time was devoted on the floor of the House include the Estate Duty Bill, 1953 (92½ hours), the Preventive Detention Bill, 1952 (57½ hours), the Press (Incitement to Crime) Bill, 1951 (52 hours), and the Representation of the People (No. 2) Bill, 1950 (39 hours). In considering Bill procedure,[2] it was already noted that there was a pressure of Bills on available time and that this seemed to demand greater use of a committee stage. Much of the time of the House is taken with work which could better be done in committee. Yet the tendency to refer Bills to Select Committees shows little signs of developing. The volume of legislation passed by the pre-independence Assembly amounted to about 25–30 Acts annually. This figure fell somewhat in the war years, but since 1947 there has been something like a trebling of the pre-war output. Yet of the 70–80 Bills that are passed through their various stages, only some 10–15 are referred to Select Committees.[3]

Nevertheless, it cannot be said that Indian legislation is ill-considered. To begin with, the work of the civil servants in the initiating ministry and in the Ministry of Law is on the whole of a high quality. Once prepared and introduced, a Bill does not normally change very greatly from its introduction to its final stage; this might happen if committees were more used. Of course, amendments are moved and some of them are accepted by the Government. In this connection, it is interesting to note two contrasts between the Provisional Parliament and the House of the People. First, the number of amendments tabled in the Provisional Parliament was immense. In the one-party situation of that body, every member was an individual anxious to make a mark for himself. Since the General Elections introduced other parties, the framing of amendments has become a more organised activity of party groups. Thus, in the 4th Session of the Provisional Parliament 1,185 amendments were tabled to 32 Bills. In the first three Sessions of the House of the People the numbers of amendments tabled were 363, 232 and 695 (to 33, 21 and 30 Bills respectively).[4] In the second place, the proportion of amendments accepted by the Government has also dropped since the advance of opposition groups. In the 4th Session of the Provisional Parliament the

---

[1] An irresistible (but, it goes without saying, wholly misleading) example is provided by the 1950 Prevention of Corruption (Amendment) Bill which was introduced, taken into consideration, considered clause by clause, given a third reading and passed in a total of four minutes.

[2] Above, pp. 233–235.

[3] The great Estate Duty Bill, however, was so referred; the Select Committee held 21 meetings.

[4] In all cases, the number of amendments actually moved is much less.

Government accepted 155 amendments and rejected 146. In the first three Sessions of the House of the People the figures were: 1st Session: accepted, 15, rejected, 120; 2nd Session: accepted, 22, rejected, 43; 3rd Session: accepted, 44, rejected, 100. These figures should not be taken to illustrate an unduly harsh and unresponsive Government attitude; the explanation is, of course, rather that the majority of amendments now come from the Opposition groups and are usually of a substantial character. Nevertheless, the Government has on occasion shown an exceptionally open mind. To refer once more to the Estate Duty Bill, the Finance Minister in his final speech on that Bill drew attenton to the fact that no less than 52 amendments had been accepted, 32 of them substantive and at least 17 in the nature of real concessions. He said that the progress of the Bill throughout its stages had indicated the 'interest of the House and the energy, effort and consideration given' to the measure.

Statistics apart, any spectator or reader of the debates of the two Houses of the Indian Parliament will be satisfied on most points. The main issues of principle are brought out and debated. The parties are of course (as in other countries) already committed to their various views, but to an increasing extent they are learning that they must listen to others if their own contributions are to be effective, that they must debate, not merely address. Some members of Parliament who recall the days of the old Central Assembly claim that members then worked much harder and prepared their facts and arguments more carefully than is now the case. This may well be true; many of the present members lack the experience, education and intellectual capacity for intensive study of the kind that is desirable; and there is certainly little anxiety to achieve elegance and polish in speeches.[1] Nevertheless, the parties are doing their best to give opportunities to the able members and to shame even the others into some efforts. In the meantime, no doubt, the valuable ideas and the forceful, documented arguments must continue to come from rather a small minority of the five hundred members. This has not, however, prevented the Parliament from achieving a not unimpressive record of legislation on a wide variety of social and economic matters; and even if the bulk of the work behind such legislation has been done by the civil service, the contribution of Parliament has not been negligible—in getting the big issues stated, the details scrutinised and the interests of affected parties heard.

3. Control of Executive

Parliament has the job, we have said, of sustaining and controlling a leadership. It might be thought that in the situation of party strengths in

---

[1] Language has a lot to do with this feature: most of the members, even if at home with conversational English, do not treat it with the delicate love that the previous generation felt. Appendix II may serve to show this.

the Indian Parliament (and in most of the State Assemblies) there was no need to emphasise the sustaining role. This, however, is not quite the case. A majority must be not only secure but also nourished. In this sense, the Congress governments are not as well sustained as they might be. That is to say, they are not strongly supported by the work and thought of their followers. The experience and equipment of the majority of members does not enable them to contribute a great deal, and one consequence is that Ministers often feel somewhat lonely and isolated, dependent for encouragement, stimulus, ideas and argument not on their back-benchers but on their civil servants. This may be more true than one likes to imagine of even England, but it is certainly too true of India. Nevertheless, as has already been stressed, the new members are being steadily trained by their parties and by the Parliament and State legislature secretariats, and there is every reason to expect an improvement in this respect in the next parliaments.

In the next parliaments it is of course very possible that the Congress Party will have a much less dominating position than at present. In that event, the more usual sense in which the word 'sustain' is used will come to have significance: that is, it will become important that majorities of a size adequate to secure stable government are produced by the elections. Such a result cannot easily be guaranteed by any electoral system, but the chances in India are not unfavourable. For one thing, there is no disposition to depart from the system of mainly single-member constituencies which tends to translate even small majorities in votes into adequate majorities of seats. Moreover, there has been a tendency for some integration of parties since the last General Elections. No doubt it would be rash to predict the future party structure in India, and it would be wise to expect at least some multiplication of parties for the election struggle, but the general tendency towards coherence is fairly sure.[1]

In any event, the main emphasis at present and for some time to come rests on the legislature as controller of the executive. On this point, opinion in India and outside has expressed itself anxiously. In the absence of a proper Opposition, with adequate strength and enjoying due recognition, there can be, it is said, no healthy parliamentary government, for the government will be uncontrolled and unresponsive. On this, little need be added to what has already been pointed out earlier. It is an error, as we have seen, to imagine that the Government of India is uncontrolled. From two directions—the party and the parliamentary committees—come criticisms and suggestions which cannot too easily be brushed aside; and there is every indication that both these channels

---

[1] The role of prophet is risky and one hastens to add that the special position of Pandit Nehru is such that a decision on his part to break the Congress into 'Right' and 'Left' groups, the latter joining the Socialists, could transform the picture. Even in such an event, however, it is not easy to see a very large number of parties as a permanent feature of Indian politics.

of control are being steadily improved. There is much to be done at the State level in both respects, but even here the movement is unmistakable. It is also worth mentioning that even though the opposition groups in the House are weak, the Government to an appreciable extent is learning to behave as if they were strong.

There remains one aspect of parliamentary control which has not been separately discussed in the preceding chapters: control of the public corporations. This is a matter of some difficulty in India as elsewhere. A résumé of an important discussion in the House of the People will serve to introduce the problem. The discussion was raised by an Independent member, Dr. Lanka Sundaram.[1] He claimed that the question was one of importance and urgency, and his general argument was that the corporations were in effect accountable to no one. Each had become a monopoly which could forget the consumer with impunity, a veritable *imperium in imperio*. The Estimates and Public Accounts Committees could do something, but not enough and usually only too late. The control by the Minister was ineffective, the control by Parliament virtually non-existent. The remedy, he suggested, was to walk courageously along the path that England seemed to be about to take—to set up a Parliamentary Committee for the control and supervision of all public corporations. The Finance Minister replied to this speech by saying that it must be appreciated that the whole conception of public corporations necessarily implied some degree of self-abnegation on the part of Parliament as well as of the Executive. So far as executive control was concerned, they would with experience learn the best pattern of Minister–Corporation relations. To improve forms of financial control characteristic of the regular departments and ministries would clearly be wrong. The Minister had power to issue directives, and the senior appointments could be controlled. Parliamentary control was bound to be even more limited. He thought that the very real influence of the Public Accounts Committee was not realised. He believed that it would certainly be unwise to set up a special Parliamentary Committee which, whatever the intentions might be, could only result in tying the corporations with red tape.

There, for the present, the matter rests. Questions relating to public corporations may be asked—but only if they are not on matters of day-to-day administration. Debates are held on the annual reports and also, of course, when the statutes setting up new corporations are before the House. The discussions on Demands for Grants afford opportunities for criticism and suggestion. For the rest, parliamentary control depends on such probing as the financial committees may be able to carry out. As to executive control, its extent is by no means clear, since it appears to be mainly exercised in informal ways. One thing is certain: the protests of

[1] It was raised under the Half-an-Hour Discussion Rule (H.P. Deb., 10 Dec. 1953).

the Auditor-General and the Public Accounts Committee have made Parliament vigilant to see that proper audit provisions are inserted in all statutes constituting new boards and corporations.

Observers who have studied the administration of the Indian River Valley Projects have concluded that, on the whole, such parliamentary control as exists has been of definite value and might with advantage be in some manner extended.[1] They point out, for example, that debates in Parliament have often had a useful clarifying effect; the contrast between the confusion of Centre and State roles in the case of Hirakud and the firm division of labour in the case of the Damodar Scheme is said to be in good part due to the debates which took place on the latter. Again, the 5th Report of the Estimates Committee and 6th Report of the Public Accounts Committee are held to have been helpful to all concerned. The value of Question Time is less certain; the scope of questions is limited, the questions are often based on ill-founded rumours, while the answers given by Ministers are often deliberately or unintentionally vague and evasive. Yet even this device is not without its worth, for at least the Minister will be anxious to inform himself so that he cannot be completely surprised by a supplementary. Perhaps the greatest difficulty in the case of many of the corporations is that which arises out of the shared responsibility of States and Centre: both Central and State legislators are liable to aim their criticisms in the wrong direction.

4. Public Forum

It has been noted earlier that, even in the days of the British when the Assemblies and Councils were intended by nationalists to be far from the centre of political gravity, these bodies attracted a good deal of public attention. Once independence was gained, there was little to prevent Parliament from stepping into its proper place at the centre of the stage. Of course, Congress as the former nationalist movement still has a special position. It is also natural that, as in every federal state, public attention has to be in some measure divided between unit and central legislatures. It is true, too, that when one speaks of 'public' attention, it must be remembered that the reference is to something much less than the total adult population. Nevertheless, when all the qualifications have been made, Parliament in India can still be properly described as a public forum. During the 72-day Budget session of 1953, fifty thousand tickets were issued for the visitors' galleries, and there is no sign of a falling off of interest. A glance at the tightly packed, attentive crowds in the galleries at Poona and Trivandrum will reassure the observer that interest in State legislatures can be even more lively. An analysis of many different

---

[1] Professor Henry Hart of the University of Wisconsin is in no way responsible for the views here expressed, but many of the points made in this paragraph owe something to instructive conversations with him.

kinds of newspapers would surely demonstrate that the press recognises and encourages this interest; in India, a much greater proportion of news space is generally devoted to parliamentary reporting than is the case with most English newspapers.

The potential virtue of a public forum is two-fold. First, it can benefit the spectators, who may by watching learn. Second, it can improve the participants, who may have at least to find reasons with which to clothe the interests they represent. These are no more than possibilities—each with corresponding vices. But, so far at least, the good in India out-weighs the harm. A very wide range of views finds expression in parliament, and parliament is accepted as the platform on which views are to be expressed and exchanged. As one comment put it, 'The Indian Parliament, a mirror and educator of popular feeling, performing its duties in the public eye, has proved that Britain's work in India lives on.'[1] Moreover, there is a very real sense in which it can be said that the impact of parliament is more than political. The habit of orderly public discussion, once established, helps to set the tone of public life in general. Parliamentary behaviour can communicate as well as embody an understanding of how leadership can be combined with fairness, adherence to principles with toleration of different views. These ideas have already become part of the outlook of many sections in India. Their expression in an institution helps to ensure that they will be passed on to new generations.

5. Conclusion

The *Manchester Guardian* wrote recently in praise of the Indian Parliament: 'Parliamentary institutions have not had a very good time in Asia. . . . All that is happening in Asia throws a spotlight on the Parliament in Delhi as the one institution of the kind which is working in an exemplary way. . . . Pericles said that Athens was the school of Hellas. Mr. Nehru without boasting may say that Delhi is the school of Asia.'[2] This is confident language, but is it not justified and supported by the evidence brought together in the preceding chapters?

The three main charges that have been levelled against parliament in India may be restated and briefly answered. First, parliament is un-Indian and will therefore not last. To this, it must be admitted that in its origins it certainly was alien to India. 'Except on the local level, democratic institutions have not been known in South-East Asia, where government has been something embodied in and run by the few far above the heads of the mass of the people'—and even village democracy probably expressed only 'the intimate ties of a small and old-established community in which everyone has a fixed place'.[3] It can be further admitted that 'to

[1] *Indian Express*, 7 Mar. 1952.   [2] 5 June 1954.
[3] R. Emerson, 'Problems of Representative Government in South-East Asia', in *Pacific Affairs*, Dec. 1953.

extend democracy from the local face-to-face relation to the great national scene of unknown masses of men may well prove to be not an extension at all but the introduction of a new and quite different principle'.[1] But, as we have seen, even if it is a new principle it is one which has developed steadily and firmly, so that the 1952 Parliament elected on adult franchise is only the latest of a long line. It is grounded in modern Indian experience. Moreover, is there any other institutional pattern which is similarly grounded and at the same time equally serviceable for the purposes of the modern state? The Bhoodan movement is of incalculable significance, but it is surely more likely to supplement than to supplant the political institutions. Even the most sober view must conclude that parliamentary institutions have a better chance of success than any other.[2] What is true, however, is that parliament's success as an institution can be hindered by a failure wholeheartedly to accept it as having by now become India's own. Publicists who continue to hanker after a mythical 'institution of the soil' do disservice to the country's political development.

Parliament in India has been described, in the second place, as a façade which barely conceals an authoritarian dictatorship. This view owes something, of course, to the peculiarly dominating position of the Congress Party. But its plausibility is reinforced by other factors. It is connected, for example, with the previous view, in that an *a priori* conviction that parliamentary democracy is unsuitable for India leads easily to the conclusion that there is bound to be an element of illusion in any appearance that it is working well. Again, the fact that in some respects the quasi-parliamentary institutions of the pre-independence period did constitute a façade has encouraged the habit of believing that parliament in India must always have about it a quality of unreality.[3] Moreover, the 'façade' theory seems to fit in very well with the view that 'the Indian mentality' is accustomed to and feels the need for unquestioning obedience to authority.[4] This receives reinforcement, of course, from the

[1] *Ibid.*

[2] Compare A. Appadorai, *Democracy in India* (Oxford Pamphlet on Indian Affairs, 1942), p. 21: 'The real question for India is not whether democracy will work successfully —for she has no desirable alternative. What she must ask herself rather is how and how quickly she can create those conditions under which democracy can start and continue to work successfully.'

[3] The 'façade' aspect of the Assemblies and Councils before 1947 refers to the fact that the British Government of India was irremovable and, in the technical sense, non-responsible; also to the fact that, during 1937–39, Congress ministries were not quite what they seemed, since they were responsible in peculiar degree to the all-India party. Recognition of these limitations in pre-war experience is by no means inconsistent with emphasis on the vital value of that experience.

[4] Compare, for example, Dr. Ambedkar's views of the dangers of the 'Bhakti' spirit of devotion (as above, p. 89n.). It has similarly been alleged, as we noted, that the attitude of the electors in 1951–52 was not one of genuine choice. R. Emerson (*loc. cit.*) for example quotes the opinion that the elections merely showed 'the obedience by the mass of the voters to commands or counsels which came to them authoritatively from above'. But this both underestimates the educative effect of the Indian General Elections and by implication overestimates the rational character of elections in the West.

special position which Pandit Nehru has enjoyed since independence. Parliament on this view is no more than Pandit Nehru's 'durbar'. Now it must be admitted that the answer that can be given to all this is not a complete one. It does need to be pointed out, however, that the charge of cabinet dictatorship is a very familiar one even outside India; those who were accustomed to think of independence as synonymous with the removal of a strong direction of affairs have to learn that the British parliamentary system does encourage powerful governments. The question of personal domination, too, requires to be seen more carefully. The effective leader in a parliamentary system is often the man who is so sensitive to currents of opinion that he never calls for obedience except on those issues when he knows he will get it; and Pandit Nehru has this quality of shrewdness. Moreover, British experience does not seem to show that the unchallenged supremacy of one man need distort too much the working of parliament. The institution's life is longer than the man's, and even if Pandit Nehru's prestige and influence has been outstanding during a crucial period of the development of parliament, it is more likely than not that the institution is strong enough to assume in time its more usual shape. The authority-loving character of the Indian temperament is also a matter more complex than at first appears.[1] It is combined—in modern India at least—with a usefully critical and sceptical approach. It seems, too, that the 'oppositionist' tradition born of nationalist struggle has a persistence in many ways fortunate. A durbar without the prince is nonsense, but the Indian Parliament, for all the valuable influence of the Prime Minister, will still make very adequate sense when Pandit Nehru is no longer there.

The third charge against parliament in India is related to the first two. It holds that the institution is unreal because it cannot operate properly with the political categories that are relevant in India. That is to say, parliament presumes a discussion of political principles, but the forces that move people in India and which account for their views and actions are the loyalties of caste and of locality. Here, again, it must be said that this seems to attribute to parliamentary institutions greater limitations of inflexibility than in fact they possess. The parliament in which nothing takes place but the debate of principles has not yet existed, and every parliament has to accommodate itself to the interests and passions of its members. The interests and passions of Indian members are no doubt different from those of the British M.P., and it may even be admitted that the process of 'accommodation' is especially difficult.[2] It is

---

[1] See discussion above, pp. 33–37.

[2] In 1933, Sardar K. M. Panikkar wrote of the difficulty of marrying caste with democracy. Caste was, he said, still 'the dominating influence in Indian social life'. Yet it would have to go if democracy was to be real and not simply 'another system of social tyranny' (*Caste and Democracy* (1933), pp. 8, 37). Whatever may be the present strength of caste, it is certain that it is already less powerful now than it was even twenty years ago.

practically impossible to detect with certainty the influence of caste and regional loyalties in the political process and therefore difficult to assess their total importance. Yet the trend is surely clear: these loyalties have to compete with other newer loyalties, and the working of parliamentary institutions is one factor among many acting in the direction of weakening their hold. The partial submergence of caste and region in the course of nationalist struggle was in a way unreal and unlasting; the present gradual submergence of these factors in the business of facing the economic and social problems of independent India is more firm and certain.[1]

If these charges can in the main be rebutted, this is not to say that parliamentary institutions in India are confronted with no problems. Some of these may be mentioned again at this stage. Of the technical, institutional problems, three are perhaps outstanding: the need for an improved Bill procedure which takes up less time of the House while permitting an adequate discussion of details; the discovery of an adequate and distinct role for the Upper House; and the improvement of methods of control over public corporations. Only the last of these is perhaps sufficiently recognised at present.[2] More substantial and obvious are the wider political problems. Foremost among these may be reckoned the absence of an established and constitutional Opposition. The conclusion reached here on this point has been that, while it is no doubt unfortunate from many points of view that the Socialist movement appears to be unable to move beyond a promising beginning, the defect is far from fatal to parliamentary government. It can be, and is, compensated for in large measure by the development of an alert and vigorous parliamentary committee system and by the growth of instruments of internal discussion and criticism within the main party. Also, its worst effects can be, and in large measure are, overcome by governments behaving as if they were confronted with a formally established Opposition.[3] It is equally unfortunate that the main opposition group in the parliamentary life of India should be the essentially non-parliamentary Communist Party. But here, too, the picture is not as black as the pessimists would have it painted. It is far better that the Communists should be inside the parliaments than that they should be driven by frustration to their other 'fronts' of campaign. Moreover, it is not wholly unrealistic to hope that

[1] The process will become even more rapid as the Congress Party ceases to enjoy such a strong position; the absence of big political cleavage has permitted regional and caste loyalties to have greater scope within the party than would have been the case if a substantial challenge existed.

[2] For example, K. M. Panikkar in *The Indian Journal of Political Science*, Jan.–Mar. 1952: 'In normal parliamentary democracies, the boundaries between political control and service administration are fairly clear and well-defined. Today the boundaries are shifting. We have to discover the nature and extent of popular authority over autonomous statutory bodies set up by the State to administer great enterprises started in the public interest but run on commercial principles.'

[3] It must be confessed that this is not yet true of all State legislatures. The result is a much more frustrated feeling among opposition groups at the State level than at the Centre.

in the case of the Indian Communist Party, experience of Parliament may have a mellowing effect. We have already quoted the French discovery that 'there is more in common between two deputies, one of whom is a revolutionary and the other who is not, than there is between two revolutionaries, one of whom is a deputy and the other who is not'; the element of truth in this may come to be important in India.[1] For the present, it is enough to note that the Communists, though so significant a group in parliament in India, have so far been able to do little damage to the working of the institution or to its reputation.

A less obvious but equally important problem is that of the relation between government and administration when the government is a party with the character of the Congress. A great deal of 'constructive work' awaits voluntary labour, for there is more to be done than the administration can hope to do; at the same time, Congress has precisely the required tradition of social service; what more natural than that supply should meet demand? But this forges links between party and administration to the prejudice of other political groups. The dilemma would have been avoided if Congress had in 1948 become, as Gandhi suggested, a social service organisation divorced from politics. That is hardly possible, but some similar divorce of functions will have to be shaped.[2]

The importance of 'educating the new masters' of India is one to which reference has already been made in several places above. At present there is admittedly too great a gap, in range of experience and degree of ability, between the front and back benches. The result is a tendency for each to live in a separate world of ideas and categories, for policy-making and policy-criticism to be insufficiently in touch with each other, for the Minister to be lonely and overworked, the back-bencher idle, frustrated and usually docile. The remedies already being put into effect to close this gap as far as it is reasonably possible to do so are the same remedies which help to overcome the absence of a recognised Opposition: parliamentary committees and party committees. The change wrought by these has been perceptible in half a lifetime of one parliament alone.

More difficult to locate—and certainly more difficult to remedy—is another 'gap' which affects the working of parliamentary institutions: the absence of an adequate body of 'independent political thinking'. Mr. Panikkar has well pointed out:

[1] It must not, of course, be exaggerated. Mr. Masani is quite right to point out that the basic Communist attitude to parliament is that they must 'use it to destroy it' and that they must never forget that they are 'not legislators but agitators' (*The Communist Party of India* (1954), p. 166). He is also right to show that even the party's parliamentary leaders have not hesitated to talk of 'not believing in the ballot as a way of changing governments' and 'desiring to wreck the Indian Constitution' (*ibid.*, p. 170).

[2] The Bharat Sevak Sangh might have been such a device, but it has—almost inevitably —become tarred with the Congress brush and is suspect to other parties. The Bhoodan movement offers a possible alternative.

Political leaders can hardly be expected to devote time to think out the complex problems of the modern State. In every country where democracy flourishes, this function is performed by voluntary associations of scholars, public men and others interested in special subjects. The numerous societies and associations which function in England . . . are in fact essential parts of the democratic system of politics. It is they who, by unremitting research, by constant public discussion, by innumerable publications do the thinking for democracy.[1]

This is as yet very deficient in India. The Indian Council of World Affairs, a few university departments of economic and social research, a handful of serious journalists, perhaps the new Institute of Public Administration—these are the only agents through which at present any long-range non-partisan thinking outside the ministries themselves can be done. Nevertheless this gap, however serious, is one that can be closed. There is every possibility that, as a greater proportion of suitable talent finds employment outside 'government service', the amount of independent thinking will increase.

Finally it must be said that almost every problem here mentioned is more serious at the State level than at the Centre, and that this constitutes a separate problem in itself. However, given the all-India character of the political parties and the growing leadership of the central Parliament, it is a problem which will in time solve itself. Nevertheless, a survey of parliamentary institutions which looked at the States alone would at the moment present a less happy picture than the one given here.

India has received an inheritance from the period of British rule; she has taken full possession of it and is adapting it to her own needs. The 'experiment' is working and parliamentary institutions are more firmly established in the way of life of the Indian people than they are in that of many a country in Europe. One writer has referred to 'the totally novel stresses which may develop when the existing generation of Indian politicians and officials, nurtured in British ways of thought and government, has disappeared'.[2] There would be more to fear in this if it did not seem much more likely that experience of both parliament and civil service has been so continuous that the 'ways of thought and government' are being passed on from one generation to the next—and passed on as Indian, not British.

The British observer who sets out to describe and assess Indian development in the period since independence has to beware of many contradictory temptations. Britain and India have been and are too close for the relationship to be devoid of emotion of one kind or another. The former critic of India's nationalist aspirations must tend to look for

1 K. M. Panikkar in *The Indian Journal of Political Science*, Jan.–Mar. 1952.
2 Mr. Ian Stephens in a review in *The Listener*, 8 Oct. 1953.

failures to support his earlier doubts; the former friend must with equal force and for similar reasons find himself drawn to emphasise the good points. And each, in attempting to correct for bias, may fall into the other's error. The wise Indian will be disappointed with the Englishman who has not changed at all, but he will be properly distrustful of one who has changed too much. It will be primarily for the Indian reader to judge whether the present author has kept a balance.

In any event, the story here told is unmistakably a story of success. As such, it is less exciting than a story of crisis and failure. But then, in politics if nowhere else, excitement is not a virtue.

APPENDIX I

Certain portions of the Constitution of India of special relevance to the working of Parliament are here reproduced for reference. The principal amendments up to May 1955 have been incorporated. Sections not reproduced are denoted by three stars, thus. * * *

Preamble.* * *

Part. I. The Union and its Territory.* * *

Part II. Citizenship.* * *

Part III. Fundamental Rights.* * *

Part IV. Directive Principles of State Policy.* * *

Part V. The Union.

Chapter I. The Executive * * *

Chapter II. Parliament

General

79.—There shall be a Parliament for the Union which shall consist of the President and two Houses to be known respectively as the Council of States and the House of the People.

80.—(1) The Council of States shall consist of:—

(a) twelve members to be nominated by the President in accordance with the provisions of clause (3); and

(b) not more than two hundred and thirty-eight representatives of the States.

(2) The allocation of seats in the Council of States to be filled by representatives of the States shall be in accordance with the provisions in that behalf contained in the Fourth Schedule.

(3) The members to be nominated by the President under sub-clause (a) of clause (1) shall consist of persons having special knowledge or practical experience in respect of such matters as the following, namely:—

Literature, science, art and social service.

(4) The representatives of each State specified in Part A or Part B of the First Schedule in the Council of States shall be elected by the elected members of the Legislative Assembly of the State in accordance with the system of proportional representation by means of the single transferable vote.

(5) The representatives of the States specified in Part C of the First Schedule in the Council of States shall be chosen in such manner as Parliament may by law prescribe.

81.[1]—(1) (*a*) Subject to the provisions of clause (2) and of articles 82 and 331, the House of the People shall consist of not more than five hundred members directly elected by the voters in the States.

(*b*) For the purpose of sub-clause (a), the States shall be divided, grouped or formed into territorial constituencies and the number of members to be allotted to each such constituency shall be so determined as to ensure that there shall be[2] not more than one member for every 500,000 of the population.

(*c*) The ratio between the number of members allotted to each territorial constituency and the population of that constituency as ascertained at the last preceding census of which the relevant figures have been published shall, so far as practicable, be the same throughout the territory of India.

(2) The representation in the House of the People of the territories comprised within the territory of India but not included within any State shall be such as Parliament may by law provide.

(3) Upon the completion of each census, the representation of the several territorial constituencies in the House of the People shall be readjusted by such authority, in such manner and with effect from such date as Parliament may by law determine;

Provided that such readjustment shall not affect representation in the House of the People until the dissolution of the then existing House.

82.—Notwithstanding anything in clause (1) of article 81, Parliament may by law provide for the representation in the House of the People of any State specified in Part C of the First Schedule or of any territories comprised within the territory of India but not included within any State on a basis or in a manner other than that provided in that clause.

83.—(1) The Council of States shall not be subject to dissolution, but as nearly as possible one-third of the members thereof shall retire as soon as may be on the expiration of every second year in accordance with the provisions made in that behalf by Parliament by law.

(2) The House of the People, unless sooner dissolved, shall continue for five years from the date appointed for its first meeting and no longer and the expiration of the said period of five years shall operate as a dissolution of the House:—

Provided that the said period may, while a Proclamation of Emergency is in operation, be extended by Parliament by law for a period not exceeding one year at a time and not extending in any case beyond a period of six months after the Proclamation has ceased to operate.

84.—A person shall not be qualified to be chosen to fill a seat in Parliament unless he:—

(a) is a citizen of India;

[1] Article 81 applies to the State of Jammu and Kashmir subject to the modification that the representatives of that State in the House of the People shall be appointed by the President on the recommendation of the Legislature of the State. Paragraph 2 of the Constitution (Removal of Difficulties) Order No. VIII makes special provision for Tribal Areas.

[2] The words 'Not less than one member for every 750,000 of the population and' were omitted by the Constitution (2nd Amendment) Act, 1952.

(b) is, in the case of a seat in the Council of States, not less than thirty years of age and, in the case of a seat in the House of the People, not less than twenty-five years of age; and

(c) possesses such other qualifications as may be prescribed in that behalf by or under any law made by Parliament.

85.[1]—(1) The President shall from time to time summon each House of Parliament to meet at such time and place as he thinks fit, but six months shall not intervene between its last sitting in one session and the date appointed for its first sitting in the next session.

(2) The President may from time to time:—

(a) prorogue the Houses or either House

(b) dissolve the House of the People.

86.—(1) The President may address either House of Parliament or both Houses assembled together, and for that purpose require the attendance of members.

(2) The President may send messages to either House of Parliament, whether with respect to a Bill then pending in Parliament or otherwise, and a House to which any message is so sent shall with all convenient despatch consider any matter required by the message to be taken into consideration.

87.—(1) At the commencement of the first session after each general election to the House of the People and at the commencement of the first session of each year[2] the President shall address both Houses of Parliament assembled together and inform Parliament of the causes of its summons.

(2) Provision shall be made by the rules regulating the procedure of either House for the allotment of time for discussion of the matters referred to in such address.[3]

88.—Every Minister and the Attorney-General of India shall have the right to speak in, and otherwise to take part in the proceedings of, either House, any joint sitting of the Houses, and any committee of Parliament of which he may be named a member—but shall not by virtue of this article be entitled to vote.

Officers of Parliament

89.—(1) The Vice-President of India shall be ex-officio Chairman of the Council of States.

(2) The Council of States shall, as soon as may be, choose a member of the Council to be Deputy Chairman thereof and, so often as the office of Deputy Chairman becomes vacant, the Council shall choose another member to be Deputy Chairman thereof.

---

[1] Substituted by the Constitution (First Amendment) Act, 1951, S.6, for the original article.

[2] This phrase was substituted for 'every session' by the Constitution (First Amendment) Act, 1951, S.7.

[3] The words 'and for the precedence of such discussion over other business of the House' were omitted by the Constitution (First Amendment) Act, 1951, S.8.

90.—A member holding office as Deputy Chairman of the Council of States:—

    (a) shall vacate his office if he ceases to be a member of the Council;

    (b) may at any time, by writing under his hand addressed to the Chairman, resign his office; and

    (c) may be removed from his office by a resolution of Council passed by a majority of all the then members of the Council:

Provided that no resolution for the purpose of clause (c) shall be moved unless at least fourteen days' notice has been given of the intention to move the resolution.

91.—(1) While the office of Chairman is vacant, or during any period when the Vice-President is acting as, or discharging the functions of, President, the duties of the office shall be performed by the Deputy Chairman, or, if the office of Deputy Chairman is also vacant, by such member of the Council of States as the President may appoint for the purpose.

(2) During the absence of the Chairman from any sitting of the Council of States the Deputy Chairman, or, if he is also absent, such person as may be determined by the rules of procedure of the Council, or, if no such person is present, such other person as may be determined by the Council, shall act as Chairman.

92.—(1) At any sitting of the Council of States, while any resolution for the removal of the Vice-President from his office is under consideration, the Chairman, or while any resolution for the removal of the Deputy Chairman from his office is under consideration, the Deputy Chairman, shall not, though he is present, preside, and the provisions of clause (2) of article 91 shall apply in relation to every such sitting as they apply in relation to a sitting from which the Chairman, or, as the case may be, the Deputy Chairman, is absent.

(2) The Chairman shall have the right to speak in, and otherwise to take part in the proceedings of, the Council of States while any resolution for the removal of the Vice-President from his office is under consideration in the Council, but, notwithstanding anything in article 100, shall not be entitled to vote at all on such resolution or on any other matter during such proceedings.

93.—The House of the People shall, as soon as may be, choose two members of the House to be respectively Speaker and Deputy Speaker thereof and so often as the office of Speaker or Deputy Speaker becomes vacant, the House shall choose another member to be Speaker or Deputy Speaker, as the case may be.

94.—A member holding office as Speaker or Deputy Speaker of the House of the People:—

    (a) shall vacate his office if he ceases to be a member of the House of the People;

    (b) may at any time, by writing under his hand addressed, if such member is the Speaker, to the Deputy Speaker, and if such member is the Deputy Speaker, to the Speaker, resign his office; and

(c) may be removed from his office by a resolution of the House of the People passed by a majority of all the then members of the House:

Provided that no resolution for the purpose of clause (c) shall be moved unless at least fourteen days' notice has been given of the intention to move the resolution:

Provided further that, whenever the House of the People is dissolved, the Speaker shall not vacate his office until immediately before the first meeting of the House of the People after the dissolution.

95.—(1) While the office of Speaker is vacant, the duties of the office shall be performed by the Deputy Speaker or, if the office of Deputy Speaker is also vacant, by such member of the House of the People as the President may appoint for the purpose.

(2) During the absence of the Speaker from any sitting of the House of the People the Deputy Speaker or, if he is also absent, such person as may be determined by the rules of procedure of the House, or, if no such person is present, such other person as may be determined by the House, shall act as Speaker.

96.—(1) At any sitting of the House of the People, while any resolution for the removal of the Speaker from his office is under consideration, the Speaker, or while any resolution for the removal of the Deputy Speaker from his office is under consideration, the Deputy Speaker, shall not, though he is present, preside, and the provisions of clause (2) of article 95 shall apply in relation to every such sitting as they apply in relation to a sitting from which the Speaker, or, as the case may be, the Deputy Speaker, is absent.

(2) The Speaker shall have the right to speak in, and otherwise to take part in the proceedings of, the House of the People while any resolution for his removal from office is under consideration in the House and shall, notwithstanding anything in article 100, be entitled to vote only in the first instance on such resolution or on any other matter during such proceedings but not in the case of an equality of votes.

97.—There shall be paid to the Chairman and the Deputy Chairman of the Council of States, and to the Speaker and the Deputy Speaker of the House of the People, such salaries and allowances as may be respectively fixed by Parliament by law and, until provision in that behalf is so made, such salaries and allowances as are specified in the Second Schedule.

98.—(1) Each House of Parliament shall have a separate secretarial staff:

Provided that nothing in this clause shall be construed as preventing the creation of posts common to both Houses of Parliament.

(2) Parliament may by law regulate the recruitment, and the conditions of service of persons appointed, to the secretarial staff of either House of Parliament.

(3) Until provision is made by Parliament under clause (2) the President may, after consultation with the Speaker of the House of the People or the Chairman of the Council of States, as the case may be, make rules regulating the re-

cruitment, and the conditions of service of persons appointed, to the secretarial staff of the House of the People or the Council of States, and any rules so made shall have effect subject to the provisions of any law made under the said clause.

Conduct of Business

99.—Every member of either House of Parliament shall, before taking his seat, make and subscribe before the President, or some person appointed in that behalf by him, an oath or affirmation according to the form set out for the purpose in the Third Schedule.

100.—(1) Save as otherwise provided in this Constitution, all questions at any sitting of either House or joint sitting of the Houses shall be determined by a majority of votes of the members present and voting, other than the Speaker or person acting as Chairman or Speaker.

The Chairman or Speaker, or person acting as such, shall not vote in the first instance, but shall have and exercise a casting vote in the case of an equality of votes.

(2) Either House of Parliament shall have power to act notwithstanding any vacancy in the membership thereof, and any proceedings in Parliament shall be valid notwithstanding that it is discovered subsequently that some person who was not entitled so to do sat or voted or otherwise took part in the proceedings.

(3) Until Parliament by law otherwise provides, the quorum to constitute a meeting of either House of Parliament shall be one-tenth of the total number of members of the House.

(4) If at any time during a meeting of a House there is no quorum, it shall be the duty of the Chairman or Speaker, or person acting as such, either to adjourn the House or to suspend the meeting until there is a quorum.

Disqualifications of Members

101.—(1) No person shall be a member of both Houses of Parliament and provision shall be made by Parliament by law for the vacation by a person who is chosen a member of both Houses of his seat in one House or the other.

(2) No person shall be a member both of Parliament and of a House of the Legislature of a State specified in Part A or Part B of the first Schedule, and if a person is chosen a member both of Parliament and of a House of the Legislature of such a State, then, at the expiration of such period as may be specified in rules[1] made by the President, that person's seat in Parliament shall become vacant, unless he has previously resigned his seat in the Legislature of the State.

(3) If a member of either House of Parliament—
(a) becomes subject to any of the disqualifications mentioned in clause (1) of article 102, or

---

[1] See the 'Prohibition of Simultaneous Membership Rules, 1950', published with the Ministry of Law Notification No. F. 46/50-C dated 26 Jan. 1950, *Gazette of India Extraordinary*, p. 678.

(b) resigns his seat by writing under his hand addressed to the Chairman or the Speaker, as the case may be,

his seat shall thereupon become vacant.

(4) If for a period of sixty days a member of either House of Parliament is without permission of the House absent from all meetings thereof, the House may declare his seat vacant:

Provided that in computing the said period of sixty days no account shall be taken of any period during which the House is prorogued or is adjourned for more than four consecutive days.

102.—(1) A person shall be disqualified for being chosen as, and for being, a member of either House of Parliament—

(a) if he holds any office of profit under the Government of India or the Government of any State, other than an office declared by Parliament by law not to disqualify its holder;

(b) if he is of unsound mind and stands so declared by a competent court;

(c) if he is an undischarged insolvent;

(d) if he is not a citizen of India, or has voluntarily acquired the citizenship of a foreign State, or is under any acknowledgment of allegiance or adherence to a foreign State;

(e) if he is so disqualified by or under any law made by Parliament.

(2) For the purposes of this article a person shall not be deemed to hold an office of profit under the Government of India or the Government of any State by reason only that he is a Minister, either for the Union or for such State.

103.—(1) If any question arises as to whether a member of either House of Parliament has become subject to any of the disqualifications mentioned in clause (1) of article 102, the question shall be referred for the decision of the President and his decision shall be final.

(2) Before giving any decision on any such question, the President shall obtain the opinion of the Election Commission and shall act according to such opinion.

104.—If a person sits or votes as a member of either House of Parliament before he has complied with the requirements of article 99, or when he knows that he is not qualified or that he is disqualified for membership thereof, or that he is prohibited from so doing by the provisions of any law made by Parliament, he shall be liable in respect of each day on which he so sits or votes to a penalty of five hundred rupees to be recovered as a debt due to the Union.

Powers, Privileges and Immunities of Parliament and its Members

105.—(1) Subject to the provisions of this Constitution and to the rules and standing orders regulating the procedure of Parliament, there shall be freedom of speech in Parliament.

(2) No member of Parliament shall be liable to any proceedings in any court in respect of anything said or any vote given by him in Parliament or any

committee thereof, and no person shall be so liable in respect of the publication by or under the authority of either House of Parliament of any report, paper, votes or proceedings.

(3) In other respects, the powers, privileges and immunities of each House of Parliament, and of the members and the committees of each House, shall be such as may from time to time be defined by Parliament by law, and, until so defined, shall be those of the House of Commons of the Parliament of the United Kingdom, and of its members and committees, at the commencement of this Constitution.

(4) The provisions of clauses (1), (2) and (3) shall apply in relation to persons who by virtue of this Constitution have the right to speak in, and otherwise to take part in the proceedings of, a House of Parliament or any committee thereof as they apply in relation to members of Parliament.

106.—Members of either House of Parliament shall be entitled to receive such salaries and allowances as may from time to time be determined by Parliament by law and, until provision in that respect is so made, allowances at such rates and upon such conditions as were immediately before the commencement of this Constitution applicable in the case of members of the Constituent Assembly of the Dominion of India.

Legislative Procedure

107.—(1) Subject to the provisions of articles 109 and 117 with respect to Money Bills and other financial Bills, a Bill may originate in either House of Parliament.

(2) Subject to the provisions of articles 108 and 109 a Bill shall not be deemed to have been passed by the Houses of Parliament unless it has been agreed to by both Houses, either without amendment or with such amendments only as are agreed to by both Houses.

(3) A Bill pending in Parliament shall not lapse by reason of the prorogation of the Houses.

(4) A Bill pending in the Council of States which has not been passed by the House of the People shall not lapse on a dissolution of the House of the People.

(5) A Bill which is pending in the House of the People, or which having been passed by the House of the People is pending in the Council of States, shall subject to the provisions of article 108, lapse on a dissolution of the House of the People.

108.—(1) If after a Bill has been passed by one House and transmitted to the other House—

(a) the Bill is rejected by the other House; or
(b) the Houses have finally disagreed as to the amendments to be made in the Bill; or
(c) more than six months elapse from the date of the reception of the Bill by the other House without the Bill being passed by it,

the President may, unless the Bill has lapsed by reason of a dissolution of the House of the People, notify to the Houses by message if they are sitting or by public notification if they are not sitting, his intention to summon them to meet in a joint sitting for the purpose of deliberating and voting on the Bill:

Provided that nothing in this clause shall apply to a Money Bill.

(2) In reckoning any such period of six months as is referred to in clause (1), no account shall be taken of any period during which the House referred to in sub-clause (c) of that clause is prorogued or adjourned for more than four consecutive days.

(3) Where the President has under clause (1) notified his intention of summoning the Houses to meet in a joint sitting, neither House shall proceed further with the Bill, but the President may at any time after the date of his notification summon the Houses to meet in a joint sitting for the purpose specified in the notification and, if he does so, the Houses shall meet accordingly.

(4) If at the joint sitting of the two Houses the Bill, with such amendments, if any, as are agreed to in joint sitting, is passed by a majority of the total number of members of both Houses present and voting, it shall be deemed for the purposes of this Constitution to have been passed by both Houses:

Provided that at a joint sitting—

    (a) if the Bill, having been passed by one House, has not been passed by the other House with amendments and returned to the House in which it originated, no amendment shall be proposed to the Bill other than such amendments (if any) as are made necessary by the delay in the passage of the Bill;

    (b) if the Bill has been so passed and returned, only such amendments as aforesaid shall be proposed to the Bill and such other amendments as are relevant to the matters with respect to which the Houses have not agreed;

and the decision of the person presiding as to the amendments which are admissible under this clause shall be final.

(5) A joint sitting may be held under this article and a Bill passed thereat, notwithstanding that a dissolution of the House of the People has intervened since the President notified his intention to summon the Houses to meet therein.

109.—(1) A Money Bill shall not be introduced in the Council of States.

(2) After a Money Bill has been passed by the House of the People it shall be transmitted to the Council of States for its recommendations and the Council of States shall within a period of fourteen days from the date of its receipt of the Bill return the Bill to the House of the People with its recommendations and the House of the People may thereupon either accept or reject all or any of the recommendations of the Council of States.

(3) If the House of the People accepts any of the recommendations of the Council of States, the Money Bill shall be deemed to have been passed by both

Houses with the amendments recommended by the Council of States and accepted by the House of the People.

(4) If the House of the People does not accept any of the recommendations of the Council of States, the Money Bill shall be deemed to have been passed by both Houses in the form in which it was passed by the House of the People without any of the amendments recommended by the Council of States.

(5) If a Money Bill passed by the House of the People and transmitted to the Council of States for its recommendations is not returned to the House of the People within the said period of fourteen days, it shall be deemed to have been passed by both Houses at the expiration of the said period in the form in which it was passed by the House of the People.

110.—(1) For the purposes of this Chapter, a Bill shall be deemed to be a Money Bill if it contains only provisions dealing with all or any of the following matters, namely—

(a) the imposition, abolition, remission, alteration or regulation of any tax;
(b) the regulation of the borrowing of money or the giving of any guarantee by the Government of India, or the amendment of the law with respect to any financial obligations undertaken or to be undertaken by the Government of India;
(c) the custody of the Consolidated Fund or the Contingency Fund of India, the payment of moneys into or the withdrawal of moneys from any such Fund;
(d) the appropriation of moneys out of the Consolidated Fund of India;
(e) the declaring of any expenditure to be expenditure charged on the Consolidated Fund of India or the increasing of the amount of any such expenditure;
(f) the receipt of money on account of the Consolidated Fund of India or the public account of India or the custody or issue of such money or the audit of the accounts of the Union or of a State; or
(g) any matter incidental to any of the matters specified in sub-clauses (a) to (f).

(2) A Bill shall not be deemed to be a Money Bill by reason only that it provides for the imposition of fines or other pecuniary penalties, or for the demand or payment of fees for licences or fees for services rendered, or by reason that it provides for the imposition, abolition, remission, alteration or regulation of any tax by any local authority or body for local purposes.

(3) If any question arises whether a Bill is a Money Bill or not, the decision of the Speaker of the House of the People thereon shall be final.

(4) There shall be endorsed on every Money Bill when it is transmitted to the Council of States under article 109, and when it is presented to the President for assent under article 111, the certificate of the Speaker of the House of the People signed by him that it is a Money Bill.

111.—When a Bill has been passed by the Houses of Parliament, it shall be presented to the President and the President shall declare either that he assents to the Bill, or that he withholds assent therefrom:

Provided that the President may, as soon as possible after the presentation to him of a Bill for assent, return the Bill if it is not a Money Bill to the Houses with a message requesting that they will reconsider the Bill or any specified provisions thereof and, in particular, will consider the desirability of introducing any such amendments as he may recommend in his message and when a Bill is so returned, the Houses shall reconsider the Bill accordingly, and if the Bill is passed again by the Houses with or without amendment and presented to the President for assent, the President shall not withhold assent therefrom.

Procedure in Financial Matters

112.—(1) The President shall in respect of every financial year cause to be laid before both the Houses of Parliament a statement of the estimated receipts and expenditure of the Government of India for that year, in this Part referred to as the 'annual financial statement'.

(2) The estimates of expenditure embodied in the annual financial statement shall show separately—
   (a) the sums required to meet expenditure described by this Constitution as expenditure charged upon the Consolidated Fund of India; and
   (b) the sums required to meet other expenditure proposed to be made from the Consolidated Fund of India,
and shall distinguish expenditure on revenue account from other expenditure.

(3) The following expenditure shall be expenditure charged on the Consolidated Fund of India—
   (a) the emoluments and allowances of the President and other expenditure relating to his office;
   (b) the salaries and allowances of the Chairman and the Deputy Chairman of the Council of States and the Speaker and the Deputy Speaker of the House of the People;
   (c) debt charges for which the Government of India is liable including interest, sinking fund charges and redemption charges, and other expenditure relating to the raising of loans and the service and redemption of debt;
   (d)   (i) the salaries, allowances and pensions payable to or in respect of Judges of the Supreme Court;
            (ii) the pensions payable to or in respect of Judges of the Federal Court;
            (iii) the pensions payable to or in respect of Judges of any High Court which exercises jurisdiction in relation to any area included in the territory of India or which at any time before the commencement of this Constitution exercised jurisdiction in relation to any area included in a Province corresponding to a State specified in Part A of the First Schedule;
   (e) the salary, allowances and pension payable to or in respect of the Comptroller and Auditor-General of India;
   (f) any sums required to satisfy any judgment, decree or award of any court or arbitral tribunal;

(g) any other expenditure declared by this Constitution or by Parliament by law to be so charged.

113.—(1) So much of the estimates as relates to expenditure charged upon the Consolidated Fund of India shall not be submitted to the vote of Parliament, but nothing in this clause shall be construed as preventing the discussion in either House of Parliament of any of those estimates.

(2) So much of the said estimates as relates to other expenditure shall be submitted in the form of demands for grants to the House of the People, and the House of the People shall have power to assent, or to refuse to assent, to any demand, or to assent to any demand subject to a reduction of the amount specified therein.

(3) No demand for a grant shall be made except on the recommendation of the President.

114.—(1) As soon as may be after the grants under article 113 have been made by the House of the People, there shall be introduced a Bill to provide for the appropriation out of the Consolidated Fund of India of all moneys required to meet—

(a) the grants so made by the House of the People; and
(b) the expenditure charged on the Consolidated Fund of India but not exceeding in any case the amount shown in the statement previously laid before Parliament.

(2) No amendment shall be proposed to any such Bill in either House of Parliament which will have the effect of varying the amount or altering the destination of any grant so made or of varying the amount of any expenditure charged on the Consolidated Fund of India, and the decision of the person presiding as to whether an amendment is inadmissible under this clause shall be final.

(3) Subject to the provisions of articles 115 and 116, no money shall be withdrawn from the Consolidated Fund of India except under appropriation made by law passed in accordance with the provisions of this article.

115.—(1) The President shall—

(a) if the amount authorised by any law made in accordance with the provisions of article 114 to be expended for a particular service for the current financial year is found to be insufficient for the purposes of that year or when a need has arisen during the current financial year for supplementary or additional expenditure upon some new service not contemplated in the annual financial statement for that year, or
(b) if any money has been spent on any service during a financial year in excess of the amount granted for that service and for that year,

cause to be laid before both the Houses of Parliament another statement showing the estimated amount of that expenditure or cause to be presented to the House of the People a demand for such excess, as the case may be.

(2) The provisions of articles 112, 113 and 114 shall have effect in relation to any such statement and expenditure or demand and also to any law to be made

authorising the appropriation of moneys out of the Consolidated Fund of India to meet such expenditure or the grant in respect of such demand as they have effect in relation to the annual financial statement and the expenditure mentioned therein or to a demand for a grant and the law to be made for the authorisation of appropriation of moneys out of the Consolidated Fund of India to meet such expenditure or grant.

116.—(1) Notwithstanding anything in the foregoing provisions of this Chapter, the House of the People shall have power—

    (a) to make any grant in advance in respect of the estimated expenditure for a part of any financial year pending the completion of the procedure prescribed in article 113 for the voting of such grant and the passing of the law in accordance with the provisions of article 114 in relation to that expenditure;

    (b) to make a grant for meeting an unexpected demand upon the resources of India when on account of the magnitude or the indefinite character of the service the demand cannot be stated with the details ordinarily given in an annual financial statement;

    (c) to make an exceptional grant which forms no part of the current service of any financial year;

and Parliament shall have power to authorise by law the withdrawal of moneys from the Consolidated Fund of India for the purposes for which the said grants are made.

(2) The provisions of articles 113 and 114 shall have effect in relation to the making of any grant under clause (1) and to any law to be made under that clause as they have effect in relation to the making of a grant with regard to any expenditure mentioned in the annual financial statement and the law to be made for the authorisation of appropriation of moneys out of the Consolidated Fund of India to meet such expenditure.

117.—(1) A Bill or amendment making such provision for any of the matters specified in sub-clauses (a) to (f) of clause (1) of article 110 shall not be introduced or moved except on the recommendation of the President and a Bill making such provision shall not be introduced in the Council of States:

Provided that no recommendation shall be required under this clause for the moving of an amendment making provision for the reduction or abolition of any tax.

(2) A Bill or amendment shall not be deemed to make provision for any of the matters aforesaid by reason only that it provides for the imposition of fines or other pecuniary penalties, or for the demand or payment of fees for licences or fees for services rendered, or by reason that it provides for the imposition, abolition, remission, alteration or regulation of any tax by any local authority or body for local purposes.

(3) A Bill which, if enacted and brought into operation, would involve expenditure from the Consolidated Fund of India shall not be passed by either House of Parliament unless the President has recommended to that House the consideration of the Bill.

Procedure Generally

118.—(1) Each House of Parliament may make rules for regulating, subject to the provisions of this Constitution, its procedure and the conduct of its business.

(2) Until rules are made under clause (1), the rules of procedure and standing orders in force immediately before the commencement of this Constitution with respect to the Legislature of the Dominion of India shall have effect in relation to Parliament subject to such modifications and adaptations as may be made therein by the Chairman of the Council of States or the Speaker of the House of the People, as the case may be.

(3) The President, after consultation with the Chairman of the Council of States and the Speaker of the House of the People, may make rules as to the procedure with respect to joint sittings of, and communications between, the two Houses.

(4) At a joint sitting of the two Houses the Speaker of the House of the People, or in his absence such person as may be determined by rules of procedure made under clause (3), shall preside.

119.—Parliament may, for the purpose of the timely completion of financial business, regulate by law the procedure of, and the conduct of business in, each House of Parliament in relation to any financial matter or to any Bill for the appropriation of moneys out of the Consolidated Fund of India, and, if and so far as any provision of any law so made is inconsistent with any rule made by a House of Parliament under clause (1) of article 118 or with any rule or standing order having effect in relation to Parliament under clause (2) of that article, such provision shall prevail.

120.—(1) Notwithstanding anything in Part XVII, but subject to the provisions of article 348, business in Parliament shall be transacted in Hindi or in English:

Provided that the Chairman of the Council of States or Speaker of the House of the People, or person acting as such, as the case may be, may permit any member who cannot adequately express himself in Hindi or in English to address the House in his mother tongue.

(2) Unless Parliament by law otherwise provides this article shall, after the expiration of a period of fifteen years from the commencement of this Constitution, have effect as if the words 'or in English' were omitted therefrom.

121.—No discussion shall take place in Parliament with respect to the conduct of any Judge of the Supreme Court or of a High Court in the discharge of his duties except upon a motion for presenting an address to the President praying for the removal of the Judge as hereinafter provided.

122.—(1) The validity of any proceedings in Parliament shall not be called in question on the ground of any alleged irregularity of procedure.

(2) No officer or member of Parliament in whom powers are vested by or under this Constitution for regulating procedure or the conduct of business, or for maintaining order, in Parliament shall be subject to the jurisdiction of any court in respect of the exercise by him of those powers.

Chapter III. Legislative Powers of the President

123.—(1) If at any time, except when both Houses of Parliament are in session, the President is satisfied that circumstances exist which render it necessary for him to take immediate action, he may promulgate such ordinances as the circumstances appear to him to require.

(2) An Ordinance promulgated under this article shall have the same force and effect as an Act of Parliament, but every such Ordinance—

(a) shall be laid before both Houses of Parliament and shall cease to operate at the expiration of six weeks from the reassembly of Parliament or, if before the expiration of that period resolutions disapproving it are passed by both Houses, upon the passing of the second of those resolutions; and

(b) may be withdrawn at any time by the President.

Explanation—Where the Houses of Parliament are summoned to reassemble on different dates, the period of six weeks shall be reckoned from the later of those dates for the purposes of this clause.

(3) If and so far as an Ordinance under this article makes any provision which Parliament would not under this Constitution be competent to enact, it shall be void.

Chapter IV. The Union Judiciary

* * *

Chapter V. Comptroller and Auditor-General of India

148.—(1) There shall be a Comptroller and Auditor-General of India who shall be appointed by the President by warrant under his hand and seal and shall only be removed from office in like manner and on like grounds as a Judge of the Supreme Court.

(2) Every person appointed to be the Comptroller and Auditor-General of India shall, before he enters upon his office, make and subscribe before the President, or some person appointed in that behalf by him, an oath or affirmation according to the form set out for the purpose in the Third Schedule.

(3) The salary and other conditions of service of the Comptroller and Auditor-General shall be such as may be determined by Parliament by law and, until they are so determined, shall be as specified in the Second Schedule:

Provided that neither the salary of a Comptroller and Auditor-General nor his rights in respect of leave of absence, pension or age of retirement shall be varied to his disadvantage after his appointment.

(4) The Comptroller and Auditor-General shall not be eligible for further office either under the Government of India or under the Government of any State after he has ceased to hold his office.

(5) Subject to the provisions of this Consitution and of any law made by Parliament, the conditions of service of persons serving in the Indian Audit and Accounts Department and the administrative powers of the Comptroller

and Auditor-General shall be such as may be prescribed by rules made by the President after consultation with the Comptroller and Auditor-General.

(6) The administrative expenses of the office of the Comptroller and Auditor-General, including all salaries, allowances and pensions payable to or in respect of persons serving in that office, shall be charged upon the Consolidated Fund of India.

149.[1]—The Comptroller and Auditor-General shall perform such duties and exercise such powers in relation to the accounts of the Union and of the States and of any other authority or body as may be prescribed by or under any law made by Parliament and, until provision in that behalf is so made, shall perform such duties and exercise such powers in relation to the accounts of the Union and of the States as were conferred on or exercisable by the Auditor-General of India immediately before the commencement of this Constitution in relation to the accounts of the Dominion of India and of the Provinces respectively.

150.[1]—The accounts of the Union and of the States shall be kept in such form as the Comptroller and Auditor-General of India may, with the approval of the President, prescribe.

151.—(1) The reports of the Comptroller and Auditor-General of India relating to the accounts of the Union shall be submitted to the President, who shall cause them to be laid before each House of Parliament.

(2)[1] The reports of the Comptroller and Auditor-General of India relating to the accounts of a State shall be submitted to the Governor or Rajpramukh of the State, who shall cause them to be laid before the Legislature of the State.

Part VI. The States in Part A of the First Schedule

Chapter I. General.***
Chapter II. The Executive.***
Chapter III. The State Legislature.

168.—(1) For every State there shall be a Legislature which shall consist of the Governor, and
(a) in the States of Bihar, Bombay, Madras, Punjab, Uttar Pradesh and West Bengal, two Houses;
(b) in other States, one House.

(2) Where there are two Houses of the Legislature of a State, one shall be known as the Legislative Council and the other as the Legislative Assembly, and where there is only one House, it shall be known as the Legislative Assembly.

169.—(1) Notwithstanding anything in article 168, Parliament may by law provide for the abolition of the Legislative Council of a State having such a Council or for the creation of such a Council in a State having no such Council,

---

[1] In Articles 149 and 150 references to States shall be construed as not including the State of Jammu and Kashmir, and in its application to that State clause (2) of Article 151 shall be omitted.

if the Legislative Assembly of the State passes a resolution to that effect by a majority of the total membership of the Assembly and by a majority of not less than two-thirds of the members of the Assembly present and voting.

(2) Any law referred to in clause (1) shall contain such provisions for the amendment of this Constitution as may be necessary to give effect to the provisions of the law and may also contain such supplemental, incidental and consequential provisions as Parliament may deem necessary.

(3) No such law as aforesaid shall be deemed to be an amendment of this Constitution for the purposes of article 368.

170.[1]—(1) Subject to the provisions of article 333, the Legislative Assembly of each State shall be composed of members chosen by direct election.

(2) The representation of each territorial constituency in the Legislative Assembly of a State shall be on the basis of the population of that constituency as ascertained at the last preceding census of which the relevant figures have been published and shall save in the case of the autonomous districts of Assam and the constituency comprising the cantonment and municipality of Shillong be on a scale of not more than one member for every seventy-five thousand of the population:
Provided that the total number of members in the Legislative Assembly of a State shall in no case be more than five hundred or less than sixty.

(3) The ratio between the number of members to be allotted to each territorial constituency in a State and the population of that constituency as ascertained at the last preceding census of which the relevant figures have been published shall, so far as practicable, be the same throughout the State.

(4) Upon the completion of each census, the representation of the several territorial constituencies in the Legislative Assembly of each State shall be re-adjusted by such authority, in such manner and with effect from such date as Parliament may by law determine:
Provided that such readjustment shall not affect representation in the Legislative Assembly until the dissolution of the then existing Assembly.

171.—(1) The total number of members in the Legislative Council of a State having such a Council shall not exceed one-fourth of the total number of members in the Legislative Assembly of that State:
Provided that the total number of members in the Legislative Council of a State shall in no case be less than forty.

(2) Until Parliament by law otherwise provides, the composition of the Legislative Council of a State shall be as provided in clause (3).

(3) Of the total number of members of the Legislative Council of a State—
(a) as nearly as may be, one-third shall be elected by electorates consisting of members of municipalities, district boards and such other local authorities in the State as Parliament may by law specify;
(b) as nearly as may be, one-twelfth shall be elected by electorates consisting of persons residing in the State who have been for at least three years

---

[1] Paragraph 2 of the Constitution (Removal of Difficulties) Order, No. VIII provides for the application of this article to tribal areas.

graduates of any university in the territory of India or have been for at least three years in possession of qualifications prescribed by or under any law made by Parliament as equivalent to that of a graduate of any such university.

(c) as nearly as may be, one-twelfth shall be elected by electorates consisting of persons who have been for at least three years engaged in teaching in such educational institutions within the State, not lower in standard than that of a secondary school, as may be prescribed by or under any law made by Parliament;

(d) as nearly as may be, one-third shall be elected by the members of the Legislative Assembly of the State from amongst persons who are not members of the Assembly;

(e) the remainder shall be nominated by the Governor in accordance with the provisions of clause (5).

(4) The members to be elected under sub-clauses (a), (b) and (c) of clause (3) shall be chosen in such territorial constituencies as may be prescribed by or under any law made by Parliament, and the elections under the said sub-clauses and under sub-clause (d) of the said clause shall be held in accordance with the system of proportional representation by means of the single transferable vote.

(5) The members to be nominated by the Governor under sub-clause (e) of clause (3) shall consist of persons having special knowledge or practical experience in respect of such matters as the following, namely:

Literature, science, art, co-operative movement and social service.

172.—(1) Every Legislative Assembly of every State, unless sooner dissolved, shall continue for five years from the date appointed for its first meeting and no longer and the expiration of the said period of five years shall operate as a dissolution of the Assembly:

Provided that the said period may, while a Proclamation of Emergency is in operation, be extended by Parliament by law for a period not exceeding one year at a time and not extending in any case beyond a period of six months after the Proclamation has ceased to operate.

(2) The Legislative Council of a State shall not be subject to dissolution, but as nearly as possible one-third of the members thereof shall retire as soon as may be on the expiration of every second year in accordance with the provisions made in that behalf by Parliament by law.

173.—A person shall not be qualified to be chosen to fill a seat in the Legislature of a State unless he—

(a) is a citizen of India;

(b) is, in the case of a seat in the Legislative Assembly, not less than twenty-five years of age and, in the case of a seat in the Legislative Council, not less than thirty years of age; and

(c) possesses such other qualifications as may be prescribed in that behalf by or under any law made by Parliament.

174.[1]—(1) The Governor shall from time to time summon the House or each

[1] Amended as in Article 85.

House of the Legislature to meet at such time and place as he thinks fit, but six months shall not intervene between its last sitting in one session and the date appointed for its first sitting in the next session.

(2) The Governor may from time to time:—
    (a) prorogue the House or either House
    (b) dissolve the Legislative Assembly.

175.—(1) The Governor may address the Legislative Assembly or, in the case of a State having a Legislative Council, either House of the Legislature of the State, or both Houses assembled together, and may for that purpose require the attendance of members.

(2) The Governor may send messages to the House or Houses of the Legislature of the State, whether with respect to a Bill then pending in the Legislature or otherwise, and a House to which any message is so sent shall with all convenient despatch consider any matter required by the message to be taken into consideration.

176.—(1) At the commencement of the first session after each general election to the Legislative Assembly and at the commencement of the first session of each year[1], the Governor shall address the Legislative Assembly or, in the case of a State having a Legislative Council, both Houses assembled together and inform the Legislature of the causes of its summons.

(2) Provision shall be made by the rules regulating the procedure of the House or either House for the allotment of time for discussion of the matters referred to in such address.[2]

177.—Every Minister and the Advocate-General for a State shall have the right to speak in, and otherwise to take part in the proceedings of, the Legislative Assembly of the State or, in the case of a State having a Legislative Council, both Houses, and to speak in, and otherwise to take part in the proceedings of, any committee of the Legislature of which he may be named a member, but shall not, by virtue of this article, be entitled to vote.

Officers of the State Legislature

[Articles 178–212 mainly repeat for the State Legislatures the provisions of Articles 89–122 above. One important difference is contained in Article 197 which differs from Article 108:]

197.—(1) If after a Bill has been passed by the Legislative Assembly of a State having a Legislative Council and transmitted to the Legislative Council—
    (a) the Bill is rejected by the Council; or
    (b) more than three months elapse from the date on which the Bill is laid before the Council without the Bill being passed by it; or
    (c) the Bill is passed by the Council with amendments to which the Legislative Assembly does not agree,
the Legislative Assembly may, subject to the rules regulating its procedure, pass the Bill again in the same or in any subsequent session with or without

---

1 This phrase was substituted by the Constitution (First Amendment) Act, 1951, S. 9 for 'every session'.
2 Amended as in Article 87(2) above.

such amendments, if any, as have been made, suggested or agreed to by the Legislative Council and then transmit the Bill as so passed to the Legislative Council.

(2) If after a Bill has been so passed for the second time by the Legislative Assembly and transmitted to the Legislative Council—

(a) the Bill is rejected by the Council; or

(b) more than one month elapses from the date on which the Bill is laid before the Council without the Bill being passed by it; or

(c) the Bill is passed by the Council with amendments to which the Legislative Assembly does not agree,

the Bill shall be deemed to have been passed by the Houses of the Legislature of the State in the form in which it was passed by the Legislative Assembly for the second time with such amendments, if any, as have been made or suggested by the Legislative Council and agreed to by the Legislative Assembly.

(3) Nothing in this article shall apply to a Money Bill.

[The provision equivalent to Article 111 is also somewhat different and is contained in Articles 200 and 201.]

200.—When a Bill has been passed by the Legislative Assembly of a State or, in the case of a State having a Legislative Council, has been passed by both Houses of the Legislature of the State, it shall be presented to the Governor and the Governor shall declare either that he assents to the Bill or that he withholds assent therefrom or that he reserves the Bill for the consideration of the President:

Provided that the Governor may, as soon as possible after the presentation to him of the Bill for assent, return the Bill if it is not a Money Bill together with a message requesting that the House or Houses will reconsider the Bill or any specified provisions thereof and, in particular, will consider the desirability of introducing any such amendments as he may recommend in his message and, when a Bill is so returned, the House or Houses shall reconsider the Bill accordingly, and if the Bill is passed again by the House or Houses with or without amendment and presented to the Governor for assent, the Governor shall not withhold assent therefrom:—

Provided further that the Governor shall not assent to, but shall reserve for the consideration of the President, any Bill which in the opinion of the Governor would, if it became law, so derogate from the powers of the High Court as to endanger the position which that Court is by this Constitution designed to fill.

201.—When a Bill is reserved by a Governor for the consideration of the President, the President shall declare either that he assents to the Bill or that he withholds assent therefrom:

Provided that, where the Bill is not a Money Bill the President may direct the Governor to return the Bill to the House or, as the case may be, the Houses of the Legislature of the State together with such a message as is mentioned in the first proviso to article 200 and, when a Bill is so returned, the House or Houses shall reconsider it accordingly within a period of six months from the date of receipt of such message and, if it is again passed by the House or

23—P.I.

Houses with or without amendment, it shall be presented again to the President for his consideration.

Chapter IV. Legislative Power of the Governor

213.—(1) If at any time, except when the Legislative Assembly of a State is in session, or where there is a Legislative Council in a State, except when both Houses of the Legislature are in session, the Governor is satisfied that circumstances exist which render it necessary for him to take immediate action, he may promulgate such Ordinances as the circumstances appear to him to require:

Provided that the Governor shall not, without instructions from the President, promulgate any such Ordinance if—

(a) a Bill containing the same provisions would under this Constitution have required the previous sanction of the President for the introduction thereof into the Legislature; or

(b) he would have deemed it necessary to reserve a Bill containing the same provisions for the consideration of the President; or

(c) an Act of the Legislature of the State containing the same provisions would under this Constitution have been invalid unless, having been reserved for the consideration of the President, it had received the assent of the President.

(2) An Ordinance promulgated under this article shall have the same force and effect as an Act of the Legislature of the State assented to by the Governor, but every such Ordinance—

(a) shall be laid before the Legislative Assembly of the State, or where there is a Legislative Council in the State, before both the Houses, and shall cease to operate at the expiration of six weeks from the reassembly of the Legislature, or if before the expiration of that period a resolution disapproving it is passed by the Legislative Assembly and agreed to by the Legislative Council, if any, upon the passing of the resolution or, as the case may be, on the resolution being agreed to by the Council; and

(b) may be withdrawn at any time by the Governor.

Explanation: Where the Houses of the Legislature of a State having a Legislative Council are summoned to reassemble on different dates, the period of six weeks shall be reckoned from the later of those dates for the purposes of this clause.

(3) If and so far as an Ordinance under this article makes any provision which would not be valid if enacted in an Act of the Legislature of the State assented to by the Governor, it shall be void:

Provided that for the purposes of the provisions of this Constitution relating to the effect of an Act of the Legislature of a State which is repugnant to an Act of Parliament or an existing law with respect to a matter enumerated in the Concurrent List, an Ordinance promulgated under this article in pursuance of instructions from the President shall be deemed to be an Act of the Legislature of the State which has been reserved for the consideration of the President and assented to by him.

Chapter V. The High Courts in the States***

Chapter VI. Subordinate Courts***

PART VII.[1] THE STATES IN PART B OF THE FIRST SCHEDULE

[This part applies the provisions of Part VI to Part B States. Relevant clauses are:]

238.—(7) In article 168, for clause (1) the following clause shall be substituted, namely:—

'(I) For every State there shall be a Legislature which shall consist of the Rajpramukh and

(a) in the State of Mysore, two Houses;

(b) in other States, one House.'

(8) In article 186, for the words 'as are specified in the Second Schedule' the words 'as the Rajpramukh may determine' shall be substituted.

(9) In article 195, for the words 'as were immediately before the commencement of this Constitution applicable in the case of members of the Legislative Assembly of the corresponding Province' the words 'as the Rajpramukh may determine' shall be substituted.

(10) In clause (3) of article 202—

(i) for sub-clause (a) the following sub-clause shall be substituted, namely:—

'(a) the allowances of the Rajpramukh and other expenditure relating to his office as determined by the President by general or special order;'

(ii) for sub-clause (f) the following sub-clauses shall be substituted, namely:—

'(f) in the case of the State of Travancore-Cochin, a sum of fifty-one lakhs of rupees required to be paid annually to the Devaswom fund under the covenant entered into before the commencement of this Constitution by the Rulers of the Indian States of Travancore and Cochin for the formation of the United State of Travancore and Cochin;

(g) any other expenditure declared by this Constitution or by the Legislature of the State by law, to be so charged.'

(11) In article 208, for clause (2), the following clause shall be substituted, namely:—

'(2) Until rules are made under clause (1), the rules of procedure and standing orders in force immediately before the commencement of this Constitution with respect to the Legislature for the State, or, where no House of the Legislature for the State existed, the rules of procedure and standing orders in force immediately before such commencement with respect to the Legislative Assembly of such Province as may be specified in that behalf by the Rajpramukh of the State, shall have effect in relation to the Legislature of the State subject to such modifications and adaptations as may be made therein by the Speaker of the Legislative Assembly or the Chairman of the Legislative Council, as the case may be.'

[1] Not applicable to the State of Jammu and Kashmir.

PART VIII. THE STATES IN PART C OF THE FIRST SCHEDULE

239.—(1) Subject to the other provisions of this Part, a State specified in Part C of the First Schedule shall be administered by the President acting, to such extent as he thinks fit, through a Chief Commissioner or a Lieutenant-Governor to be appointed by him or through the Government of a neighbouring State:

Provided that the President shall not act through the Government of a neighbouring State save after—

(a) consulting the Government concerned; and

(b) ascertaining in such manner as the President considers most appropriate the views of the people of the State to be so administered.

(2) In this article, references to a State shall include references to a part of a State.

240.—(1) Parliament may by law create or continue for any State specified in Part C of the First Schedule and administered through a Chief Commissioner or Lieutenant-Governor:

(a) a body, whether nominated, elected or partly nominated and partly elected, to function as a Legislature for the State; or

(b) a Council of Advisers or Ministers,

or both with such constitution, powers and functions, in each case, as may be specified in the law.

(2) Any such law as is referred to in clause (1) shall not be deemed to be an amendment of this Constitution for the purposes of article 368 notwithstanding that it contains any provision which amends or has the effect of amending the Constitution.

241.—(1) Parliament may by law constitute a High Court for a State specified in Part C of the First Schedule or declare any court in any such State to be a High Court for all or any of the purposes of this Constitution.

(2) The provisions of Chapter V of Part VI shall apply in relation to every High Court referred to in clause (1) as they apply in relation to a High Court referred to in article 214 subject to such modifications or exceptions as Parliament may by law provide.

(3) Subject to the provisions of this Constitution and to the provisions of any law of the appropriate Legislature made by virtue of powers conferred on that Legislature by or under this Constitution, every High Court exercising jurisdiction immediately before the commencement of this Constitution in relation to any State specified in Part C of the First Schedule or any area included therein shall continue to exercise such jurisdiction in relation to that State or area after such commencement.

(4) Nothing in this article derogates from the power of Parliament to extend or exclude the jurisdiction of a High Court in any State specified in Part A or Part B of the First Schedule to, or from, any State specified in Part C of that Schedule or any area included within that State.

242.—(1) Until Parliament by law otherwise provides, the constitution, powers and functions of the Coorg Legislative Council shall be the same as they were immediately before the commencement of this Constitution.

(2) The arrangements with respect to revenues collected in Coorg and expenses in respect of Coorg shall, until other provision is made in that behalf by the President by order, continue unchanged.

PART IX. TERRITORIES IN PART D OF THE FIRST SCHEDULE.***

PART X. THE SCHEDULED AND TRIBAL AREAS.***

PART XI. RELATIONS BETWEEN THE UNION AND THE STATES.

Chapter I. Legislative Relations

245.—(1) Subject to the provisions of this Constitution, Parliament may make laws for the whole or any part of the territory of India, and the Legislature of a State may make laws for the whole or any part of the State.

(2) No law made by Parliament shall be deemed to be invalid on the ground that it would have extra-territorial operation.

246.—(1) Notwithstanding anything in clauses (2) and (3), Parliament has exclusive power to make laws with respect to any of the matters enumerated in List I in the Seventh Schedule (in this Constitution referred to as the 'Union List').

(2) Notwithstanding anything in clause (3), Parliament, and, subject to clause (1), the Legislature of any State specified in Part A or Part B of the First Schedule also, have power to make laws with respect to any of the matters enumerated in List III in the Seventh Schedule (in this Constitution referred to as the 'Concurrent List').

(3) Subject to clauses (1) and (2), the Legislature of any State specified in Part A or Part B of the First Schedule has exclusive power to make laws for such State or any part thereof with respect to any of the matters enumerated in List II in the Seventh Schedule (in this Constitution referred to as the 'State List').

(4) Parliament has power to make laws with respect to any matter for any part of the territory of India not included in Part A or Part B of the First Schedule notwithstanding that such matter is a matter enumerated in the State List.

247.—Notwithstanding anything in this Chapter, Parliament may by law provide for the establishment of any additional courts for the better administration of laws made by Parliament or of any existing law with respect to a matter enumerated in the Union List.

248.[1]—(1) Parliament has exclusive power to make any law with respect to any matter not enumerated in the Concurrent List or State List.

(2) Such power shall include the power of making any law imposing a tax not mentioned in either of those Lists.

[1] Not applicable to the State of Jammu and Kashmir.

249.[1]—(1) Notwithstanding anything in the foregoing provisions of this Chapter, if the Council of States has declared by resolution supported by not less than two-thirds of the members present and voting that it is necessary or expedient in the national interest that Parliament should make laws with respect to any matter enumerated in the State List specified in the resolution, it shall be lawful for Parliament to make laws for the whole or any part of the territory of India with respect to that matter while the resolution remains in force.

(2) A resolution passed under clause (1) shall remain in force for such period not exceeding one year as may be specified therein:

Provided that, if and so often as a resolution approving the continuance in force of any such resolution is passed in the manner provided in clause (1), such resolution shall continue in force for a further period of one year from the date on which under this clause it would otherwise have ceased to be in force.

(3) A law made by Parliament which Parliament would not but for the passing of a resolution under clause (1) have been competent to make shall, to the extent of the incompetency, cease to have effect on the expiration of a period of six months after the resolution has ceased to be in force, except as respects things done or omitted to be done before the expiration of the said period.

250.—(1) Notwithstanding anything in this Chapter, Parliament shall, while a Proclamation of Emergency is in operation, have power to make laws for the whole or any part of the territory of India with respect to any of the matters enumerated in the State List.

(2) A Law made by Parliament which Parliament would not but for the issue of a Proclamation of Emergency have been competent to make shall, to the extent of the incompetency, cease to have effect on the expiration of a period of six months after the Proclamation has ceased to operate, except as respects things done or omitted to be done before the expiration of the said period.

251.—Nothing in articles 249 and 250 shall restrict the power of the Legislature of a State to make any law which under this Constitution it has power to make, but if any provision of a law made by the Legislature of a State is repugnant to any provision of a law made by Parliament which Parliament has under either of the said articles power to make, the law made by Parliament, whether passed before or after the law made by the Legislature of the State, shall prevail, and the law made by the Legislature of the State shall to the extent of the repugnancy, but so long only as the law made by Parliament continues to have effect, be inoperative.

252.—(1) If it appears to the Legislatures of two or more States to be desirable that any of the matters with respect to which Parliament has no power to make laws for the States except as provided in articles 249 and 250 should be regulated in such States by Parliament by law, and if resolutions to that effect are passed by all the Houses of the Legislatures of those States it shall be lawful for Parliament to pass an Act for regulating that matter accordingly, and any Act so passed shall apply to such States and to any other State by which it is adopted afterwards by resolution passed in that behalf by the House or,

[1] Not applicable to the State of Jammu and Kashmir.

where there are two Houses, by each of the Houses of the Legislature of that State.

(2) Any Act so passed by Parliament may be amended or repealed by an Act of Parliament passed or adopted in like manner but shall not, as respects any State to which it applies, be amended or repealed by an Act of the Legislature of that State.

253.[1]—Notwithstanding anything in the foregoing provisions of this Chapter, Parliament has power to make any law for the whole or any part of the territory of India for implementing any treaty, agreement or convention with any other country or countries or any decision made at any international conference, association or other body.

254.—(1) If any provision of a law made by the Legislature of a State is repugnant to any provision of a law made by Parliament which Parliament is competent to enact, or to any provision of an existing law with respect to one of the matters enumerated in the Concurrent List, then, subject to the provisions of clause (2), the law made by Parliament, whether passed before or after the law made by the Legislature of such State, or, as the case may be, the existing law, shall prevail and the law made by the Legislature of the State shall, to the extent of the repugnancy, be void.

(2) Where a law made by the Legislature of a State specified in Part A or Part B of the First Schedule with respect to one of the matters enumerated in the Concurrent List contains any provision repugnant to the provisions of an earlier law made by Parliament or an existing law with respect to that matter, then, the law so made by the Legislature of such State shall, if it has been reserved for the consideration of the President and has received his assent, prevail in that State:

Provided that nothing in this clause shall prevent Parliament from enacting at any time any law with respect to the same matter including a law adding to, amending, varying or repealing the law so made by the Legislature of the State.

255.[2]—No Act of Parliament or of the Legislature of a State specified in Part A or Part B of the First Schedule, and no provision in any such Act, shall be invalid by reason only that some recommendation or previous sanction required by this Constitution was not given, if assent to that Act was given—

(a) where the recommendation required was that of the Governor, either by the Governor or by the President;

(b) where the recommendation required was that of the Rajpramukh, either by the Rajpramukh or by the President.

(c) where the recommendation or previous sanction required was that of the President, by the President.

Chapter II. Administrative Relations
PART XII. FINANCE, PROPERTY, CONTRACTS, SUITS.*******

---

[1] Provided that after the commencement of the Constitution (Application to Jammu and Kashmir) Order, 1954, no decision affecting the disposition of the State of Jammu and Kashmir shall be made by the Government of India without the consent of that State.

[2] Not applicable to the State of Jammu and Kashmir.

PART XIII. TRADE, COMMERCE AND INTERCOURSE WITHIN THE TERRITORY OF INDIA.***

PART XIV. SERVICES UNDER THE UNION AND THE STATES.***

PART XV. ELECTIONS

324.[1]—(1) The superintendence, direction and control of the preparation of the electoral rolls for, and the conduct of, all elections to Parliament and to the Legislature of every State and of elections to the offices of President and Vice-President held under this Constitution, including the appointment of election tribunals for the decision of doubts and disputes arising out of or in connection with elections to Parliament and to the Legislatures of States shall be vested in a Commission (referred to in this Constitution as the Election Commission).

(2) The Election Commission shall consist of the Chief Election Commissioner and such number of other Election Commissioners if any, as the President may from time to time fix and the appointment of the Chief Election Commissioner and other Election Commissioners shall, subject to the provisions of any law made in that behalf by Parliament, be made by the President.

(3) When any other Election Commissioner is so appointed the Chief Election Commissioner shall act as the Chairman of the Election Commission.

(4) Before each general election to the House of the People and to the Legislative Assembly of each State, and before the first general election and thereafter before each biennial election to the Legislative Council of each State having such Council, the President may also appoint after consultation with the Election Commission such Regional Commissioners as he may consider necessary to assist the Election Commission in the performance of the functions conferred on the Commission by clause (1).

(5) Subject to the provisions of any law made by Parliament, the conditions of service and tenure of office of the Election Commissioners and the Regional Commissioners shall be such as the President may by rule determine:

Provided that the Chief Election Commissioner shall not be removed from his office except in like manner and on the like grounds as a Judge of the Supreme Court and the conditions of service of the Chief Election Commissioner shall not be varied to his disadvantage after his appointment:

Provided further that any other Election Commissioner or a Regional Commissioner shall not be removed from office except on the recommendation of the Chief Election Commissioner.

(6) The President, or the Governor or Rajpramukh of a State, shall, when so requested by the Election Commission, make available to the Election Commission or to a Regional Commissioner such staff as may be necessary for the discharge of the functions conferred on the Election Commission by clause (1).

325.[2]—There shall be one general electoral roll for every territorial consti-

---

[1] Applicable to the State of Jammu and Kashmir only in so far as it relates to elections to Parliament and to the offices of President and Vice-President.
[2] Not applicable to the State of Jammu and Kashmir.

tuency for election to either House of Parliament or to the House or either House of the Legislature of a State and no person shall be ineligible for inclusion in any such roll or claim to be included in any special electoral roll for any such constituency on grounds only of religion, race, caste, sex or any of them.

326.[1]—The elections to the House of the People and to the Legislative Assembly of every State shall be on the basis of adult suffrage; that is to say, every person who is a citizen of India and who is not less than twenty-one years of age on such date as may be fixed in that behalf by or under any law made by the appropriate Legislature and is not otherwise disqualified under this Constitution or any law made by the appropriate Legislature on the ground of non-residence, unsoundness of mind, crime or corrupt or illegal practice, shall be entitled to be registered as a voter at any such election.

327.[1]—Subject to the provisions of this Constitution, Parliament may from time to time by law make provision with respect to all matters relating to, or in connection with, elections to either House of Parliament or to the House or either House of the Legislature of a State including the preparation of electoral rolls, the delimitation of constituencies and all other matters necessary for securing the due constitution of such House or Houses.

328.[1]—Subject to the provisions of this Constitution and in so far as provision in that behalf is not made by Parliament, the Legislature of a State may from time to time by law make provision with respect to all matters relating to, or in connection with, the elections to the House or either House of the Legislature of the State including the preparation of electoral rolls and all other matters necessary for securing the due constitution of such House or Houses.

329.[1]—Notwithstanding anything in this Constitution—
   (a) the validity of any law relating to the delimitation of constituencies or the allotment of seats to such constituencies, made or purporting to be made under article 327 or article 328, shall not be called in question in any court;
   (b) no election to either House of Parliament or to the House or either House of the Legislature of a State shall be called in question except by an election petition presented to such authority and in such manner as may be provided for by or under any law made by the appropriate Legislature.

PART XVI. SPECIAL PROVISIONS RELATING TO CERTAIN CLASSES

330.—(1) Seats shall be reserved in the House of the People for—
   (a) the Scheduled Castes;
   (b) the Scheduled Tribes except the Scheduled Tribes in the tribal areas of Assam; and
   (c) the Scheduled Tribes in the autonomous districts of Assam.

(2) The number of seats reserved in any State for the Scheduled Castes or the Scheduled Tribes under clause (1) shall bear, as nearly as may be, the same

[1] Not applicable to the State of Jammu and Kashmir.

proportion to the total number of seats allotted to that State in the House of the People as the population of the Scheduled Castes in the State or of the Scheduled Tribes in the State or part of the State, as the case may be, in respect of which seats are so reserved, bears to the total population of the State.

331.[1]—Notwithstanding anything in article 81, the President may, if he is of opinion that the Anglo-Indian community is not adequately represented in the House of the People, nominate not more than two members of that community to the House of the People.

332.[1]—(1) Seats shall be reserved for the Scheduled Castes and the Scheduled Tribes, except the Scheduled Tribes in the tribal areas of Assam, in the Legislative Assembly of every State specified in Part A or Part B of the First Schedule.

(2) Seats shall be reserved also for the autonomous districts in the Legislative Assembly of the State of Assam.

(3) The number of seats reserved for the Scheduled Castes or the Scheduled Tribes in the Legislative Assembly of any State under clause (1) shall bear, as nearly as may be, the same proportion to the total number of seats in the Assembly as the population of the Scheduled Castes in the State or of the Scheduled Tribes in the State or part of the State, as the case may be, in respect of which seats are so reserved, bears to the total population of the State.

(4) The number of seats reserved for an autonomous district in the Legislative Assembly of the State of Assam shall bear to the total number of seats in that Assembly a proportion not less than the population of the district bears to the total population of the State.

(5) The constituencies for the seats reserved for any autonomous district of Assam shall not comprise any area outside that district except in the case of the constituency comprising the cantonment and municipality of Shillong.

(6) No person who is not a member of a Scheduled Tribe of any autonomous district of the State of Assam shall be eligible for election to the Legislative Assembly of the State from any constituency of that district except from the constituency comprising the cantonment and municipality of Shillong.

333.[1]—Notwithstanding anything in article 170, the Governor or Rajpramukh of a State may, if he is of opinion that the Anglo-Indian community needs representation in the Legislative Assembly of the State and is not adequately represented therein, nominate such number of members of the community to the Assembly as he considers appropriate.

334.—Notwithstanding anything in the foregoing provisions of this Part, the provisions of this Constitution relating to—

(a) the reservation of seats for the Scheduled Castes and the Scheduled Tribes in the House of the People and in the Legislative Assemblies of the States; and

(b) the representation of the Anglo-Indian community in the House of the People and in the Legislative Assemblies of the States by nomination,

1 Not applicable to the State of Jammu and Kashmir.

shall cease to have effect on the expiration of a period of ten years from the commencement of this Constitution:

Provided that nothing in this article shall affect any representation in the House of the People or in the Legislative Assembly of a State until the dissolution of the then existing House or Assembly, as the case may be.

* * *

PART XVII. OFFICIAL LANGUAGE

Chapter I. Language of the Union

343.—(1) The official language of the Union shall be Hindi in Devanagari script.

The form of numerals to be used for the official purposes of the Union shall be the international form of Indian numerals.

(2) Notwithstanding anything in clause (1), for a period of fifteen years from the commencement of this Constitution, the English language shall continue to be used for all the official purposes of the Union for which it was being used immediately before such commencement:

Provided that the President may, during the said period, by order authorise the use of the Hindi language in addition to the English language and of the Devanagari form of numerals in addition to the international form of Indian numerals for any of the official purposes of the Union.

(3) Notwithstanding anything in this article, Parliament may by law provide for the use, after the said period of fifteen years, of—

(a) the English language, or

(b) the Devanagari form of numerals,

for such purposes as may be specified in the law.

344.—(1) The President shall, at the expiration of five years from the commencement of this Constitution and thereafter at the expiration of ten years from such commencement, by order constitute a Commission which shall consist of a Chairman and such other members representing the different languages specified in the Eighth Schedule as the President may appoint, and the order shall define the procedure to be followed by the Commission.

(2) It shall be the duty of the Commission to make recommendations to the President as to—

(a) the progressive use of the Hindi language for the official purposes of the Union;

(b) restrictions on the use of the English language for all or any of the official purposes of the Union;

(c) the language to be used for all or any of the purposes mentioned in article 348;

(d) the form of numerals to be used for any one or more specified purposes of the Union;

(e) any other matter referred to the Commission by the President as regards the official language of the Union and the language for communication between the Union and a State or between one State and another and their use.

(3) In making their recommendations under clause (2), the Commission shall have due regard to the industrial, cultural and scientific advancement of India, and the just claims and the interests of persons belonging to the non-Hindi speaking areas in regard to the public services.

(4) There shall be constituted a Committee consisting of thirty members, of whom twenty shall be members of the House of the People and ten shall be members of the Council of States to be elected respectively by the members of the House of the People and the members of the Council of States in accordance with the system of proportional representation by means of the single transferable vote.

(5) It shall be the duty of the Committee to examine the recommendations of the Commission constituted under clause (1) and to report to the President their opinion thereon.

(6) Notwithstanding anything in article 343, the President may, after consideration of the report referred to in clause (5) issue directions in accordance with the whole or any part of that report.

Chapter II. Regional Languages

345.—Subject to the provisions of articles 346 and 347, the Legislature of a State may by law adopt any one or more of the languages in use in the State or Hindi as the language or languages to be used for all or any of the official purposes of that State:

Provided that, until the Legislature of the State otherwise provides by law, the English language shall continue to be used for those official purposes within the State for which it was being used immediately before the commencement of this Constitution.

346.—The language for the time being authorised for use in the Union for official purposes shall be the official language for communication between one State and another State and between a State and the Union:

Provided that if two or more States agree that the Hindi language should be the official language for communication between such States, that language may be used for such communication.

347.—On a demand being made in that behalf, the President may, if he is satisfied that a substantial proportion of the population of a State desire the use of any language spoken by them to be recognised by that State, direct that such language shall also be officially recognised throughout that State or any part thereof for such purpose as he may specify.

Chapter III. Language of the Supreme Court, High Courts, etc.

348.—(1) Notwithstanding anything in the foregoing provisions of this Part, until Parliament by law otherwise provides—
(a) all proceedings in the Supreme Court and in every High Court,

(b) the authoritative texts—

(i) of all Bills to be introduced or amendments thereto to be moved in either House of Parliament or in the House or either House of the Legislature of a State,

(ii) of all Acts passed by Parliament or the Legislature of a State and of all Ordinances promulgated by the President or the Governor or Rajpramukh of a State, and

(iii) of all orders, rules, regulations and bye-laws issued under this Constitution or under any law made by Parliament or the Legislature of a State, shall be in the English language.

(2) Notwithstanding anything in sub-clause (a) of clause (1), the Governor or Rajpramukh of a State may, with the previous consent of the President, authorise the use of the Hindi language, or any other language used for any official purposes of the State, in proceedings in the High Court having its principal seat in that State:

Provided that nothing in this clause shall apply to any judgment, decree or order passed or made by such High Court.

(3) Notwithstanding anything in sub-clause (b) of clause (1), where the Legislature of a State has prescribed any language other than the English language for use in Bills introduced in, or Acts passed by, the Legislature of the State or in Ordinances promulgated by the Governor or Rajpramukh of the State or in any order, rule, regulation or bye-law referred to in paragraph (iii) of that sub-clause, a translation of the same in the English language published under the authority of the Governor or Rajpramukh of the State in the Official Gazette of that State shall be deemed to be the authoritative text thereof in the English language under this article.

349.—During the period of fifteen years from the commencement of this Constitution, no Bill or amendment making provision for the language to be used for any of the purposes mentioned in clause (1) of article 348 shall be introduced or moved in either House of Parliament without the previous sanction of the President, and the President shall not give his sanction to the introduction of any such Bill or the moving of any such amendment except after he has taken into consideration the recommendations of the Commission constituted under clause (1) of article 344 and the report of the Committee constituted under clause (4) of that article.

Chapter IV. Special Directives

350.—Every person shall be entitled to submit a representation for the redress of any grievance to any officer or authority of the Union or a State in any of the languages used in the Union or in the State, as the case may be.

351.—It shall be the duty of the Union to promote the spread of the Hindi language, to develop it so that it may serve as a medium of expression for all the elements of the composite culture of India and to secure its enrichment by assimilating without interfering with its genius, the forms, style and expressions used in Hindustani and in the other languages of India specified in the

Eighth Schedule, and by drawing, wherever necessary or desirable, for its vocabulary, primarily on Sanskrit and secondarily on other languages.

PART XVIII. EMERGENCY PROVISIONS.***

PART XIX. MISCELLANEOUS.***

PART XX. AMENDMENT OF THE CONSTITUTION

368.[1]—An amendment of this Constitution may be initiated only by the introduction of a Bill for the purpose in either House of Parliament, and when the Bill is passed in each House by a majority of the total membership of that House and by a majority of not less than two-thirds of the members of that House present and voting, it shall be presented to the President for his assent and upon such assent being given to the Bill, the Constitution shall stand amended in accordance with the terms of the Bill:

Provided that if such amendment seeks to make any change in—

(a) article 54, article 55, article 73, article 162 or article 241, or

(b) Chapter IV of Part V, Chapter V of Part VI, or Chapter I of Part XI, or

(c) any of the Lists in the Seventh Schedule, or

(d) the representation of States in Parliament, or

(e) the provisions of this article,

the amendment shall also require to be ratified by the Legislatures of not less than one-half of the States specified in Parts A and B of the First Schedule by resolutions to that effect passed by those Legislatures before the Bill making provision for such amendment is presented to the President for assent.

PART XXI. TEMPORARY AND TRANSITIONAL PROVISIONS.***

PART XXII. SHORT TITLE, COMMENCEMENT AND REPEALS.***

First Schedule

PART A

Names of States	*Names of corresponding Provinces*
Andhra[2]	
Assam	Assam
Bihar	Bihar
Bombay	Bombay
Madhya Pradesh	The Central Provinces and Berar
Madras	Madras
Orissa	Orissa
Punjab	East Punjab
Uttar Pradesh	The United Provinces
West Bengal	West Bengal

[1] In its application to the State of Jammu and Kashmir the following proviso shall be added: Provided further that no such amendment shall have effect in relation to the State of Jammu and Kashmir unless applied by order of the President under clause (1) of Article 370.

[2] The name of the new State of Andhra was added by the Andhra State Act, 1953.

Territories of States

The territory of the State of Andhra shall comprise the territories specified in sub-section (1) of section 3 of the Andhra State Act, 1953.

The territory of the State of Assam shall comprise the territories which immediately before the commencement of this Constitution were comprised in the Province of Assam, the Khasi States and the Assam Tribal Areas.

The territory of each of the other States in this Part shall comprise the territories which immediately before the commencement of this Constitution were comprised in the corresponding Province and the territories which, by virtue of an order made under section 290A of the Government of India Act, 1935, were immediately before such commencement being administered as if they formed part of that Province.

* * *

PART B

Names of States

Hyderabad
Jammu and Kashmir
Madhya Bharat
Mysore
Patiala and East Punjab States Union
Rajasthan
Saurashtra
Travancore-Cochin.

Territories of States

The territory of each of the States in this Part shall comprise the territory which immediately before the commencement of this Constitution was comprised in or administered by the Government of the corresponding Indian State, and in the case of the State of Madhya Bharat, shall also comprise the territory which immediately before such commencement was comprised in the Chief Commissioner's Province of Panth Piploda.

PART C

Names of States

Ajmer
Bhopal
Coorg
Delhi
Himachal Pradesh
· Kutch
Manipur
Tripura
Vindhya Pradesh

Territories of States

The territory of each of the States of Ajmer, Coorg and Delhi shall comprise the territory which immediately before the commencement of this

Constitution was comprised in the Chief Commissioners' Provinces of Ajmer-Merwara, Coorg and Delhi, respectively.

The territory of each of the other States in this Part shall comprise the territories which, by virtue of an order made under section 290A of the Government of India Act, 1935, were immediately before the commencement of this Constitution being administered as if they were a Chief Commissioner's Province of the same name.

PART D

The Andaman and Nicobar Islands.

Second Schedule

PART A***

PART B***

PART C

Provisions as to the Speaker and the Deputy Speaker of the House of the People and the Chairman and the Deputy Chairman of the Council of States and the Speaker and the Deputy Speaker of the Legislative Assembly of a State in Part A of the First Schedule and the Chairman and the Deputy Chairman of the Legislative Council of any such State.

7.—There shall be paid to the Speaker of the House of the People and the Chairman of the Council of States such salaries and allowances as were payable to the Speaker of the Constituent Assembly of the Dominion of India immediately before the commencement of this Constitution, and there shall be paid to the Deputy Speaker of the House of the People and to the Deputy Chairman of the Council of States such salaries and allowances as were payable to the Deputy Speaker of the Constituent Assembly of the Dominion of India immediately before such commencement.

8.—There shall be paid to the Speaker and the Deputy Speaker of the Legislative Assembly of a State specified in Part A of the First Schedule and to the Chairman and the Deputy Chairman of the Legislative Council of such State such salaries and allowances as were payable respectively to the Speaker and the Deputy Speaker of the Legislative Assembly and the President and the Deputy President of the Legislative Council of the corresponding Province immediately before the commencement of this Constitution and, where the corresponding Province had no Legislative Council immediately before such commencement, there shall be paid to the Chairman and the Deputy Chairman of the Legislative Council of the State such salaries and allowances as the Governor of the State may determine.

PART D***

PART E

Provisions as to the Comptroller and Auditor-General of India

12.—(1) There shall be paid to the Comptroller and Auditor-General of India a salary at the rate of four thousand rupees per mensem.

(2) The person who was holding office immediately before the commencement of this Constitution as Auditor-General of India and has become on such commencement the Comptroller and Auditor-General of India under article 377 shall in addition to the salary specified in sub-paragraph (1) of this paragraph be entitled to receive as special pay an amount equivalent to the difference between the salary so specified and the salary which he was drawing as Auditor-General of India immediately before such commencement.

(3) The rights in respect of leave of absence and pension and the other conditions of service of the Comptroller and Auditor-General of India shall be governed or shall continue to be governed, as the case may be, by the provisions which were applicable to the Auditor-General of India immediately before the commencement of this Constitution and all references in those provisions to the Governor-General shall be construed as references to the President.

Third Schedule***

Fourth Schedule

Allocation of Seats in the Council of States

To each State or group of States specified in the first column of the table of seats appended to this Schedule there shall be allotted the number of seats specified in the second column of the said table opposite to that State or group of States, as the case may be.

The Council of States

Representatives of States specified in Part A of the First Schedule

1 States	2 Total Seats
Andhra[1]	12
Assam	6
Bihar	21
Bombay	17
Madhya Pradesh	12
Madras	18
Orissa	9
Punjab	8
Uttar Pradesh	31
West Bengal	14
	148

[1] Andhra was inserted by the Andhra State Act, 1953. The previous allocation for Madras was 27 so that the new total of 148 represents an increase of 3.

24—P.I.

Representatives of States specified in Part B of the First Schedule

1	2
States	Total Seats
Hyderabad	11
Jammu and Kashmir	4
Madhya Bharat	6
Mysore	6
Patiala and East Punjab States Union .	3
Rajasthan	9
Saurashtra	4
Travancore-Cochin	6
	—
	49

Representatives of States specified in Part C of the First Schedule

1	2
States	Total Seats
Ajmer⎱ Coorg⎰	1
Bhopal	1
Himachal Pradesh . . .	1
Delhi	1
Kutch	1
Manipur⎱ Tripura ⎰	1
Vindhya Pradesh . . .	4
	—
	10

Total of seats . . 207

Fifth Schedule*

Sixth Schedule*

Seventh Schedule*

Eighth Schedule*

Ninth Schedule*

APPENDIX II

THE CHANGING ASSEMBLY (See p. 50 n.)

The following extracts from the proceedings of the Central Assemblies of India may serve to illustrate the changing tone of discussion. Extracts have been made from each of the main periods following the introduction of fresh legislature reforms in 1861, 1892, 1909, 1919, 1952. The extracts are from 'Budget debates':

1. *Extract from 'Abstract of the Proceedings of the Council of the Governor-General of India assembled for the purpose of making Laws and Regulations, 1862'*:

The Council met at Government House, on Wednesday, the 16th April 1862.

PRESENT:

His Excellency the Viceroy and Governor-General of India, Presiding.
His Honor the Lieutenant-Governor of Bengal.
The Hon'ble Cecil Beadon.
Major-General the Hon'ble Sir R. Napier, K.C.B.
The Hon'ble S. Laing.
The Hon'ble H. B. Harrington.
The Hon'ble H. Forbes.
The Hon'ble C. J. Erskine.
The Hon'ble W. S. Fitzwilliam.
The Hon'ble D. Cowie.
The Hon'ble Rajah Deo Narain Singh Bahadoor.

The Hon'ble Mr. Laing having 'brought forward the Budget of the Government of India for 1862–63' in a fairly lengthy speech, the debate began:

'The Hon'ble Mr. Cowie said that, as an unofficial Member, he felt it to be his duty to express the gratification with which he had listened to the Statement which had just been made, respecting the Surplus Revenue and the objects to which it was to be devoted. To the high Duties on Imports he had always objected as wholly indefensible, except upon the ground of necessity, and he regarded their reduction as a simple act of justice, quite irrespectively of any pressure from Manchester or any other quarter. He also cordially approved of the abolition of the 2 per cent Income Tax. At the time of the introduction of the Tax by the late Mr. Wilson, he [Mr. Cowie] thought that the limit had been fixed too low, and two years' experience as an Income Tax Commissioner had convinced him that the greater part of the oppression of which complaint was made in the collection of the Income Tax, was exercised in respect of the 2 per cent levied on the smaller Incomes. With reference to the continuance of the remainder of the Tax for three years more, he trusted that the prosperity of the country would be so progressive that the Council might be able to remove it altogether before the expiration of that period.

371

The Hon'ble Mr. Fitzwilliam said that he was happy to join in the congratulations of his colleague on the Financial Statement which the Council had just heard. He considered that the reduction of the Import Duties would afford an important relief to the country, and especially to its commerce. He fully concurred with Mr. Cowie in his views of the Income Tax, and could, in like manner, speak from experience as a Commissioner for its collection. The Tax had the effect of promoting both oppression and immorality, more particularly in its operation, on the large class who would now be relieved. As a Member of that Council, he felt happy to give his cordial assent to the present partial remission of the Tax, and he hoped that the time might soon arrive when the Tax could be dispensed with altogether.

His Honor the Lieutenant-Governor said that, as his views on the Import Duties had been alluded to by Mr. Laing, it might be necessary to explain them for the satisfaction of those Members of the Council who were not Members of the Executive Council, and therefore had not seen the papers on the subject. No Member of the Council objected more strongly than he did to all Duties in the nature of protective Duties; and if he had thought that the question of protection was involved in the difference between a 5 per cent. and 10 per cent. Duty, he should have considered that the additional 5 per cent. should be the first to be remitted, or if the whole Tax partook of the character of a protective Duty, he should have been in favor of its being taken off altogether. But looking at the Tax merely as one for Revenue, in preference to the License Tax which was then about to be imposed, he thought that it was free from objection. The License Tax, however, had been given up, and thereby a considerable burden of anxiety had been removed from his mind. His impression was that the next Tax to be assailed, should be the Income Tax, in preference to the Duties on Importations. But if practical men said that those Duties acted as protective Duties, then no one more heartily approved of their remission than himself.

The Motion was then put and agreed to.

The Hon'ble Mr. Laing then applied to His Excellency the President to suspend Rules 15 and 16 for the conduct of business, in order that he might introduce the Bill.

His Excellency the President declared the Rules in question suspended.

The Hon'ble Mr. Laing then introduced the Bill, and moved that it be referred to a Select Committee with instructions to report in a week.

The Motion was put and agreed to.'

At the next meeting of the Council, a week later,—

'The Hon'ble Mr. Laing presented the Report of the Select Committee on the Bill to amend Act X of 1860 (to amend Act VII of 1859, to alter the Duties of Customs on foods imported or exported by Sea), and applied to His Excellency the President to suspend Rule 23 for the conduct of business. He said that the alterations in the Bill were simply to add the words "Silk Chussum," after the words "Raw Silk", and to strike out words that were unnecessary.

His Excellency the President declared the Rule in question suspended.

The Hon'ble Mr. Laing then moved that the Report of the Select Committee be taken into consideration, and that the Bill, as settled by the Select

Committee, be passed. He said that it was desirable that the new Duties should come into operation without delay.

The Hon'ble Rajah Deo Narain Singh said that he gladly availed himself of this opportunity to express his warm admiration of the Financial Statement submitted by the Hon'ble Mr. Laing at the last Meeting of the Council. In that Statement it was shown that owing to the excellent management of the Hon'ble Member, the expenditure had been considerably diminished, while the Income had at the same time improved, and a large increase of treasure had accumulated in the Government Treasuries. This was no easy task, and its accomplishment, while giving new strength to the Empire, had greatly benefited the people by occasioning the repeal of the two per cent. Income Tax, the License Tax, and the abolition or diminution of sundry Customs Duties. The following advantages too, would on consideration, be found to have resulted therefrom:

1st.—The two per cent. Duty bore most heavily on Incomes of not more than 500 Rupees, and the relief occasioned by its repeal would be sensibly felt. The License Tax was most oppressively felt by Artizans, etc., and was a source of daily annoyance to them, and its repeal would restore to them their peace of mind and fill their hearts with gratitude to their Sovereign, for the continuance of whose reign they would offer up hearty prayers.

2nd.—Although Act XXXII of 1860 imposed the Income Tax for a specified term of five years, people did not believe it would ever be taken off again; many instancing that, though in England the Tax had been first imposed for a limited period, it had since become permanent. The partial repeal of the Tax within the period authorized by law would have the immediate effect of driving such false surmises out of the heads of the people, and of convincing them that the Tax would really be taken off on the expiry of the five years for which it was imposed, and they would be ashamed of their former doubts.

3rd.—When Act XXXII was published, it was stated that Government was forced to impose the Tax for the purpose of equalizing the Income and Expenditure, and to make good losses incurred by the Mutiny. This statement was by most people looked upon as a mere excuse for raising money, the fact of Government having suffered any loss being denied. The falseness of these doubts would now be proved by the fact of Government having taken off the Tax as soon as the state of the finances would permit, and people would see that its imposition was forced on the Government, and that the Government was not actuated by a desire to screw money out of the people. The most important result, however, would be that the people would place entire confidence in their Sovereign in whose service they would be ready to lay down their lives.

Finally, too much could not be said in praise of Mr. Laing who, undeterred by several serious attacks of illness, had labored unceasingly and to such good purpose as in a short time to produce results quite unlooked for by the Natives of this country, who could not but feel the heavy debt of gratitude they all owed him. The Native Members of that Council were specially under obligation to him, for as these remissions of taxation had been made since they had had the honor of occupying seats in the Council, they had risen high in the estimation of their fellow subjects.

The Secretary read the Report of the Select Committee, and the Motion was then put and agreed to.'

2. *At the Council that 'met at Government House on Thursday, 21 March 1895'*, twenty members were present to hear 'the Financial Statement of the Hon'ble Sir James Westland'. Discussion of the Statement began on the following Thursday. More Members took part than in 1862. One of them, Mr. James, devoted his attention to the Post Office, urging that the main effort should be to cheapen and improve the postal service rather than to produce surpluses. Another, Sir Griffith Evans, concentrated on the importance of developing opium cultivation as a source of government revenue—in spite of the 'useless and improper agitation' of the 'opium faddists' in England—and on the doubtful wisdom of the Chitral Expedition. Mr. Playfair advocated the purchase of an increased proportion of Government stores from India instead of England, partly for reasons of economy and partly 'in justice to the important industrial interests of India'. But the most noteworthy change from 1862 is to be found in the contributions of the Indian Members. The following extracts are from the speech of Gangadhar Rao Madhar Chitnavis:

'I am aware, my Lord, that the view is urged in certain quarters that the financial arrangements of the Government of India are, as a policy, so regulated as to exhaust the very last resources of the tax-payer and to further foreign interests in total disregard of the interests of the children of the soil. My Lord, it is an opinion against which I would give the most emphatic possible protest, for with such a policy as a whole no Government in the world could have more than a most ephemeral existence. Rightly or wrongly, India is sometimes likened to the goose that used to lay golden eggs, but who would be so foolish, my Lord, after the fable has grown pretty old in the world, as to kill the goose for the sake of enriching one's self all in one day? The best interests of England and the English Government can only be served by looking first to the interests of the ruled and then to those of the ruling country, and if any Government in power reverses this policy, or disregards it even for a moment, future Governments have to pay the penalty, and I am not sure that the present straits of the Government are not said to be to some extent the inevitable result of overlooking this far-sighted policy some time in the past.

The policy, however, which has mainly guided the English Government in this country hitherto, and which will continue to guide it so long as England can produce such far-sighted statesmen as we see at the present day, will, I venture to hope, be that policy which was well defined some twenty years ago by the late Prime Minister. "Our title to be in India", said Mr. Gladstone, "depends on a first condition, that our being there is profitable to the Indian nations; and on a second condition that we can make them see and understand it to be profitable"—a statement which calls to my mind the words of another great statesman, a former Viceroy of India, I mean Lord Lawrence, who said that "light taxation is the panacea for foreign rule in India".

When, therefore, my Lord, the Government is able to announce that it has to impose no further burdens upon its subjects, I feel that the pleasure is shared by both governed and governors alike.

At the same time, my Lord, I cannot but think that, despite the best wishes of the Government, the Indian tax-payer is well nigh bent double with his burden, and that any additional pressure could only break his back. The best proof of this, I believe, is the imposition of the cotton-duties, a measure which secured for the Secretary of State such strong opposition from a very influential section of the British public, and which, I believe, he would have held on refusing to accede to, had there been open to him any further ways of taxing the Indian people without a marked and glaring injustice.

I cannot but feel concerned at the gathering clouds in the North–West horizon, which, I am afraid, bursting ere long, will bring back all his troubles in an aggravated form and scatter his surplus of Rs.46,200 to the winds.

I am glad to observe from the Financial Statement that the Government of India recognised the necessity of suspending the collections of land-revenue in the Central Provinces during 1894–95 owing to failure of crops in parts of those Provinces. Yet I read with no little concern that the whole revenue which was thus postponed, re-appears not in instalments but all at once in the Budget Estimate for the coming year, together with the entire revenue for that year.

So far as I am informed, and I have good opportunities of being well informed, the state of crops this year has by no means improved, if it has not on the contrary grown worse than last year. It was only the other day that a deputation of the leading citizens of Saugor, on behalf of the people of the Saugor District, waited upon the Chief Commissioner to represent to him the state of the kharif crops in their district, which had been entirely ruined through excessive rain. They showed that there was no hope of the outturn being more than two annas in the rupee, and also that the prospects of the rabi crop were not hopeful either. A considerable area of land has remained untilled for want of seed and funds for payment of labour. The linseed crop and, in many cases, the wheat crop has already been damaged by rust. What has been said about Saugor might be said with equal truth about Wardha, Bhandara and some other districts of the province. The people, it is said in the local paper just to hand, have a very gloomy future before them, and they are likely to suffer another famine more terrible in its effects than the previous one.

Such being the prospects of crops in my Provinces, I am quite confident that postponements of revenue will be still more urgently needed in this coming year than in the one about to expire, and that the Budget Estimate of the land-revenue in my Provinces has been fixed at rather an impossible figure. This figure alone, if properly estimated, would, in my opinion, convert the surplus into a deficit.

With this question of failure of crops is intimately connected the question of the indebtedness of the agricultural population, which has of late years attracted deserved attention from the Government. There has been continued failure of crops for some years, and the Government considered it needful to suspend the collection of revenue. This year the Government comes forward to realize its past dues all in one year, and that a year of scarcity. The only recourse open to the agricultural population to pay their dues is therefore to borrow at high rates of interest and ruin themselves beyond recovery. Under the circumstances such as these the idea occurs to me of going back to the old Indian methods of remission of Government revenue in part and realization of rent in kind. This, I think, is a very possible means of saving the agricultural population from further indebtedness and improving their condition.

My Lord, I would not like to take up the time of the Council with any further criticisms in reference to the Financial Statement presented this year: so far as it goes, it is no doubt a very favourable one. It is perhaps very unkind for a non-official member to criticise the Budget Statements of such critical years as we are passing through, for while he is almost by nature inclined to point out that there might be greater savings in every department of expenditure, the Government perhaps thinks that it had already done its best to effect it. A non-official member is perhaps too inclined to think that the ever-increasing military expenditure of the country ought to be effectually reduced, and that the internal reforms of the country should be taken up in right earnest, such questions as, for instance, the separation of the executive and the judicial, which I believe would tend (though it may sound paradoxical) to strengthen the executive, better prospects of pay and promotion to the police, greater aids to education, longer periods of settlements, etc., etc. The importance of questions such as these, in a financial crisis like the present, are necessarily lost upon the Government, and a non-official member thus performs a somewhat thankless task. His views are resented by the Government as inopportune, and he is unable to secure any benefit for the people he represents.

But, whether or not the Government be in a position to accept the suggestions of non-official members given out in this chamber from year to year, it is easy to see that the position is this. Our expenditure is every year increasing, and there seems to be no limit to the increase. On the other hand, the sources of income as at present constituted seem to have reached very nearly their last limit. India has been known through ages to be a very rich country, perhaps the richest country in the world. But today she is hardly able to bear the costs of government; for surely it means nothing else when year after year we find ourselves face to face with liabilities greater than our assets and the Finance Minister at his wit's end to make expenditure and income meet. What would a private individual under such circumstances be driven to? Either he would seek asylum in the Insolvency Court, or, if he had any hopes of solvency, he would reduce his expenditure. One only hope there seems to be, namely, in making the internal resources of the country ten times more productive that she may be able to pay her expenses. The importation of machinery and capital, the spread of commerce and improved methods of cultivation would seem to have done a good deal in the right direction; but much more must yet be done, and it would be idle to expect our financial situation to be based upon anything like a permanent and natural foundation, so long as this has not been fully effected by the Government.

In conclusion, my Lord, I would like to add that, in offering such criticisms of the Financial Statement as I have been able to make, I have acted in no carping spirit, but with an earnest desire to fulfil my duty to my people and to effectuate the object of my presence here in Your Lordship's advisory Council. I would not do Your Excellency's Government the injustice, my Lord, to believe that, in summoning to an enlarged Council natives of the country conversant with the feelings of particular provinces or classes of the population, you do not earnestly wish for the real expression of their views, and I should in fact be guilty of a want of confidence in the Government if I did not speak plainly the thoughts that pass through our minds. Finance is so intimately connected with taxation and taxation with good government and policy that I have deemed the present the best moment to give my views. Evil we know is done by want of thought as well as want of heart, and I and the people whom I have the honour to represent feel that many, if not most, of the misunderstandings which arise between the rulers and ruled in this country are the result rather of ignorance than want of sympathy and that such ignorance is often a matter of the sincerest regret on the part of the Government. It is therefore in the best spirit of loyalty that I have said what I had to say, a spirit expressed so nobly in the words of Milton that I can scarcely end better than by quoting them as an expression of my views:

"For he who freely magnifies what hath been nobly done and fears not to declare as freely what might be done better, gives ye the best covenant of his fidelity and that his loyalest affection and his hope waits on your proceedings.'''

Even more striking was the speech of Mr. Mehta from which the following passages are taken:

'I propose to offer a few observations on the Financial Statement that has been explained to the Council with a clearness and ability for which we cannot but be thankful. There can be do doubt that the right of discussing it, which has been bestowed upon this Council by the Indian Councils Act, 1892, is a most valuable privilege with large possibilities for the future. At the same time it is difficult not to feel that there is an element of unreality about it, arising from the peculiar position occupied by the Financial Member in Your Excellency's Executive Council. In a very recent debate in the House of Lords, Lord Salisbury is reported to have borne testimony to the preponderating influence of the British Treasury and the Chancellor of the Exchequer in the counsels of the Ministry, and to have said that "when the Treasury lays its hand upon any matter concerning the future development of the British Empire, the chances of an Imperial policy are small." The position of the Indian Finance Minister seems to be very nearly the reverse of that of the British Chancellor of the Exchequer. The vulgar gaze is not allowed to penetrate behind the thick curtains that enshroud the sanctuary, but the priests of the tabernacle are sometimes human enough to disclose partial glimpses of the mysteries within. In a valuable paper on "The Perilous Growth of Indian State Expenditure", which may well be styled the Confessions of an Indian Finance Minister, Sir Auckland Colvin says that "a Financial Member of Council is not at liberty to express in his annual Financial Statement his personal point of view on the collective policy of the Government of which he is a member". But, freed from official chains, both Sir David Barbour and Sir Auckland Colvin, who between them represent the financial period between 1883–1892-3, have recently acknowledged that the constitution of the Government of India is such that there is no efficient control over expenditure, and that every Member of the Council, except the Financial Minister, is not only irresponsible for financial equilibrium, but is directly interested in spending, and as a matter of fact overpower all his appeals for economy and reduction.
These are not the views of clumsy and pretentious Native would-be politicians, who audaciously presume to think that they could govern the Empire

better, but those of distinguished men whose mature and tried knowledge and experience must command respect, confirming in the most remarkable manner the contention of the Association that it is the enormous increase of expenditure since 1885–6 which is more responsible even than the depreciated rupee for the embarrassed and critical state of Indian finance. But it has been argued that, though it is perfectly true that the expenditure has increased, the increase is justified by the needs of an expanding and progressive Empire.

But the real question is whether the items of military and civil expenditure bear any just and reasonable proportion to the revenue that can be possibly realized from the country without incurring peril and exhaustion. Altogether something like seven crores of fresh taxation have been imposed since 1885.

What these figures mean is that military expenditure more than fully absorbs one-half of the whole net revenue of the country, or, to put it in another way, if you leave out of account the opium revenue, which cannot be relied on as stable owing to the competition of the home-grown drug in China, the military expenditure absorbs the whole of what has been called taxation revenue proper, derived from salt, stamps, excise, provincial rates, customs as now fully revived, income and other assessed taxes, forest, registration and tributes from Native States. Such a situation cannot but be regarded with serious anxiety, but its gravity is immeasurably enhanced when we remember how the land-revenue is raised to the amount at which it stands. I admit that there are excellent rules laid down by Government for preventing undue severity in settlement and revision proceedings. But the ingenuity of Revenue-officers is wonderful, and in spite of limits against over-enhancement the individual cultivator finds the settlement heavy beyond measure. Except in Bengal, four-fifths of the agricultural population is steeped in debt and poverty. If the saukar presses heavily against the raiyat, it is the Revenue-officer who has driven the raiyat into the hands of the saukar. But the tale does not end here. Heavy as the assessment mostly is, the rigidity and inelasticity of the system of collection is more crushing still. The Commission appointed to enquire into the Dekkan Agriculturists' Relief Act advocated a more liberal practice with regard to remissions and suspensions of revenue; but the Bombay Government actually resented the recommendation as uncalled for and imprudent. The serious import of this state of things arises from the consideration that grand military preparations for protection against foreign invasion, or indeed anything else, are nothing to the cultivator unless he has got something appreciable to protect. It has also been argued that the Indian raiyat is the most lightly taxed subject in the whole world. But, apart from the circumstance that the assessment he has to pay is both rent and tax combined, is it true that he pays no other tax than the salt-tax? In debt all his life, does he not pay in stamps and court-fees for every application he makes to a Revenue-officer, for every process that is issued by or against him in the endless resort to Courts of one sort or another, and does he not pay registration fees for his perpetual transactions of bonds and mortgages and transfers? Insufficiently fed all the year round, does he not pay the excise-duty on liquor and opium, raising the abkari revenue by leaps and bounds? In a recent discussion in the Belgian Chambers Mons. Lejeune, former Minister of Justice, pointed out from statistics that the consumption of spirits in Belgium had increased to an alarming extent, raising the excise-revenue from four millions of francs in 1851 to thirty-three millions in the present year, and that the principal reason for the increase was the insufficiency of food procurable by the labouring classes. It is a well-known fact that the cultivating labourer ekes out nourishment by the use of alcohol and opium. If he does not pay the income-tax, does he not pay the road and other cesses? Has he not, since the new forest policy was introduced, contributed to the forest-revenue by paying grazing and other fees and charges which he never had to pay before? As a matter of fact, the Indian raiyat goes through life carrying a load of many burdens on his back. My object in referring to these matters is to try to show that, if revenue can only be raised in this manner, the expenditure for which this revenue is required to be raised, however academically reasonable or incontrovertible in itself, is beyond the capacity and resources of the country.

My Lord, I have spoken freely in the firm consciousness of a true and sincere loyalty, for if by loyalty is meant a keen solicitude for the safety and permanence of the Indian Empire in which I am persuaded lie implanted the roots of the welfare, prosperity and regeneration of this country, then I claim to be more loyal than Englishmen and Anglo-Indians themselves, who are sometimes led to subordinate the interests of that safety and that permanence to the impetuous impulses of a singularly brave spirit, to the seductions of conquest and imperial vain glory, or to the immediate gains and temptations of commercial enterprise.

Sir James Westland was last year pleasantly sarcastic over "the united wisdom of the Native gentlemen interested in politics, who met at Christmas at Lahore to show us how we ought to govern India", and enjoyed a hearty laugh over their proposals to reduce revenue and increase expenditure at one and the same time. Though of course they could not bear comparison with members of the most distinguished service in the world, these gentlemen are still not altogether devoid of logic and sense in their suggestions. It is not very difficult to understand that, if you economise in the right directions, you can reduce revenue and increase expenditure in others. If you could reduce your military expenditure to reasonable proportions, if you could steady your "forward" policy so as not to lead to incessant costly expeditions, if you could get your inflated Army Home Estimates moderated, if you could devise ways by which the huge burdens of salaries and pensions could be lightened, then it is not chimerical to imagine that you could improve your judicial machinery, strengthen your police, develop a sounder system of education, cover the country with useful public works and railways, undertake larger sanitary measures, cheapen the post and telegraph, and still be in a position to relieve small incomes, to press less heavily on the land, to give the cultivators breathing time and to reduce the salt-tax.'

This contribution drew replies not only from the Financial Member but also from the Commander-in-Chief, the Lieutenant-Governor of Bengal and from the Governor-General himself.

3. *The Financial Statement for 1913–14 was presented to the new enlarged 'Morley-Minto' Council in Delhi on 1 March 1913.* The Viceroy, Lord Hardinge, presided and 47 members attended to hear Sir Guy Fleetwood Wilson. A week later, the discussion began and it now takes the form of a debate on a

series of resolutions moved by Members. 64 members were present and 24 spoke. A list of these resolutions indicates the scope of the discussion:

'That this Council recommends to the Governor General in Council that the Provincial Settlement with the Government of Madras be revised so as to increase the Provincial share of the excise revenue from one-half to three-fourths.'

'That this Council recommends to the Governor General in Council that the additional assignment for recurring expenditure on Education for the United Provinces of Agra and Oudh, announced in the Financial Statement, be raised by Rs.1,200,000 a year.'

'That this Council recommends to His Excellency the Governor General in Council that the amount allotted to Bihar and Orissa under the head of non-recurring grants for education, sanitation and other beneficial purposes, be increased by five lakhs of rupees.'

'That this Council recommends to His Excellency the Governor General in Council that the amount allotted to Bihar and Orissa in the distribution of the recurring grants for the promotion of education and the improvement of sanitation be increased by five lakhs of rupees.'

'That this Council recommends to the Governor General in Council that the grant of 85 lakhs proposed to be distributed to the Major Provinces for recurring expenditure on Education and Sanitation in the Budget, be increased by an additional sum of Rs.15 lakhs from the Imperial Revenue which should be specially allotted for the development of Technical Education.'

'That this Council recommends to the Governor General in Council that an additional grant of Rs.20 lakhs be given for Sanitation in Bengal.'

'That this Council recommends to the Governor General in Council that the grants made to Local Governments be increased by such allotments as the Government of India may think fit with a view to enable them to carry out the experiment of the separation of judicial and executive functions in the administration of criminal justice in areas to be selected by them with the approval of the Government of India.'

On this resolution sixteen members spoke and a division (25 Ayes, 37 Noes) was taken.

'That this Council recommends to the Governor General in Council the desirablity, in view of the loss of opium revenue, of considering financial measures for strengthening the resources of the Government, with special reference to the possibility of increasing the revenue under a system of preferential tariffs with the United Kingdom and the Colonies.'

'That this Council recommends to the Governor General in Council that an additional customs duty of R.5 per cent. be levied on sugar imported into India from foreign countries.'

The final budget debate took place on 24 March. The opening speech, that of Babu Surendra Nath Banerjee, is fairly typical of the general tone:

'Sir, my first words on this occasion will be words of congratulation to the Hon'ble Finance Minister on the Budget which he has presented to us. Our feelings today, Sir, are of the mixed order. While we rejoice over the financial prosperity of the country and grasp with gratitude the hand that has contributed to it, so far as it lies in the power of a Finance Minister to do so, we are filled with a sense of profound sorrow at his impending retirement and his approaching departure from this country. This feeling, I find is shared by Sir Guy Fleetwood Wilson himself. He says, in the speech with which he prefaced the Financial Statement on the 1st March last, that he views the severance of his connection with the Government of India with great sorrow. If he is sorry to leave us, we are also deeply sorry to part with him. If at the present moment India is prosperous and happy, the result is, in some degree at least, due to the successful financial administration over which Sir Guy Fleetwood Wilson presided with such conspicuous ability and such pre-eminent sympathy for the people. For, Sir, the Department of Finance covers every other Department and colours it with its hue. When Sir Guy Fleetwood Wilson came out to this country towards the end of 1908, the financial horizon was overcast with dark and ominous clouds. The budget which was presented in the course of the next three months disclosed a heavy deficit to the extent of nearly four millions. Today, Sir, we have a surplus of seven millions. True, some new taxes have been imposed to which nobody in India has seriously objected, but the public expenditure has been well-maintained, the progressive requirements of the country met, and the prospects of steady and continuous advancement assured. In bidding Sir Guy Fleetwood Wilson good-bye, we wish him long life and prosperity in the old country, and may we couple this wish with the hope that he may continue to feel an abiding interest in that country whose prosperity and welfare he so sedulously tried to advance during the period of his official connection with India? He will be remembered, Sir, as one of the ablest and one of the most sympathetic of Finance Ministers whose outlook extended beyond the range of his own particular department and whose sympathies were co-extensive with the entire circle of our varied and multitudinous interests.

Sir, there is one passage in the speech of Sir Guy Fleetwood Wilson to which I have already referred which will linger in our memories and will appeal to our imagination long after he has left these shores. While dwelling to the necessity of establishing a gold mint in this country, he made the observation that we are all united by the common bond, that we are fellow-citizens of one great Empire. Sir, no nobler sentiment could have been uttered, for it points to the essential equality of status on the part of His Majesty's Indian subjects; and here may I be permitted to make an appeal, if I am allowed to do so without impertinence or irreverence, to the Hon'ble Members who occupy those benches and who constitute the Government of India, that they may so discharge their exalted duties that this sentiment may be deepened and accentuated and that we may all feel and realise, no matter whether we are Englishmen or Scotchmen or Irishmen or Indians, that we are Britishers; fellow-citizens, participating in the privileges and also in the obligations of a common Empire, the greatest, perhaps the world has ever seen?

Sir, sanitation and education are the watchwords of modern India. They have been accepted by the Government with alacrity and enthusiasm. Sir Guy

Fleetwood Wilson, in the speech to which I have referred, says that they are twins of phenomenal development. So they are. Sanitation is the first of our needs. We must live before we can be educated, and we must be educated in order that we may realise the commonest hygienic needs so indispensable for the purposes of effective sanitation. The interdependence between sanitation and education is recognised by the Government of India, which has made them the concern of a common Department. You, Sir, as the head of the Education and Sanitary Department are responsible for the health and the education of the millions of our fellow-countrymen. I can conceive of no higher duty or more exalted trust, and I may be permitted to add that educated India is watching the operations of your Department with interest and expectancy. Sir, we are grateful to the Government of India for the grants which it has made to the Local Governments in respect of sanitation, education and other matters, and here perhaps, I may be permitted to utter a word of complaint. There has been, perhaps, too great a disposition on the part of the Government to earmark these grants, and the Local Governments, confronted with resolutions and interpellations, often find themselves in the difficult position that they have to refuse reasonable proposals put forward by non-official members on the ground that they are handicapped by the instructions of the Government of India. Sir, I do not for one moment dispute that the Government of India, having made these grants, ought to have a voice in their disposal; but I beg to submit, Sir, that in accordance with the spirit of the great Despatch of the 25th August, 1911, which holds out to us in prospect the boon of provincial autonomy, a greater and larger measure of discretion should be allowed to the Local Governments in the disposal of these funds. Sir, if sanitation and education are the watchwords of the Government of India, they are matters of absorbing interest to the Local Governments. Thus for instance, the Government of Bengal has taken up the question of rural sanitation and of village water-supply with a degree of earnestness and a measure of practical sagacity which have won for that Government the unstinted gratitude of the people. In matters of sanitation and education the policy of the Government of India is the policy of the Local Governments. I, therefore, may be permitted in this Council Chamber to plead for the independence of the Local Governments in these matters: they have to carry out the instructions of the Government of India, varied by local conditions of which they are best cognisant.

Sir, the release of the local cesses for local purposes has been an unspeakable boon to the people and is greatly appreciated by them. In Bengal, we get 25 lakhs a year, which, I understand, is to be devoted to village sanitation and rural water-supply. Thousands and hundreds of thousands of lives are lost every year through such preventible diseases as cholera and malarial fever. Good water-supply, a good system of drainage will go far to protect the people against the ravages of these diseases. The Government of Bengal has already started anti-malarial operations, and with admirable results. I can bear my personal testimony to the success of these operations in one particular area with which I happen to be connected. Sir, if the 25 lakhs of rupees to which I have referred be devoted to the digging and repairing of tanks, taking the average cost of each tank to be Rs.1,000, in the course of four years, we shall have about 10,000 tanks in Bengal, an unspeakable boon to the people in the rural areas.

Sir, the Hon'ble Finance Minister has been pleased to speak in terms of sympathy with local self-government. He says the encouragement and development of local self-government is an object about which all are agreed, and he adds that these grants have been made with a view to strengthening their resources. Sir, I am perfectly certain that these grants will enormously add to the usefulness of local bodies. But, Sir, something more is needed for the encouragement and development of local self-government. With added funds larger powers should be vested in them. I think their constitution ought to be recast; they ought to be reorganised upon a more popular and liberal basis. With greater independence, with larger powers of initiative, with less of official control, these local bodies would be quickened into a new sense of awakened responsibility. I rejoice, Sir, that the recommendations of the Decentralisation Commission have been forwarded to the Secretary of State and are under his consideration. I hope early orders will be passed, and I hope and trust these orders will include the establishment of a Local Government Board in each province. Sir, this is a proposal which was made in the time of Lord Ripon. For some reason or another it was abandoned. I find, on reading through the Report of the Decentralisation Commission, that Mr. Romesh Chandra Dutt made this recommendation. I really hope, Sir, that this part of the recommendations of Mr. Dutt will be accepted. At the present moment the local bodies are supervised by hard-worked Magistrate-Collectors and Commissioners of Divisions. I think, Sir, the organisation of a central body supervising the self-governing institutions will have the effect of co-ordinating their labours, and helping forward their development along normal and natural lines.

Sir, we rejoice to find that the military expenditure is practically at a standstill, a sum of about £552,000 having been added in 1913–14 to the expenditure side over the expenditure of the current year. Sir, it is further expected that as the result of the labours of the Nicholson Committee there will be reductions. But, Sir, there is an ominous note of warning in the speech of the Hon'ble the Finance Minister. He says that a Committee has been appointed to inquire into what he calls the Marine expenditure.

I should like to know what this marine expenditure is. I do hope that this Committee will not make recommendations to add to the contribution which we pay at the present moment to the British Navy. Hon'ble Members will remember the discussion which took place in the English newspapers regarding the alleged inadequate grant which India makes in support of the British Navy. We were reminded of the Dreadnoughts—of the gift of Dreadnoughts made by the Colonies, and we were told that our contribution was below that of the Colonies. That is so, so far as this particular matter is concerned; but in regard to other matters, our contribution has been far in excess of that of the Colonies—and I may add far in excess, in some cases at any rate, of the requirements of justice and fair-play. The India Office—that magnificent pile of buildings which attracts the gaze of the beholder in Whitehall—was built by our money, and its establishment is maintained by us. The Colonial Office is maintained by the Home Government. The Indian Army is maintained on a footing so that it serves the purpose of an Imperial Reserve for which the

Imperial Government does not pay a farthing. In 1899, we sent 10,000 troops to (South) Africa which saved the situation. In the Chinese War we sent an Indian Contingent which did admirable service. Formerly the charges of foreign expeditions in which Indian troops took part—both ordinary and extraordinary—were paid out of the Indian revenues. Happily things have altered for the better now. Lord Morley—then Mr. Morley—speaking in connection with the Sudan War—described this policy as "a policy of melancholy meanness". But, as I have said, there has been an improvement in this direction. The conscience of the British authorities has been stirred to a sense of justice to the financial claims of India. In any case, Sir, I hope and trust, in view of our contributions in the past, and in view of the poverty of our people that no addition will be made in the shape of Marine charges.

The Hon'ble the Finance Minister refers to the improvements in communications as a source of revenue in which the Government of India is interested. Probably those remarks apply to roads; but they might as well hold good in respect of waterways. Sir, these waterways form an important branch of our communications. In a country like ours with its long distances, with its fine and magnificent rivers, the maintenance of waterways in a high state of efficiency I conceive to be one of the greatest duties of Government. Sir, these waterways provide facilities for cheap transport; they help the development of inland trade; they constitute a perennial source of water-supply and thus further the interests of sanitation. Sir, the German Government pays the greatest possible attention to their canals and waterways, notwithstanding their magnificent railways, for the purposes of industrial development. I hold in my hand a book on Modern Germany written by Mr. Barker, who is an authority on German affairs and with your permission, Sir, I will read a short extract from it:

> "Recognising the importance of a cheap transport system, which would bring with it wholesome competition, Germany has steadily extended, enlarged, and improved her natural and artificial waterways, and keeps on extending and improving them year by year, and if a man would devote some years solely to the study of the German waterways, and make the necessary but very extensive and exceedingly laborious calculations, he would probably be able to prove that Germany's industrial success is due chiefly to cheap transport, and especially to the wise development of her waterways."

Well, Sir, we find in paragraph 187 of the Secretary's memorandum that only a sum of 2 and two-thirds lakhs of rupees has been provided for the Madaripur Bheel in the Faridpur district. The provision is wholly inadequate. Many of our rivers—I am speaking of Bengal, and I am sure what is true of Bengal is true of the rest of India—many of our rivers are fast silting up and need dredging. My Hon'ble friend on the left, Maharaja Ranajit Singh, has been urging in the Local Council the need for dredging the Bhagirathi river. The silting up of these rivers is a serious matter, even from the sanitary point of view; as it obstructs drainage and constitutes a menace to the health of the surrounding country. Therefore, Sir, from whatever point of view you choose to view the matter—from the point of view of sanitation, of public convenience or of the development of inland trade—it seems to me that the maintenance of our waterways in a state of the greatest possible efficiency is an Imperial duty of the utmost importance and magnitude; and I desire to press this consideration upon the attention of the Government of India with all the emphasis that I can command.

Sir, we find that the Government of India have made grants of a non-recurring character out of the surplus of this year. I hope, Sir—and I have reason to believe—that that surplus will be recurring. An analysis of the situation fortifies me in this hope. Sir, the railway revenue has of recent years developed a distinct tendency to grow and expand. From 1909 up till now there has been an increase in railway revenue year after year at the annual rate of from $2\frac{1}{2}$ to $3\frac{1}{2}$ million pounds. I cannot help thinking that the Finance Minister has been exceedingly cautious—I was going to say over-cautious—in his estimate. He has actually put the revenue of 1913–14 at 90 lakhs of rupees less than the revenue of this year. My countrymen do not share this pessimistic view. Railway revenue depends upon trade conditions as well as upon social causes working in the bosom of the community. So far as trade conditions are concerned, I am not competent to speak, and I think very few are in a position to make a confident forecast. But so far as these social causes are concerned, I may say this, that the greater the facilities offered by the Railway Administrations the greater the attention paid to the comfort and convenience of railway passengers —especially of the third-class passengers, the greater will be the volume of passenger traffic; and if passenger traffic goes on increasing, the goods traffic is bound to increase too. The one will re-act on the other, and by their mutual interaction strengthen each other. I am therefore optimistic in the view that the railway receipts are likely to grow and expand year by year. And, Sir, if the surplus is a recurring surplus, as I believe it will be, it seems to me that the best, the wisest, the most economical thing for Government to do is, instead of making these non-recurring grants, to revise the provincial settlements and to give the Provincial Governments a larger share in the expanding revenues. This is the view which was urged by Sir William Duke on behalf of the Bengal Government from his place in the local Legislative Council.'

4. *The atmosphere in the Central Legislative Assembly of 1928 can be illustrated by a few excerpts from the general discussion of the Budget on 8 March of that year.* In a large Assembly of over 100 members, the irremovable executive now found itself confronted with a vigorous and hostile Opposition:

MR. R. K. SHANMUKHAM CHETTY (*Salem and Coimbatore cum North Arcot: Non-Muhammadan Rural*): Mr. President, my Honourable friend Mr. Birla made some very serious charges against the Honourable the Finance Member in his speech yesterday. The substance of his charge is this, that the Honourable the Finance Member in presenting to this House the nation's balance sheet has presented it in such a way that if it were a company's balance sheet, the person responsible for that balance sheet would be hauled up before a court of law. My Honourable friend Mr. Birla gave some facts and'figures in support of his contention.

THE HONOURABLE SIR BASIL BLACKETT (*Finance Member*): He mentioned none.

MR R. K. SHANMUKHAM CHETTY: He mentioned at least the accrued

25—P.I.

liability on the Post Office cash certificate bonus. At least that is substantially accepted. Well, Sir, today, in the short time at my disposal, I propose to show that in the Budget that the Honourable the Finance Member has presented he had perpetrated two of the most serious fallacies known to logic, *suppressio veri* and *suggestio falsi*.

SIR WALTER WILLSON (*Associated Chambers of Commerce—Nominated Non-Official*): That is not fallacy.

MR. R. K. SHANMUKHAM CHETTY: I am afraid my Honourable friend has not read logic. In support of my contention I will take into consideration the analysis of the debt position of the Government of India as presented by the Honourable the Finance Member. In the Explanatory Memorandum of the Financial Secretary it is stated at page 14 that:

'in the five years ending the 31st March, 1929, the reduction (that is, in interest charges) is fully 40% and is, among other things, an indication of the extent of the replacement of unproductive by productive debt.'

In the speech of the Honourable the Finance Member, at page 31, he draws attention to the fact that during the five years from the 31st March 1923, the unproductive debt has been reduced by 76 crores. . . . What is the meaning of reducing the unproductive debt? There is no such thing as replacement of unproductive debt by productive debt. (The HONOURABLE SIR BASIL BLACKETT: Why not?) When an unproductive debt has been incurred for certain purposes, until that unproductive debt has been wiped off, it does remain as an unproductive debt. It is absurd to say that 'I have replaced my unproductive debt by productive debt.' Such a statement has absolutely no meaning. My Honourable friend is certainly entitled to utilise the resources in his hands in investing them for productive purposes. I am not finding fault with him for that, but to say that by this means he has reduced the unproductive debt is, to say the least, absolutely misleading. The only way by which you can reduce your unproductive debt is by setting apart a sinking fund for that purpose and paying off that unproductive debt. That is the only way in which an unproductive debt can be reduced; and if that criterion is applied, the unproductive debt during the last 5 years has been reduced to the extent of Rs.22·50 crores and not to the extent of Rs.76 crores. (AN HON. MEMBER: Quite right.) . . . If it is the intention of my Honourable friend, the Finance Member, to give an accurate presentation of the debt position of the Government of India, then it was his duty to show all the obligations of the Government of India on which he has to pay interest. This figure he has given as Rs.107·21 crores on the 31st March 1927, whereas on page 297 of the Finance and Revenue Accounts of the Government of India for 1926–7 I find that this figure is Rs.133·05 crores. Rs.133·05 crores represents the obligations of the Government of India bearing interest. Therefore the total liability of the Government of India in the matter of other obligations is Rs.133 crores and not Rs.107 crores. He has omitted to show Rs.26 crores of the obligations of the Government of India from the debt statement that he presented in his speech. I say that comes under *suppressio veri*.

In paragraph 29 of his speech, speaking about surpluses he says that in future also:

'Substantial savings may be expected to accrue in future, as they have done in the past, under interest on deadweight debt.'

This statement, I submit is *suggestio falsi*, and it is for this reason. My Honourable friend says that there will be a surplus in future years because there will be a substantial reduction in the interest on deadweight charges. I submit that if there has been a substantial reduction in the interest on deadweight debt in the last five years, it is because there have been surpluses, and it is because he has utilised these surpluses in productive enterprises. Therefore, the reduction in interest on deadweight debt was a result of the surpluses and the surpluses were not the result of a reduction in the interest on deadweight debt. I suppose it is too much for the Honourable the Finance Member to understand.

THE HONOURABLE SIR BASIL BLACKETT: I have entirely failed to follow.

MR. R. K. SHANMUKHAM CHETTY: I can explain it to you once more because it is a very serious point. My Honourable friend says in his speech that in future he feels confident there will be a surplus and he gives as one of his reasons for his belief the fact that there would be a substantial saving in the interest on deadweight debt. My point is this. In the past there has been a substantial saving in the interest on deadweight debt because there have been surpluses and these surpluses he has utilised in increasing the productive enterprises. Therefore the savings in interest were a result of the surpluses and the surpluses were not a result of the savings in interest. I hope my Honourable friend the Finance Member has understood my point.

THE HONOURABLE SIR BASIL BLACKETT: No.

MR. R. K. SHANMUKHAM CHETTY: Then I pity him. I am afraid I cannot make myself more intelligible than this.

MR. GAYA PRASAD SINGH (*Muzaffarpur cum Champaran, Non-Muhammadan*): Give him one more chance.

MR. R. K. SHANMUKHAM CHETTY: This is *suggestio falsi*. It suggests as the effect what is the cause. Surpluses are the cause of the reduction of interest and not the effect.

THE HONOURABLE SIR BASIL BLACKETT: What is the cause of the surplus?

MR. R. K. SHANMUKHAM CHETTY: Heavy taxation. I am going presently to prove how you got your surpluses. As I stated the only way by which you can reduce your unproductive debt is to lay aside a sinking fund for the purpose and pay off the unproductive debt.

MR. M. A. JINNAH (*Bombay City, Muhammadan Urban*): It does not require brains to produce a surplus. You have to tax.

MR. R. K. SHANMUKHAM CHETTY: In this connection I would just like to make an observation on the way in which the accounts of the Government are kept in this respect. So far as I have been able to understand the Finance and Revenue Accounts, the Government of India do not keep a separate account of their unproductive debt. They keep an account which shows the total volume of their debt and they have got another account which shows the various items of productive enterprise in which their debts are being utilised. Now from year to year they deduct from their total debt the amount of debt they have invested in productive enterprise and whatever balance remains is called unproductive debt. I submit that is not the proper way of maintaining accounts.

THE HONOURABLE SIR BASIL BLACKETT: Why?

MR. R. K. SHANMUKHAM CHETTY: That does not enable this House to appreciate the real position of the Government of India with regard to unproductive debt. What ought to be done is this. A separate account must be maintained for unproductive debt and the amount that you set apart for sinking fund and the amount that you get by your realised surpluses must be utilised in purchasing off securities and cancelling them. That is the only way of reducing unproductive debt.

THE HONOURABLE SIR BASIL BLACKETT: Why?

MR. R. K. SHANMUKHAM CHETTY: What is the other legitimate source that you have got for reducing unproductive debt? You are not going to utilise the railway depreciation fund to write off your unproductive debt. You are not going to utilise the reduction in cash balances to wipe off your unproductive debt. Surely that does not mean wiping off unproductive debt. I therefore maintain, Sir, that the way in which the debt position has been presented is, to say the least, absolutely misleading.

A speech by H. E. the Commander-in-Chief was followed by the following from Pandit Motilal Nehru:

PANDIT MOTILAL NEHRU (*Cities of the United Provinces, Non-Muhammadan Urban*): Sir, I have listened with great attention to the long expected announcement which has just been made by His Excellency the Commander-in-Chief. I am sorry I have to confess that it leaves me cold. It is to my mind in perfect keeping with the policy to which we owe the Statutory Commission which is now doing wonders in the Madras Presidency. We know what those wonders are. It has entered into an alliance with all the Government Publicity Departments and also with that great new agency, whose worthy representative we have in my friend, Mr. K. C. Roy, in this House. That alliance is for the purpose of throwing dust in the eyes of the world. Sir, I have not the remotest doubt in my own mind that the announcement made this morning is a further step in the same direction. But I wish to tell all whom it may concern that it will no more deceive the public than have the glowing accounts which this mutual admiration society of seven has been issuing from the Madras side. Throughout the very graphic description of the great concessions that have been made to the public demand and especially to the recommendations of the Skeen Committee, we find no real substance. The real thing which we wanted is to be found nowhere. Now, Sir, so far as the recommendations of the Skeen Committee are concerned, I must admit that I am one of those who found little reason to enthuse over them. I had once the honour of being on that Committee, and I may say, without meaning any disrespect and with due deference to my friend Mr. Jinnah, that I felt a sense of relief at having had no hand in those recommendations when I saw them in print after my having retired from the Committee at an earlier stage.

MR. M. A. JINNAH: What do you feel now?

PANDIT MOTILAL NEHRU: I have the same feeling now; the feeling is more enhanced than it was, because even if everything suggested by the Skeen Committee had been given effect to, even if a Sandhurst had been founded in India, we would have been where we were for some generations to come. But that was not to be. The insatiable greed of the Government for domination would not contemplate even at a remote date the contingency of India's standing on her own feet. As far as I have been able to understand His Excellency the Commander-in-Chief and the programme that he has laid before us, it is simply a case of what is usually described as Indianization, at perhaps a brisker pace than it has been in the past. Now, I may say at once that the word 'Indianization' is a word that I hate from the bottom of my heart. I cannot understand that word. What do you mean by Indianizing India? I think His Excellency himself was surprised at the use of the word. The Army is ours; we have to officer our own Army; there is no question of Indianizing there. What we want is to get rid of the Europeanization of the Army (Hear, hear, from the Congress Party benches.) Now, what are the chances of our doing so. No Sandhurst is to be given to India, which means a great variety of propositions. First of all, it will be said that without a Sandhurst of the precise type and of the standard of the real Sandhurst, there can be no proper military education, a proposition which I deny. The next argument is that even the ten cadets that are required for the real Sandhurst are not available. The third ground is that it must take a long time to have such an institution in India. Now, Sir, I submit that not one of these propositions is sound. So far as the dearth of men and cadets in India is concerned, I have no difficulty in saying that it is a calumny on the manhood of India to say that there is any such dearth. (Hear, hear.) During the short period that I was on the Committee, I was convinced that it was not the dearth of men but the want of inclination to get at the proper men suitable for the purpose. What did we find? There were men sent to Sandhurst who were turned back because they could not even follow the language in which the lectures were delivered. And what do we find in this country? Thousands upon thousands of men who certainly are quite able to follow the English language, whoever the professor and whatever the strange tongue that pronounces it. But they were not to be taken. What was the greatest recommendation for selection was whether the father, grandfather or great-grandfather of the candidate had served in the Indian Army. (Laughter from the Congress Party benches.) That was the chief recommendation. However, I think that part of the case will be dealt with by my friend Mr. Jinnah who was on the Committee all through and has certainly superior knowledge to my own from the material that was placed before the Committee. I base my position upon the single circumstance that you have provided nothing for the training of our men whom you can find in any numbers you like, provided you have the inclination to find them. An Indian Sandhurst is not to come into existence! What is to happen? Well, there are some more places for cadets to be thrown open at Woolwich, Cranwell and Sandhurst, and the process of what is called 'Indianization' is to take its own course. Then the question formulated by His Excellency was: 'Perhaps some Members would ask me—what about the future?' He raised India to the position of gods when he said: 'The future is on the lap of India; it lies with India.' What is poor, emasculated, helpless India to do with its teeming millions, with its thousands and thousands of capable, ablebodied and intelligent young men who are ready and willing to join the Army if they were given the chance, unless there is some means of training provided for them, unless they are admitted on their own merits and not on the merits or demerits of their fathers and grandfathers? Sir, the whole thing is that there is no intention of putting India on her feet at an early date. That is the whole truth of the matter. However sugar-coated the announcement may be, however tempting the offer of admission into Woolwich, Cranwell and Sandhurst, the fact remains that no substantive advance has been made towards giving us a national army in the sense of its being officered by Indians.

Now coming to the question of expense of founding training schools and colleges, I say that if we can afford over 50 crores of rupees every year for the normal expenses of keeping up this large army, it is sheer hypocrisy to say that we cannot afford a quarter of that amount which I have no doubt will suffice to provide military schools and colleges all over the country. In order to meet our annual requirements we must find the 50 crores, but we can find no money for these training colleges. I submit that, if His Excellency and Commander-in-Chief were really to turn his attention to the military budget, he will find in that very budget enough funds to devote to purposes of training. However, as I have said elsewhere and here, I see no sign whatever in British statesmen of a real desire to give India what by word of mouth they say they intend to give. There is no real desire, and unless there is that real desire, India cannot progress.

I was rather amused at certain parallels drawn by His Excellency. One of them was that the Soviet Budget was much larger than the Indian Budget, that it had increased by 50%. I have recently been in Soviet Russia, and I know why they are increasing their military budget, at least the reason which they gave me. They are living in perpetual danger of England provoking a war with them. (Laughter from the Treasury Benches.) It is very easy to laugh, but I think many of those who laugh have not been admitted into the confidence of the War Office and know nothing about what the designs of the War Office are. What a comparison this is. What is the army in Russia? It is a national army. It is the army of Russian peasants officered by Russians. Any amount of expenditure in face of a common danger will not be grudged. What is our army? I have not the slightest hesitation in saying that our army is a mercenary army employed by foreigners to put down their own countrymen, and to keep them under foreign heels. Surely no self-respecting nation will without compulsion contemplate such a contingency as having to pay for a mercenary army in order to remain under control by an alien Government.

Then His Excellency said that some of the Indian soliders who were sent to China made large remittances home. That again was a very interesting piece of information to give. Where did these remittances come from? Was it the savings from their salaries, or was it loot which they were allowed to make from the poor Chinese? If it was . . .

THE HONOURABLE SIR BASIL BLACKETT: The savings of their salaries, Sir.

PANDIT MOTILAL NEHRU: What about their savings in India then? Why should they be able to save money in China, in a foreign country and not in India?

His Excellency the Commander-in-Chief: I do not know why; but I can assure you they did save.

Pandit Motilal Nehru: I am sure they did; but probably they were let loose upon the Chinese who . . . (Cries of: 'Withdraw' from the Government Benches). I am not going to withdraw. I repeat a thousand times that our soldiers were not used . . . (Cries of: 'Order' and 'Withdraw'.) You may shout yourselves hoarse. I will not withdraw. I say that our soldiers were not used for the honourable purposes for which a soldier should be used. (Cries of: 'Hear, hear' from the Congress Party benches.) They were used in order to humiliate the nationals of another country who wanted to assert their independence against . . .

Mr. G. M. Young: (Army Secretary): You said they looted.

Pandit Motilal Nehru: You exacted from them a duty which, if they had been independent, they would have refused to perform.

The Honourable Sir Basil Blackett: A lie.

Pandit Motilal Nehru: Am I to substantiate what is human nature to my learned friends over there? I say it is human nature and I repeat it a thousand times over in spite of all the noise that has been made on the other side.

The Honourable Sir Basil Blackett: I say it is a foul slander.

Pandit Motilal Nehru: Then you are so full of animal nature that you have no idea of what human nature is or ought to be. It is nothing but animal nature which prompted the sending of these troops there in spite of the protest we made in India. However, Sir, leaving that alone, it is no consolation to any Indian that his countrymen who were soldiers sent to China were able to make remittances home from China.

Then His Excellency said that we will get advance in Indianization—that is his word again—in proportion to the advance in responsible government. Now, what are the steps that are being taken for any substantial advance in responsible government? There is the Statutory Commission; as I said, it is assiduously busy in circulating glowing accounts of its own proceedings and in suppressing the real kind of reception that they are having. And what will they do? They have now given out the procedure which they mean to follow. That is a procedure, Sir, which we of the Congress Party at any rate will not submit to for a single moment. How is responsible government to be granted to India? The Army is kept apart. The Army is no part of responsible government. There is a separate Committee to go into the question of the Indian States. They are not in India. And yet any responsible government is to be granted by some miracle by this Statutory Commission to India. It is not pretended that responsible government is to be given; it is only a progressive advance that is going to be made; just as His Excellency the Commander-in-Chief has said increasing responsibility in the Army, corresponding to progressive responsibility in government . . .

Lala Lajpat Rai (Jullunder Divison; Non-Muhammadan): There is nothing to prevent them saying that we should go back on the existing reforms.

Pandit Motilal Nehru: I thought you said going back without doing anything; I am sure they will go back after doing some mischief. However, Sir, this is an age-long affair. There have been Empires before this which have done the same thing. They have ignored the lessons of history, and the British Empire is doing the same. I will not say more on this occasion but sit down after again repeating the warning that the day of reckoning is not very far.

5. *An illustration may be taken from independent India. In the Provisional Parliament on 5 March 1952* (just prior to the summoning of the newly elected House of the People) the Finance Minister replied to the debate on the Finance Bill. The following extract from the debates will perhaps show that the House was lively without being hostile to the Government:

SHRI C. D. DESHMUKH: The first point that I wish to deal with is that of cotton prices, especially in Berar. From the speech made by Dr. Deshmukh, the House might gather the impression that cotton prices were threatening to tumble below the floor levels that have been fixed. That actually is not the case. From time to time the ceiling has been raised during the last two years, according to the classification and gradation of cottons, in order to encourage the cultivation of cotton, and control was exercised not only for the purpose of keeping down the price of cloth, but also for safeguarding the interests of the cultivator, so that he could obtain the proper price for certain specific genuine qualities of the cottons that he was encouraged to grow. It is true that there has been a recession in the world prices of cotton, just as there has been a recession in the prices of other raw materials and commodities, and in many cases the spot market prices are below the ceiling. But the point that I wish to make is that in no case have the prices fallen to or anywhere near the floor, and as I shall show you, the current price is still well above the floor prices . . .

SHRI SONDHI: Much below the ceiling.

SHRI C. D. DESHMUKH: That is not the relevant consideration here for the purposes of the debate. I cannot pretend to be sorry that they are below the ceiling. The ceiling is the maximum.

SHRI SONDHI: That is the point we raised.

SHRI C. D. DESHMUKH: The point raised, as I understood it, was that they were tumbling and that the time had come when Government should do something about it, which was a circumlocutory way of saying that there should be a floor.

To return to the figures which I was proposing to give, Sir, for Jerila, the ceiling is 820 and the floor is 495 and the latest available quotations will run between 700 to 880. Then Vijay: the ceiling is 925, the floor is 565 and prices are slightly below the ceilings in 920. Then C.P. Desi; here there is no floor. Gaorani 990, floor is 625 and present price is around about 900 and so on. So the ceilings and floor prices are fixed in terms of section 3 of the Cotton Control Order, 1950, and in terms of a Notification and a Press Note issued on 24 August 1946. Government have given an assurance in the following terms:

'When the prices are at the floor rates for any or all of the descriptions for which such rates are specified in the Schedule annexed to the said general permission, the Government of India undertake to buy such cotton of grade and staples, specified for those rates in Bombay on terms set out in the notes appended to the said Schedule and at equivalent prices elsewhere.'

In terms of this undertaking Government have actually purchased cotton, as, for instance, in 1943 and in 1945, and Government stand committed to this undertaking and will be closely watching the situation.

Now, one reason why prices are falling, apart from a sympathetic fall together with other commodity prices is that the mills seem to be reluctant to lift their quotas. This has been brought to our notice, but it is not so very easy to think of a remedy. If you were to say: 'Well, penalize the mills; they would forfeit their quota in case they do not lift it within a stipulated time', the result might be that the mills might cease to work for lack of cotton. That is not going to help the cotton grower. It would certainly castigate the millowner but does not improve the position. So instead of penalizing, we are considering whether we should not try admonition and the Textile Commission has been instructed to try and persuade the mills to lift their quotas within a stated period, that is to say, in effect to stagger their purchases instead of waiting till the end of the half-year and perhaps the prices might have gone down further.

All these developments are constantly being brought to the notice of Government by the interests concerned. One Dr. Deshmukh raised a point; there is another Deshmukh who has written to the Commerce and Industry Ministry at Berar and a third Deshmukh is trying to explain the situation. So you can see how alert and interested the Deshmukhs are to deal with this problem.

MR. DEPUTY SPEAKER:
Brahmarpanam Brahma havir
Brahmagnau Brahmna hutam.
Brahmaiva tena gantavyam
Brahma-Karma-samadhina.

[The offering-spoon is Brahma (the Omnipresent God), the oblation is Brahma, it is offered to the fire that is Brahma; through all these deeds done for Brahma, it is to reach the Brahma.]

SHRI KAMATH: Om Shantih, Shantih, Shantih.

SHRI C. D. DESHMUKH: From this incantation it is time for me to pass from cotton to agriculturists about which Chaudhuri Ranbir Singh spoke. He raised some fundamental issues, that is to say, justice and equality as between the town dweller and the village dweller. Now, that is an issue on which one could not hope to throw light in the course of an answer to a debate of this kind. It is my impression that the denizen of the rural areas has not done so badly during the last few years. Although I have no statistical evidence, I should imagine that at least the producer is better off relatively than the middle-class man in the urban areas.

SHRI ALEXANDER (*Travancore-Cochin*): What about the producer of foodgrains?

SHRI C. D. DESHMUKH: That is precisely the person I referred to. He has not done so badly.

SHRI BHARATI (*Madras*): That is not correct.

SHRI C. D. DESHMUKH: That can be proved. In 1947, for instance, in my district, the grower was getting Rs.125 per kandy for his paddy. In six months' time, he started getting Rs.185.

SHRI BHARATI: What about the cost of production?

SHRI C. D. DESHMUKH: In six months, there was no change in the cost of production. It was just a windfall due to decontrol. Apart from the jute grower, I cannot think of anyone else who has received that kind of accretion to his profits. I think that by and large, till very recently, the grower of food and cash crops has not been too badly off. The particular point of taxation to which Ch. Ranbir Singh referred is a matter not within the field of the Central Government. He referred to land revenue and the absence of any exempted minimum of income. That again involves the question of agricultural income-tax. I dare say that when land revenue is placed on a more uniform footing in the country, that is to say, when it is replaced by an agricultural income-tax, there might emerge some such minimum as is contemplated by the hon. Member. But, in any case, as I said, so far as the Central Government is concerned, there is nothing that one can do about it. Since most of the other taxes are indirect taxes and since the purchases made by the rural population are not so considerable as compared with the purchases made by the inhabitants of urban areas, I do not think the average agriculturist bears a disproportionately large share of the general taxation in the country.

I next come to the vexed question of subsidies. I can assure the hon. Member that any tears that we may have shed were not crocodile tears. Nor was there any intention to juggle with figures.

SHRI SONDHI: Were there any tears at all?

SHRI VENKATARAMAN: Yes.

SHRI C. D. DESHMUKH: There were plenty of figures.

SHRI VENKATARAMAN: He was asking about tears.

SHRI C. D. DESHMUKH: The point made by the hon. Member was that what was said about the time-lag as between the curve of wholesale price indices and the cost of living indices is not true. On the other hand, he seemed to imply that the opposite was the case. That, I fail to understand. It is possible that there is no parallelism after a time-lag; that is to say, that the other curve does not follow the first one after an interval of three months. But, since some of the items are common to both the indices to the extent to which the prices of those articles are affected, the shape of the curve is bound to be affected. That was the only point which it was my intention to make. The weightage that has been given to food articles is not as high as 50 or 60, but is nearer 33. Food articles include various other things besides cereals. If the hon. Member is interested, I can show him the working of the Chief of the Economic Division in the Planning Commission, on whose authority I quoted the figure the other day of three per cent. I said three points. I am afraid it is wrong. It is three per cent increase. So, we have these two figures that between 1948 and December 1951 there has been an increase of ten per cent in the cost of living indices.

Secondly, if the subsidies are taken away, the middle class representative may have to pay three per cent more and his cost of living may go up by three per cent. The hon. Member quoted certain figures to show what the cost of the cereals would be if no subsidy were given. That brings out the point that I have made, that even with the existing subsidy we cannot hold the situation because of the progressively increasing prices of imported foodgrains. That costs us more and the freight on it is greater. Therefore, the work that was done by a subsidy of say 35 crores one year would require 60 crores next year and perhaps 90 crores: that was the maximum figure that we calculated. However sympathetic one may be—and one is genuinely so to the middle classes—our Budget just cannot bear the impact of a figure of that dimension when it is devoted just to subsidies, namely a figure of 90 crores. All that we could at one time afford was 25 crores of which about 10 or 12 crores will be retained in any case. The point that I made the other day was that the sum of 15 crores is not going to make such a material difference to the population affected.

On the other hand, there are certain indications which could be regarded as hopeful by the middle classes, and that is, if we can find additional money for our development projects, it will mean additional employment for the representatives of what we recognise as the middle classes. It is not strictly true to say that only one person in a middle class family works. Actually, I referred to the figures and I find that 1·68 person works.

SHRI VENKATARAMAN: Is that in the middle class family budget report prepared by Mr. Subramaniam of the Government of India? A statistical enquiry has been conducted by the Government. A statistician went into the middle class family budgets all over India and his figure was 1·68 for the working classes and 1 or less for the middle classes.

SHRI C. D. DESHMUKH: I am quoting from 'War on Middle Classes: An Enquiry into the Effects of War-time Inflation on Middle Classes in Bombay City,' by J. J. Anjaria.

SHRI VENKATARAMAN: Why not refer to your own statistician?

SHRI C. D. DESHMUKH: He is one of our statisticians.

SHRI VENKATARAMAN: The Government appointed a statistician to go into the question and Government has conducted an enquiry into the cost of living of the middle classes. The report is there before the Government.

PROF. K. T. SHAH (Bihar): May I ask what is the definition of 'middle class'?

SHRI TYAGI: Unemployed.

SHRI C. D. DESHMUKH: That is trenching into the time that has been allotted to me, but, I have no doubt that if one goes through this pamphlet he can find out what the definition of 'middle class' is. Anyway, if we do not know the definition, it is no use discussing the subject. If we understand something in common by 'middle class' . . .

PROF. K. T. SHAH: It is not a question of not knowing the definition. It is a question of knowing what you have adopted as the middle class.

MR. DEPUTY SPEAKER: It is a question of categories. Anyhow, it will be opening a new chapter.

SHRI C. D. DESHMUKH: I do not lay any great stress on this point that it is 1·68. It may be one and a half. All I am saying is that there is a tendency for greater employment being available as a result of the development plans undertaken by the Centre and the State Governments. And the condition of the middle-classes would be very much worse if these development plans were not to be there. For the rest they could only be helped by our general efforts to increase production and to counter inflation by monetary and fiscal and other means rather than by these somewhat artificial means of subsidising living.

Then there was another point made by the hon. Member and that is that it might be practicable to give a subsidy to people whose income was Rs.300 per mensem and below. Now, that means that the subsidy should be given to 90 per cent of the people instead of to 100 per cent. It does not really make any difference in this country, in a country where incomes are so low. That really is no solution of the problem. It is after giving anxious thought to all these considerations that we came to the conclusion in issue. It is not as if the middle-class has been forgotten entirely and throughout. After all, take the history of the income-tax over the last few years. In 1947 the taxable minimum was raised from Rs.2,000 to Rs.2,500. In 1948 it was raised to Rs.3,000 and in 1949 the minimum for a Hindu undivided family about which we might hear a little more, was raised from Rs.3,000 to Rs.5,000.

PANDIT THAKUR DAS BHARGAVA: Their minimum is about Rs.900.

SHRI C. D. DESHMUKH: The hon. Member will have an opportunity to say a lot about the Hindu undivided family. Well then, in 1950, the taxable income for a person within the Hindu divided family was raised from Rs.3,000 to Rs.3,600 and for the Hindu undivided family to Rs.7,200. And then the rate of income-tax on the slab between Rs.10,000 and Rs.15,000 was reduced from five annas to four annas. Now, it may be said that these are small mercies: but these are all that one could afford from time to time. I give this information in order to prove that it is not out of neglect that a larger extent of relief is not available to the middle-classes.

SHRI SONDHI: Does it compare favourably with the price index?

SHRI C. D. DESHMUKH: We have not tried to establish any correlation between price indices and the income-tax relief; but I do believe, Sir, that if we get the better of inflation, we shall have taken some effective step towards helping the middle classes both in reducing the cost of living and in making more money available for development expenditure.

Then there was the question of food self-sufficiency. An attractive scheme was put forward by an hon. Member who at one time had a great deal to do with food production, and I find tube-wells cannot be dug in all parts of the country for they depend on subsoil water levels. Neither the machinery nor the equipment nor the technical personnel is available for constructing 30,000 tube-wells in six months—or nine months—I forget which (an Hon. Member: Six months). And, then, at present the experiment is being carried on for sinking 1,000 tube-wells in the Punjab, U.P. and Bihar and it will take about two years to complete these. Therefore, 30,000 tube-wells will take 30 times two, that is, 60 years, and the cost will be about 100 crores. I am not referring to the cost if the thing is worth doing. If the money can be found and if some one were to say you can complete this thing in six months and you have a million tons waiting for you, well, I for my part, would take the risk, because it is the quickest form of return to projects that anyone would turn to. But, alas, that is not the case.

SHRI SONDHI: But he himself offered his services.

SHRI C. D. DESHMUKH: That is not enough. One has to consider the circumstances of the case. Actually the water table is not considered high enough or plentiful enough to sustain 30,000 tube-wells. Anyway, it will require a great deal of elaborate surveying before we can come to the conclusion that one could embark upon the construction of so many tube-wells. Otherwise it might become one of those muddles about which we might be asked to start an enquiry, if we give a contract for 30,000 tube-wells in our excessive enthusiasm. I am told, however, that the estimated cost of one tube-well including equipments is Rs.60,000. Therefore, 30,000 will cost Rs.180 crores or 378 million dollars and not 160 million dollars—I think that was the figure that the hon. Member gave. And the average output per tube-well is estimated at 60 tons per year and therefore, 30,000 tube-wells will give 1·8 million tons and not four million tons. Therefore there is a great deal of difference when you examine it prosaically between the scheme put forward by the hon. Member and the facts as they are. But taking his points in general, we are prepared to agree that if one could concentrate within the limits of one's resources, on minor works of irrigation and so on, one could get the quickest return and both the Planning Commission and the State Governments as well as the Ministry of Food and Agriculture are very well seized of the importance of his point.

Then coming to the next few less important points like prohibition (SHRI KAMATH: Less important? It is very important). I will not enter into an elaborate defence of what is being done, but by and large, we are committed to bringing about prohibition some time and the whole question is, what exactly is the objective diagnosis on which our experiments are based, and I myself would be inclined to agree with the hon. Member that if one finds as a result of experience that one has taken a premature step, that certain very serious sociological consequences have come about, then one ought to review the situation and see if some other step could be taken or if propaganda could be strengthened or if in the last resort, one should draw back. One cannot make a general statement. Apart from stating these principles, each case would have to be examined on its own merits. I understand—I have not seen the report, but I am prepared to accept the hon. Member's statement—that in Madhya Pradesh they seem to have come to the conclusion that they perhaps acted in too much of a hurry. That in a sense touches me, because the first prohibition experiment was in my time when I was Secretary in the separate Revenue Department (SHRI KAMATH: Yes.) and I hope it is not there that the failure has been made.

SHRI KAMATH: May I know whether the other State Governments have been advised to review and report to the Centre, following the example of Madhya Pradesh?

SHRI C. D. DESHMUKH: I think it is an important matter and the final draft of the Planning Commission is getting ready. We have not yet finalised it. We have had discussions with various people interested in the question and I am not sure if we have heard the Chairman of the Committee which went into this matter in Madhya Pradesh. We were trying to arrange an interview with him. I can assure the hon. Member that we are considering this point, though categorically the reply to the question is that no directive has gone from the Central Government so far.

DR. DESHMUKH: Are there similar Committees in Bombay and Madras?

SHRI C. D. DESHMUKH: There is a Committee in Bombay but I would not call it a similar Committee. Its terms of reference differ slightly.

MR. DEPUTY SPEAKER: A Committee was appointed in Madras also.

SHRI C. D. DESHMUKH: That was many years ago. I do not know what the findings and results of that Committee are.

Then there is the question of the election which crops up again and again. I am informed that it is wrong to say that in U.P. and Madhya Pradesh the Election Commissioner's instructions were not observed. No ballot boxes used by any State were unapproved by the Election Commission. A ballot box which is not closed and sealed properly can of course be opened with a hair pin or any other pin. But merely because a ballot box is tamperable one need not necessarily draw the conclusion that in all cases over whole States the boxes were tampered with.

SHRI KAMATH: Nobody says that.

SHRI SONDHI: That is not the allegation.

PANDIT KUNZRU: May I know whether the Election Commission has sent for the Presiding Officers and asked them how they sealed their boxes as soon as the voting was over?

SHRI C. D. DESHMUKH: I could not say what action the Election Commission has taken. This is the information that I have received from him.

SHRI KAMATH: In all the States other than U.P. and Madhya Pradesh the ballot boxes used were manufactured by Godrej or Allwyn. In these two States the boxes were manufactured locally.

SHRI C. D. DESHMUKH: I did not deny that, but that does not necessarily mean that they were tamperable.

MR. DEPUTY SPEAKER: Were they not steel boxes? In Madras wooden boxes or plywood ones were used and no such thing happened. I was myself a candidate.

SHRI KAMATH: In Madhya Pradesh the boxes used were cottage industry products.

SHRI C. D. DESHMUKH: I am sorry I shall not be able to throw any more light.

THE MINISTER OF WORKS, PRODUCTION AND SUPPLY (SHRI GADGIL): Veritable Pandora's box!

SHRI KAMATH: Where is Pandora?

SHRI C. D. DESHMUKH: There was the question of aerodromes. I had some notes here, which I have lost, showing the provision made in the next year's Budget. There is provision in accordance with a programme for the improvement of aerodromes, especially in regard to lighting. That matter is receiving attention.

Then there was some reference to smuggling of goods from Pondicherry,

Goa and so on. Questions have been frequently asked in the House and replies given as to what precautions are taken from time to time, but if the conclusion is that because there is smuggling we should reduce the import duties and allow these goods in, I do not think that that conclusion is right. Even if you remove all duties there are people who would be risking their lives or self-respect for bringing the goods in, if there is money in it.

Lastly, there was reference to death-bed bequests, parting kicks, swan song by an hon. Member who is not here.

SHRI NAZIRUDDIN AHMAD: I am here.

SHRI C. D. DESHMUKH: Those also are in very general terms, that one has done nothing about corruption, blackmarketing or one has not solved the question of controls, etc. These questions have been discussed very frequently on the floor of this House and I am inclined to think that there is a far greater awareness now and consequently a far greater degree of success in dealing with both corruption and blackmarketing, and to the extent to which it flourished in money supply, action has been taken to reduce money supply to them. Today you will find that our money supply in contrast to many other countries in the world is 100 crores down. I think gradually we are getting the better of these problems.

Sir, I have tried to meet the criticisms made by hon. Members and would now commend my motion to the House.

MR. DEPUTY SPEAKER: The question is:

'That the Bill to continue for the financial year 1952–53 the existing rates of income-tax and super-tax and additional duties of customs and excise, and to provide for the discontinuance of the duty on salt for the said year, be taken into consideration.'

The motion was adopted.

APPENDIX III

DATES OF SESSIONS (See p. 129)

	Date of Commence-ment	Date of Termination	Actual No. of days on which House sat	
			Per Session	Per Annum
First Legislative Assembly				
First Session	3.2.1921	29.3.1921	28	43
Second Session	1.9.1921	30.9.1921	15	
Third Session	10.1.1922	28.3.1922	44	59
	5.9.1922	26.9.1922	15	
	15.1.1923	27.3.1923	51	68
	2.7.1923	28.7.1923	17	
Second Legislative Assembly				
First Session	30.1.1924	25.3.1924	38	60
	27.5.1924	11.6.1924	8	
	3.9.1924	24.9.1924	14	
Second Session	20.1.1925	24.3.1925	41	59
Third Session	20.8.1925	17.9.1925	18	
Fourth Session	20.1.1926	25.3.1926	39	51
Fifth Session	17.8.1926	2.9.1926	12	
Third Legislative Assembly				
First Session	19.1.1927	28.3.1927	45	65
	18.8.1927	20.9.1927	20	
Second Session	1.2.1928	27.3.1928	36	53
Third Session	4.9.1928	25.9.1928	17	
Fourth Session	28.1.1929	12.4.1929	45	62
Fifth Session	2.9.1929	26.9.1929	17	
Sixth Session	20.1.1930	31.3.1930	46	56
Seventh Session	7.7.1930	18.7.1930	10	
Fourth Legislative Assembly				
First Session	14.1.1931	1.4.1931	51	84
Second Session	7.9.1931	3.10.1931	20	
	4.11.1931	20.11.1931	13	
Third Session	25.1.1932	6.4.1932	46	88
Fourth Session	5.9.1932	30.9.1932	19	
	7.11.1932	15.12.1932	23	
Fifth Session	1.2.1933	12.4.1933	48	97
Sixth Session	22.8.1933	21.9.1933	23	
	20.11.1933	22.12.1933	26	
Seventh Session	24.1.1934	21.4.1934	61	92
Eighth Session	16.7.1934	31.8.1934	31	
Fifth Legislative Assembly				
First Session	21.1.1935	9.4.1935	49	68
Second Session	2.9.1935	26.9.1935	19	
Third Session	3.2.1936	23.4.1936	52	87
Fourth Session	31.8.1936	16.10.1936	35	
Fifth Session	25.1.1937	3.4.1937	44	79
Sixth Session	23.8.1937	7.10.1937	35	

	Date of Commencement	Date of Termination	Actual No. of days on which House sat	
			Per Session	Per Annum
Fifth Legislative Assembly—continued				
Seventh Session . .	31.1.1938	12.4.1938	45 ⎱	
Eighth Session . .	8.8.1938	20.9.1938	30 ⎰	96
	10.11.1938	12.12.1938	21	
Ninth Session . .	3.2.1939	15.4.1939	47 ⎱	
Tenth Session . .	30.8.1939	22.9.1939	15 ⎰	62
Eleventh Session . .	6.2.1940	6.4.1940	37 ⎱	
Twelfth Session . .	5.11.1940	27.11.1940	16 ⎰	53
Thirteenth Session .	11.2.1941	1.4.1941	34 ⎱	
Fourteenth Session .	27.10.1941	18.11.1941	14 ⎰	48
Fifteenth Session . .	11.2.1942	2.4.1942	32 ⎱	
Sixteenth Session . .	14.9.1942	24.9.1942	9 ⎰	41
Seventeenth Session .	10.2.1943	2.4.1943	36 ⎱	
Eighteenth Session .	26.7.1943	25.8.1943	23 ⎰	69
Nineteenth Session .	8.11.1943	19.11.1943	10	
Twentieth Session .	7.2.1944	5.4.1944	37 ⎱	
Twenty-first Session .	1.11.1944	21.11.1944	15 ⎰	52
Twenty-second Session .	8.2.1945	12.4.1945	43	43
Sixth Legislative Assembly				
First Session . .	21.1.1946	18.4.1946	60 ⎱	
Second Session . .	28.10.1946	18.11.1946	16 ⎰	76
Third Session . .	3.2.1947	12.4.1947	47	
Dominion Legislature— Constituent Assembly (Legislative)				68
First Session . .	17.11.1947	12.12.1947	21	
Second Session . .	28.1.1948	9.4.1948	52 ⎱	
Third Session . .	9.8.1948	7.9.1948	22 ⎰	74
Fourth Session . .	1.2.1949	9.4.1949	51	
Fifth Session . .	5.10.1949	6.10.1949	2 ⎱	75
Sixth Session . .	28.11.1949	24.12.1949	22 ⎰	
Provisional Parliament				
First Session . .	28.1.1950	20.4.1950	60 ⎱	
Second Session . .	31.7.1950	14.8.1950	12 ⎰	101
Third Session . .	14.11.1950	22.12.1950	29	
	5.2.1951	9.6.1951	99 ⎱	
Fourth Session . .	6.8.1951	16.10.1951	51 ⎰	150
Fifth Session . .	5.2.1952	5.3.1952	23	
House of the People				
First Session . .	13.5.1952	12.8.1952	66	· 125
Second Session . .	5.11.1952	20.12.1952	36	
Third Session . .	11.2.1953	15.5.1953	72 ⎱	
Fourth Session . .	3.8.1953	18.9.1953	35 ⎰	137
Fifth Session . .	16.11.1953	24.12.1953	30	
Sixth Session . .	15.2.1954	21.5.1954	74 ⎱	
Seventh Session . .	23.8.1954	30.9.1954	31 ⎰	137
Eighth Session . .	15.11.1954	24.12.1954	32	
Ninth Session . .	21.2.1955	7.5.1955	58 ⎱	
Tenth Session . .	25.7.1955	1.10.1955	54 ⎰	137
Eleventh Session . .	21.11.1955	23.12.1955	25	

APPENDIX IV (See p. 105)

FREQUENCY OF DIVISIONS AND VOTING FIGURES

| | Record of Divisions | |
	Date	Vote
Constituent Assembly (*Legislative*) Six Sessions (1947–49)	Nil	
Provisional Parliament 1st Session, 28 Jan.–20 April 1950 . .	Nil	
2nd Session, 31 July–14 Aug. 1950 . .	Nil	
3rd Session, (1st part) 14 Nov.–22 Dec. 1950 .	Nil	
	15.3.51	74:23
	1.5.51	84:34
	31.5.51	246:14
	1.6.51	243:5
	1.6.51	228:19
	1.6.51	239:6
	1.6.51	238:7
	1.6.51	238:7
	2.6.51	229:7
3rd Session (2nd part), 5 Feb.–9 June 1951 .	2.6.51	225:7
	2.6.51	228:8
	2.6.51	229:8
	2.6.51	227:7
	2.6.51	232:6
	2.6.51	232:9
	2.6.51	234:12
	2.6.51	234:12
	2.6.51	228:20
	22.8.51	89:13
	29.8.51	91:25
4th Session, 6 Aug.–16 Oct. 1951 . . .	22.9.51	63:34
	1.10.51	110:28
	3.10.51	95:31
5th Session, 5 Feb.–5 Mar. 1952 . . .	Nil	
House of the People		
	15.5.52	394:55
	6.6.52	257:74
	11.6.52	303:65
	12.6.52	296:72
	18.6.52	280:72
	25.6.52	227:68
	9.7.52	279:84
1st Session, 13 May–12 Aug. 1952 . .	10.7.52	254:89
	10.7.52	262:88
	12.7.52	261:77
	23.7.52	312:68
	4.8.52	211:58
	6.8.52	186:55
	6.8.52	296:61

	Record of Divisions	
	Date	Vote
House of the People—continued		
	15.11.52	216:59
	27.11.52	149:41
	3.12.52	156:51
2nd Session, 5 Nov.–20 Dec. 1952 . .	4.12.52	152:42
	15.12.52	366:26
	15.12.52	364:24
	15.12.52	351:23
	19.12.52	286:62
	18.2.53	284:64
	27.2.53	255:74
	12.3.53	208:60
	13.3.53	129:55
3rd Session, 11 Feb.–15 May 1953 . .	17.3.53	278:49
	10.4.53	174:52
	30.4.53	186:49
	12.5.53	212:64
	12.5.53	214:60
4th Session, 3 Aug.–18 Sept. 1953 . . .	26.8.53	246:54
	3.9.53	195:51
	18.11.53	118:12
	30.11.53	186:45
5th Session, 16 Nov.–24 Dec. 1953 . .	4.12.53	115:29
	17.12.53	181:27
	23.12.53	286:91
	18.2.54	259:66
	26.2.54	147:39
	9.3.54	168:47
6th Session, 15 Feb.–21 May 1954. . .	12.3.54	226:67
	12.3.54	117:23
	13.3.54	185:49
	30.4.54	117:34
	14.5.54	208:42
	7.9.54	118:106
	13.9.54	294:43
	15.9.54	161:47
7th Session 23 Aug.–30 Sept. 1954 . .	23.9.54	283:33
	23.9.54	288:35
	23.9.54	286:33
	24.9.54	68:37
	19.11.54	154:35
	22.11.54	141:38
	23.11.54	146:36
8th Session 15 Nov.–24 Dec. 1954 . . .	30.11.54	172:28
	7.12.54	132:39
	8.12.54	133:31
	13.12.54	135:38
	15.3.55	322:9
	2.4.55	95:12
	12.4.55	280:16
	12.4.55	297:8
9th Session 21 Feb.—7 May 1955 . .	12.4.55	301:9
	12.4.55	295:8
	12.4.55	300:7
	12.4.55	302:5
	4.5.55	150:20

Bill No. 64 of 1953

THE PRESS (OBJECTIONABLE MATTER) AMENDMENT BILL, 1953

(As introduced in the House of the People)

A

BILL

to amend the Press (Objectionable Matter) Act, 1951.

Be it enacted by Parliament as follows:—

1. Short title.—This Act may be called the Press (Objectionable Matter) Amendment Act, 1953.

2. Amendment of section 1, Act LVI of 1951.—In section 1 of the Press (Objectionable Matter) Act, 1951 (hereinafter referred to as the principal Act), in sub-section (*3*), for the words 'two years' the words 'four years' shall be substituted.

3. Amendment of section 2, Act LVI of 1951.—In section 2 of the principal Act, in clause (*k*), the following words shall be inserted at the end, namely:

'or any news-sheet which does not contain the name of the printer and the publisher.'

4. Amendment of section 20, Act LVI of 1951.—In section 20 of the principal Act,

(*a*) in sub-section (*3*), for the words 'a list of persons', the words 'a list for the entire State of persons' shall be substituted;

(*b*) after sub-section (*4*), the following sub-section shall be inserted, namely:

'(*4A*) In any inquiry under this section, it is the duty of the jury to decide whether any newspaper, news-sheet, book or other document placed before it contains any objectionable matter and it is the duty of the Sessions Judge to decide whether there are sufficient grounds for making an order for the demanding of security or for directing any security which has been deposited or any part thereof to be forfeited to the Government or for directing further security to be deposited.'

5. Amendment of section 23, Act LVI of 1951.—In section 23 of the principal Act, for the words and figures 'Any person against whom an order is passed by a Sessions Judge under section 4, section 5, section 7 or section 8 may, within sixty days of the date of such order, prefer an appeal to the High Court,' the following shall be substituted, namely:

'The competent authority or any other person aggrieved by an order passed by a Sessions Judge under section 4, section 5, section 7 or section 8 may, within sixty days of the date of such order, prefer an appeal to the High Court,'.

6. Amendment of section 29, Act LVI of 1951.—In section 29 of the principal Act, in sub-section (2), the words 'in the territories to which this Act extends' shall be inserted at the end.

STATEMENT OF OBJECTS AND REASONS

The Press (Objectionable Matter) Act is due to expire on the 31st January, 1954. In view of the fact that the Press Commission will, among other things, examine the existing Press legislation and make recommendations relating thereto, it is proposed to defer a detailed examination of the issues involved until after the Press Commission's recommendations have been received. At the same time, Government feel that it would be undesirable to allow the Act to lapse. The Bill seeks to extend the life of the Act by two years. Opportunity is being taken to make certain minor amendments at the same time.

NEW DELHI;
The 10*th December*, 1953.   K. N. KATJU.

ANNEXURE

EXTRACTS FROM THE PRESS (OBJECTIONABLE MATTER) ACT, 1951
(LVI OF 1951).

* * * *

1. Short title, extent and commencement.—(1) This Act may be called the Press (Objectionable Matter) Act, 1951.

* * * *

(3) It shall come into force on such date as the Central Government may, by notification in the Official Gazette, appoint and shall remain in force for a period of two years from the date of its commencement.

* * * *

2. Definitions.—In this Act, unless the context otherwise requires,

* * * *

(k) 'unauthorised news-sheet' means any news-sheet in respect of which security has been required under this Act but has not been furnished as required;

* * * *

20. Jury.—(1) If in any inquiry before a Sessions Judge under this Act, the respondent claims to have the matter determined with the aid of a jury, the provisions hereinafter contained shall apply.

* * * *

(3) Such officer as may be appointed by the State Government in this behalf shall prepare and make out in alphabetical order a list of persons residing within the State who by reason of their journalistic experience or of their connection with printing presses or newspapers or of their experience in public affairs are qualified to serve as jurors.

* * * *

23. Appeal to High Court against orders of Sessions Judges.—Any person against whom an order is passed by a Sessions Judge under section 4, section 5, section 7, or section 8 may, within sixty days of the date of such order, prefer an appeal to the High Court, and upon such appeal, the High Court may pass such orders as it deems fit confirming, varying or reversing the order appealed from and may pass such consequential or incidental orders as may be necessary.

* * * *

29. Issue of search warrants in certain cases.—(1) Where any press is, or any copies of any newspaper, news-sheet, book or other document are, declared forfeited to Government under this Act, the State Government may direct a Magistrate to issue a warrant empowering any police officer, not below the rank of sub-inspector, to seize and detain any property ordered to be forfeited and to enter upon and search for such property in any premises—

* * * *

(2) Without prejudice to the provisions contained in sub-section (1), where any newspaper, news-sheet, book or other document is declared forfeited to Government, it shall be lawful for any police officer to seize the same wherever found.

* * * *

HOUSE OF THE PEOPLE

A

BILL

to amend the Press (Objectionable Matter) Act, 1951

(Shri Kailas Nath Katju,
Minister for Home Affairs)

SELECT BIBLIOGRAPHY

A. OFFICIAL RECORDS AND REPORTS

(i) *Before 1947*

Legislative Council, Proceedings, 1862–1920.

Legislative Assembly, Debates, 1921–1947.

Council of State, Debates, 1921–1947.

Report of the Decentralisation Commission, 1909 (Cmd. 4360).

Report on Indian Constitutional Reforms (Montagu-Chelmsford), 1918 (Cmd. 9109).

East India Constitutional Reforms: Report of the Franchise Committee (Southborough), 1919 (Cmd. 141).

Report of the Reforms Enquiry Committee (Muddiman), 1925 (Cmd. 2360).

Report of the Indian Central Committee, 1929 (Cmd. 3451).

Report of the Indian Statutory Commission (Simon), 1930 (Cmd. 3568–9).

Proceedings of the Round Table Conference (3 Sessions, 1931–32) (Cmd. 3778; Cmd. 3997; Cmd. 4238).

Report of the Indian Franchise Committee (Lothian), 1932 (Cmd. 4086).

Report of the Joint Committee on Indian Constitutional Reform, 1934 (H.C. 5).

Manual of Business and Procedure in the Legislative Assembly, 1945.

(ii) *Since 1947—Government of India*

Constituent Assembly Debates, 1946–49 (twelve volumes).

Constituent Assembly, Reports of Committees (in three volumes).

Constituent Assembly (Legislative) Debates, 1947–49.

> NOTE: These cover six sessions. From the 3rd Session, the volumes are in two 'Parts': Part I containing Questions and Answers; Part II the rest of the proceedings.

Provisional Parliament Debates, 1950–52.

> NOTE: From 1950, Statements laid on the Table of the House in elaboration of answers to Questions are published in separate Appendices.

House of the People Debates, 1952 onwards.

Council of States Debates, 1952 onwards.

State Legislative Assembly Debates.

The Constitution of India, 1949, and reprinted with amendments, 1955.

White Paper on Communist Violence in India, 1949.

White Paper on Indian States, 1950.

Reports of the Commissioner for Scheduled Castes and Scheduled Tribes (annual from 1951).

Report of the Finance Commission, 1953.

Report on Public Administration in India, by P. H. Appleby, 1953.

Report on the First General Elections in India, 1951–52 (1955).

Report of the Taxation Enquiry Commission (3 volumes), 1955.

Report of the Press Commission, 1954.

Report of the States Reorganisation Commission, 1955.

Planning Commission:
   Report on Public Administration, by A. D. Gorwala, 1951.

   Report on the Efficient Conduct of State Enterprises, by A. D. Gorwala, 1951.

   The First Five-Year Plan, 1953.
   Progress Reports on the Plan, from 1953.
   Community Projects Administration, Evaluation Reports.

(iii) *Since 1947—Parliament Secretariat*

NOTE: The following is only a part of the total list of publications prepared and issued by the Parliament Secretariat. It does not include, for example, several pamphlets, designed to give Indian M.P.s information about the House of Commons. Certain other publications (e.g. Rules, Committee Minutes, Speakers' Conference Minutes) are confidential.

(a) *General:*
Journal of the House (sessional from 1950).

Parliament of India, Who's Who, 1950.

Parliament of India, Who's Who (2nd Edition), 1951.

House of the People, Who's Who, 1952.

Council of States, Who's Who, 1952.

A Guide to Parliament House.

A Guide to the Parliament Library.

(b) *Procedure*
Constituent Assembly (Legislative), Rules of Procedure and Standing Orders, 1947.

Rules of Procedure and Conduct of Business in Parliament, 1950.

Rules of Procedure and Conduct of Business in the House of the People, 1952.

Rules of Procedure and Conduct of Business in the House of the People (2nd Edition), 1952.

Council of States Manual, 1952.

Decisions from the Chair (House of the People) (irregular to 1949, sessional from 1950).

Observations from the Chair (House of the People) (sessional from 1950).

(c) *Statistical*

Chart showing Hourly Count and Total Attendance of Members (sessional from 1950).

Statistical Information relating to Business (sessional from 1951).

Statement showing Time involved in Various Kinds of Business (sessional from 1950).

Brief Summary of Work relating to Legislation (sessional from 1950).

Statement showing Time involved in Various Stages of Bills (sessional from 1950).

Statistical Information relating to Questions (sessional from 1950).

(d) *Committees*

Financial Committees, A Review (annual).

Estimates Committee:
    Select Documents on the Estimates Committee (3 series).
    Minutes of the Estimates Committee (sessional).
    Recommendations of the Estimates Committee and Action taken thereon by Government (occasional).
    First Report, 1950–51, Ministry of Industry and Supply.
    Second Report, 1950–51, Reorganisation of the Secretariat and Departments of Government.
    Third Report, 1950–51, Ministry of Commerce.
    Fourth Report, 1950–51, Ministry of Works, Mines and Power.
    Fifth Report, 1951–52, Central Water and Power Commission and Multi-purpose River Valley Schemes.
    Sixth Report, 1952–53, Ministry of Food and Agriculture.
    Seventh Report, 1953–54, Ministry of Food and Agriculture.
    Eighth Report, 1953–54, Damodar Valley Corporation.
    Ninth Report, 1953–54, Administrative, Financial and other Reforms.
    Tenth Report, 1953–54, Ministry of Food and Agriculture.
    Eleventh Report, 1953–54, Ministry of Information and Broadcasting.

Public Accounts Committee:
    Select Documents on the Public Accounts Committee (2 series).
    1950–51, First Report, Accounts of 1947–48 (post-partition).
    1951–52, First Report, Accounts of 1948–49.
    1951–52, Second Report, Accounts of 1948–49.
    1952–53, Third Report, Exchequer Control over Public Expenditure.
    1952–53, Fourth Report, Import and Sale of Japanese Cloth.
    1952–53, Fifth Report, Appropriation Accounts (Railways) and (Posts and Telegraphs), 1949–50.
    1952–53, Sixth Report, Hirakud Dam Project.
    1952–53, Seventh Report, Appropriation Accounts (Civil), 1949–50.

26*

1952–53, *Eighth Report, Disposal of Tyres and Tubes.*

1953–54, *Ninth Report, Appropriation Accounts (Defence Services), 1949–50 and 1950–51.*

1953–54, *Tenth Report, Appropriation Accounts (Railways) and (Posts and Telegraphs), 1950–51.*

1953–54, *Eleventh Report, Hirakud Dam Project.*

1953–54, *Twelfth Report, Fertilizer Deal and Pashabhai Patel Implements.*

1954–55, *Thirteenth Report, Appropriation Accounts (Posts and Telegraphs) and (Railways), 1951–52 and 1952–53.*

1954–55, *Fourteenth Report, Appropriation Accounts (Defence Services) 1951–52 and 1952–53.*

1954–55, *Fifteenth Report, Appropriation Accounts (Civil), 1950–51 and Audit Report (Civil), 1952.*

Committee of Privileges:
The Deshpande Case, 1952.
The Dasartha Deb Case, 1952.
The Sinha Case, 1952.
The Sundarayya Case, 1952.

Committee on the Conduct of a Member:
The Mudgal Case, 1951.

Committee on Subordinate Legislation:
Select Documents on Delegated Legislation.
Reports.

Committee on Private Members' Bills:
Reports.

Committee on Government Assurances:
Reports.

Joint Committee on payment of salary:
Report (1953).

B. Books and Pamphlets

Note: Place of publication, if not stated, is London

(i) *Constitutional and Political Development*

ALL-PARTIES CONFERENCE, *Report of a Committee to Determine Principles of the Constitution for India* (Allahabad, 1928).

APPADORAI, A., *Dyarchy in Practice* (1937).

BANJERJEE, A. C., *Constituent Assembly of India* (1947).

CHINTAMANI, SIR C. Y., and MASANI, M. R., *India's Constitution at Work* (Bombay, 1940).

CHAMIER, D., *Parliamentary Procedure in India* (Bombay, 1925).

COUPLAND, SIR R., *Report on the Constitutional Problem in India*, Vol. I, *The Indian Problem, 1833–1935* (1942); Vol. II, *Indian Politics* (1943); Vol. III, *The Future of India* (1944).

CURTIS, L., *Dyarchy* (1920).

EGGAR, A., *The Government of India* (Rangoon, 1924).

ILBERT, SIR C., *The Government of India* (3rd Edition, 1915).

ILBERT, SIR C., and LORD MESTON, *The New Constitution of India* (1923).
KEITH, A. B., *A Constitutional History of India* (2nd Ed., 1937).
'KERALA PUTRA' (K. M. PANIKKAR), *The Working of Dyarchy in India* (Bombay, 1928).
KRISHNA, K. B., *The Problem of Minorities* (1939).
LUMBY, E. W. R., *The Transfer of Power* (1954).
MASALDAN, P., *The Evolution of Provincial Autonomy in India, 1858-1950* (Bombay, 1953).
MONTAGU, E. S., *An Indian Diary* (1930).
SCHUSTER, SIR G., and WINT, G., *India and Democracy* (1941).
SINGH ROY, B. P., *Parliamentary Government in India* (Calcutta, 1943).
SYMONDS, R., *The Making of Pakistan* (1950).

(ii) *The Indian Constitution*

BASU, D. D., *Commentary on the Constitution of India* (2nd Ed., Calcutta, 1952).
GADGIL, D. R., *Some Observations on the Draft Constitution* (Poona, 1948).
GLEDHILL, A., *The Republic of India* (1951).
— —, *Fundamental Rights in India* (1955).
JENNINGS, SIR W. I., *Some Characteristics of the Indian Constitution* (1952).
MISRA, B. R., *Economic Aspects of the Indian Constitution* (Calcutta, 1952).
SRINIVASAN, N., *Democratic Government in India* (Calcutta, 1954).

(iii) *Modern Indian Politics*

APPADORAI, A., *Democracy in India* (1942).
ANDREWS, C. F., and MUKHERJI, G., *The Rise and Growth of Congress* (1938).
BAILEY, S. D., *Parliamentary Government in South Asia* (1953).
CHAUDHURI, N. C., *The Autobiography of an Unknown Indian* (1952).
CURRAN, J. A., *Militant Hinduism in Indian Politics* (1951).
DARLING, SIR M. L., *At Freedom's Door* (1949).
DESAI, A. R., *The Social Background of Indian Nationalism* (Bombay, 1948).
DUBE, S. C., *The Indian Village* (1955).
GORWALA, A. D., *The Role of the Administrator* (Gokhale Institute, Poona, 1952).
INDIAN NATIONAL CONGRESS, *Congress Bulletin* (Delhi, Monthly).
— —, *The Constitution of the Indian National Congress* (Delhi, 1953).
— —, *The Development of the Congress Constitution*, by N. V. Rajkumar (Delhi, 1949).
— —, *Indian Political Parties*, by N. V. Rajkumar (Delhi, 1948).
— —, *The Pilgrimage and After*, Ed. N. V. Rajkumar (Delhi, 1952).
— —, *Reports of the Congress Party in Parliament* (Sessional).
— —, *Reports of the General Secretaries* (Annual).
— —, *Report of the Linguistic Provinces Committee* (1949).
JENNINGS, SIR W. I., *The Commonwealth in Asia*.
KHUSHWANT SINGH, *The Sikhs* (1953).
KRIPALANI, J. B., *Towards Sarvodaya* (New Delhi, 1951).
LAL, A. B. (Ed.), *The Indian Parliament* (Allahabad, 1956).
LOHIA, R. M., *Aspects of Socialist Philosophy* (Bombay, 1952).

MASANI, M., *The Communist Party of India* (1954).

MEHTA, A., *The Political Mind of India* (Bombay, 1952).

MELLOR, A., *India since Partition* (1951).

MOON, P., *Strangers in India* (1943).

MURPHY, G., *In the Minds of Men: The Study of Human Behaviour and Social Tensions in India* (New York, 1953).

NANAVATI, SIR M. B., and VAKIL, C. N., *Group Prejudices in India* (Bombay, 1951).

NARAYAN, J. P., *Why Socialism?* (Bombay, 1936).

NEHRU, J., *Autobiography* (1936).

— —, *The Unity of India* (1942).

— —, *Speeches, 1949–53* (Delhi, 1954).

PANIKKAR, K. M., *Caste and Democracy* (1933).

SINGH SUD, S. P., *Indian Elections and Legislators* (Ludhiana, 1953).

SPEAR, T. G. P., *India, Pakistan and the West* (1949).

TENNYSON, H., *Saint on the March* (1955).

TINKER, H., *The Foundations of Local Self-Government in India, Pakistan and Burma* (1954).

VENKATARANGAIYA, M., *The General Election in Bombay City* (Bombay, 1953).

WATTAL, P. K., *Parliamentary Financial Control in India* (Simla, 1953).

WINT, G., *The British in Asia* (1947).

ZINKIN, M., *Asia and the West* (1951).

C. JOURNALS

Asian Review.

Asian Recorder.

Eastern Economist.

Economic Weekly.

Far Eastern Survey.

Far Eastern Quarterly.

Indian Journal of Political Science.

India Quarterly.

Journal of the Society of Clerks-at-the-Table in Empire Parliaments.

Pacific Affairs.

Parliamentary Affairs.

INDEX

Act, Indian Councils (1861), 16 n., 46–7
—, — — (1892), 16 n., 47-8
—, — — (1909), 16 n., 48–9, 114, 201
—, Government of India (1919), 5, 17, 53–9, 201, 264
—, — — (1935), 5, 16–17, 19, 59–71, 91, 114, 202, 245, 281
Adjournment Motion, 226–7, 228, 319, 321
Advisory Committees. *See* Committees, Standing Advisory
Akali Party, 13, 28, 106–7
Ambedkar, Dr, 64, 85–9, 152 n., 156–7, 159
Amendments. *See* Bill Procedure
Andhra State, 5, 21–3, 110–12, 136, 178 n., 184
Appropriation Bill. *See* Bill, Appropriation
Assembly, Central Legislative (1919–47), under 1919 Act, 55–9, 71, 201–2; under 1935 Act, 59–60, 71, 117–18, 126, 129–31, 154 n., 185, 226, 238, 239 n., 245–6, 264–6, 270, 279–80, 296, 323, 328. *See* also Council, Central Legislative (1861–1919); Council of State (1919–47)
—, Constituent (1946–49), 17, 21, 43, 71, 81–9, 115, 152, 185, 202–4, 280, 296, 309
Assemblies, Provincial Legislative (1935–50), 5, 17, 59–72, 81, 245–6, 279–80, 296, 328 n. *See* also Councils, Provincial Legislative (1861–1935)
—, State Legislative (1950 onwards), constitutional status, 92–5; parties in, 106; members of, 114–20, 123–8, 137; sessions, 129, 136; sittings, 132; languages of debate, 146; constituency pressures, 150, 320; Congress Party members of, 192, 198–9; procedure, 209, 231 n., 236 n.; privilege, 246, 253–5; Speaker, 269–271; Secretariat, 277; Committees,

295, 300, 308, 311 n.; control of public corporations, 326; general comment, 330 n., 332
Auditor-General. *See* Comptroller and Auditor-General

Balfour, Lord, 74
Bhave, Vinoba. *See* Bhoodan
Bhoodan (Land-Gifts) Movement, 2, 37–40, 42 n., 328, 331 n.
Bill, 92, 187, 191, 203, 204, 205, 207, 211–12, 218–19, 277, 319, 320–3; Appropriation, 204, 237, 242–3; Finance, 244–5; Money, 92, 229, 243, 258; Private Members', 206, 212–18. *See* also Committee on Private Members' Bills.
— procedure, 229–36, 257–8, 320–3, 330
Blitz Case, The, 255
Bombay State, 15, 24, 115–20, 127–8, 136, 139, 141, 146, 160, 165, 198, 253–4, 262–3
Budget, 143 n., 237–9, 242, 245, 321. *See* also Demands; Votes; etc.
Business, List of, 209–19. *See* also Committee, Business Advisory
By-elections. *See* Elections

Cabinet, 150–65. *See* Ministers
— Parliamentary Affairs Committee. *See* Committee, Cabinet Parliamentary Affairs
Campion, Lord, 150–53, 246 n.
Caste, 28–31, 36–7, 75–6, 98–9, 110, 148, 180, 183, 329–30. *See* also Communalism; Scheduled Castes
Central Hall, 130, 132–3
Chatterjee, N. C., 104, 185, 261
Christians, 26, 27, 72, 85
Civil Servants, 6, 11–12, 19, 135, 152, 286–93, 295, 305–7, 313, 323, 324
Closure, 233–5, 244